Contemporary Moral Issues

Contemporary Moral Issues

DIVERSITY AND CONSENSUS

THIRD EDITION

Lawrence M. Hinman

UNIVERSITY OF SAN DIEGO

PEARSON
Prentice
Hall

Upper Saddle River, New Jersey 07458

Library of Congress Cataloging-in-Publication Data

Hinman, Lawrence M.
  Contemporary moral issues : diversity and consensus / Lawrence M. Hinman.—3rd ed.
    p. cm.
  Includes bibliographical references.
  ISBN 0-13-182997-1
  1. Ethical problems—Textbooks.   I. Title.

  BJ1031.H65 2005
  170–dc22

                                                      2004030499

Editorial Director: Charlyce Jones-Owen
Senior Acquisitions Editor: Ross Miller
Assistant Editor: Wendy B. Yurash
Editorial Assistant: Carla Worner
Marketing Manager: Kara Kindstrom
Marketing Assistant: Jennifer Lang
Production Liaison: Joanne Hakim
Manufacturing Buyer: Christina Helder
Cover Art Director: Jayne Conte
Cover Design: Bruce Kenselaar
Manager, Cover Visual Research & Permissions: Karen Sanatar
Cover Photo/Illustration: Diana Ong/Superstock, Inc.
Composition/Full-Service Project Management: Jessica Balch/Pine Tree Composition, Inc.
Printer/Binder: Phoenix Book Tech Park

Credits and acknowledgments borrowed from other sources and reproduced, with permission, in this textbook
appear on the appropriate pages within the text.

Pearson Education LTD., London
Pearson Education Singapore, Pte. Ltd
Pearson Education, Canada, Ltd
Pearson Education—Japan
Pearson Education Australia PTY, Limited

Pearson Education North Asia Ltd
Pearson Educación de Mexico, S.A. de C.V.
Pearson Education Malaysia, Pte. Ltd
Pearson Education, Upper Saddle River, New Jersey

10 9 8 7 6 5 4 3 2 1
ISBN 0-13-182997-1

Contents

PART ONE

Matters of Life and Death

PART TWO

Matters of Diversity and Equality

6   RACE AND ETHNICITY   207

7   GENDER   259

PART THREE

Expanding the Circle

ABCNEWS

Videotape: Topic: Inundated by E-mail Spam
              Source: ABC *20/20,* August 1, 2003   **ABC**NEWS

Preface

The third edition of *Contemporary Moral Issues* contains over twenty new articles and, for instructors, is accompanied with a free set of ABC videos, with many new segments. A new chapter on War, Terrorism, and Counterterrorism has been added to Part One and a new chapter on Cyberethics has been added to Part Three. The bibliographical essays have been updated throughout the book. The book has also been shortened by nearly 100 pages.

Even with these changes, the book retains the strengths that characterized the first edition: narratives that position the issues within the context of lived experience, overviews of the issues, bibliographical essays, and pre- and post-tests.

Issues of diversity play an important role in questions of social policy and in the stories of individual lives. Throughout this book, I have tried to provide the opportunity for as many voices of diversity as possible to be heard. In addition to this, one third of this book—Part Two: Issues of Diversity and Equality—is explicitly devoted to a number of specific issues about diversity and equality in regard to race, gender, and sexual orientation.

This book is "user-friendly" for students. *Critical introductions* to each chapter provide a conceptual map of the moral terrain to be covered, whereas a short *Introduction to the Moral Issues* helps to specify some of the common issues that arise in each chapter. Each selection is introduced with *prereading questions* to focus the students' attention. *Discussion questions* at the end of each selection are designed to help students develop their own positions on the issues raised, whereas journal questions—in italics—explore more personal issues raised by the readings. A *bibliographic essay* at the end of each chapter highlights key works and points the way to valuable resources for students. A guide about critical reading in philosophy and writing philosophical papers on moral issues is now available on Ethics Updates (http://ethics.sandiego.edu). It includes tips on choosing and refining a topic, developing a bibliography, refining arguments, and using counterexamples.

I have retained the *Moral Problems Self-Quiz* at the beginning of this book that surveys your position on a number of issues discussed throughout the book. At the end of each chapter, there is a retest of the relevant questions. Take the initial quiz before you read any of the individual chapters, and then revisit the relevant questions at the end of each chapter. Check your responses against your initial answers and see in what ways—if any—you've changed.

Finally, the integration with the World Wide Web that was begun with the first edition is even more extensive in this third edition. Two sites now provide support for this book: Prentice Hall has developed an excellent site (http://www.prenhall.com/hinman), and my own site, Ethics Updates (http://ethics.sandiego.edu), continues to provide extensive resources on all the topics covered in this book. These resources are increasingly multimedia and interactive and contain several types of sources. First, continually updated versions of the bibliographic essays in this book will be available online, with references to the latest work in each area. Second, hypertext links to numerous Web sites will provide additional resources for the book. For example, the section on abortion contains links to the Web pages of both pro-choice and pro-life groups, and also contains links to the full texts of major court decisions about abortion. Third, there are both PowerPoints and streaming video of lectures. Finally, discussion groups are available on each of the main topics in this book. Please come, visit, and contribute.

This book, like Caesar's Gaul, is divided into three parts. Part One centers around issues of life and death, including *in vitro* fertilization, abortion, euthanasia, the death penalty, and war. Central to this section is the question of the right to life and the sanctity of human life. Part Two deals explicitly with questions of diversity and equality, including issues of race, ethnicity, gender, and sexual orientation. Here one of the central issues is how we balance the recognition of diversity with the demands for community. Part Three turns to a consideration of the boundaries of the moral domain. Morality may begin at home, but how far from home does it extend? Do our moral obligations extend to the poor and starving of other countries? To animals? To the environment? To the virtual world? These four questions provide the basis for the final four chapters of this book.

For instructors who are interested in using it, a videotape is available with segments dealing with the topics in most of the chapters. The segments are intended to stimulate discussion of the issues. They are drawn from ABC News sources, primarily *Nightline*.

I wish to thank, first of all, the authors who kindly allowed their work to be reprinted in this book, for their contributions, which form the heart of this work. Moreover, I would like to thank the following reviewers for their comments and suggestions for making this a better book: James A. Pietrovito, New Hampshire Technical Institute; Gerald A. McBeath, University of Alaska, Fairbanks; and Jennifer K. Berenson Maclean, Roanoke College; any shortcomings are my own. At Prentice Hall, I am especially grateful to Ross Miller, for his patience and support in a project that took longer than either of us anticipated, and for Wendy Yurash's careful editorial support. At the University of San Diego, many contributed to the success of this project: Patrick Drinan, Dean of the College of Arts and Sciences, for his support for computer resources that saved me countless hours on this project; Leeanna Cummings, our departmental secretary, for invaluable assistance in managing permissions requests and generally making my life much less chaotic than it would otherwise be; Andy Khoury, for extraordinarily careful work on the manuscript; and many of my colleagues, including Mike Soroka, George Bryjak, Beth Simon, and Mark Woods, and my students in my Social Ethics course. Most of all, I would like to thank my wife, Virginia, for her continued love as well as her support. Without her, this book would not have been written.

Finally, I would greatly appreciate comments from readers, both students and professors. Please feel free to write to me either via e-mail (hinman@sandiego.edu) or the old fashioned way to Lawrence M. Hinman, Department of Philosophy, University of San Diego, 5998 Alcalá Park, San Diego, CA 92110-2492. Your comments and suggestions are most welcome.

Lawrence M. Hinman

A Pluralistic Approach to Contemporary Moral Issues

Moral Disagreement

As we move through the chapters of this book, we see one area of moral disagreement after another. Abortion, stem cell research, euthanasia, the death penalty, racism, sexism, homosexuality, welfare, world hunger, animal rights, and environmental issues—all are areas characterized by fundamental disagreements, often intense, sometimes bitter and acrimonious.

This situation is made even more perplexing by the fact that in all of these debates, each side has good arguments in support of its position. In other words, these are not debates in which one side is so obviously wrong that only moral blindness or ill will could account for its position. Thus, we cannot easily dismiss such disagreements by just saying that one side is wrong in some irrational or malevolent way. Ultimately, these are disagreements among intelligent people of good will. It is precisely this fact that makes them so disturbing. Certainly part of moral disagreement can be attributed to ignorance or ill will, but the troubling part is the moral disagreement among informed and benevolent people.

What kind of sense can we make of such disagreement? Three possible responses deserve particular attention.

Moral Absolutism

The first, and perhaps most common, response to such disagreements is to claim that there is a single, ultimate answer to the questions being posed. This is the answer of the moral absolutists, those who believe there is a single Truth with a capital "T." Usually, absolutists claim to know what that truth is—and it usually corresponds, not surprisingly, to their own position.

Moral absolutists are not confined to a single position. Indeed, absolutism is best understood as much as a way of holding certain beliefs as it is an item of such belief. Religious fundamentalists—whether Christian, Muslim, or some other denomination—are usually absolutists. Some absolutists believe in communism, others believe just as absolutely in free-market economics. Some moral philosophers are absolutists, believing that their moral viewpoint is the only legitimate one. But what characterizes all absolutists is the conviction that their truth is *the* truth.

Moral absolutists may be right, but there are good reasons to be skeptical about their claims. If they are right, how do they explain the persistence of moral disagreement? Certainly there are disagreements and disputes in other areas (including the natural sciences), but in ethics there seems to be persistence to these disputes that we usually do not find in other areas. It is hard to explain this from an absolutist standpoint without saying such disagreement is due to ignorance or ill will. Certainly this is part of the story, but can it account for all moral disagreement? Absolutists are unable to make sense out of the fact that sometimes we have genuine moral disagreements among well-informed and good-intentioned people who are honestly and openly seeking the truth.

Moral Relativism

The other common response to such disagreement effectively denies that there is a truth in this area, even with a lower case "t." Moral relativists maintain that moral disagreements stem from the fact that what is right for one is not necessarily right for another. Morality is like beauty, they claim—purely relative to the beholder. There is no ultimate standard in terms of which perspectives can be judged. No one is wrong; everyone is right within his or her own sphere.

Notice that these relativists do more than simply acknowledge the existence of moral disagreement. Just to admit that moral disagreement exists is called descriptive relativism, and this is a comparatively uncontroversial claim. There is plenty of disagreement in the moral realm, just as there is in most other areas of life. However, normative relativists go further. They not only maintain that such disagreement exists; they also say that each is right relative to his or her own culture. Incidentally, it is also worth noting that relativists disagree about precisely what morality is relative to. When we refer to moral relativists here, we will be talking about normative relativists, including both cultural moral relativists and moral subjectivists.

Although moral relativism often appears appealing at first glance, it proves to be singularly unhelpful in the long run. It provides an explanation of moral disagreement, but it fails to provide a convincing account of how moral agreement could be forged. In the fact of disagreement, what practical advice can relativists offer us? All they can say, it would seem, is that we ought to follow the customs of our society, our culture, our age, or our individual experience. Thus cultural moral relativists tell us, in effect, "When in Rome, do as the Romans do." Moral subjectivists tell us that we should be true, not to our culture, but to our individual selves. But relativists fail to offer us help in how to resolve disputes when they arise. To say that each is right unto itself is of no help, for the issue is what happens when they come together.

Although this might be helpful advice in an age of moral isolationism when each society (or individual) was an island unto itself, it is of little help today. In our contemporary world, the pressing moral question is how we can live together, not how we can live apart. Economies are mutually interdependent; corporations are often multinational; products such as cars are seldom made in a single country. Communications increasingly cut across national borders. Satellite-based telecommunication systems allow international television (MTV is worldwide and news networks are sure to follow) and international telephone communications. Millions of individuals around the world dial into the Internet, establishing a virtual community. In such a world, relativism fails to provide guidance for resolving disagreements. All it can tell us is that everyone is right in his or her own world. But the question for the future is how to determine what is right when worlds overlap.

Moral Pluralism

Let's return to our problem: in some moral disputes, there seem to be well-informed and good-intentioned people on opposing sides. Absolutism fails to offer a convincing account of how opposing people could be both well informed and good intentioned. It says there is only one answer, and those who do not see it are either ignorant or ill willed. Relativism fails to offer a convincing account of how people can agree. It says no one is wrong, that each culture (or individual) is right unto itself. However, it offers no help about how to resolve these moral disputes.

There is a third possible response here, which I call moral pluralism. Moral pluralists maintain that there are moral truths, but they do not form a body of coherent and consistent truths in the way that one finds in the science or mathematics. Moral truths are real, but partial. Moreover, they are inescapably plural. There are many moral truths, not just one—and they may conflict with one another.

Let me borrow an analogy from government. Moral absolutists are analogous to old-fashioned monarchists: there is one leader, and he or she has the absolute truth. Moral relativists are closer to anarchists: each person or group has its own truth. The U.S. government is an interesting example of a tripartite pluralist government. We don't think that the president, the Congress, or the judiciary alone has an exclusive claim to truth. Each has a partial claim, and each provides a check on the other two. We don't—at least not always—view conflict among the three branches as a bad thing. Indeed, such a system of overlapping and at times conflicting responsibilities is a way of hedging our bets. If we put all of our hope in only one of the branches of government, we would be putting ourselves at greater risk. If that one branch is wrong, then everything is wrong. However, if there are three (at least partially conflicting) branches of government, then the effects of one branch's being wrong are far less catastrophic. Moreover, the chance that mistakes will be uncovered earlier is certainly increased when each branch is being scrutinized by the others.

We have an analogous situation in the moral domain. As we shall see, there are conflicting theories about goodness and rightness. Such conflict is a good thing. Each theory contains important truths about the moral life and none of them contains the whole truth. Each keeps the others honest, as it were, curbing the excesses of any particular moral absolutism. Yet each claims to have the truth, and refuses the relativist's injunction to avoid making judgments about others. Judgment—both making judgments and being judged—is crucial to the moral life, just as it is to the political life. We have differing moral perspectives, but we must often inhabit a common world.

It is precisely this tension between individual viewpoints and living in a common world that lies at the heart of this book. The diversity of viewpoints is not intended to create a written version of those television news shows where people constantly shout at one another. Rather, these selections indicate the range of important and legitimate insights with which we approach the issue in question. The challenge, then, is for us—as individuals, and as a society—to forge a common ground that acknowledges the legitimacy of the conflicting insights but also establishes a minimal area of agreement so that we can live together with our differences. The model this book strives to emulate is not the one-sided monarch who claims to have the absolute truth, nor is it the anarchistic society that contains no basis for consensus. Rather, it is the model of a healthy government in which diversity, disagreement, compromise, and consensus are signs of vitality.

A Pluralistic Approach to Moral Theories

Just as in the political realm there are political parties and movements that delineate the main contours of the political debate, so also in philosophy there are moral theories that provide characteristic ways of understanding and resolving particular moral issues. In the readings throughout this book, we see a number of examples of these theories in action. It is helpful to look at some of the main characteristics of each of these theories. Just as Republicans and Democrats, liberals and conservatives, libertarians and socialists all have important, and often conflicting, insights about the political life, so too does each of these theories have valuable insights into the moral life. Yet none of them has the whole story. Let's look briefly at each of these approaches.

Morality as Consequences

What makes an action morally good? For many of us, what counts are consequences. The right action is the one that produces good consequences. If I give money to Oxfam to help starving people, and if Oxfam saves the lives of starving people and helps them develop a self-sustaining economy, then I have done something good. It is good because it produced good consequences. For this reason, it is the right thing to do. Those who subscribe to this position are called consequentialists. All consequentialists share a common belief that it is consequences that make an action good, but they differ among themselves about precisely which consequences.

Ethical Egoism

Some consequentialists, called ethical egoists, maintain that each of us should look only at the consequences that affect us. In their eyes, each person ought to perform those actions that contribute most to his or her own self-interest. Each person is the best judge of his or her own self-interest and each person is responsible for maximizing his or her own self-interest. The political expression of ethical egoism occurs most clearly in libertarianism and the best-known advocate of this position was probably Ayn Rand.

Utilitarianism

Once we begin to enlarge the circle of those affected by the consequences of our actions, we move toward a utilitarian position. At its core, utilitarianism believes that we ought to do what produces the greatest overall good consequences for everyone, not just for me. We determine this by examining the various courses of action open to us, calculating the consequences associated with each, and then deciding on the one that produces the greatest overall good consequences for everyone. It is consequentialist and computational. It holds out the promise that moral disputes can be resolved objectively by computing consequences. Part of the attraction of utilitarianism is precisely this claim to objectivity based on a moral calculus.

Utilitarians disagree among themselves about what the proper standard is for judging consequences. What are "good" consequences? Are they the ones that produce the most pleasure? The most *happiness?* The most truth, beauty, and the like? Or simply the consequences that satisfy the most people? Each of these standards of utility has its strengths and weaknesses. Pleasure is comparatively easy to measure, but in many people's eyes it seems to be a rather base standard. Can't we increase pleasure just by putting electrodes in the proper location in a person's brain? Presumably we want something more, and better, than that. Happiness seems a more plausible candidate, but the difficulty with happiness is that it is both elusive to define and extremely difficult to measure. This is particularly a problem for utilitarianism because its initial appeal rests in part on its claim to objectivity. Ideals such as truth and beauty are even more difficult to measure. Preference satisfaction is more measurable, but it provides no foundation for distinguishing between morally acceptable preferences and morally objectionable preferences such as racism.

The other principal disagreement that has plagued utilitarianism centers on the question of whether we look at the consequences of each individual act—this is called act utilitarianism—or the consequences that would result from everyone following a particular rule—this is called rule utilitarianism. The danger of act utilitarianism is that it may justify some particular acts that most of us would want to condemn, particularly those that sacrifice individual life and liberty for the sake of the whole. The classic problem occurs in regard to punishment. We could imagine a situation in which punishing an innocent person—while concealing his innocence, of course—would have the greatest overall good consequences. If doing so would result in the greatest overall amount of pleasure or happiness, then it would not only be permitted by act utilitarianism, it would be morally required. Similar difficulties arise in regard to an issue such as euthanasia. It is conceivable that overall utility might justify active euthanasia of the elderly and infirm, even involuntary euthanasia, especially of those who leave no one behind to mourn their passing. Yet are there things we cannot do to people, even if utility seems to require it? Many of us would answer such a question affirmatively.

Feminist Consequentialism

During the past 20 years, much interesting and valuable work has been done in the area of feminist ethics. It would be misleading to think of feminist approaches to ethics as falling into a single camp, but certainly some feminist moral philosophers have sketched out consequentialist accounts of the moral life in at least two different ways.

First, some feminists have argued that morality is a matter of consequences, but that consequences are not best understood or evaluated in the traditional computational model offered by utilitarianism. Instead, they focus primarily on the ways in which particular actions have consequences for relationships and feelings. Negative consequences are those that destroy relationships and that hurt others, especially those that hurt others emotionally. Within this tradition, the morally good course of action is the one that preserves the greatest degree of connectedness among all those affected by it. Carol Gilligan has described this moral voice in her book *In a Different Voice.*

Second, other feminists have accepted a roughly utilitarian account of consequences, but have paid particular attention to—and often given special weight to—the consequences that affect women. Such consequences, they argue, have often been overlooked by traditional utilitarian calculators, supposedly impartial but often insensitive to harming women. Unlike the work of Gilligan and others mentioned in the previous paragraph, feminists in this tradition do not question the dominant utilitarian paradigm, but rather question whether it has in fact been applied impartially.

Conclusion: Consequentialism

Despite these disagreements about the precise formulation of utilitarianism, most people would admit that utilitarianism contains important insights into the moral life. Part of the justification for morality, and one of the reasons people accept the burdens of morality, is that it promises to produce a better world than we would have without it. This is undoubtedly part of the picture. But is it the whole picture?

Morality as Act and Intention

Critics of utilitarianism point out that, for utilitarianism, no actions are good or bad in themselves. All actions in themselves are morally neutral, and for pure consequentialists no action is intrinsically evil. Yet this seems to contradict the moral intuition of many people, people who believe that some actions are just morally wrong, even if they have good results. Killing innocent human beings, torturing people, raping them—these are but a few of the actions that many would want to condemn as wrong in themselves, even if in unusual circumstances they may produce good consequences.

How can we tell if some actions are morally good or bad in themselves? Clearly, we must have some standard against which they can be judged. Various standards have been proposed, and most of these again capture important truths about the moral life.

Conformity to God's Commands

In a number of fundamentalist religious traditions, including some branches of Judaism, Christianity, and Islam, what makes an act right is that it is commanded by God and what makes an act wrong is that it is forbidden by God. In these traditions, certain kinds of acts are wrong just because God forbids them. Usually such prohibitions are contained in sacred texts such as the Bible or the Koran.

There are two principal difficulties with this approach, one external and one internal. The external problem is that, although this may provide a good reason for believers to act in particular ways, it hardly gives a persuasive case to nonbelievers. The internal difficulty is that it is often difficult, even with the best of intentions, to discern what God's commands actually are. Sacred texts, for example, contain numerous injunctions, but it is rare that any religious tradition takes all of them seriously. (The Bible tells believers to pick up venomous vipers, but only a handful of Christians engage in this practice.) How do we decide which injunctions to take seriously and which to ignore or interpret metaphorically?

Natural Law

There is a long tradition, beginning with Aristotle and gaining great popularity in the Middle Ages, that maintains that acts that are "unnatural" are always evil. The underlying premise of this view is that the natural is good, and therefore what contradicts it is bad. Often, especially in the Middle Ages, this was part of a larger Christian worldview that saw nature as created by God, who then was the ultimate source of its goodness. Yet it has certainly survived in 20th century moral and legal philosophy quite apart from its theological underpinnings. This appeal to natural law occurs at a number of junctures in our readings, but especially in the discussions of reproductive technologies and those of homosexuality. Natural law arguments lead quite easily into considerations of human nature, again with the implicit claim that human nature is good.

Natural law arguments tend to be slippery for two, closely interrelated reasons. First, for natural law arguments to work, one has to provide convincing support for the claim that the "natural" is (the only) good—or at least for its contrapositive, the claim that the "unnatural" is bad. Second, such arguments presuppose that we can clearly differentiate between the natural and the unnatural. Are floods and earthquakes natural? Is disease natural? Either the natural is not always good, or else we have to adopt a very selective notion of natural.

Proper Intention

A second way in which acts can be said to be good or bad is that they are done from the proper motivation, with the correct intention. Indeed, intentions are often built into our vocabulary for describing actions. The difference between stabbing a person and performing surgery on that person may well reside primarily in the intention of the agent.

Acting for the sake of duty.   Again, there is no shortage of candidates for morally acceptable intentions. A sense of duty, universalizability, a respect for other persons, sincerity or authenticity, care and compassion—these are but a few of the acceptable moral motivations. Consider, first of all, the motive of duty. Immanuel Kant argued that what gives an action moral worth is that it is done for the sake of duty. In his eyes, the morally admirable person is the one who, despite inclinations to the contrary, does the right thing solely because it is the right thing to do. The person who contributes to charities out of a sense of duty is morally far superior to the person who does the same thing to look good in the eyes of others, despite the fact that the consequences may be the same.

Universalizability.   How do we know what our duty is? Kant avoided saying duty was simply a matter of "following orders." Instead, he saw duty as emanating from the nature of reason itself. And because reason is universal, duty is also universal. Kant suggested an important test of whether our understanding of duty was rational in any particular instance. We always act, he maintained, with a subjective rule or maxim that guides our decision. Is this maxim one that we can will that everyone accept, or is it one that fails this test of universalizability?

Consider cheating. If you cheat on an exam, it's like lying: you are saying something is your work when it is not. Imagine you cheat on all the exams in a course and finish with an average of 98 percent. The professor then gives you a grade of "D." You storm into the professor's office, demanding an explanation. The professor calmly says, "Oh, I lied on the grade sheet." Your reply would be, "But you can't lie about my grade!" Kant's point is that, by cheating, you've denied the validity of your own claim. You've implicitly said that it is morally all right for people to lie. But of course you don't believe it's permissible for your professor to lie—only for you yourself to do so. This, Kant says, fails the test of universalizability.

Notice that Kant's argument isn't a consequentialist one. He's not asking what would happen to society if everyone lied. Rather, he's saying that certain maxims are inconsistent and thus irrational. You cannot approve of your own lying without approving of everyone else's, and yet the advantage you get depends precisely on other people's honesty. It is the irrationality of making an exception of my own lying in this way that Kant feels violates the moral law. We have probably all had the experience of acting in a morally sleazy way, of making an exception for ourselves that (at least in retrospect) we know isn't justified.

Kant's argument captured something valuable about the moral life: the insight that what's fair for one is fair for all. Yet critics were quick to point out that this can hardly be the entire story. Consequences count, and intentions are notoriously slippery. A given act can be described with many different intentions—to cheat on a test, to try to excel, to try to meet your parents' expectations, to be the first in the class—and not all of them necessarily fail the test of universalizability.

Respect for other persons.   Kant offered another formulation of his basic moral insight, one that touches a responsive chord in many of us. We should never treat people merely as things, Kant argued. Rather, we should always respect them as autonomous (i.e., self-directing) moral agents. Both capitalism and technology pressure us to treat people merely as things, and many have found Kant's refusal to do this to be of crucial moral importance.

It is easy to find examples at both ends of this spectrum. We use people merely as things when we do not let them make their own decisions and when we harm them for our own benefit without respect for their rights. Consider the now infamous Tuskegee experiment, in which medical researchers tracked the development of syphilis in a group of African American men for over 30 years, never telling them the precise nature of their malady and never treating them—something that would have been both inexpensive and effective. Instead, the researchers let the disease proceed through its ultimately fatal course to observe more closely the details of its progress. These men were used merely as means to the researchers' ends.

Similarly, we have all, hopefully, experienced being treated as ends in ourselves. If I am ill, and my physician gives me the details of my medical condition, outlines the available options for treatment (including nontreatment), and is supportive of whatever choice I finally make in this matter, then I feel as though I have been treated with respect. Timothy Quill's selection in the chapter on euthanasia offers a good, real-life example of such respect in the doctor–patient relationship.

The difficulty with this criterion is that there is a large middle ground where it is unclear if acting in a particular way is really using other people merely as things. Indeed, insofar as our economic system is based on commodification, we can be assured that this will be a common phenomenon in our society. To what extent is respect for persons attainable in a capitalist and technological society?

Compassion and caring.   Some philosophers, particularly but not exclusively feminists, have urged the moral importance of acting out of motives of care and compassion. Many of these philosophers have argued that caring about other persons is the heart of the moral life, and that a morality of care leads to a refreshingly new picture of morality as centering on relationships, feelings, and connectedness rather than impartiality, justice, and fairness. The justice-oriented person in a moral dispute will ask what the fair thing to do is, and then proceed to follow that course of action, no matter what effect that has on others. The care-oriented individual, on the other hand, will try to find the course of action that best preserves the interests of all involved and that does the least amount of damage to the relationships involved.

Many in this tradition have seen the justice orientation as characteristically male, and the care orientation as typically female. (Notice that this is not the same as claiming that these orientations are exclusively male or female.) Critics have argued that such correlations are simplistic and misleading. Both orientations may be present to some degree in almost everyone and particular types of situations may be responsible for bringing one or the other to the fore.

Respect for Rights

Kant, as we have just seen, told us that we ought to respect other persons. Yet what specific aspects of other persons ought we to respect? One answer, which has played a major political as well as philosophical role during the past two centuries, has been framed in terms of human rights. The Bill of Rights was the first set of amendments to the U.S. Constitution. At approximately the same time, the French were drafting the Declaration of the Rights of Man and Citizen. Concern for human rights has continued well into the 20th century and the past 40 years in the United States have been marked by an intense concern with rights—the civil rights movement for racial equality, the equal rights movement for women, the animal rights movement, the gay rights movement, and equal rights for Americans with disabilities. Throughout the selections in this book, we see continual appeals to rights, debates about the extent and even the existence of rights, and attempts to adjudicate conflicts of rights.

Rights provide the final criterion to be considered here for evaluating acts. Those acts that violate basic human rights are morally wrong, this tradition suggests. Torture, imprisoning, and executing the innocent; denial of the right to vote; denial of due process—these are all instances of actions that violate human rights. (The fact that an act does not violate basic human rights does not mean that it is morally unobjectionable; there may be other criteria for evaluating it as well as rights.) Human rights, defenders of this tradition maintain, are not subject to nationality, race, religion, class, or any other such limitation. They cannot be set aside for reasons of utility, convenience, or political or financial gain. We possess them simply by virtue of being human beings and they thus exhibit a universality that provides the foundation for a global human community.

Criticisms of the rights tradition abound. First, how do we determine which rights we have? Rights theorists often respond that we have a right to those things—such as life, freedom, and property—that are necessary to human existence itself. Yet many claim that such necessities are contextual, not universal. Moreover, they maintain that there is something logically suspicious about proceeding from the claim that "I need something" to the claim that "I have a right to it." Needs, these critics argue, do not entail rights. Second, critics have asked whether these rights are negative rights (i.e., freedoms from certain kinds of interference) or positive rights (i.e., entitlements). This is one of the issues at the core of the welfare debate currently raging in the United States. Do the poor have any positive rights to welfare, or do they only have rights not to be discriminated against in various ways? Finally, some critics have argued that the current focus on rights has obscured other morally relevant aspects of our lives. Rights establish a moral minimum for the ways in which we interact with others, especially strangers we do not care about. But when we are dealing with those we know and care about, more may be demanded of us morally than just respecting their rights.

Morality as Character

It is rare that a philosophy anthology reaches the bestseller lists and it is even more unusual when that book is a relatively traditional work about character. William Bennett's *The Book of Virtues,* however, has done just that. Staying on the bestseller list for week after week, Bennett's book indicates a resurgence of interest in a long-neglected tradition of ethic: Aristotelian virtue theory.

The Contrast between Act-Oriented Ethics and Character-Oriented Ethics

This Aristotelian approach to ethic, sometimes called character ethics or virtue ethics, is distinctive. In contrast to the preceding act-oriented approaches, it does not focus on what makes acts right or wrong. Rather, it focuses on people and their moral character. Instead of asking, "What should I do?", those in this tradition ask, "What kind of person should I strive to be?" This gives a very different focus to the moral life.

An analogy with public life may again be helpful. Consider the American judiciary system. We develop an elaborate set of rules through legislation and these rules are often articulated in excruciating detail. However, when someone is brought to trial, we do not depend solely on the rules to guarantee justice. Ultimately, we place the fate of accused criminals in the hands of people—a judge and jury. As a country, we bet on both rules and people.

A similar situation exists in ethics. We need good rules—and the preceding sections have described some attempts to articulate those rules—but we also need good people to have the wisdom and good will to interpret and apply those rules. Far from being in conflict with each other, act-oriented and character-oriented approaches to ethics complement one another.

Human Flourishing

The principal question that character-oriented approaches to ethics asks is the following: What strengths of character (i.e., virtues) promote human flourishing? Correlatively, what weaknesses of character (i.e., vices) impede human flourishing? Virtues are thus those strengths of character that contribute to human flourishing, whereas vices are those weaknesses that get in the way of flourishing.

To develop an answer to these questions, the first thing that those in this tradition must do is to articulate a clear notion of human flourishing. Here they depend as much on moral psychology as moral philosophy. Aristotle had a vision of human flourishing, but it was one that was clearly limited to his time—one that excluded women and slaves. In contemporary psychology, we have seen much interesting work describing flourishing in psychological terms—Carl Rogers and Abraham Maslow are two of the better known psychologists who attempt to describe human flourishing. The articulation of a well-founded and convincing vision of human flourishing remains one of the principal challenges of virtue ethics today.

Virtue Ethics as the Foundation of Other Approaches to Ethics

We can conclude this section by reflecting once again on the relationship between virtue ethics and act-oriented approaches to ethics. One of the principal problems faced by moral philosophers has been how to understand the continuing disagreement among the various ethical traditions described earlier. It seems implausible to say that one is right and all the rest are wrong, but it also seems impossible to say that they are all right, for they seem to contradict each other. If we adopt a pluralistic approach, we may say that each contains partial truths about the moral life, but none contains the whole truth. But then the question is: How do we know which position should be given precedence in a particular instance?

There is no theoretical answer to this question, no meta-theory that integrates all these differing and at times conflicting theories. However, there is a practical answer to this question: We ultimately have to put our trust in the wise person to know when to give priority to one type of moral consideration over another. Indeed, it is precisely this that constitutes moral wisdom.

Analyzing Moral Problems

As we turn to consider the various moral problems discussed in this book, each of these theories will help us to understand aspects of the problem that we might not originally have noticed, to see connections among apparently unconnected factors, and to formulate responses that we might not previously have envisioned. Ultimately, our search is a personal one, a search for wisdom.

But it is also a social approach, one that seeks to discern how to live a good life with other people, how to live well together in the community. As we consider the series of moral issues that follow in this book, we will be attempting to fulfill both the individual and the communal goals. We will be seeking to find the course of action that is morally right for us as individuals, and we will be developing our own account of how society as a whole ought to respond to these moral challenges.

An Initial Self-Quiz

Drawing on your current moral beliefs, answer the following questions as honestly as possible. You may feel that these check boxes do not allow you to state your beliefs accurately enough. Please feel free to add notes, qualifications, and so on, in the margins. You will be asked to return to reassess your answers to these questions throughout the semester.

To participate in an online version of this self-quiz, and to see how others have responded, visit the Ethics Surveys section of Ethics Updates (http://ethics.sandiego.edu).

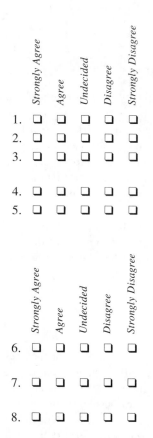

Chapter 1: Cloning and Reproductive Technologies

1. *In vitro* fertilization is morally wrong.

2. Any procedure that helps infertile couples to have children is good.

3. Surrogate mothers should never have to give up their babies if they don't want to do so.

4. Surrogate motherhood should be illegal.

5. Genetic manipulation of embryos should be forbidden.

Chapter 2: Abortion

6. The principal moral consideration about abortion is the question of whether the fetus is a person or not.

7. The principal moral consideration about abortion is the question of the rights of the pregnant woman.

8. The only one who should have a voice in making the decision about an abortion is the pregnant woman.

9. Abortion should be legal but morally discouraged.

10. Abortion protesters are justified in breaking the law to prevent abortions.

Strongly Agree	Agree	Undecided	Disagree	Strongly Disagree	

Chapter 3: Euthanasia

11. ❑ ❑ ❑ ❑ ❑   Euthanasia is always morally wrong.

12. ❑ ❑ ❑ ❑ ❑   Euthanasia should be illegal under almost all circumstances.

13. ❑ ❑ ❑ ❑ ❑   The principal moral consideration about euthanasia is the question of whether the person freely chooses to die or not.

14. ❑ ❑ ❑ ❑ ❑   Actively killing someone is always morally worse than just letting them die.

15. ❑ ❑ ❑ ❑ ❑   Sometimes we have a duty to die.

Chapter 4: Punishment and the Dealth Penalty

16. ❑ ❑ ❑ ❑ ❑   The purpose of punishment is primarily to pay back the offender.

17. ❑ ❑ ❑ ❑ ❑   The purpose of punishment is primarily to deter the offender and others from committing future crimes.

18. ❑ ❑ ❑ ❑ ❑   Capital punishment is always morally wrong.

19. ❑ ❑ ❑ ❑ ❑   The principal moral consideration about capital punishment is the question of whether it is administered arbitrarily or not.

20. ❑ ❑ ❑ ❑ ❑   The principal moral consideration about capital punishment is that it doesn't really deter criminals.

Chapter 5: War, Terrorism, and Counterterrorism

21. ❑ ❑ ❑ ❑ ❑   It is always morally wrong to strike first in a war.

22. ❑ ❑ ❑ ❑ ❑   Captured terrorists should be treated like prisoners of war.

23. ❑ ❑ ❑ ❑ ❑   Sometimes we must go to war to save innocent people from being killed.

24. ❑ ❑ ❑ ❑ ❑   Terrorists should be hunted down and killed.

25. ❑ ❑ ❑ ❑ ❑   Torture is always wrong and should be forbidden.

	Strongly Agree	Agree	Undecided	Disagree	Strongly Disagree	
26.	❑	❑	❑	❑	❑	

Chapter 6: Race and Ethnicity

	Strongly Agree	Agree	Undecided	Disagree	Strongly Disagree	
26.	❑	❑	❑	❑	❑	African Americans are still often discriminated against in employment.
27.	❑	❑	❑	❑	❑	African Americans should be paid reparations for past injustices against them.
28.	❑	❑	❑	❑	❑	Racial separatism is wrong.
29.	❑	❑	❑	❑	❑	Hate speech should be banned.
30.	❑	❑	❑	❑	❑	We should encourage the development of racial and ethnic identity.

Chapter 7: Gender

	Strongly Agree	Agree	Undecided	Disagree	Strongly Disagree	
31.	❑	❑	❑	❑	❑	Women's moral voices are different from men's.
32.	❑	❑	❑	❑	❑	Women are still discriminated against in the workplace.
33.	❑	❑	❑	❑	❑	Sexual harassment should be illegal.
34.	❑	❑	❑	❑	❑	Affirmative action helps women.
35.	❑	❑	❑	❑	❑	Genuine equality for women demands a restructuring of the traditional family.

Chapter 8: Sexual Orientation

	Strongly Agree	Agree	Undecided	Disagree	Strongly Disagree	
36.	❑	❑	❑	❑	❑	Gays and lesbians should be allowed to serve openly in the military.
37.	❑	❑	❑	❑	❑	Gays and lesbians should not be discriminated against in hiring or housing.
38.	❑	❑	❑	❑	❑	Homosexuality is unnatural.
39.	❑	❑	❑	❑	❑	Same-sex marriages should be legal.
40.	❑	❑	❑	❑	❑	Homosexuality is a matter of personal choice.

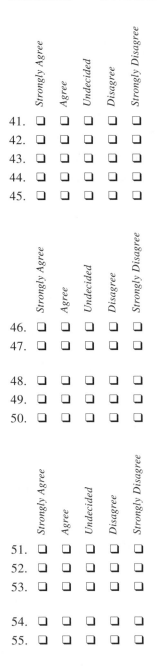

Chapter 9: World Hunger and Poverty

41. ❏ ❏ ❏ ❏ ❏   Only the morally heartless would refuse to help the starving.
42. ❏ ❏ ❏ ❏ ❏   We should help starving nations until we are as poor as they are.
43. ❏ ❏ ❏ ❏ ❏   In the long run, relief aid to starving nations does not help them.
44. ❏ ❏ ❏ ❏ ❏   Overpopulation is the main cause of world hunger and poverty.
45. ❏ ❏ ❏ ❏ ❏   The world is gradually becoming a better place.

Chapter 10: Living Together with Animals

46. ❏ ❏ ❏ ❏ ❏   There's nothing morally wrong with eating veal.
47. ❏ ❏ ❏ ❏ ❏   It's morally permissible to cause animals pain to do medical research that benefits human beings.
48. ❏ ❏ ❏ ❏ ❏   All animals have the same moral standing.
49. ❏ ❏ ❏ ❏ ❏   Zoos are a morally good thing.
50. ❏ ❏ ❏ ❏ ❏   There is nothing morally wrong with hunting.

Chapter 11: Environmental Ethics

51. ❏ ❏ ❏ ❏ ❏   Nature is just a source of resources for us.
52. ❏ ❏ ❏ ❏ ❏   The government should strictly regulate toxic waste.
53. ❏ ❏ ❏ ❏ ❏   We should make every effort possible to avoid infringing on the natural environment any more than we already have.
54. ❏ ❏ ❏ ❏ ❏   We owe future generations a clean and safe environment.
55. ❏ ❏ ❏ ❏ ❏   We should not impose our environmental concerns on developing nations.

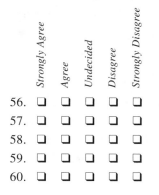

Chapter 12: CyberEthics

	Strongly Agree	Agree	Undecided	Disagree	Strongly Disagree	
56.	❏	❏	❏	❏	❏	All spam should be outlawed.
57.	❏	❏	❏	❏	❏	Hackers only want to cause trouble.
58.	❏	❏	❏	❏	❏	Cyberstalking is not really different from regular stalking.
59.	❏	❏	❏	❏	❏	There's nothing wrong with downloading music from the Internet.
60.	❏	❏	❏	❏	❏	We should ban cyborgs.

PART ONE

Matters of Life and Death

In the following four chapters, we are concerned primarily with matters of life and death. In abortion, cloning, euthanasia, and the death penalty, we are faced time after time with decisions in which lives hang in the balance. Before looking at any of these specific issues, it is helpful to look at the general background issue in all these chapters—the question of the value of life.

The Value of Life

Immanuel Kant, one of the most influential moral philosophers of modern times, said that human life was priceless. His insight was a tremendously important one. He argued that human beings are fundamentally different from mere objects. Objects or things have a price. It is entirely appropriate to buy and sell things. I might purchase a new book or sell an old car, and all of that is entirely morally appropriate. I cannot, however, buy or sell human beings, because human beings—if Kant is right—are not the kind of entities that can have a price or be bought and sold. Human beings are ends in themselves, not mere means to be used to an end.

Although Kant thought human life was priceless, he was not a pacifist. Some, however, go even further than Kant and maintain that all human life is sacred and, as a result, no one is ever justified in taking a human life. There are strains of this in Christianity, Buddhism, and other religions as well. What these positions have in common is a belief that human life is sacred and inviolable, a gift given by God and not to be taken away by human beings. In the Catholic tradition, this position translates into an opposition to abortion, active euthanasia, war, the death penalty, and other forms of killing human beings. Respect for life becomes a "seamless garment."

These perspectives contrast starkly with utilitarian accounts of the value of human life. Utilitarianism is about weighing things, comparing the suffering and happiness that various alternatives might produce. As such, it has to put a price tag on human life.

At first glance, the utilitarian approach may seem morally noxious and we may be inclined to dismiss it out of hand. However, we often place a value on human lives, even innocent human lives. Consider such a simple matter as speed limits. If we lower the speed limit, there will be fewer traffic-related fatalities. Yet there is a trade-off here. When the speed limit is lowered, it takes longer to get from one place to another. The price of shipped goods goes up. Commuting takes longer, perhaps with more pollution as a by-product. We are able to save a number of lives by reducing the speed limit to 55 mph. What about reducing it to 45 mph? Perhaps 35 mph? In each case, we would (presumably) save additional innocent lives, but we may be unwilling to make the trade-off. Whether we like it or not, we often think in utilitarian terms, even about matters of life and death.

As you work through the following four chapters, you will continually be asked to weigh the value of human life against other values, including safety, medical progress, suffering, and justice. As you develop your position on this issue, look for issues of consistency and inconsistency in your thinking about the value of life across a range of different issues.

CHAPTER 1 · Cloning and Reproductive Technologies

Videotape

Topic:	To Preserve or Defend: Does the Gift of Life Cost Life Itself? Stem Cell Research
Source:	*Nightline,* June 20, 2001
Anchors:	Ted Koppel, Michel Martin
Guests:	Sen. Orin Hatch, Richard Doerflinger (National Council of Catholic Bishops), David Prentice (Indiana State University), George W. Bush, Dr. John Gearhart (Johns Hopkins)

An Introduction to the Moral Issues

Many of the moral problems we face today—such as euthanasia, punishment, hunger, and discrimination—have been perennial issues for humanity. In the past few decades, however, we have been faced with a new range of moral problems—problems arising out of the advance of medical technology. Perhaps nowhere are these more pressing and more complex than in the areas of cloning and reproductive technology. The past two decades of scientific advances have now turned fiction into fact. Indeed, so-called "test-tube babies"—more precisely, babies conceived in a petrie dish from human sperm and eggs and then implanted in a woman's uterus—used to be the stuff of science fiction. Now the question is more likely to be whether the cost of such procedures should be covered by health insurance.

In this chapter, we look at a number of the moral issues raised by this and other advances in reproductive technology. Some of these relate directly to the moral status of what is variously called the embryo, the pre-embryo, or the conceptus. To a large extent, the issues here repeat those explored in our discussion of abortion. However, some completely new issues arise as well. For example, there have been several cases in which divorcing couples have gone to court to settle disagreements about the disposition of frozen embryos from their own eggs and sperm.

A quite different set of issues arises in those situations where a surrogate mother carries the embryo to term and these issues center primarily on the relationship among three parties: (a) the couple—or, occasionally, the single individual—who wants to raise the child; (b) the surrogate mother who carries the baby to term; and (c) the baby that the surrogate mother bears.

A third set of issues arises through the intersection of reproductive technologies and genetic manipulation. We are only on the verge of confronting such issues, but they are sure to become more pressing as medical science becomes increasingly skilled at genetic manipulation and as the Human Genome Project maps out the genetic code with increasing precision. The questions are primarily hypothetical at present. What if we can decide whether a given embryo develops as a male or a female? What if we can select physical characteristics? Personality traits? Sexual orientation? The specter of "designer babies" looms, if not in the immediate future, at least in the not-too-distant future. How should such choices be made, if at all? The final step in this process is cloning.

Let's consider each of these three areas in more detail.

In Vitro Fertilization (IVF)

Current estimates suggest that 1 in 12 American couples who want to have a child experience significant medical barriers to fertility. For such couples, once the nature of the medical problem(s) has been diagnosed, there are often initial therapeutic techniques, such as hormone therapy or surgery, that can enable the couple to have children without further medical assistance. However, this is not possible for all. For some couples, it is still impossible to conceive. In those cases, it is necessary to turn to more radical means. If conception cannot take place in the woman, then the next step is to try to bring about conception externally—in a glass laboratory dish, *in vitro*. The man's sperm and the woman's egg are combined in a glass dish (*in vitro* just means "in glass" in Latin) in a way that allows the sperm to fertilize the egg, producing the embryo. This creates a double separation. First, the act of creating a human life is separated from sexual intercourse. Second, and even more important, the embryo itself is separate (if only for a short period of time) from the mother. At this point, the embryo is implanted, either in the woman whose egg was fertilized or in another woman who will bear the baby.

The Moral Status of the Pre-Embryo

We discuss many of the arguments about the moral status of the fetus in the introduction to the chapter on abortion. However, when we are dealing with IVF, we are dealing with what is sometimes called a *pre-embryo,* which arguably has a different moral status than an embryo.

What is a pre-embryo? Some have argued that it is simply an embryo at its earliest stage of development, and that the attempt to call it a pre-embryo is simply an attempt to make anything relating to it appear morally unobjectionable. Yet giving something a new name does not change its moral status. We will follow common usage and employ the term pre-embryo, but note that this does not entail any judgment about its moral status.

At least two points are relevant here to the moral status of the pre-embryo. First, at this early stage, the pre-embryo is microscopic, smaller than the period at the end of this sentence. Usually, it is implanted or frozen when it has reached eight cells. There is nothing visually resembling a human being, although the pre-embryo certainly contains the coded genetic information for a full human being. Second, in contrast to its situation when it is *in utero,* the pre-embryo in a Petrie dish will not develop into a human being unless someone takes positive steps to implant it. This is very different from the situation of abortion, where someone has to intervene to prevent the pre-embryo from developing. Of course, the positive steps necessary when the pre-embryo is *ex utero* are only necessary because the woman's eggs have been artificially removed and fertilized.

One of the principal moral issues here is that it is standard procedure during IVF to harvest a number of eggs, to fertilize them outside of the uterus, and then to implant the pre-embryo most likely to thrive. What happens to the remaining pre-embryos? In some instances, they may be frozen to be used later by the couple if this attempt is unsuccessful or if they want additional children. Otherwise they are usually destroyed. Some people are opposed to IVF primarily because it produces pre-embryos that are then discarded.

Access to IVF

Unusual cases often find their way into the newspaper headlines, and unusual cases involving *in vitro* fertilization are no exception. In 1995 in Italy, a woman in her early 60s gave birth to a healthy baby boy, with the help of donor eggs and her husband's sperm. She decided to try IVF after the death of their 17-year-old son and after they were told that they were too old to adopt. Such a case inevitably raises questions. Should there be age limits on couples seeking IVF? Moreover, should there be any restrictions about motivation? In the Italian case, the woman gave her new baby the same name as her deceased son. In another case in 1995, a black woman in Italy with a husband of mixed race obtained IVF using the eggs of a white woman. One of the reasons she gave was her belief that a light-skinned child would have an easier time in life than a dark-skinned one, given the existence of racism. Again, questions about motivation immediately arise.

What interest, if any, does the state have in regulating such IVF? Although we might raise questions about the motives of the women mentioned in the preceding paragraph, we could certainly raise questions about the motives of many parents, and yet that is not sufficient grounds for state intervention. The situation changes significantly if public money is used to finance such procedures; but as long as they are done with private funds, it seems that the state has little basis for questioning the motivation of the couples involved.

Conflicting Claims: The Embryos of Divorcing Couples

One of the more perplexing issues arising out of the fact that embryos can—at least temporarily—exist outside the mother's womb is that couples, when in the process of divorcing, make competing claims for custody of the embryos. Usually, such embryos are frozen and this allows such battles to be protracted. Several issues are intertwined here.

The first of these issues is the moral status of the pre-embryo, which we have already considered. If the pre-embryo has the moral status of a person, then it has a right to life. If one member of the couple wants the embryos destroyed, this would not be morally permissible if they have a right to life. If, on the other hand, they do not yet have this moral status, then destroying embryos would be morally permissible.

Second, what kind of rights and responsibilities do the genetic parents have toward the embryo as *parents?* Is it a relationship of ownership? Of parenthood? In the case of one divorcing couple, the woman wanted possession of the embryos to have them implanted in herself and to bring them to term. The divorcing husband did not want to be the (genetic) father, with its accompanying responsibilities, when he and his wife were getting a divorce. Does the wife have the right to go ahead and have the embryos implanted? Does the husband have the right to have the embryos destroyed because he no longer wants to be their father? What role should the courts play in settling such disputes?

Conservative Objections to IVF

Some critics of the current rise in IVF recognize that it may be effective in achieving its goal, but that it ought not to be used anyway. Several motives come into play in such criticisms.

Religiously based critiques of assisted reproduction.   Many religious traditions are profoundly opposed to the development of reproductive technologies. At its deepest level, just as we have seen in our discussion of abortion, this view questions the technological society's presumption that we can control our destiny. Instead, it believes that our fates are ultimately in divine hands, and that intrusive technological procedures are *hubris.*

The second principal concern within religious traditions is that reproductive technologies almost always involve manipulating and destroying embryos. Embryos, many religious thinkers maintain, are persons and thus are not the proper objects of manipulation. Certainly, it is immoral to destroy them. Because IVF almost inevitably involves such destruction of embryos, many religious thinkers believe it should be condemned.

Anti-technology critiques of assisted reproduction.   Not all critics of assisted reproduction are motivated solely by religious concerns. Many are concerned with the way in which technology distorts the reproductive process, as our selection from Paul Lauritzen, "What Price Parenthood?," indi-

The debate unfolded over the week of March 18–22, with each participant responding within hours of the other's posting. Readers interested in more information can visit www.reason.com/biclone.shtml, which includes links to *Reason*'s voluminous coverage of cloning and biotechnology. Of special interest is "Criminalizing Science," in which a transpartisan coalition of thinkers and commentators respond to a left–right alliance to outlaw "therapeutic cloning" and stigmatize genetic research.

Go Ahead and Clone

Gregory Stock: "Don't cause real damage to assuage phantom fears."

There has been a lot of hand wringing recently about cloning. Considering that not a single viable cloned human embryo has yet been created, that the arrival of a clinical procedure to do so seems quite distant, and that having a delayed identical twin (which is, after all, what a clone is) has limited appeal, why all the fuss?

The fuss arises because cloning has become a proxy for broader fears about the new technologies emerging from our unraveling of human biology. Critics like Francis Fukuyama imagine that if we can stop cloning we can head off possibilities like human enhancement, but they're dreaming. As we decipher our biology and learn to modify it, we are learning to modify ourselves—and we will do so. No laws will stop this.

Embryo selection, for example, is a mere spin-off from widely supported medical research of a sort that leaves no trail and is feasible in thousands of labs throughout the world. Any serious attempt to block such research will simply increase the potential dangers of upcoming technologies by driving the work out of sight, blinding us to early indications of any medical or social problems.

The best reason not to curb interventions that many people see as safe and beneficial, however, is not that such a ban would be dangerous but that it would be wrong. A ban would prevent people from making choices aimed at improving their lives that would hurt no one. Such choices should be allowed. It is hard for me to see how a society that pushes us to stay healthy and vital could justify, for instance, trying to stop people from undergoing a genetic therapy or consuming a drug cocktail aimed at retarding aging. Imposing such a ban requires far more compelling logic than the assertion that we should not play God or that, as Fukuyama has suggested, it is wrong to try to transcend a "natural" human life span.

What's more, a serious effort to block beneficial technologies that might change our natures would require policies so harsh and intrusive that they would cause far greater harm than is feared from the technologies themselves. If the War on Drugs, with its vast resources and sad results, has been unable to block people's access to deleterious substances, the government has no hope of withholding access to technologies that many regard as beneficial. It would be a huge mistake to start down this path, because even without aggressive enforcement, such bans would effectively reserve the technologies for the affluent and privileged. When abortion was illegal in various states, the rich did not suffer; they just traveled to more-permissive locales.

Restricting emerging technologies for screening embryos would feed deep class divisions. Laboratories can now screen a six-cell human embryo by teasing out a single cell, reading its genes, and letting parents use the results to decide whether to implant or discard the embryo. In Germany such screening is criminal. But this doesn't deny the technology to affluent Germans who want it: They take a trip to Brussels or London, where it is legal. As such screenings become easier and more informative, genetic disease could be gradually relegated to society's disadvantaged. We need to start thinking about how to make the tests more, not less, accessible.

But let's cut to the chase. If parents can easily and safely choose embryos, won't they pick ones with predispositions toward various talents and temperaments, or even enhanced performance? Of course. It is too intrusive to have the government second-guessing such decisions. British prohibitions of innocuous choices like the sex of a child are a good example of undesirable government intrusion. Letting parents who strongly desire a girl (or boy) be sure to have one neither injures the resulting child nor causes gender imbalances in Western countries.

Sure, a few interventions will arise that virtually everyone would find troubling, but we can wait until actual problems appear before moving to control them. These coming reproductive technologies are not like nuclear weapons, which can suddenly vaporize large numbers of innocent bystanders. We have the luxury of feeling our way forward, seeing what problems develop, and carefully responding to them.

The real danger we face today is not that new biological technologies will occasionally cause injury but that opponents will use vague, abstract threats to our values to justify unwarranted political incursions that delay the medical advances growing out of today's basic research. If, out of concern over cloning, the U.S. Congress succeeds in criminalizing embryonic stem cell research that might bring treatments for Alzheimer's disease or diabetes—and Fukuyama lent his name to a petition supporting such laws—there would be real victims: present and future sufferers from those diseases.

We should hasten medical research, not stop it. We are devoting massive resources to the life sciences not out of idle curiosity but in an effort to penetrate our biology and learn to use this knowledge to better our lives. We should press ahead. Of course, the resultant technologies will pose challenges: They stand to revolutionize health care and medicine, transform great swaths of our economy, alter the way we conceive our children, change the way we manage our moods, and even extend our life spans.

The possibilities now emerging will force us to confront the question of what it means to be a human being. But however uneasy these new technologies make us, if we wish to continue to lead the way in shaping the human future we must actively explore them. The challenging question facing us is: Do we have the courage to continue to embrace the possibilities ahead, or will we succumb to our fears and draw back, leaving this exploration to braver souls in other regions of the world?

Sensible Restrictions

Francis Fukuyama: "There are good reasons to regulate future biotechnologies."

Gregory Stock offers two sets of arguments against restricting future biotechnologies: first, that such rules are unnecessary as long as reproductive choices are being made by individual parents rather than states, and second, that they cannot be enforced and will be ineffective even if they were to be enacted. Let me respond to each in turn.

While genetic choices made by parents (either in the short run, via pre-implantation genetic diagnosis, or in the more distant future, through germline engineering) are on the whole likely to be better than those made by coercive states, there are several grounds for not letting individuals have complete freedom of choice in this regard.

The first two are utilitarian. When we get into human germline engineering, in which modifications will be passed on to successive generations, safety problems will multiply exponentially over what we today experience with drug approval. Genetic causation is highly complex, with multiple genes interacting to create one outcome or behavior and single genes having multiple effects. When a long-term genetic effect may not show up for decades after the procedure is administered, parents will risk a multitude of unintended and largely irreversible consequences for their children. This would seem to be a situation calling for strict regulation.

A second utilitarian concern has to do with possible negative externalities, which is the classic ground for state regulation, accepted by even the most orthodox free market economists. An example is sex selection. Today in Asia, as a result of cheap sonograms and abortion, cohorts are being born with extremely lopsided sex ratios—117 boys for every 100 girls in China and at one point 122 boys for every 100 girls in Korea. Sex selection is rational from the standpoint of individual parents, but it imposes costs on society as a whole in terms of the social disruption that a large number of unattached and unmarriageable young males can produce. Similar negative externalities can arise from individual choices to, for example, prolong life at the cost of a lower level of cognitive and physical functioning.

A further set of concerns about the ability to "design" our children has to do with the ambiguity of what constitutes improvement of a human being, particularly when we get into personality traits and emotional makeup. We are the product of a highly complex evolutionary adaptation to our physical and social environment, which has created an equally complex whole human being. Genetic interventions made out of faddishness, political correctness, or simple whim might upset that balance in ways that we scarcely understand—in the interest, for example, of making boys less violent and aggressive, girls more assertive, people more or less competitive, etc. Would an African American's child be "improved" if we could genetically eliminate his or her skin pigmentation?

The final issue concerns human nature itself. Human rights are ultimately derived from human nature. That is, we assign political rights to ourselves based on our understanding of the ways members of our species are similar to one another and different from other species. We are fortunate to be a relatively homogenous species. Earlier views that blacks were not intelligent enough to vote, or that women were too emotional to be granted equal political rights, proved to be empirically false. The final chapter of Greg Stock's book opens up the prospect of a future world in which this human homogeneity splinters, under the impact of genetic engineering, into competing human biological kinds. What kind of politics do we imagine such a splintering will produce? The idea that our present-day tolerant, liberal, democratic order will survive such changes is farfetched: Nietzsche, not John Stuart Mill or John Rawls, should be your guide to the politics of such a future.

Stock's second set of arguments is based on his belief that no one can stop this technology. He is certainly right that if some future biotechnology proves safe, cheap, effective, and highly desirable, government would not be able to stop it and probably should not try. What I am calling for, however, is not a ban on wide swaths of future technology but rather their strict regulation in light of the dangers outlined above.

Today we regulate biomedical technology all the time. People can argue whether that technology is properly regulated and where exactly to draw various regulatory lines. But the argument that procedures that will be as potentially unsafe and ethically questionable as, say, germline engineering for enhancement purposes cannot in principle be regulated has no basis in past experience.

We slow the progress of science today for all sorts of ethical reasons. Biomedicine could advance much faster if we abolished our rules on human experimentation in clinical trials, as Nazi researchers did, and allowed doctors to deliberately inject infectious substances into their subjects. Today we enforce rules permitting the therapeutic use of drugs like Ritalin, while prohibiting their use for enhancement or entertainment.

The argument that these technologies will simply move to more favorable jurisdictions if they are banned in any one country may or may not carry weight; it all depends on what they are and what the purpose of the regulation is. I regard a ban on reproductive cloning to be analogous to current legislation banning incest, which is based on a similar mix of safety and ethical considerations. The purpose of such a ban would not be undermined if a few rich people could get themselves cloned outside the country. In any event, the world seems to be moving rather rapidly toward a global ban on reproductive cloning. The fact that the Chinese may not be on board shouldn't carry much weight; the Chinese also involuntarily harvest organs from executed prisoners and are hardly an example we would want to emulate.

I don't think that a set of regulations designed to focus future biomedicine on therapeutic rather than enhancement purposes constitutes oppressive state intervention or goes so far beyond the realm of what is done today that we can declare its final failure in advance. By Greg Stock's reasoning, since rules against doping in athletic competitions don't work 100 percent of the time, we should throw them out altogether and have our athletes compete not on the basis of their natural abilities but on the basis of who has the best pharmacologist. I'd rather watch and participate in competitions of the old-fashioned kind.

Biotech Tyranny

Gregory Stock: "Banning enhancement would be massively invasive."

I have no problem with attempts to address serious externalities that arise from otherwise harmless personal activities. But if government does not bear a heavy burden of proof when justifying such intrusions into our lives, it can employ vague arguments about social harm to take away our basic freedoms. Francis Fukuyama would push us toward just such intrusions by erecting a powerful regulatory structure charged with ensuring the ethical and social desirability of future technologies.

Fukuyama is so suspicious of change in general and new technology in particular that he won't even acknowledge the desirability of allowing people to use safe and beneficial interventions that would almost certainly improve their lives. He will admit only that if a technology is "safe, cheap, effective, and highly desirable," government "probably [my emphasis] should not try" to stop it. If he won't even embrace technologies that meet this high threshold, he would never allow the far more problematic possibilities of the real world. But facing such possibilities is precisely what has improved our health and raised our standard of living so greatly during the last century.

Fukuyama speaks of safety, but his reluctance about even safe and highly desirable technologies suggests that his major concern is neither safety nor aberrant misuse. Moreover, he admits that these dangers are well covered by existing agencies and institutions. He makes his primary focus explicit in his book when he complains that the Food and Drug Administration is charged only with establishing "safety and efficacy," while we need institutions that can look at ethical consequences.

For the most part, Fukuyama is vague when it comes to precisely what we should prevent. This may be good strategy, because notions of safety, caution, and minimized externalities are so appealing. But it is deceptive because it is in the details that the rubber meets the road.

In fairness, Fukuyama is specific about banning human cloning, which in today's climate is about as risky as coming out for motherhood. His reasoning here is faulty, however. To liken a blanket ban on reproductive cloning to a ban on incest is not even fathomable if one considers the cloning of a deceased child or someone other than the parent. But as I said, cloning is a sideshow.

A more interesting situation is sex selection. I argued that in the U.S. such selection—which can be done by sorting sperm, so that no embryos are destroyed—is innocuous. Sex selection does not harm children; indeed, it likely benefits them when a child of the "wrong" sex would seriously disappoint his or her parents. Fukuyama brings up the lopsided sex ratio in China, but this does not justify regulating the practice here, where such imbalances do not arise from the practice. Moreover, the problem in China is hardly an argument for government regulation, since sex selection there has long been illegal. Indeed, government regulation in China—namely, its one-child policy—exacerbates the problem of gender balance by pushing parents who want a boy toward aborting a girl, since they can't try again. Fukuyama opposes sex selection here and has proposed the formation of a review board like the one in Britain that has barred this procedure. But does he have anything better to offer than a fear that the practice would be a step down a slippery slope? If he sees a serious externality to sex selection in the U.S., it would be worth hearing about.

In response to my comments about the obvious appeal and benefit of future anti-aging medications, Fukuyama points out that "negative externalities can arise from individual choices to . . . prolong life at the cost of a lower level of cognitive and physical functioning." This is true, but it is a frightening basis for legislation (as opposed to decisions regarding government funding). I shudder to think about regulatory boards tasked with balancing the additional years that an individual seeks against the social cost of those years. To see the peril, we need only apply Fukuyama's logic to medicine generally.

If he does not want to allow interventions to slow the onset of aging and bring longer lives of relative health (though presumably not matching the vitality of youth), then why not block all treatments for the aged and debilitated? Their extra years are a net cost, and withholding medical treatment for those over 65 would work wonders for our ailing Social Security system. It isn't much of a step to go even further and block medical interventions that save accident victims who suffer crippling injuries.

Fukuyama no doubt feels that a sharp line between therapy and enhancement will avoid such perversions, but this distinction does not stand up to scrutiny. This line will increasingly blur in the years ahead. Anti-aging interventions, for example, fall in a large realm that is best labeled therapeutic enhancement. If we could gain an extra decade by strengthening our immune system or our anti-oxidation and cellular repair mechanisms, this would clearly be a human enhancement. But it would also be a preventive therapy, because it would delay cardiovascular disease, senile dementia, cancer, and other illnesses of aging, which we spend billions trying to treat.

Banning enhancement from sports competitions can obviously be justified as a way of enforcing the agreed-upon rules of the game. But neither Fukuyama nor our democratic political institutions have a recognized right to set the rules of life. Outlawing a whole realm of benefits that are not injuring others is not just impractical; it is tyranny. Enhancement is not wrong, and when such possibilities become safe and reliable large numbers of people will seek them. Fukuyama is right about the ambiguities of "improvement," but I have not suggested some grandiose government project that seeks human perfection. I have spoken only of freely made parental choices, and I argue that such choices are likely to lead toward great diversity.

I do not argue that parents need no oversight in the use of advanced technology for the conception of children, just that it should be minimal, should address real rather than imagined problems, and should be concerned with the child's safety rather than the social order or the personhood of embryos. When it comes to children, I trust the judgment of individual parents more than that of political or judicial panels. Most parents are deeply concerned with the welfare of their own children, whereas such panels are composed of individuals who are more oriented toward larger social and philosophical concerns than the well-being of particular individuals.

Upholding Norms

Francis Fukuyama: "Our laws should be updated to take account of technological advances."

I think Greg Stock has misunderstood a couple of the points I was trying to make in my initial response. The issue with regard to sex selection is not that it would be a serious problem in this country; it's possible now, after all, but not widely practiced. The point is that individual choice coupled with the spread of cheap biomedical technologies can quickly produce population-level effects with serious social consequences. In other words, the problem with eugenics is not simply that it is state-sponsored and coercive; if practiced by enough individuals, it can also have negative consequences for the broader society.

I suspect that if the U.S. ever gets into something like this in the future, it will have to do with potential "enhancement" targets other than sex. One I speculate about in my book is sexual preference: It seems pretty clear to me that if parents, including ones who are perfectly accepting of gays today, had the choice, they would select against their children being gay, if for no other reason than their desire to have grandchildren. (Contrary to Stock, by the way, gays can't reproduce, so I'm not quite sure how they'd do germ-line intervention to produce gay children.) The proportion of gays in the population could drop quite dramatically, and I'm not at all sure that society as a whole (let alone gays as a persecuted minority) would be enhanced as a result.

Governments can intervene successfully to correct individual choices like these. The severe sex-ratio imbalance in Korea that emerged in the early 1990s was noticed, and the government took measures to enforce existing laws against sex selection so that today the ratio is much closer to 50-50. If the government of a young democracy like Korea can do this, I don't see why we can't.

The reason I noted that life extension coupled with diminished capability can create negative externalities was not to suggest that we should ban or regulate such procedures. Stock is perfectly right that we already have adopted a lot of medical innovations that produce this tradeoff, and that we can't stop future advances for this reason. The reason this is an important issue is that in contemporary debates over stem cells and cloning there is an unquestioned assumption that anything that will prolong life or cure disease is obviously desirable and automatically trumps other ethical concerns.

This is not obvious to me. Anyone who has walked around a nursing home recently (as I have) can see that past advances in biomedicine have created a horrible situation for many elderly people who can't function at anything close to the levels they'd like but who also can't die. Of course, new advances in biotechnology may provide cures for degenerative, age-related diseases such as Alzheimer's or Parkinson's, but the research community is in effect just cleaning up the mess it created. So when we are balancing near-term rights and wrongs, the argument that more medical advance is necessarily good needs to be treated with some skepticism. At the hearing on Florida Republican Dave Weldon's bill banning cloning last summer, a representative of a patients' advocacy group said the baby boomers were getting older and desperately needed cures for a variety of diseases with which they would soon be afflicted—as if research cloning would prevent them from ever having to die. If you want a real nightmare scenario, consider one in which we double life spans but increase periods of debility by a few decades.

Stock is correct in saying that much of my interest in having new regulatory institutions in place has to do with ethical and social consequences of new technology and not simply safety. States intervene all the time to shape norms and produce certain social outcomes. Incest is an example, and it seems to me a very apt analogy to reproductive cloning. Of course, you can find sympathetic situations where an individual might want to clone, say, a dead child. But you can also find sympathetic situations where you might want a brother and sister to marry and have children (e.g., they have grown up apart, have no dangerous recessive genes, etc.).

But the fact that there are certain sympathetic cases does not mean that society would be better off without a ban on incest. The possible benefits of cloning need to be balanced against social harms. Consider the following scenario: A wife decides to clone herself because a couple cannot otherwise have children. As their daughter grows up to be a teenager, the husband will find his wife growing older and less sexually attractive. In the meantime, his daughter, who will be a physical duplicate of her mother, will blossom into sexual maturity and increasingly come to resemble the younger woman the husband fell in love with and married. It is hard to see how this situation would not produce an extremely unhealthy situation within the family; in a certain number of cases, it would lead to incest.

Stock is using a rhetorical ploy in suggesting that I am recommending new, tyrannical government intrusion into private lives. Rather, I am recommending an extension of existing institutions to take account of the new possibilities that will be put before us as a result of technological advance. This may result in regulation irksome to industry and to certain individuals, but it will be no more tyrannical than existing rules banning incest or, in the case of the Koreans, banning sex selection. All societies control social behavior through a complex web of norms, economic incentives, and laws. All I am suggesting is that the law part of the mix will need to be updated and strengthened in light of what is to come.

Clones, Gays, and the Elderly

Gregory Stock: "Overestimating the threats posed by technology—and underestimating the threats posed by regulation."

I'm glad Francis Fukuyama agrees that sex selection here poses no serious threat. To me, this means it should not be regulated. Moreover, we should also hold off on passing legislative protections against other such technologies until actual problems show up. Fukuyama may worry about rapid "population-level effects with serious social consequences," but his example of Korea's success at handling the sex-ratio imbalances that arose there is not an invitation to regulate, but evidence that we can afford to wait.

Outlawing a whole realm of benefits not injurious to others—namely enhancements—would be tyranny. Potent regulatory structures that pass judgment on the morality and social cost of future technologies would move us in this direction. Judging from the composition of President Bush's Bioethics Advisory Commission, many potential regulators would be less moderate than Fukuyama and quite willing to abridge people's choices.

Consider Fukuyama's argument about cloning. It is one thing to worry about the obvious medical dangers of so unproven a technology, another to justify a complete ban with stories about a future father's possible sexual attraction for his wife's budding clone-daughter. Kids hardly need to resemble a parent to inspire incest, as many adoptees and stepchildren can no doubt confirm. If we start regulating families on the basis of hypothetical sexual attractions and perversions—and we can conjure ones more lurid and likely than Fukuyama's clone love—we will ultimately damage rather than protect the family. We have laws governing child abuse; let's content ourselves with enforcing them.

As to gays, if there are fewer in the future because of people's choices about the genetics or rearing of their kids, so be it. But I am not at all convinced it would play out that way. Fukuyama asserts that gays can't reproduce, but they do so all the time using donor eggs or sperm, surrogate mothers, and partners of the opposite sex. Moreover, such reproduction will get ever easier. If we want to be sure to maintain our gay population, additional AIDS research would accomplish more than bans on embryo screening.

I'm glad to hear that Fukuyama doesn't oppose anti-aging interventions; I've previously heard him say only that government would be unable to block such enhancements. He is right, of course, that advances in health care bring many challenges, and that the needless prolongation of a dying loved one's pain and decrepitude is nothing to boast about. But my reaction is not to deny the value of the good added years that modern medicine has brought so many of us, but to recognize that we must find better ways for individuals to reach death with dignity when it draws near. Why must so many of our elderly try to squirrel away a stash of lethal drugs in case they might be captured by a medical system that would torture them for their final few weeks or months? The issue of cloning pales alongside this cruelty.

Fukuyama says he is urging only a harmless extension of existing institutions. I disagree. The relegation of decisions about human reproduction to a political process typically driven by impassioned zealots on either side would invite disaster. New agencies with the power to project abstract philosophy, social theory, and even religious dogma into family life would be a frightening development. And when lawmakers on Capital Hill start telling medical researchers not to do certain types of embryonic stem cell research because adult stem cells will work just as well, something is very wrong. These legislators are micromanaging a realm they do not understand, assaulting our freedom of inquiry, and ignoring the entreaties of those afflicted with serious diseases. These steps are not small.

Nietzschean Endgame

Francis Fukuyama: "Self-enhancement and 'immense wars of the spirit.'"

I think that one of the great virtues of Greg Stock's book is that he is willing to take some risks in predicting what kinds of changes might be in store in the long-run future in terms of enhancement technology. Most people in the scientific community are not willing to speculate out beyond the next five to 10 years. I urge people to read the last chapter of *Redesigning Humans* if you want to understand why I'm worried about biotechnology.

There, Stock suggests a number of things that might happen in a future world in which various forms of enhancement become safe, effective, and inexpensive. Among other things, he suggests that reproduction via sex may disappear altogether as a result of the difficulties of handling artificial chromosomes in vivo. Reproduction could not happen outside a lab. We could freely alter our personalities and moods through a combination of drugs and genetics.

But most importantly, the human race disappears. He suggests that there will be differentiation within our species, and, in effect, new speciation. Some groups of people may decide to enhance their children for musical ability, some for athletic prowess, others for math or literary ability. There will be a basic social divide between the enhanced and the unenhanced, and in the competitive situation that will emerge, it will be difficult for people not to join into this genetic arms race. Moreover, genetic differentiation will become a cornerstone of international politics. If we and the Germans decide not to take part, the Chinese will charge ahead with self-enhancement, and then we as a nation will be challenged to follow suit.

What I don't understand is why anyone thinks that in this kind of world—one in which the existing genetic homogeneity of the human race is being undermined—we will be able to continue to live within the nice, liberal democratic framework that we currently enjoy. Stock argues as if we can presume the continuity of that political world and fully enjoy the technological paradise opening before us, and that the biggest arguments we will have will concern whether we have a little more regulation and less progress, or the reverse.

But as I noted earlier, in this kind of world Nietzsche is the best guide to what politics will be like. What is going to happen to equality of opportunity when a non-musically enhanced child aspires to be a musician, which has become not just the territory of a guild of musicians, but of a subspecies of musicians whose total genetic identity is tied up in that form of life? Why shouldn't the enhanced start demanding superior political rights for themselves, and seek to dominate the unenhanced, since they will in fact be superior not just as a result of acquired social status and education, but of genetic enhancements as well? What is going to happen to international conflict, when other, hostile societies are not just culturally different, but not fully human either?

The fact is that there will be no theoretical or practical reason at that point not to abandon the principle of universal human equality (i.e., the one enshrined in the Declaration of Independence). It is strongly believed in today in part as a matter of faith, but also in part because it is empirically supported. When the principle was enunciated in 1776, blacks and women were not granted political rights in North America because it was believed that they were too stupid, or too emotional, or otherwise lacking in some essential human characteristic to be granted equal rights. This view resurfaced as scientific racism in the early 20th century, and one of the great achievements of our time is that both the empirical doctrine and the politics built on it have been discredited.

So if we are going to embrace this technology and the prospect of human self-enhancement, we ought to do it with our eyes open. We should say, with Nietzsche, that this is a wonderful opportunity because we can finally transcend liberal democracy, and reestablish the possibility of natural aristocracy, of social hierarchy, of the pathos of distance (i.e., the inability to empathize with the suffering of others), and otherwise usher in an era of "immense wars of the spirit."

As I said, I'm grateful that Greg Stock has clarified all of these issues for us.

Journal/Discussion Questions

1. Do Stock and Fukuyama have factual disagreements about the state of current technology? If so, what are these disagreements?

2. Leaving aside questions of disagreements about factual matters, on what other points do Stock and Fukuyama disagree?

3. Explain the differences between Stock and Fukuyama in regard to government regulation and intervention.

Glenn McGee
"Parenting in an Era of Genetics"

Glenn McGee is the Associate Director of the Center for Bioethics at the University of Pennsylvania. He is the author of numerous works in bioethics, including Beyond Genetics: Putting the Power of DNA to Work in Your Life *(New York: William Morrow, 2003) and* The Perfect Baby: Parenthood in the New World of Cloning and Genetics, *2nd ed. (Latham: Rowman & Littlefield, 2000).*

In this article, McGee explores the various ways in which the road to human enhancement is paved with some deadly (and no-so-deadly) sins that ought to be avoided: calculativeness, overbearingness, shortsightedness, hasty judgment, and pessimism.

As You Read, Consider This:

1. McGee discusses five deadly sins that form dangers on the road to genetic enhancement. Explain the principal problem McGee finds with each of these five dangers.

2. Why does McGee maintain that "bioethicists' conversation about expensive and sophisticated genetic technologies must be connected to public conversations about parenthood"? How does he develop this theme throughout his article?

Lately it seems a whole commercial culture and social conversation has grown up around "enhancements." Some are quite controversial: Prozac and other antidepressants have been increasingly reported to be performance-enhancers, and, as Peter Kramer points out, are even prescribed for that purpose.[1] Lawrence Diller's recent essay highlights an increase in enhancement-based rationale for use of the stimulant Ritalin, originally prescribed to combat attention deficit disorder.[2] Some enhancements only barely raise our collective ire, such as the now well-established use of cosmetic surgery to modify appearance, the selection of offspring gender, or the sale of "genius" germ-line cells by one California sperm bank. Still others seem uncontroversial, or seem not to count as "enhancements" at all, such as the use of private schools, vaccinations, and vitamin supplements.

Hastings Center Report, Vol. 27, no. 2 (1997), pp. 16–24.

Bioethicists have attempted to draw distinctions between enhancements and the conventional development of genetically determined potential, and to differentiate enhancement from restoration or therapy. In the former case, struggling for a rationale as to why cosmetic surgery is fundamentally different from and more objectionable than a new haircut, Kathy Davis argues that through cosmetic surgery patients attempt to change the kind of person that they are.[3] In the latter case, Norman Daniels and others attempt to distinguish enhancement from therapy or restoration with an idea they term "species-typical functioning."[4] In an era of limited resources, species-typical functioning is the attempt to divine from aggregate medical data and data "in society a theoretical account of the design of the organism" that describes "the natural functional organization of a typical member of the species." Bringing an organism to within species-typical parameters is therapy or restoration, while improving on those norms is enhancement.

Elsewhere I argue at length that attempts to distinguish between conventional development of potential and artificial enhancement rely on an outmoded account of human nature and of genetic causality, and that species-typical functioning misses the point that health and illness are experienced and defined in terms of their meaning in human social experience.[5] Parents and others engage in a variety of attempts to enhance human life, and the important differences between these enhancements seem tied to their social context. In the present essay I focus on the ethical implications of genetic enhancement in parenting. The reason for this focus is partially technological: many current and proposed genetic services will primarily, or first, be useful in a reproductive context or for children. For example, most genetic tests have immediate implications for would-be parents. As tests, technologies, and gene therapies begin to move into the less conventional realm of improvement, parents will be the first to make choices about the best means and most appropriate ends of enhancement. My reasoning is also personal. Parenthood can feel like a laboratory in enhancement. All of us with children experience the pressure to develop the life of an infant, a young person, a young adult. Children present themselves to us as so many interwoven needs: for support, for care, for attention. The struggle to parent feels like a perilous and wonderful dance as we balance the need to transmit and inculcate values and culture with the need to give children what Joel Feinberg terms "an open future." As we make choices about our children, we pick up some cultural lessons that work not only for mundane parental decision-making but also for the radical possibility of making, perhaps sooner than we think, some systematic choices about the enhancement of our children through genetic technologies.

It may turn out, in this quest for some social improvement, that genes are among the least effective tools for advancing personal, familial, and social goals. Technical failings in all previously initiated trials of gene therapy suggest that our powers to induce genetic modification have perhaps been exaggerated. Is it likely that even an effective genetic therapy would revamp the human species? Not especially nor is it likely, conversely, that altered genes will destroy our human natures. Conventional social institutions, such as schools and churches, have a much more immediate effect on who we become, and we "conventional" parents can botch up child-making quite well without gene therapy.

There is plenty, though, to be frightened about when conversation turns to eugenics. The fear is not of genetic control but of socially prescribed blueprints of perfection, enforced by intolerant scientists-cum-bureaucrats. We have seen the results in our own century, and can at least glean from the misadventures chronicled by Daniel Kevles and others that a scientifically styled "perfect society," stratified by genes, makes little sense in a world where genetic variability turns out to be a virtue—and in which specialization and rigidity spell extinction. There are also plenty of practical examples of the danger of replacing parental responsibility with overarching social control.[6]

How then can we put history's lessons to work in making responsible use of our social aim of improvement? First, we have to separate the dreams of eugenics from the hopes of families. The quest to improve humanity is not mere aberration, the deluded dream of social engineers. The *Newsweek* description of perfection (tall, blonde, powerful, smart children, made-to-order) is shocking, in part, because it is lifted directly from fashion magazines and television. Our culture pursues notions of perfection, from eye color to weight to "swagger." We invest billions of dollars in the attempt to make people more intelligent and less aggressive. We call this attempt public education. As with eugenics, the goal of education is to design and inculcate skills and norms in the behaviors of offspring, from sexual mores through beliefs about history to respect for the law. Athletic activity and school lunches are designed so that children will grow up to be stronger, more capable, and smarter. Those who do not perform well in school are "failed," and miss out on college, better paying work, or social success. That families and the social order should abandon the aim at the improvement of children is unthinkable. Libraries, nutritional and environmental regulations, and the matrix of social and political institutions we have crafted testify to the necessity of this goal.

Because we make big social blunders, our programs, visionary plans, and political ambitions often do not provide the New World Order that is promised. Great plans for our children's futures can also be doomed by shortsightedness, avarice, and cowardice, or merely turn out to be unworkable or inapplicable to environmental and cultural conditions. Nonetheless, the hope for continuing improvement, "making the world better for our children," remains central to human progress and is present in the rhetoric of markets, politics, religion, and even medicine. We learn from our mistakes and work for a better future. Thus the deadly and not-so-deadly sins[7] we need to avoid along the road to enhancement are not all related to genes, test tubes, or the Nazis. The five I explore here are instead sins we learn to avoid as parents and social stewards: Calculativeness, Overbearingness, Shortsightedness, Hasty Judgment, and Pessimism.

The Sin of Calculativeness

Consider, for a moment, your memories of childhood. Parents (or guardians) send children thousands of messages about appropriate behavior, communicating their hopes and fears. Some give an inordinate amount of advice and counseling.[8] Some even set up elaborate systems of rules and procedures to instill certain habits and values. You might have been awarded two dollars for mowing the lawn, cleaning your room, and washing the dishes. You might have lost your driving or entertaining privileges for misbehaving. These thoughtful, organized systems provide a network of beliefs and structure the developmental environment. But they are not the whole experience of being a child. In fact, you may have learned much more from the character, rules, and goals of your parents by watching what they in fact did than by obeying or disobeying the rules they set for you. Or, the most vital and formative experiences of your childhood may not have had anything at all to do with the detailed plans that your parents agonized over. A brief, unpredictable outburst from a parent may outweigh years of regimented education. The sudden death of a grandparent or parent may change the entire family ethos. We commit the sin of calculativeness when we overemphasize the importance of planning and systematic choices in parenthood.

Like most sins, calculativeness is as much impractical as it is immoral. It is extraordinarily difficult to know what actions and words will register in the minds of our children. How will the whole package fit together: the way we treat them, the food we feed them, the genes we give them, and the rules we set for them? The most complex and sophisticated plans for a child's future can turn out to be the least effective, and we may send messages that are much more mixed than we know.

At times, we cannot even be sure what we want for (and from) our children. Children can be instruments in our own efforts to work out our childhood insecurities, ambitions, and fears. Our own frustrated effort to get to Harvard may become our child's yoke. The abuse of a father becomes a son's abuse of his own child. The approval of friends and neighbors can influence the way that we dress and teach our children. Parents can effortlessly create tortuous paradigms that children are expected to meet.

Our beliefs about the "perfection" of our expected child may be much simpler or grander than we can articulate. The hopeful, infertile couple who expresses the fervent wish for any biological child, saying "all we want is a healthy baby" may not be fully conscious of the reasons why they seek not only health but also biological relation. A father who spends weeks teaching baseball to his son might actually prefer (at some deeper and more inarticulate level) that he and his son be able to have a nice conversation, or share a common goal. Because parenting is subtle, sophisticated, and enormously complicated, it is not at all surprising that we should be unaware of our own motivations—or even that we should act in ways contrary to our deeply held desires. Parenting habits are as complex as any human patterns of behavior, and can be malleable or rigid, conscientious or the thoughtless repetition of our own parents' behaviors.

Though genetic tests and therapies may not have the capacity to advance the intelligence and attractiveness of our children, faith in the efficacy of genetic technologies could lead parents to de-emphasize important parts of parental responsibility. In addition, a faith in genetic modifications of offspring could encourage the emphasis by parents on narrow, artificially defined traits. Parents could have hopes of transmitting, in a simple and systematic way, all of the currently fashionable traits to their children, relying on the common images of "perfection" in the public. These images of perfection are not taken from the dreams of dictators or science-fiction novels. They are present in advertisements, polls, television programs, and movies.[9] The perfect baby of *Cosmopolitan* or *Men's Health* might grow to be six feet tall, 185 pounds, and disease-free. His IQ is 150, with special aptitudes in biomedical science. He has blonde hair, blue eyes. He is aggressive and can play NFL football, NHL hockey, and NBA basketball, but also enjoys poetry and fine wine.

The parent who opts for such systematic control over the creation of a child puts faith in the ability of "genetic parenthood" to create a child that has particular traits. The more ordinary ways of parenting offer no such systematic options. The hereditary possibilities in "conventional" parenthood revolve around a mixture of similarities (traits already in our family), over which we have little control. Will she have my ears or hers? Our toes? We don't know, and we have little control over the answer. By contrast, genetic parenthood seems to offer a different kind of control. Here, parents could utterly abandon similarities, replacing them with choices that are reasoned in advance. If we thought that we could systematically impart an IQ of 150 instead of whatever mental traits we carry, we might opt to change our hereditary gift.

The "sin" of these calculated choices is not rooted in the idea that they might actually work, giving our kids 150 IQs or the appearances of gods. That much is unlikely to emerge from the polymerase chain reaction, gene-splicing, and vector technology of 1997, and may be conceptually impossible for reasons we described above. The sin is in understanding a child to be the result of systematic choices, and thus allowing genetic choices to define the child's telos. The faith that genetic enhancements can alter character (removing homosexuality or increasing thoughtfulness) lends itself to a parenthood of oppressive control. Parents that choose traits as calculative consumers might come to devalue the essential connections of relatedness and sameness in the family relationship.

Though it may not be articulated in the fashion of the day, parents also want their children to be like themselves. This is evidenced by the celebration of every child as a "perfect" child, beautiful and appropriate exactly because it represents the particular union of two particular people.[10] We share names and houses and values with our children, as well as important biological and cultural habits. The essential fact of this sharing is not its biological element. Adoptive parents also appreciate similarities in their children, and secure it through familial patterns of value-transmission. The sharing of similarities among members of a family could be diluted by genetic choices. A parent who is expecting a "brilliant child" could value that child only for her accomplishments, rather than for her struggles and growth.

And there is the problem of efficacy in our calculations: whatever our social goals, the likelihood of achieving them through genetic interventions does—or should—figure in calculations about how to spend money. This propensity should then be measured against other means of dealing with the problem. In the case of intelligence, it is amazing that we are willing to spend millions of dollars on the search for genes that code for calculative efficiency, while Head Start programs go unfunded, teachers are underpaid and overworked, and even smart kids graduate ill prepared for the job market and uninspired by democracy.

The Sin of Being Overbearing

Hans Jonas and Joel Feinberg refer to a child's right to be open to as much freedom of identity as possible. They fear that genetic engineering, by stylizing children along the lines of rigid parental expectations, could steal this right. Children would be born into a world where their ultimate choices have been made by parents before the moment of their birth. While Jonas's fear hinges, in part, on the power of genetics to accomplish this feat, his insistence on children's continuing need for freedom is important. Generic expectations, we noted above, could carry tremendous weight, as parents hope that children will become the sort of person whom they engineered. Already, parents who use in vitro fertilization technologies to implant the sperm of especially intelligent or athletic donors have expressed expectations of greatness from such children, insisting on endless piano lessons or daily tennis practice.

How do we distinguish between responsible hopes and overbearing ambitions in reproductive enhancement? A pragmatic answer begins with the recognition of essential continuity between hopes connected to genetic engineering and everyday hopes. The parent who wants a beautiful ballerina will want one whether or not genetic technologies are in the picture. Likewise, parents whose guiding motivation is that a child find and pursue some kind of flourishing career will be reluctant to use genetic improvements or conventional means of overdetermining identity through reproduction. The decisions of parenthood are not always explicit, and take place in a social context, so that parents are constantly exposed to suggestions from all quarters about the kind of baby that is "good." Fortunately, there are also extensive pressures in society that push for the maintenance of randomness and the celebration of hereditary difference. The sentiment that each baby is "perfect" conveys this pressure, as does the choice many parents make to refuse unnecessary ultrasound exams, waiting to see about a baby's gender until birth.

We have to emphasize the responsibility that comes with new information before we spill it onto the table and write it into the chart. Parents must ask themselves of each new test and procedure, "Why do I want to know about X?" Honest answers may turn up more than parental curiosity. If tests for gender, intelligence, and other traits cultivate a parental mentality in which traits take center stage, it pays to consider the danger of such planning and expectations. However, as J. S. Mill, William James, and Derek Parfit have made so plain, there must be tolerance to different ways of approaching human natures. Wherever tests and procedures do not compromise the child, plural approaches to genetic modifications must be allowed. No simple, single solution will work. It makes no sense, and is generally counterproductive, to issue wholesale policy restrictions of any genetic research that is "positive" or "enhancing" in character.

Experiments in biological engineering must be tempered by respect for diversity and for each individual child. Overbearing parents can reduce the child to an instrument of their own ambitions or insecurities. This is no more appropriate when exercised through genetic technologies than when implemented by a parent who insists that a child accompany him to Klan meetings or refuse appropriate medical treatment in the name of religious beliefs a child cannot endorse. Children must be allowed to imagine and grow, and the balance to be struck is between instilling the values that parents hold and allowing the growth that could pull children away from those values. The desire for sameness can be a crippling expression of parental ego, just as the desire for a fashionably beautiful child can express self-loathing in the parent. The key is to avoid extreme measures through biological or any other means, and to temper decisions before birth with the recognition that every child has a right to make some decisions about her own identity.

The Sin of Shortsightedness

As much as we plan for and anticipate the future, we cannot be sure what our children should or will become. We simply cannot anticipate the world of tomorrow. Within the past decade, an empire has been destroyed, Europe has formed an economic alliance, genetic testing has been developed, and computer speed has increased 10,000-fold. Economic and political prophets failed to predict a major market crash, the United States went to war with a third world country, and a U.S. physician began an assisted suicide delivery service. Fashions have changed, as have language, science, philosophy, psychology, and secondary education. Our heroes have also changed: Alan Alda was in, then out; George Bush moved from an 80 percent to 34 percent approval rating in less than a year. What will the next decade, a mere ten years in the life of a child, hold in store? If you think you know, odds are you have a shortsightedness problem. Which is fine, unless it becomes the basis for designing your descendants.

One advantage of the conventional uncertainties in parenting is that just about all of our rules and practices can be changed to fit the exigencies of a changing world. For example, business schools grew to their apex during the early 1980s, then began to shrink as fewer employers recruited business majors. Savvy students quickly transferred from "entrepreneurship" into the humanities and environmental sciences. Parents with stubborn, outmoded commitments to business school for their kids ended up with unemployed progeny or children on Prozac. Younger children are even more malleable than college students, and infants will accept the most conditioning of all. A child is receptive to language, math, rules, values, and abstract ideas. If conditions change, a child adapts. One danger of genetic engineering for positive traits, then, is the sin of shortsightedness: how can we know which traits to lock in through genetics in a world where fashions fade quickly and rigidity is a disadvantage?

An intelligent approach will militate against hasty and acontextual decisions. Just as it is difficult to plan the inculcation of values and character in children, hard to know what action or word will register, so too is it difficult to single out characteristics that will make a child's life better. In the first edition of Mueller's *Out of the Night,* one of the most important eugenic treatises, the geneticist favored breeding children who embodied the traits of Lenin and Marx. In his later lectures, Lenin was dropped for Descartes; Marx for Lincoln. Political currency plays a role in our nations of perfection.

When we examine contemporary genetic optimists' plans for a gradual but total revision of human natures, what is most striking is their confidence that we already have the wisdom to select the best traits. Like Plato, writers such as Leroy Hood and Brian Stableford assume that human natures are immutable and determined prior to birth, so that genetic engineers have merely to figure out how to manipulate stable biological materials in order to accomplish wondrous things.[11] A human with scales and gills would help us to live in the sea, Stableford writes, where we would be able to exploit its unending resources. But to which oceans does Stableford refer? We have turned much of the sea into a colossal dump for industrial and commercial waste. How much would we have to give up to live in this deep, dark ocean? Why would we want to live there? The description of genetic engineering as a one-stop shop for human improvement sometimes depends on wildly unrealistic political and scientific plans. Such grand schemes are not only difficult from a genetic standpoint, they can simply be icons of poorly thought-through political visions for human growth.

A parent who desires a smart child might actually be able, at some point, to increase the calculative speed of that child's brain. At present, scientists often compare the power of our minds to the power of computers. Computers are better when they are faster, so much of this research has focused on a faster brain. In ten years, though, it may turn out that calculative speed is a hindrance to thoughtfulness, imagination, and vision. A child could thus be robbed of the ability to adapt and be stuck with a trait that hinders her ability to work with flexibility in the changing world. All this while expected by her parents to be brilliant.

Moreover, it is not always wise to assume that "more of a good thing is better." Genetic diversity has tremendous value because it provides the opportunity for those of many hereditary backgrounds to employ differing approaches toward maximization of the potential of a given environment. If dozens of children were created from the genes of an Einstein, would the world be a better place? Einstein was the product of a particular set of parents, experiences, and inspirations. In suburban Dallas, child of an oil baron, a cloned Einstein might as easily end up driving a truck or selling horizontal drilling rigs. He might live alone and homeless. Even with an optimal environment, young Clonestein would find that his progenitor's approach has been all but replaced by a different mode of analysis, as differing approaches to problems rendered his style of physics less capable of explanation and control in physics.

Just as it is important for parents to allow children to develop in individual ways, there is reason for parental plans to allow for a changing world. Highly directed parental ambitions for children, such as success in a particular sport or with a particular musical instrument, can result in crushed hopes for parent and child. There are only so many slots on college and professional basketball teams, and not many will go to 5′ 7″ men. Only one in a million musicians attends Julliard. It would be no advantage to choose male offspring, which most Americans report that they would, if suddenly 60 percent of live births were male.[12]

Children need support—not pressure—in pursuing their own dreams within the context of family and culture. Diffuse parental hopes are more appropriate. Children need to learn courage and self-esteem, and need to be critical and functionally literate. They should have the support of their parents as they learn and grow.

The Sin of Hasty Judgment

In College Station, Texas, there are acres and acres of "test fields." In these fields the so-called Aggies of Texas A&M see to it that there are more hybridized and genetically engineered crops than in any other region on earth. It is here that the super-tomato was born. Cantaloupes are genetically crossed with watermelons, and cows have been cloned and genetically modified in literally thousands of ways. College Station is also home to amazing new strains of disease, which began to thrive on these same new crops. Genetic engineering in agriculture has been a proving ground for the possibilities of modification of humans. The results are somewhat revealing: genetically engineered fruits and vegetables are frequently much more vulnerable to diseases and parasites, and rarely taste as good as nonhybridized, nonengineered strains.[13] Engineering of plants and animals can also result in the transmission of dangerous materials into the human and animal food supply.

The perfect baby, like perfect soybeans and perfect corn, could turn out to be markedly imperfect. How difficult would it be to live an engineered life? Hans Jonas cautions of the danger of freakish accidents in genetic engineering, of the kind discussed in Cambridge, Massachusetts and at Asilomar. Ironically, the more important accidents may be more likely to occur after the birth of an apparently healthy, improved baby. While medical technologies could make alterations in the physical characteristics of a newborn, we can hardly hope for the viability of those traits in our complex world. For example, wild strawberries have a much better chance of surviving against infection and parasites than engineered strawberries. The reason is that while genetic engineers controlled for particular traits, they could not control for the dozens of conditions that face a strawberry. Wild strawberries pack a variety of genetic habits. These "resistances" help them to have stable interaction with a range of circumstances. A genetically engineered strawberry, on the other hand, is a hit-or-miss proposition, with engineering emphasis placed only on particular traits.

A child who is engineered to possess positive traits might end up suffering unexpected and disastrous ills. It is extremely dangerous to move too quickly in the direction of changing human traits, lest we forget to control, or forget that we can't control, for the vast variety of human environmental conditions. Just as the gene that presumably causes sickle cell anemia codes for resistance to malaria, the gene for sonar hearing might interfere with the genetic pattern that codes for opposable thumbs or sex organs. In a strawberry, such mistakes can lead to new diseases and bad tasting fruit—in a human child, such errors become the sin of hasty judgment, and could be much more catastrophic for families.

There is also a more general point to be gleaned from our recent experience with agricultural engineering. The genetically enhanced tomato was delicious and tender when raised in lab conditions, but turned out to taste rubbery in real life. Seedless watermelons also suffer from diminished flavor. By analogy, imagine the beautiful, intelligent, even-tempered girl developed by genetic engineering. Could she survive in an imperfect world, with bad water and fatty foods? Would others hate or envy her? On paper, genetic engineering's traits look enticing. In practice, the attractiveness of other people is more random and depends on their quirks as well as assets. A perfect child would find the world of imperfection, disease, disasters, and emotions deadly or unsatisfying.

A pragmatic approach urges more cautious progress toward improving humans. Just as parents should promote malleability in their parenting, there must be room for imperfections and developmental choices. The child who is genetically crafted to 1997's models of perfection may find the world of 2014 intolerable. Instead, parents should aim to continue to update their style of parenting to match the demands of natural and social conditions.

This means that some modifications may indeed become advisable, but only on condition of reversibility. It might be to our advantage to have access to Rostand's "built-in cheek headlights" at some point during our lives. However, we would want to insist on the reversibility of the modification and to carefully examine its side-effects prior to clinical trials.

The Sin of Pessimism

In his essay, "The Moral Equivalent of War," William James argues that while war is to be avoided at all costs, humans seem to need to exercise aggression and domination during their lives. He termed the channeling of these powerful impulses into other activities, "the moral equivalent" of war. This notion of moral equivalency is useful here. Reproductive genetic enhancement may present new choices, but these choices are suffused with the "moral equivalence" of activities already present in the context of parenthood. The moral dominion of parenthood creates the context for reproductive genetic interventions. Thus while caution is intelligent, we need not treat genetics as a radically different endeavor, a slippery slope to biological castes and Frankenstein. The categorical opponents of genetic enhancement, Paul Ramsey and Jeremy Rifkin being the most notable, have utilized rigid rules to enforce the sanctity of human genetic coding. Such an ethic does little to guide our actions—it is simply naive in the light of other social pressures to apply scientific results, obtain improvements in life, and have healthy children. Ethics cannot ignore science: the problem with putting the values that are present in our culture to use in our culture is that those values can sometimes be "undermined by the conclusions of modern science."[14]

We also would do well to consider John Dewey's charge that "if intelligent method is lacking, prejudice, the pressure of immediate circumstance, self-interest and class interest, traditional customs, institutions of accidental historical origin, are not lacking, and they tend o take the place of intelligence."[15] For example, the few fetal diagnoses available now are so expensive that only the wealthy use them. As a consequence, a disproportionate number of children with Downs syndrome are "almost certainly born to the less affluent" (p. 583). Our claim that some eugenic selection is already present in social engineering intimates another danger, then, of uncritical genetic research: it may be engineering that benefits only the powerful and wealthy. If society chooses not to concern itself with reproductive enhancement, we too have made a choice: to leave science to the scientists, and its application to political pressure and happenstance. Consider the application of genetic research in its political and economic context: where there are therapies, there will always be pressures on a physician to offer them. The day that a gene for homosexuality is announced is too late for bioethics to put a "spin" on whether or not that gene is useful. We need to join the conversation about appropriate research before it becomes technology.

If pessimism is sinful, though, abject optimism is not its antidote. Even assuming that certain isolable ailments could be dealt with by genetic engineering, the approach to avoiding the not-so-deadly sins must be intelligent and cautious; we work toward developing protocols and therapies experimentally and gradually. This approach takes seriously the caution implicit in the "hands-off" attitude of those who would leave genetics to nature without surrendering the hope to make our condition and our nature better a little at a time. Social conversation concerning the enhancement of children is possible, and technological advancement is desirable in pediatrics. First, though, bioethicists' conversation about expensive and sophisticated genetic technologies must be connected to public conversations about parenthood. This requires us to abandon the search for an exotic ethics of enhancement, and get our hands dirty in the mundane world of the ordinary parents who will make decisions about genetic interventions and the meaning of growth and flourishing in their family and community.

Acknowledgments

The author acknowledges Peter Ubel, Arthur Caplan, Bette-Jane Crigger, Dan Brock, Eric Juengst, James Gustafson, Monica Arruda, and Erik Parens for comments on early drafts, and support from Vanderbilt Center for Social and Political Thought, the University of Iowa, S.U.N.Y. Downstate Medical Center, Miami University, and The Hastings Center project, "On the Prospect of Technologies Aimed at the Enhancement of Human Capacities."

References

1. Peter Kramer, *Listening to Prozac* (New York: HarperCollins, 1994).

2. Lawrence H. Diller, "The Run on Ritalin: Attention Deficit Disorder and Stimulant Treatment in the 1990s," Hastings Center Report 26, No. 2 (1996), p. 12.

3. Kathy Davis, *Reshaping the Female Body: The Dilemma of Cosmetic Surgery* (New York: Routledge, 1995).

4. Norman Daniels, *Just Health Care* (New York: Cambridge University Press, 1986), p. 28.

5. Glenn McGee, *The Perfect Baby: A Pragmatic Approach to Genetics* (Lanham: Rowman & Littlefield, 1997).

6. C. K. Chan, "Eugenics on the Rise: A Report from Singapore," in *Ethics, Reproduction, and Genetic Control,* Ed. Ruth Chadwick (London: Croon Helm, 1987), pp. 210–223.

7. Paul Ramsey also makes mention of deadly sins of a different kind in his *Fabricated Man* (New Haven: Yale University Press, 1970).

8. Obviously, this advice and counsel takes many forms in many different groups, varying with language, folkways, and styles of communication. One parent's advice may come in the form of constant reassurances and encouragement, while another may scold and demean a child when it misbehaves.

9. Susan Bordo, *Unbearable Weight: Feminism, Western Culture, and the Body* (Berkeley: University of California Press, 1993).

10. McGee, *The Perfect Baby.*

11. Brian Stableford, *Future Man* (New York: Crown Publishers, 1984), pp. 13–15.

12. We have only to look at the tragic results of the introduction of ultrasound to India to see what thoughtless application of reproductive technologies can mean. Indian women are forced to abort their female fetuses despite the effect on the population and the women. Thus the very technology that was created to bring more of reproduction under the control of women came to

be an instrument for the oppression of women—it is not the maldistribution of technology that is at issue, but the actual rearticulation of the purposes of that technology.

12. Glenn McGee, "Consumers, Land, and Food: In Search of Food Ethics," in *The Agricultural and Food Sector in the New Global Era,* Ed. A. Bonanno (New Delhi: Concept, 1993); Jack Doyle, *Altered Harvest: Agriculture, Genetics, and the Fate of the World's Food Supply* (New York: Viking, 1985); David Goodman, *From Farming to Biotechnology: A Theory of Agro-Industrial Development* (New York: Basil Blackwell, 1987); and House Hearings, "Field Testing Genetically-Engineered Organisms," Hearing before the Subcommittee on Natural Resources, Agricultural Research, and Environment of the Committee on Science, Space, and Technology, U.S. House of Representatives, One Hundredth Congress, Second Session (Washington, DC: Government Publications Office, 1988).

14. "The Construction of the Good," in *The Philosophy of John Dewey,* Ed. J. McDermott (Chicago: University of Chicago Press, 1981), p. 577.

15. Richard Lewontin, *Biology as Ideology: The Doctrine of DNA* (New York: HarperCollins, 1993).

Journal/Discussion Questions

1. Many people feel that the dangers of genetic enhancement are far outweighed by the potential benefits. What would McGee say to such an argument? How would you evaluate such a claim?

2. Which of the dangers McGee discusses are the most pressing in your view? Why?

3. What role, if any, should the state play in the regulation of genetic enhancements?

F. M. Kamm
"Embryonic Stem Cell Research: A Moral Defense"

Frances M. Kamm is the Littauer Professor of Philosophy and Public Policy, Kennedy School of Government and Professor of Philosophy, Department of Philosophy, Harvard University. She is the author of numerous works including Morality, Mortality *(2 vols., Harvard, 1993, 1994) and* Creation and Abortion *(Oxford, 1992).*

Kamm looks at the principal moral justifications offered for limiting embryonic stem cell research and argues that none of these succeeds in justifying the types of limitations proposed by many conservatives.

As You Read, Consider This:
1. What does Kamm mean by the *Mere Means* thesis? What follows from that thesis?
2. What does Kamm mean by the principle of *Alternate Destruction?*
3. Kamm introduces the No-Potential Solution. What does she mean by this?

Boston Review, Vol. 27, No. 5 (October/November 2002).

4. Kamm argues against *Mere Means, Noncreation,* and *Alternate Destruction.* What arguments does she give against each? Why did she select these three principles to argue against?
5. Kamm introduces a comparison with a magic wand. What is the point of that comparison? Do you agree with her point?

Should scientists seeking to cure human diseases be permitted to use stem cells from human embryos in their research? Proponents of embryonic stem cell (ESC) research emphasize that it may help in finding cures for diabetes, Parkinson's disease, heart disease, Lou Gehrig's disease, and other devastating disabilities and illnesses. Critics acknowledge the possible medical benefits but point out that ESC research destroys embryos. Such destruction, they say, shows insufficient respect for the embryo and, more broadly, insufficient regard for the value of human life. Human embryos, the critics argue, are morally important, and that importance imposes substantial limits on permissible research.

Last summer, President Bush came down close to the critics. He announced that taxpayer dollars could be used only to finance ESC research on stem-cell lines that had already been extracted from human embryos; federal money could not be used, he said, to "sanction or encourage further destruction of human embryos." Interpretation of this policy has softened recently, making it easier for scientists who accept federal funds to use ESCs in their research, but the debate has grown in intensity because of connections between the use of ESCs and the controversial issue of human cloning. Cloning is one possible source of embryos. And with a bill before the U.S. Senate that seeks to prohibit human cloning for all purposes, including biomedical research, and a majority of the President's Council on Bioethics recently recommending a four-year moratorium on all cloning of human embryos,[1] we urgently need to assess the permissibility of using ESCs.

The moral problems with ESC research have been exaggerated, I believe. But to answer the critics, it is not enough to show that many lives may well be saved and much suffering avoided by new breakthroughs from ESC-based research. Critics acknowledge those benefits—although sometimes with considerable hesitation about their likelihood—but rightly deny that the magnitude of the benefits suffices to justify the research. After all, experimentation on infants is impermissible even if it generates socially valuable results. To respond, then, we need to address the moral criticism head-on, either by showing that human embryos are devoid of moral importance—like a human fingernail or an appendix or a small clump of human cells—or that the kind of moral importance they have is consistent with using them in biomedical research.

The idea that human embryos have no moral importance at all strikes me as wrong, so my case for the permissibility of ESC research assumes that embryos are morally important. I will, however, challenge the conception of that importance endorsed by the majority on the President's Council in their report on cloning and in an earlier government commission report on stem-cell research.[2]

The Sources of ESCs

When a human sperm fertilizes a human ovum, a single cell is created with the potential to grow into a human person. A few days after fertilization, a blastocyst develops, comprising an outer layer of cells that forms the placenta and other tissues needed for the fetus to develop and a hollow sphere that contains an inner cell mass. Cells in the inner mass are called "stem cells," and they can go on to form nearly all tissues and specialized cells in the human body (e.g., organs and blood cells). Because of this unusual potential, stem cells—sometimes called *pluripotential cells*—may be useful in treating many illnesses. From this early stage in development until it is nine to ten weeks old, the organism is called an embryo. The embryo passes through a pre-implanted zygote stage, which lasts about seven to fourteen days, and the first eight weeks of gestation. Only after significant cell differentiation has occurred does the organism become known as the fetus. Stem cells can be gathered from the embryo's inner cell mass; thus originates the term *embryonic stem cells.*

ESCs can be obtained from three sources: aborted embryos and early fetuses that still have some such cells; embryos generated for in vitro fertilization (IVF) but not implanted; and embryos created by cloning. However the embryos are obtained, they die when the stem cells are removed. A 1999 government report on guidelines for federally funded research involving ESCs acquired through abortion or IVF (that is, not through cloning)[3] took the view that while human embryos do not have the moral status of human persons, they should be treated with respect. Treating human embryos with respect entails not using them simply as a means for achieving some further goal. I shall call this the *Mere Means Thesis.* According to the government report, *Mere Means* has two important corollaries, one concerning the creation of embryos, the other concerning their destruction.

1. *Noncreation:* Embryos should not be created for the purpose of conducting research that will destroy them. In particular, embryos should not be created for stem cell research because removing stem cells destroys the embryo. An embryo should only be used in stem cell research if it was created for some other purpose. Otherwise, it is treated as a mere means.

2. *Alternate Destruction:* Even embryos not created for the purpose of conducting research that will destroy them should not be destroyed in research *unless they would have been destroyed in any case.* Consider, for example, an embryo left over from an IVF project that will be stored in a freezer. *Alternate Destruction* says that a researcher should not acquire that embryo and use it to acquire stem cells. That, too, would be to treat it merely as a means and would not show respect.

Together, *Noncreation* and *Alternate Destruction* very substantially restrict morally permissible ways to acquire ESCs; they should only be obtained from embryos that were not created for the purpose of being destroyed but that will in any case be destroyed.

To appreciate the force of these restrictions, consider how they apply to the case of cloning as a source of ESCs. Many people assume that *reproductive* cloning—that is, cloning that results in a new human person—should be banned, but suppose we clone embryos. If reproductive cloning is wrong, then we have a duty to prevent the cloned embryos from developing into full human beings. So if a scientist clones ten embryos for the purpose of acquiring ESCs but draws ESCs from only five, then the remaining five must not be allowed to survive and grow into cloned human persons. Unless we can freeze the embryos, we will have a duty to destroy any that can develop further.[4] Development of cloned embryos, however, violates *Noncreation,* and destroying them violates *Alternate Destruction.* The result closes off the cloning option altogether.

In a recent *New York Times* interview,[5] Harold T. Shapiro, the chair of the federal panel that produced the original report on the use of ESCs in federally funded research, said that cloning embryos for the purpose of reproduction poses no unique moral problems. *Mere Means* and *Noncreation,* however, appear in his panel's report—theses that conflict with cloning for the purpose of obtaining ESCs for research if, as seems to be the case, destruction of cloned embryos will occur and indeed be required.[6]

Perhaps, however, *Mere Means* does not apply to cloned embryos. How might one arrive at that exemption? One reason for thinking that embryos ought not to be treated as means is that the embryo has the potential to develop into a person. Embryos, however, could be created that lack the genetic potential to develop beyond a few days. Some scientists think that using such embryos for research would obviate many moral problems in using ESCs from cloned embryos. Let us call this the *No-Potential Solution.* In this scenario, *Mere Means, Noncreation,* and *Alternate Destruction* do not apply to embryos with such limited genetic potential, even if they apply to embryos with the genetic potential to develop into a person. After all, by destroying an embryo lacking the potential to develop into a human being, we would not be taking away its future because it could have no future.

An alternative way to reopen the option of cloning as a source of ESCs is to say that an embryo's potential to develop into a human person depends on its environment. Thus Senator Orrin Hatch, an opponent of abortion, came out in favor of ESC research because "life begins in a woman's womb, not in a petri dish."[7] Hatch's view seems to be that when an embryo is already in a sustaining environment such as the womb, it has the potential to develop into a person. In a petri dish or a freezer, however, it does not have the potential to develop until someone puts it in a sustaining environment. Hence, even cloned embryos that could develop if put in a sustaining environment do not have the potential to develop when they are not and will not be placed in such an environment. Creating and using embryos in laboratories (as is done in IVF) would create no problem according to this view because they would not have the potential for further development. Interestingly, bioethicist Arthur Caplan—who is no opponent of abortion—also holds this view.[8]

Notice that in the view proposed by Hatch and Caplan, we achieve the *No-Potential Solution* without creating embryos that are genetically unable to develop. If ESCs are taken from embryos deliberately created outside a sustaining environment such as the womb, then *Mere Means, Noncreation,* and *Alternate Destruction* may not apply. The fact that an embryo will not develop because we never put it in a sustaining environment is crucial. Achieving the *No-Potential Solution* in this way would, it might be thought,[9] allow us to obtain ESCs from cloned embryos and from leftover embryos generated for IVF.

Because he is pro-choice, Caplan may also believe that when an embryo is aborted, it may be destroyed for its ESCs. Senator Hatch, however, may not share this view, for he thinks that abortion, which fatally interferes with an embryo that is in a sustaining environment, is morally wrong. He may believe it is impermissible to take advantage of an immorally aborted embryo. Therefore, depending on one's beliefs, the *No-Potential Solution* may or may not allow us to obtain ESCs from aborted fetuses.

Problems with Current Policies and Positions

Mere Means and its corollaries impose large restrictions on using ESCs. Unless we endorse some form of the *No-Potential* view, they appear to close off completely the option of obtaining ESCs from cloning. I want now to offer some reasons for rejecting *Mere Means, Noncreation,* and *Alternate Destruction* and for thinking that the *No-Potential Solution* is incomplete and even unnecessary. In this section, I will offer some hypothetical cases that suggest that the first three ideas are implausible. In the next section, I will challenge a view that makes the moral importance of embryos depend on their potential to develop into human persons, and I will propose an alternative view of their importance. The upshot is that ESC research is morally much less troubling than much current discussion suggests.

Mere Means.   The government report that presents *Mere Means* seems to be founded on an idea that traces to Immanuel Kant's moral philosophy. The second formulation of Kant's categorical imperative says that we should treat rational humanity, "whether in [our] own person or in that of another, always as an end and never as a means only."[10] The embryo is not rational humanity, however, but pre-rational humanity. A pre-rational embryo may have *some* moral value, but why suppose that the strong Kantian principle applies to it?

To see the force of the question, consider a couple in an IVF clinic. The couple has produced three embryos for implantation and cannot produce any more. The couple hopes for at least two children. Two of the embryos run into trouble, but both could be saved by sustaining them with parts of the third embryo. The third embryo is not in any trouble, is about to be implanted in the womb and would have developed without problems. Still, it seems permissible to use that one embryo to save the other two, even though it is impermissible to kill one person in order to save two people.[11] Thus, the couple may use one embryo to save two, but they may not, for example, take organs from one infant child to save two others. If this is so, it is not true that human embryos should never be used as mere means. Embryos have a different moral status than human persons.

Noncreation.   According to *Noncreation,* we must not create embryos we intend to destroy.[12] But suppose that a woman dying of heart disease learns that if she becomes pregnant and has a very early abortion that kills the embryo, her body's reaction to the embryo's death will prompt a cure for her disease. Would it be morally permissible for her to become pregnant with the aim of aborting the embryo immediately? *Noncreation* implies that she should not do it, yet it seems permissible.[13] To be sure, the example is very odd, but ask yourself what you think. Now suppose instead that the woman could cure her heart disease by carrying her pregnancy to term and having the infant's heart valves transplanted into her body. In this case, the woman's conduct is plainly wrong. Once more, moral thought distinguishes embryos from other living human beings—a difference obscured by *Noncreation.*

Suppose it is permissible for a woman to create an embryo that will be destroyed to cure her heart disease. Why may she not create it in order to give it to a scientist who will destroy it in an attempt to find a cure? Why may she not help create the embryo outside her body, in a laboratory, for the same purpose? If a doctor may help her have an abortion, why may a scientist not help her through ESC research in a laboratory? Perhaps the likelihood of finding a cure is important for assessing the permissibility of these acts, but this should hold whether or not a scientist is involved. Why should it matter that a cure is sought for the very woman whose embryo is donated? Why should she be permitted to help herself but barred from trying to help someone else in the same way?

Another problem with *Noncreation* is raised by the possibility that one might need to *create* a spare embryo for IVF in order to use it to keep other embryos alive. (This is an extension of the three-embryo case discussed above.)[14] This case reminds us that creating an embryo in order to have a baby does not necessarily mean an embryo must become—or even have a possibility of becoming—a baby. Though *Noncreation* rules out creating an extra embryo for this purpose, it strikes me as morally permissible.

Alternate Destruction.   According to *Alternate Destruction,* we may not destroy an embryo in research unless it would have been destroyed anyway for nonresearch reasons. Suppose, however, a woman is pregnant and discovers early in the pregnancy that she has fatal breast cancer. She has every intention of going through with the pregnancy, as this is her chance to leave a child behind for her family. She is then told that if she aborts the embryo and gives it to a scientist, a drug can be developed that will cure her cancer. According to *Alternate Destruction,* aborting this embryo is impermissible because the embryo would not otherwise have been destroyed. But it seems permissible for the woman to save her life this way. It seems permissible, too, for her to abort the early embryo to save someone else's life or to use an embryo in laboratory research even if it would have been implanted had the research not been possible.

The Moral Importance of Embryos

The basic principles underlying the 1999 government report on federally funded stem cell research— *Mere Means, Noncreation,* and *Alternate Destruction*—all seem misguided. These principles are founded on the plausible idea that human embryos are morally important, but they misrepresent that moral importance. How, then, *should* we understand the moral importance of embryos? I will come at this question a little bit indirectly through a problem raised by cloning.

My criticisms of *Mere Means, Noncreation,* and *Alternate Destruction* imply that it is *permissible* to destroy embryos in more circumstances than if these theses were true. But cloning raises a special problem with these theses. It is widely thought that allowing a cloned embryo to develop into a human person would be wrong.[15] To avoid that wrong, we would have a *duty* to destroy any cloned embryo that might develop into a human person. Even if it is permissible to destroy an embryo for research purposes, it might be thought wholly objectionable to produce embryos that we subsequently have a duty to kill. An embryo has the potential to develop into a human person and, it might be said, we cannot have a duty to kill an entity with such potential. Hatch and Caplan deny that an embryo in a laboratory has any such potential. Imagine, however, that this embryo has been mistakenly implanted in the womb (or some external gestation device)[16]—as might happen—and is otherwise fine. Everyone would agree that this cloned and implanted embryo has the potential to develop into a person. Could we nevertheless have a duty to kill it? And is it permissible to start projects that might lead to such mistakes and result in such a duty?

The answer to both questions is "yes" because of the kind of moral importance the embryo has. An embryo is not the sort of entity that can be harmed by the loss of its future. An embryo may have some moral value in the sense that its continued existence, *in its own right* (even if it is frozen and will never develop into a person), gives us a reason not to destroy it. This value could only be overridden by some good that we can achieve in destroying it, thus ruling out the useless or gratuitous killing of embryos. This is very different from saying that we should not destroy the embryo because that is bad *for the embryo.*

Consider, by way of analogy, a valuable work of art: say, a painting. A painting is valuable in its own right and therefore should not be wantonly destroyed. But we do not preserve paintings for the sake of the paintings themselves, because their continued existence cannot be good *for them.* After all, a painting cannot sense, perceive, or experience anything. Likewise, an embryo does not have and never had the capacity to sense, perceive, or experience anything. In contrast, when we refrain from destroying a bird—even if it is less valuable in its own right than a painting—we may be acting for its sake, for it may be good *for the bird* to continue to exist.[17]

By not destroying the embryo, can we be acting for its sake because it has the *potential* to become a human person able to think, perceive, and experience? I do not think so, because even if it is good to be a person and even if there is some sense in which the embryo loses out on becoming a person (from which it is very different), I do not think that the embryo itself is harmed by this loss. I do not think that an embryo is the sort of entity that can benefit from transformation into a person or be harmed by not so transforming. This has something to do with its not being (and never having been) capable of consciousness or sentience,[18] and so not capable of being benefited at all, even by turning into the kind of being that can be benefited. Analogously, suppose that a table could, by magic, be made capable of turning into a person. The table is not harmed if it is destroyed instead of being allowed to transform.[19] (Harming an entity is not the only way to treat it disrespectfully, of course. For example, overriding a person's will for his or her own good can be disrespectful. But embryos do not have wills, and so cannot be treated disrespectfully in this way either.)

Notice that the reasons I have given for the permissibility of destroying embryos for research do not yield a principled distinction between embryos in the first two weeks of life and older embryos. Researchers on stem cells intend to use embryos in the first two weeks, before the "primitive streak" appears and marks the first point at which the clump of cells begins to be an individual coordinated embryo. It is possible that other research might find it useful to use older embryos. Some have argued that because an embryo can split before the primitive streak appears and form the bases of identical twins, it does not merit the same protection as the embryo that is the basis for a definite individual person.

I am not convinced this is a morally crucial distinction. Suppose it were possible for children to split into identical twins before age four. A child who will not split still merits protection against destruction. What justifies such protection are the characteristics of the entity. A person has the necessary characteristics, but embryos before or after the primitive streak may not have them. Nor would it be correct to conclude that a child who will split can permissibly be killed on the grounds that the child will soon be replaced by two other people and thus cease to exist.

For these reasons, I do not think that it would be wrong to involve ourselves in a project that would result in a duty to destroy a cloned embryo with the potential to become a human person. I also think that many of my judgments about the permissibility of killing the embryo in the hypothetical cases I explored earlier can be justified by this understanding of the moral importance of a human embryo.

Let us now consider in more detail the question of what has the potential to be a person and whether creating an embryo without the potential to develop into a person is a plausible solution to the many moral issues that surround ESC research. Is it correct to say that an embryo that is not and will not be in a sustaining environment has no more potential for development than an embryo created with a genetic makeup that prohibits development? I do not think so. Consider an embryo that could develop if placed in a sustaining environment but will be frozen instead. Even if it never develops, its genetic capacity for development makes it more valuable in its own right than an embryo without such a capacity. The potential for development into a human person counts for *something*.

Imagine a magic wand, capable of producing a great effect, that is locked in a museum case and will never be used. Compare it with a nonmagic wand in the same case. Though neither will ever produce any great effects, the former wand has greater intrinsic value in virtue of its potential even though both wands have the same instrumental value. The human embryo that could develop into a human person if it were placed in a sustaining environment is like an unused magic wand.

The difference between embryos with no genetic potential and embryos lacking potential because of their environment can also explain why some antiabortionists object to Hatch's position. If one believes that the embryo with genetic potential is very important, a possible response is to call for it to be placed in a sustaining environment. This is analogous to how one would treat a child who was in a nonsustaining environment: one would not say that it was permissible to kill the child because the child was in a nonsustaining environment; one would instead try to move the child into a better environment. However, such a position concerning the embryo also implies that frozen leftover embryos from IVF should be adopted and transferred to a sustaining environment at reasonable cost. If this is, in fact, not morally necessary, it is because the value of an embryo with genetic potential does not imply that its potential must be developed or even that it cannot be killed for the sake of an important good. What is most important for the permissibility of using human embryos for biomedical research is not that genetically normal embryos in a nonsustaining environment will not have a chance to develop, but that such embryos need not be placed in a sustaining environment.

Finally, is the creation of human embryos that will die naturally soon after being created a solution to the current controversies? I believe not. The problem here is that we first need to show why embryos can be used in research projects before we can permissibly create entities that are otherwise like human embryos but lack the potential to develop into persons or to live beyond a few days.

To see why, suppose that an embryo already exists with potential to develop, and we seek to take away that genetic potential (without destroying the embryo) in order that we may then destroy it because it lacks genetic potential. Doing this is problematic if we do not first justify our action by showing that embryos are not the sort of entities that have a right to retain their genetic potential or are harmed by having this potential taken away. But if we show these things to be true, we will have gone a long way in proving that it is the sort of entity that can be destroyed.

Now suppose we could create an embryo without genetic potential for continuing life rather than removing such potential. To show that this is permissible, we must first show that it would be permissible to kill the embryo even if it has potential. The following analogy may help. Suppose someone wanted to experiment on human persons but it was objected that this is impermissible because it would lead them to lose the rest of their lives. Creating a human person with a genetic modification that will produce an early death, just so that we could experiment on him without thereby causing him any loss of life, is not a solution, for the sort of entity he would be—a person—would thereby lose out on life, and thus be denied something that is a basic good for him. Hence, it is only permissible to make such a genetic modification to an entity that would not be harmed to a great degree by losing out on more life. If, as I argued earlier, the human embryo is such an entity, then we have already gone a long way in showing that it is the sort of entity that we may destroy even if it has potential for development. To defend the permissibility of creating an embryo without potential, then, we have to defend the very same theses that are crucial to the permissibility of killing an embryo *with potential*.

In conclusion, I want to recall the context of my argument. The discussion of biomedical research using ESCs begins from two basic considerations: first, that such research may have very large benefits; and second, that the research requires the destruction of embryos. Critics argue that we must forgo the benefits of ESC research because destroying embryos fails to show respect for their moral importance.

I have argued that this conclusion is founded on an implausible view of the moral importance of embryos. A proper understanding of that importance must take seriously the fact that the destruction of an embryo is not bad *for the embryo*. The grave evil that we associate with the destruction of human life—and more broadly with using people as means to an end—reflects the fact that such destruction—and such use—is either bad *for the persons whose lives are destroyed or who are used,* or contrary to their will. Embryos, however, have no will, and their destruction is not bad *for them.* The conclusion is not that we can use human embryos however we want, but that we have no reason to forgo the large benefits that doctors and scientists expect will follow from research on ESCs.[20]

Notes

1. President's Council on Bioethics, "Human Cloning and Human Dignity: An Ethical Inquiry," available on-line under "Reports" at: http://www.bioethics.gov.

2. See National Bioethics Advisory Commission, "Ethical Issues in Human Stem Cell Research, Executive Summary," September 1999.

3. National Bioethics Advisory Commission, "Ethical Issues."

4. Charles Krauthammer—a columnist, M.D., and member of the President's Commission on Bioethics—points to this as a decisive reason not to allow cloning for research purposes, even though he agrees that the embryo does not have the same moral status as a person. See his "Crossing Lines: A Secular Argument Against Research Cloning," *The New Republic,* 29 April 2002. He also supports *Noncreation,* arguing that we must not create human life while intending to destroy it.

5. Howard Markel, "A Conversation with Harold Shapiro: Weighing Medical Ethics for Many Years to Come,"*New York Times,* 2 July 2002.

6. Of course, Shapiro may not have agreed personally with the panel's report, though no dissent was published. Reports by government panels that aim to provide reasons for their conclusions may well be compromises in their conclusions as well as their reasoning. Such reports appear to propose philosophical rationales, but no one on the panel fully endorses the rationale. It is there as window dressing. If this is so, it may not be wise to treat the reasoning in these reports as intended to be correct and so rightly subject to critical examination in the search for truth. On the other hand, such a critical examination is important in order to show that these reports do not embody correct, but only compromise, window-dressing reasoning. I have examined the reasoning provided in other government reports, on organ transplantation and brain death, and also found them wanting. See my "Reflections on the Report of the U.S. Task Force on Organ Transplantation," *The Mount Sinai Journal of Medicine* (May 1989): 207–20, and my "Brain Death and Spontaneous Breathing," *Philosophy and Public Affairs* 30:3 (Summer 2001). For a philosopher's discussion of the compromises that are made in serving as advisors to government deliberative panels, see Dan Brock, "Truth or Consequences: The Role of Philosophers in Policymaking," *Ethics,* 97:4 (July 1987): 786–91; and the last part of D. Green and D. Wikler, "Brain Death and Personal Identity," *Philosophy and Public Affairs,* 9:2 (Winter 1980). On some of the issues they raise, see my "The Philosopher as Insider and Outsider," *Journal of Medicine and Philosophy* 15 (August 1990).

7. Sheryl Gay Stolberg, "Key Republican Backs Cloning in Research," *New York Times,* 1 May 2002.

8. See his discussion of these issues in "Attack of the Anti-Cloners," *The Nation,* 17 June 2002.

9. The reasons for the qualification will be clear later: I do not think that the No-Potential solution is really a solution at all.

10. *Groundwork of the Metaphysics of Morals,* trans. Lewis White Beck, p. 47.

11. On why we should not kill one person in order to save two, see my *Morality, Mortality,* Vol. 2 (New York: Oxford University Press, 1996).

12. I shall assume in what follows that creating embryos with the intention to use them for research with foresight of the fact that they will certainly die from such use is as contrary to *Noncreation* as is creating embryos while intending their destruction or creating embryos foreseeing that we will intend their destruction.

13. Notice that those who endorse *Noncreation* and would support its implication for this case could also think that it is, in general, morally permissible to have abortions. For in most abortions, a woman does not get pregnant *in order to* have an abortion. Furthermore, one of the reasons given to support the moral permissibility of most abortions is that the embryo (or fetus) is imposing on the woman's body and its presence is presenting some problem for her. In extreme cases, the embryo may pose a threat to her life, just as heart disease does in the case above. So a person may believe, with no inconsistency, that it is permissible to destroy an embryo that presents a (morally innocent) threat to a woman but that it is impermissible to create and use an embryo (that is not itself presenting a threat to her) simply because destroying it will help the woman avoid *another* threat, like heart disease.

14. Krauthammer also presents such a case. He thinks that it is analogous to what is involved in cloning and that it is clearly morally impermissible.

15. I shall not here try to contest this assumption that reproductive cloning is wrong, though it can possibly be contested.

16. For discussion of the moral relevance of such external gestation devices for the permissibility of abortion, see F. M. Kamm, *Creation and Abortion* (New York: Oxford University Press, 1993).

17. Notice that even creatures, such as birds, for whose sake we can act in keeping them alive do not necessarily have a right not to be killed.

18. A being that is capable of sentient experience or consciousness is not one that merely has the capacity to develop into a being that is capable of sentience or consciousness. Also, it is not necessarily a being that has already had sentient experience or consciousness. For example, a being that has never experienced pleasure can still be capable of it, and so it is the sort of being for whose sake I can act in giving it pleasure for the first time and in not depriving it of future life from which it will get pleasure. Here I differ with the view in Bonnie Steinbock, *Life Before Birth: The Moral and Legal Status of Embryos and Fetuses* (New York: Oxford University Press, 1992), and Mary Ann Warren in *Moral Status: Obligations to Persons and Other Living Things* (Oxford: Clarendon Press, 1998). They both require that a being have already experienced in order for it to be possible to harm it by killing it.

19. Although it is not a harm to the embryo to lose its potential, it would be an indication of the value of an embryo if we would try to correct a defect in it that interfered with its potential rather than dispose of it and create a new embryo without a defect. Similarly, it can be an indication of the value of a painting if we try to rescue it from damage rather than have an equally good painting created in its stead. If a person suffered damage that made her incapable of consciousness (for example, total destruction of the brain), we could have a strong duty to restore the capacity if this resulted in the same individual. This duty would be owed to the person who once existed; it would be a duty to restore her, if possible, to being a person. An alternative to the view that an embryo cannot be harmed if it is destroyed is that it can be harmed but harm

to it has no moral signifcance given what it is and has always been. These two views would have similar implications for stem cell research.

20. I am grateful to Derek Parfit and Jeff McMahan for comments on earlier drafts.

Journal/Discussion Questions

1. To what extent does Kamm's article provide a critique of Outka's position in our reading?

2. Kamm maintains that embryos have a different status than human beings. What do you think her strongest argument is in this respect? Do you agree?

3. Kamm likens an embryo to a work of art. What point does she want to make with this analogy?

4. According to Kamm, is there a morally significant line between embryos less than two weeks old and older embryos? Why or why not? Do you agree with her position?

Concluding Discussion Questions

Where Do You Stand Now?

Instructions

You have already answered the following questions in your moral problems self-quiz at the beginning of this book. Now that you have studied the material in this section, take a moment to answer the same questions again.

Chapter 1: Cloning and Reproductive Technologies

	Strongly Agree	Agree	Undecided	Disagree	Strongly Disagree	
1.	❑	❑	❑	❑	❑	*In vitro* fertilization is morally wrong.
2.	❑	❑	❑	❑	❑	Any procedure that helps infertile couples to have children is good.
3.	❑	❑	❑	❑	❑	Surrogate mothers should never have to give up their babies if they don't want to do so.
4.	❑	❑	❑	❑	❑	Surrogate motherhood should be illegal.
5.	❑	❑	❑	❑	❑	Genetic manipulation of embryos should be forbidden.

Compare your answers to this self-quiz with the answers to the initial self-quiz. How, if at all, have your answers changed? How have the *reasons* for your answers changed?

Journal/Discussion Questions

✍ *If you were going to have a baby, to what extent would you want to select its characteristics in advance? Which characteristics, if any, would you not want to consciously select? Physical characteristics? Physical and mental capabilities? Personality traits? Sex? Sexual orientation?*

1. In light of the readings in this chapter, what new issues about reproductive technologies were most interesting to you? Which ones do you think will be most difficult for us as a society to resolve?

2. Should there be any limits on couples who wish to use artificial means to have children? Should there be any limits on individuals who wish to do so?

3. Should society regulate the practice of surrogacy? In what ways? How should it deal with surrogate mothers who change their minds?

For Further Reading

Web Resources

The Reproductive Technologies page of Ethics Updates (http://ethics.sandiego.edu) contains numerous resources relating to reproductive technologies and cloning. This includes numerous articles, court decisions, and reports of the National Bioethics Advisory Committee and the President's Council on Bioethics, which is located at http://bioethics.gov. Also see the Bioethics section of Bio-Med Central (http://www.biomedcentral.com/bmcmedethics/) for a number of excellent online, full-text articles.

Journals

See the *Hastings Center Reports, BioEthics, Kennedy Institute of Ethics, Journal of Medicine and Philosophy, Biomedical Ethics Reviews, Journal of Medical Humanities,* and *Law, Medicine & Health Care* for discussion of issues relating specifically to biomedical ethics. Some of the best articles in the *Hastings Center Reports* have been gathered together in *Life Choices: A Hastings Center Introduction to Bioethics,* edited by Joseph H. Howell and William Frederick Sale (Washington, DC: Georgetown University Press, 1995).

Review Articles and Reports

There are a number of helpful bibliographies available on issues relating to the topics in this chapter. See the ScopeNotes from the Kennedy Institute of Ethics, Georgetown University, at http://www.georgetown.edu/research/nrcbl/scopenotes/index.htm, as well as their directory of bioethics resources on the Web (http://www.georgetown.edu/research/nrcbl/scopenotes/sn38.htm). The *Bibliography of Bioethics,* begun at the Kennedy Institute of Ethics, Georgetown University, is available online at http://www.csu.edu.au/learning/ncgr/gpi/grn/edures/elsi.tc.html.

There have been a number of national commissions, both here and in England, that have prepared reports and policy recommendations on these issues. In the United States, The President's Council on Bioethics (http://bioethics.gov/) has prepared a number of helpful reports; the National Bioethics Advisory Commission reports, which are available online at http://www.georgetown.edu/research/nrcbl/nbac/, contain extensive resources and provide an excellent point of departure. Also see Mary Warnock, *A Question of Life: The Warnock Report on Human Fertilization and Embryology* (Oxford, England: Basil Blackwell, 1985); Jonathan Glover et al., *Fertility and the Family: The Glover Report on Reproductive Technologies to the European Commission* (London: Fourth Estate, 1989); for a religious response to the Warnock report, see Oliver O'Donovan, *Begotten or Made?* (Oxford, England: Clarendon Press, 1984).

For a review of some of the moral issues raised by new reproductive technologies, see Helen Bequaert Holmes, "Reproductive Technologies," *Encyclopedia of Ethics,* edited by Lawrence C.

Becker and Charlotte B. Becker (New York: Garland, 1992), Vol. II, pp. 1083–1089; several of the articles in *A Companion to Bioethics,* edited by Helga Kuhse and Peter Singer (Oxford: Blackwell, 2001); Robert Wachbroit and David Wasserman, "Reproductive Technology," *The Oxford Handbook of Practical Ethics,* edited by Hugh LaFollette (New York: Oxford University Press, 2003), pp. 136-160; and the various articles in the *Encyclopedia of Applied Ethics,* edited by Dan Callahan, Peter Singer, and Ruth Chadwick (San Diego: Academic Press, 1998).

Anthologies and Books

There are a number of excellent anthologies available in the area of reproductive technologies. Among the general anthologies on issues in bioethics, see the excellent *Contemporary Issues in Bioethics,* edited by Tom L. Beauchamp, LeRoy Walters, and Les L. Johnston, 6th edition (Belmont, CA: Wadsworth, 2003); for an excellent selection of both philosophical and nonphilosophical authors, see *Genetic Engineering: Opposing Viewpoints,* edited by James D. Torr (San Diego: Greenhaven Press, 2000) and *Taking Sides: Clashing View on Controversial Bioethical Issues,* edited by Carol Levine, 10th ed. (Guilford, CT: Dushkin, 2003). On the issue of the family, see especially *Kindred Matters: Rethinking the Philosophy of the Family,* edited by Diana Tietjens Meyers, Kenneth Kipnis, and Cornelius F. Murphy, Jr. (Ithaca: Cornell University Press, 1993).

Cloning.   In regard to cloning, see the excellent anthology by Glenn McGee, *The Human Cloning Debate,* 3rd edition (Albany, CA: Berkeley Hills Books, 2002); *Clones and Clones: Facts and Fantasies About Human Cloning,* edited by Martha C. Nussbaum and Cass R. Sunstein (New York: W.W. Norton & Company, 1999); Gregory E. Pence, *Who's Afraid of Human Cloning?* (Lanham, MD: Rowman & Littlefield Publishing (via NBN, January 1, 1998); *Ethical Issues in Human Cloning: Cross-Disciplinary Perspectives,* edited by Michael C. Brannigan (Seven Bridges Press, 2000); *The Human Embryonic Stem Cell Debate: Science, Ethics, and Public Policy* (Basic Bioethics Series), edited by Suzanne Holland, Karen Lebacqz , and Laurie Zoloth (Boston: MIT Press, 2001); Leon R. Kass and James Q. Wilson, *The Ethics of Human Cloning* (Washington, DC: AEI Press, 1998). The report on cloning of the President's Commission on Bioethics is available at http://bioethics.gov/topics/cloning_index.html. On religious perspectives, see Ronald Cole-Turner, *Human Cloning: Religious Responses* (Westminster John Knox Press, 1997); *Cloning: For and Against,* edited by M. L. Rantala and Arthur J. Milgram (Chicago: Open Court, 1999); *Flesh of My Flesh: The Ethics of Cloning Humans: A Reader,* edited by Gregory E. Pence (Totowa, NJ: Rowman & Littlefield, 1998); Leon R. Kass and James Q. Wilson, *The Ethics of Human Cloning* (Washington, DC: The AEI Press, 1998). In addition, see *The Cloning Sourcebook,* edited by Arlene Judith Klotzko (New York: Oxford University Press, 2003); *Cloning and the Future of Human Embryo Research,* edited by Paul Lauritzen (New York: Oxford University Press, 2001).

Genetic Manipulation.   If you are doing research on the ethics of genetic manipulation, begin with the President's Council on Bioethics (http://bioethics.gov/topics/beyond_index.html); it has a number of excellent papers and discussions, as well as its report *Beyond Therapy.* With the success in decoding the human genome, genetic manipulation has come within our grasp and spawned countless books on this topic. Among the best are Glenn McGee, *Beyond Genetics: Putting the Power of DNA to Work in Your Life* (New York: William Morrow, 2003), which provides a balanced and pragmatic assessment of the possibilities of genetic manipulation; *Improving Nature? The Science and Ethics of Genetic Engineering,* edited by Michael Jonathan Reiss and Roger Straughan (Cambridge, England: Cambridge University Press, 2001). Gregory Stock's *Redesigning Humans: Choosing Our Genes, Changing Our Future* (New York: Houghton Mifflin Company, 2003) offers a strong defense of the possibilities of genetic engineering; Leon Kass's *Beyond Therapy: Biotechnology and the Pursuit of Happiness* (New York: HarperCollins, 2003) sees a quite different future than the one that Stock envisions, as does Francis Fukuyama's *Our Posthuman Future: Consequences of the Biotechnology Revolution* (New York: Farrar, Straus & Giroux, 2002). Also see John Harris, *Clones, Genes, and Immortality: Ethics and the Genetic Revolution* (New York: Oxford University Press, 1998); *Ethical Issues in the New Reproductive Technologies,* edited by Richard Hull (Belmont, CA: Wadsworth, 1990); Kenneth D. Alpern, *The Ethics of Reproductive Technology* (New York: Oxford University Press, 1992); *Ethics, Reproduction, and Genetic Control,* rev. ed. (London: Routledge, 1994). For a well-argued and balanced approach to these issues, see Glenn McGee, *The Perfect Baby: A Pragmatic Approach to Genetics* (Totowa, NJ: Rowman & Littlefield, 1997). Also see the anthology, *The Future of Human Reproduction,* edited by John Harris and Søren Holm (New York: Oxford, 1998) and Peter Singer et al., eds., *Embryo Experimentation* (New York: Cambridge University Press).

Stem Cell Research.   Again, the best place to start research on the ethics of stem cells is the stem cell site of the President's Council on Bioethics (http://bioethics.gov/topics/stemcells_index.html); not only does it contain the Council's report, but it also has numerous presentations and working papers on the topic, including several that deal with religious aspects. For an excellent anthology, see *The Human Embryonic Stem Cell Debate: Science, Ethics, and Public Policy,* edited by Suzanne Holland, Karen Lebacqz, and Laurie Zoloth (Boston: MIT Press, 2001); Ronald M. Green's *Human Embryo Research Debates: Bioethics in the Vortex of Controversy* (New York: Oxford University Press, 2001); and Bonnie Steinbock, *Life before Birth: The Moral and Legal Status of Embryos and Fetuses* (New York: Oxford University Press, 1996). For a strong defense of the moral permissibility of stem cell research, see Frances Myrna Kamm, "Embryonic Stem Cell Research: A Moral Defense," *Boston Review,* Vol. 27, No. 5 (October–November, 2002), online at http://www.bostonreview.net/BR27.5/kamm.html.

CHAPTER 2

Abortion

    Topic: Civil War (*Roe v. Wade*)

    Source: *Nightline*, January 22, 2003

    Anchor: Chris Bury

    Guests: Interviews with four college students: Sarah Butler (University of
               Chicago), Vinita Ahuja (Georgetown University), Kate Lesker (George
               Washington University), and Lauren Anderson (Howard University)

Experiential Accounts

Linda Bird Francke
"There Just Wasn't Room in Our Lives Now for Another Baby"

Linda Bird Francke is a journalist whose articles have appeared in The New York Times, Harper's Bazaar, The Washington Post, Esquire, Ms., *and* McCalls. *Her books include* The Ambiguity of Abortion *and* Growing Up Divorced. *She has three children and lives in Sagaponack, New York.*

The present selection originally appeared anonymously in the Letters to the Editor section of The New York Times. *The article itself brought forth a number of letters in reply. Eventually her concern with the issue of abortion led to her book on* The Ambivalence of Abortion, *which presents first-hand accounts of the decision about abortion from women in numerous positions in life.*

We were sitting in a bar on Lexington Avenue when I told my husband I was pregnant. It is not a memory I like to dwell on. Instead of the champagne and hope that had heralded the impending births of the first, second and third child, the news of this one was greeted with shocked silence and Scotch. "Jesus," my husband kept saying to himself, stirring the ice cubes around and around. "Oh, Jesus."

Oh, how we tried to rationalize it that night as the starting time for the movie came and went. My husband talked about his plans for a career change in the next year, to stem the staleness that fourteen years with the same investment-banking firm had brought him. A new baby would preclude that option.

The timing wasn't right for me either. Having juggled pregnancies and child care with what freelance jobs I could fit in between feedings, I had just taken on a full-time job. A new baby would put me right back in the nursery just when our youngest child was finally school age. It was time for us, we tried to rationalize. There just wasn't room in our lives now for another baby. We both agreed. And agreed. And agreed.

How very considerate they are at the Women's Services, known formally as the Center for Reproductive and Sexual Health. Yes, indeed, I could have an abortion that very Saturday morning and be out in time to drive to the country that afternoon. Bring a first morning urine specimen, a sanitary belt and napkins, a money order for $125 cash—and a friend.

My friend turned out to be my husband, standing awkwardly and ill at ease as men always do in places that are exclusively for women, as I checked in at 9 A.M. Other men hovered around just as anxiously, knowing they had to be there, wishing they weren't. No one spoke to each other. When I would be cycled out of there four hours later, the same men would be slumped in their same seats, locked downcast in their cells of embarrassment.

The Saturday morning women's group was more dispirited than the men in the waiting room. There were around fifteen of us, a mixture of races, ages and backgrounds. Three didn't speak English at all and a fourth, a pregnant Puerto Rican girl around eighteen, translated for them.

New York Times, op. ed. page, May 14, 1976. Appears under the pseudonym "Jane Doe." Reprinted in Linda Bird Francke, *The Ambiguity of Abortion* (New York: Random House, 1978), pp. 3–7.

There were six black women and a hodgepodge of whites, among them a T-shirted teenager who kept leaving the room to throw up and a puzzled middle-aged woman from Queens with three grown children.

"What form of birth control were you using?" the volunteer asked each one of us. The answer was inevitably "none." She then went on to describe the various forms of birth control available at the clinic, and offered them to each of us.

The youngest Puerto Rican girl was asked through the interpreter which she'd like to use: the loop, diaphragm, or pill. She shook her head "no" three times. "You don't want to come back here again, do you?" the volunteer pressed. The girl's head was so low her chin rested on her breastbone. "Si," she whispered.

We had been there two hours by that time, filling out endless forms, giving blood and urine, receiving lectures. But unlike any other group of women I've been in, we didn't talk. Our common denominator, the one which usually floods across language and economic barriers into familiarity, today was one of shame. We were losing life that day, not giving it.

The group kept getting cut back to smaller, more workable units, and finally I was put in a small waiting room with just two other women. We changed into paper bathrobes and paper slippers, and we rustled whenever we moved. One of the women in my room was shivering and an aide brought her a blanket.

"What's the matter?" the aide asked her. "I'm scared," the woman said. "How much will it hurt?" The aide smiled. "Oh, nothing worse than a couple of bad cramps," she said. "This afternoon you'll be dancing a jig."

I began to panic. Suddenly the rhetoric, the abortion marches I'd walked in, the telegrams sent to Albany to counteract the Friends of the Fetus, the Zero Population Growth buttons I'd worn, peeled away, and I was all alone with my microscopic baby. There were just the two of us there, and soon, because it was more convenient for me and my husband, there would be one again.

How could it be that I, who am so neurotic about life that I step over bugs rather than on them, who spends hours planting flowers and vegetables in the spring even though we rent out the house and never see them, who makes sure the children are vaccinated and inoculated and filled with vitamin C, could so arbitrarily decide that this life shouldn't be?

"It's not a life," my husband had argued, more to convince himself than me. "It's a bunch of cells smaller than my fingernail."

But any woman who has had children knows that certain feeling in her taut, swollen breasts, and the slight but constant ache in her uterus that signals the arrival of a life. Though I would march myself into blisters for a woman's right to exercise the option of motherhood, I discovered there in the waiting room that I was not the modern woman I thought I was.

When my name was called, my body felt so heavy the nurse had to help me into the examining room. I waited for my husband to burst through the door and yell "stop," but of course he didn't. I concentrated on three black spots in the acoustic ceiling until they grew in size to the shape of saucers, while the doctor swabbed my insides with antiseptic.

"You're going to feel a burning sensation now," he said, injecting Novocaine into the neck of the womb. The pain was swift and severe, and I twisted to get away from him. He was hurting my baby, I reasoned, and the black saucers quivered in the air. "Stop," I cried. "Please stop." He shook his head, busy with his equipment. "It's too late to stop now," he said. "It'll just take a few more seconds."

What good sports we women are. And how obedient. Physically the pain passed even before the hum of the machine signaled that the vacuuming of my uterus was completed, my baby sucked up like ashes after a cocktail party. Ten minutes start to finish. And I was back on the arm of the nurse.

There were twelve beds in the recovery room. Each one had a gaily flowered draw sheet and a soft green or blue thermal blanket. It was all very feminine. Lying on these beds for an hour or more were the shocked victims of their sex, their full wombs now stripped clean, their futures less encumbered.

It was very quiet in that room. The only voice was that of the nurse, locating the new women who had just come in so she could monitor their blood pressure, and checking out the recovered women who were free to leave.

Juice was being passed about, and I found myself sipping a Dixie cup of Hawaiian Punch. An older woman with tightly curled bleached hair was just getting up from the next bed, "That was no goddamn snap," she said, resting before putting on her miniskirt and high white boots. Other women came and went, some walking out as dazed as they had entered, others with a bounce that signaled they were going right back to Bloomingdale's.

Finally then, it was time for me to leave. I checked out, making an appointment to return in two weeks for an IUD insertion. My husband was slumped in the waiting room, clutching a single yellow rose wrapped in a wet paper towel and stuffed into a baggie.

We didn't talk the whole way home, but just held hands very tightly. At home there were more yellow roses and a tray in bed for me and the children's curiosity to divert.

It had certainly been a successful operation. I didn't bleed at all for two days just as they had predicted, and then I bled only moderately for another four days. Within a week my breasts had subsided and the tenderness vanished, and my body felt mine again instead of the eggshell it becomes when it's protecting someone else.

My husband and I are back to planning our summer vacation and his career switch.

And it certainly does make more sense not to be having a baby right now—we say that to each other all the time. But I have this ghost now. A very little ghost that only appears when I'm seeing something beautiful, like the full moon on the ocean last weekend. And the baby waves at me. And I wave at the baby. "Of course, we have room," I cry to the ghost. "Of course, we do."

Journal/Discussion Questions

🖉 Write about your reactions to the case just described. What, if anything, touched you the most in Francke's essays? What would be the questions that would run through your mind in this situation? What would you do if you were in this situation?

1. Was there anything about the Francke selection that surprised you? If so, what was it? Explain.

2. Francke says that she does not regret having an abortion. Does that claim seem consistent with the rest of what she says? Explain.

3. Francke says that she is still as strongly "pro-choice" as she ever was. Yet she depicts abortion as a profoundly ambiguous moral experience. Is this consistent? Explain.

4. Do you think that Francke and her husband made the right decision? What do you mean by "the right decision"? Explain.

An Introduction to the Moral Issues

Abortion: The Two Principal Moral Concerns

The ongoing discussion of abortion in American society is often framed as a debate between two sides, usually called *pro-life* and *pro-choice.* The labels themselves are instructive. Whereas one label points our attention toward the fetus, the other emphasizes the pregnant woman. Each position highlights a different aspect of the situation as the principal focus of moral concern. Pro-life supporters emphasize the issue of the rights of the unborn, whereas pro-choice advocates stress the importance of the rights of the pregnant woman.

Notice that these two moral concerns are not immediately mutually exclusive in the same way that, for example, the pro- and anti-capital-punishment positions are. (They may, of course, be secondarily exclusive insofar as the consequences of one exclude the other.) This results in a certain murkiness in debates about abortion, because the opposing sides are often talking primarily about quite different things, either the moral status of the fetus or the rights of the pregnant woman. Let's examine each of these issues.

The Moral Status of the Fetus

Initially, much of the debate about abortion centered around the question of the moral status of the fetus—in particular, if and when the fetus is a person. Most participants in the discussion took for granted that if the fetus can be shown to be a person, then abortion is morally wrong. Thus the discussion focused primarily on whether the fetus could be shown to be a person or not. To answer this question, it was necessary to specify what we meant by *a person.*

Criteria of Personhood

In attempting to define personhood, philosophers have looked for the criteria by means of which we determine whether a being is a person or not. This is a search for *sufficient conditions;* that is, conditions that if present would guarantee personhood. The argument moves in the following way: Some criterion is seen as conferring personhood, and personhood is seen as conferring certain rights, including the right to life. Thus the overall structure of the argument looks like this:

Criterion ⇨ Personhood ⇨ Right to life

We can see the two critical junctures in the argument just by looking at this diagram. The first is in the transition from the criterion to personhood. What justification is there for claiming that this criterion (or group of criteria) justifies the claim that a being is a person? The second transition has sometimes been seen as less problematic, but it may have more difficulties than are initially apparent. The issue in this transition is whether personhood always justifies the right to life.

A number of criteria have been advanced for personhood. Some of these result in conferring personhood quite early in fetal development, sometimes from the moment of conception.

The *conceived-by-humans* criterion is, at least on the surface, the most straightforward: anyone conceived by human parents is a human being. But this straightforwardness turns out to be misleading. We obviously acknowledge the personhood of anyone *born of human parents.* This is the indisputably true sense of "conceived-by-humans." However, we do not obviously and necessarily acknowledge the personhood of everything "conceived-by-humans" in the strict sense. This either equivocates or begs the question.

The *genetic structure* argument maintains that a human genetic code is a sufficient condition for personhood. All the genetic information for the fully formed human being is present in the fetus at the time of conception; therefore, it has the rights of a person. Nothing more needs to be added, and if nothing interferes with the development of the fetus, it will emerge as a full-fledged human baby.

The *physical resemblance* criterion claims that something that looks human is human. Advocates of this criterion then claim that the fetus is a person because of its physical resemblance to a full-term baby. Movies such as *The Silent Scream* (which graphically depicts the contortions of a fetus during an abortion) depend strongly on such a criterion. This criterion seems rhetorically more powerful than the appeal to DNA (since DNA lacks the same visual and emotive impact), but less rigorous, because resemblance can be more strongly in the eye of the beholder than DNA structures.

The *presence-of-a-soul* criterion is often evoked by religious thinkers. The criterion is then used in an argument maintaining that God gives an immortal soul to the fetus at a particular moment, at which time the fetus becomes a person. Although contemporary versions of this argument usually maintain that the implantation of a soul takes place at the time of conception, St. Thomas Aquinas— one of the most influential of modern theologians—claimed that implantation usually occurs at quickening, around the third month. (Aquinas also thought that this event occurred later for females than it did for males.) The principal difficulty with this argument is that it attempts to clarify the opaque by an appeal to the utterly obscure: God's will, at least in matters such as the implantation of a soul, is even more difficult to discern than the personhood of the fetus.

The *viability* criterion sees personhood as inextricably tied to the ability to exist independently of the mother's womb. A fetus is thus seen as a person and having a right to life when it could survive (even with artificial means) outside the body of the mother. This criterion is clearly dependent on developments in medical technology that make it possible to keep increasingly young premature babies alive. If artificial wombs are eventually developed, then viability might be pushed back to a much earlier stage in fetal development.

Finally, the *future-like-ours* criterion maintains that fetuses have a future, just as adult human beings have a future. Just as the killing of adults is wrong because it deprives them of everything that comprises their future, so too the killing of a fetus deprives it of its future. Don Marquis develops this argument in his selection, "Why Abortion Is Immoral."

Some philosophers have argued that there are other criteria that are *necessary* conditions of personhood and that fetuses usually lack these characteristics. These are criteria that we usually associate with adult human beings: *reasoning, a concept of self, use of language,* and so on. (These criteria are often particularly relevant in discussions of the end of life: at what point, if any, does a breathing human being cease to be a person?) There are several dangers with appeals to such criteria. Most notably, such criteria may set the standard of personhood too high and justify not only abortion, but also infanticide, the killing of brain-damaged adults, and involuntary euthanasia.

There are a number of possible responses to this lack of consensus in regard to the conditions of personhood. Two arguments have been advanced which see this lack of consensus as supporting a conservative position on the morality of abortion. The *Let's Play It Safe* argument states that we cannot be absolutely sure when the fetus becomes a person, so let's be careful and err on the safe side. This is often coupled with the *Let's Not Be Arbitrary* argument, which states that because we do not know precisely the moment at which a fetus assumes personhood, we should assume that it becomes a person at the moment of conception and act accordingly. The moment of conception provides, according to this argument, the only nonarbitrary point of demarcation.

Other philosophers have taken a quite different tack in the face of this disagreement about the conditions of personhood. They have argued that it is impossible to define the concept of a person with the necessary precision. Instead, we should turn to other moral considerations to determine whether and when abortion is morally justified.

Relevance of Personhood

There was a widespread assumption that if the fetus is a person, then abortion is morally wrong. The first major article to challenge this assumption was Judith Jarvis Thomson's "A Defense of Abortion" (1971), which presented an intriguing example. Imagine that, without your prior knowledge or consent, you are sedated in your sleep and surgically connected to a famous violinist, who must share the use of your kidneys for nine months until he is able to survive on his own. Even granting that the violinist is obviously a full-fledged person, Thomson argues that you are morally justified in disconnecting yourself from the violinist, even if it results in his death. Going back to our diagram of the two main stages of the abortion argument, we can see that Thomson's strategy is to question the transition from "personhood" to "right to life." Even granting that the dependent entity is a full person (whether fetus or violinist), we may still be morally justified in cutting off support and thereby killing that person. Thus, Thomson argues, the morality of abortion does not depend on our answer to the question of whether the fetus is a person or not. A more developed version of Thomson's example is to be found in Jane English's selection, "Abortion and the Concept of a Person."

Thomson's article has been criticized on many fronts, but despite these criticisms, the major impact of her piece has been to open the door to the possibility that the answer to the question of abortion does not depend solely on the moral status of the fetus. This opened the door to a more extensive consideration of the other principal moral consideration in this situation, the rights of the pregnant woman.

The Rights of the Pregnant Woman

The second principal focus of moral concern is on the rights of the pregnant woman. Yet what precisely are these rights? At least four main arguments have been advanced: the right to privacy, the right to ownership and control over one's own body, the right to equal treatment, and the right to self-determination.

The Right to Privacy

In *Roe v. Wade* (1973), the Supreme Court based its support for a woman's right to abortion in part on the claim that the woman has a right to privacy. In constitutional law, the right to privacy seems to have two distinct senses. First, certain behaviors—such as sexual intercourse—are usually thought to be private; the government may not infringe upon these behaviors unless there is some particularly compelling reason (such as preventing the sexual abuse of children) for doing so. Second, some decisions in an individual's life—such as the choice of a mate or a career—are seen as matters of individual autonomy or self-determination; these are private in the sense that the government has no right to tell an individual what to do in such areas. This second sense of privacy will be discussed below in the section on the right to self-determination. In this section, we confine our attention to the first sense of privacy.

The Right to Ownership of One's Own Body

Some have argued that the right to abortion is based on a woman's right to control her own body and in some instances this is seen as a property right. This approach also seems wide of the mark. To be sure, no one else owns our bodies and, in this sense, there seems to be a right to control our own bodies. However, it is doubtful whether the relationship we have with our own bodies is best understood in terms of ownership, nor is the presence of the fetus most perceptively grasped as the intrusion onto private property.

The Right to Equal Treatment

Some jurists, most notably Ruth Bader Ginsburg, have suggested that a woman's right to abortion may be best justified constitutionally through an appeal to the right to equal protection under the law. Pregnancy results from the combined actions of two people, yet the woman typically bears a disproportionate amount of the responsibility and burden. This line of reasoning certainly seems highly relevant to striking down laws and regulations that discriminate against women because of pregnancy, but it is unclear whether it alone is sufficient to support a right to abortion. In fact, it would seem that there must be some other, more fundamental right that is at stake here.

The Right to Self-Determination

When we consider the actual conflict that many women experience in making the decision about abortion, it would seem that it centers primarily around the effects that an unwanted pregnancy and child would have on their lives. The most fundamental right at issue for the pregnant woman in this context would seem to be the right to determine the course of her own life. In this context, it is relevant to ask *how much* the pregnancy would interfere with the woman's life. As John Martin Fisher pointed out, one of the misleading aspects of Thomson's violinist example is that it suggests pregnancy would virtually eliminate one's choices for nine months. In actuality, the violinist case would be comparable only to the most difficult of pregnancies, those that require months of strict bed rest. Yet in most cases, pregnancy does not involve such an extreme restriction on the woman's everyday life; the restrictions on self-determination are much less.

In what ways do pregnancy and childbirth potentially conflict with self-determination? Consider, first of all, the extremes on the spectrum. On the one hand, imagine a most grave threat to self-determination: a rape that results in an extremely difficult pregnancy that required constant bed rest, childbirth that contained a high risk of the mother's death, and the likelihood that the child would require years of constant medical attention. Conception, pregnancy, delivery, and the child would all severely limit (if not destroy) the mother's choices in life. These carry enormous moral weight. On the other hand, an easy pregnancy and birth of a perfectly healthy baby are potentially much less restrictive to a woman's power of self-determination. Raising a child, of course, is potentially quite restrictive to self-determination, but in those cases where adoption is a reasonable option, raising the child is not necessary.

There is a further perplexity about self-determination. It is reasonable, as Fisher and others have done, to distinguish between what is central to one's self-determination and what is peripheral to it. We intuitively recognize this when we hear, for example, of a pianist whose hands have been crushed. Although such an accident would be terrible for anyone, it is especially terrible for a person whose life is devoted to making music with his or her hands. If the pianist were to become color-blind, this would be much less serious because it would not strike as centrally at the pianist's sense of self. (We would have a quite different assessment of color-blindness in a painter, however.) Yet the perplexity centers around those cases in which people make something central to their sense of identity that we, as outsiders, would consider peripheral at best. For example, the couple who want an abortion because bearing a child would force them to postpone a vacation for two months seems to be giving undue weight to the timing of their vacation. What if, to take an even more extreme case, a woman bank robber decided on an abortion because pregnancy would interfere with robbing banks? Are there any limits to what can legitimately be taken as central to self-determination?

The Principle of Double Effect

Centuries of Christian theology and philosophy have finely honed what is known as the *Principle of the Double Effect,* which allows us to perform certain actions that would otherwise be immoral. Typically, four conditions have to be met for an action to be morally permissible: (a) the action itself must be either morally good or at least morally neutral, (b) the bad consequences must not be intended, (c) the good consequences cannot be the direct causal result of the bad consequences, and (d) the good consequences must be proportionate to the bad consequences. For example, the principle of the double effect allows a physician to remove a cancerous uterus from a pregnant woman, even if the fetus is thereby killed. Removal of the uterus is in itself morally neutral; it is not done to abort the fetus; the elimination of the cancer does not result from the killing of the fetus; and the saving of the woman's life is proportionate to the termination of the pregnancy.

Abortion and Compromise: Seeking a Common Ground

Initially, it might seem that there is no room for compromise in matters of abortion. If it is the intentional killing of an innocent human being, then it cannot be countenanced. If it does not involve killing a human being, then it should not be prohibited. It is either wrong or right, and there seems to be little middle ground. Yet as we begin to reflect on the issue, we see that there are indeed areas of potential cooperation. Let's briefly consider several such areas.

Reducing Unwanted Pregnancies

One of the striking aspects of the abortion issue is its potential avoidability. Abortions occur when there are unwanted pregnancies. To the extent that we can reduce unwanted pregnancies, we can reduce abortions. Certainly there are cases of unwanted pregnancy due to rape or incest and there are certainly other cases due to the failure of contraceptive devices. Unfortunately, despite our best efforts, none of these types of cases will probably be completely eliminated in the future. Yet they comprise only a small percentage of the cases of unwanted pregnancies; moreover, there is already agreement that these should be further reduced.

The single most common cause of unwanted pregnancies is sexual intercourse without contraception. To the extent that this can be reduced, the number of abortions can be reduced. Conservatives, liberals, and strong feminists can agree on this goal, although they may emphasize quite different ways of achieving it. Conservatives will stress the virtue of chastity and the value of abstinence. Liberals will stress the importance of contraceptives and family planning. Strong feminists will urge social and political changes that will ensure that women have at least an equal voice in decisions about sexual intercourse. Some will respond to the conservative call, others to the liberal program, still others to the feminist concerns. Yet the common result may be the reduction of unwanted pregnancies and, with that, the reduction of abortions. In addition to this, an increase in responsibility in the area of sexuality may help to reduce the spread of AIDS and other sexually communicated diseases.

Ensuring Genuinely Free and Informed Choice

There is widespread agreement among almost all parties that a choice made freely is better than one made under pressure or duress. There are several ways of increasing the likelihood of a genuinely free and informed choice. First, *the earlier the choice, the better.* Many people maintain that the more the fetus is developed, the more morally serious is the abortion decision. Although conservatives would maintain that all abortions are equally wrong, encouraging an early decision would not contradict their beliefs. Second, *women should have the opportunity to make the choice without undue outside pressure.* There are a number of ways in which undue outside pressure can be reduced, most notably through providing genuinely impartial counseling in an atmosphere devoid of coercion (demonstrations, etc.). Third, *alternatives to abortion should be available.* These include adoption (for those who wish to give their baby up for adoption), aid to dependent children (for those who wish to raise their own babies), day care (for those who work full-time and raise children), and adequate maternity leave.

Abortion and Sorrow

Naomi Wolf refers to a Japanese practice that honors the memory of departed fetuses. This is called *Mizuko Kuyo.* I have gathered together a number of resources relating to this practice on the Web page on abortion at http://ethics.sandiego.edu/abortion.html. Philosophically, one of the most interesting aspects of this practice is that it unites two elements that are rarely brought together in the American philosophical discussion of abortion. In the practice of *Mizuko Kuyo,* couples who have had an abortion dedicate a doll at a temple to the memory of the departed fetus. To some extent, this is analogous to the practice of lighting a votive candle in Christian churches. What is noteworthy is that Japanese society both permits abortion and at the same time recognizes that it is a sorrowful occasion. In most instances, American philosophical literature chooses one or the other of these elements, but not both simultaneously.

Living Together with Moral Differences

Abortion is a particularly interesting and important moral issue in contemporary America, for it poses most clearly to us as a society the question of how we can live together with deep moral differences. People on all sides of the abortion controversy are intelligent people of good will, genuinely trying to do what they believe is right. The challenge for all of us in such situations is to view one another in this light and seek to create a community that embraces and respects our differences while at the same time preserving our moral integrity. It is in this spirit that you are urged to approach the articles contained in this section. None provides the final answer to all our questions about the morality of abortion, but each helps to shed light on the moral complexity of the situation and the differing moral insights with which we as a society approach this difficult issue. Even if none of these articles provides the complete answer to the problem of abortion, each does help us to better understand ourselves and others.

The Arguments

Jane English
"Abortion and the Concept of a Person"

Jane English (1947–1978) received her doctorate from Harvard University. She authored several articles in the field of ethics before her untimely death in a mountain climbing accident on the Matterhorn at the age of 31.

English challenges a common belief often shared by both advocates and critics of abortion. Both sides often claim that the permissibility of abortion turns on the question of whether the fetus is a person or not. English argues that (1) the notion of personhood is not precise enough to offer a decisive criterion for judging whether the fetus is a person and (2) there are a number of cases in which we can reasonably conclude that (a) abortion is permissible even if the fetus is a person and (b) abortion is not permissible even if the fetus is not a person. The issue of abortion, in other words, does not turn on the issue of the personhood of the fetus.

As You Read, Consider This:

1. What reasons does English offer for claiming that the notion of personhood is not precise enough to serve as a foundation for deciding the abortion issue? Do you agree with her reasons?

2. Why, according to English, do we need "an additional premise" to move from the claim that the fetus is a person to the conclusion that abortion is always morally wrong?

The abortion debate rages on. Yet the two most popular positions seem to be clearly mistaken. Conservatives maintain that a human life begins at conception and that therefore abortion must be wrong because it is murder. But not all killings of humans are murders. Most notably, self-defense may justify even the killing of an innocent person.

Liberals, on the other hand, are just as mistaken in their argument that since a fetus does not become a person until birth, a woman may do whatever she pleases in and to her own body. First, you cannot do as you please with your own body if it affects other people adversely.[1] Second, if a fetus is not a person, that does not imply that you can do to it anything you wish. Animals, for example, are not persons, yet to kill or torture them for no reason at all is wrong.

At the center of the storm has been the issue of just when it is between ovulation and adulthood that a person appears on the scene. Conservatives draw the line at conception, liberals at birth. In this paper, I first examine our concept of a person and conclude that no single criterion can capture the concept of a person and no sharp line can be drawn. Next I argue that if a fetus is a person,

Canadian Journal of Philosophy, Vol. 5, No. 2 (October, 1975).

abortion is still justifiable in many cases; and if a fetus is not a person, killing it is still wrong in many cases. To a large extent, these two solutions are in agreement. I conclude that our concept of a person cannot and need not bear the weight that the abortion controversy has thrust upon it.

I

The several factions in the abortion argument have drawn battle lines around various proposed criteria for determining what is and what is not a person. For example, Mary Anne Warren[2] lists five features (capacities for reasoning, self-awareness, complex communication, etc.) as her criteria for personhood and argues for the permissibility of abortion because a fetus falls outside this concept. Baruch Brody[3] uses brain waves. Michael Tooley[4] picks having-a-concept-of-self as his criterion and concludes that infanticide and abortion are justifiable, while the killing of adult animals is not. On the other side, Paul Ramsey[5] claims a certain gene structure is the defining characteristic. John Noonan[6] prefers conceived-of-humans and presents counterexamples to various other candidate criteria. For instance, he argues against viability as the criterion because the newborn and infirm would then be non-persons, since they cannot live without the aid of others. He rejects any criterion that calls upon the sorts of sentiments a being can evoke in adults on the grounds that this would allow us to exclude other races as non-persons if we could just view them sufficiently unsentimentally.

These approaches are typical: foes of abortion propose sufficient conditions for personhood which fetuses satisfy, while friends of abortion counter with necessary conditions for personhood which fetuses lack. But these both presuppose that the concept of a person can be captured in a straightjacket of necessary and/or sufficient conditions.[7] Rather, "person" is a cluster of features, of which rationality, having a self-concept and being conceived of humans are only part.

What is typical of persons? Within our concept of a person we include, first, certain biological factors: descended from humans, having a certain genetic make-up, having a head, hands, arms, eyes, capable of locomotion, breathing, eating, sleeping. There are psychological factors: sentience, perception, having a concept of self and of one's own interests and desires, the ability to use tools, the ability to use language or symbol systems, the ability to joke, to be angry, to doubt. There are rationality factors: the ability to reason and draw conclusions, the ability to generalize and to learn from past experience, the ability to sacrifice present interests for greater gains in the future. There are social factors: the ability to work in groups and respond to peer pressures, the ability to recognize and consider as valuable the interests of others, seeing oneself as one among "other minds," the ability to sympathize, encourage, love, the ability to evoke from others the responses of sympathy, encouragement, love, the ability to work with others for mutual advantage. Then there are legal factors: being subject to the law and protected by it, having the ability to sue and enter contracts, being counted in the census, having a name and citizenship, the ability to own property, inherit, and so forth.

Now the point is not that this list is incomplete, or that you can find counterinstances to each of its points. People typically exhibit rationality, for instance, but someone who was irrational would not thereby fail to qualify as a person. On the other hand, something could exhibit the majority of these features and still fail to be a person, as an advanced robot might. There is no single core of necessary and sufficient features which we can draw upon with the assurance that they constitute what really makes a person; there are only features that are more or less typical.

This is not to say that no necessary or sufficient conditions can be given. Being alive is a necessary condition for being a person, and being a U.S. Senator is sufficient. But rather than falling inside a sufficient condition or outside a necessary one, a fetus lies in the penumbra region where our concept of a person is not so simple. For this reason I think a conclusive answer to the question whether a fetus is a person is unattainable. Here we might note a family of simple fallacies that proceed by stating a necessary condition for personhood and showing that a fetus has that characteristic. This is a form of the fallacy of affirming the consequent. For example, some have mistakenly reasoned from the premise that a fetus is human (after all, it is a human fetus rather than, say, a canine fetus), to the conclusion that it is a human. Adding an equivocation of "being," we get the fallacious argument that since a fetus is something both living and human, it is a human being.

Nonetheless, it does seem clear that a fetus has very few of the above family of characteristics, whereas a newborn baby exhibits a much larger proportion of them—and a two-year old has even more. Note that one traditional anti-abortion argument has centered on pointing out the many ways in which a fetus resembles a baby. They emphasize its development ("It already has ten fingers. . .") without mentioning its dissimilarities to adults (it still has gills and a tail). They also try to evoke the sort of sympathy on our part that we only feel toward other persons ("Never to laugh. . .or feel the sunshine?"). This all seems to be a relevant way to argue, since its purpose is to persuade us that a fetus satisfies so many of the important features on the list that it ought to be treated as a person. Also note that a fetus near the time of birth satisfies many more of these factors than a fetus in the early months of development. This could provide reason for making distinctions among the different stages of pregnancy, as the U.S. Supreme Court has done.[8]

Historically, the time at which a person has been said to come into existence has varied widely. Muslims date personhood from fourteen days after conception. Some medievals followed Aristotle in placing ensoulment at forty days after conception for a male fetus and eighty days for a female fetus.[9] In European common law since the seventeenth century, abortion was considered the killing of a person only after quickening, the time when a pregnant woman first feels the fetus move on its own. Nor is this variety of opinions surprising. Biologically, a human being develops gradually. We shouldn't expect there to be any specific time or sharp dividing point when a person appears on the scene.

For these reasons I believe our concept of a person is not sharp or decisive enough to bear the weight of a solution to the abortion controversy. To use it to solve that problem is to clarify *obscurum per obscurius.*

II

Next let us consider what follows if a fetus is a person after all. Judith Jarvis Thomson's landmark article, "A Defense of Abortion,"[10] correctly points out that some additional argumentation is needed at this point in the conservative argument to bridge the gap between the premise that the fetus in an innocent person and the conclusion that killing it is always wrong. To arrive at this conclusion, we would need the additional premise that killing an innocent person is always wrong. But killing an innocent person is sometimes permissible, most notably in self-defense. Some examples may help draw out our intuitions or ordinary judgments about self-defense.

Suppose a mad scientist, for instance, hypnotized innocent people to jump under the bushes and attack innocent passers-by with knives. If you are so attacked, we agree you have a right to kill the attacker in self-defense, if killing him is the only way to protect your life or to save yourself from serious injury. It does not seem to matter here that the attacker is not malicious but himself an innocent pawn, for your killing of him is not done in a spirit of retribution but only in self-defense.

How severe an injury may you inflict in self-defense? In part this depends upon the severity of the injury to be avoided: you may not shoot someone merely to avoid having your clothes torn. This might lead one to the mistaken conclusion that the defense may only equal the threatened injury in severity; that to avoid death you may kill, but to avoid a black eye you may only inflict a black eye or the equivalent. Rather, our laws and customs seem to say that you may create an injury somewhat, but not enormously, greater than the injury to be avoided. To fend off an attack whose outcome would be as serious as rape, a severe beating or the loss of a finger, you may shoot; to avoid having your clothes torn, you may blacken an eye.

Aside from this, the injury you may inflict should only be the minimum necessary to deter or incapacitate the attacker. Even if you know he intends to kill you, you are not justified in shooting him if you could equally well save yourself by the simple expedient of running away. Self-defense is for the purpose of avoiding harms rather than equalizing harms.

Some cases of pregnancy present a parallel situation. Though the fetus is itself innocent, it may pose a threat to the pregnant woman's well-being, life prospects or health, mental or physical. If the pregnancy presents a slight threat to her interests, it seems self-defense cannot justify abortion. But if the threat is on a par with a serious beating or the loss of a finger, she may kill the fetus that poses such a threat, even if it is an innocent person. If a lesser harm to the fetus could have the same defensive effect, killing it would not be justified. It is unfortunate that the only way to free the woman from the pregnancy entails the death of the fetus (except in very late stages of pregnancy). Thus a self-defense model supports Thomson's point that the woman has a right only to be freed from the fetus, not a right to demand its death.[11]

The self-defense model is most helpful when we take the pregnant woman's point of view. In the pre-Thomson literature, abortion is often framed as a question for a third party: do you, a doctor, have a right to choose between the life of the woman and that of the fetus? Some have claimed that if you were a passer-by who witnessed a struggle between the innocent hypnotized attacker and his equally innocent victim, you would have no reason to kill either in defense of the other. They have concluded that the self defense model implies that a woman may attempt to abort herself, but that a doctor should not assist her. I think the position of the third party is somewhat more complex. We do feel some inclination to intervene on behalf of the victim rather than the attacker, other things equal. But if both parties are innocent, other factors come into consideration. You would rush to the aid of your husband whether he was attacker or attackee. If a hypnotized famous violinist were attacking a skid row bum, we would try to save the individual who is of more value to society. These considerations would tend to support abortion in some cases.

But suppose you are a frail senior citizen who wishes to avoid being knifed by one of these innocent hypnotics, so you have hired a body-guard to accompany you. If you are attacked, it is clear we believe that the bodyguard, acting as your agent, has a right to kill the attacker to save you from a serious beating. Your rights of self-defense are transferred to your agent. I suggest that we should similarly view the doctor as the pregnant woman's agent in carrying out a defense she is physically incapable of accomplishing herself.

Thanks to modern technology, the cases are rare in which a pregnancy poses as clear a threat to a woman's bodily health as an attacker brandishing a switchblade. How does self-defense fare when more subtle, complex and long-range harms are involved?

To consider a somewhat fanciful example, suppose you are a highly trained surgeon when you are kidnapped by the hypnotic attacker. He says he does not intend to harm you but to take you back to the mad scientist who, it turns out, plans to hypnotize you to have a permanent mental block against all your knowledge of medicine. This would automatically destroy your career which would in turn have a serious adverse impact on your family, your personal relationships and your happiness. It seems to me that if the only way you can avoid this outcome is to shoot the innocent attacker, you are justified in so doing. You are defending yourself from a drastic injury to your life prospects. I think it is no exaggeration to claim that unwanted pregnancies (most obviously among teenagers) often have such adverse life-long consequences as the surgeon's loss of livelihood.

Several parallels arise between various views on abortion and the self-defense model. Let's suppose further that these hypnotized attackers only operate at night, so that it is well known that they can be avoided completely by the considerable inconvenience of never leaving your house after dark. One view is that since you could stay home at night, therefore if you go out and are selected by one of these hypnotized people, you have no right to defend yourself. This parallels the view that abstinence is the only acceptable way to avoid pregnancy. Others might hold that you ought to take along some defense such as Mace which will deter the hypnotized person without killing him, but that if this defense fails, you are obliged to submit to the resulting injury, no matter how severe it is. This parallels the view that contraception is all right but abortion is always wrong, even in cases of contraceptive failure.

A third view is that you may kill the hypnotized person only if he will actually kill you, but not if he will only injure you. This is like the position that abortion is permissible only if it is required to save a woman's life. Finally we have the view that it is all right to kill the attacker, even if only to avoid a very slight inconvenience to yourself and even if you knowingly walked down the very street where all these incidents have been taking place without taking along any Mace or protective escort. If we assume that a fetus is a person, this is the analogue of the view that abortion is always justifiable, "on demand."

The self-defense model allows us to see an important difference that exists between abortion and infanticide, even if a fetus is a person from conception. Many have argued that the only way to justify abortion without justifying infanticide would be to find some characteristic of personhood that is acquired at birth. Michael Tooley, for one, claims infanticide is justifiable because the really significant characteristics of a person are acquired some time after birth. But all such approaches look to characteristics of the developing human and ignore the relation between the fetus and the woman. What if, after birth, the presence of an infant or the need to support it posed a grave threat to the woman's sanity or life prospects? She could escape this threat by the simple expedient of running away. So a solution that does not entail the death of the infant is available. Before birth, such solutions are not available because of the biological dependence of the fetus on the woman. Birth is the crucial point not because of any characteristics the fetus gains, but because after birth the woman can defend herself by a means less drastic than killing the infant. Hence self-defense can be used to justify abortion without necessarily thereby justifying infanticide.

III

On the other hand, supposing a fetus is not after all a person, would abortion always be morally permissible? Some opponents of abortion seem worried that if a fetus is not a full-fledged person, then we are justified in treating it in any way at all. However, this does not follow. Non-persons do get some consideration in our moral code, though of course they do not have the same rights as persons have (and in general they do not have moral responsibilities), and though their interests may be overridden by the interests of persons. Still, we cannot just treat them in any way at all.

Treatment of animals is a case in point. It is wrong to torture dogs for fun or to kill wild birds for no reason at all. It is wrong Period, even though dogs and birds do not have the same rights persons do. However, few people think it is wrong to use dogs as experimental animals, causing them considerable suffering in some cases, provided that the resulting research will probably bring discoveries of great benefit to people. And most of us think it all right to kill birds for food or to protect our crops. People's rights are different from the consideration we give to animals, then, for it is wrong to experiment on people, even if others might later benefit a great deal as a result of their suffering. You might volunteer to be a subject, but this would be supererogatory; you certainly have a right to refuse to be a medical guinea pig.

But how do we decide what you may or may not do to non-persons? This is a difficult problem, one for which I believe no adequate account exists. You do not want to say, for instance, that torturing dogs is all right whenever the sum of its effects on people is good—when it doesn't warp the sensibilities of the torturer so much that he mistreats people. If that were the case, it would be all right to torture dogs if you did it in private, or if the torturer lived on a desert island or died soon afterward, so that his actions had no effect on people. This is an inadequate account, because whatever moral consideration animals get, it has to be indefeasible, too. It will have to be a general proscription of certain actions, not merely a weighing of the impact on people on a case-by-case basis.

Rather, we need to distinguish two levels on which consequences of actions can be taken into account in moral reasoning. The traditional objections to Utilitarianism focus on the fact that it operates solely on the first level, taking all the consequences into account in particular cases only. Thus Utilitarianism is open to "desert island" and "lifeboat" counterexamples because these cases are rigged to make the consequences of actions severely limited.

Rawls's theory could be described as a teleological sort of theory, but with teleology operating on a higher level.[12] In choosing the principles to regulate society from the original position, his hypothetical choosers make their decision on the basis of the total consequences of various systems. Furthermore, they are constrained to choose a general set of rules which people can readily learn and apply. An ethical theory must operate by generating a set of sympathies and attitudes toward others which reinforces the functioning of that set of moral principles. Our prohibition against killing people operates by means of certain moral sentiments including sympathy, compassion and guilt. But if these attitudes are to form a coherent set, they carry us further: we tend to perform supererogatory actions, and we tend to feel similar compassion toward person-like non-persons.

It is crucial that psychological facts play a role here. Our psychological constitution makes it the case that for our ethical theory to work, it must prohibit certain treatment of non-persons which are significantly person-like. If our moral rules allowed people to treat person-like non-persons in ways we do not want people to be treated, this would undermine the system of sympathies and attitudes that makes the ethical system work. For this reason, we would choose in the original position to make mistreatment of some sorts of animals wrong in general (not just wrong in the cases with public impact), even though animals are not themselves parties in the original position. Thus it makes sense that it is those animals whose appearance and behavior are most like those of people that get the most consideration in our moral scheme.

It is because of "coherence of attitudes," I think, that the similarity of a fetus to a baby is very significant. A fetus one week before birth is so much like a newborn baby in our psychological space that we cannot allow any cavalier treatment of the former while expecting full sympathy and nutritive support for the latter. Thus, I think that anti-abortion forces are indeed giving their strongest arguments when they point to the similarities between a fetus and a baby, and when they try to evoke our emotional attachment to and sympathy for the fetus. An early horror story from New York about nurses who were expected to alternate between caring for six-week premature infants and disposing of viable 24-week aborted fetuses is just that—a horror story. These beings are so much alike that no one can be asked to draw a distinction and treat them so very differently.

Remember, however, that in the early weeks after conception a fetus is very much unlike a person. It is hard to develop these feelings for a set of genes which doesn't yet have a head, hands, beating heart, response to touch or the ability to move by itself. Thus it seems to me that the alleged "slippery slope" between conception and birth is not so very slippery. In the early stages of pregnancy, abortion can hardly be compared to murder for psychological reasons, but in the latest stages it is psychologically akin to murder.

Another source of similarity is the bodily continuity between fetus and adult. Bodies play a surprisingly central role in our attitudes toward persons. One has only to think of the philosophical literature on how far physical identity suffices for personal identity or Wittgenstein's remark that the best picture of the human soul is the human body. Even after death when all agree the body is no longer a person, we still observe elaborate customs of respect for the human body; like people who torture dogs, necrophilics are not to be trusted with people.[13] So it is appropriate that we show respect to a fetus as the body continuous with the body of a person. This is a degree of resemblance to persons that animals cannot rival.

Michael Tooley also utilizes a parallel with animals. He claims that it is always permissible to drown newborn kittens and draws conclusions about infanticide.[14] But it is only permissible to drown kittens when their survival would cause some hardship. Perhaps it would be a burden to feed and house six more cats or to find other homes for them. The alternative of letting them starve produces even more suffering than the drowning. Since the kittens get their rights secondhand, so to speak, via the need for coherence in our attitudes, their interests are often overridden by the interests of full-fledged persons. But if their survival would be no inconvenience to people at all, then it is wrong to drown them, contra Tooley.

Tooley's conclusions about abortion are wrong for the same reason. Even if a fetus is not a person, abortion is not always permissible, because of the resemblance of a fetus to a person. I agree with Thomson that it would be wrong for a woman who is seven months pregnant to have an abortion just to avoid having to postpone a trip to Europe. In the early months of pregnancy when the fetus hardly resembles a baby at all, then, abortion is permissible whenever it is in the interests of the pregnant woman or her family. The reasons would only need to outweigh the pain and inconvenience of the abortion itself. In the middle months, when the fetus comes to resemble a person, abortion would be justifiable only when the continuation of the pregnancy or the birth of the child would cause harm—physical, psychological, economic or social—to the woman. In the last months of pregnancy, even on our current assumption that a fetus is not a person, abortion seems to be wrong except to save a woman from significant injury or death.

The Supreme Court has recognized similar gradations in the alleged slippery slope stretching between conception and birth. To this point, the present paper has been a discussion of the moral status of abortion only, not its legal status. In view of the great physical, financial and sometimes psychological costs of abortion, perhaps the legal arrangement most compatible with the proposed moral solution would be the absence of restrictions, that is, so-called abortion "on demand."

So I conclude, first, that application of our concept of a person will not suffice to settle the abortion issue. After all, the biological development of a human being is gradual. Second, whether a fetus is a person or not, abortion is justifiable early in a pregnancy to avoid modest harms and seldom justifiable late in pregnancy except to avoid significant injury or death.

Endnotes

1. We also have paternalistic laws which keep us from harming our own bodies even when no one else is affected. Ironically, anti-abortion laws were originally designed to protect pregnant women from a dangerous but tempting procedure.

2. Mary Anne Warren, "On the Moral and Legal Status of Abortion," *Monist* 5 (1973), p. 55.

3. Baruch Brody, "Fetal Humanity and the Theory of Essentialism" in Robert Baker and Frederick Elliston (eds.) *Philosophy and Sex* (Buffalo, NY, 1975).

4. Michael Tooley, "Abortion and Infanticide." *Philosophy and Public Affairs* I (1971).

5. Paul Ramsey, "The Morality of Abortion," in James Rachels (ed.), *Moral Problems* (New York, 1971).

6. John Noonan, "Abortion and the Catholic Church: A Summary History," *Natural Law Forum* 12 (1967), pp. 125–131.

7. Wittgenstein has argued against the possibility of so capturing the concept of a game, *Philosophical Investigations* (New York, 1958), §66–71.

8. Not because the fetus is partly a person and so has some of the rights of persons but rather because of the rights of person-like non-persons. This I discuss in part III.

9. Aristotle himself was concerned, however, with the different question of when the soul takes form. For historical data, see Jimmye Kimmey "How the Abortion Laws Happened," *Ms.* I (April, 1973), p. 48 ff. and John Noonan, *loc. cit.*

10. J.J. Thomson, "A Defense of Abortion," *Philosophy and Public Affairs* I (1971).

11. *Ibid.*, p. 52.

12. John Rawls, *A Theory of Justice* (Cambridge, MA, 1971), §§3–4.

13. On the other hand, if they can be trusted with people, then our moral customs are mistaken. It all depends on the facts of psychology.

14. *Op. cit.*, pp. 40, 60–61.

Journal/Discussion Questions

✍ *In your own experience, do you think of the fetus as a person? In what sense(s)? In what ways did English's remarks shed light on your moral feelings toward the unborn?*

1. English indicates that it is not always morally wrong to kill an innocent person. What support does she give for this claim? Do you agree with her?

2. What does English mean by "coherence of attitudes"? What role does this term play in the development of her argument?

3. Under what circumstances would English hold that abortion is morally wrong? What are her reasons? Do you agree with her? Why or why not?

Roy W. Perrett
"Buddhism, Abortion, and the Middle Way"

Roy Perrett is Professor of Philosophy, University of Hawai'i at Manoa. Prior to that, he taught in New Zealand and Australia. His has published numerous articles and five books, including Death and Immortality *(1987);* Hindu Ethics: A Philosophical Study *(1998); and* Indian Philosophy: A Collection of Readings *(5 vols., ed., 2001); as well as numerous articles.*

In this article, Perrett explores whether Japanese Buddhism offers a response to the dilemma of abortion, a middle way between the pro-choice and pro-life extremes found in the Western debate about abortion. He sketches out that middle way and offers a defense of it.

As You Read, Consider This:
1. What is the First Precept in Buddhism? How does this relate to abortion?
2. What is meant by a moral dilemma? Are genuine moral dilemmas possible in Perrett's view?
3. What does Perrett mean by a "moral remainder?" What role does that concept play in his analysis?
4. What role does the concept of compassion play in Perrett's analysis?

Abortion is clearly one of the most controversial and divisive contemporary moral problems, a problem that has of late greatly exercised western religious ethicists. What, however, have modern Buddhist ethicists to say about the issue, and is there anything to be learned from it? A number of writers have suggested that Buddhism does indeed have something important to offer here: a response to the dilemma of abortion that is a "middle way" between the pro-choice and pro-life extremes that have polarised the western debate. I begin with a brief review of some features of the contemporary situation in Buddhist Asia (particularly Japan), then seek to analyse this material with respect to claims that Buddhism offers a viable "middle way" on abortion. This analysis will in turn require some consideration of the nature of moral dilemmas, of the significance of moral remainders and the emotions of self-assessment, and of the possibility of conflicts between moral requirements and moral ideals.

I

Central to traditional Buddhist ethics are the Five Precepts (pancasila), the first of which is an undertaking to observe the rule to abstain from taking life. Notwithstanding this prohibition on killing and a traditional embryology that implies that the fetus is a living being from the point of conception, there is—surprisingly enough—no explicit prohibition of abortion to be found in the most ancient Pali scriptures of the Theravadin school, though the monastic disciplinary code in the later

Asian Philosophy Vol. 10, No. 2, (2000), pp. 101–114.

Vinayapitaka does explicitly forbid the involvement of monks and nuns in the practice, and the Jatakas and other mythological texts warn of the dire karmic consequences attendant upon abortion.[1] Nevertheless it is certainly true that many contemporary Theravadin Buddhists, particularly monastics, disapprove of abortion as a violation of the precept against taking life. Moreover, the situation is not too different in the Mahayana traditions of Tibetan Buddhism, even though the Tibetans follow an alternative Mulasarvastivadin Vinaya.[2] (As we shall see, this general pattern is rather less marked in East Asian Mahayana Buddhism.)

When we turn from text to context, however, we find in modern Buddhist Asia a remarkable toleration of the practice of abortion.[3] In Thailand, for example, where over 90 per cent of the population are Theravadin Buddhists, the abortion rate is some 50 per cent higher than the US figure for the equivalent number of citizens. True, most of these abortions, though readily available, are technically illegal. But opinion polls also indicate that the majority of Thais believe both that abortion is immoral and that it ought to be more extensively legalized.[4]

The situation in Mahayana Taiwan is analogous in many respects: a traditional Buddhist disapproval of abortion, very restrictive abortion laws, but a widespread and tolerated practice of abortion.[5] Much the same situation obtains in Korea, where not only is the national abortion rate very high, but the rate among Buddhists is as high or higher than that of the rest of the population.[6] In Japan, the abortion rate is also very high (officially 22.6 per 1000 women of child-bearing age, though probably in reality nearer 65–90). However, there abortion laws are very liberal too, while contraception (especially the Pill) is not so readily available.

This apparent discrepancy between text and context may seem unremarkable: after all, Buddhists would be by no means unique if they sometimes do what they ought not to according to their own religious precepts. But modern advocates of a Buddhist middle way on abortion seem to want to claim that something deeper is happening here. The Thai bioethicist Pinit Ratanakul, for instance, refers to "the Thai 'middle way' . . . between the extreme positions found in Western views," a view which recognises that "in some situations . . . abortion cannot be perceived as an either/or option."[7] Helen Tworkov, editor of the Buddhist magazine *Tricycle,* suggests that Buddhism involves "taking both sides" on the anti-abortion/pro-choice issue.[8] Ken Jones' popular book *The Social Face of Buddhism* describes abortion as a "dilemma" involving Buddhism's dual commitment, on the one hand, to refraining from killing and, on the other hand, to expressing compassion for the pregnant woman.[9]

The Japanese Buddhist tradition has been particularly influential here. The American Zen master Robert Aitken criticizes "over-simplified positions of pro-life and pro-choice" that fail to "touch the depths of the dilemma," referring approvingly to the Japanese practice of mizuko kuyo, a Buddhist memorial service for aborted children.[10] William LaFleur, a scholar who has extensively studied this practice in recent years, enthusiastically commends it as a response to the abortion issue from which the West might learn.[11] LaFleur suggests it is an interesting exemplar of the way in which Japanese "societal pragmatism" has achieved a consensus on abortion, forefronting the need for a solution without tearing the social fabric apart. In contrast to the western tendency to represent the abortion issue as involving only two irreconcilable alternatives (pro-life or pro-choice), Japanese Buddhism offers a "third option—perhaps a middle way between the others."[12]

The Japanese practice of mizuko kuyo is a Buddhist memorial service for children (mizuko is literally "water-child") who have died before their parents, including children who have died as a result of spontaneous or induced abortion, as well as stillborn children or those who have died prematurely.[13] Given the huge number of abortions performed in Japan since the post-war legalization of such operations, the majority of these mizuko are aborted fetuses. Ritual prayers and offerings are made in memory of the departed "water-children" and parents (particularly mothers) offer apologies to them. The practice permits a ritualized expression of guilt for the regrettable, though perhaps unavoidable, act of abortion.

Although the upsurge in the present day form of the ritual dates only from the 1950s and the practice came in for some public criticism in the 1980s, today it occurs everywhere in Japan and goes largely unremarked. In this way, a kind of public consensus on abortion has been reached in Buddhist Japan, whereby the act is neither forbidden nor treated lightly. In the West the abortion debate has often polarized into a pro-life camp which insists that the fetus is a being with a moral status equivalent to that of a fully grown child, and a pro-choice camp which consequently feels compelled to refuse to acknowledge that the fetus is anything but so much living tissue. In contrast, the Japanese regard the aborted fetus as a kind of "child" that, due to other pressing circumstances, has been "returned." Consequently they are able to make room for the ritual public acknowledgment of the strong emotions of regret and guilt that a woman may feel after an abortion, even when that abortion is thought to have been unavoidable. In other words, Japanese Buddhists seek to walk a kind of "middle way" between the conflicting pro-life and pro-choice alternatives, a way that attempts to give full moral weight to the competing values of both life and choice.

The practice of mizuko kuyo is nowadays so well established in Japan that Buddhists elsewhere have begun to follow suit. As already mentioned, the Zen master Robert Aitken has taken over the ritual for use by American practitioners, skillfully reinterpreting it for the western context.[14] Moreover in Korea Buddhists have recently begun to express a concern for aborted fetuses and demand Buddhist memorial services for them, though of a distinctively Korean form.[15] The practice does not seem to have caught on yet in the Theravadin world, but Thai Buddhists already have available to them more private rituals to acknowledge guilt and improve the karmic situation of the aborted fetus.[16]

Not everyone, however, is unreservedly impressed by all this.[17] Few would want to dispute the potential psychological utility of mizuko kuyo as an aid in the grieving and healing process, but it is much less clear how the ritual acknowledgement of the strong emotions a woman might have about her aborted fetus represents a morally significant "middle way" with respect to the supposed "dilemma" of abortion. Indeed, if the First Precept prohibits taking life and the fetus is conceded to be a living being, then where is the moral dilemma? And does not the guilt acknowledged by the grieving woman in the ritual itself imply her belief that she has acted wrongly?

Clearly it is important here to begin by clarifying just what the dilemma of abortion is supposed to be, such that Buddhism offers a middle way. In ordinary usage the term "moral dilemma" may just mean any kind of moral problem. But philosophers usually understand a moral dilemma to be a situation in which an agent morally ought to do two (or more) alternate actions, but cannot do both (or all) of them together. That there are apparent moral dilemmas is indisputable: persuasive arguments can often be given for incompatible alternatives on a number of moral issues, including abortion. But to show there are moral conflicts in this sense does not establish that there are genuine moral dilemmas, i.e. conflicting moral obligations which cannot be resolved by one of the requirements being justifiably overridden by another.

But perhaps when the authors cited earlier refer to the "dilemma" of abortion they mean no more than the apparent dilemma of abortion; after all, the moral philosopher's special use of "dilemma" is very much a term of art. This understanding of our authors' meaning, however, would imply that they are really making much less interesting claims for the Buddhist contribution to the abortion debate than it might have appeared at first sight. Correspondingly, I suggest it is first worth pursuing a bit further the proposal that there really is a "dilemma" of abortion to which Buddhism is responding.

It is interesting to note in this connection that the philosopher and logician, Ruth Barcan Marcus, herself perfectly familiar with the special philosophical use of "dilemma," has argued that the controversies surrounding non-spontaneous abortion suggest the issue is indeed a genuine dilemma:

> Philosophers are often criticized for inventing bizarre examples and counterexamples to make a philosophical point. But no contrived example can equal the complexity and the puzzles generated by the actual circumstances of foetal conception, parturition, and the ultimate birth of a human being . . . There are arguments that recognize competing claims . . . [and] various combinations of such arguments are proposed . . . What all the arguments seem to share is the assumption that there is, despite uncertainty, a resolution without residue; that there is a correct set of metaphysical claims, principles, and priority rankings of principles which will justify the choice. Then, given the belief that one choice is justified, assignment of guilt relative to the overridden alternative is seen as inappropriate, and feelings of guilt or pangs of conscience are viewed as, at best sentimental. But as one tries to unravel the tangle of arguments, it is clear that to insist that there is in every case a solution without residue is false to the moral facts.[18]

Notable here is Marcus' appeal to the supposed existence of moral residues (including emotions like guilt or remorse) after every choice in the matter as evidence that abortion is a genuine dilemma, a situation where each alternative violates a moral requirement. But these emotions of self-assessment are apparently the very same sorts of emotions involved in the mizuko kuyo ritual. Does the existence of such emotions there too support the claim that the Buddhist ritual is a response to a genuine dilemma of abortion? To answer this question we need to investigate further the nature of moral dilemmas.

II

The first point to note is that Marcus' claim that abortion represents a genuine moral dilemma is one that runs counter to the majority tradition in western ethics. Most western moral philosophers, whatever their disagreements on other matters, have agreed that there can be no moral dilemmas.[19] . . . To show conclusively that moral dilemmas are impossible we need to be more confident of the truth of the relevant deontic principles here than of the thesis that there are moral dilemmas. But it is by no means obvious that there is such a general confidence.

III

To argue thus for the inconclusiveness of these two arguments for the impossibility of moral dilemmas, however, does not do anything to demonstrate that there are such dilemmas. In a much discussed paper Bernard Williams has tried to argue from the existence of moral residues like regret (or remorse or guilt) to the existence of moral dilemmas.[22] Williams begins by pointing out that moral conflicts are more like conflicts of desire than conflicts of (non-moral) belief. When we act on one of two conflicting desires, the rejected desire is not always abandoned, for we may still regret what we have thereby missed. This contrasts with the case of (non-moral) belief, where we do not regret our abandoned false belief. Now when two moral oughts conflict and we act on only one of them, we may well still regret what was not done: i.e. we may hold on to the unactioned ought as a "moral remainder," rather than totally reject it. Even if we are convinced that we acted for the best, we may still regret that we failed to honour one of our conflicting oughts. In other words, the phenomenon of regret shows it is mistaken to suppose that in situations of moral conflict it is always the case that "one ought must be totally rejected in the sense that one becomes convinced that it did not actually apply."[23] But this dubious supposition is essential to traditional scepticism about the possibility of moral dilemmas.

Obviously the argument requires some clarification of the nature of the regret appealed to here. After all, it may be that such regret, if it does exist, is just irrational or non-moral. First of all, we need to understand that Williams is alluding to a particular kind of regret: what some have called agent regret, where one morally regrets an action one has done.[24] Thus I may regret the Holocaust, but unless I believe that I was implicated in it as an agent, I cannot experience agent regret with respect to it. Secondly, it is not a condition of such regret that the agent would undo the action if she could. The agent may believe she acted for the best, but nevertheless still regret that course of action. Thirdly, agent regret is a species of moral regret: it is not just, for instance, regret at having to do something unpleasant (though agent regret will typically involve the agent experiencing some sort of unpleasant feeling). Finally, agent regret can be rational. What Williams is claiming, then, is that there are cases where an agent reasonably experiences agent regret with respect to an action, even though (through no fault of her own) she could not have done otherwise.

The argument from moral remainders to the existence of moral dilemmas needs to proceed with care. The only sort of moral remainder that would be direct evidence for moral dilemmas is an agent's justified (i.e. morally appropriate) feeling that she has violated a moral requirement. But her feeling can only be so justified if she has indeed violated one of two (or more) conflicting moral requirements—which is what the argument from regret is supposed to establish. In other words, the argument threatens to beg the question of whether there ever are conflicting moral requirements.

The most that the apparent existence of moral remainders can establish is that, insofar as these emotions seem morally appropriate, then a putative explanation for them is that the agent has violated a moral requirement. Thus the inference runs not from the existence of regret to the existence of dilemma, but from dilemma to regret: if there are dilemmas, then regret is a morally appropriate response to their practical resolution. This inference does not by itself show that any particular case of regret is both morally appropriate and a response to a dilemma. But insofar as the particular regret seems morally appropriate, then one possible explanation for that appropriateness is that it may be a response to the violation of one of the moral requirements involved in a dilemma. The plausibility of this putative explanation in any particular case then has to be evaluated relative to competing explanations, as is usual when we search for an inference to the best explanation.

It is also important to be careful about how we characterize the emotions that are the moral remainders. I have already indicated that the relevant kind of regret is agent regret, not the kind of impersonal regret which implies no responsibility. Some writers prefer to use the term "regret" in such a way that an agent's experiencing regret does not imply a belief that a moral requirement was violated.[25] Regret is then contrasted with remorse or guilt, both of which do imply such a belief. Other writers allow a sense of "guilt" such that the experience of guilt need not imply a belief that one has committed any blameworthy offence. On this usage an agent can appropriately feel guilty provided merely that she is causally responsible for bringing about a terrible state of affairs: e.g. killing a child in a traffic accident, where there is no question of driver negligence.[26] Other putative examples of morally appropriate and blameless guilt are survivor guilt (or guilt over unjust enrichment), vicarious guilt for one's country's actions (where one had no effective power over those actions), and guilt for feelings and desires that one did not act upon.[27]

Given this diversity of usage, it seems unlikely that the concepts of guilt and related emotions are susceptible to precise analyses that entirely square with all the usages of ordinary language. Moreover, it is important that skepticism about moral dilemmas does not turn upon a merely verbal point about which name we attach to the emotion that is the moral remainder. But perhaps all that we require for our present purposes are the following claims. First, that we need to acknowledge the existence of rectificatory responses of feeling rather than action—including emotions like guilt, remorse, regret, and shame—and that these responses reveal relevant positive values of an agent who has acted wrongly or is identified with a bad action or state of affairs. Second, that such emotions often seem morally appropriate. Finally, that if there are moral dilemmas, then such emotions may well be a morally appropriate response to their practical resolution.

Why would such emotions be a morally appropriate response to a dilemma? One reason is that emotions like guilt are unpleasant to experience and this unpleasantness is likely to motivate us to avoid dilemmatic situations in the future.[28] But that is not the whole story. Consider in this regard a fictional case sometimes offered as a paradigmatic tragic dilemma: Agamemnon's choice to sacrifice his daughter Iphigenia in order to save the becalmed Greek expedition and allow their passage to Troy to recover Helen. As that choice is represented in Aeschylus's Agamemnon, it is a choice to violate one moral requirement (a father's duties to his child) in order to fulfill another moral requirement (a leader's duties to protect the members of a morally justified military expedition). The tragedy of Agamemnon's situation is that either course of action involves him in guilt: clearly he ought not to slaughter his daughter and yet clearly he ought not to allow the members of the expedition (including Iphigenia) to starve to death on a becalmed ship. For Aeschylus, however, what is most blameworthy about Agamemnon is not that he opted to sacrifice Iphigenia (an unwelcome choice which is nonetheless accepted as preferable to its alternative), but that he experiences no remorse about his actions.[29] The absence of any such emotion is taken to say something important about Agamemnon's moral character: his complacency because he takes himself to have obviously done the right thing, his failure to acknowledge the horror involved in (justifiably) sacrificing his own daughter, are quite properly condemned by the play's Chorus.

In other words, Aeschylus insists that there was a genuine moral dilemma involved in Agamemnon's choice: even if Agamemnon justifiably chose to fulfill only one of the conflicting moral claims, the force of the losing claim still has to be acknowledged and good character expresses this demand through pain and remorse. As Martha Nussbaum eloquently puts it:

> in the depiction of these cases Aeschylus has shown how thoroughly, in fact, the pain and remorse that are part of the intuitive picture are bound up with ethical goodness in other areas of life; with a seriousness about value, a constancy in commitment, and a sympathetic responsiveness that we wish to maintain and develop in others and ourselves.[30]

More generally, we need to acknowledge the moral importance of emotions like guilt as emotions of self-assessment. Gabriele Taylor argues, for example, that when a person feels guilt she is concerned with herself as the doer of a wrong deed. The repayment that is now due from her is required that she should be able to live with herself again.[31] The presence or absence of such emotions, their depth or shallowness, are indicators of the kind of person the agent is. Correspondingly the experience of an emotion of self-assessment changes the view the agent takes of herself.

Herbert Morris makes related points about the way in which a capacity to feel guilt is bound up with an agent's sense of empathy—with her sense of caring for others. A person who refuses to inflict upon herself the pain of guilt is a person who fails to acknowledge others' pain, a person with no sense of herself as someone who cares.[32] It is this feature that also helps explain the phenomena of justified "non-moral guilt" (survivor guilt, vicarious guilt, or guilt for states of mind alone). Such cases involve one's (morally praiseworthy) sense of identification with others and hence while non-moral, derive from a moral posture towards others.[33]

IV

What is the relevance of all this to the practice of mizuko kuyo? Briefly, that the emotions involved in this Japanese practice are the very emotions of self-assessment that would be appropriate to the practical resolution of a moral dilemma. Moreover the participants themselves often speak of their practice in a way that is thoroughly consonant with the claim that they are responding to their previous actions in the face of a perceived moral dilemma.

For example: respondents to a 1987 survey of Japanese mizuko kuyo participants conducted by Elizabeth Harrison described their loss of a child as "regrettable (nasakenai and kuyashii), unavoidable (yamu naku), and the result of selfishness on their part (watashi no mikatte), all terms from ordinary language which they might have used about any unfortunate event in their lives for which they felt some responsibility."[34] Many respondents expressed grief at the unavoidability of aborting a child, feeling that they were in a situation where there was no justifiable choice other than abortion. But very few of the respondents indicated that, given the chance to relive their decision to have an abortion, they would give birth to the child instead. Rather, they expressed regret that they had conceived a child in the first place, hoped never to repeat that irresponsibility, and thought it only right to do something for the absent child.[35]

In other words, the respondents' ritual apology to the aborted fetus is plausibly understood as an acknowledgement of the moral force of the losing claim in the practical resolution of a perceived dilemma. The guilt involved need not mean that the agent would now act differently if she had to choose again; only that she wishes to testify to her sense of the pain and remorse involved in the decision and thereby hold on to her sense of herself as a caring person, a person possessed of that prized sensitivity the Japanese call kokoro. As William LaFleur puts it:

> the majority of those who do mizuko kuyo may do so, at least in part, because they want to keep on believing that they are sensitive, conscience-controlled persons—even though in undergoing an abortion they have felt virtually compelled to do something that would seem to fly in the face of that self-assessment.[36,37]

For Japanese Buddhists, then, abortion is neither absolutely forbidden nor treated lightly. In this respect, the Japanese Buddhist response is a kind of "middle way" between two extreme positions, both present in contemporary Japan. One of these is the "liberationist" camp which strongly supports legalized abortion and which opposes as victimizing of women any practice that legitimizes "abortion guilt." The other is the neo-Shinto camp which invokes a rhetoric that makes much of "life," views abortion as an unmitigated evil and would like to recriminalize it. (The former position is obviously reminiscent of the western "pro-choice" movement, the latter of the "pro-life" movement.) The Buddhist position accepts that the fetus is "life" in some morally significant sense (pace the liberationists). It also accepts that abortion is a locus of pain and suffering for both the fetus and its parents. Hence whereas neo-Shintoists refer to abortion as a sin (tsumi) or an evil (aku), Buddhists prefer to talk of the suffering (ku) or sadness (kanashimi) involved. Insofar as abortion necessarily harms another living being, regret and guilt are natural and morally appropriate emotions for a person who has chosen abortion to experience. But Buddhism also recognizes the importance of showing compassion to women pregnant with unwanted fetuses, of the regrettable need at times to take life out of compassion for the woman bearing it. Thus the widespread Buddhist tolerance of abortion in Japan.

If abortion really is a genuine moral dilemma where an agent faces conflicting moral demands which cannot be simply resolved by one of the claims being justifiably overridden by another, then the Buddhist "middle way" here is arguably a morally appropriate response to the situation. It gives full moral weight to the conflicting "pro-life" and "pro-choice" values, accepting the demands of both but acknowledging that any practical resolution of the dilemma will entail that one of the conflicting moral claims will perforce lose. However, the force of the losing claim still has to be acknowledged and good character expresses this demand through pain and remorse, publicly addressed in the mizuko kuyo ritual. I take this to be the sense in which Buddhism does indeed have something important to offer on the abortion issue: a response to "the dilemma of abortion" that is a "middle way" between the pro-choice and pro-life extremes that have polarised the Western debate.

V

So far I have argued that if abortion is a moral dilemma, then we should expect that any action in the face of it will give rise to the existence of moral remainders, emotions like regret and guilt. Furthermore, Buddhists in modern Japan who have opted for abortion do indeed exhibit such emotions, emotions that the practice of mizuko kuyo deals directly with. A plausible interpretation of this phenomenon, then, is that these Buddhists are responding appropriately to abortion as a perceived moral dilemma. But is it correct to represent abortion as a genuine dilemma for Buddhists?

Damien Keown has vigorously defended a negative answer to this question. Keown rejects the suggestion that Buddhists can properly acknowledge a "dilemma of abortion" representable as a conflict between two moral requirements: the requirement not to take life and the requirement to be compassionate. Insofar as Buddhism is unequivocally committed to the First Precept forbidding the taking of life and has also traditionally held that human life begins at conception, there can be no doubt that abortion is prohibited for Buddhists. Hence Keown claims that "Buddhism may be regarded as holding what is known as a 'consistent' (i.e., exceptionless) pro-life position."[38]

Keown acknowledges that one way to challenge his position would be to concede that the First Precept prohibits killing, but to argue that killing in certain circumstances may be justifiable because compassion requires it. He speculates that "the likely direction this argument would take would be to suggest that the rule against taking human life is of a prima facie nature and can be overridden when circumstances require," perhaps invoking the Buddhist notion of upaya-kausalya or "skilful means." However, such an argument, he suggests, has yet to be made at any length.

Although I think it would be very interesting to see such an argument developed at some length, it is not the argument I am defending here. To invoke the notion of prima facie duties in order to defend the permissibility of abortion is to give up the claim that there is a genuine dilemma of abortion.

Instead any apparent conflict of two moral obligations would be dissolved into a situation where only one of those obligations is actual. The other obligation would then be merely prima facie (i.e. certainly overrideable, and perhaps not even a real moral obligation at all). A moral dilemma, in contrast, involves conflicting moral obligations which cannot be resolved by one of the requirements being justifiably overridden by another.

Can abortion be plausibly represented as such a dilemma for Buddhists? To answer this question we need to be clearer about the status of the apparently conflicting principles involved, i.e. the First Precept and the demands of compassion.

The First Precept is uncontroversially fundamental to traditional Buddhist ethics since taking the Three Refuges and the Five Precepts has traditionally been seen as the mark of becoming a Buddhist. The Five Precepts are incumbent on all Buddhists, both lay and monastic. In its Pali version, the First Precept says, "I undertake the rule of training to refrain from taking life (panatipata veramani sikkhapadam samadiyami)." Like the other precepts, the First Precept is thus a rule of training, a personal commitment rather than a commandment. As such it creates for those who endorse it a genuine moral requirement, but the requirement does not have the kind of "moral necessity" that some have thought to be characteristic of moral prescriptions.

When Kant claimed that "obligation includes necessitation," he meant to imply that moral prescriptions must be obeyed no matter what. Unsurprisingly, then, he also went on to endorse the "ought" implies "can" principle and declare a conflict of obligations impossible. Buddhists are not committed to anything as uncompromising as this. While it is true that if an agent takes the First Precept she ought to refrain from taking life, it does not follow that this ought cannot conflict with another ought. But then when an agent acts on only one of these oughts because acting on both is impossible, the other ought persists as a moral remainder, with resultant agent regret and a felt need to compensate.

The conflicting ought here is supposed to be the obligation of Buddhists to show compassion. However, while it is true that compassion (karuna) is explicitly recognized as a virtue in Buddhism (particularly in the Mahayana), it certainly does not feature among the Five Precepts. This suggests an obvious objection to the claim that abortion can be represented as a dilemma for Buddhists involving a conflict between the moral requirement to refrain from taking life and the requirement to be compassionate: there is no moral requirement on Buddhists to be compassionate in the way that there is a fundamental moral requirement to keep the First Precept. Hence if the two demands come into collision, the First Precept presumably overrides the other.

To respond to this objection we need to make a distinction between moral requirements and moral ideals.[39,40,41] Moral requirements are those moral reasons (including obligations, duties and rights) for adopting an alternative such that it would be morally wrong of us not to adopt that alternative, unless there is moral justification for not doing so. For instance: a moral reason not to kill is plausibly a requirement because killing is morally wrong, unless there is an adequate justification for doing so. Another way to put the matter is to say that someone who fails to adopt a moral requirement without justification is thereby liable to punishment (i.e. it would not be morally wrong to punish him). Typically, moral requirements are those moral reasons associated with the moral rules.

But although the moral rules are an essential part of morality, they are not the whole of it, for morality includes moral ideals as well as rules. Moral ideals are those moral reasons for adopting an alternative such that, although it would be morally good or ideal to do so, it need not be morally wrong to refrain (even when there is no moral justification for so refraining). Thus it might be morally ideal to exhibit compassion without it being the case that it is morally wrong not to do so on every occasion (even if there is no moral justification on those occasions for failing to exhibit compassion). A person who acted so would not thereby be liable to punishment.

With this distinction between requirements and ideals in hand we can distinguish three kinds of moral conflict: (i) between ideals and ideals, (ii) between requirements and requirements, and (iii) between ideals and requirements. Conflicts between ideals are surely possible, but not usually what people have in mind when they dispute the possibility of moral dilemmas. Instead the paradigm example of a moral dilemma is typically taken to be a conflict between two moral requirements. This point now enables us to sharpen the objection against representing abortion as a dilemma involving the incompatible requirements of harmlessness and compassion: although there is a moral requirement in Buddhism to refrain from taking life, there is no requirement to be compassionate (it would be morally wrong, for instance, to punish a person for failing to be compassionate). Hence insofar as dilemmas are conflicts of requirements, abortion cannot be a moral dilemma for Buddhists.

I reply to this objection by invoking the third kind of possible moral conflict distinguished above: that between an ideal and a requirement. For instance, I might promise to do something (thus creating a moral requirement) and then be asked to assist with some worthy activity that would promote a moral ideal. If it would be impossible for me to fulfil the demands of both the requirement and the ideal on this occasion, then we have a situation which would often also be counted as a moral dilemma. Certainly the structure of the situation is much the same as that of the standard moral dilemma involving a conflict of requirements. Moreover it is surely as plausible to suppose that such ideal-requirement conflicts are sometimes irresolvable (in the sense that neither demand is overridden in any morally relevant way) as it is to suppose that requirement-requirement conflicts are sometimes irresolvable.

Unsurprisingly Buddhist ethics exhibits the presence of both requirements and ideals. The basic moral rules enshrined in the Five Precepts are moral requirements in our sense: in the absence of justification, it is wrong for a Buddhist to kill, steal, indulge in illicit sex, lie or take intoxicants. But these rules do not capture all of Buddhist ethics: there are also the Buddhist ideals, one of which is compassion. Moreover, Buddhism insists that its supreme value, the state of nirvana, is not to be attained merely by following the rather minimal demands of the moral rules.[42,43] Abortion, then, could indeed be a genuine moral dilemma for Buddhists: an irresolvable conflict between the demands of the moral requirement of the First Precept and the moral ideal of compassion. If it is such a dilemma, then whichever option we choose we violate one sort of moral claim, leaving us with a moral remainder that has to be acknowledged. The mizuko kuyo ritual allows those who have opted for abortion to acknowledge their sense of the moral weight of the losing value of harmlessness.

Of course, this does not mean that Buddhists are thereby committed to holding that every decision to abort is the reasoned practical resolution of a genuine moral dilemma; nor do the emotions of regret and guilt experienced by the mizuko kuyo participants entail that they are responding to the practical resolution of an actual, rather than an apparent, dilemma. But insofar as those involved in an abortion choice have reasonably taken themselves to have been involved in a situation with the structure of a dilemma, their subsequently opting for mizuko kuyo while continuing to insist that they would not undo what they have done is entirely morally appropriate. Faced with such a perceived dilemma, the mizuko kuyo ritual provides for a Buddhist "middle way" with respect to abortion, a way that gives full moral weight to the irresolvably conflicting demands of both pro-choice and pro-life values.

One final point. Some Japanese feminists have been highly critical of mizuko kuyo and the significance of the suffering it highlights? They argue that the high rate of abortion in Japan and the attendant guilt women often feel about opting for abortion are a direct result of masculine resistance to making contraception and sex education freely available to women. But Buddhists should surely accept this too. If abortion is ever a genuine moral dilemma, then it is obvious that it would be morally preferable to avoid being put in such a position, since whichever way the agent acts she violates some sort of moral claim. Moreover, although Buddhism has traditionally disapproved of abortion, there is no such traditional disapproval of contraception.[44] Hence, Buddhists should freely grant that it is important to promote sex education and birth control in order to minimize the prospects of women being placed in an abortion dilemma, as unfortunately has not been done in Japan. However, this is entirely compatible with it also being true that if women do find themselves in such a dilemma, then mizuko kuyo represents a morally appropriate Buddhist response.

Notes

1. McDermott, James P. (1998), Abortion in the Pali Canon and early Buddhist thought. In D. Keown (Ed.), *Buddhism and Abortion* (London, Macmillan).

2. Stott, David (1992), Buddhadharma and contemporary ethics: Some notes on the attitude of Tibetan Buddhism to abortion and related procedures, *Religion,* 22, pp. 171–182.

3. Florida, R. E. (1991), Buddhist approaches to abortion. *Asian Philosophy,* 1, pp. 39–50; Keown, Damien (1998), (Ed.), *Buddhism and abortion* (London, Macmillan).

4. Florida, R. E. (1998), *Abortion in Buddhist Thailand.* In: Keown, op. cit., note 3, p. 24.

5. Florida, op. cit., note 3, p. 44.

6. Tedesco, Frank (1998), *Abortion in Korea.* In Keown, op. cit., note 3.

7. Ratanakul, Pinit (1998), *Socio-medical aspects of abortion in Thailand.* In Keown, op. cit., note 3, pp. 63–64.

8. Tworkov, Helen (1992), Anti-abortion/pro-choice: Taking both sides, *Tricycle,* 1(3), pp. 60–69.

9. Jones, Ken (1989), *The social face of Buddhism* (London, Wisdom), p. 176.

10. Aitken, Robert (1984), The mind of clover: Essays in Zen Buddhist ethics (San Francisco, North Point), p. 21.

11. LaFleur, William R. (1990), Contestation and confrontation: The morality of abortion in Japan, *Philosophy East and West,* 40, pp. 529–542; LaFleur, William R. (1992), *Liquid life: Buddhism and abortion in Japan* (Princeton, NJ: Princeton University Press); LaFleur, William R. (1995), The cult of Jizo: Abortion practices in Japan and what they can teach the West, *Tricycle,* 4(4), pp. 41–44.

12. LaFleur (1992), op. cit., note 11, p. 213.

13. For further information about the practice see (in addition to the works by LaFleur, op. cit., note 11), Brooks, Anne Page (1981), "Mizuko kuyo" and Japanese Buddhism, *Japanese Journal of Religious Studies,* 8, pp. 119–147; Miura, Domyo (1983), *The forgotten child: An ancient Eastern answer to a modern problem* (Henley-on-Thames, Aidan Ellis); Hoshino, Eiki & Takada, Dosho (1987), Indebtedness and comfort: The undercurrents of mizuko kuyo in contemporary Japan, *Japanese Journal of Religious Studies,* 14, pp. 305–320; Smith, Bardwell (1992), Bud-

dhism and abortion in contemporary Japan: Mizuko kuyo and the confrontation with death, in J. Cabezon (Ed.), *Buddhism, Sexuality, and Gender* (Albany, State University of New York Press); Harrison, Elizabeth G. (1995), Women's responses to child loss in Japan: the case of mizuko kuyo, *Journal of Feminist Studies in Religion,* 11, pp. 67–93; Harrison, Elizabeth G. (1998), *"I can only move my feet towards mizuko kuyo": memorial services for dead children in Japan,* in: Keown, op. cit., note 3.

14. LaFleur (1992), op. cit., note 11, pp. 198–201.

15. Tedesco, op. cit., note 6.

16. Florida, op. cit., note 4, pp. 25–26.

17. See, for instance, Keown, Damien (1995), *Buddhism and Bioethics* (London, Macmillan), pp. 100–118; Keown, Damien (1998), *Buddhism and abortion: Is there a "middle way"?,* in Keown, op. cit., note 3.

18. Marcus, Ruth Barcan (1987), Moral dilemmas and consistency, in C. Gowans (Ed.), *Moral dilemmas* (New York, Oxford University Press), p. 198.

19. See Gowans, Christopher W. (Ed.), (1987), *Moral dilemmas* (New York, Oxford University Press); Sinnott-Armstrong, Walter (1988), *Moral dilemmas* (Oxford, Blackwell); Mason, H. E. (Ed.), (1996), *Moral dilemmas and moral theory* (New York, Oxford University Press). . . .

22. Williams, Bernard (1987), Ethical consistency, in Gowans, op. cit., note 19.

23. Ibid., p. 134.

24. Rorty, Amelie Oksenberg (1980), Agent regret, in A. Rortv (Ed.), Explaining emotions (Berkeley, University of California Press).

25. For example, McConnell, Terrance C. (1987), Moral dilemmas and consistency in ethics, in Gowans, op. cit., note 19, p. 161.

26. Taylor, Gabriele (1985), Pride, shame and guilt: Emotions of self-assessment (Oxford, Clarendon Press), p. 91.

27. Morris, Herbert (1987), Nonmoral guilt, in F. Schoeman (Ed.), *Responsibility, character and the emotions: New essays in moral psychology* (Cambridge, Cambridge University Press).

28. Marcus, op. cit., note 18.

29. Nussbaum, Martha C. (1986), *The fragility of goodness: Luck and ethics in Greek tragedy and philosophy* (Cambridge, Cambridge University Press), ch. 2.

30. Ibid., p. 50.

31. Taylor, op. cit., note 26, pp. 97–98.

32. Morris, Herbert (1976), On *guilt and innocence: Essays in legal philosophy and moral psychology* (Berkeley, University of California Press).

33. Morris, op. cit., note 27.

34. Harrison (1998), op. cit., note 13, p. 105.

35. Ibid., p. 107.

36. LaFleur (1992), op. cit., note 11, p. 155.

37. Ibid., pp. 191–197.

38. Keown (1998), op. cit., note 17, p. 209.

39. Ibid.

40. Kant, Immanuel (1987), Moral duties, in Gowans, op. cit., note 19, p. 38.

41. Sinnott-Armstrong, op. cit., note 19, pp. 11–15; Gert, Bernard (1988), *Morality: A new justification of the moral rules* (New York, Oxford University Press).

42. "Or to put it in Buddhist terms: Merely moral practices will never bring a man to sainthood or Nibbana" (King, Winston L. (1964), In *The Hope of Nibbana: An essay on Theravada Buddhist ethics* (LaSalle, Open Court), p. 31.)

43. See, for instance, Igeta, Midori (1995) A response, *Journal of Feminist Studies in Religion,* 11, pp. 95–100.

44. See Keown (1995), op. cit., note 17, pp. 122–132.

Don Marquis
"Why Abortion Is Immoral"

Don Marquis is a professor of philosophy at the University of Kansas who specializes in medical ethics. He originally became interested in the issue of abortion while teaching medical ethics. He was also motivated by his belief that American involvement in the Vietnam War was profoundly immoral and he wanted to understand why that was so in a philosophically respectable way.

To demonstrate precisely what is wrong with abortion, Marquis first develops a theory of what is wrong with killing in general. The principal moral objection to killing is that it deprives beings of their futures—hopes, projects, dreams. If this is what is objectionable about killing, it is easy to see that abortion is morally wrong, for it deprives a living being of its future.

As You Read, Consider This:

1. Marquis considers several possible answers to the question of why killing is wrong. Which of these is closest to your own?

2. On what basis does Marquis support his claim that the fetus is an innocent human being?

The view that abortion is, with rare exceptions, seriously immoral has received little support in the recent philosophical literature. No doubt most philosophers affiliated with secular institutions of higher education believe that the anti-abortion position is either a symptom of irrational religious dogma or a conclusion generated by seriously confused philosophical argument. The purpose of this essay is to undermine this general belief. This essay sets out an argument that purports to show, as well as any argument in ethics can show, that abortion is, except possibly in rare cases, seriously immoral, that it is in the same moral category as killing an innocent adult human being.

Journal of Philosophy, Vol. 86 (April, 1989), pp. 183–202.

The argument is based on a major assumption. Many of the most insightful and careful writers on the ethics of abortion—such as Joel Feinberg, Michael Tooley, Mary Ann Warren, H. Tristram Engelhardt, Jr., L.W. Sumner, John T. Noonan, Jr., and Philip Devine[1]—believe that whether or not abortion is morally permissible stands or falls on whether or not a fetus is the sort of being whose life it is seriously wrong to end. The argument of this essay will assume, but not argue, that they are correct.

Also, this essay will neglect issues of great importance to a complete ethics of abortion. Some anti-abortionists will allow that certain abortions, such as abortion before implantation or abortion when the life of a woman is threatened by a pregnancy or abortion after rape, may be morally permissible. This essay will not explore the casuistry of these hard cases. The purpose of this essay is to develop a general argument for the claim that the overwhelming majority of deliberate abortions are seriously immoral.

I

A sketch of standard anti-abortion and pro-choice arguments exhibits how those arguments possess certain symmetries that explain why partisans of those positions are so convinced of the correctness of their own positions, why they are not successful in convincing their opponents, and why, to others, this issue seems to be unresolvable. An analysis of the nature of this standoff suggests a strategy for surmounting it.

Consider the way a typical anti-abortionist argues. She will argue or assert that life is present from the moment of conception or that fetuses look like babies or that fetuses possess a characteristic such as a genetic code that is both necessary and sufficient for being human. Anti-abortionists seem to believe that (1) the truth of all of these claims is quite obvious, and (2) establishing any of these claims is sufficient to show that abortion is morally akin to murder.

A standard pro-choice strategy exhibits similarities. The pro-choicer will argue or assert that fetuses are not persons or that fetuses are not rational agents or that fetuses are not social beings. Pro-choicers seem to believe that (1) the truth of any of these claims is quite obvious, and (2) establishing any of these claims is sufficient to show that an abortion is not a wrongful killing.

In fact, both the pro-choice and the anti-abortion claims do seem to be true, although the "it looks like a baby" claim is more difficult to establish the earlier the pregnancy. We seem to have a standoff. How can it be resolved?

As everyone who has taken a bit of logic knows, if any of these arguments concerning abortion is a good argument, it requires not only some claim characterizing fetuses, but also some general moral principle that ties a characteristic of fetuses to having or not having the right to life or to some other moral characteristic that will generate the obligation or the lack of obligation not to end the life of a fetus. Accordingly, the arguments of the anti-abortionist and the pro-choicer need a bit of filling in to be regarded as adequate.

Note what each partisan will say. The anti-abortionist will claim that her position is supported by such generally accepted moral principles as "It is always prima facie seriously wrong to take a human life" or "It is always prima facie seriously wrong to end the life of a baby." Since these are generally accepted moral principles, her position is certainly not obviously wrong. The pro-choicer will claim that her position is supported by such plausible moral principles as "Being a person is what gives an individual intrinsic moral worth" or "It is only seriously prima facie wrong to take the life of a member of the human community." Since these are generally accepted moral principles, the pro-choice position is certainly not obviously wrong. Unfortunately, we have again arrived at a standoff.

Now, how might one deal with this standoff? The standard approach is to try to show how the moral principles of one's opponent lose their plausibility under analysis. It is easy to see how this is possible. On the one hand, the anti-abortionist will defend a moral principle concerning the wrongness of killing which tends to be broad in scope in order that even fetuses at an early stage of pregnancy will fall under it. The problem with broad principles is that they often embrace too much. In this particular instance, the principle "It is always prima facie wrong to take a human life" seems to entail that it is wrong to end the existence of a living human cancer-cell culture, on the grounds that the culture is both living and human. Therefore, it seems that the anti-abortionist's favored principle is too broad.

On the other hand, the pro-choicer wants to find a moral principle concerning the wrongness of killing which tends to be narrow in scope in order that fetuses will *not* fall under it. The problem with narrow principles is that they often do not embrace enough. Hence, the needed principles such as "It is prima facie seriously wrong to kill only persons" or "It is prima facie wrong to kill only rational agents" do not explain why it is wrong to kill infants or young children or the severely retarded or even perhaps the severely mentally ill. Therefore, we seem again to have a standoff. The anti-abortionist charges, not unreasonably, that pro-choice principles concerning killing are too narrow to be acceptable; the pro-choicer charges, not unreasonably, that anti-abortionist principles concerning killing are too broad to be acceptable.

Attempts by both sides to patch up the difficulties in their positions run into further difficulties. The anti-abortionist will try to remove the problem in her position by reformulating her principle concerning killing in terms of human beings. Now we end up with: "It is always prima facie seriously wrong to end the life of a human being." This principle has the advantage of avoiding the problem of the human cancer-cell culture counterexample. But this advantage is purchased at a high price. For although it is clear that a fetus is both human and alive, it is not at all clear that a fetus is a human *being*. There is at least something to be said for the view that something becomes a human being only after a process of development, and that therefore first trimester fetuses and perhaps all fetuses are not yet human beings. Hence, the anti-abortionist, by this move, has merely exchanged one problem for another.[2]

The pro-choicer fares no better. She may attempt to find reasons why killing infants, young children, and the severely retarded is wrong which are independent of her major principle that is supposed to explain the wrongness of taking human life, but which will not also make abortion immoral. This is no easy task. Appeals to social utility will seem satisfactory only to those who resolve not to think of the enormous difficulties with a utilitarian account of the wrongness of killing and the significant social costs of preserving the lives of the unproductive.[3] A pro-choice strategy that extends the definition of "person" to infants or even to young children seems just as arbitrary as an anti-abortion strategy that extends the definition of "human being" to fetuses. Again, we find symmetries in the two positions and we arrive at a standoff.

There are even further problems that reflect symmetries in the two positions. In addition to counterexample problems, or the arbitrary application problems that can be exchanged for them, the standard anti-abortionist principle "It is prima facie seriously wrong to kill a human being," or one of its variants, can be objected to on the grounds of ambiguity. If "human being" is taken to be a *biological* category, then the anti-abortionist is left with the problem of explaining why a merely biological category should make a moral difference. Why, it is asked, is it any more reasonable to base a moral conclusion on the number of chromosomes in one's cells than on the color of one's skin?[4] If "human being," on the other hand, is taken to be a *moral* category, then the claim that a fetus is a human being cannot be taken to be a premise in the anti-abortion argument, for it is precisely what needs to be established. Hence, either the anti-abortionist's main category is a morally irrelevant, merely biological category, or it is of no use to the anti-abortionist in establishing (noncircularly, of course) that abortion is wrong.

Although this problem with the anti-abortionist position is often noticed, it is less often noticed that the pro-choice position suffers from an analogous problem. The principle "Only persons have the right to life" also suffers from an ambiguity. The term "person" is typically defined in terms of psychological characteristics, although there will certainly be disagreement concerning which characteristics are most important. Supposing that this matter can be settled, the pro-choicer is left with the problem of explaining why *psychological* characteristics should make a *moral* difference. If the pro-choicer should attempt to deal with this problem by claiming that an explanation is not necessary, that in fact we do treat such a cluster of psychological properties as having moral significance, the sharp-witted anti-abortionist should have a ready response. We do treat being both living and human as having moral significance. If it is legitimate for the pro-choicer to demand that the anti-abortionist provide an explanation of the connection between the biological character of being a human being and the wrongness of being killed (even though people accept this connection), then it is legitimate for the anti-abortionist to demand that the pro-choicer provide an explanation of the connection between psychological criteria for being a person and the wrongness of being killed (even though that connection is accepted).[5]

Feinberg has attempted to meet this objection (he calls psychological personhood "commonsense personhood"):

> The characteristics that confer commonsense personhood are not arbitrary bases for rights and duties, such as race, sex or species membership; rather they are traits that make sense out of rights and duties and without which those moral attributes would have no point or function. It is because people are conscious; have a sense of their personal identities; have plans, goals, and projects; experience emotions; are liable to pains, anxieties, and frustrations; can reason and bargain, and so on—it is because of these attributes that people have values and interests, desires and expectations of their own, including a stake in their own futures, and a personal well-being of a sort we cannot ascribe to unconscious or nonrational beings. Because of their developed capacities they can assume duties and responsibilities and can have and make claims on one another. Only because of their sense of self, their life plans, their value hierarchies, and their stakes in their own futures can they be ascribed fundamental rights. There is nothing arbitrary about these linkages. (*op. cit.,* p. 270)

The plausible aspects of this attempt should not be taken to obscure its implausible features. There is a great deal to be said for the view that being a psychological person under some description is a necessary condition for having duties. One cannot have a duty unless one is capable of behaving morally, and a being's capability of behaving morally will require having a certain psychology. It is far from obvious, however, that having rights entails consciousness or rationality, as Feinberg suggests. We speak of the rights of the severely retarded or the severely mentally ill, yet some of these persons are not rational. We speak of the rights of the temporarily unconscious. The New Jersey Supreme Court based their decision in the Quinlan case on Karen Ann Quinlan's right to privacy, and she was known to be permanently unconscious at that time. Hence, Feinberg's claim that having rights entails being conscious is, on its face, obviously false.

Of course, it might not make sense to attribute rights to a being that would never in its natural history have certain psychological traits. This modest connection between psychological personhood and moral personhood will create a place for Karen Ann Quinlan and the temporarily unconscious. But then it makes a place for fetuses also. Hence, it does not serve Feinberg's pro-choice purposes. Accordingly, it seems that the pro-choicer will have as much difficulty bridging the gap between psychological personhood and personhood in the moral sense as the anti-abortionist has bridging the gap between being a biological human being and being a human being in the moral sense.

Furthermore, the pro-choicer cannot any more escape her problem by making person a purely moral category than the anti-abortionist could escape by the analogous move. For if person is a moral category, then the pro-choicer is left without the resources for establishing (noncircularly, of course) the claim that a fetus is not a person, which is an essential premise in her argument. Again, we have both a symmetry and a standoff between pro-choice and antiabortion views.

Passions in the abortion debate run high. There are both plausibilities and difficulties with the standard positions. Accordingly, it is hardly surprising that partisans of either side embrace with fervor the moral generalizations that support the conclusions they preanalytically favor, and reject with disdain the moral generalizations of their opponents as being subject to inescapable difficulties. It is easy to believe that the counterexamples to one's own moral principles are merely temporary difficulties that will dissolve in the wake of further philosophical research, and that the counterexamples to the principles of one's opponents are as straightforward as the contradiction between A and O propositions in traditional logic. This might suggest to an impartial observer (if there are any) that the abortion issue is unresolvable.

There is a way out of this apparent dialectical quandary. The moral generalizations of both sides are not quite correct. The generalizations hold for the most part, for the usual cases. This suggests that they are all *accidental* generalizations, that the moral claims made by those on both sides of the dispute do not touch on the *essence* of the matter.

This use of the distinction between essence and accident is not meant to invoke obscure metaphysical categories. Rather, it is intended to reflect the rather atheoretical nature of the abortion discussion. If the generalization a partisan in the abortion dispute adopts were derived from the reason why ending the life of a human being is wrong, then there could not be exceptions to that generalization unless some special case obtains in which there are even more powerful countervailing reasons. Such generalizations would not be merely accidental generalizations; they would point to, or be based upon, the essence of the wrongness of killing, what it is that makes killing wrong. All this suggests that a necessary condition of resolving the abortion controversy is a more theoretical account of the wrongness of killing. After all, if we merely believe, but do not understand, why killing adult human beings such as ourselves is wrong, how could we conceivably show that abortion is either immoral or permissible?

II

In order to develop such an account, we can start from the following unproblematic assumption concerning our own case: it is wrong to kill us. Why is it wrong? Some answers can be easily eliminated. It might be said that what makes killing us wrong is that a killing brutalizes the one who kills. But the brutalization consists of being inured to the performance of an act that is hideously immoral; hence, the brutalization does not explain the immorality. It might be said that what makes killing us wrong is the great loss others would experience due to our absence. Although such hubris is understandable, such an explanation does not account for the wrongness of killing hermits, or those whose lives are relatively independent and whose friends find it easy to make new friends.

A more obvious answer is better. What primarily makes killing wrong is neither its effect on the murderer nor its effect on the victim's friends and relatives, but its effect on the victim. The loss of one's life is one of the greatest losses one can suffer. The loss of one's life deprives one of all the experiences, activities, projects, and enjoyments which would otherwise have constituted one's future. Therefore, killing someone is wrong, primarily because the killing inflicts (one of) the greatest possible losses on the victim. To describe this as the loss of life can be misleading, however. The change in my biological state does not by itself make killing me wrong. The effect of the loss of my biological life is the loss to me of all those activities, projects, experiences, and enjoyments which would otherwise have constituted my future personal life. These activities, projects, experiences, and enjoyments are either valuable for their own sakes or are means to something else that is valuable for its own sake. Some parts of my future are not valued by me now, but will come to be valued by me as I grow older and as my values and capacities change. When I am killed, I am deprived both of what I now value which would have been part of my future personal life, but also what I would come to value. Therefore, when I die, I am deprived of all of the value of my future. Inflicting this loss on me is ultimately what makes killing me wrong. This being the case, it would seem that what makes killing *any* adult human being prima facie seriously wrong is the loss of his other future.[6]

How should this rudimentary theory of the wrongness of killing be evaluated? It cannot be faulted for deriving an "ought" from an "is," for it does not. The analysis assumes that killing me (or you, reader) is prima facie seriously wrong. The point of the analysis is to establish which natural property ultimately explains the wrongness of the killing, given that it is wrong. A natural property will ultimately explain the wrongness of killing, only if (1) the explanation fits with our intuitions about the matter and (2) there is no other natural property that provides the basis for a better explanation of the wrongness of killing. This analysis rests on the intuition that what makes killing a particular human or animal wrong is what it does to that particular human or animal. What makes killing wrong is some natural effect or other of the killing. Some would deny this. For instance, a divine command theorist in ethics would deny it. Surely this denial is, however, one of those features of divine-command theory which renders it so implausible.

The claim that what makes killing wrong is the loss of the victim's future is directly supported by two considerations. In the first place, this theory explains why we regard killing as one of the worst of crimes. Killing is especially wrong, because it deprives the victim of more than perhaps any other crime. In the second place, people with AIDS or cancer who know they are dying believe, of course, that dying is a very bad thing for them. They believe that the loss of a future to them that they would otherwise have experienced is what makes their premature death a very bad thing for them. A better theory of the wrongness of killing would require a different natural property associated with killing which better fits with the attitudes of the dying. What could it be?

The view that what makes killing wrong is the loss to the victim of the value of the victim's future gains additional support when some of its implications are examined. In the first place, it is incompatible with the view that it is wrong to kill only beings who are biologically human. It is possible that there exists a different species from another planet whose members have a future like ours. Since having a future like that is what makes killing someone wrong, this theory entails that it would be wrong to kill members of such a species. Hence, this theory is opposed to the claim that only life that is biologically human has great moral worth, a claim which many anti-abortionists have seemed to adopt. This opposition, which this theory has in common with personhood theories, seems to be a merit of the theory.

In the second place, the claim that the loss of one's future is the wrong-making feature of one's being killed entails the possibility that the futures of some actual nonhuman mammals on our own planet are sufficiently like ours and it is seriously wrong to kill them also. Whether some animals do have the same right to life as human beings depends on adding to the account of the wrongness of killing some additional account of just what it is about my future or the futures of other adult human beings which makes it wrong to kill us. No such additional account will be offered in this essay. Undoubtedly, the provision of such an account would be a very difficult matter. Undoubtedly, any such account would be quite controversial. Hence, it surely should not reflect badly on this sketch of an elementary theory of the wrongness of killing that it is indeterminate with respect to some very difficult issues regarding animal rights.

In the third place, the claim that the loss of one's future is the wrong-making feature of one's being killed does not entail, as sanctity of human life theories do, that active euthanasia is wrong. Persons who are severely and incurably ill, who face a future of pain and despair, and who wish to die will not have suffered a loss if they are killed. It is, strictly speaking, the value of a human's future which makes killing wrong in this theory. This being so, killing does not necessarily wrong some persons who are sick and dying. Of course, there may be other reasons for a prohibition of active euthanasia, but that is another matter. Sanctity-of-human-life theories seem to hold that active euthanasia is seriously wrong even in an individual case where there seems to be good reason for it independently of public policy considerations. This consequence is most implausible, and it is a plus for the claim that the loss of a future of value is what makes killing wrong that it does not share this consequence.

In the fourth place, the account of the wrongness of killing defended in this essay does straightforwardly entail that it is prima facie seriously wrong to kill children and infants, for we do presume that they have futures of value. Since we do believe that it is wrong to kill defenseless little babies, it is important that a theory of the wrongness of killing easily account for this. Personhood theories of the wrongness of killing, on the other hand, cannot straightforwardly account for the wrongness of killing infants and young children.[7] Hence, such theories must add special ad hoc accounts of the wrongness of killing the young. The plausibility of such ad hoc theories seems to be a function of how desperately one wants such theories to work. The claim that the primary wrong-making feature of a killing is the loss to the victim of the value of its future accounts for the wrongness of killing young children and infants directly; it makes the wrongness of such acts as obvious as we actually think it is. This is a further merit of this theory. Accordingly, it seems that this value of a future-like-ours theory of the wrongness of killing shares strengths of both sanctity-of-life and personhood accounts while avoiding weaknesses of both. In addition, it meshes with a central intuition concerning what makes killing wrong.

The claim that the primary wrong-making feature of a killing is the loss to the victim of the value of its future has obvious consequences for the ethics of abortion. The future of a standard fetus includes a set of experiences, projects, activities, and such which are identical with the futures of adult human beings and are identical with the futures of young children. Since the reason that is sufficient to explain why it is wrong to kill human beings after the time of birth is a reason that also applies to fetuses, it follows that abortion is prima facie seriously morally wrong.

This argument does not rely on the invalid inference that, since it is wrong to kill persons, it is wrong to kill potential persons also. The category that is morally central to this analysis is the category of having a valuable future like ours; it is not the category of personhood. The argument to the conclusion that abortion is prima facie seriously morally wrong proceeded independently of the notion of person or potential person or any equivalent. Someone may wish to start with this analysis in terms of the value of a human future, conclude that abortion is, except perhaps in rare circumstances, seriously morally wrong, infer that fetuses have the right to life, and then call fetuses "persons" as a result of their having the right to life. Clearly, in this case, the category of person is being used to state the *conclusion* of the analysis rather than to generate the *argument* of the analysis.

The structure of this anti-abortion argument can be both illuminated and defended by comparing it to what appears to be the best argument for the wrongness of the wanton infliction of pain on animals. This latter argument is based on the assumption that it is prima facie wrong to inflict pain on me (or you, reader). What is the natural property associated with the infliction of pain which makes such infliction wrong? The obvious answer seems to be that the infliction of pain causes suffering and that suffering is a misfortune. The suffering caused by the infliction of pain is what makes the wanton infliction of pain on me wrong. The wanton infliction of pain on other adult humans causes suffering. The wanton infliction of pain on animals causes suffering. Since causing suffering is what makes the wanton infliction of pain wrong and since the wanton infliction of pain on animals causes suffering, it follows that the wanton infliction of pain on animals is wrong.

This argument for the wrongness of the wanton infliction of pain on animals shares a number of structural features with the argument for the serious prima facie wrongness of abortion. Both arguments start with an obvious assumption concerning what it is wrong to do to me (or you, reader). Both then look for the characteristic or the consequence of the wrong action which makes the action wrong. Both recognize that the wrong-making feature of these immoral actions is a property of actions sometimes directed at individuals other than postnatal human beings. If the structure of the argument for the wrongness of the wanton infliction of pain on animals is sound, then the structure of the argument for the prima facie serious wrongness of abortion is also sound, for the structure of the two arguments is the same. The structure common to both is the key to the explanation of how the wrongness of abortion can be demonstrated without recourse to the category of person. In neither argument is that category crucial.

This defense of an argument for the wrongness of abortion in terms of a structurally similar argument for the wrongness of the wanton infliction of pain on animals succeeds only if the account regarding animals is the correct account. Is it? In the first place, it seems plausible. In the second place, its major competition is Kant's account. Kant believed that we do not have direct duties to animals at all, because they are not persons. Hence, Kant had to explain and justify the wrongness of inflicting pain on animals on the grounds that "he who is hard in his dealings with animals becomes hard also in his dealing with men."[8] The problem with Kant's account is that there seems to be no reason for accepting this latter claim unless Kant's account is rejected. If the alternative to Kant's account is accepted, then it is easy to understand why someone who is indifferent to inflicting pain on animals is also indifferent to inflicting pain on humans, for one is indifferent to what makes inflicting pain wrong in both cases. But, if Kant's account is accepted, there is no intelligible reason why one who is hard in his dealings with animals (or crabgrass or stones) should also be hard in his dealings with men. After all, men are persons: animals are no more persons than crabgrass or stones. Persons are Kant's crucial moral category. Why, in short, should a Kantian accept the basic claim in Kant's argument?

Hence, Kant's argument for the wrongness of inflicting pain on animals rests on a claim that, in a world of Kantian moral agents, is demonstrably false. Therefore, the alternative analysis, being more plausible anyway, should be accepted. Since this alternative analysis has the same structure as the anti-abortion argument being defended here, we have further support for the argument for the immorality of abortion being defended in this essay.

Of course, this value of a future-like-ours argument, if sound, shows only that abortion is prima facie wrong, not that it is wrong in any and all circumstances. Since the loss of the future to a standard fetus, if killed, is, however, at least as great a loss as the loss of the future to a standard adult human being who is killed, abortion, like ordinary killing, could be justified only by the most compelling reasons. The loss of one's life is almost the greatest misfortune that can happen to one. Presumably abortion could be justified in some circumstances, only if the loss consequent on failing to abort would be at least as great. Accordingly, morally permissible abortions will be rare indeed unless, perhaps, they occur so early in pregnancy that a fetus is not yet definitely an individual. Hence, this argument should be taken as showing that abortion is presumptively very seriously wrong, where the presumption is very strong—as strong as the presumption that killing another adult human being is wrong. . . .

VI

The purpose of this essay has been to set out an argument for the serious presumptive wrongness of abortion subject to the assumption that the moral permissibility of abortion stands or falls on the moral status of the fetus. Since a fetus possesses a property, the possession of which in adult human beings is sufficient to make killing an adult human being wrong, abortion is wrong. This way of dealing with the problem of abortion seems superior to other approaches to the ethics of abortion, because it rests on an ethics of killing which is close to self-evident, because the crucial morally relevant property clearly applies to fetuses, and because the argument avoids the usual equivocations on "human life," "human being," or "person." The argument rests neither on religious claims nor on Papal dogma. It is not subject to the objection of "speciesism." Its soundness is compatible with the moral permissibility of euthanasia and contraception. It deals with our intuitions concerning young children.

Finally, this analysis can be viewed as resolving a standard problem—indeed, *the* standard problem—concerning the ethics of abortion. Clearly, it is wrong to kill adult human beings. Clearly, it is not wrong to end the life of some arbitrarily chosen single human cell. Fetuses seem to be like arbitrarily chosen human cells in some respects and like adult humans in other respects. The problem of the ethics of abortion is the problem of determining the fetal property that settles this moral controversy. The thesis of this essay is that the problem of the ethics of abortion, so understood, is solvable.

Endnotes

1. Feinberg, "Abortion," in *Matters of Life and Death: New Introductory Essays in Moral Philosophy,* Tom Regan, ed. (New York: Random House, 1986), pp. 256–293; Tooley, "Abortion and Infanticide," *Philosophy and Public Affairs,* Vol. 11, No. 1 (1972), pp. 37–65, Tooley, *Abortion and Infanticide* (New York: Oxford, 1984); Warren, "On the Moral and Legal Status of Abortion," *The Monist* LVIX, Vol. 1 (1973), p. 4361; Engelhardt, "The Ontology of Abortion," *Ethics* LXXXIV, Vol. 3 (1974), pp. 217–234; Sumner, *Abortion and Moral Theory* (Princeton: University Press, 1981); Noonan "An Almost Absolute Value in History," in *The Morality of*

Abortion: Legal and Historical Perspectives, Noonan, ed. (Cambridge: Harvard, 1970); and Devine, *The Ethics of Homicide* (Ithaca: Cornell, 1978).

2. For interesting discussions of this issue, see Warren Quinn, "Abortion: Identity and Loss," *Philosophy and Public Affairs,* Vol. XIII, No. 1 (1984), pp. 24–54; and Lawrence C. Becker, "Human Being: The Boundaries of the Concept," *Philosophy and Public Affairs,* Vol. IV, No. 4 (1975), pp. 334–359.

3. For example, see my "Ethics and the Elderly: Some Problems," in Stuart Spicker, Kathleen Woodward, and David van Tassel, eds., *Aging and the Elderly: Humanistic Perspectives in Gerontology* (Atlantic Highlands, NJ: Humanities, 1978), pp. 341–355.

4. See Warren, *op. cit.,* and Tooley "Abortion and Infanticide."

5. This seems to be the fatal flaw in Warren's treatment of this issue.

6. I have been most influenced on this matter by Jonathan Glover, *Causing Death and Saving Lives* (New York: Penguin, 1977), ch. 3; and Robert Young, "What Is So Wrong with Killing People?" *Philosophy,* Vol. LIV, No. 210 (1979), pp. 515–528.

7. Feinberg, Tooley, Warren, and Engelhardt have all dealt with this problem.

8. "Duties to Animals and Spirits," in *Lectures on Ethics,* Louis Infeld, trans. (New York: Harper, 1963), p. 239.

Journal/Discussion Questions

✍ *Take some time to reflect on what makes killing wrong for you. Why do you think it is wrong? Is it because you believe people have a right to life? If so, what is the basis for that right? Is it because of the suffering that the person being killed experiences? What if the killing were sudden and painless? Would that make it less objectionable?*

1. Marquis maintains that what's wrong with killing someone is that the person who is killed suffers the loss of his or her life and "the loss of one's life deprives one of all the experiences, activities, projects, and enjoyments that would otherwise have constituted one's future." Do you agree that this is what makes killing wrong?

2. At the beginning of his article, Marquis dismisses two proposed candidates for explaining the wrongness of killing—the effects on the perpetrator and the effects on the victim's family and friends—in favor of his own analysis. Why do you think that Marquis considers and rejects these two particular claims? Can there be more than one thing that is wrong with killing people or must wrongness always be reduced to a single factor?

3. Imagine that you are the First Officer of the U.S.S. Enterprise and head of a landing party being beamed down to a planet that you don't have any previous knowledge of. How would you decide which beings on the planet ought not to be killed? Marquis suggests that it would be morally wrong to kill any being that has a future like ours. Is this the criterion that you would use?

4. Marquis argues that "personhood theories of the wrongness of killing. . .cannot straightforwardly account for the wrongness of killing infants and young children." Recall the discussion of personhood theories presented in Jane English's article. Do

you think that Marquis's criticism of such theories is justified? Why?

5. The future-like-ours argument, Marquis maintains, does not entail the claim that contraception is morally wrong. Do you think that Marquis is justified in this claim? Does it depend on the kind of contraception? At what point does an entity have a future like ours? At the moment of conception? Implantation? Or later?

6. Do you think that abortion involves killing an innocent human being? If it does, is it murder?

Concluding Discussion Questions

Where Do You Stand Now?

Instructions

You have already answered the following questions in your moral problems self-quiz at the beginning of this book. Now that you have studied the material in this section, take a moment to answer the same questions again.

	Strongly Agree	Agree	Undecided	Disagree	Strongly Disagree	*Chapter 2: Abortion*
6.	❑	❑	❑	❑	❑	The principal moral consideration about abortion is the question of whether the fetus is a person or not.
7.	❑	❑	❑	❑	❑	The principal moral consideration about abortion is the question of the rights of the pregnant woman.
8.	❑	❑	❑	❑	❑	The only one who should have a voice in making the decision about an abortion is the pregnant woman.
9.	❑	❑	❑	❑	❑	Abortion should be legal but morally discouraged.
10.	❑	❑	❑	❑	❑	Abortion protesters are justified in breaking the law to prevent abortions.

Now compare your answers to this self-quiz with the answers to the initial self-quiz. How, if at all, have your answers changed? How have the *reasons* for your answers changed?

Journal/Discussion Questions

✍ *You have now read, thought, and discussed a number of aspects of the morality of the abortion decision. How have your views changed and developed? What idea had the greatest impact on your thinking about abortion?*

✍ *Imagine that a close friend at another college just called you to tell you that she was pregnant and that she didn't know what to*

do. Although she is not asking you to tell her what to do, she does ask you to tell her what you believe about abortion. Write her a letter in which you tell her what your own beliefs are. Talk, among other things, about what sorts of factors should be taken into consideration.

✍ *If you were going to have a baby, to what extent would you want to select its charac-*

teristics in advance? Which characteristics, if any, would you not want to consciously select? Physical characteristics? Physical and mental capabilities? Personality traits? Sex? Sexual orientation?

1. What, in the readings in this chapter, was the most thought-provoking idea you encountered? In what ways did it prompt you to reconsider some of your previous beliefs?

2. Has your overall position on the morality of abortion changed? If so, in what way(s)? If your position has not changed, have your reasons developed in any way? If so, in what way(s)? Has your understanding *changed* of the reasons supporting other positions that are different from your own changed? If so, in what way(s)?

For Further Reading

Web Resources

For an overview of Web-based resources relating to abortion, including relevant Supreme Court decisions, see the abortion page of *Ethics Updates* (http://ethics.sandiego.edu). Among the resources listed there on abortion is an excellent article in the *Boston Review* on abortion by Judith Jarvis Thomson and comments by Philip L. Quinn, Donald Regan, Douglas Laycock, Drucilla Cornell, Peter de Marneffe, and a rejoinder by Judith Jarvis Thomson. A link to George McKenna's "On Abortion: A Lincolnian Position," on the *Atlantic Monthly* site is also provided. Steven Schwartz's *The Moral Question of Abortion* is also available online. I have also included a set of online resources on Mizuko Kuyo, the memorial rites for the spirits of departed fetuses in Japan.

Journals

There are a number of excellent journals in ethics that contain articles on virtually all of the topics treated in this book. These include *Ethics,* the oldest and arguably the finest of the ethics journals; *Philosophy and Public Affairs,* which—as its name implies—places special emphasis on questions of public rather than private morality; *Journal of Social Philosophy,* which often contains articles on the cutting edge of social controversies; *Social Philosophy and Policy,* which is devoted to a particular topic each issue (such as Liberalism and the Economic Order; Altruism; Property Rights; and Crime, Culpability, and Remedy); and *Public Affairs Quarterly,* which contains a number of articles on the ethical dimensions of public policy issues. In addition to these, see the *Hastings Center Reports, BioEthics, Kennedy Institute of Ethics, Journal of Medicine and Philosophy, Biomedical Ethics Reviews,* and *Law, Medicine & Health Care* for discussion of issues relating specifically to biomedical ethics.

Review Articles and Reports

For a comprehensive bibliographical guide to abortion, see Diane E. Fitzpatrick, *A History of Abortion in the United States: A Working Bibliography of Journal Articles* (Monticello, IL: Vance Bibliographies, 1991). For excellent surveys of the philosophical issues, see Nancy (Ann) Davis, "Abortion," *Encyclopedia of Ethics,* edited by Lawrence C. Becker and Charlotte B. Becker (New York: Garland, 1992), Vol. I, pp. 2–6; Mary Ann Warren, "Abortion," Blackwell Companion to Bioethics, edited by Helga Kuhse and Peter Singer (Oxford: Blackwell, 2001), pp. 127–134; and especially John Harris and Soren Holm, "Abortion," *The Oxford Handbook of Practical Ethics,* edited by Hugh LaFollette, ed. (New York: Oxford University Press, 2003), pp. 112–135.

Anthologies and Books

There are a number of excellent anthologies of selections dealing solely with the issue of abortion. *The Abortion Controversy—25 Years After* Roe v. Wade, *A Reader,* 2nd ed. edited by Louis P. Pojman and Francis J. Beckwith (Belmont: Wadsworth, 1998) has a number of excellent articles with a very balanced selection of viewpoints. *The Problem of Abortion,* 3rd ed., edited by Susan Dwyer and Joel Feinberg (Belmont, CA: Wadsworth, 1996) contains a number of important pieces covering a wide range of positions, as does *The Ethics of Abortion: Pro-Life vs. Pro-Choice,* rev. ed., edited by Robert M. Baird and Stuart E. Rosenbaum (Buffalo: Prometheus Books, 1993). Lewis M. Schwartz's *Arguing about Abortion* (Belmont, CA: Wadsworth, 1993) not only contains a number of important essays, but also (a) provides a well-done introduction to reconstructing and evaluating argumentative discourse and (b) offers an outline and analysis of six of the essays contained in the anthology. *Abortion: Moral and Legal Perspectives,* edited by Jay L. Garfield and Patricia Hennessey (Amherst: University of Massachusetts Press, 1984), contains several original essays as well as reprints of some previously published pieces. Also see Marshall Cohen, Thomas Nagel, and Thomas Scanlon, eds., *Rights and Wrongs of Abortion* (Princeton: Princeton University Press, 1974) and John T. Noonan, Jr., ed., *The Morality of Abortion: Legal and Historical Perspectives* (Cambridge: Harvard University Press, 1970). The anthology, *Abortion: Understanding Differences,* edited by Sidney Callahan and Daniel Callahan (New York: Plenum Press, 1984) contains a number of perceptive essays. For an excellent selection of both philosophical and popular articles, see *Abortion: Opposing Viewpoints,* edited by Mary Williams (San Diego, CA: Greenhaven Press, 2001).

Among the many excellent books on the morality of abortion, see Jeff McMahon's *The Ethics of Killing: Problems at the Margins of Life* (New York: Oxford University Press, 2002), which presents an account of the ethics of killing in cases in which the metaphysical or moral status of the individual killed is uncertain or controversial; he deals with not only with embryos and fetuses, but also anencephalic infants, persons in irreversible comas, and other difficult cases at the margins of life. Laurie Shrage's *Abortion and Social Responsibility: Depolarizing the Debate* (New York: Oxford, 2003) argues for a reduction of the current six-month period of abortion on demand but only if there is a significant increase in services to ensure universal access to abortion in earlier months of pregnancy. Jeffrey Reiman's *Abortion and the Ways We Value Human Life* (Lanham: Rowman and Littlefield, 1999) argues that the foundation of opposition to abortion is to be found in the way in which we value human lives "irreplaceably;" he provides an interesting critique of Don Marquis as well. Mary Ann Warren's *Moral Status: Obligations to Persons and Other Living Things* (New York: Oxford University Press, 1997) argues against the claim that there is any single criterion of moral status and instead presents a set of seven properties that affect moral status. Laura M. Purdy's *Reproducing Persons: Issues in Feminist Bioethics* (Ithaca: Cornell University Press, 1996) develops a feminist version of utilitarianism to deal with a number of issues in reproductive ethics, including abortion.

Bonnie Steinbock's *Life Before Birth: The Moral and Legal Status of Embryos and Fetuses* (New York: Oxford, 1992) concentrates primarily on the issue of the status of embryos and fetuses, whereas F. M. Kamm's *Creation and Abortion* (New York: Oxford, 1992) develops a broader theory of creating new people responsibility and explores the issue of abortion within this context; these themes are extended in her *Morality, Mortality: Rights, Duties, and Status* (New York: Oxford, 2001). See L.W. Sumner, *Abortion and Moral Theory* (Princeton: Princeton University Press, 1981), for a carefully reasoned moderate view on the permissibility of abortion. Rosiland Hursthouse's *Beginning Lives* (Oxford: Basil Blackwell, 1987) includes a perceptive account of the issue of abortion. John T. Noonan, Jr., who represents a conservative Catholic view, has several books on this issue, including *How to Argue About Abortion* (New York, 1974) and *A Private Choice: Abortion in America in the Seventies* (New York: The Free Press, 1979); Germain G. Grisez's *Abortion: The Myths, the Realities, and the Arguments* (New York: Corpus Books, 1970) also argues for a strongly conservative view. Baruch Brody's *Abortion and the Sanctity of Human Life: A Philosophical View* (Cambridge, MA: The MIT Press, 1975) defends a fairly conservative view, arguing that the fetus becomes a person when brain activity begins. Michael Tooley's *Abortion and Infanticide* (Oxford: Clarendon Press, 1983) presents some controversial arguments in support of abortion and situates the issue within the larger context of infanticide and the killing of nonhuman animals. Also see Stephen D. Schwarz, *The Moral Question of Abortion* (Chicago: Loyola University Press, 1990). For an excellent CD-ROM introduction to this issue, see *The Issue of Abortion in America,* by Robert Cavalier, Liz Style, Preston Covey, and Andrew Thompson (Routledge, 1998).

Key Essays

Among philosophers, there are several key essays that have set the stage for the philosophical discussion of abortion. The most reprinted essay in contemporary philosophy is probably Judith Jarvis Thomson's "A Defense of Abortion," which originally appeared in the inaugural issue of *Philosophy and Public Affairs* Vol. 1, No. 1 (Fall 1971), pp. 47–66 and is reprinted in her *Rights, Restitution, & Risk: Essays in Moral Theory* (Cambridge: Harvard University Press, 1986)—which also contains her "Rights and Deaths," a reply to several critics of her initial essay—and in both the Feinberg and the Schwarz anthologies cited earlier. Thomson's article has elicited a vast number of replies; one of the more insightful of these is John Martin Fisher, "Abortion and Self-Determination," *Journal of Social Philosophy* XXII, 2 (Fall 1991), pp. 5–13. On the issue of responsibility for pregnancy in Thomson's example, see David Boonin-Vail, "A Defense of 'A Defense of Abortion': On the Responsibility Objection to Thomson's Argument," *Ethics* Vol. 107, No. 2 (January 1997), pp. 286–313.

Don Marquis's "Why Abortion Is Immoral," *Journal of Philosophy,* Vol. 86 (1989) is one of the most philosophically sophisticated arguments against abortion, and it too has generated a number of replies, including Walter Sinnott-Armstrong "You Can't Lose What You Ain't Never Had: A Reply to Marquis on Abortion," *Philosophical Studies,* Vol. 96, No. 1, (October, 1999), pp. 59–72. Elizabeth Harman's "Creation Ethics: The Moral Status of Early Fetuses and the Ethics of Abortion," *Philosophy and Public Affairs,* Vol. 28, No. 4 (Fall, 1999), pp. 310–324, argues in favor of a very liberal theory of early abortion while addressing such issues as early miscarriages, love for early fetuses, and regret over abortions.

John T. Noonan, Jr.'s "An Almost Absolute Value in History," is also widely reprinted (including in Noonan's *The Morality of Abortion,* cited earlier) and is a strong, classic statement of the conservative view. Joel Feinberg's "Abortion," in *Matters of Life and Death,* edited by Tom Regan (New York: Random House, 1980), pp. 183–217, is a careful and nuanced discussion of the question of the moral status of the fetus. Roger Wertheimer's "Understanding the Abortion Argument," *Philosophy and Public Affairs,* Vol. 1, No. 1 (Fall, 1971), pp. 67–95, presents strong arguments for a fairly conservative view. Mary Anne Warren's "On the Moral and Legal Status of Abortion," *The Monist,* Vol. 57 (1973) argues for a strongly liberal position, maintaining that the fetus is not a person.

For a good collection of essays on the status of the fetus, see *Biomedical Ethics Reviews: Bioethics and the Fetus: Medical, Moral, and Legal Issues,* edited by James M. Humber and Robert Almeder (Clifton, NJ: Humana Press, 1991) and Peter Singer et al., eds., *Embryo Experimentation*

(New York: Cambridge University Press). For a critique of the philosophical viability of the notion of the "pre-embryo," see A. A. Howsepian, "Who or What Are We?" *Review of Metaphysics,* Vol. 45, No. 3 (March 1992), pp. 483–502, which replied to Richard McCormick's "Who or What is the Preembryo?" in the *Kennedy Institute of Ethics Journal,* Vol. 1 (1991), pp. 1–15; Alan Holland, "A Fortnight of My Life Is Missing: A Discussion of the Status of the Human 'Pre-Embryo,'" *Applied Philosophy,* edited by Brenda Almond and Donald Hill (London: Routledge, 1991), pp. 299–311.

For background on the principle of double effect, see Joseph T. Mangan, "An Historical Analysis of the Principle of Double Effect," *Theological Studies,* Vol. 10 (1949), pp. 41–61. G. E. M. Anscombe's "Modern Moral Philosophy," *Philosophy,* Vol. 33 (1958), pp. 26–42, raises important questions about the distinction between intended consequences and foreseen consequences. Phillipa Foot expresses doubts about the moral significance of this distinction in her article, "Abortion and the Doctrine of Double Effect," in her *Virtues and Vices and Other Essays* (Berkeley: University of California Press, 1978), pp. 19–32. For a short survey of the philosophical issues surrounding this principle, see William David Solomon, "Double Effect," *Encyclopedia of Ethics,* edited by Lawrence C. Becker and Charlotte B. Becker (New York: Garland, 1992), Vol. I, pp. 268–269.

Abortion and Religion

Abortion has been a controversial issue within the Christian tradition, and this debate has generated countless resources, a number of which have been mentioned earlier. For the "seamless garment" doctrine of respect for life, see Joseph Cardinal Bernardin, *Selected Works of Joseph Cardinal Bernardin: Church and Society,* Vol. 2 (Collegeville, MN: Liturgical Press, 2000). In addition, abortion has been an issue in other religious traditions. See *Islamic Ethics of Life: Abortion, War, and Euthanasia,* Studies in Comparative Religion, edited by Jonathan E. Brockopp and Gene Outka (Columbia, SC: University of South Carolina Press, 2003); Harold G. Coward, Julius J. Lipner, and Katherine K. Young, *Hindu Ethics: Purity, Abortion, and Euthanasia* (Albany, NY: State University of New York Press, 1989); William R. La Fleur, *Liquid Life: Abortion and Buddhism in Japan* (Princeton: Princeton University Press, 2000); Damien Keown, ed., *Buddhism and Abortion* (Honolulu, Hawai'i: University of Hawaii Press, 1998); Daniel Schiff, *Abortion in Judaism* (Cambridge: Cambridge University Press, 2002).

On Finding a Common Ground

Several recent contributions to the search for common ground in the abortion discussion are Laurence H. Tribe, *Abortion: The Clash of Absolutes* (New York: Norton, 1992); Roger Rosenblatt, *Life Itself* (New York: Vintage Books, 1992); Ronald Dworkin, *Life's Dominion: An Argument about Abortion, Euthanasia, and Individual Freedom* (New York: Knopf, 1993); and Elizabeth Mensch and Alan Freeman, *The Politics of Virtue. Is Abortion Debatable?* (Durham: Duke University Press, 1993). For an excellent review of Tribe's book, see Nancy (Ann) Davis, "The Abortion Debate: The Search for Common Ground," *Ethics,* Vol. 103, No. 3 (April, 1993), pp. 516–539, and Vol. 103, No. 4 (July, 1993), pp. 731–778. For a discussion of abortion within the general context of a theory of compromise, see Martin Benjamin, *Splitting the Difference: Compromise and Integrity in Ethics and Politics* (Lawrence, KS: University of Kansas Press, 1990), especially pp. 151–171; and Georgia

Warnke, *Legitimate Differences: Interpretation in the Abortion Controversy and Other Public Debates* (Berkeley: University of California Press, 1999).

For a model of how to conduct a fruitful dialogue on this issue, see the Boston Public Conversations Project (http://www.publicconversations.org), which brings together committed activists on various sides of controversial issues to engage in genuine dialogue. Their project initially arose in response to an abortion clinic shooting in Boston at the end of 1994.

CHAPTER 3

Euthanasia

Narrative Accounts

Anonymous
"It's Over, Debbie"

The author of this essay remains anonymous; at the time this was written, he or she was a gynecology resident. After the publication of this essay in The Journal of the American Medical Association, *unsuccessful attempts were made to indict the resident for murder.*

This article describes an actual instance of euthanasia by a physician who at that time was a resident in gynecology. The case of Debbie, as it has come to be known, is discussed in several selections later in this chapter.

The call came in the middle of the night. As a gynecology resident rotating through a large, private hospital, I had come to detest telephone calls, because invariably I would be up for several hours and would not feel good the next day. However, duty called, so I answered the phone. A nurse informed me that a patient was having difficulty getting rest, could I please see her. She was on 3 North. That was the gynecologic-oncology unit, not my usual duty station. As I trudged along, bumping sleepily against walls and corners and not believing I was up again, I tried to imagine what I might find at the end of my walk. Maybe an elderly woman with an anxiety reaction, or perhaps something particularly horrible.

I grabbed the chart from the nurses' station on my way to the patient's room, and the nurse gave me some hurried details: a twenty-year-old girl named Debbie was dying of ovarian cancer. She was having unrelenting vomiting apparently as the result of an alcohol drip administered for sedation. Hmmm, I thought. Very sad. As I approached the room I could hear loud, labored breathing. I entered and saw an emaciated, dark-haired woman who appeared much older than twenty. She was receiving nasal oxygen, had an IV, and was sitting in bed suffering from what was obviously severe air hunger. The chart noted her weight at eighty pounds. A second woman, also dark-haired but of middle age, stood at her right, holding her hand. Both looked up as I entered. The room seemed filled with the patient's desperate effort to survive. Her eyes were hollow, and she had suprasternal and intercostal retractions with her rapid inspirations. She had not eaten or slept in two days. She had not responded to chemotherapy and was being given supportive care only. It was a gallows scene, a cruel mockery of her youth and unfulfilled potential. Her only words to me were, "Let's get this over with."

I retreated with my thoughts to the nurses' station. The patient was tired and needed rest. I could not give her health, but I could give her rest. I asked the nurse to draw 20 mg. of morphine sulfate into a syringe. Enough, I thought, to do the job. I took the syringe into the room and told the two women I was going to give Debbie something that would let her rest and to say good-bye. Debbie

Journal of the American Medical Association, Vol. 259 (1988), p. 272.

96

looked at the syringe, then laid her head on the pillow with her eyes open, watching what was left of the world. I injected the morphine intravenously and watched to see if my calculations would be correct. Within seconds her breathing slowed to a normal rate, her eyes closed, and her features softened as she seemed restful at last. The older woman stroked the hair of the now-sleeping patient. I waited for the inevitable next effect of depressing the respiratory drive. With clocklike certainty, within four minutes the breathing rate slowed even more, then became irregular, then ceased. The dark-haired woman stood erect and seemed relieved.

It's over, Debbie.

Journal/Discussion Questions

✍ *As you develop your own position on the morality and legality of euthanasia, in what ways does this article help you to develop your own thinking?*

1. If you had been the resident in this situation, what would you have done? Why?

2. One of the major issues in euthanasia is the question of informed consent. Do you think the resident had informed consent? What more, if anything, should have been done to ensure informed consent?

3. If you were the district attorney for the city in which this took place, would you seek to charge the resident with a crime? Why or why not?

Timothy E. Quill, M.D.
"Death and Dignity: A Case of Individualized Decision Making"

Timothy Quill, M.D., specializes in internal medicine, has had experience as a hospice director, and is an associate professor of medicine and psychiatry at the University of Rochester School of Medicine and Dentistry. His book, Death and Dignity: Making Choices and Taking Charge *argues in favor of physician-assisted euthanasia.*

In sharp contrast to the previous selection, this piece depicts a strong and long relationship between a physician and his patient. As the patient, Diane, confronts her terminal cancer, she decides that she does not want extraordinary medical care. Her doctor, Timothy Quill, must then face crucial issues about how willing he is to help to alleviate Diane's suffering and support her choice to die.

Diane was feeling tired and had a rash. A common scenario, though there was something subliminally worrisome that prompted me to check her blood count. Her hematocrit was 22, and the white-cell count was 4.3 with some metamyelocytes and unusual white cells. I wanted it to be viral, trying to deny what was staring me in the face. Perhaps in a repeated count it would disappear. I called Diane and told her it might be more serious than I had initially thought—that the test needed to be repeated and that

New England Journal of Medicine, Vol. 324 (1991), pp. 691–694. Copyright © The Massachusetts Medical Society.

if she felt worse, we might have to move quickly. When she pressed for the possibilities, I reluctantly opened the door to leukemia. Hearing the word seemed to make it exist. "Oh, shit!" she said. "Don't tell me that." Oh, shit! I thought, I wish I didn't have to.

Diane was no ordinary person (although no one I have ever come to know has been really ordinary). She was raised in an alcoholic family and had felt alone for much of her life. She had vaginal cancer as a young woman. Through much of her adult life, she had struggled with depression and her own alcoholism. I had come to know, respect, and admire her over the previous eight years as she confronted these problems and gradually overcame them. She was an incredibly clear, at times brutally honest, thinker and communicator. As she took control of her life, she developed a strong sense of independence and confidence. In the previous 3½ years, her hard work had paid off. She was completely abstinent from alcohol, she had established much deeper connections with her husband, college-age son, and several friends, and her business and her artistic work were blossoming. She felt she was really living fully for the first time.

Not surprisingly, the repeated blood count was abnormal, and detailed examination of the peripheral-blood smear showed myelocytes. I advised her to come into the hospital, explaining that we needed to do a bone marrow biopsy and make some decisions relatively rapidly. She came to the hospital knowing what we would find. She was terrified, angry, and sad. Although we knew the odds, we both clung to the thread of possibility that it might be something else.

The bone marrow confirmed the worst: acute myelomonocytic leukemia. In the face of this tragedy, we looked for signs of hope. This is an area of medicine in which technological intervention has been successful, with cures 25 percent of the time—long-term cures. As I probed the costs of these cures, I heard about induction chemotherapy (three weeks in the hospital, prolonged neutropenia, probable infectious complications, and hair loss; 75 percent of patients respond, 25 percent do not). For the survivors, this is followed by consolidation chemotherapy (with similar side effects; another 25 percent die, for a net survival of 50 percent). Those still alive, to have a reasonable chance of long-term survival, then need bone marrow transplantation (hospitalization for two months and whole-body irradiation, with complete killing of the bone marrow, infectious complications, and the possibility for graft-versus-host disease—with a survival of approximately 50 percent, or 25 percent of the original group). Though hematologists may argue over the exact percentages, they don't argue about the outcome of no treatment—certain death in days, weeks, or at most a few months.

Believing that delay was dangerous, our oncologist broke the news to Diane and began making plans to insert a Hickman catheter and begin induction chemotherapy that afternoon. When I saw her shortly thereafter, she was enraged at his presumption that she would want treatment, and devastated by the finality of the diagnosis. All she wanted to do was go home and be with her family. She had no further questions about treatment and in fact had decided that she wanted none. Together we lamented her tragedy and the unfairness of life. Before she left, I felt the need to be sure that she and her husband understood that there was some risk in delay, that the problem was not going to go away, and that we needed to keep considering the options over the next several days. We agreed to meet in two days.

She returned in two days with her husband and son. They had talked extensively about the problem and the options. She remained very clear about her wish not to undergo chemotherapy and to live whatever time she had left outside the hospital. As we explored her thinking further, it became clear that she was convinced she would die during the period of treatment and would suffer unspeakably in the process (from hospitalization, from lack of control over her body, from the side effects of chemotherapy, and from pain and anguish). Although I could offer support and my best effort to minimize her suffering if she chose treatment, there was no way I could say any of this would not occur. In fact, the last four patients with acute leukemia at our hospital had died very painful deaths in the hospital during various stages of treatment (a fact I did not share with her). Her family wished she would choose treatment but sadly accepted her decision. She articulated very clearly that it was she who would be experiencing all the side effects of treatment and that odds of 25 percent were not good enough for her to undergo so toxic a course of therapy, given her expectations of chemotherapy and hospitalization and the absence of a closely matched bone marrow donor. I had her repeat her understanding of the treatment, the odds, and what to expect if there were no treatment. I clarified a few misunderstandings, but she had a remarkable grasp of the options and implications.

I have been a longtime advocate of active, informed patient choice of treatment or nontreatment, and of a patient's right to die with as much control and dignity as possible. Yet there was something about her giving up a 25 percent chance of long-term survival in favor of almost certain death that disturbed me. I had seen Diane fight and use her considerable inner resources to overcome alcoholism and depression, and I half expected her to change her mind over the next week. Since the window of time in which effective treatment can be initiated is rather narrow, we met several times that week. We obtained a second hematology consultation and talked at length about the meaning and implications of treatment and nontreatment. She talked to a psychologist she had seen in the past. I gradually understood the decision from her perspective and became convinced that it was the right decision for her. We arranged for home hospice care (although at that time Diane felt reasonably well, was active, and looked healthy), left the door open for her to change her mind, and tried to anticipate how to keep her comfortable in the time she had left.

Just as I was adjusting to her decision, she opened up another area that would stretch me profoundly. It was extraordinarily important to Diane to maintain control of herself and her own dignity during the time remaining to her. When this was no longer possible, she clearly wanted to die. As a former director of a hospice program, I know how to use pain medicines to keep patients comfortable and lessen suffering. I explained the philosophy of comfort care, which I strongly believe in. Although Diane understood and appreciated this, she had known of people lingering in what was called relative comfort, and she wanted no part of it. When the time came, she wanted to take her life in the least painful way possible. Knowing of her desire for independence and her decision to stay in control, I thought this request made perfect sense. I acknowledged and explored this wish but also thought that it was out of the realm of currently accepted medical practice and that it was more than I could offer or promise. In our discussion, it became clear that preoccupation with her fear of a lingering death would interfere with Diane's getting the most out of the time she had left until she found a safe way to ensure her death. I feared the effects of a violent death on her family, the consequences of an ineffective suicide that would leave her lingering in precisely the state she dreaded so much, and the possibility that a family member would be forced to assist her, with all the legal and personal repercussions that would follow. She discussed this at length with her family. They believed that they should respect her choice. With this in mind, I told Diane that information was available from the Hemlock Society that might be helpful to her.

A week later she phoned me with a request for barbiturates for sleep. Since I knew that this was an essential ingredient in a Hemlock Society suicide, I asked her to come to the office to talk things over. She was more than willing to protect me by participating in a superficial conversation about her insomnia, but it was important to me to know how she planned to use the drugs and to be sure that she was not in despair or overwhelmed in a way that might color her judgment. In our discussion, it was apparent that she was having trouble sleeping, but it was also evident that the security of having enough barbiturates available to commit suicide when and if the time came would leave her secure enough to live fully and concentrate on the present. It was clear that she was not despondent and that in fact she was making deep, personal connections with her family and close friends. I made sure that she knew how to use the barbiturates for sleep, and also that she knew the amount needed to commit suicide. We agreed to meet regularly, and she promised to meet with me before taking her life, to ensure that all other avenues had been exhausted. I wrote the prescription with an uneasy feeling about the boundaries I was exploring—spiritual, legal, professional, and personal. Yet I also felt strongly that I was setting her free to get the most out of the time she had left, and to maintain dignity and control on her own terms until her death.

The next several months were very intense and important for Diane. Her son stayed home from college, and they were able to be with one another and say much that had not been said earlier. Her husband did his work at home so that he and Diane could spend more time together. She spent time with her closest friends. I had her come into the hospital for a conference with our residents, at which she illustrated in a most profound and personal way the importance of informed decision making, the right to refuse treatment, and the extraordinarily personal effects of illness and interaction with the medical system. There were emotional and physical hardships as well. She had periods of intense sadness and anger. Several times she became very weak, but she received transfusions as an outpatient and responded with marked improvement of symptoms. She had two serious infections that responded surprisingly well to empirical courses of oral antibiotics. After three tumultuous months, there were two weeks of relative calm and well-being, and fantasies of a miracle began to surface.

Unfortunately, we had no miracle. Bone pain, weakness, fatigue, and fevers began to dominate her life. Although the hospice workers, family members, and I tried our best to minimize the suffering and promote comfort, it was clear that the end was approaching. Diane's immediate future held what she feared the most—increasing discomfort, dependence, and hard choices between pain and sedation. She called up her closest friends and asked them to come over to say good-bye, telling them that she would be leaving soon. As we had agreed, she let me know as well. When we met, it was clear that she knew what she was doing, that she was sad and frightened to be leaving, but that she would be even more terrified to stay and suffer. In our tearful good-bye, she promised a reunion in the future at her favorite spot on the edge of Lake Geneva, with dragons swimming in the sunset.

Two days later her husband called to say that Diane had died. She had said her final good-byes to her husband and son that morning, and asked them to leave her alone for an hour. After an hour, which must have seemed an eternity, they found her on the couch, lying very still and covered by her favorite shawl. There was no sign of struggle. She seemed to be at peace. They called me for advice about how to proceed. When I arrived, her husband and son were quiet. We talked about what a remarkable person she had been. They seemed to have no doubts about the course she had chosen or about their cooperation, although the unfairness of her illness and the finality of her death were overwhelming to us all.

I called the medical examiner to inform him that a hospice patient had died. When asked about the cause of death, I said, "acute leukemia." He said that was fine and that we should call a funeral director. Although acute leukemia was the truth, it was not the whole story. Yet any mention of suicide would have given rise to a police investigation and probably brought the arrival of an ambulance crew for resuscitation. Diane would have become a "coroner's case," and the decision to perform an autopsy would have been made at the discretion of the medical examiner. The family or I could have been subject to criminal prosecution, and I to professional review, for our roles in support of Diane's choices. Although I truly believe that the family and I gave her the best care possible, allowing her to define her limits and directions as much as possible, I am not sure the law, society, or the medical profession would agree. So I said "acute leukemia" to protect all of us, to protect Diane from an invasion into her past and her body, and to continue to shield society from the knowledge of the degree of suffering that people often undergo in the process of dying. Suffering can be lessened to some extent, but in no way eliminated or made benign, by the careful intervention of a competent, caring physician, given current social constraints.

Diane taught me about the range of help I can provide if I know people well and if I allow them to say what they really want. She taught me about life, death, and honesty and about taking charge and facing tragedy squarely when it strikes. She taught me that I can take small risks for people that I really know and care about. Although I did not assist in her suicide directly, I helped indirectly to make it possible, successful, and relatively painless. Although I know we have measures to help control pain and lessen suffering, to think that people do not suffer in the process of dying is an illusion. Prolonged dying can occasionally be peaceful, but more often the role of the physician and family is limited to lessening but not eliminating severe suffering.

I wonder how many families and physicians secretly help patients over the edge into death in the face of such severe suffering. I wonder how many severely ill or dying patients secretly take their lives, dying alone in despair. I wonder whether the image of Diane's final aloneness will persist in the minds of her family, or if they will remember more the intense, meaningful months they had together before she died. I wonder whether Diane struggled in that last hour, and whether the Hemlock Society's way of death by suicide is the most benign. I wonder why Diane, who gave so much to so many of us, had to be alone for the last hour of her life. I wonder whether I will see Diane again, on the shore of Lake Geneva at sunset, with dragons swimming on the horizon.

Journal/Discussion Questions

✍ *Have you ever known anyone in a situation similar to Diane's? How did they deal with it? How would you have dealt with it?*

1. Do you think that Dr. Quill made the right decision in this case? Why or why not? How would you have responded to Diane's decision?

2. Do you think physicians should ever be allowed to assist patients in ending their own lives? What guidelines, if any, would you propose for physicians who face this choice?

An Introduction to the Moral Issues

As we consider the details of the issue of euthanasia, it is helpful to begin by realizing the pervasiveness of the issue. Increasingly, people die in a medical context—often a hospital—that is unfamiliar to them and populated primarily by strangers. Currently, 85 percent of Americans die in some kind of health-care facility (this includes not only hospitals, but nursing homes, hospices, etc.); of this group, 70 percent (which is equivalent to almost 60 percent of the population as a whole) choose to withhold some kind of life-sustaining treatment.[1] It is highly likely that each of us will eventually face that same decision about ourselves; it is even more likely that we will indirectly be involved in that decision as family members and loved ones face death.

Dying in a hospital is particularly difficult, for there is nothing within medicine itself—which is tenaciously committed to winning every possible battle with death, even though there is no hope of ever winning the war—that helps physicians to let go, to allow an individual to die peacefully. There are certainly many physicians who show great wisdom in dealing with this issue (the selection from Dr. Quill is a good example of this), but their wisdom flows primarily from their character as persons rather than from their medical knowledge. Medical knowledge alone does not tell us when to let go, and medical practice—perhaps quite rightly—is often committed to fighting on and on, no matter what the odds. Yet this means that each of us as patients must face this question squarely.

Some Initial Distinctions

Recent discussions of euthanasia have been dominated by several important distinctions—and by disagreement over exactly how the distinctions are to be drawn and what significance they should have. The three most important of these are the distinction between active and passive euthanasia, voluntary and involuntary euthanasia, and assisted and unassisted euthanasia. Let's consider each of these in turn.

Active versus Passive Euthanasia

The distinction between active and passive euthanasia seems, on the surface, easy enough. *Active euthanasia* occurs in those instances in which someone takes active means, such as a lethal injection, to bring about someone's death; *passive euthanasia* occurs in those instances in which someone simply refuses to intervene to prevent someone's death. In a hospital setting, a Do Not Resuscitate (DNR) order is one of the most common means of passive euthanasia.

Conceptual clarity. This distinction has been attacked in at least two ways. First, some have attacked the *conceptual clarity* of the distinction, arguing that the line between active and passive is much more blurred than one might initially think. One reason this distinction becomes conceptually slippery, especially in regard to the notion of passive euthanasia, is that it is embedded in a background set of assumptions about what constitutes normal care and what the normal duties of care givers are. In typical hospital settings, there is a distinction between ordinary and extraordinary care. At one end of the spectrum, giving someone food and water is clearly ordinary care; at the other end of the spectrum, giving someone an emergency heart and lung transplant to save that person's life is clearly extraordinary care. Refusing to give food and water seems to be different than refusing to perform a transplant. Both are passive, but one involves falling below the expectations of normal care whereas the other does not. Typically, DNRs would fall somewhere in the middle ground on this scale. The source of this bit of conceptual slipperiness comes from the fact that we need to distinguish between two levels of passive euthanasia: (a) refusing to provide extraordinary care and (b) refusing to provide any life-sustaining care at all. Just as in daily life, we would distinguish between the person who refuses to jump into a turbulent sea to save a drowning child and the person who refuses to reach into a bathtub to save a baby drowning there, so, too, in medical contexts we must distinguish between refusing to take extraordinary means to prevent death and refusing to provide normal care (such as nutrition and hydration) to sustain life.

There is at least a second reason why this distinction is conceptually slippery, especially in regard to the notion of active euthanasia. As we have already seen in our discussion of abortion, philosophers distinguish between the intended consequences of an action and the unintended (but foreseeable) consequences of an action. This distinction is crucial to the principle of the double effect, which under certain specifiable conditions morally permits an individual to perform an action that would otherwise not be allowed. Many Catholic ethicians, for example, would argue that a physician might be morally permitted to perform a surgical procedure such as a hysterectomy to remove a cancerous uterus even if this results in the death of a fetus, as long as the intention was not to kill the fetus, the cause was serious, and there was no other means to that end. Similarly, physicians might give certain terminal patients painkillers in large dosages, realizing that such dosages might cause death but having no other way of alleviating the patient's extreme pain.

Moral significance. In addition to attacking the conceptual clarity of the active/passive distinction, some ethicists have attacked the *moral significance* of this distinction. The standard view is that active euthanasia is morally much more questionable than passive euthanasia, because it involves actively choosing to bring about the death of a human being. Critics of the moral significance of this distinction have argued that active euthanasia is often more compassionate than passive euthanasia and morally preferable to it. The typical type of case they adduce is one in which (a) there is no doubt that the patient will die soon, (b) the option of passive euthanasia causes significantly more pain for the patient (and often the family as well) than active euthanasia and does nothing to enhance the remaining life of the patient, and (c) passive measures will not bring about the death of the patient. Certain types of cancers are not only extremely painful, but also very resistant to painkilling medications in dosages that still permit patients to be aware of themselves and those around them. It is not uncommon for situations to occur in which patients will undoubtedly die (within several days, if not hours) and in which their remaining time will be filled either with extreme pain or unconsciousness resulting from pain medication. Removal of life-support may not bring about the death of such patients if their heart and respiratory systems have not been seriously compromised. In such situations, passive euthanasia seems to be *crueler* than active euthanasia and therefore morally less preferable.

Voluntary, Nonvoluntary, and Involuntary Euthanasia

The second crucial distinction in discussion of euthanasia is among voluntary, nonvoluntary, and involuntary euthanasia. Voluntary euthanasia occurs when the individual chooses to die; nonvoluntary euthanasia occurs when the individual's death is brought about (either actively or passively) without the individual's choosing to die; involuntary euthanasia occurs when the individual's death is brought about against the individual's wishes. Several points need to be made about this distinction.

The distinction between nonvoluntary and involuntary.   Involuntary euthanasia covers those cases in which an individual does not want to be euthanized; nonvoluntary euthanasia refers to those in which the individual cannot make an expressed choice at all. The former class of cases is clearly troubling: the individual wishes to live and someone else intentionally terminates that individual's life. Most would say that this is simply murder. The latter class of cases is more common and morally more ambiguous. How do we treat those individuals, usually terminally ill and unable to choose (due to coma or some other medical condition), who may be in great pain and who have never clearly expressed their wishes about euthanasia in the past? Similarly, infants are unable to express their wishes about this (or any other) matter. If euthanasia is employed in such cases, it is not voluntary, but not in the same sense as it is involuntary when the patient has expressed a clear wish not to be euthanized. Thus, we get the following type of division:

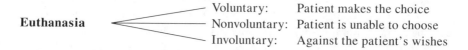

Euthanasia	Voluntary:	Patient makes the choice
	Nonvoluntary:	Patient is unable to choose
	Involuntary:	Against the patient's wishes

The morally most troubling of these cases will be those of involuntary euthanasia where the patient is unable to choose.

Assisted versus Unassisted Euthanasia

The final important distinction in the discussion of euthanasia centers around the fact that many instances of euthanasia occur when an individual is no longer physically able to carry out the act. Assistance becomes necessary, either to perform the action at all or at least to die in a relatively painless and nonviolent way. Several important points need to be noted about this distinction.

The following chart helps us to see the ways in which these basic distinctions relate to one another, the types of acts they designate, and their current legal status in the United States:

Euthanasia: Some Fundamental Distinctions

	Passive	Active: Not Assisted	Active: Assisted
Voluntary	Currently legal; often contained in living wills	Equivalent to suicide for the patient	Equivalent to suicide for the patient; possibly equivalent to murder for the assistant
Nonvoluntary: Patient not able to choose	Sometimes legal, but only with court permission	Not possible	Equivalent to either suicide or being murdered for the patient; legally equivalent to murder for the assistant
Involuntary: Against patient's wishes	Not legal	Not possible	Equivalent to being murdered for the patient; equivalent to murder for the assistant

Equipped with these distinctions, let's now turn to a consideration of the fundamental moral issues raised by euthanasia, looking first at the justifications that have been offered for and against euthanasia and then considering the three most typical types of cases: defective newborns, adults with profoundly diminished lives, and those in the final and painful phase of a terminal illness.

Euthanasia as the Compassionate Response to Suffering

One of the principal moral motives that moves some of us toward euthanasia is compassion: we see needless suffering, whether in ourselves or others, we want to alleviate or end it, and euthanasia is the only means of doing so. The paradigmatic situation here is that of a patient who is near death, who is in great pain that is not responsive to medication, and who has made an informed choice to die. At that juncture, those who care about the patient simply want the patient's suffering to end— there seems to be no point in further suffering, for there is no hope of recovery—and euthanasia becomes the way of ending it.

The Sanctity of Life and the Right to Die

There are very few villains in the debate over euthanasia, but there are disagreements about the interpretation and relative place of certain fundamental values and rights. One of the most prominent areas of conflict centers around the relationship between the sanctity of life and the right to die.

The Sanctity of Life

Human life, many of us believe, is sacred. In its original form, this belief is a religious one; the sanctity of life is an indication that life is a gift from God and therefore cannot be ended by human hand without violating God's law or rejecting God's love. Moreover, in its original form—one sees this most clearly in Buddhism, but also in other religious traditions—this belief encompasses *all* life, not just human life. In this form, it is not only a tradition that encompasses pacifism and opposes capital punishment, abortion, and euthanasia, but also one that respects the lives of animals and the living environment as a whole. Life is a sacred gift from God, and it is not the proper role of human beings to take it away from anyone. Respect for life, in the words of one Catholic bishop, is a "seamless garment" that covers the entire fabric of living creation. No distinction is drawn about the quality of life. All life is to be respected, loved, and cared for. It is this tradition that leads to the compassion of the Buddha and of Mother Theresa.

Followers of this tradition do not support either active or passive euthanasia in the sense discussed here. However, they certainly are committed to the broader sense of "dying well" and spiritual discipline is often part of that commitment. Their alternative to active or passive euthanasia in the Western sense is not neglect, but compassion and love and ministering to the sick, the infirm, and the dying.

The Right to Die

Those who argue that human beings have a right to die usually differ from those who stress the sanctity of life on two principal points. First, and more important, they do not see life as a gift from God that cannot be disposed of at will; instead, they often see life ontologically as an accident and almost always morally as the possession of an individual. The dominant metaphor here is of life as property rather than gift. In this tradition, each person is seen as *owning* his or her own life and owners are allowed to do whatever they want with their property. Second, respect for life in this tradition entails allowing the proper owner (i.e., the individual) to decide for himself or herself whether to continue living. Notice that this tradition does not deny respect for life; rather, it has a different view of the source of life and of who holds proper dominion over life.

Those in this tradition respond quite differently to illnesses that profoundly reduce the quality of an individual's life or produce great and needless pain. Their focus is on reducing suffering, maintaining a minimal threshold of quality for the individual's life, and encouraging individuals to make their own decisions about the termination of their own life. The focus is thus on the quality of life and individual autonomy. The types of cases that those in this tradition point to are usually cases in which individuals want to die to end their suffering but are kept alive against their own wishes because a family member, the court, or in some cases the administrators of health care facilities—ever fearful of suits and federal investigations—are unwilling to let them die.

The Conflict of Traditions

It is important to understand the nature of this disagreement—and it is especially important to avoid certain easy ways of misunderstanding it. This is not a conflict between those who respect life and those who do not, nor is it a conflict between those who are indifferent to suffering and those who seek to eliminate it. Rather, it is a conflict between two types of traditions, both of which respect life and both of which encourage compassion and the reduction of suffering. The differences between them center on how they understand life and what they accept as legitimate ways of reducing suffering.

The Value of Life and the Cost of Caring

In the *Groundwork of a Metaphysics of Morals,* Immanuel Kant drew a crucial moral distinction between rational beings and mere things.[2] Everything, Kant maintains, has either a *price* or a *dignity.* Mere things always have a price; that is, an equivalent value of some kind (usually a monetary one)—they can be exchanged one for the other. Rational beings, however, have dignity, for the value of a human being is such that it is beyond all calculations of price; they cannot be exchanged, one for the other. In drawing this distinction, Kant articulated a moral insight that remains powerful today: the belief that human life is priceless and that we therefore ought not to put a price tag on it. Human life is to be preserved at all costs, for the value of human life is beyond that of any costs. Indeed, this may well be one of the motivations in critical care situations when the full arsenal of medicine's skill and technology is brought to bear on a frail, old, dying person to prolong his or her life for a few days, weeks, or even months. We cannot put a price tag on human life, the Kantian inside us says. There is something morally odious about thinking that a human life can be traded for something else.

Slippery Slopes

Even among those who are not opposed to euthanasia in principle, there are serious reservations about the possibility that legalizing euthanasia could lead to abuses. Once the door is opened even a little, the danger is that more will be permitted—either through further legalization or because of objectionable but common abuses that although not permitted by the new proposal, could not be effectively curbed—than we originally wanted. History makes us cautious. Euthanasia of the physically and mentally handicapped was part of Hitler's plan, and by some estimates as many as 200,000 handicapped people were killed as part of the Nazi eugenics program. Not surprisingly, many are watching the Netherlands very carefully now, for active euthanasia has been tolerated there for a number of years and legalized in 1994.

Undervalued Groups

The slippery slope argument has an added dimension when placed within a social context of discrimination. In a society in which the lives of certain classes of people are typically undervalued, legalized euthanasia could become a further instrument of discrimination. The classes discriminated against may vary from society to society, and the classes may be based on race, ethnicity, gender, social orientation, religious beliefs, social class, age, or some other characteristic. However the classes are determined, the point remains the same: legalized euthanasia would be more likely to encourage the early deaths of members of those classes that are discriminated against in society. For this argument to work, it must either presuppose that euthanasia is bad in itself or else that it would encourage certain morally unjustified kinds of euthanasia such as involuntary euthanasia. The latter line of argument seems to be plausible; namely, that the legalization of voluntary euthanasia would result in undue pressure on certain segments of society to "choose" euthanasia when they did not really want to do so.

There is certainly no shortage of undervalued groups in the United States. Some groups are racially constituted: some Native Americans and some African Americans feel that their people have been treated in ways that have genocidal overtones. Similar issues exist for the poor and the homeless, but they are often less able to advance their own interests in public forums. Finally, and perhaps most pervasively, the elderly in the United States (and elsewhere as well) form a group that is highly undervalued.

Endnotes

1. Miles, S., and Gomez, C., *Protocols for Elective Use of Life-Sustaining Treatment.* (New York: Springer-Verlag, 1988). Cited in Margaret Battin, "Euthanasia: The Way We Do It, the Way They Do It," *Journal of Pain and Symptom Management,* 6, no. 5, 298–305.
2. Immanuel Kant, *The Moral Law: Kant's Groundwork of the Metaphysic of Morals,* trans. and anal. by H.J. Paton (London: Hutchinson University Library, 1969), pp. 96–97.

Journal/Discussion Questions

1. Under what conditions, if any, would you want others to withhold medical treatment from you? To withhold fluids and nutrition? To actively terminate your life?

2. Write your own living will, including in it all instructions and requests you think are relevant.

The Arguments

John Hardwig
"Is There a Duty to Die?"

John Hardwig is professor of philosophy at East Tennessee State University. He has published widely in the area of ethics.

   Hardwig maintains that modern medicine and American individualistic culture have encouraged us to think that we have an almost unlimited right to life and to health care. Hardwig argues that there are circumstances in which we have a duty to die and that this will become a more common scenario as a result of the advances of modern medicine and technology.

As You Read, Consider This:

1. Under what circumstances, according to Hardwig, do we have a duty to die?
2. How does Hardwig deal with the case of someone who has a duty to die but does not want to die?
3. What does Hardwig mean by "the individualistic fantasy"?

When Richard Lamm made the statement that old people have a duty to die, it was generally shouted down or ridiculed. The whole idea is just too preposterous to entertain. Or too threatening. In fact, a fairly common argument against legalizing physician-assisted suicide is that if it were legal, some people might somehow get the idea that they have a duty to die. These people could only be the victims of twisted moral reasoning or vicious social pressure. It goes without saying that there is no duty to die.

   But for me the question is real and very important. I feel strongly that I may very well some day have a duty to die. I do not believe that I am idiosyncratic, morbid, mentally ill, or morally perverse in thinking this. I think many of us will eventually face precisely this duty. But I am first of all concerned with my own duty. I write partly to clarify my own convictions and to prepare myself. Ending my life might be a very difficult thing for me to do.

   This notion of a duty to die raises all sorts of interesting theoretical and metaethical questions. I intend to try to avoid most of them because I hope my argument will be persuasive to those holding a wide variety of ethical views. Also, although the claim that there is a duty to die would

Hastings Center Report, Vol. 27, No. 2 (1997), pp. 34–42.

ultimately require theoretical underpinning, the discussion needs to begin on the normative level. As is appropriate to my attempt to steer clear of theoretical commitments, I will use "duty," "obligation," and "responsibility" interchangeably, in a pre-theoretical or preanalytic sense.[1]

Circumstances and a Duty to Die

Do many of us really believe that no one ever has a duty to die? I suspect not. I think most of us probably believe that there is such a duty, but it is very uncommon. Consider Captain Oates, a member of Admiral Scott's expedition to the South Pole. Oates became too ill to continue. If the rest of the team stayed with him, they would all perish. After this had become clear, Oates left his tent one night, walked out into a raging blizzard, and was never seen again.[2] That may have been a heroic thing to do, but we might be able to agree that it was also no more than his duty. It would have been wrong for him to urge—or even to allow—the rest to stay and care for him.

This is a very unusual circumstance—a "lifeboat case"—and lifeboat cases make for bad ethics. But I expect that most of us would also agree that there have been cultures in which what we would call a duty to die has been fairly common. These are relatively poor, technologically simple, and especially nomadic cultures. In such societies, everyone knows that if you manage to live long enough, you will eventually become old and debilitated. Then you will need to take steps to end your life. The old people in these societies regularly did precisely that. Their cultures prepared and supported them in doing so.

Those cultures could be dismissed as irrelevant to contemporary bioethics; their circumstances are so different from ours. But if that is our response, it is instructive. It suggests that we assume a duty to die is irrelevant to us because our wealth and technological sophistication have purchased exemption for us . . . except under very unusual circumstances like Captain Oates's.

But have wealth and technology really exempted us? Or are they, on the contrary, about to make a duty to die common again? We like to think of modern medicine as all triumph with no dark side. Our medicine saves many lives and enables most of us to live longer. That is wonderful, indeed. We are all glad to have access to this medicine. But our medicine also delivers most of us over to chronic illnesses and it enables many of us to survive longer than we can take care of ourselves, longer than we know what to do with ourselves, longer than we even are ourselves.

The costs—and these are not merely monetary of prolonging our lives when we are no longer able to care for ourselves—are often staggering. If further medical advances wipe out many of today's "killer diseases"—cancers, heart attacks, strokes, ALS, AIDS, and the rest—then one day most of us will survive long enough to become demented or debilitated. These developments could generate a fairly widespread duty to die. A fairly common duty to die might turn out to be only the dark side of our life-prolonging medicine and the uses we choose to make of it.

Let me be clear. I certainly believe that there is a duty to refuse life-prolonging medical treatment and also a duty to complete advance directives refusing life-prolonging treatment. But a duty to die can go well beyond that. There can be a duty to die before one's illnesses would cause death, even if treated only with palliative measures. In fact, there may be a fairly common responsibility to end one's life in the absence of any terminal illness at all. Finally, there can be a duty to die when one would prefer to live. Granted, many of the conditions that can generate a duty to die also seriously undermine the quality of life. Some prefer not to live under such conditions. But even those who want to live can face a duty to die. These will clearly be the most controversial and troubling cases; I will, accordingly, focus my reflections on them.

The Individualistic Fantasy

Because a duty to die seems such a real possibility to me, I wonder why contemporary bioethics has dismissed it without serious consideration. I believe that most bioethics still shares in one of our deeply embedded American dreams: the individualistic fantasy. This fantasy leads us to imagine that lives are separate and unconnected, or that they could be so if we chose. If lives were unconnected, things that happened in my life would not or need not affect others. And if others were not (much) affected by my life, I would have no duty to consider the impact of my decisions on others. I would then be free morally to live my life however I please, choosing whatever life and death I prefer for myself. The way I live would be nobody's business but my own. I certainly would have no duty to die if I preferred to live.

Within a health care context, the individualistic fantasy leads us to assume that the patient is the only one affected by decisions about her medical treatment. If only the patient were affected, the relevant questions when making treatment decisions would be precisely those we ask: What will benefit the patient? Who can best decide that? The pivotal issue would always be simply whether the patient wants to live like this and whether she would consider herself better off dead.[3] "Whose life is it, anyway?" we ask rhetorically.

But this is morally obtuse. We are not a race of hermits. Illness and death do not come only to those who are all alone. Nor is it much better to think in terms of the bald dichotomy between "the interests of the patient" and "the interests of society" (or a third-party payer), as if we were isolated individuals connected only to "society" in the abstract or to the other, faceless members of our health maintenance organization.

Most of us are affiliated with particular others and most deeply, with family and loved ones. Families and loved ones are bound together by ties of care and affection, by legal relations and obligations, by inhabiting shared spaces and living units, by interlocking finances and economic prospects, by common projects and also commitments to support the different life projects of other family members, by shared histories, by ties of loyalty. This life together of family and loved ones is what defines and sustains us; it is what gives meaning to most of our lives. We would not have it any other way. We would not want to be all alone, especially when we are seriously ill, as we age, and when we are dying.

But the fact of deeply interwoven lives debars us from making exclusively self-regarding decisions, as the decisions of one member of a family may dramatically affect the lives of all the rest. The impact of my decisions upon my family and loved ones is the source of many of my strongest obligations and also the most plausible and likeliest basis of a duty to die. "Society," after all, is only very marginally affected by how I live, or by whether I live or die.

A Burden to My Loved Ones

Many older people report that their one remaining goal in life is not to be a burden to their loved ones. Young people feel this, too: when I ask my undergraduate students to think about whether their death could come too late, one of their very first responses always is, "Yes, when I become a burden to my family or loved ones." Tragically, there are situations in which my loved ones would be much better off—all things considered, the loss of a loved one notwithstanding—if I were dead.

The lives of our loved ones can be seriously compromised by caring for us. The burdens of providing care or even just supervision twenty-four hours a day, seven days a week are often overwhelming.[4] When this kind of caregiving goes on for years, it leaves the caregiver exhausted, with no time for herself or life of her own. Ultimately, even her health is often destroyed. But it can also be emotionally devastating simply to live with a spouse who is increasingly distant, uncommunicative, unresponsive, foreign, and unreachable. Other family members' needs often go unmet as the caring capacity of the family is exceeded. Social life and friendships evaporate, as there is no opportunity to go out to see friends and the home is no longer a place suitable for having friends in.

We must also acknowledge that the lives of our loved ones can be devastated just by having to pay for health care for us. One part of the recent SUPPORT study documented the financial aspects of caring for a dying member of a family. Only those who had illnesses severe enough to give them less than a 50 percent chance to live six more months were included in this study. When these patients survived their initial hospitalization and were discharged about one-third required considerable caregiving from their families; in 20 percent of cases a family member had to quit work or make some other major lifestyle change; almost one-third of these families lost all of their savings; and just under 30 percent lost a major source of income.[5]

If talking about money sounds venal or trivial, remember that much more than money is normally at stake here. When someone has to quit work, she may well lose her career. Savings decimated late in life cannot be recouped in the few remaining years of employability, so the loss compromises the quality of the rest of the caregiver's life. For a young person, the chance to go to college may be lost to the attempt to pay debts due to an illness in the family, and this decisively shapes an entire life.

A serious illness in a family is a misfortune. It is usually nobody's fault; no one is responsible for it. But we face choices about how we will respond to this misfortune. That's where the responsibility comes in and fault can arise. Those of us with families and loved ones always have a duty not to make selfish or self-centered decisions about our lives. We have a responsibility to try to protect the lives of loved ones from serious threats or greatly impoverished quality, certainly an obligation not to make choices that will jeopardize or seriously compromise their futures. Often, it would be wrong to do just what we want or just what is best for ourselves; we should choose in light of what is best for all concerned. That is our duty in sickness as well as in health. It is out of these responsibilities that a duty to die can develop.

I am not advocating a crass, quasi-economic conception of burdens and benefits, nor a shallow, hedonistic view of life. Given a suitably rich understanding of benefits, family members sometimes do benefit from suffering through the long illness of a loved one. Caring for the sick or aged can foster growth, even as it makes daily life immeasurably harder and the prospects for the future much bleaker. Chronic illness or a drawn-out death can also pull a family together, making the care for each other stronger and more evident. If my loved ones are truly benefiting from coping with my illness or debility, I have no duty to die based on burdens to them.

But it would be irresponsible to blithely assume that this always happens, that it will happen in my family, or that it will be the fault of my family if they cannot manage to turn my illness into a positive experience. Perhaps the opposite is more common: a hospital chaplain once told me that he could not think of a single case in which a family was strengthened or brought together by what happened at the hospital.

Our families and loved ones also have obligations, of course—they have the responsibility to stand by us and support us through debilitating illness and death. They must be prepared to make significant sacrifices to respond to an illness in the family. I am far from denying that. Most of us are aware of this responsibility and most families meet it rather well. In fact, families deliver more than 80 percent of the long-term care in this country, almost always at great personal cost. Most of us who are a part of a family can expect to be sustained in our time of need by family members and those who love us.

But most discussions of an illness in the family sound as if responsibility were a one-way street. It is not, of course. When we become seriously ill or debilitated, we, too, may have to make sacrifices. To think that my loved ones must bear whatever burdens my illness, debility, or dying process might impose upon them is to reduce them to means to my well-being. And that would be immoral. Family solidarity, altruism, bearing the burden of a loved one's misfortune, and loyalty are all important virtues of families, as well. But they are all also two-way streets.

Objections to a Duty to Die

To my mind, the most serious objections to the idea of a duty to die lie in the effects on my loved ones of ending my life. But to most others, the important objections have little or nothing to do with family and loved ones. Perhaps the most common objections are: (1) there is a higher duty that always takes precedence over a duty to die; (2) a duty to end one's own life would be incompatible with a recognition of human dignity or the intrinsic value of a person; and (3) seriously ill, debilitated, or dying people are already bearing the harshest burdens and so it would be wrong to ask them to bear the additional burden of ending their own lives.

These are all important objections; all deserve a thorough discussion. Here I will only be able to suggest some moral counterweights—ideas that might provide the basis for an argument that these objections do not always preclude a duty to die.

An example of the first line of argument would be the claim that a duty to God, the giver of life, forbids that anyone take her own life. It could be argued that this duty always supersedes whatever obligations we might have to our families. But what convinces us that we always have such a religious duty in the first place? And what guarantees that it always supersedes our obligations to try to protect our loved ones?

Certainly, the view that death is the ultimate evil cannot be squared with Christian theology. It does not reflect the actions of Jesus or those of his early followers. Nor is it clear that the belief that life is sacred requires that we never take it. There are other theological possibilities.[6] In any case, most of us—bioethicists, physicians, and patients alike—do not subscribe to the view that we have an obligation to preserve human life as long as possible. But if not, surely we ought to agree that I may legitimately end my life for other-regarding reasons, not just for self-regarding reasons.

Secondly, religious considerations aside, the claim could be made that an obligation to end one's own life would be incompatible with human dignity or would embody a failure to recognize the intrinsic value of a person. But I do not see that in thinking I had a duty to die I would necessarily be failing to respect myself or to appreciate my dignity or worth. Nor would I necessarily be failing to respect you in thinking that you had a similar duty. There is surely also a sense in which we fail to respect ourselves if in the face of illness or death, we stoop to choosing just what is best for ourselves. Indeed, Kant held that the very core of human dignity is the ability to act on a self-imposed moral law, regardless of whether it is in our interest to do so.[7] We shall return to the notion of human dignity.

A third objection appeals to the relative weight of burdens and thus, ultimately, to considerations of fairness or justice. The burdens that an illness creates for the family could not possibly be great enough to justify an obligation to end one's life—the sacrifice of life itself would be a far greater burden than any involved in caring for a chronically ill family member.

But is this true? Consider the following case:

An 87-year-old woman was dying of congestive heart failure. Her APACHE score predicted that she had less than a 50 percent chance to live for another six months. She was lucid, assertive, and terrified of death. She very much wanted to live and kept opting for rehospitalization and the most aggressive life-prolonging treatment possible. That treatment successfully prolonged her life (though with increasing debility) for nearly two years. Her 55-year-old daughter was her only remaining family, her caregiver, and the main source of her financial support. The daughter duly cared for her mother. But before her mother died, her illness had cost the daughter all of her savings, her home, her job, and her career.

This is by no means an uncommon sort of case. Thousands of similar cases occur each year. Now, ask yourself which is the greater burden:

(a) To lose a 50 percent chance of six more months of life at age 87?
(b) To lose all your savings, your home, and your career at age 55?

Which burden would you prefer to bear? Do we really believe the former is the greater burden? Would even the dying mother say that (a) is the greater burden? Or has she been encouraged to believe that the burdens of (b) are somehow morally irrelevant to her choices?

I think most of us would quickly agree that (b) is a greater burden. That is the evil we would more hope to avoid in our lives. If we are tempted to say that the mother's disease and impending death are the greater evil, I believe it is because we are taking a "slice of time" perspective rather than a "lifetime perspective."[8] But surely the lifetime perspective is the appropriate perspective when weighing burdens. If (b) is the greater burden, then we must admit that we have been promulgating an ethic that advocates imposing greater burdens on some people in order to provide smaller benefits for others just because they are ill and thus gain our professional attention and advocacy.

A whole range of cases like this one could easily be generated. In some, the answer about which burden is greater will not be clear. But in many it is. Death or ending your own life is simply not the greatest evil or the greatest burden.

This point does not depend on a utilitarian calculus. Even if death were the greatest burden (thus disposing of any simple utilitarian argument), serious questions would remain about the moral justifiability of choosing to impose crushing burdens on loved ones in order to avoid having to bear this burden oneself. The fact that I suffer greater burdens than others in my family does not license me simply to choose what I want for myself, nor does it necessarily release me from a responsibility to try to protect the quality of their lives.

I can readily imagine that, through cowardice, rationalization, or failure of resolve, I will fail in this obligation to protect my loved ones. If so, I think I would need to be excused or forgiven for what I did. But I cannot imagine it would be morally permissible for me to ruin the rest of my partner's life to sustain mine or to cut off my sons' careers, impoverish them, or compromise the quality of their children's lives simply because I wish to live a little longer. This is what leads me to believe in a duty to die.

Who Has a Duty to Die?

Suppose, then, that there can be a duty to die. Who has a duty to die? And when? To my mind, these are the right questions, the questions we should be asking. Many of us may one day badly need answers to just these questions.

But I cannot supply answers here, for two reasons. In the first place, answers will have to be very particular and contextual. Our concrete duties are often situated, defined in part by the myriad details of our circumstances, histories, and relationships. Though there may be principles that apply to a wide range of cases and some cases that yield pretty straightforward answers, there will also be many situations in which it is very difficult to discern whether one has a duty to die. If nothing else, it will often be very difficult to predict how one's family will bear up under the weight of the burdens that a protracted illness would impose on them. Momentous decisions will often have to be made under conditions of great uncertainty.

Second and perhaps even more importantly, I believe that those of us with family and loved ones should not define our duties unilaterally, especially not a decision about a duty to die. It would be isolating and distancing for me to decide without consulting them what is too much of a burden for my loved ones to bear. That way of deciding about my moral duties is not only atomistic, it also treats my family and loved ones paternalistically. They must be allowed to speak for themselves about the burdens my life imposes on them and how they feel about bearing those burdens.

Some may object that it would be wrong to put a loved one in a position of having to say, in effect, "You should end your life because caring for you is too hard on me and the rest of the family." Not only will it be almost impossible to say something like that to someone you love, it will carry with it a heavy load of guilt. On this view, you should decide by yourself whether you have a duty to die and approach your loved ones only after you have made up your mind to say good-bye to them. Your family could then try to change your mind, but the tremendous weight of moral decision would be lifted from their shoulders.

Perhaps so. But I believe in family decisions. Important decisions for those whose lives are interwoven should be made together, in a family discussion. Granted, a conversation about whether I have a duty to die would be a tremendously difficult conversation. The temptations to be dishonest could be enormous. Nevertheless, if I am contemplating a duty to die, my family and I should, if possible, have just such an agonizing discussion. It will act as a check on the information, perceptions, and reasoning of all of us. But even more importantly, it affirms our connectedness at a critical juncture in our lives and our life together. Honest talk about difficult matters almost always strengthens relationships.

However, many families seem unable to talk about death at all, much less a duty to die. Certainly most families could not have this discussion all at once, in one sitting. It might well take a number of discussions to be able to approach this topic. But even if talking about death is impossible, there are always behavioral clues—about your caregiver's tiredness, physical condition, health, prevailing mood, anxiety, financial concerns, outlook, overall well-being, and so on. And families unable to talk about death can often talk about how the caregiver is feeling, about finances, about tensions within the family resulting from the illness, about concerns for the future. Deciding whether you have a duty to die based on these behavioral clues and conversation about them honors your relationships better than deciding on your own about how burdensome you and your care must be.

I cannot say when someone has a duty to die. Still, I can suggest a few features of one's illness, history, and circumstances that make it more likely that one has a duty to die. I present them here without much elaboration or explanation.

1. A duty to die is more likely when continuing to live will impose significant burdens—emotional burdens, extensive caregiving, destruction of life plans, and, yes, financial hardship—on your family and loved ones. This is the fundamental insight underlying a duty to die.

2. A duty to die becomes greater as you grow older. As we age, we will be giving up less by giving up our lives, if only because we will sacrifice fewer remaining years of life and a smaller portion of our life plans. After all, it's not as if we would be immortal and live forever if we could just manage to avoid a duty to die. To have reached the age of, say, seventy-five or eighty years without being ready to die is itself a moral failing, the sign of a life out of touch with life's basic realities.[9]

3. A duty to die is more likely when you have already lived a full and rich life. You have already had a full share of the good things life offers.

4. There is greater duty to die if your loved ones' lives have already been difficult or impoverished, if they have had only a small share of the good things that life has to offer (especially if through no fault of their own).

5. A duty to die is more likely when your loved ones have already made great contributions—perhaps even sacrifices—to make your life a good one. Especially if you have not made similar sacrifices for their well-being or for the well-being of other members of your family.

6. To the extent that you can make a good adjustment to your illness or handicapping condition, there is less likely to be a duty to die. A good adjustment means that smaller sacrifices will be required of loved ones and there is more compensating interaction for them. Still, we must also recognize that some diseases—Alzheimer or Huntington chorea—will eventually take their toll on your loved ones no matter how courageously, resolutely, even cheerfully you manage to face that illness.

7. There is less likely to be a duty to die if you can still make significant contributions to the lives of others, especially your family. The burdens to family members are not only or even primarily financial, neither are the contributions to them. However, the old and those who have terminal illnesses must also bear in mind that the loss their family members will feel when they die cannot be avoided, only postponed.

8. A duty to die is more likely when the part of you that is loved will soon be gone or seriously compromised. Or when you soon will no longer be capable of giving love. Part of the horror of dementing disease is that it destroys the capacity to nurture and sustain relationships, taking away a person's agency and the emotions that bind her to others.

9. There is a greater duty to die to the extent that you have lived a relatively lavish lifestyle instead of saving for illness or old age. Like most upper middle-class Americans, I could easily have saved more. It is a greater wrong to come to your family for assistance if your need is the

result of having chosen leisure or a spendthrift lifestyle. I may eventually have to face the moral consequences of decisions I am now making.

These, then, are some of the considerations that give shape and definition to the duty to die. If we can agree that these considerations are all relevant, we can see that the correct course of action will often be difficult to discern. A decision about when I should end my life will sometimes prove to be every bit as difficult as the decision about whether I want treatment for myself.

Can the Incompetent Have a Duty to Die?

Severe mental deterioration springs readily to mind as one of the situations in which I believe I could have a duty to die. But can incompetent people have duties at all? We can have moral duties we do not recognize or acknowledge, including duties that we never recognized. But can we have duties we are unable to recognize? Duties when we are unable to understand the concept of morality at all? If so, do others have a moral obligation to help us carry out this duty? These are extremely difficult theoretical questions. The reach of moral agency is severely strained by mental incompetence.

I am tempted to simply bypass the entire question by saying that I am talking only about competent persons. But the idea of a duty to die clearly raises the specter of one person claiming that another—who cannot speak for herself—has such a duty. So I need to say that I can make no sense of the claim that someone has a duty to die if the person has never been able to understand moral obligation at all. To my mind, only those who were formerly capable of making moral decisions could have such a duty.

But the case of formerly competent persons is almost as troubling. Perhaps we should simply stipulate that no incompetent person can have a duty to die, not even if she affirmed belief in such a duty in an advance directive. If we take the view that formerly competent people may have such a duty, we should surely exercise extreme caution when claiming a formerly competent person would have acknowledged a duty to die or that any formerly competent person has an unacknowledged duty to die. Moral dangers loom regardless of which way we decide to resolve such issues.

But for me personally, very urgent practical matters turn on their resolution. If a formerly competent person can no longer have a duty to die (or if other people are not likely to help her carry out this duty), I believe that my obligation may be to die while I am still competent, before I become unable to make and carry out that decision for myself. Surely it would be irresponsible to evade my moral duties by temporizing until I escape into incompetence. And so I must die sooner than I otherwise would have to. On the other hand, if I could count on others to end my life after I become incompetent, I might be able to fulfill my responsibilities while also living out all my competent or semi-competent days. Given our society's reluctance to permit physicians, let alone family members, to perform aid-in-dying, I believe I may well have a duty to end my life when I can see mental incapacity on the horizon.

There is also the very real problem of sudden incompetence—due to a serious stroke or automobile accident, for example. For me, that is the real nightmare. If I suddenly become incompetent, I will fall into the hands of a medical-legal system that will conscientiously disregard my moral beliefs and do what is best for me, regardless of the consequences for my loved ones. And that is not at all what I would have wanted!

Social Policies and a Duty to Die

The claim that there is a duty to die will seem to some a misplaced response to social negligence. If our society were providing for the debilitated, the chronically ill, and the elderly as it should be, there would be only very rare cases of a duty to die. On this view, I am asking the sick and debilitated to step in and accept responsibility because society is derelict in its responsibility to provide for the incapacitated.

This much is surely true: there are a number of social policies we could pursue that would dramatically reduce the incidence of such a duty. Most obviously, we could decide to pay for facilities that provided excellent long-term care (not just health care!) for all chronically ill, debilitated, mentally ill, or demented people in this country. We probably could still afford to do this. If we did, sick, debilitated, and dying people might still be morally required to make sacrifices for their families. I might, for example, have a duty to forgo personal care by a family member who knows me and really does care for me. But these sacrifices would only rarely include the sacrifice of life itself. The duty to die would then be virtually eliminated.

I cannot claim to know whether in some abstract sense a society like ours should provide care for all who are chronically ill or debilitated. But the fact is that we Americans seem to be unwilling to pay for this kind of long-term care, except for ourselves and our own. In fact, we are moving in precisely the opposite direction—we are trying to shift the burdens of caring for the seriously and chronically ill onto families in order to save costs for our health care system. As we shift the burdens of care onto families, we also dramatically increase the number of Americans who will have a duty to die.

I must not, then, live my life and make my plans on the assumption that social institutions will protect my family from my infirmity and debility. To do so would be irresponsible. More likely, it will be up to me to protect my loved ones.

A Duty to Die and the Meaning of Life

A duty to die seems very harsh, and often it would be. It is one of the tragedies of our lives that someone who wants very much to live can nevertheless have a duty to die. It is both tragic and ironic that it is precisely the very real good of family and loved ones that gives rise to this duty. Indeed, the genuine love, closeness, and supportiveness of family members is a major source of this duty: we could not be such a burden if they did not care for us. Finally, there is deep irony in the fact that the very successes of our life-prolonging medicine help to create a widespread duty to die. We do not live in such a happy world that we can avoid such tragedies and ironies. We ought not to close our eyes to this reality or pretend that it just doesn't exist. We ought not to minimize the tragedy in any way.

And yet, a duty to die will not always be as harsh as we might assume. If I love my family, I will want to protect them and their lives. I will not want to make choices that compromise their futures. Indeed, I can easily imagine that I might want to avoid compromising their lives more than I would want anything else. I must also admit that I am not necessarily giving up so much in giving up my life: the conditions that give rise to a duty to die would usually already have compromised the quality of the life I am required to end. In any case, I personally must confess that at age fifty-six, I have already lived a very good life, albeit not yet nearly as long a life as I would like to have.

We fear death too much. Our fear of death has led to a massive assault on it. We still crave after virtually any life-prolonging technology that we might conceivably be able to produce. We still too often feel morally impelled to prolong life—virtually any form of life—as long as possible. As if the best death is the one that can be put off longest.

We do not even ask about meaning in death, so busy are we with trying to postpone it. But we will not conquer death by one day developing a technology so magnificent that no one will have to die. Nor can we conquer death by postponing it ever longer. We can conquer death only by finding meaning in it.

Although the existence of a duty to die does not hinge on this, recognizing such a duty would go some way toward recovering meaning in death. Paradoxically, it would restore dignity to those who are seriously ill or dying. It would also reaffirm the connections required to give life (and death) meaning. I close now with a few words about both of these points.

First, recognizing a duty to die affirms my agency and also my moral agency. I can still do things that make an important difference in the lives of my loved ones. Moreover, the fact that I still have responsibilities keeps me within the community of moral agents. My illness or debility has not reduced me to a mere moral patient (to use the language of the philosophers). Though it may not be the whole story, surely Kant was onto something important when he claimed that human dignity rests on the capacity for moral agency within a community of those who respect the demands of morality.

By contrast, surely there is something deeply insulting in a medicine and an ethic that would ask only what I want (or would have wanted) when I become ill. To treat me as if I had no moral responsibilities when I am ill or debilitated implies that my condition has rendered me morally incompetent. Only small children, the demented or insane, and those totally lacking in the capacity to act are free from moral duties. There is dignity, then, and a kind of meaning in moral agency, even as it forces extremely difficult decisions upon us.

Second, recovering meaning in death requires an affirmation of connections. If I end my life to spare the futures of my loved ones, I testify in my death that I am connected to them. It is because I love and care for precisely these people (and I know they care for me) that I wish not to be such a burden to them. By contrast, a life in which I am free to choose whatever I want for myself is a life unconnected to others. A bioethics that would treat me as if I had no serious moral responsibilities does what it can to marginalize, weaken, or even destroy my connections with others.

But life without connection is meaningless. The individualistic fantasy, though occasionally liberating, is deeply destructive. When life is good and vitality seems unending, life itself and life lived for yourself may seem quite sufficient. But if not life, certainly death without connection is meaningless. If you are only for yourself, all you have to care about as your life draws to a close is yourself and your life. Everything you care about will then perish in your death. And that—the end of everything you care about—is precisely the total collapse of meaning. We can, then, find meaning in death only through a sense of connection with something that will survive our death.

This need not be connections with other people. Some people are deeply tied to land (for example, the family farm), to nature, or to a transcendent reality. But for most of us, the connections that sustain us are to other people. In the full bloom of life, we are connected to others in many ways—through work, profession, neighborhood, country, shared faith and worship, common leisure pursuits, friendship. Even the guru meditating in isolation on his mountaintop is connected to a long tradition of people united by the same religious quest.

But as we age or when we become chronically ill, connections with other people usually become much more restricted. Often, only ties with family and close friends remain and remain important to us. Moreover, for many of us, other connections just don't go deep enough. As Paul Tsongas has reminded us, "When it comes time to die, no one says, 'I wish I had spent more time at the office.'"

If I am correct, death is so difficult for us partly because our sense of community is so weak. Death seems to wipe out everything when we can't fit it into the lives of those who live on. A death motivated by the desire to spare the futures of my loved ones might well be a better death for me than the one I would get as a result of opting to continue my life as long as there is any pleasure in it for me. Pleasure is nice, but it is meaning that matters.

I don't know about others, but these reflections have helped me. I am now more at peace about facing a duty to die. Ending my life if my duty required might still be difficult. But for me, a far greater horror would be dying all alone or stealing the futures of my loved ones in order to buy a little more time for myself. I hope that if the time comes when I have a duty to die, I will recognize it, encourage my loved ones to recognize it, too, and carry it out bravely.

Acknowledgments

I wish to thank Mary English, Hilde Nelson, Jim Bennett, Tom Townsend, the members of the Philosophy Department at East Tennessee State University, and anonymous reviewers of the *Report* for many helpful comments on earlier versions of this paper. In this paper, I draw on material in John Hardwig, "Dying at the Right Time; Reflections on (Un)Assisted Suicide" in *Practical Ethics,* edited by H. LaFollette (London: Blackwell, 1996), with permission.

Endnotes

1. Given the importance of relationships in my thinking, "responsibility"—rooted as it is in "respond"—would perhaps be the most appropriate word. Nevertheless, I often use "duty" despite its legalistic overtones, because Lamm's famous statement has given the expression "duty to die" a certain familiarity. But I intend no implication that there is a law that grounds this duty, nor that someone has a right corresponding to it.

2. For a discussion of the Oates case, see Tom L. Beauchamp, "What Is Suicide?" in *Ethical Issues in Death and Dying,* edited by Tom L. Beauchamp and Seymour Perlin (Englewood Cliffs, NJ: Prentice-Hall, 1978).

3. Most bioethicists advocate a "patient-centered ethics"—an ethics which claims only the patients' interests should be considered in making medical treatment decisions. Most health care professionals have been trained to accept this ethic and to see themselves as patient advocates. For arguments that a patient-centered ethics should be replaced by a family-centered ethics, see John Hardwig, "What About the Family?" *Hastings Center Report* 20, no. 2 (1990): 5–10; Hilde L. Nelson and James L. Nelson, *The Patient in the Family* (New York: Routledge, 1995).

4. A good account of the burdens of caregiving can be found in Elaine Brody, *Women in the Middle: Their Parent-Care Years* (New York: Springer, 1990). Perhaps the best article-length account of these burdens is Daniel Callahan, "Families as Caregivers; the Limits of Morality" in *Aging and Ethics: Philosophical Problems in Gerontology,* edited by Nancy Jecker (Totowa, NJ: Humana Press, 1991).

5. Kenneth E. Covinsky et al., "The Impact of Serious Illness on Patients' Families," *Journal of the American Medical Association* 272 (1994): 1839–1844.

6. Larry Churchill, for example, believes that Christian ethics takes us far beyond my present position: "Christian doctrines of stewardship prohibit the extension of one's own life at a great cost to the neighbor. . . . And such a gesture should not appear to us a sacrifice, but as the ordinary virtue entailed by a just, social conscience." Larry Churchill, *Rationing Health Care in America* (South Bend, IN: Notre Dame University Press, 1988), p. 112.

7. Kant, as is well known, was opposed to suicide. But he was arguing against taking your life out of self-interested motives. It is not clear that Kant would or we should consider taking your life out of a sense of duty to be wrong. See Hilde L. Nelson, "Death with Kantian Dignity," *Journal of Clinical Ethics* 7 (1996): 215–221.

8. Obviously, I owe this distinction to Norman Daniels. Norman Daniels, *Am I My Parents' Keeper? An Essay on Justice Between the Young and the Old* (New York: Oxford University Press, 1988). Just as obviously, Daniels is not committed to my use of it here.

9. Daniel Callahan, The *Troubled Dream of Life* (New York: Simon & Schuster, 1993).

Journal/Discussion Questions

✎ *Can you ever imagine a circumstance in which you personally would feel that you had a duty to die? What would you do?*

1. What is the fundamental insight that underlies Hardwig's claim that we may have a duty to die in certain circumstances?

2. What specific circumstances would increase the likelihood that a person would have a duty to die, according to Hardwig? Do you agree with his analysis?

3. How does Hardwig answer the question of whether the incompetent have a duty to die? Do you agree with him? Explain.

4. How does Hardwig see the relationship between the duty to die and questions about the meaning of life?

James Rachels
"Active and Passive Euthanasia"

James Rachels was one of the most prominent of contemporary moral philosophers, especially in the area of applied ethics. His books include Created From Animals: The Moral Implications of Darwinism, The Elements of Moral Philosophy, *and* The End of Life: The Morality of Euthanasia.

This article, originally published in a medical journal and directed toward physicians, was the first major challenge to the moral significance of the distinction between active and passive euthanasia.

New England Journal of Medicine, Vol. 292, No. 2 (January 9, 1975), pp. 78–80.

As You Read, Consider This:

1. Why, according to Rachels, is active euthanasia morally preferable to passive euthanasia in some cases?

2. What, according to Rachels, is the difference between killing and letting die?

The distinction between active and passive euthanasia is thought to be crucial for medical ethics. The idea is that it is permissible, at least in some cases, to withhold treatment and allow a patient to die, but it is never permissible to take any direct action designed to kill the patient. This doctrine seems to be accepted by most doctors, and it is endorsed in a statement adopted by the House of Delegates of the American Medical Association on December 4, 1973:

> The intentional termination of the life of one human being by another—mercy killing—is contrary to that for which the medical profession stands and is contrary to the policy of the American Medical Association.
>
> The cessation of the employment of extraordinary means to prolong the life of the body when there is irrefutable evidence that biological death is imminent is the decision of the patient and/or his immediate family. The advice and judgment of the physician should be freely available to the patient and/or his immediate family.

However, a strong case can be made against this doctrine. In what follows I will set out some of the relevant arguments, and urge doctors to reconsider their views on this matter.

To begin with a familiar type of situation, a patient who is dying of incurable cancer of the throat is in terrible pain, which can no longer be satisfactorily alleviated. He is certain to die within a few days, even if present treatment is continued, but he does not want to go on living for those days since the pain is unbearable. So he asks the doctor for an end to it, and his family joins in the request.

Suppose the doctor agrees to withhold treatment, as the conventional doctrine says he may. The justification for his doing so is that the patient is in terrible agony, and since he is going to die anyway, it would be wrong to prolong his suffering needlessly. But now notice this. If one simply withholds the treatment, it may take the patient longer to die, and so he may suffer more than he would if more direct action were taken and a lethal injection given. This fact provides strong reason for thinking that, once the initial decision not to prolong his agony has been made, active euthanasia is actually preferable to passive euthanasia, rather than the reverse. To say otherwise is to endorse the option that leads to more suffering rather than less, and is contrary to the humanitarian impulse that prompts the decision not to prolong his life in the first place.

Part of my point is that the process of being "allowed to die" can be relatively slow and painful, whereas being given a lethal injection is relatively quick and painless. Let me give a different sort of example. In the United States about one in 600 babies is born with Down's syndrome. Most of these babies are otherwise healthy—that is, with only the usual pediatric care, they will proceed to an otherwise normal infancy. Some, however, are born with congenital defects such as intestinal obstructions that require operations if they are to live. Sometimes, the parents and the doctor will decide not to operate, and let the infant die. Anthony Shaw describes what happens then:

When surgery is denied [the doctor] must try to keep the infant from suffering while natural forces sap the baby's life away. As a surgeon whose natural inclination is to use the scalpel to fight off death, standing by and watching a salvageable baby die is the most emotionally exhausting experience I know. It is easy at a conference, in a theoretical discussion, to decide that such infants should be allowed to die. It is altogether different to stand by in the nursery and watch as dehydration and infection wither a tiny being over hours and days. This is a terrible ordeal for me and the hospital staff—much more so than for the parents who never set foot in the nursery.[1]

I can understand why some people are opposed to all euthanasia, and insist that such infants must be allowed to live. I think I can also understand why other people favor destroying these babies quickly and painlessly. But why should anyone favor letting "dehydration and infection wither a tiny being over hours and days"? The doctrine that says that a baby may be allowed to dehydrate and wither, but may not be given an injection that would end its life without suffering, seems so patently cruel as to require no further refutation. The strong language is not intended to offend, but only to put the point in the clearest possible way.

My second argument is that the conventional doctrine leads to decisions concerning life and death made on irrelevant grounds.

Consider again the case of the infants with Down's syndrome who need operations for congenital defects unrelated to the syndrome to live. Sometimes, there is no operation, and the baby dies, but when there is no such defect, the baby lives on. Now, an operation such as that to remove an intestinal obstruction is not prohibitively difficult. The reason why such operations are not performed in these cases is, clearly, that the child has Down's syndrome and the parents and doctor judge that because of that fact it is better for the child to die.

But notice that this situation is absurd, no matter what view one takes of the lives and potentials of such babies. If the life of such an infant is worth preserving, what does it matter if it needs a simple operation? Or, if one thinks it better that such a baby should not live on, what difference does it make that it happens to have an unobstructed intestinal tract? In either case, the matter of life and death is being decided on irrelevant grounds. It is the Down's syndrome, and not the intestines, that is the issue. The matter should be decided, if at all, on that basis, and not be allowed to depend on the essentially irrelevant question of whether the intestinal tract is blocked.

What makes this situation possible, of course, is the idea that when there is an intestinal blockage, one can "let the baby die," but when there is no such defect there is nothing that can be done, for one must not "kill" it. The fact that this idea leads to such results as deciding life or death on irrelevant grounds is another good reason why the doctrine should be rejected.

One reason why so many people think that there is an important moral difference between active and passive euthanasia is that they think killing someone is morally worse than letting someone die. But is it? Is killing, in itself, worse than letting die? To investigate this issue, two cases may be considered that are exactly alike except that one involves killing whereas the other involves letting someone die. Then, it can be asked whether this difference makes any difference to the moral assessments. It is important that the cases be exactly alike, except for this one difference, since otherwise one cannot be confident that it is this difference and not some other that accounts for any variation in the assessments of the two cases. So, let us consider this pair of cases:

In the first, Smith stands to gain a large inheritance if anything should happen to his six-year-old cousin. One evening while the child is taking his bath, Smith sneaks into the bathroom and drowns the child, and then arranges things so that it will look like an accident.

In the second, Jones also stands to gain if anything should happen to his six-year-old cousin. Like Smith, Jones sneaks in planning to drown the child in his bath. However, just as he enters the bathroom Jones sees the child slip and hit his head, and fall face down in the water. Jones is delighted; he stands by, ready to push the child's head back under if it is necessary, but it is not necessary. With only a little thrashing about, the child drowns all by himself, "accidentally," as Jones watches and does nothing.

Now Smith killed the child, whereas Jones "merely" let the child die. That is the only difference between them. Did either man behave better, from a moral point of view? If the difference between killing and letting die were in itself a morally important matter, one should say that Jones's behavior was less reprehensible than Smith's. But does one really want to say that? I think not. In the first place, both men acted from the same motive, personal gain, and both had exactly the same end in view when they acted. It may be inferred from Smith's conduct that he is a bad man, although that judgment may be withdrawn or modified if certain further facts are learned about him—for example, that he is mentally deranged. But would not the very same thing be inferred about Jones from his conduct? And would not the same further considerations also be relevant to any modification of this judgment? Moreover, suppose Jones pleaded, in his own defense, "After all, I didn't do anything except just stand there and watch the child drown. I didn't kill him; I only let him die." Again, if letting die were in itself less bad than killing, this defense should have at least some weight. But it does not. Such a "defense" can only be regarded as a grotesque perversion of moral reasoning. Morally speaking, it is no defense at all.

Now, it may be pointed out, quite properly, that the cases of euthanasia with which doctors are concerned are not like this at all. They do not involve personal gain or the destruction of normal, healthy children. Doctors are concerned only with cases in which the patient's life is of no further use to him, or in which the patient's life has become or will soon become a terrible burden. However, the point is the same in these cases: The bare difference between killing and letting die does not, in itself, make a moral difference. If a doctor lets a patient die, for humane reasons, he is in the same moral position as if he had given the patient a lethal injection for humane reasons. If his decision was wrong—if, for example, the patient's illness was in fact curable—the decision would be equally regrettable no matter which method was used to carry it out. And if the doctor's decision was the right one, the method used is not in itself important.

The AMA policy statement isolates the crucial issue very well; the crucial issue is "the intentional termination of the life of one human being by another." But after identifying this issue, and forbidding "mercy killing," the statement goes on to deny that the cessation of treatment is the intentional termination of a life. This is where the mistake comes in, for what is the cessation of treatment, in these circumstances, if it is not "the intentional termination of the life of one human being by another." Of course it is exactly that, and if it were not, there would be no point to it.

Many people will find this judgment hard to accept. One reason, I think, is that it is very easy to conflate the question of whether killing is, in itself, worse than letting die, with the very different question of whether most actual cases of killing are more reprehensible than most actual cases of letting die. Most actual cases of killing are clearly terrible (think, for example, of all the murders reported in the newspapers), and one hears of such cases every day. On the other hand, one hardly ever hears of a case of letting die, except for the actions of doctors who are motivated by humanitarian reasons. So one learns to think of killing in a much worse light than of letting die. But this does not mean that there is something about killing that makes it in itself worse than letting die, for it is not the bare difference between killing and letting die that makes the difference in these cases. Rather, the other factors—the murderer's motive of personal gain, for example, contrasted with the doctor's humanitarian motivation—account for different reactions to the different cases.

I have argued that killing is not in itself any worse than letting die; if my contention is right, it follows that active euthanasia is not any worse than passive euthanasia. What arguments can be given on the other side? The most common, I believe, is the following:

> The important difference between active and passive euthanasia is that, in passive euthanasia, the doctor does not do anything to bring about the patient's death. The doctor does nothing, and the patient dies of whatever ills already afflict him. In active euthanasia, however, the doctor does something to bring about the patient's death: he kills him. The doctor who gives the patient with cancer a lethal injection has himself caused his patient's death; whereas if he merely ceases treatment, the cancer is the cause of the death.

A number of points need to be made here. The first is that it is not exactly correct to say that in passive euthanasia the doctor does nothing, for he does do one thing that is very important: he lets the patient die. "Letting someone die" is certainly different, in some respects, from other types of action—mainly in that it is a kind of action that one may perform by way of not performing certain other actions. For example, one may let a patient die by way of not giving medication, just as one may insult someone by way of not shaking his hand. But for any purpose of moral assessment, it is a type of action nonetheless. The decision to let a patient die is subject to moral appraisal in the same way that a decision to kill him would be subject to moral appraisal: it may be assessed as wise or unwise, compassionate or sadistic, right or wrong. If a doctor deliberately let a patient die who was suffering from a routinely curable illness, the doctor would certainly be to blame for what he had done, just as he would be to blame if he had needlessly killed the patient. Charges against him would then be appropriate. If so, it would be no defense at all for him to insist that he didn't "do anything." He would have done something very serious indeed, for he let his patient die.

Fixing the cause of death may be very important from a legal point of view, for it may determine whether criminal charges are brought against the doctor. But I do not think that this notion can be used to show a moral difference between active and passive euthanasia. The reason why it is considered bad to be the cause of someone's death is that death is regarded as a great evil—and so it is. However, if it has been decided that euthanasia—even passive euthanasia—is desirable in a given case, it has also been decided that in this instance death is no greater an evil than the patient's continued existence. And if this is true, the usual reason for not wanting to be the cause of someone's death simply does not apply.

Finally, doctors may think that all of this is only of academic interest—the sort of thing that philosophers may worry about but that has no practical bearing on their own work. After all, doctors must be concerned about the legal consequences of what they do, and active euthanasia is clearly forbidden by the law. But even so, doctors should also be concerned with the fact that the law is forcing upon them a moral doctrine that may well be indefensible, and has a considerable effect on their practices. Of course, most doctors are not now in the position of being coerced in this matter, for they do not regard themselves as merely going along with what the law requires. Rather, in statements such as the AMA policy statement that I have quoted, they are endorsing this doctrine as a central point of medical ethics. In that statement, active euthanasia is condemned not merely as illegal but as "contrary to that for which the medical profession stands," whereas passive euthanasia is approved.

However, the preceding considerations suggest that there is really no moral difference between the two, considered in themselves (there may be important moral differences in some cases in their consequences, but, as I pointed out, these differences may make active euthanasia, and not passive euthanasia, the morally preferable option). So, whereas doctors may have to discriminate between active and passive euthanasia to satisfy the law, they should not do any more than that. In particular, they should not give the distinction any added authority and weight by writing it into official statements of medical ethics.

Endnote

1. A. Shaw, "Doctor, Do We Have a Choice?" *The New York Times Magazine* (January 30, 1972): 54.

Journal/Discussion Questions

✍ *Rachels maintains that active euthanasia is sometimes justified on the basis of a desire to alleviate suffering, and that it is more humane than passive euthanasia. What limits are there on compassionate action? Can compassion ever be a legitimate reason for ending someone's life?*

1. Rachels offers two principal arguments against the distinction between active and passive euthanasia. What are these arguments?

2. What objections to his position does Rachels consider? Are you convinced by his replies to those objections? Can you think of any objections that Rachels does not consider? What are they?

3. Rachels claims that "killing is not in itself any worse than letting die." What support does he offer for this claim? Do you agree? Why or why not?

Richard Doerflinger
"Assisted Suicide: Pro-Choice or Anti-Life?"

Richard Doerflinger is associate director of the Office for Pro-Life Activities of the National Conference of Catholic Bishops, Washington, DC.

In this article, Doerflinger argues that respect for life is incompatible with assisting in active euthanasia. He argues, furthermore, that liberalization of the euthanasia laws is dangerous because it could combine with other factors at work in society to threaten the value of individual lives.

As You Read, Consider This:

1. On what basis does Doerflinger claim that arguments in favor of assisted suicide presuppose a viewpoint on the value of life?
2. What, according to Doerflinger, are the two kinds of slippery slope arguments? Why is this distinction crucial for understanding the euthanasia issue?

Hastings Center Report, Vol. 19, Supplement (January/February, 1989), pp. 16–19.

The intrinsic wrongness of directly killing the innocent, even with the victim's consent, is all but axiomatic in the Jewish and Christian worldviews that have shaped the laws and mores of Western civilization and the self-concept of its medical practitioners. This norm grew out of the conviction that human life is sacred because it is created in the image and likeness of God, and called to fulfillment in love of God and neighbor.

With the pervasive secularization of Western culture, norms against euthanasia and suicide have to a great extent been cut loose from their religious roots to fend for themselves. Because these norms seem abstract and unconvincing to many, debate tends to dwell not on the wrongness of the act as such but on what may follow from its acceptance. Such arguments are often described as claims about a "slippery slope," and debate shifts to the validity of slippery slope arguments in general.

Since it is sometimes argued that acceptance of assisted suicide is an outgrowth of respect for personal autonomy, and not lack of respect for the inherent worth of human life, I will outline how autonomy-based arguments in favor of assisting suicide do entail a statement about the value of life. I will also distinguish two kinds of slippery slope argument often confused with each other, and argue that those who favor social and legal acceptance of assisted suicide have not adequately responded to the slippery slope claims of their opponents.

Assisted Suicide versus Respect for Life

Some advocates of socially sanctioned assisted suicide admit (and a few boast) that their proposal is incompatible with the conviction that human life is of intrinsic worth. Attorney Robert Risley has said that he and his allies in the Hemlock Society are "so bold" as to seek to "overturn the sanctity of life principle" in American society. A life of suffering, "racked with pain," is "not the kind of life we cherish."[1]

Others eschew Risley's approach, perhaps recognizing that it creates a slippery slope toward practices almost universally condemned. If society is to help terminally ill patients to commit suicide because it agrees that death is objectively preferable to a life of hardship, it will be difficult to draw the line at the seriously ill or even at circumstances where the victim requests death.

Some advocates of assisted suicide therefore take a different course, arguing that it is precisely respect for the dignity of the human person that demands respect for individual freedom as the noblest feature of that person. On this rationale a decision as to when and how to die deserves the respect and even the assistance of others because it is the ultimate exercise of self-determination—"ultimate" both in the sense that it is the last decision one will ever make and in the sense that through it one takes control of one's entire self. What makes such decisions worthy of respect is not the fact that death is chosen over life but that it is the individual's own free decision about his or her future.

Thus Derek Humphry, director of the Hemlock Society, describes his organization as "pro-choice" on this issue. Such groups favor establishment of a constitutional "right to die" modeled on the right to abortion delineated by the U.S. Supreme Court in 1973. This would be a right to choose whether or not to end one's own life, free of outside government interference. In theory, recognition of such a right would betray no bias toward choosing death.

Life versus Freedom

This autonomy-based approach is more appealing than the straightforward claim that some lives are not worth living, especially to Americans accustomed to valuing individual liberty above virtually all else. But the argument departs from American traditions on liberty in one fundamental respect.

When the Declaration of Independence proclaimed the inalienable human rights to be "life, liberty, and the pursuit of happiness," this ordering reflected a long-standing judgment about their relative priorities. Life, a human being's very earthly existence, is the most fundamental right because it is the necessary condition for all other worldly goods including freedom; freedom in turn makes it possible to pursue (without guaranteeing that one will attain) happiness. Safeguards against the deliberate destruction of life are thus seen as necessary to protect freedom and all other human goods. This line of thought is not explicitly religious but is endorsed by some modern religious groups:

> The first right of the human person is his life. He has other goods and some are more precious, but this one is fundamental—the condition of all the others. Hence it must be protected above all others.[2]

On this view suicide is not the ultimate exercise of freedom but its ultimate self-contradiction: A free act that by destroying life, destroys all the individual's future earthly freedom. If life is more basic than freedom, society best serves freedom by discouraging rather than assisting self-destruction. Sometimes one must limit particular choices to safeguard freedom itself, as when American society chose over a century ago to prevent people from selling themselves into slavery even of their own volition.

It may be argued in objection that the person who ends his life has not truly suffered loss of freedom, because unlike the slave he need not continue to exist under the constraints of a loss of freedom. But the slave does have some freedom, including the freedom to seek various means of liberation or at least the freedom to choose what attitude to take regarding his plight. To claim that a slave is worse off than a corpse is to value a situation of limited freedom less than one of no freedom whatsoever, which seems inconsistent with the premise of the "pro-choice" position. Such a claim also seems tantamount to saying that some lives (such as those with less than absolute freedom) are objectively not worth living, a position that "pro-choice" advocates claim not to hold.

It may further be argued in objection that assistance in suicide is only being offered to those who can no longer meaningfully exercise other freedoms due to increased suffering and reduced capabilities and lifespan. To be sure, the suffering of terminally ill patients who can no longer pursue the simplest everyday tasks should call for sympathy and support from everyone in contact with them. But even these hardships do not constitute total loss of freedom of choice. If they did, one could hardly claim that the patient is in a position to make the ultimate free choice about suicide. A dying person capable of making a choice of that kind is also capable of making less monumental free choices about coping with his or her condition. This person generally faces a bewildering array of choices regarding the assessment of his or her past life and the resolution of relationships with family and friends. He or she must finally choose at this time what stance to take regarding the eternal questions about God, personal responsibility, and the prospects of a destiny after death.

In short, those who seek to maximize free choice may with consistency reject the idea of assisted suicide, instead facilitating all choices *except* that one which cuts short all choices.

In fact proponents of assisted suicide do not consistently place freedom of choice as their highest priority. They often defend the moderate nature of their project by stating, with Derek Humphry, that "we do not encourage suicide for any reason except to relieve unremitting suffering." It seems their highest priority is the "pursuit of happiness" (or avoidance of suffering) and not "liberty" as such. Liberty or freedom of choice loses its value if one's choices cannot relieve suffering and lead to happiness; life is of instrumental value insofar as it makes possible choices that can bring happiness.

In this value system, choice as such does not warrant unqualified respect. In difficult circumstances, as when care of a suffering and dying patient is a great burden on family and society, the individual who chooses life despite suffering will not easily be seen as rational, thus will not easily receive understanding and assistance for this choice.

In short, an unqualified "pro-choice" defense of assisted suicide lacks coherence because corpses have no choices. A particular choice, that of death, is given priority over all the other choices it makes impossible, so the value of choice as such is not central to the argument.

A restriction of this rationale to cases of terminal illness also lacks logical force. For if ending a brief life of suffering can be good, it would seem that ending a long life of suffering may be better. Surely the approach of the California "Humane and Dignified Death Act"—where consensual killing of a patient expected to die in six months is presumably good medical practice, but killing the same patient a month or two earlier is still punishable as homicide—is completely arbitrary.

Slippery Slopes, Loose Cannons

Many arguments against sanctioning assisted suicide concern a different kind of "slippery slope": Contingent factors in the contemporary situation may make it virtually inevitable in practice, if not compelling at the level of abstract theory, that removal of the taboo against assisted suicide will lead to destructive expansions of the right to kill the innocent. Such factors may not be part of euthanasia advocates' own agenda; but if they exist and are beyond the control of these advocates, they must be taken into account in judging the moral and social wisdom of opening what may be a Pandora's box of social evils.

To distinguish this sociological argument from our dissection of the conceptual *logic* of the rationale for assisted suicide, we might call it a "loose cannon" argument. The basic claim is that socially accepted killing of innocent persons will interact with other social factors to threaten lives that advocates of assisted suicide would agree should be protected. These factors at present include the following:

The Psychological Vulnerability of Elderly and Dying Patients

Theorists may present voluntary and involuntary euthanasia as polar opposites; in practice there are many steps on the road from dispassionate, autonomous choice to subtle coercion. Elderly and disabled patients are often invited by our achievement-oriented society to see themselves as useless burdens on younger, more vital generations. In this climate, simply offering the option of "self-deliverance" shifts a burden of proof, so that helpless patients must ask themselves why they are not availing themselves of it. Society's offer of death communicates the message to certain patients that they *may* continue to live if they wish but the rest of us have no strong interest in their survival. Indeed, once the choice of a quick and painless death is officially accepted as rational, resistance to this choice may be seen as eccentric or even selfish.[3]

The Crisis in Health Care Costs

The growing incentives for physicians, hospitals, families, and insurance companies to control the cost of health care will bring additional pressures to bear on patients. Curt Garbesi, the Hemlock Society's legal consultant, argues that autonomy-based groups like Hemlock must "control the public debate" so assisted suicide will not be seized upon by public officials as a cost-cutting device. But simply basing one's own defense of assisted suicide on individual autonomy does not solve the problem. For in the economic sphere also, offering the option of suicide would subtly shift burdens of proof.

Adequate health care is now seen by at least some policymakers as a human right, as something a society owes to all its members. Acceptance of assisted suicide as an option for those requiring expensive care would not only offer health care providers an incentive to make that option seem attractive—it would also demote all other options to the status of strictly private choices by the individual. As such they may lose their moral and legal claim to public support—in much the same way that the U.S. Supreme Court, having protected abortion under a constitutional "right of privacy," has quite logically denied any government obligation to provide public funds for this strictly private choice. As life-extending care of the terminally ill is increasingly seen as strictly elective, society may become less willing to appropriate funds for such care, and economic pressures to choose death will grow accordingly.

Legal Doctrines on "Substituted Judgment"

American courts recognizing a fundamental right to refuse life-sustaining treatment have concluded that it is unjust to deny this right to the mentally incompetent. In such cases the right is exercised on the patient's behalf by others, who seek either to interpret what the patient's own wishes might have been or to serve his or her best interests. Once assisted suicide is established as a fundamental right, courts will almost certainly find that it is unjust not to extend this right to those unable to express their wishes. Hemlock's political arm, Americans Against Human Suffering, has underscored continuity between "passive" and "active" euthanasia by offering the Humane and Dignified Death Act as an amendment to California's "living will" law, and by including a provision for appointment of a proxy to choose the time and manner of the patient's death. By such extensions our legal system would accommodate nonvoluntary, if not involuntary, active euthanasia.

Expanded Definitions of Terminal Illness

The Hemlock Society wishes to offer assisted suicide only to those suffering from terminal illnesses. But some Hemlock officials have in mind a rather broad definition of "terminal illness." Derek Humphry says "two and a half million people alone are dying of Alzheimer's disease."[4] At Hemlock's 1986 convention, Dutch physician Pieter Admiraal boasted that he had recently broadened the meaning of terminal illness in his country by giving a lethal injection to a young quadriplegic woman—a Dutch court found that he acted within judicial guidelines allowing euthanasia for the terminally ill, because paralyzed patients have difficulty swallowing and could die from aspirating their food at any time.

The medical and legal meaning of terminal illness has already been expanded in the United States by professional societies, legislatures, and courts in the context of so-called passive euthanasia. A Uniform Rights of the Terminally Ill Act proposed by the National Conference of Commissioners on Uniform State Laws in 1986 defines a terminal illness as one that would cause the patient's death in a relatively short time if life-preserving treatment is not provided—prompting critics to ask if all diabetics, for example, are "terminal" by definition. Some courts already see comatose and vegetative states as "terminal" because they involve an inability to swallow that will lead to death unless artificial feeding is instituted. In the Hilda Peter case, the New Jersey Supreme Court declared that the traditional state interest in "preserving life" referred only to "cognitive and sapient life" and not to mere "biological" existence, implying that unconscious patients are terminal, or perhaps as good as dead, so far as state interests are concerned. Is there any reason to think that American law would suddenly resurrect the older, narrower meaning of "terminal illness" in the context of active euthanasia?

Prejudice Against Citizens with Disabilities

If definitions of terminal illness expand to encompass states of severe physical or mental disability, another social reality will increase the pressure on patients to choose death: long-standing prejudice, sometimes bordering on revulsion, against people with disabilities. While it is seldom baldly claimed that disabled people have "lives not worth living," able-bodied people often say they could not live in a severely disabled state or would prefer death. In granting Elizabeth Bouvia a right to refuse a feeding tube that preserved her life, the California Appeals Court bluntly stated that her physical handicaps led her to "consider her existence meaningless" and that "she cannot be faulted for so concluding." According to disability rights expert Paul Longmore, in a society with such attitudes toward the disabled, "talk of their 'rational' or 'voluntary' suicide is simply Orwellian newspeak."[5]

Character of the Medical Profession

Advocates of assisted suicide realize that most physicians will resist giving lethal injections because they are trained, in Garbesi's words, to be "enemies of death." The California Medical Association firmly opposed the Humane and Dignified Death Act, seeing it as an attack on the ethical foundation of the medical profession.

Yet California appeals judge Lynn Compton was surely correct in his concurring opinion in the *Bouvia* case, when he said that a sufficient number of willing physicians can be found once legal sanctions against assisted suicide are dropped. Judge Compton said this had clearly been the case with abortion, despite the fact that the Hippocratic Oath condemns abortion as strongly as it condemns euthanasia. Opinion polls of physicians bear out the judgment that a significant number would perform lethal injections if they were legal.

Some might think this division or ambivalence about assisted suicide in the medical profession will restrain broad expansions of the practice. But if anything, Judge Compton's analogy to our experience with abortion suggests the opposite. Most physicians still have qualms about abortion, and those who perform abortions on a full-time basis are not readily accepted by their colleagues as paragons of the healing art. Consequently, they tend to form their own professional societies, bolstering each other's positive self-image and developing euphemisms to blunt the moral edge of their work.

Once physicians abandon the traditional medical self-image, which rejects direct killing of patients in all circumstances, their new substitute self-image may require ever more aggressive efforts to make this killing more widely practiced and favorably received. To allow killing by physicians in certain circumstances may create a new lobby of physicians in favor of expanding medical killing.

The Human Will to Power

The most deeply buried yet most powerful driving force toward widespread medical killing is a fact of human nature: Human beings are tempted to enjoy exercising power over others; ending another person's life is the ultimate exercise of that power. Once the taboo against killing has been set aside, it becomes progressively easier to channel one's aggressive instincts into the destruction of life in other contexts. Or as James Burtchaell has said: "There is a sort of virginity about murder; once one has violated it, it is awkward to refuse other invitations by saying, 'But that would be murder!'"[6]

Some will say assisted suicide for the terminally ill is morally distinguishable from murder and does not logically require termination of life in other circumstances. But my point is that the skill and the instinct to kill are more easily turned to other lethal tasks once they have an opportunity to exercise themselves. Thus Robert Jay Lifton has perceived differences between the German "mercy killings" of the 1930s and the later campaign to annihilate the Jews of Europe, yet still says that "at the heart of the Nazi enterprise . . . is the destruction of the boundary between healing and killing."[7] No other boundary separating these two situations was as fundamental as this one, and thus none was effective once it was crossed. As a matter of historical fact, personnel who had conducted the "mercy killing" program were quickly and readily recruited to operate the killing chambers of the death camps.[8] While the contemporary United States fortunately lacks the anti-Semitic and totalitarian attitudes that made the Holocaust possible, it has its own trends and pressures that may combine with acceptance of medical killing to produce a distinctively American catastrophe in the name of individual freedom.

These "loose cannon" arguments are not conclusive. All such arguments by their nature rest upon a reading and extrapolation of certain contingent factors in society. But their combined force provides a serious case against taking the irreversible step of sanctioning assisted suicide for any class of persons, so long as those who advocate this step fail to demonstrate why these predictions are wrong. If the strict philosophical case on behalf of "rational suicide" lacks coherence, the pragmatic claim that its acceptance would be a social benefit lacks grounding in history or common sense.

Endnotes

1. Presentation at the Hemlock Society's Third National Voluntary Euthanasia Conference, "A Humane and Dignified Death," September 2–27, 1986, Washington, DC. All quotations from Hemlock Society officials are from the proceedings of this conference unless otherwise noted.

2. Vatican Congregation for the Doctrine of the Faith, *Declaration on Procured Abortion* (1974), para. 11.

3. I am indebted for this line of argument to Dr. Eric Chevlen.

4. Denis Herbstein, "Campaigning for the Right to Die," *International Herald Tribune,* September 11, 1986.

5. Paul K. Longmore, "Elizabeth Bouvia, Assisted Suicide, and Social Prejudice," *Issues in Law and Medicine* Vol. 3, No. 2 (1987), p. 168.

6. James T. Burtchaell, *Rachel Weeping and Other Essays on Abortion* (Kansas City: Andrews & McMeel, 1982), p. 188.

7. Robert Jay Lifton, *The Nazi Doctors: Medical Killing and the Psychology of Genocide* (New York: Basic Books, 1986), p. 14.

8. Yitzhak Rad, *Belzec, Sobibor, Treblinka* (Bloomington, IN: Indiana University Press, 1987), pp. 11, 16–17.

Journal/Discussion Questions

✍ *Doerflinger's analysis takes place within the larger context of a Christian worldview. Do you share this worldview? Do you agree with Doerflinger's conclusions about euthanasia?*

1. According to Doerflinger, the prohibition against killing the innocent is grounded in the Judeo-Christian conviction that life is sacred. Do you think that the religious belief that human life is sacred necessarily leads to the conclusion that voluntary euthanasia is always morally wrong? Do other religious traditions permit euthanasia? Discuss.

2. Doerflinger argues that proponents of euthanasia claim that liberty is their highest value, but this claim is misleading. Why, according to Doerflinger, is it misleading?

3. In the "loose cannon" argument, Doerflinger maintains that legalizing euthanasia will interact with seven other factors in our society in ways that are ultimately harmful. What are these other factors? How plausible do you think each of these seven arguments is? Which of the seven factors do you think is the greatest threat?

4. Doerflinger sees euthanasia as related to "the human will to power." What does he mean by this? Are you convinced by his analysis? Discuss.

Concluding Discussion Questions

Where Do You Stand Now?

Instructions

You have already answered the following questions in your moral problems self-quiz at the beginning of this book. Now that you have studied the material in this section, take a moment to answer the same questions again.

Chapter 3: Euthanasia

	Strongly Agree	Agree	Undecided	Disagree	Strongly Disagree	
11.	❏	❏	❏	❏	❏	Euthanasia is always morally wrong.
12.	❏	❏	❏	❏	❏	Euthanasia should be illegal at least under almost all circumstances.
13.	❏	❏	❏	❏	❏	The principal moral consideration about euthanasia is the question of whether the person freely chooses to die or not.
14.	❏	❏	❏	❏	❏	Actively killing someone is always morally worse than just letting them die.
15.	❏	❏	❏	❏	❏	Sometimes we have a duty to die.

Compare your answers to this self-quiz with the answers to the initial self-quiz. How, if at all, have your answers changed? How have the *reasons* for your answers changed?

Journal/Discussion Questions

1. Under what conditions, if any, would you want others to withhold medical treatment from you? To withhold fluids and nutrition? To actively terminate your life?

2. Review the living will you wrote at the beginning of this chapter. What changes, if any, would you make in it after reading this chapter?

3. You have now read, thought, and discussed a number of aspects of the morality of the euthanasia decision. How have your views *changed* and developed? Has your understanding of the reasons supporting other positions that are different from your own changed? What issue(s) remain unresolved for you at this point?

4. What, in the readings is this section, was the most thought-provoking idea you encountered? In what ways did it prompt you to reconsider some of your previous beliefs?

5. In light of the preceding readings, what do you think is the single most compelling reason for legalizing euthanasia? What do you think is the single most compelling reason for *not* doing so? If euthanasia were to be legalized, what do you think would be the most important safeguard that should accompany it?

For Further Reading

Web Resources

For Web-based resources, including the major Supreme Court decisions on end-of-life decisions, see the Euthanasia page of *Ethics Updates* (http://ethics.sandiego.edu). Among the resources are: the Amicus Brief, Assisted Suicide: The Brief by Ronald Dworkin, Thomas Nagel, Robert Nozick, John Rawls, Thomas Scanlon, and Judith Jarvis Thomson; Frances M. Kamm's "A Right to Choose Death" in the *Boston Review;* Robert Young's "Voluntary Suicide"; *Stanford Encyclopedia of Philosophy;* and links to several important documentaries on end-of-life decisions. *Ethics Videos* (http://ethics.sandiego.edu/video) contains several videos of presentations relating to euthanasia, including video of a conference on "Medical Ethics and the Humanities in End-of-Life Care" sponsored by San Diego Hospice. This includes sessions by Tom Beauchamp, Rita Marker, and Larry Schneiderman. Additional video resources include Daniel Callahan on end-of-life issues and Karma Lekshe Tsomo on "Living and Dying in Buddhist Cultures."

Journals

In addition to the standard journals on ethics mentioned in Chapter 1, see *The Hastings Center Reports, The Journal of Medicine and Philosophy, Bioethics,* and *The Kennedy Institute of Ethics Journal.*

Review Articles

For an excellent survey of the philosophical issues (and a very helpful annotated bibliography), see Margaret P. Battin, "Euthanasia and Physician-Assisted Suicide," *The Oxford Handbook of Practical Ethics,* edited by Hugh LaFollette (New York: Oxford, 2003); Michael Tooley, "Euthanasia and Assisted Suicide," in *A Companion to Applied Ethics: Blackwell Companions to Philosophy,* edited by R. G. Frey (Malden, MA: Blackwell Publishing, 2003), pp. 326–341; Marvin Kohl, "Euthanasia," *Encyclopedia of Ethics,* edited by Lawrence C. Becker and Charlotte B. Becker (New York: Garland, 1992), pp. 335–339; and Part VII of *A Companion to Bioethics,* edited by Helga Kahse and Peter Singer (Oxford: Blackwell, 1998), including Dan W. Brock, "Medical Decisions at the End of Life," Jeff McMahan, "Brain Death, Cortical Death, and Persistent Vegetative State," and Alexander Morgan Capron, "Advance Directives." For an overview of Buddhist perspectives, see Damien Keown, "Suicide, Assisted Suicide, and Euthanasia: A Buddhist Perspective" in *Varieties of Ethical Reflection: New Directions for Ethics in a Global Context,* edited by Michael G. Barnhart (New York: Lexington Books, 2002), pp. 263-282.

Anthologies

There are several very helpful anthologies that deal with euthanasia. *Beneficent Euthanasia,* edited by Marvin Kohl (Buffalo: Prometheus Books, 1975) contains a very good range of pieces; *Ethical Issues Relating to Life and Death,* edited by John Ladd (New York: Oxford University Press, 1979);

Euthanasia: The Moral Issues, edited by Robert M. Baird and Stuart E. Rosenbaum (Buffalo: Prometheus Books, 1989) contains a nice balance of philosophical and popular pieces; *Euthanasia: Opposing Viewpoints,* edited by Carol Wekesser (San Diego: Greenhaven Press, 1995), also contains a good balance of philosophical and popular pieces, all in relatively short segments, as does *Terminal Illness: Opposing Viewpoints,* edited by Mary Williams (San Diego: Greenhaven, 2001). Also see, *Voluntary Euthanasia,* edited by A.B. Downing and Barbara Smoker (London: Peter Owen, 1986), which includes a number of important essays, including an exchange between Yale Kamisar and Glanville Williams; *The Dilemmas of Euthanasia,* edited by J. A. Behnke and Sissela Bok (New York, 1975); *Suicide and Euthanasia,* edited by Baruch Brody (Dordrecht: Kluwer); and *Euthanasia Examined,* edited by John Keown (Cambridge: Cambridge University Press, 1995). On cross-cultural perspectives, see especially *Ethnic Variations in Dying, Death, and Grief,* edited by Donald P. Irish et al. (Philadelphia: Taylor & Francis, 1993).

On the distinction between killing and letting die, see *Killing and Letting Die,* edited by Bonnie Steinbock and Alastair Norcross, 2nd ed. (New York: Fordham University Press, 1994), which contains virtually all the major essays on this topic; it also contains an excellent bibliography.

Punishment and the Death Penalty

Narrative Account

Helen Prejean, C.S.J.
"Crime Victims on the Anvil of Pain"

Sister Helen Prejean, C.S.J., is a native of Louisiana, a member of the Sisters of St. Joseph of Medaille, and a spiritual counselor both to inmates on death row and to the families of their victims. Her book and the movie based on it, Dead Man Walking: An Eyewitness Account of the Death Penalty in the United States, *quickly became one of the most influential works questioning the morality of the death penalty.*

In the following newspaper article from 1988, Helen Prejean tries to do justice both to her firm conviction that the death penalty is wrong and her compassion for those who have lost a family member to a violent crime. She describes, briefly but graphically, the pain of both and the effects of their pain on her.

As You Read, Consider This:

1. Do you think that Sister Prejean perceives the death row inmates clearly? The families of the victims?

2. What moves you about Sister Prejean's account of her ministry to death row inmates and to the families of their victims?

I stand outside the door and take a deep breath. It's my first meeting with the New Orleans Chapter of Parents of Murdered Children, a support group for people whose children have met violent deaths.

Vernon Harvey, my nemesis of sorts, waits for me on the other side of the door. His stepdaughter, Faith, was murdered by Robert Lee Willie. I was Robert's spiritual adviser. Both of us witnessed Robert's execution in the electric chair.

Prior to the execution, both of us had appeared at the Pardon Board hearing—he, urging Robert's death; I, pleading for his life. He was furious at me.

"You should be helping victims' families," he had told me.

Finally, at his urging I was coming to this meeting.

People ask me how I got involved in all this. Good question. I ask it of God sometimes when I pray.

For 20 years I did what most other Catholic nuns were doing—teaching the young, conducting religious education programs in a suburban church parish. But in 1981, I moved into a steamy public

St. Petersburg Times, May 15, 1988, Sunday, City Edition, Section: Perspective, p. 1D.

housing project in New Orleans and for the first time in my life tasted the struggle of those who live on the "underside of history."

One day a friend in prison ministry asked me to become a pen pal to someone on death row. "Sure," I said, having no idea what lay in store for me. I wrote to Elmo Patrick Sonnier, then I became his spiritual adviser, then I watched him die in the electric chair. I became a strong advocate for death row inmates and their families.

I am with Elmo Patrick Sonnier in the death house. The guards are in his cell, shaving his head, his left ankle. . . .

He returns to the metal door where I sit on the other side. His body sags in the chair. He looks naked, stripped. He smokes cigarettes and drinks black coffee.

I've known him for two years. As a child he alternated between divorced parents and he was out on his own by the time he was 16. He had done his share of settling life's challenges with his fists, but never anything like Nov. 5, 1977, when he and his brother killed a teen-age couple. The fathers of the victims will be there to witness his execution.

He's talking non-stop . . . snatches from the past . . . how good it felt to go hunting when the weather was cool . . . driving 18 wheelers . . . "thank you for your love . . . please take care of my Mama . . ."

We pray together. "God, just give me the strength to make that last walk." He starts to shiver. A guard puts a denim jacket over his shoulders.

It's midnight. "Time to go, Sonnier," the warden says.

We walk to the electric chair, my hand on his shoulder as I read from the Bible. We stop. I look up and see the chair. The guards are leading me away. "Pray for me, Pat." He turns around. "I will, Sister Helen, I will."

His last words . . . he looks at the parents of the murdered teen-agers. "Forgive me for what me and my brother did."

He sits in the chair. The guards move quickly, strapping his arms, his legs. He finds my face among the witnesses. "I love you," he says.

I turn the doorknob and enter the room where the Parents of Murdered Children are meeting. Vernon comes over to greet me. His eyes say, "You're coming around—at last."

The meeting begins. The motto of the group is "Give sorrow words."

> "Laura was stabbed by my son's best friend one week before her 12th birthday. Her skiing outfit is still hanging in the closet . . . five years now. I just can't give it away."

> "When my child was killed, it took over a week to find her body. The police treated us like we were the criminals. They brushed us off whenever we phoned."

> "I got to witness the son of a b— fry who killed our daughter. The chair is too quick. I hope he's burning in hell."

> "I'm beginning to let my anger go. I put John's picture on the Christmas tree. My Christmas angel, I call him."

> "Friends avoid us. If you try to bring up your child's death, they change the subject."

I leave the meeting stunned by the pain I have been allowed to touch. On the anvil of that pain I forge a new commitment to expend my energies for victims' families as well as death row inmates. Now I work on a task force to see that victims' families get state-allotted funds for counseling, unemployment compensation, funeral expenses. Only a handful of sheriff's offices in Louisiana bother to appoint the personnel to administer these funds. Related, I think, to a mind-set prevalent in our criminal justice system: big on recrimination; short on healing.

As I see it, the death penalty is just another killing (and a highly selective one at that; two-thirds of all executions happen in four southern states). Obviously executions don't do anything for the criminal, and, from what I've seen, they don't do much for victims' families either.

Our need to protect ourselves from killers is real. When I walk to my car at night I glance often over my shoulder. I know now that really bad things can happen to really good people. But surely in 1988 we who purport to be the most civilized of societies can find a way to incapacitate dangerous criminals without imitating their tragic, violent behavior.

Journal/Discussion Questions

🖉 *Sister Prejean's reactions to both the death row inmates and to the families of their victims are probably different from our own—certainly the combination is most unusual, for she seems able to appreciate the humanity of both without idealizing either. Do you think that her perceptions are correct? If they are different from your own and you think they are correct, what makes it difficult for you fully to perceive the humanity of these murderers? Of their victims?*

1. How does Sister Prejean reconcile her commitment to the death row inmates and to the families of their victims? Does this have more moral force than if she were just committed to one or the other alone? Why?

2. Why is Sister Prejean opposed to the death penalty? What does she suggest as an alternative?

An Introduction to the Moral Issues

A Life for a Life

Advocates of the death penalty often invoke the *lex talionis,* the law of "an eye for an eye, a tooth for a tooth," as their justification for the death penalty. If we take that law literally, then it becomes "a death for a death." It is, however, more helpful to take this law metaphorically as one of proportionality: our harshest punishment for our worst crimes. This is in fact the way in which it has been interpreted in the United States, where the death penalty is reserved for aggravated murder and a handful of other, similarly egregious crimes.

Yet the legitimacy of this metaphorical interpretation raises interesting questions. Why don't we take the *lex talionis* literally? Why shouldn't a torturer be tortured as punishment? Why shouldn't a rapist endure the agony of being raped as punishment? Why shouldn't someone who has raped, tortured, and killed a person be punished in the same way? As we reflect on these questions, we discover that capital punishment isn't the worst possible punishment—there are other punishments, such as torture and rape and mutilation, which are worse *in some way*. When we try to specify the exact way in which they are worse, we get an interesting answer. They aren't worse in the sense that they are more final, that they destroy more possibilities. Clearly the death penalty is the worst in this respect, because it eliminates any further possibilities for the person being executed. Rather, it is worse in the sense that it is *crueler.* If we ranked punishments along a continuum according to their *level of cruelty,* we might get something like this:

Punishments: Scale of Cruelty

Monetary Fines ⇨ Day Service ⇨ Imprisonment ⇨ Execution ⇨ Rape and Torture

This is a different scale than we might get if we ranked punishments according to the *extent to which they destroyed a person's future possibilities.* Then we might get something like this:

Punishments: Scale of Destruction of Life Possibilities

Monetary Fines ⇨ Day Service ⇨ Imprisonment ⇨ Rape and Torture ⇨ Execution

The metaphorical interpretation of the *lex talionis* comes into play when the literal interpretation results in a punishment that is too far to the right on the cruelty scale. Clearly, everyone admits that some punishments are too cruel. The issue then becomes one of drawing the line: at what point do we say that the literal interpretation of the *lex talionis* results in a punishment that is too cruel? The claim of opponents of the death penalty is that the line should be drawn before execution; advocates of the death penalty draw the line after execution.

We now can see that there is a sense in which the death penalty is the worst possible punishment (it completely destroys all future life possibilities) and a sense in which it isn't the worst (other punishments may be crueler). Although literal interpretations of the *lex talionis* would seem to justify crueler punishments such as torture for convicted torturers, we are barred from such punishments because of their cruelty; yet the death penalty seems acceptable for the most heinous of crimes because it is the worst possible punishment in another sense.

The Sanctity of Life

Opponents of the death penalty are often motivated by a moral concern for the sanctity of life. We can distinguish three versions of this concern. First, the *strong version,* such as we find among Quakers and Buddhists, maintains an absolute prohibition on the taking of *any* human life. It is thus opposed to the death penalty because it involves intentionally killing a human being, just as it would be opposed to war and even killing in self-defense. Second, the *moderate version,* which we find in many religious traditions, is opposed to any taking of *innocent* human life. This version would also be opposed to practices such as active euthanasia as well as the death penalty. It would be opposed to the death penalty insofar as its administration inevitably involves inadvertently executing innocent people occasionally. Finally, the *weak version* of this view maintains that any practice involving the intentional killing of other human beings must have an extremely strong justification—and that the justification of the death penalty instead of life imprisonment simply isn't strong enough to warrant its use.

For those who support the strong or moderate versions of the sanctity of life, the potential deterrent effect of capital punishment is not really an issue. In their eyes, even if capital punishment deters more effectively than alternative punishments, it still is not justified, for it involves the intentional taking of a human life.

Hope and the Possibility of Change

Opponents of the death penalty are often motivated by another, less articulated concern. For many of them, the death penalty is a sign of giving up, a sign that we have concluded—at least in this particular instance—that there is nothing salvageable about this criminal, that there is nothing that redeems this person's life and justifies his (and it is almost always "his," not "hers") continued existence. Sometimes this is part of a larger religious worldview that sees hope for all human beings, no matter what their situation; sometimes it is part of a purely humanistic worldview that sees human beings as fundamentally good at the core and only brutalized and deformed through external influences.

For those who share this belief, in whatever form, the death penalty is an act of breaking faith with ourselves, with our humanity, an act of despair from people who no longer know what else to do.

The Effect of the Death Penalty: Deterrence or Brutalization?

What effect does the death penalty have? Two competing and incompatible claims have been advanced in answer to this question. On the one hand, some have argued that it has a deterrence effect, that is, that it reduces the number of potential future crimes for which it is a punishment. On the other hand, others have argued that it results in what has been called the *brutalization effect,* that is, that the number of capital crimes actually *increases* as a result of executions.

The Empirical Findings

There are two distinct issues here: an empirical one and a normative one. The *empirical question* is in the domain of social scientists and their answer is by no means univocal. This is hardly surprising, given the complexity of the issue. One not only has to show that the death penalty deters, but that it deters more effectively than alternative punishments such as life imprisonment. Moreover, even if the death penalty as presently administered doesn't deter more effectively than the alternatives, there is still the question of whether it might be a more effective deterrent if it were administered differently (more often, more quickly, etc.).

The empirical findings on the effects of capital punishment have been mixed. They range between two extremes. On the one hand, some researchers have argued that the death penalty was responsible for saving seven or eight lives (of innocent potential victims) per year in the United States while it was being used.[1] On the other hand, others have claimed that the number of capital offenses goes up immediately following an execution.[2] One of the more interesting studies has compared *contiguous states,* such as North and South Dakota, where one has the death penalty and the other does not, but which in many other respects are similar. If the death penalty were an effective deterrent, one would expect that the rate of capital crimes would decline in the state with the death penalty, but this has not been the case.

The Argument from Common Sense

Some theorists have argued that we need not be bothered by these contradictory findings; all we need to do is to reflect for a moment, and common sense will give us the answer to our question about the deterrent effects of capital punishment. When prisoners are given a choice between life in prison and the death penalty, they inevitably choose life in prison. We don't find "lifers" trying to get their sentence changed to death; on the other hand, we find there are plenty of prisoners on death row who are trying to get their sentences changed to life in prison. Common sense and a moment's reflection tell us that virtually everyone considers execution to be worse than life in prison. And if everyone considers it to be worse, then they will be more deterred by it than by a life sentence.

The common sense argument, at least in its initial version, falls short of the mark in at least two respects. First, granting the premises of the argument, we still have an additional question: Do potential criminals, when contemplating a capital offense, think that they will receive the death penalty rather than life in prison? For deterrence to work, it must be effective *before* the crime is committed, and the argument from common sense does not assure us that it is. Second, the argument ignores any other factors as influencing the situation. (This is a problem with hypothetical examples in general: often we only discover in them the factors that we wanted to be there in the first place; real life cases are messier, more surprising, and consequently more instructive.) For example, it ignores the possibility that potential criminals might feel that because the state kills (through executions), it's okay for them to kill.

The Moral Issue

The *moral issue* on which deterrence turns is distinct from the empirical question: If it turns out that capital punishment deters significantly more effectively than alternative punishments, then should we employ it? After all, the death penalty is the intentional killing of another human being—in the eyes of some, murder by the state. It is certainly consistent to say that capital punishment deters and still be opposed to it because it violates the sanctity of human life (as we have already seen), because of the high probability that some innocent people will be executed, or because it is administered in our society in an unavoidably arbitrary manner.

Deterrence and Publicity

If capital punishment is justified in terms of its deterrent effect, then it would seem to follow that it should be administered in such a way as to maximize its potential as a deterrent. If we are executing criminals in order to deter other (potential) criminals from committing the same crime, then shouldn't we execute them in such a way as to have the greatest possible impact on anyone else who might commit such a crime? Two possible changes might increase the deterrent effect.

First, as mentioned earlier, punishments that are administered quickly and surely are, all other things being equal, more likely to be effective deterrents than punishments that are administered long after the fact and sporadically. In capital punishment cases, every effort should be made to hasten the judicial process and the execution if the point of such punishment is deterrence.

Second, the more vivid the realization of the consequences, the more effectively they influence behavior. In the case of capital punishment, this would seem to justify public, televised executions, presuming that they increase the deterrent effect of capital punishment. Indeed, if deterrence is the justification for such punishment, then it seems to be wasting an individual's execution if the government does not maximize its potential deterrent effects. Of course, this would have to be done in a way that properly shelters children, and so forth, and at the same time is most likely to reach those most likely to commit capital crimes.

The Irrevocability of Capital Punishment

One of the common objections to capital punishment is that it is irrevocable: once an innocent person is executed, there is no way to bring that person back to life again. Yet when we reflect on this argument, we see that it is not stated very precisely, for *all* punishment (except, perhaps, monetary fines, which can be returned with interest) is in a very real sense irrevocable. Twenty years in prison cannot be given back to someone who was falsely convicted. The real issue is that there is no way of even attempting to compensate for the injustice when someone has been executed, because the person is no longer alive to receive the compensation.

The Demand for Certitude

The high stakes in capital punishment create an additional demand in terms of the level of certitude required to carry out the punishment. Precisely because there is no way to undo a mistake in capital punishment, we must be more certain than would otherwise be required that we are in fact executing the guilty party.

How often do mistakes get made? One recent estimate claimed that in the United States since 1900, 57 innocent persons—or, more precisely, persons whose innocence can be *proved* in retrospect—have been executed.[3] The further claim is that, if this number can be shown to have been innocent, how many more were innocent that we did not know about? This is a difficult empirical matter, but it seems reasonable to conclude that at least some times, innocent persons are executed, even if we are not certain how many. This situation is exacerbated by the increase in executions in recent years and by the Supreme Court decisions that exclude the uncovering of new evidence of innocence as a basis for reconsideration of a case. However, DNA tests have offered new, scientific evidence that has helped to exonerate a number of inmates on death row. Since capital punishment again became legal in 1976, 82 convicts—one out of every seven waiting to be executed—have been exonerated.[4]

Diversity and Consensus

As always in this book, each of us has to come to a considered, reflective judgment that weighs complex and competing claims. Indeed, that's the very nature of the problems selected for this book—the easy problems have been omitted, because we need little help in resolving them. We can, however, draw some conclusions that may provide part of the common ground we need here to reach a societal consensus on the issue of the death penalty.

First, many people on both sides of this debate agree that the *empirical evidence about the deterrent effect of capital punishment is inconclusive.* There is no incontrovertible evidence that the death penalty is a more effective deterrent than life imprisonment, but neither is there clear evidence that it is not. Moreover, this remains such an empirically tricky question to settle that there is little likelihood that there will be an indisputable empirical answer to the question of the death penalty's deterrent effect.

Second, most people agree that human life is sacred or at least extremely valuable (for those who do not frame the issue in religious terms), but this shared belief leads to opposite conclusions. For some, it leads to a prohibition against capital punishment because it involves the intentional taking of human life. For others, it leads to support of the death penalty as either the proper penalty for violating the sanctity of life or as the deterrent most likely to preserve the sanctity of innocent life.

Third, almost everyone would agree that a society in which capital crimes do not occur is better than one in which they occur and are punished. Our long-range focus needs to be on reducing the number of crimes that could be classified as capital, and the most effective long-term use of our resources is toward that end. It is an empirical question what will most effectively promote that goal—some suggestions include more community-based policing, more rehabilitation in and out of prison, more programs that reduce drug and alcohol use (which are often associated with crime), more programs that strengthen family and community values, and more research into which programs are most effective in reducing crime—and it is a question well worth pursuing.

Finally, I would hope—and this is a personal hope rather than a statement of societal consensus—that many will agree that capital punishment, no matter how deserved it is on the basis of the crime (and surely there are crimes that justify it), is unworthy of us. It diminishes us, the ones in whose name it is administered. And it is, finally, an act of despair, a declaration that the person to be executed is beyond hope, beyond redemption. This may in fact be a realistic assessment of that individual, but there is moral merit in living in the area between realism and hope.

Endnotes

1. See Isaac Ehrlich, "The Deterrent Effect of Capital Punishment: A Question of Life or Death," *American Economic Review,* Vol. 65 (June, 1975), pp. 397–417; also see the discussion of this issue in Jeffrey Reiman's "Justice, Civilization, and the Death Penalty," and the bibliography in his Footnote 35.

2. W. Bowers and G. Pierce in "Deterrence or Brutalization: What is the Effect of Executions?" *Crime & Delinquency,* Vol. 26 (1980), pp. 453–484.

3. See especially the study by Hugo A. Bedeau and M. L. Radelet, "Miscarriages of Justice in Potentially Capital Cases," *Stanford Law Review,* Vol. 40 (1987), pp. 21–179.

4. Caitlin Lovinger, "Death Row's Living Alumni," *The New York Times,* Week in Review, August 22, 1999, p. 4.

The Arguments

David Gelernter
"What Do Murderers Deserve? The Death Penalty in Civilized Societies"

David Gelernter, a professor of computer science at Yale, was letter-bombed in June 1993 and nearly lost his life. He is the author, most recently, of Drawing Life: Surviving the Unabomber *and* Machine Beauty: Elegance and the Heart of Technology. *He is at work on a novel, portions of which have appeared in* Commentary *(August 1997 and January 1998).*

Gelernter argues that capital punishment is not only permissible, but in a certain sense it is a characteristic of a civilized society that finds murder intolerable. It is part of our communal response to an intolerable action.

As You Read, Consider This:

1. Murder, Gelernter tells us, always involves "messing in other people's problems." Why is this true? What significance does it have?
2. What role, according to Gelernter, do the emotions play in making decisions about the death penalty?

No civilized nation ever takes the death penalty for granted; two recent cases force us to consider it yet again. A Texas woman, Karla Faye Tucker, murdered two people with a pickaxe, was said to have repented in prison, and was put to death. A Montana man, Theodore Kaczynski, murdered three people with mail bombs, did not repent, and struck a bargain with the Justice Department; he pleaded guilty and will not be executed. (He also attempted to murder others and succeeded in wounding some, myself included.) Why did we execute the penitent and spare the impenitent? However we answer this question, we surely have a duty to ask it.

And we ask it—I do, anyway—with a sinking feeling, because in modern America, moral upside-downness is a specialty of the house. To eliminate race prejudice we discriminate by race. We promote the cultural assimilation of immigrant children by denying them schooling in English. We throw honest citizens in jail for child abuse, relying on testimony so phony any child could see through it. Orgasm studies are okay in public high schools but the Ten Commandments are not. We make a point of admiring manly women and womanly men. None of which has anything to do with capital punishment directly, but it all obliges us to approach any question about morality in modern America in the larger context of this country's desperate confusion about elementary distinctions.

Commentary, March/April 1999.

Why execute murderers? To deter? To avenge? Supporters of the death penalty often give the first answer, opponents the second. But neither can be the whole truth. If our main goal were deterring crime, we would insist on public executions—which are not on the political agenda, and not an item that many Americans are interested in promoting. If our main goal were vengeance, we would allow the grieving parties to decide the murderer's fate; if the victim had no family or friends to feel vengeful on his behalf, we would call the whole thing off.

In fact, we execute murderers in order to make a communal proclamation: that murder is intolerable. A deliberate murderer embodies evil so terrible that it defiles the community. Thus the late social philosopher Robert Nisbet: "Until a catharsis has been effected through trial, through the finding of guilt and then punishment, the community is anxious, fearful, apprehensive, and above all, contaminated."

Individual citizens have a right and sometimes a duty to speak. A community has the right, too, and sometimes the duty. The community certifies births and deaths, creates marriages, educates children, fights invaders. In laws, deeds, and ceremonies it lays down the boundary lines of civilized life, lines that are constantly getting scuffed and needing renewal.

When a murder takes place, the community is obliged, whether it feels like it or not, to clear its throat and step up to the microphone. Every murder demands a communal response. Among possible responses, the death penalty is uniquely powerful because it is permanent and can never be retracted or overturned. An execution forces the community to assume forever the burden of moral certainty; it is a form of absolute speech that allows no waffling or equivocation. Deliberate murder, the community announces, is absolutely evil and absolutely intolerable, period.

Of course, we could make the same point less emphatically if we wanted to—for example, by locking up murderers for life (as we sometimes do). The question then becomes: is the death penalty overdoing it? Should we make a less forceful proclamation instead?

The answer might be yes if we were a community in which murder was a shocking anomaly and thus in effect a solved problem. But we are not. Our big cities are full of murderers at large. "One can guesstimate," writes the criminologist and political scientist John J. DiIulio, Jr., "that we are nearing or may already have passed the day when 500,000 murderers, convicted and undetected, are living in American society."

DiIulio's statistics show an approach to murder so casual as to be depraved. We are reverting to a pre-civilized state of nature. Our natural bent in the face of murder is not to avenge the crime but to shrug it off, except in those rare cases when our own near and dear are involved. (And even then, it depends.)

This is an old story. Cain murders Abel and is brought in for questioning: where is Abel, your brother? The suspect's response: how should I know? "What am I, my brother's keeper?" It is one of the very first statements attributed to mankind in the Bible; voiced here by an interested party, it nonetheless expresses a powerful and universal inclination. Why mess in other people's problems? And murder is always, in the most immediate sense, someone else's problem, because the injured party is dead.

Murder in primitive societies called for a private settling of scores. The community as a whole stayed out of it. For murder to count, as it does in the Bible, as a crime not merely against one man but against the whole community and against God—that was a moral triumph that is still basic to our integrity, and that is never to be taken for granted. By executing murderers, the community reaffirms this moral understanding by restating the truth that absolute evil exists and must be punished.

Granted (some people say), the death penalty is a communal proclamation; it is nevertheless an incoherent one. If our goal is to affirm that human life is more precious than anything else, how can we make such a declaration by destroying life?

But declaring that human life is more precious than anything else is not our goal in imposing the death penalty. Nor is the proposition true. The founding fathers pledged their lives (and fortunes and sacred honor) to the cause of freedom; Americans have traditionally believed that some things are more precious than life. ("Living in a sanitary age, we are getting so we place too high a value on human life—which rightfully must always come second to human ideas." Thus E.B. White in 1938, pondering the Munich pact ensuring "peace in our time" between the Western powers and Hitler.) The point of capital punishment is not to pronounce on life in general but on the crime of murder.

Which is not to say that the sanctity of human life does not enter the picture. Taking a life, says the Talmud (in the course of discussing Cain and Abel), is equivalent to destroying a whole world. The rabbis used this statement to make a double point: to tell us why murder is the gravest of crimes, and to warn against false testimony in a murder trial. But to believe in the sanctity of human life does not mean, and the Talmud does not say it means, that capital punishment is ruled out.

A newer objection grows out of the seemingly random way in which we apply capital punishment. The death penalty might be a reasonable communal proclamation in principle, some critics say, but it has become so garbled in practice that it has lost all significance and ought to be dropped. DiIulio writes that "the ratio of persons murdered to persons executed for murder from 1977 to 1996 was in the ballpark of 1,000 to 1"; the death penalty has become in his view "arbitrary and capricious," a "state lottery" that is "unjust both as a matter of Judeo-Christian ethics and as a matter of American citizenship."

We can grant that, on the whole, we are doing a disgracefully bad job of administering the death penalty. After all, we are divided and confused on the issue. The community at large is strongly in favor of capital punishment; the cultural elite is strongly against it. Our attempts to speak with assurance as a community come out sounding in consequence like a man who is fighting off a chokehold as he talks. But a community as cavalier about murder as we are has no right to back down. That we are botching things does not entitle us to give up.

Opponents of capital punishment tend to describe it as a surrender to our emotions—to grief, rage, fear, blood lust. For most supporters of the death penalty, this is exactly false. Even when we resolve in principle to go ahead, we have to steel ourselves. Many of us would find it hard to kill a dog, much less a man. Endorsing capital punishment means not that we yield to our emotions but that we overcome them. (Immanuel Kant, the great advocate of the death penalty precisely on moral grounds, makes this point in his reply to the anti-capital-punishment reformer Cesare Beccaria—accusing Beccaria of being "moved by sympathetic sentimentality and an affectation of humanitarianism.") If we favor executing murderers it is not because we want to but because, however much we do not want to, we consider ourselves obliged to.

Many Americans, of course, no longer feel that obligation. The death penalty is hard for us as a community above all because of our moral evasiveness. For at least a generation, we have urged one another to switch off our moral faculties. "Don't be judgmental!" We have said it so many times, we are starting to believe it.

The death penalty is a proclamation about absolute evil, but many of us are no longer sure that evil even exists. We define evil out of existence by calling it "illness"—a tendency Aldous Huxley anticipated in his novel *Brave New World* (1932) and Robert Nisbet wrote about in 1982: "America has lost the villain, the evil one, who has now become one of the sick, the disturbed. . . . America has lost the moral value of guilt, lost it to the sickroom."

Our refusal to look evil in the face is no casual notion; it is a powerful drive. Thus we have, (for example) the terrorist Theodore Kaczynski, who planned and carried out a hugely complex campaign of violence with a clear goal in mind. It was the goal most terrorists have: to get famous and not die. He wanted public attention for his ideas about technology; he figured he could get it by attacking people with bombs.

He was right. His plan succeeded. It is hard to imagine a more compelling proof of mental competence than this planning and carrying out over decades of a complex, rational strategy. (Evil, yes; irrational, no; they are different things.) The man himself has said repeatedly that he is perfectly sane, knew what he was doing, and is proud of it.

To call such a man insane seems to me like deliberate perversity. But many people do. Some of them insist that his thoughts about technology constitute "delusions," though every terrorist holds strong beliefs that are wrong, and many nonterrorists do, too. Some insist that sending bombs through the mail is ipso facto proof of insanity—as if the twentieth century had not taught us that there is no limit to the bestiality of which sane men are capable.

Where does this perversity come from? I said earlier that the community at large favors the death penalty, but intellectuals and the cultural elite tend to oppose it. This is not (I think) because they abhor killing more than other people do, but because the death penalty represents absolute speech from a position of moral certainty, and doubt is the black-lung disease of the intelligentsia—an occupational hazard now inflicted on the culture as a whole.

American intellectuals have long differed from the broader community—particularly on religion, crime and punishment, education, family, the sexes, race relations, American history, taxes and public spending, the size and scope of government, art, the environment, and the military. (Otherwise, I suppose, they and the public have been in perfect accord.) But not until the late 60s and 70s were intellectuals finally in a position to act on their convictions. Whereupon they attacked the community's moral certainties with the enthusiasm of guard dogs leaping at throats. The result is an American community smitten with the disease of intellectual doubt—or, in this case, self-doubt.

The failure of our schools is a consequence of our self-doubt, of our inability to tell children that learning is not fun and they are required to master certain topics whether they want to or not. The tortured history of modern American race relations grows out of our self-doubt: we passed a civil-rights act in 1964, then lost confidence immediately in our ability to make a race-blind society work, racial preferences codify our refusal to believe in our own good faith. During the late stages of the cold war, many Americans laughed at the idea that the American way was morally superior or the Soviet Union was an "evil empire"; some are still laughing. Within their own community and the American community at large, doubting intellectuals have taken refuge (as doubters often do) in bullying, to the point where many of us are now so uncomfortable at the prospect of confronting evil that we turn away and change the subject.

Returning then to the penitent woman and the impenitent man: the Karla Faye Tucker case is the harder of the two. We are told that she repented of the vicious murders she committed. If that is true, we would still have had no business forgiving her, or forgiving any murderer. As Dennis Prager has written apropos this case, only the victim is entitled to forgive, and the victim is silent. But showing mercy to penitents is part of our religious tradition, and I cannot imagine renouncing it categorically.

Why was Cain not put to death, but condemned instead to wander the earth forever? Among the answers given by the rabbis in the Midrash is that he repented. The moral category of repentance is so important, they said, that it was created before the world itself. I would therefore consider myself morally obligated to think long and hard before executing a penitent. But a true penitent would have to have renounced (as Karla Faye Tucker did) all legal attempts to overturn the original conviction. If every legal avenue has been tried and has failed, the penitence window is closed. Of course, this still leaves the difficult problem of telling counterfeit penitence from the real thing, but everything associated with capital punishment is difficult.

As for Kaczynski, the prosecutors who accepted the murderer's plea-bargain say they got the best outcome they could, under the circumstances, and I believe them. But I also regard this failure to execute a cold-blooded impenitent terrorist murderer as a tragic abdication of moral responsibility. The tragedy lies in what, under our confused system, the prosecutors felt compelled to do. The community was called on to speak unambiguously. It flubbed its lines, shrugged its shoulders, and walked away.

Which brings me back to our moral condition as a community. I can describe our plight better in artistic than in philosophical terms. The most vivid illustrations I know of self-doubt and its consequences are the paintings and sculptures of Alberto Giacometti (who died in 1966). Giacometti was an artist of great integrity; he was consumed by intellectual and moral self-doubt, which he set down faithfully. His sculpted figures show elongated, shriveled human beings who seem corroded by acid, eaten-up to the bone, hurt and weakened past fragility nearly to death. They are painful to look at. And they are natural emblems of modern America. We ought to stick one on top of the Capitol and think it over.

In executing murderers, we declare that deliberate murder is absolutely evil and absolutely intolerable. This is a painfully difficult proclamation for a self-doubting community to make. But we dare not stop trying. Communities may exist in which capital punishment is no longer the necessary response to deliberate murder. America today is not one of them.

Journal/Discussion Questions

✍ *Gelernter sees American society as plagued by self-doubt. Do you agree with this analysis? Discuss.*

1. How would Gelernter reply to Sr. Helen Prejean's objections to the death penalty?

2. How does Gelernter think we should react to murders who genuinely repent after the murder? Do you agree? Why?

Jeffrey H. Reiman
"Against the Death Penalty"

Jeffrey Reiman is professor of philosophy and justice at the American University in Washington, DC. He is the author of several books, including The Rich Get Richer and the Poor Get Prison *and* Justice and Modern Moral Philosophy.

This article stakes out an interesting position. In contrast to most abolitionists, Reiman admits that the death penalty may well be a just punishment for murder. However, he still argues against the death penalty in states such as ours, maintaining that abolition of the death penalty is part of the process of becoming more civilized.

As You Read, Consider This:

1. Some critics of the death penalty maintain the death penalty is wrong because it is irrevocable. What reply does Reiman offer to this position?
2. According to Reiman, is the death penalty unjust? Explain.
3. What criticisms does Reiman offer of the deterrence argument?
4. What, according to Reiman, makes the death penalty so horrible? Should horribleness be part of some punishments? Why or why not?

My position about the death penalty as punishment for murder can be summed up in the following four propositions:

1. though the death penalty is a just punishment for some murderers, it is not unjust to punish murderers less harshly (down to a certain limit);
2. though the death penalty would be justified if needed to deter future murders, we have no good reason to believe that it is needed to deter future murders; and
3. in refraining from imposing the death penalty, the state, by its vivid and impressive example, contributes to reducing our tolerance for cruelty and thereby fosters the advance of human civilization as we understand it.

Taken together, these three propositions imply that we do no injustice to actual or potential murder victims, and we do some considerable good, in refraining from executing murderers. This conclusion will be reinforced by another argument, this one for the proposition:

4. though the death penalty is *in principle* a just penalty for murder, it is unjust *in practice* in America because it is applied in arbitrary and discriminatory ways, and this is likely to continue into the foreseeable future.

This fourth proposition conjoined with the prior three imply the overall conclusion *that it is good in principle to avoid the death penalty and bad in practice to impose it.* In what follows, I shall state briefly the arguments for each of these propositions.[1] For ease of identification, I shall number the first paragraph in which the argument for each proposition begins.

Before showing that the death penalty is just punishment for some murders, it is useful to dispose of a number of popular but weak arguments against the death penalty. One such popular argument contends that, if murder is wrong, then death penalty is wrong as well. But this argument proves too much! It would work against *all* punishments since all are wrong if done by a regular citizen under normal circumstances. (If I imprison you in a little jail in my basement, I am guilty of kidnapping; if I am caught and convicted, the state will lock me up in jail and will not have committed the same wrong that I did.) The point here is that what is wrong about murder is not merely that it is killing per se, but the killing of a legally innocent person by a nonauthorized individual—and this doesn't apply to executions that are the outcome of conviction and sentencing at a fair trial.

Another argument that some people think is decisive against capital punishment points to the irrevocability of the punishment. The idea here is that innocents are sometimes wrongly convicted and if they receive the death penalty there is no way to correct the wrong done to them. While there is some force to this claim, its force is at best a relative matter. To be sure, if someone is executed and later found to have been innocent, there is no way to give that him back the life that has been taken. But, if someone is sentenced to life in prison and is found to have been innocent, she can be set free and perhaps given money to make up for the years spent in prison—but those years cannot be given back. On the other hand, the innocent person who has been executed can at least be compensated in the form of money to his family and he can have his named cleared. So, it's not that the death penalty is irrevocable and other punishments are revocable; rather, all punishments are irrevocable though the death penalty is, so to speak, relatively more irrevocable than the rest. In any event, this only makes a difference in cases of mistaken conviction of the innocent, and the evidence is that such mistakes— particularly in capital cases—are quite rare. And, further, since we accept the death of innocents elsewhere, on the highways, as a cost of progress, as a necessary accompaniment of military operations, and so on, it is not plausible to think that the execution of a small number of innocent persons is so terrible as to outweigh all other considerations, especially when every effort is made to make sure that it does not occur.

Finally, it is sometimes argued that if we use the death penalty as a means to deter future murderers, we kill someone to protect others (from different people than the one we have executed), and thus we violate the Kantian prohibition against using individuals as means to the welfare of others. But the Kantian prohibition is not against using others as means, it is against using others as *mere* means (that is, in total disregard of their own desires and goals). Though you use the bus driver as a means to your getting home, you don't use him as a mere means because the job pays him a living and thus promotes his desires and goals as it does yours. Now, if what deters criminals is the existence of an effective system of deterrence, then criminals punished as part of that system are not used as mere means since their desires and goals are also served, inasmuch as they have also benefited from deterrence of other criminals. Even criminals don't want to be crime victims. Further, if there is a right to threaten punishment in self-defense, then a society has the right to threaten punishment to defend its members, and there is no more violation of the Kantian maxim in imposing such punishment then there is in carrying out any threat to defend oneself against unjust attack.[2]

1. One way to see that the death penalty is a just punishment for at least some murders (the cold-blooded, premeditated ones) is to reflect on the *lex talionis,* an eye for an eye, a tooth for a tooth, and all that. Some regard this as a primitive rule, but it has I think an undeniable element of justice. And many who think that the death penalty is just punishment for murder are responding to this element. To see what the element is consider how similar the *lex talionis* is to the Golden Rule. The Golden Rule tells us to do unto others what we would have others do unto us, and the *lex talionis* counsels that we do to others what they have done to us. Both of these reflect a belief in the equality of all human beings. Treating others as you *would* have them treat you means treating others as equal to you, because it implies that you count their suffering to be as great a calamity as your own suffering, that you count your right to impose suffering on them as no greater than their right to impose suffering on you, and so on. The Golden Rule would not make sense if it were applied to two people, one of whom was thought to be inherently more valuable than the other. Imposing a harm on the more valuable one would be worse than imposing the same harm on the less valuable one—and neither could judge her actions by what she would have the other do to her. Since *lex talionis* says that you are rightly paid back for the harm you have caused another with a similar harm, it implies that the value of what of you have done to another is the same as the value of having it done to you—which, again, would not be the case, if one of you were thought inherently more valuable than the other. Consequently, treating people according to the *lex talionis* (like treating them according to the Golden Rule) affirms the equality of all concerned—and this supports the idea that punishing according to *lex talionis* is just.

Furthermore, on the Kantian assumption that a rational individual implicitly endorses the universal form of the intention that guides his action, a rational individual who kills another implicitly endorses the idea that he may be killed, and thus, he authorizes his own execution thereby absolving his executioner of injustice. What's more, much as above we saw that acting on *lex talionis* affirms the equality of criminal and victim, this Kantian-inspired argument suggests that acting on *lex talionis* affirms the rationality of criminal and victim. The victim's rationality is affirmed because the criminal only authorizes his own killing if he has intended to kill another rational being like himself—then, he implicitly endorses the universal version of that intention, thereby authorizing his own killing. A person who intentionally kills an animal does not implicitly endorse his own being killed; only someone who kills someone like himself authorizes his own killing. In this way, the Kantian argument also invokes the equality of criminal and victim.

On the basis of arguments like this, I maintain that the idea that people deserve having done to them roughly what they have done (or attempted to do) to others affirms both the equality and rationality of human beings and for that reason is just. Kant has said: "no one has ever heard of anyone condemned to death on account of murder who complained that he was getting too much [punishment] and therefore was being treated unjustly; everyone would laugh in his face if he were to make such a statement."[3] If Kant is right, then even murderers recognize the inherent justice of the death penalty.

However, while the justice of the *lex talionis* implies the justice of executing some murderers, it does not imply that punishing less harshly is automatically unjust. We can see this by noting that the justice of the *lex talionis* implies also the justice of torturing torturers and raping rapists. I am certain and I assume my reader is as well that we need not impose these latter punishments to do justice (even if there were no other way of equaling the harm done or attempted by the criminal). Otherwise the price of doing justice would be matching the cruelty of the worst criminals, and that would effectively price justice out of the moral market. It follows that justice can be served with lesser punishments. Now, I think that there are two ways that punishing less harshly than the *lex talionis* could be unjust: it could be unjust to the actual victim of murder or to the future victims of potential murderers. It would be unjust to the actual victim if the punishment we mete out instead of execution were so slight that it trivialized the harm that the murderer did. This would make a sham out of implicit affirmation of equality that underlies the justice of the *lex talionis*. However, life imprisonment, or even a lengthy prison sentence—say, twenty years or more without parole—is a very grave punishment and not one that trivializes the harm done by the murderer. Punishment would be unjust to future victims if it is so mild that it fails to be a reasonable deterrent to potential murderers. Thus, refraining from executing murderers could be wrong if executions were needed to deter future murderers. In the following section, I shall say why there is no reason to think that this is so.

2. I grant that, if the death penalty were needed to deter future murderers, that would be a strong reason in favor of using the death penalty, since otherwise we would be sacrificing the future victims of potential murderers whom we could have deterred. And I think that this is a real injustice to those future victims, since the "we" in question is the state. Because the state claims a monopoly on the use of force, it owes its citizens protection, and thus does them injustice when it fails to provide the level of protection it reasonably could provide. However, there is no reason to believe that we need the death penalty to deter future murderers. The evidence we have strongly supports the idea that we get the same level of deterrence from life imprisonment, and even from substantial prison terms, such as twenty years without parole.

Before 1975, the most important work on the comparative deterrent impact of the capital punishment versus life in prison was that of Thorsten Sellin. He compared the homicide rates in states with the death penalty to the rates in similar states without the death penalty, and found no greater incidence of homicide in states without the death penalty than in similar states with it. In 1975, Isaac Ehrlich, a University of Chicago econometrician, reported the results of a statistical study which he claimed proved that, in the period from 1933 to 1969, each execution deterred as many as eight murders. This finding was, however, widely challenged. Ehrlich found a deterrent impact of executions in the period from 1933 to 1969, which includes the period of 1963 to 1969, a time when hardly any executions were carried out and crime rates rose for reasons that are arguably independent of the existence or nonexistence of capital punishment. When the 1963–1969 period is excluded, no significant deterrent effect shows. This is a very serious problem since the period from 1933 through to the end of the 1930s was one in which executions were carried out at the highest rate in American history—before or after. That no deterrent effect turns up when the study is limited to 1933 to 1962 almost seems evidence *against* the deterrent effect of the death penalty!

Consequently, in 1978, *after Ehrlich's study,* the editors of a National Academy of Sciences' study of the impact of punishment wrote: "In summary, the flaws in the earlier analyses (i.e., Sellin's and others) and the sensitivity of the more recent analyses to minor variation in model specification and the serious temporal instability of the results lead the panel to conclude that the available studies provide no useful evidence on the deterrent effect of capital punishment."[4] Note that, while the deterrence research commented upon here generally compares the deterrent impact of capital punishment with that of life imprisonment, the failure to prove that capital punishment deters murder more than does incarceration goes beyond life in prison. A substantial proportion of people serving life sentences are released on parole before the end of their sentences. Since this is public knowledge, we should conclude from these studies that we have no evidence that capital punishment deters murder more effectively than prison sentences that are less than life, though still substantial, such as twenty years.

Another version of the argument for the greater deterrence impact of capital punishment compared to lesser punishments is called *the argument from common sense*. It holds that, whatever the social science studies do or don't show, it is only common sense that people will be more deterred by what they fear more, and since people fear death more than life in prison, they will be deterred more by execution than by a life sentence. This argument for the death penalty, however, assumes without argument or evidence that deterrence increases continuously and endlessly with the fearfulness of threatened punishment rather than leveling out at some threshold beyond which increases in fearfulness produce no additional increment of deterrence. That being tortured for a year is worse than being tortured for six months doesn't imply that a year's torture will deter you from actions that a half-year's torture would not deter—since a half-year's torture may be bad enough to deter you from all the actions that you can be deterred from doing. Likewise, though the death penalty may be worse than life in prison, that doesn't imply that the death penalty will deter acts that a life sentence won't because a life sentence may be bad enough to do all the deterring that can be done—and that is precisely what the social science studies seem to show. And, as I suggested above, what applies here to life sentences applies as well to substantial prison sentences.

I take it then that there is no reason to believe that we save more innocent lives with the death penalty than with less harsh penalties such as life in prison or some lengthy sentence, such as twenty years without parole. But then we do no injustice to the future victims of potential murderers by refraining from the death penalty. And, in conjunction with the argument of the previous section, it follows that we do no injustice to actual or potential murder victims if we refrain from executing murderers and sentence them instead to life in prison or to some substantial sentence, say, twenty or more years in prison without parole. But it remains to be seen what good will be served by doing the latter instead of executing.

3. Here I want to suggest that, in refraining from imposing the death penalty, the state, by its vivid and impressive example, contributes to reducing our tolerance for cruelty and thereby fosters the advance of human civilization as we understand it. To see this, note first that it has long been acknowledged that the state, and particularly the criminal justice system, plays an educational role in society as a model of morally accepted conduct and an indicator of the line between morally permissible and impermissible actions. Now, consider the general repugnance that is attached to the use of torture—even as punishment for criminals who have tortured their victims. It seems to me that, by refraining from torturing even those who deserve it, our state plays a role in promoting that repugnance. That we will not torture even those who have earned it by their crimes conveys a message about the awfulness of torture, namely, that it is something that civilized people will not do even to give evil people their just desserts. Thus it seems to me that in this case the state advances the cause of human civilization by contributing to a reduction in people's tolerance for cruelty. I think that the modern state is uniquely positioned to do this sort of thing because of its size (representing millions, even hundreds of millions of citizens) and its visibility (starting with the printing press that accompanied the birth of modern nations, increasing with radio, television and the other media of instantaneous communication). And because the state can do this, it should. Consequently, I contend that if the state were to put execution in the same category as torture, it would contribute yet further to reducing our tolerance for cruelty and to advancing the cause of human civilization. And because it can do this, it should.

To make this argument plausible, however, I must show that execution is horrible enough to warrant its inclusion alongside torture. I think that execution is horrible in a way similar to (though not identical with) the way in which torture is horrible. Torture is horrible because of two of its features, which also characterize execution: intense pain and the spectacle of one person being completely subject to the power of another.[5] This latter is separate from the issue of pain, since it is something that offends people about unpainful things, such as slavery (even voluntarily entered) and prostitution (even voluntarily chosen as an occupation). Execution shares this separate feature. It enacts the total subjugation of one person to his fellows, whether the individual to be executed is strapped into an electric chair or bound like a laboratory animal on a hospital gurney awaiting lethal injection.

Moreover, execution, even by physically painless means, is characterized by a special and intense psychological pain that distinguishes it from the loss of life that awaits us all. This is because execution involves the most psychologically painful features of death. We normally regard death from human causes as worse than death from natural causes, since a humanly caused shortening of life lacks the consolation of unavoidability. And we normally regard death whose coming is foreseen by its victim as worse than sudden death because a foreseen death adds to the loss of life the terrible consciousness of that impending loss. An execution combines the worst of both: Its coming is foreseen, in that its date is normally already set, and it lacks the consolation of unavoidability, in that it depends on the will of one's fellow human beings not on natural forces beyond human control. It was on just such grounds that Albert Camus regarded the death penalty as itself a kind of torture: "As a general rule, a man is undone by waiting for capital punishment well before he dies. Two deaths are inflicted on him, the first being worse than the second, whereas he killed but once. Compared to such torture, the penalty of retaliation [the *lex talionis*] seems like a civilized law."[6]

Consequently, if a civilizing message is conveyed about torture when the state refrains from torturing, I believe we can and should try to convey a similar message about killing by having the state refrain from killing even those who have earned killing by their evil deeds. Moreover, if I am right about this, then it implies further that refraining from executing murderers will have the effect of deterring murder in the long run and thereby make our society safer. This much then shows that it would be good in principle to refrain from imposing capital punishment. I want now to show why it would be good in practice as well.

4. However just in principle the death penalty may be, it is applied unjustly in practice in America and is likely to be so for the foreseeable future. The evidence for this conclusion comes from various sources. Numerous studies show that killers of whites are more likely to get the death penalty than killers of blacks, and that black killers of whites are far more likely to be sentenced to death than white killers of blacks. Moreover, just about everyone recognizes that poor people are more likely to be sentenced to death and to have those sentences carried out than well-off people. And these injustices persist even after all death penalty statutes were declared unconstitutional in 1972[7] and only those death penalty statutes with provisions for reducing arbitrariness in sentencing were admitted as constitutional in 1976.[8] In short, injustice in the application of the death penalty persists even after legal reform, and this strongly suggests that it is so deep that it will not be corrected in the foreseeable future.

It might be objected that discrimination is also found in the handing out of prison sentences and thus that this argument would prove that we should abolish prison as well as the death penalty. But I accept that we need some system of punishment to deter crime and mete out justice to criminals, and for that reason even a discriminatory punishment system is better than none. Then, the objection based on discrimination works only against those elements of the punishment system that are not needed either to deter crime or to do justice, and I have shown above that this is true of the death penalty. Needless to say we should also strive to eliminate discrimination in the parts of the criminal justice that we cannot do without.

Other, more subtle, kinds of discrimination also affect the way the death penalty is actually carried out. There are many ways in which the actions of well-off people lead to death which are not counted as murder. For example, many more people die as a result of preventable occupational diseases (due to toxic chemicals, coal and textile dust, and the like, in the workplace) or preventable environmental pollution than die as a result of what is treated legally as homicide.[9] So, in addition to all the legal advantages that money can buy a wealthy person accused of murder, the law also helps the wealthy by not defining as murder many of the ways in which the wealthy are responsible for the deaths of fellow human beings. Add to this that many of the killings that we do treat as murders, the ones done by the poor in our society, are the predictable outcome of remediable social injustice—the discrimination and exploitation that, for example, have helped to keep African Americans at the bottom of the economic ladder for centuries. Those who benefit from injustice and who could remedy it bear some of the responsibility for the crimes that are the predictable outcome of injustice—and that implies that plenty of well-off people share responsibility with many of our poor murderers. But since these more fortunate folks are not likely to be held responsible for murder, it is unfair to hold only the poor victims of injustice responsible—and wholly responsible to boot!

Finally, we already saw that the French existentialist, Albert Camus, asserted famously that life on death row is a kind of torture. Recently, Robert Johnson has studied the psychological effects on condemned men on death row and confirmed Camus's claim. In his book *Condemned to Die,* Johnson recounts the painful psychological deterioration suffered by a substantial majority of the death row prisoners he studied.[10] Since the death row inmate faces execution, he is viewed as having nothing to lose and thus is treated as the most dangerous of criminals. As a result, his confinement and isolation are nearly total. Since he has no future for which to be rehabilitated, he receives the least and the worst of the prison's facilities. Since his guards know they are essentially warehousing him until his death, they treat him as something less than human—and so he is brutalized, taunted, powerless and constantly reminded of it. The effect of this on the death row inmate, as Johnson reports it, is quite literally the breaking down of the structures of the ego—a process not unlike that caused by brainwashing. Since we do not reserve the term "torture" only for processes resulting in physical pain, but recognize processes that result in extreme psychological suffering as torture as well (consider sleep deprivation or the so-called Chinese water torture), Johnson's and Camus's application of this term to the conditions of death row confinement seems reasonable.

It might be objected that some of the responsibility for the torturous life of death row inmates is the inmates' own fault, since in pressing their legal appeals, they delay their executions and thus prolong their time on death row. Capital murder convictions and sentences, however, are reversed on appeal with great frequency, nearly ten times the rate of reversals in noncapital cases. This strongly supports the idea that such appeals are necessary to test the legality of murder convictions and death penalty sentences. To hold the inmate somehow responsible for the delays that result from his appeals, and thus for the (increased) torment he suffers as a consequence, is effectively to confront him with the choice of accepting execution before its legality is fully tested or suffering torture until it is. Since no just society should expect (or even want) a person to accept a sentence until its legal validity has been established, it is unjust to torture him until it has and perverse to assert that he has brought the torture on himself by his insistence that the legality of his sentence be fully tested before it is carried out.

The worst features of death row might be ameliorated, but it is unlikely that its torturous nature will be eliminated, or even that it is possible to eliminate it. This is, in part, because it is linked to an understandable psychological strategy used by the guards in order to protect themselves against natural, painful, and ambivalent feelings of sympathy for a person awaiting a humanly inflicted death. Johnson writes: "I think it can also be argued . . . that humane death rows will not be achieved in practice because the purpose of death row confinement is to facilitate executions by dehumanizing both the prisoners and (to a lesser degree) their executioners and thus make it easier for both to conform to the etiquette of ritual killing."[11]

If conditions on death row are and are likely to continue to be a real form of psychological torture, if Camus and Johnson are correct, then it must be admitted that the death penalty is in practice not merely a penalty of death—it is a penalty of torture until death. Then the sentence of death is more than the *lex talionis* allows as a just penalty for murder—and thus it is unjust in practice.

I think that I have proven that it would be good in principle to refrain from imposing the death penalty and bad in practice to continue using it. And, I have proven this while accepting the two strongest claims made by defenders of capital punishment, namely, that death is just punishment for at least some murderers, and that, if the death penalty were a superior deterrent to murder than imprisonment that would justify using the death penalty.

Notes

1. The full argument for these propositions, along with supporting data, references, and replies to objections is in Louis Pojman and Jeffrey Reiman, *The Death Penalty: For and Against* (Lanham, MD: Rowman & Littlefield Publishers, Inc., 1998), pp. 67–132, 151–163. That essay in turn is based upon and substantially revises my "Justice, Civilization, and the Death Penalty: Answering van den Haag," *Philosophy and Public Affairs* 14, no. 2 (Spring 1985): 115–48, and my "The Justice of the Death Penalty in an Unjust World," in *Challenging Capital Punishment: Legal and Social Science Approaches,* ed. K. Haas & J. Inciardi (Beverly Hills, CA: Sage, 1988), pp. 29–48.

2. Elsewhere I have argued at length that punishment needed to deter reasonable people is *deserved* by criminals. See Pojman and Reiman, *The Death Penalty,* pp. 79–85.

3. Immanuel Kant, "The Metaphysical Elements of Justice," pt. 1 of *The Metaphysics of Morals,* trans. J. Ladd (Indianapolis, Ind.: Bobbs-Merrill, 1965; originally published 1797), p. 104, see also p. 133.

4. Alfred Blumstein, Jacqueline Cohen, and Daniel Nagin, eds., *Deterrence and Incapacitation: Estimating the Effects of Criminal Sanctions on Crime Rates* (Washington, DC: National Academy of Sciences, 1978), p. 9.

5. Hugo Bedau has developed this latter consideration at length with respect to the death penalty. See Hugo A. Bedau, "Thinking about the Death Penalty as a Cruel and Unusual Punishment," *U.C. Davis Law Review* 18 (Summer 1985): 917ff. This article is reprinted in Hugo A. Bedau, *Death Is Different: Studies in the Morality, Law, and Politics of Capital Punishment* (Boston:

Northeastern University Press, 1987); and Hugo A. Bedau, ed., *The Death Penalty in America: Current Controversies* (New York: Oxford University Press, 1997).

6. Albert Camus, "Reflections on the Guillotine," in Albert Camus, *Resistance, Rebellion, and Death* (New York: Knopf, 1961), p. 205.

7. *Furman v Georgia,* 408 U.S. 238 (1972).

8. *Gregg v Georgia,* 428 U.S. 153 (1976).

9. Jeffrey Reiman, *The Rich Get Richer and the Poor Get Prison: Ideology, Class, and Criminal Justice,* 5th ed. (Needham Heights, MA: Allyn & Bacon, 1998), pp. 71–78, 81–87.

10. Robert Johnson, *Condemned to Die: Life under Sentence of Death* (New York: Elsevier, 1981), pp. 129ff.

11. Robert Johnson, personal correspondence to author.

Journal/Discussion Questions

1. Consider your reaction to the bombing of the Federal Building in Oklahoma City. To what extent does Reiman's analysis shed light on your feelings? What shortcomings does his analysis have in light of your own experience?

2. To what extent does Reiman succeed in recognizing the legitimate claims of both advocates and critics of the death penalty?

3. Why, according to Reiman, are we not justified in arguing that the death penalty is wrong because it uses people as a means?

Concluding Discussion Questions

Where Do You Stand Now?

Instructions

You have already answered the following questions in your moral problems self-quiz at the beginning of this book. Now that you have studied the material in this section, take a moment to answer the same questions again.

	Strongly Agree	Agree	Undecided	Disagree	Strongly Disagree	*Chapter 4: Punishment and the Death Penalty*
16.	❏	❏	❏	❏	❏	The purpose of punishment is primarily to pay back the offender.
17.	❏	❏	❏	❏	❏	The purpose of punishment is primarily to deter the offender and others from committing future crimes.
18.	❏	❏	❏	❏	❏	Capital punishment is always morally wrong.
19.	❏	❏	❏	❏	❏	The principal moral consideration about capital punishment is the question of whether it is administered arbitrarily or not.
20.	❏	❏	❏	❏	❏	The principal moral consideration about capital punishment is that it doesn't really deter criminals.

Compare your answers to this self-quiz with the answers to the initial self-quiz. How, if at all, have your answers changed? How have the *reasons* for your answers changed?

Journal/Discussion Questions

✍ *Imagine that you are on a jury. You have just found a young adult guilty of a particularly heinous rape/torture/murder of a small child. The defendant appears to be unrepentant. Now you are being asked to consider sentencing. The prosecution is asking for the death penalty, while the defense is requesting a sentence of life imprisonment. How would you vote? What factors would you consider? What would be the*
major stumbling block to changing your mind and voting the other way?

Given your answers to these questions, how does your position fit in with the positions and issues discussed in this chapter?

1. You have now read, thought, and discussed a number of aspects of punishment in general and the use of the death penalty in particular. How have your views *changed* and developed? Has your understanding of the

reasons supporting other positions that are different from your own changed? If so, in what way(s)? What idea had the greatest impact on your thinking about punishment? About the death penalty? Why?

2. Imagine that a close family member was murdered. How, if at all, would this affect your views on punishment? On capital punishment? Presuming that the murderer was caught, what would you like punishment to accomplish?

3. Imagine that you are a new member of the Senate, and that you have just been given an assignment to the Senate committee that is responsible for recommendations about criminal punishment on the state and local levels as well as nationally. Your committee is asked to determine (a) what aspects of our current punishment practices are in need of revision and (b) what changes you would recommend for the future. At the first meeting of the committee, the committee chair asks each member to state their initial general views on these two issues. What would your response be?

For Further Reading

Web Resources

For Web-based resources, including the major Supreme Court decisions on the death penalty, see the Punishment & Death Penalty page of *Ethics Updates* (http://ethics.sandiego.edu). Among the resources are extensive statistical information about the use of the death penalty in America, John Stuart Mill's speech in favor of capital punishment, John Rawls' "Two Concepts of Rules," and works by Hugo Bedeau.

Capital Punishment. Among the many books and anthologies on the death penalty, see *Debating the Death Penalty. Should America Have Capital Punishment? The Experts on Both Sides Make Their Best Case,* edited by Hugo Adam Bedau and Paul G. Cassell (New York: Oxford University Press, 2004); the selections and exchanges in Hugo Adam Bedau, *The Death Penalty in America* (New York: Oxford University Press, 1998); Ernest van den Haag and John P. Conrad, *The Death Penalty: A Debate* (New York: Plenum Press, 1983). Also see Walter Berns, *For Capital Punishment: Crime and the Morality of the Death Penalty* (New York: Basic Books, 1979); Charles Black, *Capital Punishment: The Inevitability of Caprice and Mistake,* 2nd ed. (New York: W.W. Norton, 1976); Robert Johnson, *Condemned to Die: Life Under Sentence of Death* (New York: Elsevier, 1981); Jeffrey H. Reiman, *The Rich Get Richer and the Poor Get Prison: Ideology, Class, and Criminal Justice,* 2nd ed. (New York: John Wiley, 1984); Stephen Nathanson, *An Eye for an Eye: The Morality of Punishing by Death* (Totowa, NJ: Rowman & Littlefield, 1987); and *The Death Penalty: Opposing Viewpoints,* edited by Carol Wekesser (San Diego: Greenhaven Press, 1991) contains a good balance of short pieces. For an excellent debate on this issue, see Louis P. Pojman and Jeffrey Reiman, *The Death Penalty: For and Against* (Lanthan: Rowman & Littlefield, 1998). Also see Austin Sarat, *When the State Kills: Capital Punishment and the American Condition* (Princeton: Princeton University Press, 2002); *The Killing State. Capital Punishment in Law, Politics, and Culture,* edited by Austin Sarat (New York: Oxford University Press, 2001); Franklin E. Zimring, *The Contradictions of American Capital Punishment* (New York: Oxford University Press, 2003); and Stuart Banner, *The Death Penalty. An American History* (Boston: Harvard University Press, 2003).

For an insightful as well as beautifully written treatment of mistakes and the death penalty, see Scott Turow's *Ultimate Punishment. A Lawyer's Reflections on Dealing with the Death Penalty* (New York: Farrar, Straus, and Giroux, 2003); a former federal prosecutor and novelist, Turow was a member of the commission that studied the death penalty in Illinois.

Among the many helpful articles on capital punishment, see Hugo Adam Bedau's "Capital Punishment," *The Oxford Handbook of Practical Ethics,* edited by Hugh LaFollette (Oxford: Oxford University Press, 2003), pp. 705–733 and his excellent overview, analysis, and bibliography in "Capital Punishment," *The Encyclopedia of Ethics,* edited by Lawrence C. Becker and Charlotte B. Becker (New York: Garland, 1992), Vol. I, pp. 122–125; Stanley I. Benn, "Punishment," *The Encyclopedia of Philosophy* vol. 7, edited by Paul Edwards (New York: Macmillan, 1967), p. 32 ff.;

and Richard Wasserstrom, "Capital Punishment as Punishment: Some Theoretical Issues and Objections," *Midwest Studies in Philosophy,* Vol. 7, pp. 473–502, who raises a number of objections to capital punishment, not because it is capital, but because it is punishment.

On the inhumanity of the death penalty, Michael Davis recently argued in "The Death Penalty, Civilization, and Inhumaneness," *Social Theory and Practice,* Vol. 16, No. 2 (Summer 1990), pp. 245–259, that the "argument from inhumaneness" advanced by Reiman and Bedau lacks an adequate account of inhumaneness. Jeffrey Reiman replied to Davis in "The Death Penalty, Deterrence, and Horribleness: Reply to Michael Davis," *Social Theory and Practice,* Vol. 16, No. 2 (Summer 1990), pp. 261–272. Also see Thomas A. Long, "Capital Punishment—'Cruel and Unusual'?" *Ethics,* Vol. 83 (April 1973), pp. 214–223 and the reply by Robert S. Gerstein, "Capital Punishment—'Cruel and Unusual': A Retributivist Response," *Ethics,* Vol. 85 (October 1974), pp. 75–79.

On the irrevocability of capital punishment, see Michael Davis, "Is the Death Penalty Irrevocable?" *Social Theory and Practice,* Vol. 10 (Summer 84), pp. 143–156, argues that there is no morally significant sense in which the death penalty is more irrevocable than life imprisonment; the death penalty is only distinctive in regard to the more modest claim about what we can do to correct error in application.

On the arbitrariness of the death penalty, see especially Christopher Meyers, in "Racial Bias, the Death Penalty, and Desert," *Philosophical Forum* (Winter 1990–1991), pp. 139–148, which supports *McCleskey v. Kemp* (1987), in which the Supreme Court ruled that racial bias was not sufficient ground for overturning a death sentence, as long as punishment is seen as retribution and as long as defendants do not receive more punishment than they deserve; Brian Calvert, in "Retribution, Arbitrariness and the Death Penalty," *Journal of Social Philosophy,* Vol. 23, No. 3 (Winter 92), pp. 140–165, which argues that the administration of the death penalty is arbitrary because there is not a sufficiently clear distinction in kind between murders that deserve execution and murders that deserve life imprisonment. On class bias in the criminal justice system, see especially Jeffrey Reiman, *The Rich Get Richer and the Poor Get Poorer,* 5th ed. (Boston: Allyn & Bacon, 1998).

On the international dimensions of the death penalty, see William A. Schabas, *The Abolition of the Death Penalty in International Law,* 3rd ed. (New York: Cambridge University Press, 2002) and Roger Hood, *The Death Penalty: A Worldwide Perspective,* 3rd ed. (New York: Oxford University Press, 2003); and *Capital Punishment: Strategies for Abolition,* edited by Peter Hodgkinson and William A. Schabas (New York: Cambridge University Press, 2004).

On the deterrent effect of the death penalty, see Ernest Van Den Haag, "Deterrence and the Death Penalty: A Rejoinder," *Ethics,* Vol. 81 (October 1970), pp. 74–75; Hugo Adam Bedau, "A Concluding Note," *Ethics,* Vol. 81, (October 1970), p. 76; Michael Davis, "Death, Deterrence, and the Method of Common Sense," *Social Theory and Practice,* Vol. 7 (Summer 1981), pp. 145–178, uses what he calls the "method of common sense" to show that the death penalty is the most effective humane deterrent available to us. Steven Goldberg, "On Capital Punishment," *Ethics,* Vol. 85 (October 1974), pp. 67–74, argues in favor of capital punishment for its deterrent effect on potential criminals and George Schedler, "Capital Punishment and Its Deterrent Effect," *Social Theory and Practice,* Vol. 4 (Fall 76), pp. 47–56 refutes the "innocent people" argument. David A. Conway, "Capital Punishment and Deterrence: Some Considerations in Dialogue Form," *Philosophy & Public Affairs,* Vol. 3, No. 4 (Summer 1974), pp. 433 ff.

On mercy and the death penalty, see Kathleen Dean Moore, *Pardons, Justice, Mercy, and the Public Interest* (New York: Oxford, 1989); Jeffrie G. Murphy and Jean Hampton, *Forgiveness and Mercy* (New York: Cambridge University Press, 1994), as well as Murphy's *Getting Even: Forgiveness and Its Limits* (New York: Oxford University Press, 2003). For a personal memoir about his decisions, see Edmund G. (Pat) Brown, with Dick Adler, *Public Justice, Private Mercy: A Governor's Education on Death Row* (New York: Weidenfeld & Nicolson, 1989). On the relationship between retribution and mercy, see Marvin Henberg, *Retribution: Evil for Evil in Ethics, Law, and Literature* (Philadelphia: Temple University Press, 1990). Martha Minow's *Between Vengeance and Forgiveness: Facing History after Genocide and Mass Violence* (Boston: Beacon, 1998) is an excellent consideration of these issues in a different context than our domestic one.

On alternatives to punishment, see David C. Anderson, *Sensible Justice: Alternatives to Prison* (New York: The New Press, 1998) and Elliott Currie, *Crime and Punishment in America* (New York: Metropolitan Books, 1998).

CHAPTER
5

War, Terrorism, and Counterterrorism

Videotape

    Topic: Torture

    Source: *Nightline*, May 12, 2004

    Anchor: Ted Koppel

    Guests   Ariel Dorfman (author, *Prisoner without a Name, Cell without
              a Number), Greg Hartley (former Army interrogator), Alan Dershowitz
              (Harvard Law School)

An Introduction to the Moral Issues

War and terrorist threats have become increasingly real to many Americans since September 11, 2001. Issues of life and death have been highlighted in a new way for many in the United States. In this overview, we consider two principal areas of moral concern in regard to war and peace: pacifism and just war theory.

To Kill or Not to Kill

War and killing seem to stretch back into the mist of the beginnings of human history. To many they seem not only a longstanding part of the human condition, but also one that cannot (and perhaps should not) be eliminated.

Some, however, have stood against this position and rejected killing and warfare as legitimate ways of resolving human conflicts. These are pacifists, individuals who believe that it is always wrong to kill other human beings.

In the 20th century, we witnessed several extraordinary pacifist leaders. Gandhi's pacifism, his nonviolent resistance to British rule of India, was a stunning example of the power of pacifism, and his nonviolent campaigns were probably more successful against the British than any attempt at violent resistance could have been. Martin Luther King's nonviolent resistance to segregation in the United States again provided a model of moral leadership of tremendous power.

Pacifism is often deeply rooted in religious traditions. In France during World War II, the pacifist village of Le Chambon was responsible for saving the lives of several thousand Jews, mostly children, and doing so in a way that never shed blood. (Phillip Hallie has chronicled this in his beautiful book, *Lest Innocent Blood Be Shed*). Amish, Mennonite, and Quaker traditions often reject all forms of violence. In the Catholic tradition, Joseph Cardinal Bernardin articulates the "seamless garment" doctrine of respect for human life that rejects killing in all its forms—abortion, euthanasia, capital punishment, and war—as well as the destructive conditions of poverty and racism that often were a form of violence against the poor and persons of color. The Dali Lama has provided yet another powerful model of pacifism, in this case from a Buddhist tradition.

Can pacifism be justified philosophically outside of a religious tradition? It seems that there are two main types of arguments that can be advanced in support of pacifism. The first of these is broadly utilitarian in structure and claims that killing other human beings never results in the best possible world. In other words, the path of nonviolence always produces a better world (less suffering, more happiness) than does the path of violence, killing, and war.

Yet this surely must be false. We can easily imagine some situations in which killing a few (perhaps a few who are themselves quite evil) can save the lives of the many, who may in fact be quite good people. The passengers who overpowered the September 11th hijackers and crashed the plane in a corn field in Pennsylvania in all probability saved the lives of many citizens who would have died if the hijacked plane had also crashed into a major target.

Nevertheless, there may be a lot of truth in this position. It may well be the case that in many—perhaps most—situations, the path of violence, killing, and war produces more harm than good. All too often, violence and killing simply produce more of the same, and other ways of resolving differences may produce more overall good. However, it is an empirical matter—a tricky one, to be sure—to determine when this is the case.

The other way of justifying pacifism is deontological. It claims that there are certain rules that we are never entitled to violate, even if doing so would produce greater overall utility. For example, we are never entitled to kill an innocent homeless person so that the lives of several other individuals might be saved through organ transplants. Similarly, many pacifists—Gandhi, for example—simply maintain that the rule "do not kill" is fundamental and binding irrespective of circumstances.

Among those who do sometimes accept the possibility of killing and war as legitimate, the question is: When is it justified? Just war theory attempts to answer this question in regard to conflicts among nations.

The Just War Tradition

Medieval Christian theologians and philosophers (there often wasn't a clear division in those days) were quite concerned with the application of the concept of justice to conflicts. The most influential of these was Thomas Aquinas, whose account of just war set the stage for most subsequent discussions of this issue. Much more recently, Michael Walzer's *Just and Unjust Wars* (1977) has become the definitive work on this issue. These issues have been a matter of deep concern not just to political philosophers, but also the military and political leaders who must sometimes make decisions about whether to commit their nation to war or not. The premise on which this entire discussion rests is a simple one: war is a terrible, terrible evil, and there must be much in its favor before it becomes justified.

Aquinas and many others distinguish two distinct areas where the concept of justice can be applied to issues of war: **the just conditions for entering into a war** (called *Jus ad bellum,* "justice toward war"), including the question of just cause of war; and **the just conditions for conducting a war** (*Jus in bello,* "justice in war"). Less attention has been paid to yet a third area: **the conditions of a just peace** (*Jus post bellum,* "justice after war").[1] Let's look at each of these.

Jus ad bellum: When Is It Just to Enter Into a War?

Just war theorists from Aquinas to Walzer list a number of conditions that must be met if *entrance* into a war is to be considered just. Let's look briefly at each of these conditions.

Just Cause

The first of these is that there must be a *just cause,* and this usually means that you have been attacked. Typically, starting a war is never just. The underlying assumption here is that everyone has a right to self-defense and that countries that are attacked are entitled to defend themselves.

Two important questions have been raised about just cause. First, does a country actually have to allow itself to be attacked before it can defend itself? This is particularly an issue in the age of weapons of mass destruction, when the first attack could be massively destructive. To many, it seems unreasonable to prevent a country from defending itself against the immanent threat of attack and allowing an armed response only after a devastating attack. Yet the danger, in the eyes of many critics of preemptive attacks, is that once this door is open, much more is justified than is desirable. Many countries feel seriously threatened even when attack is not in fact immanent. If the notion of just cause includes permitting countries to launch pre-emptive attacks when they feel sufficiently threatened, then it would seem to justify too much.

The second question here is this: are we justified in entering a war to defend, not ourselves, but someone else? This is the issue of humanitarian intervention, and it is discussed in more detail later. It has been a crucial issue in the Balkans, Africa, and the Middle East.

Right Intention

Second, you must have the *right intention,* and in this context the right intention involves self-defense and the restoration of a just political order. This condition excludes such actions as going to war to expand your territories or influence; it does permit going to war to stop aggression. It is very important for a country to have a clear idea of what it is trying to accomplish by going to war. Is it simply to stop the aggression?

It is important to note that having the right intention plays an important role in determining when a war is over and what constitutes a legitimate peace.

Public Declaration by Lawful Authority

Third, the war must be *publicly declared by a lawful authority* such as a head of state. Part of the rationale for this requirement is to prevent segments of a country (such as the military) from committing the nation to conflict without an adequate decision-making process. It also prevents pursuing wars in secret without the consent of the whole nation.

Last Resort

Fourth, war must be *the last resort.* If it is possible to achieve your just ends of other means such as blockades or embargoes or diplomatic pressures, then it is unjust to resort to war. This condition presupposes, incidentally, that war is always the most horrific alternative, but some critics have argued that blockades and embargos often have at least as devastating an effect on the average citizen as warfare.

Probability of Success

Fifth, there must be some *probability of success* before you are justified in going to war. Here the rationale is simple: war is such an evil that it ought not to be undertaken if there is not some chance of bringing about a significant good.

Proportionality

Sixth and finally, there must be *proportionality* between the possible benefits of war and the amount of pain and suffering and death that the war will cause. A costly war fought for a small gain fails to meet this condition.

If all of these conditions are met, then entering into a war is just.

Jus in bello: **The Just Conduct of War**

Once a country has entered into a war justly, there still remain important moral considerations about how the war may be conducted. Despite the fact that war is considered horrible, there is nonetheless a recognition that some basic standards of human decency still apply to the ways in which we conduct ourselves during a war. Let's look at the conditions typically outlined as the conditions necessary for the just conduct of war. There are three such conditions.

Discrimination

First, we must always conduct war in such a way that we *discriminate between combatants and civilians.* This is one of the most basic rules for conducting a war properly. Civilians cannot be targeted for attack, nor can they be used as human shields to deter enemy attacks. Most just war theorists interpret this condition in such a way as to permit unavoidable collateral civilian casualties, although exactly where the line is to be drawn here becomes a contentious issue.

Consider an example. In attacking an enemy, there is the least chance of civilian casualties if the attack is conducted by ground soldiers. If low-level air attacks are used, the chances of civilian casualties increases but casualties to one's own forces go down. If high-level air power is used, the chances of civilian casualties become even greater and the safety of one's own forces increases significantly. The question that then arises is this: in the conduct of war, to what extent is a country justified in trading off increased civilian casualties for increased safety of its own military personnel?

When the dividing line between combatants and civilians is clearly marked by military uniforms, this condition is comparatively easy to implement. However, the last 50 years have been marked by numerous conflicts in which one side often was not in uniform—insurgents, guerrillas, and so forth. It then becomes difficult to distinguish between combatants and noncombatants, and guerrillas often depend on this as a form of concealment.

Second, there must be a *principle of proportionality* in the conduct of war. Countries should only use as much force as is necessary for the achievement of their just goals. This excludes massive attacks when the legitimate goals of the conflict are minor. Often, when this is ignored, we see local conflicts grow into much larger wars simply by their own momentum.

Third and finally, just wars must be conducted in a way that *uses no means that are evil in themselves.* In recent decades, there has been a consensus developing among most nations that biological warfare agents such as smallpox and anthrax are forbidden because they are means that are evil in themselves. In the Balkans, we saw rape used as a means of war, intended to destroy family and civic structures and thereby destroy the enemy, and such means clearly fall into the category of means that are evil in themselves: there are no circumstances in which their use is permissible. Many would include torture among those means that are evil in themselves.

These conditions of a just war have been shaped over the years to fit the traditional model of large nation states. In the late 20th and the beginning of the 21st century, we have seen situations arise that this doctrine of just war was not originally designed to cover. Let's briefly consider two of those here.

Humanitarian Interventions

It's clear that just war theory specifies the conditions under which a nation can respond to an attack. But what do powerful nations do when they see grave injustices, such as genocide, occurring in other countries? It seems to violate our basic sense of justice and decency simply to stand by and allow such things to happen, despite the fact that the attacks are not against our own nation. Typically, diplomatic and economic pressure are the first lines of offense here, but in some situations they have relatively little impact on the situation. Nonmilitary interventions may sometimes make a difference, but at least in some cases nothing short of military intervention offers the hope of protecting the innocent in such situations.

Are nations who are not directly attacked ever justified in intervening militarily for humanitarian reasons to prevent the loss of civilian lives? Does this count as a "just cause" for entering an armed conflict? The answer that has emerged in the West is an affirmative one: sometimes third-party military intervention for humanitarian intervention may be justified in order to save the lives of innocent people. Typically, this is done under the sanction of some multinational organization such as the UN or NATO, in part to prevent it from degenerating into some kind of nationalistic campaign. Within this context, all the conditions for just war will continue to apply.

Terrorist Threats

Traditionally, war has taken place between nation states. What happens when a nation is attacked by an entity that is not a state? Consider the Taliban attacks against the United States. No nation declared war against the United States, and many would say that if the United States were to declare war on the Taliban, this would in effect raise the Taliban's level of status to that of a nation state.

So, too, terrorists typically do not distinguish between military and civilian targets. Indeed, they often prefer to attack civilian targets. They are easier to attack with fewer casualties, and attacks against civilian targets can often bring terror to the entire population. One of the principal objections to terrorism, from the standpoint of just war theory, is that it often ignores the crucial distinction between combatants and civilians. Not only does it target civilians, but terrorists themselves often hide out among civilian populations and, because they do not fight in uniform, the line between civilians and terrorists is further blurred.

Jus post bellum: A Just Peace

Although typically the discussion of justice and war has been limited to jus ad bellum and jus in bellum, the classical sources also contain a discussion of a third type of justice: justice in peace. According to Brian Orend, whose work has done much to highlight the notion of a just peace, there are five conditions for a just peace: just cause for termination; right intention; public declaration and legitimate authority; discrimination; and proportionality. A just cause for peace exists when the rights that were originally violated are now restored. The right intention excludes motives of revenge against the defeated and both victors and vanquished must be subjected to the same laws. This precludes, for example, holding the defeated accountable for war crimes but not doing the same thing for yourself and your allies. Whatever punishment is exacted must discriminate appropriately between general citizens and military personnel and, within the military, between those responsible for prosecuting the war and those not in leadership positions. Finally, a just peace is marked by proportionality, where punishments exacted are proportional to the severity of the offense.

One of the most intriguing aspects of the notion of a just peace is that it can guide the conduct of a war. Faced with difficult decisions, national leaders can ask themselves which alternative will increase the possibility of just peace at the end of the conflict. In the American Civil War, we saw the way in which certain actions, such as Sherman's march through South Carolina, left a bitter legacy that endangered the prospects of a just peace. On the other hand, the leadership that Abraham Lincoln showed, including his generous terms of surrender, promoted the possibility of a just peace. Wise leaders are able to conduct war in a way that maximizes the possibility of creating a just and lasting peace. Similarly, Allied policies toward Germany after World War II were consciously and effectively designed to produce a just peace, to promote healing rather than retribution.

Retribution and Reconciliation

Achieving a balance between retribution and reconciliation is no easy matter. Too much retribution can often lead to an unending cycle of violence. Too little retribution, in the name of reconciliation, seems to let evil go unpunished and to devalue the suffering and death of those who were persecuted. Truth and reconciliation hearings in South Africa and several Latin American countries have attempted to create precisely this delicate balance between justice (in naming the guilty and detailing the crimes publicly) and reconciliation (by not punishing those who come forward to acknowledge their crimes).

Treatment of Prisoners

Oddly, the treatment of prisoners is a topic largely neglected by traditional just war theory, presumably because it presupposed that those who surrendered had already forfeited their life and thus had few if any rights. However, the Geneva Convention has clearly articulated the rights of prisoners of war and, even when its standards have not been observed, it has been influential in setting the standard to which civilized nations should aspire.

Considerations about treatment of prisoners, if they were incorporated into the just war tradition, would seem relevant in two places. First, as part of the *jus in bello* considerations, the just treatment of prisoners would seem to be integral to the just conduct of war. One of the principal reasons for this is simply enlightened self-interest: If we want our captured military personnel to be treated humanely, then we will do well to treat those prisoners we hold with respect as well. Prisoners are in a particularly vulnerable position, easily subject to abuse against which they usually cannot defend themselves.

Considerations of *jus post bellum* are also relevant here, and we see this particularly in regard to the pictures that emerged from the American mistreatment of Iraqi prisoners of war. Mistreatment of prisoners creates bitterness and hatred, and these in turn make a lasting peace more difficult.

Endnote

1. Throughout this introduction, I am indebted to Brian Orend's excellent overview of just war theory in the Stanford Encyclopedia of Philosophy (http://plato.stanford.edu/entries/war/), especially his discussion of a just peace.

The Arguments

Michael Walzer
"The Argument about Humanitarian Intervention"

Michael Walzer is a political philosopher at the Institute for Advanced Studies, Princeton. He specializes in issues of war, peace, and justice. His books include Just and Unjust Wars, On Toleration, *and* Spheres of Justice.

In this article, Walzer examines some of the difficult ethical and political arguments about humanitarian intervention.

As You Read, Consider This:

1. According to Walzer, what are the legitimate occasions when humanitarian intervention is justified?
2. Who should be the preferred agents of humanitarian intervention?
3. How should agents act in intervening from humanitarian motives?
4. When should humanitarian intervention end?

There is nothing new about human disasters caused by human beings. We have always been, if not our own, certainly each other's worst enemies. From the Assyrians in ancient Israel and the Romans in Carthage to the Belgians in the Congo and the Turks in Armenia, history is a bloody and barbaric tale. Still, in this regard, the twentieth century was an age of innovation, first—and most important—in the way disasters were planned and organized and then, more recently, in the way they were publicized. I want to begin with the second of these innovations—the product of an extraordinary speedup in both travel and communication. It may be possible to kill people on a very large scale more efficiently than ever before, but it is much harder to kill them in secret. In the contemporary world there is very little that happens far away, out of sight, or behind the scenes; the camera crews arrive faster than rigor mortis. We are instant spectators of every atrocity; we sit in our living rooms and see the murdered children, the desperate refugees. Perhaps horrific crimes are still committed in dark places, but not many; contemporary horrors are well-lit. And so a question is posed that has never been posed before—at least never with such immediacy, never so inescapably: What is our responsibility? What should we do?

Dissent, Vol. 49, No. 1 (Winter 2002). A slightly different version of this article was given as the Theodore Mitan Lecture at Macalester College, St. Paul, Minnesota.

In the old days, "humanitarian intervention" was a lawyer's doctrine, a way of justifying a very limited set of exceptions to the principles of national sovereignty and territorial integrity. It is a good doctrine, because exceptions are always necessary, principles are never absolute. But we need to rethink it today, as the exceptions become less and less exceptional. The "acts that shock the conscience of humankind"—and, according to the nineteenth-century law books, justify humanitarian intervention—are probably no more frequent these days than they were in the past, but they are more shocking, because we are more intimately engaged by them and with them. Cases multiply in the world and in the media: Somalia, Bosnia, Rwanda, East Timor, Liberia, Sierra Leone, and Kosovo in only the past decade. The last of these has dominated recent political debates, but it isn't the most illuminating case. I want to step back a bit, reach for a wider range of examples, and try to answer four questions about humanitarian intervention: First, what are its occasions? Second, who are its preferred agents? Third, how should the agents act to meet the occasions? And fourth, when is it time to end the intervention?

Occasions

The occasions have to be extreme if they are to justify, perhaps even require, the use of force across an international boundary. Every violation of human rights isn't a justification. The common brutalities of authoritarian politics, the daily oppressiveness of traditional social practices—these are not occasions for intervention; they have to be dealt with locally, by the people who know the politics, who enact or resist the practices. The fact that these people can't easily or quickly reduce the incidence of brutality and oppression isn't a sufficient reason for foreigners to invade their country. Foreign politicians and soldiers are too likely to misread the situation, or to underestimate the force required to change it, or to stimulate a "patriotic" reaction in defense of the brutal politics and the oppressive practices. Social change is best achieved from within.

I want to insist on this point; I don't mean to describe a continuum that begins with common nastiness and ends with genocide, but rather a radical break, a chasm, with nastiness on one side and genocide on the other. We should not allow ourselves to approach genocide by degrees. Still, on this side of the chasm, we can mark out a continuum of brutality and oppression, and somewhere along this continuum an international response (short of military force) is necessary. Diplomatic pressure and economic sanctions, for example, are useful means of engagement with tyrannical regimes. The sanctions might be imposed by some free-form coalition of interested states. Or perhaps we should work toward a more established regional or global authority that could regulate the imposition, carefully matching the severity of the sanctions to the severity of the oppression. But these are still external acts; they are efforts to prompt but not to preempt an internal response. They still assume the value, and hold open the possibility, of domestic politics. The interested states or the regional or global authorities bring pressure to bear, so to speak, at the border; and then they wait for something to happen on the other side.

But when what is going on is the "ethnic cleansing" of a province or country or the systematic massacre of a religious or national community, it doesn't seem possible to wait for a local response. Now we are on the other side of the chasm. The stakes are too high, the suffering already too great. Perhaps there is no capacity to respond among the people directly at risk and no will to respond among their fellow citizens. The victims are weak and vulnerable; their enemies are cruel; their neighbors indifferent. The rest of us watch and are shocked. This is the occasion for intervention.

We will need to argue, of course, about each case, but the list I've already provided seems a fairly obvious one. These days the intervening army will claim to be enforcing human rights, and that was a plausible and fully comprehensible claim in each of the cases on my list (or would have been, since interventions weren't attempted in all of them). We are best served, I think, by a stark and minimalist version of human rights here: it is life and liberty that are at stake. With regard to these two, the language of rights is readily available and sufficiently understood across the globe. Still, we could as easily say that what is being enforced, and what should be enforced, is simple decency.

In practice, even with a minimalist understanding of human rights, even with a commitment to nothing more than decency, there are more occasions for intervention than there are actual interventions. When the oppressors are too powerful, they are rarely challenged, however shocking the oppression. This obvious truth about international society is often used as an argument against the interventions that do take place. It is hypocritical, critics say to the "humanitarian" politicians or soldiers, to intervene in this case when you didn't intervene in that one—as if, having declined to challenge China in Tibet, say, the United Nations should have stayed out of East Timor for the sake of moral consistency. But consistency isn't an issue here. We can't meet all our occasions; we rightly calculate the risks in each one. We need to ask what the costs of intervention will be for the people being rescued, for the rescuers, and for everyone else. And then, we can only do what we can do.

The standard cases have a standard form: a government, an army, a police force, tyrannically controlled, attacks its own people or some subset of its own people, a vulnerable minority, say, territorially based or dispersed throughout the country. (We might think of these attacks as examples of state terrorism and then consider forceful humanitarian responses, such as the NATO campaign in Kosovo, as instances of the "war against terrorism," avant la lettre. But I won't pursue this line of argument here.) The attack takes place within the country's borders; it doesn't require any boundary crossings; it is an exercise of sovereign power. There is no aggression, no invading army to resist and beat back. Instead, the rescuing forces are the invaders; they are the ones who, in the strict sense of international law, begin the war. But they come into a situation where the moral stakes are clear: the oppressors or, better, the state agents of oppression are readily identifiable; their victims are plain to see.

Even in the list with which I started, however, there are some nonstandard cases—Sierra Leone is the clearest example—where the state apparatus isn't the villain, where what we might think of as the administration of brutality is decentralized, anarchic, almost random. It isn't the power of the oppressors that interventionists have to worry about, but the amorphousness of the oppression. I won't have much to say about cases like this. Intervention is clearly justifiable but, right now at least, it's radically unclear how it should be undertaken. Perhaps there is not much to do beyond what the Nigerians did in Sierra Leone: they reduced the number of killings, the scope of the barbarism.

Agents

"We can only do what we can do." Who is this "we"? The Kosovo debate focused on the United States, NATO, and the UN as agents of military intervention. These are indeed three political collectives capable of agency, but by no means the only three. The United States and NATO generate suspicion among the sorts of people who are called "idealists" because of their readiness to act unilaterally and their presumed imperial ambitions; the UN generates skepticism among the sorts of people who are called "realists" because of its political weakness and military ineffectiveness. The arguments here are overdetermined; I am not going to join them. We are more likely to understand the problem of agency if we start with other agents. The most successful interventions in the last thirty years have been acts of war by neighboring states: Vietnam in Cambodia, India in East Pakistan (now Bangladesh), Tanzania in Uganda. These are useful examples for testing our ideas about intervention because they don't involve extraneous issues such as the new (or old) world order; they don't require us to consult Lenin's, or anyone else's, theory of imperialism. In each of these cases, there were horrifying acts that should have been stopped and agents who succeeded, more or less, in stopping them. So let's use these cases to address the two questions most commonly posed by critics of the Kosovo war: Does it matter that the agents acted alone? Does it matter that their motives were not wholly (or even chiefly) altruistic?

In the history of humanitarian intervention, unilateralism is far more common than its opposite. One reason for this is obvious: the great reluctance of most states to cede the direction of their armed forces to an organization they don't control. But unilateralism may also follow from the need for an immediate response to "acts that shock." Imagine a case where the shock doesn't have anything to do with human evildoing: a fire in a neighbor's house in a new town where there is no fire department. It wouldn't make much sense to call a meeting of the block association, while the house is burning, and vote on whether or not to help (and it would make even less sense to give a veto on helping to the three richest families on the block). I don't think that the case would be all that different if, instead of a fire, there was a brutal husband, no police department, and screams for help in the night. Here too, the block association is of little use; neighborly unilateralism seems entirely justified. In cases like these, anyone who can help should help. And that sounds like a plausible maxim for humanitarian intervention also: who can, should.

But now let's imagine a block association or an international organization that planned in advance for the fire, or the scream in the night, or the mass murder. Then there would be particular people or specially recruited military forces delegated to act in a crisis, and the definition of "crisis" could be determined—as best it can be—in advance, in exactly the kind of meeting that seems so implausible, so morally inappropriate, at the moment when immediate action is necessary. The person who rushes into a neighbor's house in my domestic example and the political or military commanders of the invading forces in the international cases would still have to act on their own understanding of the events unfolding in front of them and on their own interpretation of the responsibility they have been given. But now they act under specified constraints, and they can call on the help of those in whose name they are acting. This is the form that multilateral intervention is most likely to take, if the UN, say, were ever to authorize it in advance of a particular crisis. It seems preferable to the different unilateral alternatives, because it involves some kind of prior warning, an agreed-upon description of the occasions for intervention, and the prospect of overwhelming force.

But is it preferable in fact, right now, given the UN as it actually is? What makes police forces effective in domestic society, when they are effective, is their commitment to the entire body of citizens from which they are drawn and the (relative) trust of the citizens in that commitment. But the UN's General Assembly and Security Council, so far, give very little evidence of being so committed, and there can't be many people in the world today who would willingly entrust their lives to UN police. So if, in any of my examples, the UN's authorized agents or their domestic equivalents decide not to intervene, and the fire is still burning, the screams can still be heard, the murders go on—then unilateralist rights and obligations are instantly restored. Collective decisions to act may well exclude unilateral action, but collective decisions not to act don't have the same effect. In this sense, unilateralism is the dominant response when the common conscience is shocked. If there is no collective response, anyone can respond. If no one is acting, act.

In the Cambodia, East Pakistan, and Uganda cases, there were no prior arrangements and no authorized agents. Had the UN's Security Council or General Assembly been called into session, it would almost certainly have decided against intervention, probably by majority vote, in any case because of great-power opposition. So, anyone acting to shut down the Khmer Rouge killing fields or to stem the tide of Bengalese refugees or to stop Idi Amin's butchery would have to act unilaterally. Everything depended on the political decision of a single state.

Do these singular agents have a right to act or do they have an obligation? I have been using both words, but they don't always go together: there can be rights where there are no obligations. In "good Samaritan" cases in domestic society, we commonly say that passersby are bound to respond (to the injured stranger by the side of the road, to the cry of a child drowning in the lake); they are not, however, bound to risk their lives. If the risks are clear, they have a right to respond; responding is certainly a good thing and possibly the right thing to do; still, they are not morally bound to do it. But military interventions across international boundaries always impose risks on the intervening forces. So perhaps there is no obligation here either; perhaps there is a right to intervene but also a right to refuse the risks, to maintain a kind of neutrality—even between murderers and their victims. Or perhaps humanitarian intervention is an example of what philosophers call an "imperfect" duty: someone should stop the awfulness, but it isn't possible to give that someone a proper name, to point a finger, say, at a particular country. The problem of imperfect duty yields best to multilateral solutions; we simply assign responsibility in advance through some commonly accepted decision procedure.

But perhaps, again, these descriptions are too weak: I am inclined to say that intervention is more than a right and more than an imperfect duty. After all, the survival of the intervening state is not at risk. And then why shouldn't the obligation simply fall on the most capable state, the nearest or the strongest, as in the maxim I have already suggested: Who can, should? Nonintervention in the face of mass murder or ethnic cleansing is not the same as neutrality in time of war. The moral urgencies are different; we are usually unsure of the consequences of a war, but we know very well the consequences of a massacre. Still, if we follow the logic of the argument so far, it will be necessary to recruit volunteers for humanitarian interventions; the "who" who can and should is only the state, not any particular man or woman; for individuals the duty remains imperfect. Deciding whether to volunteer, they may choose to apply the same test to themselves—who can, should—but the choice is theirs.

The dominance that I have ascribed to unilateralism might be questioned—commonly is questioned—because of a fear of the motives of single states acting alone. Won't they act in their own interests rather than in the interests of humanity? Yes, they probably will or, better, they will act in their own interests as well as in the interests of humanity; I don't think that it is particularly insightful, merely cynical, to suggest that those larger interests have no hold at all (surely the balance of interest and morality among interventionists is no different than it is among noninterventionists). In any case, how would humanity be better served by multilateral decision-making? Wouldn't each state involved in the decision process also act in its own interests? And then the outcome would be determined by bargaining among the interested parties—and humanity, obviously, would not be one of the parties. We might hope that particular interests would cancel each other out, leaving some kind of general interest (this is in fact Rousseau's account, or one of his accounts, of how citizens arrive at a "general will"). But it is equally possible that the bargain will reflect only a mix of particular interests, which may or may not be better for humanity than the interests of a single party. Anyway, political motivations are always mixed, whether the actors are one or many. A pure moral will doesn't exist in political life, and it shouldn't be necessary to pretend to that kind of purity. The leaders of states have a right, indeed, they have an obligation, to consider the interests of their own people, even when they are acting to help other people. We should assume, then, that the Indians acted in their national interest when they assisted the secession of East Pakistan, and that Tanzania acted in its own interests when it moved troops into Idi Amin's Uganda. But these interventions also served human-itarian purposes, and presumably were intended to do that too. The victims of massacre or "ethnic cleansing" disasters are very lucky if a neighboring state, or a coalition of states, has more than one reason to rescue them. It would be foolish to declare the multiplicity morally disabling. If the inter-vention is expanded beyond its necessary bounds because of some "ulterior" motive, then it should be criticized; within those bounds, mixed motives are a practical advantage.

Means

When the agents act, how should they act? Humanitarian intervention involves the use of force, and it is crucial to its success that it be pursued forcefully; the aim is the defeat of the people, whoever they are, who are carrying out the massacres or the ethnic cleansing. If what is going on is awful enough to justify going in, then it is awful enough to justify the pursuit of military victory. But this simple proposition hasn't found ready acceptance in international society. Most clearly in the Bosn-ian case, repeated efforts were made to deal with the disaster without fighting against its perpetra-tors. Force was taken, indeed, to be a "last" resort, but in an ongoing political conflict "lastness" never arrives; there is always something to be done before doing whatever it is that comes last. So military observers were sent into Bosnia to report on what was happening; and then UN forces brought hu-manitarian relief to the victims, and then they provided some degree of military protection for re-lief workers, and then they sought (unsuccessfully) to create a few "safe zones" for the Bosnians. But if soldiers do nothing more than these things, they are hardly an impediment to further killing; they may even be said to provide a kind of background support for it. They guard roads, defend doctors and nurses, deliver medical supplies and food to a growing number of victims and refugees—and the number keeps growing. Sometimes it is helpful to interpose soldiers as "peacekeepers" between the killers and their victims. But though that may work for a time, it doesn't reduce the power of the killers, and so it is a formula for trouble later on. Peacekeeping is an honorable activity, but not if there is no peace. Sometimes, unhappily, it is better to make war.

In Cambodia, East Pakistan, and Uganda, the interventions were carried out on the ground; this was old-fashioned war-making. The Kosovo war provides an alternative model: a war fought from the air, with technologies designed to reduce (almost to zero!) the risk of casualties to the intervening army. I won't stop here to consider at any length the reasons for the alternative model, which have to do with the increasing inability of modern democracies to use the armies they recruit in ways that put soldiers at risk. There are no "lower orders," no invisible, expendable citizens in democratic states today. And in the absence of a clear threat to the community itself, there is little willingness even among political elites to sacrifice for the sake of global law and order or, more particularly, for the sake of Rwandans or Kosovars. But the inability and the unwillingness, whatever their sources, make for moral problems. A war fought entirely from the air, and from far away, probably can't be won without attacking civilian targets. These can be bridges and television stations, electric generators and water purification plants, rather than residential areas, but the attacks will endanger the lives of innocent men, women, and children nonetheless. The aim is to bring pressure to bear on a government acting barbarically toward a minority of its citizens by threatening to harm, or actually harming, the majority to which, presumably, the government is still committed. Obviously this isn't a strategy that would have worked against the Khmer Rouge in Cambodia, but it's probably not legitimate even where it might work—so long as there is the possibility of a more precise intervention against the forces actually engaged in the barbarous acts. The same rules apply here as in war generally: non-combatants are immune from direct attack and have to be protected as far as possible from "collateral damage"; soldiers have to accept risks to themselves in order to avoid imposing risks on the civilian population.

Any country considering military intervention would obviously embrace technologies that were said to be risk-free for its own soldiers, and the embrace would be entirely justified so long as the same technologies were also risk-free for civilians on the other side. This is precisely the claim made on behalf of "smart bombs": they can be delivered from great distances (safely), and they never miss. But the claim is, for the moment at least, greatly exaggerated. There is no technological fix currently available, and therefore no way of avoiding this simple truth: from the standpoint of justice, you cannot invade a foreign country, with all the consequences that has for other people, while insisting that your own soldiers can never be put at risk. Once the intervention has begun, it may become morally, even if it is not yet militarily, necessary to fight on the ground—in order to win more quickly and save many lives, for example, or to stop some particularly barbarous response to the intervention.

That's the moral argument against no-risk interventions, but there is also a prudential argument. Interventions will rarely be successful unless there is a visible willingness to fight and to take casualties. In the Kosovo case, if a NATO army had been in sight, so to speak, before the bombing of Serbia began, it is unlikely that the bombing would have been necessary; nor would there ever have been the tide of desperate and embittered refugees. Postwar Kosovo would look very different; the tasks of policing and reconstruction would be easier than they have been; the odds on success much better.

Endings

Imagine the intervening army fully engaged. How should it understand the victory that it is aiming at? When is it time to go home? Should the army aim only at stopping the killings, or at destroying the military or paramilitary forces carrying them out, or at replacing the regime that employs these forces, or at punishing the leaders of the regime? Is intervention only a war or also an occupation? These are hard questions and I want to begin my own response by acknowledging that I have answered them differently at different times.

The answer that best fits the original legal doctrine of humanitarian intervention, and that I defended in *Just and Unjust Wars* (1977), is that the aim of the intervening army is simply to stop the killing. Its leaders prove that their motives are primarily humanitarian, that they are not driven by imperial ambition, by moving in as quickly as possible to defeat the killers and rescue their victims and then by leaving as quickly as possible. Sorting things out afterward, dealing with the consequences of the awfulness, deciding what to do with its agents—that is not properly the work of foreigners. The people who have always lived there, wherever "there" is, have to be given a chance to reconstruct their common life. The crisis that they have just been through should not become an occasion for foreign domination. The principles of political sovereignty and territorial integrity require the "in and quickly out" rule.

But there are three sorts of occasions when this rule seems impossible to apply. The first is perhaps best exemplified by the Cambodian killing fields, which were so extensive as to leave, at the end, no institutional base, and perhaps no human base, for reconstruction. I don't say this to justify the Vietnamese establishment of a satellite regime, but rather to explain the need, years later, for the UN's effort to create, from the outside, a locally legitimate political system. The UN couldn't or wouldn't stop the killing when it was actually taking place, but had it done so, the "in and quickly out" test would not have provided a plausible measure of its success; it would have had to deal, somehow, with the aftermath of the killing.

The second occasion is exemplified by all those countries—Uganda, Rwanda, Kosovo, and others—where the extent and depth of the ethnic divisions make it likely that the killings will resume as soon as the intervening forces withdraw. If the original killers don't return to their work, then the revenge of their victims will prove equally deadly. Now "in and quickly out" is a kind of bad faith, a choice of legal virtue at the expense of political and moral effectiveness. If one accepts the risks of intervention in countries like these, one had better accept also the risks of occupation.

The third occasion is the one I called nonstandard earlier on: where the state has simply disintegrated. It's not that its army or police have been defeated; they simply don't exist. The country is in the hand of paramilitary forces and warlords—gangs, really—who have been, let's say, temporarily subdued. What is necessary now is to create a state, and the creation will have to be virtually ex nihilo. And that is not work for the short term.

In 1995, in an article called "The Politics of Rescue," published in these pages, I argued that leftist critics of protectorates and trusteeships needed to rethink their position, for arrangements of this sort might sometimes be the best outcome of a humanitarian intervention. The historical record makes it clear enough that protectors and trustees, under the old League of Nations, for example, again and again failed to fulfill their obligations; nor have these arrangements been as temporary as they were supposed to be. Still, their purpose can sometimes be a legitimate one: to open a span of time and to authorize a kind of political work between the "in" and the "out" of a humanitarian intervention. This purpose doesn't cancel the requirement that the intervening forces get out. We need to think about better ways of making sure that the purpose is actually realized and the requirement finally met. Perhaps this is a place where multilateralism can play a more central role than it does, or has done, in the original interventions. For multilateral occupations are unlikely to serve the interests of any single state and so are unlikely to be sustained any longer than necessary. The greater danger is that they won't be sustained long enough: each participating state will look for an excuse to pull its own forces out. An independent UN force, not bound or hindered by the political decisions of individual states, might be the most reliable protector and trustee—if we could be sure that it would protect the right people, in a timely way. Whenever that assurance doesn't exist, unilateralism returns, again, as a justifiable option.

Either way, we still need an equivalent of the "in and out" rule, a way of recognizing when these longstanding interventions reach their endpoint. The appropriate rule is best expressed by a phrase that I have already used: "local legitimacy." The intervening forces should aim at finding or establishing a form of authority that fits or at least accommodates the local political culture, and a set of authorities, independent of themselves, who are capable of governing the country and who command sufficient popular support so that their government won't be massively coercive. Once such authorities are in place, the intervening forces should withdraw: "in and finally out."

But this formula may be as quixotic as "in and quickly out." Perhaps foreign forces can't do the work that I've just described; they will only be dragged deeper and deeper into a conflict they will never be able to control, gradually becoming indistinguishable from the other parties. That prospect is surely a great disincentive to intervention; it will often override not only the benign intentions but even the imperial ambitions of potential interveners. In fact, most of the countries whose inhabitants (or some of them) desperately need to be rescued offer precious little political or economic reward to the states that attempt the rescue. One almost wishes that the impure motivations of such states had more plausible objects, the pursuit of which might hold them to their task. At the same time, however, it's important to insist that the task is limited: once the massacres and ethnic cleansing are really over and the people in command are committed to avoiding their return, the intervention is finished. The new regime doesn't have to be democratic or liberal or pluralist or (even) capitalist. It doesn't have to be anything, except non-murderous. When intervention is understood in this minimalist fashion, it may be a little easier to see it through. As in the argument about occasions, minimalism in endings suggests that we should be careful in our use of human rights language. For if we pursue the legal logic of rights (at least as that logic is understood in the United States), it will be very difficult for the intervening forces to get out before they have brought the people who organized the massacres or the ethnic cleansing to trial and established a new regime committed to enforcing the full set of human rights. If those goals are actually within reach, then, of course, it is right to reach for them. But intervention is a political and military process, not a legal one, and it is subject to the compromises and tactical shifts that politics and war require. So we will often need to accept more minimal goals, in order to minimize the use of force and the time span over which it is used. I want to stress, however, that we need, and haven't yet come close to, a clear understanding of what "minimum" really means. The intervening forces have to be prepared to use the weapons they carry, and they have to be prepared to stay what may be a long course. The international community needs to find ways of supporting these forces—and also, since what they are doing is dangerous and won't always be done well, of supervising, regulating, and criticizing them.

Conclusion

I have tried to answer possible objections to my argument as I went along, but there are a couple of common criticisms of the contemporary practice of humanitarian intervention that I want to single out and address more explicitly, even at the cost of repeating myself. A few repetitions, on key points, will make my conclusion. I am going to take Edward Luttwak's critical review of Michael Ignatieff's *Virtual War*[1] as a useful summary of the arguments to which I need to respond, since it is short, sharp, cogent, and typical. Ignatieff offers a stronger human rights justification of humanitarian warfare than I have provided, though he would certainly agree that not every rights violation "shocks the conscience of humankind" and justifies military intervention. In any case, Luttwak's objections apply (or fail to apply) across the board—that is, to the arguments I've made here as well as to Ignatieff's book.

First objection: the "prescription that X should fight Y whenever Y egregiously violates X's moral and juridical norms would legitimize eternal war." This claim seems somewhat inconsistent with Luttwak's further claim (see below) that the necessity of fighting not only forever but everywhere follows from the fact that there are so many violations of commonly recognized norms. But leave that aside for now. If we intervene only in extremity, only in order to stop mass murder and mass deportation, the idea that we are defending X's norms and not Y's is simply wrong. Possessive nouns don't modify morality in such cases, and there isn't a series of different moralities—the proof of this is the standard and singular lie told by all the killers and "cleansers": they deny what they are doing; they don't try to justify it by reference to a set of private norms.

Second objection: "Even without civil wars, massacres, or mutilations, the perfectly normal, everyday, functioning of armies, police forces, and bureaucracies entails constant extortion, frequent robbery and rape, and pervasive oppression"—all of which, Luttwak claims, is ignored by the humanitarian interveners. So it is, and should be, or else we would indeed be fighting all the time and everywhere. But note that Luttwak assumes now that the wrongness of the extortion, robbery, rape, and oppression is not a matter of X's or Y's private norms but can be recognized by anyone. Maybe he goes too far here, because bureaucratic extortion, at least, has different meaning and valence in different times and places. But the main actions on his list are indeed awful, and commonly known to be awful; they just aren't awful enough to justify a military invasion. I don't think the point is all that difficult, even if we disagree about exactly where the line should be drawn. Pol Pot's killing fields had to be shut down—and by a foreign army if necessary. The prisons of all the more ordinary dictators in the modern world should also be shut down-emptied and closed. But that is properly the work of their own subjects.

Third objection: "What does it mean," Luttwak asks, "for the morality of a supposedly moral rule when it is applied arbitrarily, against some but not others?" The answer to this question depends on what the word "arbitrarily" means here. Consider a domestic example. The police can't stop every speeding car. If they go after only the ones they think they will be able to catch without endangering themselves or anyone else, their arrests will be "determined by choice or discretion," which is one of the meanings of "arbitrary," but surely that determination doesn't undermine the justice of enforcing the speeding laws. On the other hand, if they only go after cars that have bumper stickers they don't like, if they treat traffic control as nothing more than an opportunity to harass political "enemies," then their actions "arise from will or caprice," another definition of "arbitrary," and are indeed unjust. It's the first kind of "arbitrariness" that ought to qualify humanitarian interventions (and often does). They are indeed discretionary, and we have to hope that prudential calculations shape the decision to intervene or not. Hence, as I have already acknowledged, there won't be an actual intervention every time the justifying conditions for it exist. But, to answer Luttwak's question, that acknowledgment doesn't do anything to the morality of the justifying rule. It's not immoral to act, or decline to act, for prudential reasons.

These three objections relate to the occasions for intervention, and rightly so. If no coherent account of the occasions is possible, then it isn't necessary to answer the other questions that I have addressed. My own answers to those other questions can certainly be contested. But the main point that I want to make is that the questions themselves cannot be avoided. Since there are in fact legitimate occasions for humanitarian intervention, since we know, roughly, what ought to be done, we have to argue about how to do it; we have to argue about agents, means, and endings. There are a lot of people around today who want to avoid these arguments and postpone indefinitely the kinds of action they might require. These people have all sorts of reasons, but none of them, it seems to me, are good or moral reasons.

References

1.   "No Score War," *Times Literary Supplement* (July 14, 2000), p. 11.

Journal/Discussion Questions

1.   Walzer speaks of a "chasm." What does he mean? Explain.

2.   How does the framework Walzer provides here apply to the U.S. invasion of Iraq? Discuss.

3.   What, according to Walzer, is the moral argument against no-risk interventions? Do you agree with his analysis? Explain.

Martin L. Cook
"Ethical Issues in Counterterrorism Warfare"

Martin Cook is a Professor of Philosophy at the United States Air Force Academy and, prior to that, was Elihu Root Professor of Military Studies and Professor of Ethics at the U.S. Army War College.
   Cook examines emerging ethical issues relating to the changing nature of contemporary warfare and the rise of terrorism in the aftermath of the September 11th attacks.

As You Read, Consider This:

1.   Cook draws a distinction between *jus ad bellum* and *jus in bello.* Explain his distinction.

2.   What constraints does the standard of just cause impose on us in regard to responding to the events of September 11, 2001?

3.   What, according to Cook, is the "reasonable person" standard of proof? How does this apply to September 11th?

4.   According to Cook, why does terrorism raise special difficulties in regard to the distinction between combatants and civilians?

Introduction

Much has been said and written about the changed nature of "warfare" as it pertains to responding to the attacks on the Pentagon and the World Trade Center. The fact that attacks of such vast scale were made directly on U.S. soil by non-state actors poses important new questions for military leaders and planners charged with conceiving an appropriate and effective response.

The established moral and legal traditions of just war are similarly challenged. Forged almost entirely in the context of interstate war, those traditions are also pressed to adapt to the new and unforeseen character of a "war against terrorism." This article is an effort to extrapolate and apply existing fundamental moral principles of just war theory to this novel military and political terrain.

Fundamental Moral Principles

The theoretical framework of the just war tradition provides two separate moral assessments of uses of military force. The first, *jus ad bellum* (right or justice *toward* war) attempts to determine which sets of political and military circumstances are sufficiently grave to warrant a military response. It focuses on the "just cause" element of war and attempts to determine whether use of force to redress a given wrong has a reasonable hope of success and whether non-violent alternatives have been attempted (the "last resort" criterion) to redress the grievance. Given the horrendous loss of innocent American (and other) life in these recent attacks, it is without serious question that a just cause exists to use military force in response to those attacks. However, legitimate questions remain regarding reasonable hope of success given the difficult and diffuse nature of the perpetrators of these events. Indeed, the very definition of success in conflict of this sort is to some degree ambiguous.

The second body of assessments concerns *jus in bello*, right conduct of military operations. The central ideas here concern *discrimination* (using force against those who are morally and legally responsible for the attack and not deliberately against others) and *proportionality* (a reasonable balance between the damage done in the responding attack and the military value of the targets destroyed).

These fundamental moral principles continue to have force, even in the quite different "war" in which we are now engaged.

Jus ad bellum Considerations

The scale and nature of the terrorist attacks on the United States without question warrant a military response. The important questions about *jus ad bellum* are confined to the other questions the just war tradition requires us to ask regarding the ability to respond to those attacks with military force that will, in fact, respond to the attackers themselves and be effective in responding to the wrong received.

Just cause requires that we identify with accuracy those responsible and hold them to be the sole objects of legitimate attack. Who are those agents? In the first instance, those directly responsible for funding and directing the activities of the now-deceased hijackers. There is a tremendous intelligence demand to identify those agents correctly. But, having identified them to a moral certainty (a standard far short of what would be required by legal criteria of proof, it should be noted), there is no moral objection to targeting them. Indeed, one of the benefits of framing these operations as "war" rather than "law enforcement" is that it does not require the ideal outcome to be the apprehension and trial of the perpetrators. Instead, it countenances their direct elimination by military means if possible.

What of the claim that we may legitimately attack those who harbor terrorists, even if they are not directly involved in authorizing their activities? The justification for attacking them has two aspects: first, it holds them accountable for activities that they knew, or should have known, were being conducted in their territories and did nothing to stop; second, it serves as a deterrent to motivate other states and sponsors to be more vigilant and aware of the activities of such groups on their soil.

How far ought the moral permission to attack parties not directly involved extend? I would propose application of a standard from American civil law: the "reasonable person" (or "reasonable man") standard of proof. This standard asks not what an individual knew, as a matter of fact, about a given situation or set of facts. Instead, it asks what a reasonable and prudent person in a similar situation should know. Thus, even if a person or government truthfully asserts that they were unaware of the activities of a terrorist cell in their territory, this does not provide moral immunity from attack. This standard asks not what they *did* know, but what they *ought to have known* had they exercised the diligence and degree of inquiry a reasonable person/nation in their circumstance would have exercised.

Also, legitimate targets include more than those who have carried out or are actively engaged in preparing to carry out attacks against U.S. citizens and forces. There will presumably be numerous individuals who, in various ways, assisted or harbored attackers, or who possessed knowledge of planned attacks. From a moral perspective, the circle of legitimate targets surely includes at least these individuals. A rough analog for the principle here is the civil law standard for criminal conspiracy: all those within the circle of the conspiracy are legitimate targets. The analogy is not perfect, but in general it justifies attacks on those who possessed information about the contemplated terrorist activity or who supplied weapons, training, funding, or safe harbor to the actors, even if they did not possess full knowledge of their intent.

Jus in bello Considerations

How do ethical considerations constrain the manner of attack against legitimate adversaries? The traditional requirements of just war continue to have application in this kind of war. Attacks must be *discriminate* and they must be *proportionate*. Discrimination requires that attacks be made on persons and military objects in ways that permit successful attack on them with a minimum of damage to innocent persons and objects. In practical terms, this requires as much precision as possible in determination of the location and nature of targets. Further, it requires choice of weapons and tactics that are most likely to hit the object of the attack accurately with a minimum of damage to surrounding areas and personnel.

Proportionality imposes an essentially common-sense requirement that the damage done in the attack is in some reasonable relation to the value and nature of the target. To use a simple example: if the target is a small cell of individuals in a single building, the obliteration of the entire town in which the structure sits would be disproportionate. Obviously, many questions of proportionality are more subtle and difficult than this example, and in many cases, reasonable persons of good will may disagree regarding proportionality calculations.

There are two important real world considerations that bear on this discussion. The first is military necessity. Military necessity permits actions that might otherwise be ethically questionable. For example, if there simply is no practical alternative means of attacking a legitimate target, weapons and tactics that are less than ideal in terms of their discrimination and proportionality may be acceptable. It is important not to confuse military *necessity* with military *convenience*. It is the obligation of military personnel to assume some risk in the effort to protect innocents. However, situations can certainly arise in which there simply is not time or any alternative means of attacking in a given situation. There, military necessity generates the permission to proceed with the attack.

The other consideration is the tendency of adversaries of this type to colocate themselves and their military resources with civilians and civilian structures to gain some sense of protection from such human shields. Obviously, when possible, every effort should be made to separate legitimate targets from such shields. But when that is not possible, it is acceptable to proceed with the attack, foreseeing that innocent persons and property will be destroyed. The moral principle underlying this judgment is known as "double effect" and permits such actions insofar as the agent sincerely can claim (as would be the case here) that the destruction of the innocents was no part of the plan or intention, but merely an unavoidable by-product of legitimate military action. However, it is obviously important to take into account the strategic impact on the overall campaign that press coverage and public reaction to such killing of civilians will produce when one makes the proportionality calculation (i.e., the target must be very important to be willing to incur such inevitable criticism and its impact on the overall strategy). Furthermore, it is critical if such attacks are to be made that a clear strategic communication plan be developed well in advance to explain the military urgency of attacking the legitimate target.

It is important to note, however, that there can be no just war justification for a response to indiscriminant terrorist attacks with attacks of a similar character on other societies. Not only would this constitute an unethical and illegal attack on innocent parties, it would almost certainly erode the moral "high ground" and widespread political support the U.S. currently enjoys.

The Moral Status of the Adversary

The individuals who initiated the terror attacks are clearly not "soldiers" in any moral or legal sense. They, and others who operate as they did from the cover of civilian identities, are not entitled to any of the protections of the war convention. This means that, if captured, they are not entitled to the benevolent quarantine of the POW convention or of domestic criminal law. For the purposes of effective response to these individuals, as well as future deterrence, it may be highly undesirable even if they are captured to carry out the extensive due process of criminal proceedings. If we can identify culpable individuals to a moral certainty, their swift and direct elimination by military means is morally acceptable and probably preferable in terms of the goals of the policy.

However, as this conflict proceeds, whenever it evolves into something resembling war against fixed targets, one may foresee that individuals and groups may come to operate against U.S. forces as organized military units (as they did in Afghanistan). It is important to keep in mind that, no matter how horrific the origins of this conflict, if and when this occurs and such groups begin to behave as organized units, to carry weapons openly, and to wear some kind of distinctive dress or badge, they become assimilated to the war convention. At that point, close moral and legal analysis will be required to determine the degree to which they become entitled to the status of "combatant" and are given the Geneva Convention protection that status provides. The previous permission for swift elimination applies to the period in which they operate with civilian "cover." Should elements of the adversary force eventually choose to operate as an organized military force, the long-term importance of universal respect for the Geneva Convention's provision would make our treating them at that point as soldiers under the law the preferred course of action. A very real legal and ethical issue will arise, however, regarding how long one may detain al Qaeda representatives. The normal Geneva standard is "for the duration of the conflict." Yet this conflict is unlikely ever to have a clear endpoint and every al Qaeda member has a valid passport from some sovereign state. How we and their home countries will balance our desire to detain them as long as possible so as to keep them from becoming a threat again with the inevitable push states are likely to make to repatriate their own citizens will be a very difficult legal and moral challenge.

Journal/Discussion Questions

1. Responses to terrorist attacks can be understood either in terms of warfare or in terms of police actions. What are the significant differences between these two frameworks? Which do you think is the better framework for the September 11th attacks?

2. Cook writes: "For the purposes of effective response to these individuals, as well as future deterrence, it may be highly undesirable even if they are captured to carry out the extensive due process of criminal proceedings. If we can identify culpable individuals to a moral certainty, their swift and direct elimination by military means is morally acceptable and probably preferable in terms of the goals of the policy?" Do you agree or disagree? Why? Discuss.

Deni Elliott
"Terrorism, Global Journalism, and the Myth of the Nation-State"

Deni Elliott is a philosopher who specializes in the area of media ethics. She is the Poynter-Jamison Professor of Journalism Ethics and Press Policy, Journalism & Media Studies at the University of South Florida at St. Petersburg.

In this article, Elliott concentrates on the question of the obligations of the press in reporting on the war on terror and argues that news media are morally prohibited from adopting a nationalistic point of view in their reporting. This is of particular relevance in regard to the war in Iraq and reporting on the abuse of Iraqi prisoners, where one of the central issues has been the role of the media in reporting events and publicizing pictures and videos.

As You Read, Consider This:
1. What, according to Elliott, is the job of journalism in reporting on issues of national interest?
2. In what ways has the notion of nation changed? How does this relate to our understanding of terrorism? How does this impact journalism?
3. In what ways has journalism been globalized? How does that affect our understanding of journalistic responsibility?

Journal of Mass Media Ethics, Vol. 19, No. 1 (2004).

September 13, 2001, President George W. Bush said, "We have just seen the first war of the 21st Century."

The term, "war" did not quite capture what we had seen. On September 11, the world had seen, not a war, but rather a far more massive suicide bombing than had been happening on the streets of Jerusalem for almost a year. What we had seen was an attack that has resulted in far fewer intentional civilian deaths than those caused during WW II or armed conflicts throughout the latter 20th Century. But, that such an attack had happened on the soil of the world's Superpower underscored a slowly emerging understanding. Armed conflict had changed; the nature of combatants had changed; governments and news media were going to have to change as well.

What the U.S. government has labelled the "war on terrorism" is clearly not metaphorical as were the previous administrations' "war on drugs" and "war on poverty," but a war that targets terrorists world wide, as well as a U.S. proclaimed "axis of evil" is a significant departure from what used to be meant by the concept of war. For the first time in history, the U.S. is engaged in a preemptive rather than retaliatory strikes.

In this paper, I am not going to argue that military intervention in Afghanistan or Iraq is morally acceptable. Nor will I argue that it is not. However, I will argue that U.S. news media should not report these conflicts or conflicts of the future from a nationalistic perspective. While I explain the motivation for the U.S. governments, as well as other governments, to adopt nationalistic arguments and descriptors, I argue that news media are morally prohibited from doing so. The job of government is to protect and promote national interests; the job of journalism is to provide citizens with a contextual understanding of their nation's interest, as that is what is necessary for educated self-governance.

National governments have the unique job of protecting citizens from suffering some harms at the hands of citizen and alien others. Governments have the unique job of keeping the peace and of supporting the overall good by promoting moral and utilitarian ideals such as educational systems and medical research. Governments, because of their unique relationship with their citizens, may act in ways different from how individuals are morally permitted to act toward other individuals. Governments can, and should, deprive individuals of freedom through incarceration under certain circumstances and require citizens to pay taxes to support the government and its work.[1]

The job of news media, on the other hand, is to provide citizens with information that they can use to make educated decisions about self-governance, which includes being able to contribute to the decisions made on their behalf by their leaders.[2] While the primary audience for a particular news organization may be a local audience, such as one in Missoula, Montana, or Sydney, New South Wales or Tehran, Iran, or the United States as a whole, the job of journalists, regardless of their national base, is to provide their citizen audiences with the global perspective needed to understand the political world of today.

The intellectual project described in this paper did not start with the attacks of 9/11. The changes in relationships between nations have been evolving so that our traditional notion of the nation-state is a dangerously outdated basis for decision making. Because the political world is in a period of transition in which national governments are attempting to apply old rules that are difficult to justify while attempting to find new models of collaboration, news media have a special obligation to step outside of nationalistic perspectives to help citizens develop a new way of understanding world conflicts and a new way of describing them. An example from the coverage of 9/11/01 makes this point.

Throughout the days following the attacks, U.S. officials and some U.S. journalists made comparisons between September 11, 2001 and those of December 7, 1941, when a U.S. military base was attacked by Japanese soldiers. The choice of this nationally-based comparison highlights the point that both attacks were made on U.S. soil. However, there are important differences between them as well.

The attack on Pearl Harbor was an attack on a military base, ordered by the legitimate government of a recognized nation. While the Pentagon was a military target on 9/11, the World Trade Center, where most of the victims died, was not. Unlike the attack on Pearl Harbor, the attack on 9/11 was not one by state-sanctioned military personnel.

Instead of fighter jets and artillery, the weapons of the recent combatants were commercial airliners, credit cards and a willingness to act in a way completely alien to what is traditionally understood as hostile enemy action.

While it is understandable why the U.S. government would use the similarity of attacks on its soil to make the comparison, news media could have used additional analogies and thus highlighted other aspects of the attacks, such as the intentional targeting of civilians. Here, comparisons with the recent suicide bombings in Israel by Palestinian militants would have provided context, as would the comparisons with the lives of 6 million civilians taken by Nazi Germany in World War II or the more than 300,000 civilian lives taken by U.S. action in Japan.

There are obviously important differences among these analogies as well. Far more lives were taken and far more property destroyed in the attack of 9/11 as compared with the suicide bombings in Jerusalem. Those killed by the Nazis were not random victims. And, the city bombings in Japan occurred during a declared war and were justified at the time by the probability that such acts might bring about an earlier end to that costly war.

However, despite the difference, targeting of civilians would have provided a certain kind of context to the world-wide discussion of 9/11, because this aspect is one of the important ways that wars have changed. Throughout the 1900s, casualties among innocents increased during armed conflicts or attacks until, ultimately, by the end of the 20th Century, it was safer to be a soldier than a civilian. In 1900, the ratio of soldier to civilian casualties in armed conflict was 9-1; nine soldiers were killed for every one civilian who was killed. By the turn of the 21st century, the ratio has switched to 1-9, that is, one soldier killed for every nine civilians.[3] The civilian designation extends to humanitarian workers and journalists as well as people who happen to be present in the wrong place at the wrong time. *Wall Street Journal* bureau chief, Daniel Pearl, was not the first, but the 10th, journalist to die covering the War on Terrorism.

The traditional definition of "war" breaks down when one seeks to include those who the U.S. governmental officials and journalists called "terrorists." Wars are traditionally acts of aggression or defence waged by recognized governments against other recognized governments, or factions within a territory fighting for recognition or geographical control. Wars traditionally use state-sanctioned or faction-sanctioned combatants.

Terrorism is aimed at inflicting indiscriminate violence and the fear of random violence on innocent civilians. Terrorism is waged by fighters who are not officially sanctioned by a recognized nation-state or by a faction seeking control of an identified nation-state. Instead, these fighters are fuelled by their allegiance to specific cultural, religious or ethnic distinctions that cross political borders. Terrorists follow no international agreements regarding just war declaration or procedures. They are often funded through multiple sources, including some recognized governments, private funding sources and renegade coalitions. Rather than seizing power or identified territory, their goal may be as amorphous as the destabilization of a particular culture or ruler. As even different governmental agencies in the U.S. disagree about what counts as the essential element of terrorism, it is probably true that, to some extent, terrorism is in the eye of the beholder. One nation's terrorist is another's freedom fighter.

The Notion of Nation

What we call "nations" are, in reality, legal fictions. They lack the characteristics of persons that we use in holding people responsible for their actions. Like corporations, nations are lacking in will and in reason. The term is used metaphorically to stand for certain types of ruling bodies that have control over certain geographical areas. The concept of "nation" as we know it, has been defined since the 17th Century. France and England, which served as home to some of the political theorists who constructed the notion, are not accidentally recognised as the oldest examples of national consciousness. What is called nation, state or nation-state is really no more than a general acceptance of a particular ruling body.[4] The state is "a system of animated institutions that govern the territory and its residents, and that administer and enforce the legal system and carry out the programs of government"[5] Nations have designated combatants to protect the nation's interests from internal and external threat. Attacking citizens in retaliation for the actions of their government is equivalent to sending rank and file employees from Enron or World Com or Arthur Anderson Accounting to prison for the actions of their bosses. Citizens have always been affected by wars, just as employees have felt the negative consequences of their managers' actions. However, traditionally, designated combatants from one nation would seek to overpower the designative combatants from another nation. Citizen deaths were generally "collateral damage"—unfortunate, unintended consequences.

Traditionally, all that has been necessary for something to be able to function as the "state" is that the ruling group be recognized by powerful people within and by ruling bodies outside of the territory. Appeal to how the government came to be in power was traditionally not considered important in determining the legitimacy of a state. The boundaries of most modern states were created by laws, war, treaties and by the imposition of colonial boundaries. Many "states were founded in a way that involved wrongful exercise of force and fraud."[6] As the initial definition of "nation" came from intellectuals in nations that had taken land that they could seize, how land was acquired was not traditionally considered important in determining the legitimacy of a "nation." What mattered was that the ruling body was recognized by powerful individuals and other nations as being legitimate.

A state that has "recognitional legitimacy" has special powers that no other group wishing to speak for that particular territory can simultaneously have. These powers include:

1. the right to territorial integrity;
2. the right to non-interference in internal affairs;
3. the power to make treaties, alliances, and trade agreements; thereby altering juridical relations with other states;
4. the right to make just war; and
5. the right to promulgate, adjudicate, and enforce legal rules on those within its territory.[7]

The primary function of government with recognitional legitimacy is to keep the peace by protecting citizens from one another and protecting the territory, its citizens, and its ruling body from outside aggressors. Through what has been called the Social Contract, citizens are expected to give up some of their freedom in return for the government's protection. British philosopher Thomas Hobbes (1588–1679) argued that it was rational for individuals to give up their individual personal sovereignty only in exchange for the protection of a larger, stronger body—that is, the state. Citizens agree to obey the laws and government agrees to protect them from some harms and to promote to general welfare.[8]

However, Hobbes' companion theory of how nations can best co-exist is not nearly as symbiotic as the citizen-state relationship. Nations, in Hobbes' view, stand in relation to one another in a state of nature, just as individuals would stand in regard to one another if not for the government's control. There is not social contract possible between states in this view, only uneasy and temporary alliances developed with mutual suspicion. In the 17th Century, there was no body larger than a nation, like our current United Nations, to protect nations from one another or to seek to create another notion of sovereign superior to any individual nation.

The obligation then, was for each state to protect itself from all of the others. All nations were seen as potentially threats to every other nation. Escalating and demonstrating military force is significant to this idea of how one state should protect its citizens from the potential aggression of another. The more fearsome one could look to potential intruders, the less fear one has of actual intrusion.

While Hobbes sought to describe and justify the the relationships between individuals and nations and between nations, Hugo Grotius, a Dutch natural law theorist, was arguing that conflicts between states needed to be regulated. Complementary to national consciousness, each government was obliged to avoid a state of war between nations, if possible. Nations were under moral obligation to first attempt to settle disputes peacefully. If battle was necessary, it had to be just in conditions in which to enter war (*jus ad bellum*) and just in the manner in which war was waged (*jus in bello*).[9]

Legitimate governments making war on other nations were said to be acting justly if the war was waged in self-defense, if the purpose of the war was to take back what was rightfully theirs, if the nation had a reasonable chance of succeeding and if the amount of force used was proportionate to the goal. Only combatants were to be targets.

A little more than a hundred years later, Immanuel Kant agreed that while it is "the desire of every state (or its ruler) to . . . dominat[e] the whole world, if it all possible," he argued that there were more positive reasons than fear of war to keep states from fighting one another.

"Nature," he says, "also unites nations . . . and does so by means of their mutual self-interest. For the spirit of commerce sooner or later takes hold of every people, and it cannot exist side by side with war. And of all the powers (or means) at the disposal of the power of the state, financial power can probably be relied on most. Thus states find themselves compelled to promote the noble cause of peace, though not exactly from motives of morality."[10]

For three hundred years or so, this reliance on hard boundaries between states seemed to work out reasonably well, with fear of aggression and the mutually compatible desire for financial stability working to generally sustain the peace. During that time, the internal affairs of a nation was considered to be a private matter. If one state acted aggressively toward another, then the aggrieved party had a recognized right to protect itself and its citizens. Otherwise, sovereign nations were to be free from interference from another. That perception has been affirmed at every peace conference since

Westphalia in 1648.[11] As philosopher Alan Goldman notes, "Observance of a rule against all foreign intervention limits internal struggles that might otherwise escalate into great power confrontations."[12]

Violence within a state is not a matter of global relevance or concern. Within the traditional understanding of relationships among sovereign states, it was morally required that the world stand by while factions fought for legitimate leadership within a country or while a government brutalized the people within its territory. Each state was a sovereign on to itself, with its citizens subject to the sovereign. An essential of the hard boundary theory is that state borders are defensible, that the only one who has the power and resources to wage war with other states is the legitimate ruling body.

The World Has Changed

From 1500 to 1900, 500 political entities devolved into the 25 that now rank among the world's most viable modern states.[13] The Hobbesian idea of hard boundaries worked in that, for a time, nations stayed out of one another's way regarding internal affairs, and also allowed only the fittest to survive. But, the tide turned in 1900.

The number of newly sovereign entities rose rather than the declined in the last century. In addition, an understanding has evolved over the past century that the legitimacy of states should be based on something other than the fact that some strong or rich nation was able to claim other territory as their own. The period of colonisation had ended. Global configurations multiplied. Through decolonisation in the 1960s, 140 new states were accorded formal recognition within the United Nations. Thirty new states were admitted in the 1990s alone. From a start of 51 original state members of the UN in 1949, the list has grown to 189.[14]

No longer do disagreements or conflicts occur mostly between recognized nations or legitimate governments. In 1995, 49 of the 50 armed conflicts in the world were wars of secession or conflicts among ethnic rivals who did not want to be controlled by a centralized or culturally different political ruling body. In the period between 1989–1996, there were 96 armed conflicts—only five were between nations.

David Hume could be reflecting on the events of today when he said, in the late 1700s, "The face of the earth is continually changing, by the increase of small kingdoms into great empires, by the dissolution of great empires into smaller kingdoms, by the planting of colonies, by the migration of tribes."[15] While Hobbes, Locke, Rousseau and Kant saw the world growing toward greater structure and stability, Hume's view of constant flux seems more accurate today.

Non-nation sanctioned fighters who have the power to create terror throughout the world has created an essential question for how it is reasonable to think about state-to-state relations. Self-declared sovereign agents threaten a return for the world from a state of society to a state of nature. First, those who are called terrorists are taking for their own the role-related responsibilities and privileges traditionally granted only to states—the ability to be an aggressor in a foreign state's territory. Next, and far more frightening, the fighters of today are showing that no state is capable of defending its citizens. The primary justification for the Social Contract is that individuals give up their power to a greater, protective power.

Hobbes tells us, "If there be no power erected, or not great enough for our security, every man will, and may, rely on his own strength and act for caution against all other men."[16]

Locke says, "Whoever uses force without right, as every one does in society who does it without law, puts himself into a state of war with those against whom he so uses it, and in that state all former ties are cancelled, all other rights cease, and every one has a right to defend himself, and to resist the aggressor."[17] Terrorism provides the ultimate contradiction to the argument for a sovereign state.

However, national governments had lost their power to protect their citizens from external aggressors and accidents long before 9/11. For decades, we have lived in a world in which political borders are increasingly meaningless in the ability of one state to impact another.

Degradation of the water, land and atmosphere happened without respect for national boundaries. A nuclear accident in one country causes death and destruction in another.

No nation is a financial isolationist. The markets of all depend on the markets of each. Popular culture from fast food to music, television and film are consumed globally. Economic or cultural aggression is viewed as equivalent to military aggression by some of the world's citizens.

States have the ability, albeit unequally shared, to access information about one's neighbors, with some of us having access through satellites that allow us to peer in one another's backyard. Global communication no longer allows citizens to remain ignorant of the plight and strife of innocents anywhere in the world.

And, of course, every nation and most terrorist groups, no matter how rich or poor, have the ability to use nuclear and chemical and biological agents to destroy not only other governments but the very world that allows for geopolitical boundaries to exist.

Accompanying these changes is a change in the global perception of the conditions under which it is morally permitted or required for a state to tolerate intervention from others. World War II dramatically illustrated the horrific results of non-intervention.

In response to the atrocities of that war, the United Nations committed all of its members to uphold a set of fundamental principles that includes "promoting and encouraging respect for human rights and for fundamental freedoms for all without distinction to race, sex, language or religion."[18] The Declaration of Human Rights, in a short preamble and 30 articles, articulates the following human rights: "the right to life, liberty and property, the right to remain free from torture, the right to a fair and public hearing, the right to remain free from slavery."[19]

The fact that some people in the world have not realized even the most basic of these rights does not change the humanitarian realization that all people are due these rights. People who have not achieved these rights are deprived world citizens. They are not getting what we realize everyone is entitled to have. But, whether or not the government that rules the territory in which they live is morally blameworthy, however, for the individual's deprivation depends on how that person's life is in regard to others in the territory. At a minimal level, the state's responsibility is to make sure only that no person or identifiable group has substantially less than others in the territory. But, it was quite a while before the UN held any state accountable for failing to meet even this minimal level of human rights claim.

The UN's Declaration of the universality of human rights was initially little more than declaration. "Only two years after the Charter was adopted, the UN Commission on Human Rights formally declared that it could not act on any reported complaints about violations of human rights. The commission refused to compromise the absolute sovereign authority of states."[20]

However, over the next 40 years, the UN and NGOs (Non-governmental Organizations) began to work together to formally and informally put pressure on nations that violated human rights.

Human rights have begun to be recognized, slowly, ever so slowly, as a legitimate standard for intervention in another nation's affairs. A new global understanding is emerging that governments are required to be just toward their subjects. The list of UN sanctioned humanitarian interventions in the late 20th Century shows that the absolute sovereignty of the hard borders era has dissolved.

The recognition of internal justice as a basic responsibility of a recognized ruling body means that a state can forfeit its legitimacy through violations of human rights. In the philosopher Allen Buchanan's words, "To be legitimate, a political order must exemplify a common good conception of justice according to which every individual's good is to count. . . . Therefore, a legitimate political order must respect the basic human rights."[21]

The legitimacy of a state can be measured by the citizens' ability to make changes within it. Within what Buchanan calls "minimal democracy," state legitimacy is based on the following criteria: "(1) there are representative, majoritarian institutions for making the most general laws, such that no competent adult is excluded from participation, (2) the highest government officials are accountable, that is, subject to being removed from office through the workings of these representative institutions, and (3) at least a minimal amount of freedom of speech and association are secured for reasonable deliberation about democratic decisions."[22]

Within an understanding of statehood based on justice, states must include in their documents of formation methods for changing the government itself. It must be possible for citizens within a legitimate state to strip the current leadership of its right to govern. If citizens have this power, then it is automatically illegitimate for a state to have its right to govern extinguished by any other means. Otherwise, external intervention on behalf of a people or a government is sometimes morally acceptable.

What we have seen since 9/11 is an even greater softening of national boundaries to yield the harboring of terrorists as yet another U.N. justification for violating state sovereignty and for nation's suppression of individual human rights.

Not surprisingly, terrorism unites U.N. member states as no other issue has. In October, 2001, an overwhelming number of states joined in a five day discussion on the problem of terrorism. "It is unprecedented in the history of the United Nations for 167 Member States and 4 Observers to participate in the debate on a single agenda item," said Assembly President Han Seung-soo of the Republic of Korea. He added that all participants had "wholeheartedly condemned the 11 September attacks against the United States."[23] While unprecedented, global agreement on this issue is not surprising. It would be irrational for legitimate governments not to agree on the threat of terrorism. Armed attack by non-nation-sanctioned zealot combatants threatens the legitimacy of all nations.

Despite the dissolving of hard borders between nations and the growing strength of the U.N., U.S. governmental rhetoric in response to the attacks of 9/11 continue to be strongly nationalistic. It is in the interest of recognized governments to have its citizens continue to believe in the myth of nations with hard borders and the ability of individual national governments to protect their citizens against any threat. It is the obligation of news media to reject that myth.

The Role of the Press in Reporting State Actions

I'll start the concluding section of my argument with the assertion that journalism is a global enterprise in that it penetrates beyond national boundaries and that it is an intentional or unintentional player in conflict situations. CNN and Al-Jazeera are at least as much a part of the global politics as is the U.N. Among other things, networks are used to provide platforms for significant parties to conflict.

According to journalist Nic Gowing, "Technology has facilitated the globalisation of the news business. In TV, international news channels like CNN, BBC World, and NBC Superchannel are lined up for battle on what this author has labelled the new Wild West broadcasting frontier via satellite and cable. In theory, this situation should allow comprehensive coverage of global issues. Again, in theory, this coverage should include early warning of conflicts that have erupted in defiance of all diplomatic efforts."[24]

Says journalism scholar Robert Picard, "The importance of the press in the democratic process has been recognized since the seventeenth century. The need to permit individuals to freely exchange ideas and information in order to promote the public interest was regularly posited by democratic theorists."[25]

While McDonalds and CNN are both worldwide U.S. exports, the corporations have different social responsibilities. News organizations have and obligation to offer, at a minimum, information that can be used by citizens for self-governance. To fulfil this purpose, the information must be balanced, accurate, relevant and complete. As I've written elsewhere, the journalistic knowledge that comes from the observing, mediating, and producing process is different, in kind, from scientific knowledge.[26] Presentations of journalistic knowledge are more like slide shows to science's landscape paintings. What counts at the moment as balanced, accurate, relevant and complete coverage is not likely to be the same at the end of a 24-hour news cycle.

In order to do their special job of educating citizens during conflict, news organizations should provide citizens with a global rather than a nationalistic perspective. Reporting from a global perspective includes providing historical and cultural context for the views expressed by governmental leaders. It includes providing the perspective of our enemies as clearly as possible, as that is the only way that citizens can truly understand the motives of those who would attack us. Reporting from a global perspective also includes the requirement that news media seek language that provides citizens alternatives to and context for governmental rhetoric. It includes the need for journalists to refrain from being the nation's cheerleaders. I'll conclude by examining these last two aspects in turn.

News organizations should not adopt governmental rhetoric or perspective as the sole way of understanding the conflict. News organizations have the responsibility to provide their audiences with messages that are alternative to governmental views. The purpose of providing alternatives is not to harm the impact of governmental messages, but to open those messages to broad examination and understanding. Support for governmental perspective, if warranted, will be stronger when citizens can understand that view against opposing alternatives.

If news media build an independent rhetoric, news coverage could avoid the reflective strategy response that mirrors the terrorists. The U.S. government has created an "us vs. them, good vs. evil" way of describing the crisis.

An alternative, non-reflective democratic rhetoric includes respect for the other, the goal of full information and intellectual honesty. Non-reflective rhetoric provides a way for news media to raise appropriate questions for governmental speakers by leading a conversation on how to judge the legitimacy of response rather than simply repeating governmental explanations for why a particular response is justified. Doing so, according to scholar Richard Leeman, "would enact democracy, a valued process that, intrinsically, terrorism cannot embody. Democratic rhetoric would thus model the process of democracy, re-creating the values of democracy at the same time that it perhaps lessened the incidence of terrorism."[27]

An example of non-reflective media coverage includes an article from November, 2001 in the *New York Times*. Here, the writer Barbara Crossette provided context for examination of U.S. strategy by quoting an authority who argued that excluding enemy voices breeds more terrorism.

In the article, a former undersecretary general of the U.N., Sir Brian Urquhart, who worked on early peace keeping missions in the Congo and Middle East, claimed that the U.S. was making a mistake in insisting that anyone associated with the Taliban be excluded from the process of rebuilding Afghanistan and that the U.N. was wrong in giving in to U.S. demands for this.

Urquhart called this exclusion reminiscent of early Mideast policy errors involving the PLO because the Taliban represents the Pashtun, Afghanistan's largest ethnic group. "You can't have a Middle East peace conference without including the PLO," he said, "but that's what we tried to do for 40 years and got into a hell of a mess. It's an old, old story. We don't deal with somebody for supposedly moral gounds and then we get something infinitely worse. We wouldn't deal with the PLO and now we've got Hamas and Islamic Jihad. Some element of the Taliban should be in these talks. They were the previous government, after all."[28]

Reporting from a global perspective requires that journalists and news organizations refrain from being the nation's cheerleaders. The mainstream coverage that followed 9/11 found the news industry in full patriotic garb. Newspapers carried flags. Television news anchors lapels sprouted ribbons and banners. Television news graphics rippled with red, white and blue and gave greater legitimacy to the administration's pet phrases, "Attack on America," and "War on Terrorism."

As was the case with the 1991 Gulf War, journalistic rhetoric became more vehement as public approval rating for military intervention soared, which resulted in higher public approval both for the action and the media. On the Fox News Channel Tuesday (a week after the aerial attacks), the anchor Jon Scott told Wolfgang Ischinger, the German ambassador to the United States, "We look forward to working with your country in wiping out these terrorists." On "Late Show with David Letterman," the same day, CBS anchor Dan Rather said, "George Bush is the president, he makes the decisions, and, you know, as just one American, he wants me to line up, just tell me where."[29] Steve Dunleavy from the *New York Post* wrote, "The response to this unimaginable 21st Century Pearl Harbor should be as simple as it is swift—kill the bastards. . . . As for cities or countries that host these worms, bomb them into basketball courts." Dave Kopel from the *National Review* wrote, "To prevent future attacks, the perpetrators of Tuesday's infamies must be utterly destroyed, even if that means infringing the territorial sovereignty of nations which harbor these war criminals." Charles Krauthammer from the *Washington Post* wrote, "War was long ago declared on us. Until we declare war in return, we will have thousands of more innocent victims."[30] And, in a November 5 column, *Newsweek* columnist Jonathan Adler suggested that a way to deal with terrorists was to use legal forms of psychological torture at home and then transfer "some suspects to our less squeamish allies" for a taste of the real thing.[31]

Journalists, like people and nations everywhere, should be outraged by violent attacks on innocent civilians, no matter where they occur or who the attackers might be. But, for self-governance, citizens, of this country and all others, need news media to play a role different from that of outraged citizen or from national government trying to figure out its role in a changing world. The appropriate role for news media in reporting 21st Century conflict necessitates distancing from a narrow, nationalistic perspective. The difference between who news media label "terrorists" and who they call "militants" should be a difference larger than the number and nationality of civilians killed in the World Trade Center and those killed on the streets of Jerusalem.

References

1. Gert, B. (1998). *Morality, Its Nature and Justification,* pp. 362–371. New York: Oxford University Press.

2. Elliott, D. (1986). "Foundations of Press Responsibility," in Deni Elliott (ed), *Responsible Journalism.* Thousand Oaks, CA: Sage Press.

3. Stremlau, J. (1998). *People in Peril, Human Rights, Humanitarian Action, and Preventing Deadly Conflict.* A Report to the Carnegie Commission on Preventing Deadly Conflict (New York: The Carnegie Corporation), p. 25.

4. Nation, nation-state, and state are used as synonymous terms in this paper.

5. Copp, D. (1998). "The Idea of a Legitimate State." *Philosophy & Public Affairs,* Vol. 28, No. 1, pp. 3–45.

6. Copp, p. 45.

7. Buchanan, A. (1998). "Recognitional Legitimacy and the State System," *Philosophy & Public Affairs,* Vol. 28, No. 1, pp. 46–78.

8. Hobbes, T. (1651). *Leviathan.*

9. Grotius, H. (1625). *On the Law of War and Peace.*

10. Kant, I. (1795). *Perpetual Peace.*

11. Stremlau, p. 8.

12. Goldman, Al. (1982). "The Moral Significance of National Boundaries," pp. 437–543 in Peter A. French, Theordore E. Uehling, Jr., and Howard K. Wettstein, (eds.), *Midwest Studies in Philosophy VII.* (Minneapolis: University of Minnesota Press), p. 441.

13. Stremlau, p. 14.

14. http://www.un.org./News/facts/setting.htm

15. Hume, D. (1758). Of the Original Contract. *Essays, Moral, Political and Literary.*

16. Hobbes, *ibid.*

17. Locke, J. (1690). *Two Treatises of Government.*

18. Universal Declaration of Human Rights.

19. Hutchins, 1998.

20. Korey, W. (1996). *Human Rights and NGO's: The Power of Persuasion.* A Report to the Carnegie Commission on Preventing Deadly Conflict (New York: The Carnegie Corporation), p. 153.

21. Buchanan, p. 53.

22. Buchanan, p. 60.

23. http://www.un.org/News/dh/20011005.htm

24. Gowing, N. (1997). *Media Coverage, Help or Hinderance in Conflict Prevention?* A Report to the Carnegie Commission on Preventing Deadly Conflict (New York: The Carnegie Corporation), p. 25.

25. Picard, R. (1985). *The Press and the Decline of Democracy.* Westport, CT: Greenwood Press, p. 12.

26. Elliott, D. (1996). "Journalistic Research," *Accountability in Research Journal,* Vol 4, pp. 103–114.

27. Leeman, R. (1991). *The Rhetoric of Terrorism and Counterterrorism.* New York: Greenwood Press, p. 115.

28. Crossette, B. (2001). "How To Put a Nation Back Together Again," *The New York Times,* 11/25.

29. Rutenberg, J, and Bill Carter (2001), "Draping Newscasts With the Flag," *The New York Times,* September 20, p. C8.

30. Kurtz, H. (2001). "Commentators Are Quick to Beat Their Pens into Swords," *The Washington Post,* September 13.

31. http://fair.org/extra/0201/pro-pain.html

Alan M. Dershowitz
"Is There a Tortuous Road to Justice?"

Alan Dershowitz is the Felix Frankfurter Professor of Law at Harvard Law School. He writes extensively in the area of criminal law and rights.

In this op-ed piece, Dershowitz argues in favor of legalizing torture in exceptional cases— what he calls the "ticking bomb" cases—and ensuring that this not be abused by requiring torture warrants.

As You Read, Consider This:

1. According to Dershowitz, do prisoners have a right to refuse truth serum? On what basis, if at all?

2. What is "use immunity?" Why is it important in Dershowitz's argument?

3. Explain what Dershowitz means by a "ticking bomb" case.

The FBI's frustration over its inability to get material witnesses to talk has raised a disturbing question rarely debated in this country: When, if ever, is it justified to resort to unconventional techniques such as truth serum, moderate physical pressure and outright torture?

Los Angeles Times, Nov 8, 2001, p. B19. Reprinted with the kind permission of the author.

The constitutional answer to this question may surprise people who are not familiar with the current U.S. Supreme Court interpretation of the 5th Amendment privilege against self-incrimination: Any interrogation technique, including the use of truth serum or even torture, is not prohibited. All that is prohibited is the introduction into evidence of the fruits of such techniques in a criminal trial against the person on whom the techniques were used. But the evidence could be used against that suspect in a non-criminal case—such as a deportation hearing—or against someone else.

If a suspect is given "use immunity"—a judicial decree announcing in advance that nothing the defendant says (or its fruits) can be used against him in a criminal case—he can be compelled to answer all proper questions. The issue then becomes what sorts of pressures can constitutionally be used to implement that compulsion. We know that he can be imprisoned until he talks. But what if imprisonment is insufficient to compel him to do what he has a legal obligation to do? Can other techniques of compulsion be attempted?

Let's start with truth serum. What right would be violated if an immunized suspect who refused to comply with his legal obligation to answer questions truthfully were compelled to submit to an injection that made him do so?

Not his privilege against self-incrimination, since he has no such privilege now that he has been given immunity.

What about his right of bodily integrity? The involuntariness of the injection itself does not pose a constitutional barrier. No less a civil libertarian than Justice William J. Brennan rendered a decision that permitted an allegedly drunken driver to be involuntarily injected to remove blood for alcohol testing. Certainly there can be no constitutional distinction between an injection that removes a liquid and one that injects a liquid.

What about the nature of the substance injected? If it is relatively benign and creates no significant health risk, the only issue would be that it compels the recipient to do something he doesn't want to do. But he has a legal obligation to do precisely what the serum compels him to do: answer all questions truthfully.

What if the truth serum doesn't work? Could the judge issue a "torture warrant," authorizing the FBI to employ specified forms of non-lethal physical pressure to compel the immunized suspect to talk?

Here we run into another provision of the Constitution—the due process clause, which may include a general "shock the conscience" test. And torture in general certainly shocks the conscience of most civilized nations.

But what if it were limited to the rare "ticking bomb" case—the situation in which a captured terrorist who knows of an imminent large-scale threat refuses to disclose it?

Would torturing one guilty terrorist to prevent the deaths of a thousand innocent civilians shock the conscience of all decent people?

To prove that it would not, consider a situation in which a kidnapped child had been buried in a box with two hours of oxygen. The kidnapper refuses to disclose its location. Should we not consider torture in that situation?

All of that said, the argument for allowing torture as an approved technique, even in a narrowly specified range of cases, is very troubling.

We know from experience that law enforcement personnel who are given limited authority to torture will expand its use. The cases that have generated the current debate over torture illustrate this problem. And, concerning the arrests made following the Sept. 11 attacks, there is no reason to believe that the detainees know about specific future terrorist targets. Yet there have been calls to torture these detainees.

I have no doubt that if an actual ticking bomb situation were to arise, our law enforcement authorities would torture. The real debate is whether such torture should take place outside of our legal system or within it. The answer to this seems clear: If we are to have torture, it should be authorized by the law.

Judges should have to issue a "torture warrant" in each case. Thus we would not be winking an eye of quiet approval at torture while publicly condemning it.

Democracy requires accountability and transparency, especially when extraordinary steps are taken. Most important, it requires compliance with the rule of law. And such compliance is impossible when an extraordinary technique, such as torture, operates outside of the law.

Journal/Discussion Questions

1. One of the classic objections to Dershowitz's argument is the "slippery slope argument"; that is, the claim that Dershowitz's position, even if not objectionable in itself, would lead to far worse abuses that would certainly be objectionable. Critically evaluate this objection.

2. What type of ethical perspective—deontological, consequentialist, virtue—does Dershowitz's position seem to exemplify? Does his position shed any light on the strengths and weaknesses of that ethical perspective?

Concluding Discussion Questions

Where Do You Stand Now?

Instructions

You have already answered the following questions in your moral problems self-quiz at the beginning of this book. Now that you have studied the material in this section, take a moment to answer the same questions again.

	Strongly Agree	Agree	Undecided	Disagree	Strongly Disagree	*Chapter 5: War, Terrorism, and Counterterrorism*
21.	❑	❑	❑	❑	❑	It is always morally wrong to strike first in a war.
22.	❑	❑	❑	❑	❑	Captured terrorists should be treated like prisoners of war.
23.	❑	❑	❑	❑	❑	Sometimes we must go to war to save innocent people from being killed.
24.	❑	❑	❑	❑	❑	Terrorists should be hunted down and killed.
25.	❑	❑	❑	❑	❑	Torture is always wrong and should be forbidden.

Compare your answers to this self-quiz with the answers to the initial self-quiz. How, if at all, have your answers changed? How have the reasons for your answers changed?

Journal/Discussion Questions

1. In light of the readings in this chapter, how would you evaluate the United States's war in Iraq?

2. Have the readings in this chapter promoted you to reconsider your views on any of these issues of war, peace, and terrorism?

3. How has terrorism transformed our understanding of warfare?

For Further Reading

Web Resources

For Web-based resources, see the War and Peace page of *Ethics Updates* (http://ethics.sandiego.edu).

Pacifism. For an overview, see Jeff McMahan, "War and Peace," *A Companion to Ethics,* edited by Peter Singer (Cambridge Blackwell, 1991). In addition, see Jenny Teichman, *Pacifism and the Just War* (Oxford, England: Blackwell, 1986); Robert L. Holmes and Marshall Cohen, *On War and Morality* (Princeton: Princeton University Press, 1989); Robert L. Holmes, *Nonviolence in Theory and Practice* (Belmont, CA: Wadsworth, 1990); Terry Nardin, *The Ethics of War and Peace: Religious and Secular Perspectives* (Princeton, NJ: Princeton University Press, 1996); Richard B. Miller, *Interpretations of Conflict: Ethics, Pacifism, and the Just-War Tradition* (Chicago: University of Chicago Press, 1991); Douglas Lackey, *The Ethics of War and Peace* (Englewood Cliffs, NJ: Prentice Hall, 1989).

Just War. On just war theory, see the excellent overview by Brian D. Orend, "War," in the *Stanford Encyclopedia of Philosophy* (http://plato.stanford.edu/entries/war/). Michael Walzer's *Just and Unjust Wars: A Moral Argument With Historical Illustrations,* 3rd ed. (New York: Basic Books, 1979, 2000) remains the classic text, while Jean B. Elstain's *Just War Theory* (New York: New York University Press, 1994) is an excellent anthology. On Walzer, see Brian Orend, *Michael Walzer on War and Justice* (Montreal: McGill-Queens University Press, 2001); also see his *War and International Justice: A Kantian Perspective* (Waterloo: Wilfrid Laurier University Press, 2001).

Humanitarian Intervention. J. L. Holzgrefe and Robert O. Keohane, eds., *Humanitarian Intervention: Ethical, Legal and Political Dilemmas* (Cambridge, England: Cambridge University Press, 2003); Simon Chesterman, *Just War or Just Peace?: Humanitarian Intervention and International Law,* Oxford Monographs in International Law (Oxford, England: Oxford University Press, 2001); Nicholas J. Wheeler, *Saving Strangers: Humanitarian Intervention in International Society* (Oxford, England: Oxford University Press, 2001). For a classic study, see Stanley Hoffmann, *Duties Beyond Borders: On the Limits and Possibilities of Ethical International Politics* (The Frank W. Abrams Lectures, Syracuse, NY: Syracuse University Press, 1981); for an excellent discussion of Hoffmann's position, see Stanley Hoffmann, Robert C. Johansen, James P. Sterba, Raimo Vayrynen, *The Ethics and Politics of Humanitarian Intervention* (Notre Dame Studies on International Peace, South Bend, IN: University of Notre Dame Press, 1996). Also see George R. Lucas and Anthony C. Zinni, *Perspectives on Humanitarian Military Intervention* (Berkeley: University of California, Institute of Governmental Studies, 2001); Jonathan Moore, ed., *Hard Choices: Moral Dilemmas in Humanitarian Intervention* (Lanham, MD: Rowman & Littlefield, 1999); Robert L. Phillips and Duane L. Cady, *Humanitarian Intervention: Just War vs. Pacifism* (Lanham, MD: Rowman & Littlefield, 1995); Alexander Moseley and Richard Norman, eds., *Human Rights and Military Intervention* (Williston, VT: Ashgate Publishing, 2002). Bruno Coppieters and Nick Fotion, eds., *Moral Constraints on War: Principles and Cases* (Lanham, MD: Lexington Books, 2002).

Terrorism.   For a short overview of the main issues, see C. A. J. Coady, "War and Terrorism," *A Companion to Applied Ethics* (Blackwell Companions to Philosophy), edited by R. G. Frey (Malden, MA: Blackwell, 2003), pp. 254–266. For philosophical analyses of terrorism, see Angelo Corlett, *Terrorism: A Philosophical Analysis* (Dordrecht: Kluwer Academic Publishers, 2003); James P. Sterba, ed., *Terrorism and International Justice* (Oxford, England: Oxford University Press, 2003) contains an excellent selection of articles; Jean Bethke Elshtain, *Just War Against Terror: The Burden of American Power in a Violent World* (New York: Basic Books, 2003); Trudy Govier, *A Delicate Balance: What Philosophy Can Tell Us about Terrorism* (Boulder, CO: Westview Press, 2002); also see the Winter 2003 issue of *Hypatia,* which is devoted to feminist analyses of terrorism. Paul Berman's *Terror and Liberalism* (New York: W.W. Norton, April 2003) provides a very insightful account of Sayyid Qutb and militant Islamic fundamentalism and the challenges it presents to Western liberal democracies. Andrew Valls's *Ethics in International Affairs: Theories and Cases* (Lanham, MD: Rowman & Littlefield, 2000) includes a number of case studies relating to terrorism.

Treatment of Prisoners.   The most influential document in regard to the treatment of prisoners is the Geneva Convention. For the online text, see: http://www.unhchr.ch/html/menu3/b/91.htm. Numerous other relevant documents are available on the Web site of the Office of the high Commissioner for Human Rights (http://www.unhchr.ch/).

PART TWO

Matters of Diversity and Equality

Conceptualizing the Issues

In the following four chapters, a wide range of issues—hate crimes, harassment, stereotyping, hate speech, and welfare, to name but a few—are raised. These issues often cut across the boundaries of the four chapters, which deal with race, gender, sexual orientation, and economic inequality.

It is possible to approach each of these issues separately, one at a time. In fact, the public discussion of these issues often occurs precisely in this fashion, with pundits and politicians singling out specific problems for comment.

There is another way of approaching these issues that places the particular issues within a larger context. Let me suggest that we ask ourselves five questions.

1. **What would the ideal society look like in regard to each of these issues?** Consider, first of all, the issue of race. What would the ideal society look like in regard to race? Would race be as unimportant as, say, eye color? Would race be important to identity, but not an object of discrimination? Would each race, as separatists urge, try to maintain its own identity? Similar questions could be asked about gender, sexual orientation, and economic status.

2. **What would the minimally acceptable society look like in regard to each of these issues?** Again, consider race. Even if we were not able to achieve ideal racial conditions of harmony and understanding, we might still say that certain conditions must be met for a society to be morally acceptable at all. Hate crimes, for example, would have to be abolished; job discrimination should be eliminated.

3. **What is the present condition of society in regard to these issues?** For example, when you consider issues about affirmative action, one of the questions to answer is what is the actual condition of minority groups in our society today? This is an empirical question and the social sciences are the disciplines that attempt to provide us with answers to this question.

4. **How do we best get from the actual condition to the minimally acceptable condition of society?** This presumes that, at least in some respects, the present situation does not meet minimal

expectations. This question is also, at least in significant measure, an empirical question about what works, and about what is effective, in moving from one condition to another. Generally speaking, this is the realm of law and rights, the area of minimal requirements that must be guaranteed to all. It is also the area in which the least amount of compromise and tolerance is present.

5. **Finally, how do we get from the minimally acceptable state of society to the ideal one?** Once we move beyond the moral minimum to a consideration of the ideals toward which we are striving, we realize two things. First, there is more room for legitimate differences in regard to ideals. Reasonable people of good will can differ widely on these. Second, as a result of the first difference, the means of reaching the ideal state are generally persuasive rather than coercive. We seek to convince others of our ideals rather than to force them to comply. Public debate, education, and incentive programs are but a few of the possible means of getting to this ideal state.

The following diagram will help to visualize these five questions and their relationship to one another:

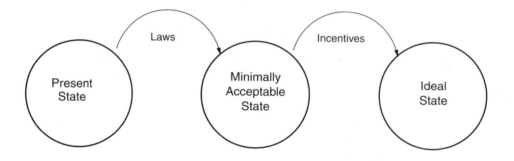

In each chapter of this section, this general framework has been converted to a specific questionnaire to help you to conceptualize your own stance on these issues and also to help to bring into focus both the similarities and the differences between your vision of society and the vision of your classmates.

CHAPTER
6

Race and Ethnicity

Videotape

   Topic: America in Black and White
   Source: *Nightline,* December 3, 2003
   Anchor: Ted Koppel, John Donvan
   Guests: Mae Miller (former slave); Antoinette Harrell-Miller (genealogist);
               Deadria Farmer-Paellmann (researcher)

An Introduction to the Moral Issues

The issues of race and ethnic identity have always been central to American society, yet at the same time our American identity as a "melting pot" has in part been forged on the basis of denying this as the principal basis of our identity.

Recall our threefold structure for analyzing these issues: the problem, the ideal, and the means for going from one to the other. We begin by considering the facts of racism, turn to a consideration of the various ideals, and then discuss which means offer the most hope of moving us from actual situation toward the ideal. But first, a few words about a basic distinction.

Race and Ethnicity

Although distinct concepts, race, and ethnicity are obviously related to one another, anthropologists generally see race as a physical characteristic. They recognize the existence of three or four major racial groups: Caucasoid, Negroid, Mongoloid, and sometimes Australoid. (The U.S. Census Bureau, on the other hand, recognizes four races, adding Native American—which anthropologists consider as part of Mongoloid—to the first three.) Ethnicity, on the other hand, refers primarily to social and cultural forms of identification and self-identification. There are many more ethnic identities than racial ones. The English, French, Italians, Germans, and Poles all share a common race, but they consider themselves ethnically different.

Several points should be noted about these concepts. First, race inevitably has a socially constituted meaning and it is at this point that the distinction between race and ethnicity is somewhat less clear-cut. Whatever race is, it isn't just a physical characteristic. Second, although we have a clear term to denote discrimination based on race (viz., racism), we lack a corresponding term to indicate discrimination based on ethnicity. However, ethnically based discrimination (witness the atavistic conflicts of Eastern Europe) is often of the same structure as racism, and sometimes masquerades as racially based when it is actually ethnically grounded. Third, it is worth noting that, at least in the United States, we tend to think of racial categories as mutually exclusive. In forms asking about race, we are usually asked to "check one of the following: white, black, Asian, or American Indian." However, some of us are either remotely (i.e., back at least two generations) or recently (i.e., our parents or grandparents) of mixed race. Forms that allow individuals to acknowledge the plurality of their racial and ethnic identities would not only be more accurate, but also less polarizing for society as a whole.

The Facts of Racism

Racism has long been a pervasive and disturbing fact of American society. The very founding of the United States is inextricably bound up with the racism that characterized our treatment of Native Americans and, soon thereafter, with the racism that helped to make slavery possible. The legacy, and in some cases the continuing reality, of that racism is still with us today. Most Americans in their 40s and older grew up in a world where racial discrimination was still legally sanctioned.

African Americans (and others as well) were legally denied access to schools, jobs, neighborhoods, churches, clubs, and the voting booth well into the middle 1960s. Although such discrimination continues to some extent today, it is no longer done under the sanction of law.

The word racism is both descriptive and evaluative. As a descriptive term, it refers to certain attitudes and actions that (a) single out certain people on the basis of their racial—or, in some cases, ethnic—heritage and (b) disadvantage them in some way on this basis. (The second element, disadvantaging someone on the basis of race, has to be present or else simple categorization—such as one finds in a census—would be racist.) College admissions policies that exclude African Americans on the basis of their race would be a clear example of racism. Yet racism also has an evaluative element: it conveys a negative value judgment that racism is morally objectionable, evil. The evaluative element may refer primarily to the intention behind the practice or to the consequences of such a practice.

This distinction between intention and consequence also provides part of the foundation for a distinction between overt racism and institutional racism. Gertrude Ezorsky, for example, sees overt racist action as grounded in "the agent's racial bias against the victim or in a willingness to oblige the racial prejudice of others" (*Racism and Justice*, p. 249). In the case of institutional racism, no negative value judgment is made about the agents' intentions. Their actions might not be intended to harm a particular racial group at all, although this may be an unintended consequence. The negative value judgment is reserved primarily for the consequences of such actions and policies.

It is important, both morally and politically, to distinguish between government-sanctioned racism and racism that occurs without such official endorsement. When our government enacts racist laws—such as separate schooling, housing—then it acts in our name as citizens, and it seems reasonable to argue that we as citizens are under an obligation to those who have been wronged. On the other hand, when an individual restaurant owner illegally discriminates against a potential patron on the basis of race, it does not seem that we as citizens are under the same kind of obligation to those who have been wronged because the restaurant owner was not acting in our names. Virtually all ethnic minorities have been subject to unfair treatment at one time or another in American history, but only a few—most notably, Native Americans, African Americans, and Japanese Americans—have been the object of governmentally sanctioned discrimination. The government would seem to have a special obligation in those cases in which groups have been wronged, not just by individuals, but by the government itself. Furthermore, we as citizens may be obligated to compensate wronged groups because such discrimination was done in our name.

Compensatory Programs

How do we respond morally to the fact of racism in our society and the role that it has played in our history? One response has been to suggest that we owe compensation to those who have been wronged. Compensatory programs, which seek to indemnify previously wronged individuals or groups, are essentially backward-looking; they seek to determine who has been wronged in the past and to make up for it in the present and future. Here the issue of governmental sanction assumes special importance. Insofar as racist discrimination was legally required in the past, it was done in our name as citizens. Consequently, we as citizens have a debt to compensate such discrimination. We do not have the same debt in the case of illegal discriminatory acts by individuals. In those cases, racist individuals may owe a debt of compensation to those they have discriminated against; but because they did not discriminate in our name, we are not under the same compensatory debt merely as citizens.

Presumably, compensatory programs are limited in scope to a repayment of the debt incurred by the wrong. There is a strong case, for example, that the United States as a whole owes a compensatory debt to many Native American tribes for the various ways in which those tribes have been mistreated by the U. S. government. Moreover, the death of those who have been wronged does not nullify the compensatory debt. It makes both moral and legal sense to compensate the descendants of those who have been wronged or the group as a whole, even if those who were originally wronged are now dead.

Similarly, compensatory programs do not necessarily demand that the current recipients be in a negative condition. Consider, for example, the Japanese Americans who were wrongfully incarcerated during World War II. It is certainly possible that we might conclude that they should be compensated for the wrong imposed upon them by our government, even if they have subsequently achieved economic success. This is little different, some would argue, from repaying a debt: the obligation to repay is not diminished by the fact that the person to whom the debt is owed has just won the lottery.

It is important to realize the morally symbolic value of such programs, which is often as important as any monetary value. When we commit ourselves as a country to compensate those who have been wronged by us as a country—the case of the indemnification of Japanese Americans interned in detention camps is an example of this—we are acknowledging our guilt as a country and stating our willingness to rectify the harm that we have caused. There is, as it were, a totaling of the public moral ledger that is often important in the process of moral reconciliation. When those who have been harmed feel that the perpetrators (a) genuinely recognize that they have done wrong and (b) are genuinely trying to make up for the actual harm they caused, then it becomes much easier for the victims to put the wrong behind them and heal the moral rift between themselves and the perpetrators.

Such compensatory programs are different, at least in their moral logic, from future-oriented programs—whether equal rights approaches or affirmative action programs—that seek to create some future goal of equality. Similarly, because compensatory programs are essentially backward-looking, differing ideals of the place of race and ethnicity in society are irrelevant to them. In future-oriented programs, on the other hand, the ideals we are striving to realize are of paramount importance. Let us now turn to a consideration of such future-oriented programs, beginning first with a consideration of the ideals that they may be striving to implement.

Ideals of the Place of Race in Society

What, precisely, is our ideal in regard to the place of race and ethnicity in our society? Several possible models suggest themselves, ranging from strongly separatist models to highly assimilationist ones. The ideal to which we are committed will have important implications for the means we choose for eradicating racism. Let's briefly consider each type of ideal.

Separatist Models

Despite claims about being a "melting pot," the United States has a long history of racial—and, often, ethnic—separatism. Sometimes separatism is imposed from outside the group and sometimes it comes from within. Racial separatism was often imposed in laws against Native Americans, African Americans, and (during World War II) Japanese and Japanese Americans. The intent of such legislation was both to keep the races separate and to maintain the supremacy of the white race in particular.

Separatism has often been a comparatively attractive option for comparatively small groups whose culture would easily be obliterated by the larger culture of the society if it were not protected in some way. Some Native American tribes (e.g., members of the Acoma Pueblo) have chosen to maintain a largely separate life, sheltered from the intrusions of outsiders, as a way of preserving their own identity. Separatist groups may be constituted along strictly ethnic lines—the major eastern cities of the United States often contained numerous ethnic neighborhoods in which residents could easily go about their day-to-day affairs without having to know English—and sometimes on the basis of religious commitments. The Amish and the Mennonites, for example, have long been committed to a largely separatist view of their place in American society as a whole, and many major religions exhibit a separatist current in monasteries, cloistered convents, and the like. Similarly, some utopian communities have preferred a separatist model of their place in society. Typically, most of these groups ask little from the larger world around them except to be left alone.

Clearly, there is no moral justification for imposing separatism on others and such attempts are almost always conjoined with either overt or covert beliefs in the racial supremacy of those in control. Self-imposed separatism is a morally more ambiguous matter and key to its evaluation are the questions of what the proponents of separatism propose to preserve and why they want to preserve it. Moreover, we must recognize that separatism is usually a matter of degree. Only a few are at the far extreme of not wanting to share anything—language, products, transportation—with the surrounding society.

The strongest argument in support of self-imposed racial or ethnic separatism is what we can call the identity argument. It maintains that a firm sense of one's race and ethnicity is a necessary component of one's identity as a person and that this sense of racial and ethnic identity can be preserved only through separatism. These issues are often discussed under the heading of "the politics of identity" or "the politics of recognition" and this has been a principal concern for many racial and ethnic groups that fear their identities will be lost through immersion in the larger society.

Critics of such separatist models maintain that, although some degree of separatism may be workable, strongly separatist models threaten to undermine the sense in which we have a national identity at all. Moreover, some argue that some separatists are inconsistent: they want both to be left alone by the larger society and at the same time be provided with the benefits of that larger society.

Assimilationist Models

The "melting pot" metaphor of American society suggests a model of American society that is primarily assimilationist. Differences are largely obliterated, melted down, and the result is a homogeneous nation of citizens. Indeed, this seems to have occurred with most immigrant groups from western and eastern Europe. Many whose ethnic background is European identify themselves primarily as American and only secondarily—and sometimes not at all—in terms of their ethnic European background. Traditional liberalism in the United States has been strongly committed to an assimilationist model, at least within the political realm.

The tension between separatist and assimilationist models comes out in various areas of daily life and public policy. For example, one of the principal issues in publicly funded education is whether it should seek to encourage such assimilation or whether it should seek to encourage the preservation and development of racial and ethnic identity.

Pluralistic Models

Somewhere between these two extremes is a middle ground that both respects diversity and at the same time tries to establish the minimal conditions necessary to a common life—a shared political life even if not a shared community. The principal thrust of a pluralistic model is to suggest, first, that there are certain minimal conditions necessary to the establishment of a common life; second, that specific groups may maintain a partially separate identity without negating that common life; and, third, that the identity of any given individual is constituted through both participation in the common life and through identification with any number of specific groups.

Pluralists do not even need to posit that different groups in society exhibit some fundamental agreement with one another. Consider an analogous issue: pacifism. I am not a pacifist. I do not believe that all killing of human beings is wrong, but I am glad that I live in a society in which some people are pacifists. Their presence reminds me of a truth, albeit a partial truth, that human life is of inestimable importance and ought not to be destroyed if that can be avoided. On the other hand, I am glad that I do not live in a society in which everyone is a pacifist. Not only would I feel morally lonely in such a world, but I would fear that it would lack the resilience to defend itself in the face of aggressive evil if faced with such a challenge. The tension between pacifists and nonpacifists is a good thing for our society as a whole and for each of us as individuals, and our lives would be diminished if we did not have one of these two opposing groups. Nor are these opposing groups without common ground. They both respect life—or, at least, most of both groups do most of the time. No one advocates indiscriminate killing and those who defend killing at all usually do so through an appeal to some core values, including the value of innocent life (which can be preserved through self-defense or whose loss can be avenged through capital punishment).

So, too, with racial and ethnic pluralism. Our world is richer for the diversity of our traditions, and there is no need to make everyone be like us. Indeed, I can feel that our world is a better place precisely because there are people who are not like me. The diversity of racial and ethnic traditions is a source of richness for the society as a whole, providing a wealth of possibilities far beyond the scope of any single ethnic tradition. That wealth of possibilities becomes especially important whenever we need help and whenever we run out of possibilities dealing with a specific issue, for we can then turn to the wisdom of other ethnic traditions to discover new and potentially better ways of dealing with that issue.

Finally, we should note that pluralism is multidimensional in the following sense. Pluralists would typically not only favor a diversity of ethnic traditions, but would also maintain that we as individuals are members of a wide range of communities, many of which may have little or nothing to do with race and ethnicity. There are many lines of affiliation in which ethnicity plays no role: computer hackers, smokers, people who hate to fly. Pluralists typically see a plurality of identities within the individual, not just within society as a whole.

The Means to Our Ideals

Let's imagine, simply for the sake of discussion, that we have general agreement about our actual situation and about the ideal condition toward which we are striving. The question that then presents itself is how we are to move from one to the other. In general, we can distinguish several kinds of approaches. First, equal rights approaches seek to ensure that previously discriminated against groups are henceforth treated in a scrupulously fair manner. Such approaches seek to eliminate discrimination in the future, but are often unable to significantly reduce the cumulative and continuing effects of past patterns of discrimination. Second, affirmative action approaches attempt to provide some kind of special support, consideration, or advantage to groups that have previously been discriminated against. These have the advantage of seeking to undo the residual effects of past discrimination, but they run the risk of being viewed as further discrimination. Finally, special protection approaches provide selected groups with stronger-than-usual protection of the law in specific areas relating to their identity as a group. Regulations banning hate speech, for example, give extra protection of law to certain groups. Such approaches stand midway between equal rights approaches and affirmative action approaches, providing more than extra protection but less than affirmative action in protection of certain groups.

Equal Rights Approaches

Since *Brown v. Board of Education* in 1954, the United States has increasingly committed itself to equal rights for all citizens, regardless of race. The Civil Rights Act of 1964 extended and deepened this commitment, and there are few today who would argue publicly that some citizens ought to be denied their civil rights on the basis of race or discriminated against because of race. Such a commitment was implicit in our Constitution and is increasingly central to our identity as a nation.

It is important to note, however, that there is often a huge gulf between commitment to the general principle of equal rights and commitment to the specific means of ensuring such equality. This is particularly the case where there are existing, often deeply ingrained patterns of discrimination. To what extent does the government take an active role in (a) discouraging such attitudes of discrimination and (b) punishing acts of discrimination? Consider, for example, the issue of discrimination in housing. Is the cause of equal rights in this area adequately served by simply passing a law forbidding such discrimination? Should special enforcement agencies be established?

Affirmative Action Programs

Four senses of affirmative action. Affirmative action is a notoriously slippery term, and it is important to define precisely what we mean when we use it. There are several possible senses of the term. If we consider it just within the context of hiring potential employees, we can distinguish four senses, two of which are weak, the other two of which are strong.

Weak senses of affirmative action:

1. Encouraging the largest possible number of minority applications in the applicant pool, and then choosing the best candidates regardless of gender, race, and so on.
2. When the two best candidates are equally qualified and one is a minority candidate, choosing the minority candidate.

Strong senses of affirmative action:

3. From a group of candidates, all of whom are qualified, choosing the minority candidate over better-qualified nonminority ones.
4. Choosing an unqualified minority candidate over a qualified nonminority one.

The third and fourth alternatives involve choosing a minority candidate over a better qualified non-minority one. Almost no one advocates the fourth alternative, although critics sometimes claim that support for the third alternative in theory leads, in practice, to the fourth alternative. Many are willing to support the third alternative. Proponents of affirmative action often argue that the first two types of affirmative action, although commendable, are often insufficient to break the cycle of past discrimination and that a more active program—that is, the third type of program—is necessary if affirmative action is to achieve its goal.

Special Protection Programs

In recent years, some attempts have been made to provide special protection to particular groups on the basis of race. Such programs do not qualify as affirmative action programs, but they clearly go beyond simple equal rights guarantees. Consider the example of hate speech laws.

Hate speech.   Another area in which attempts at special protection have been made is hate speech. Advocates of such protection maintain that racist speech is often deeply damaging to minorities and that the government ought to provide special protection to them against such speech. This special protection has been criticized on three grounds. First, it severely limits the right of free speech, which has a very strong constitutional foundation in the United States. In the eyes of the critics of such restrictions, it is not clear that the possible benefits outweigh the accompanying loss of freedom. Second, such restrictions are usually framed in such a way as to protect minorities in particular from such speech, but in the interests of equality shouldn't such protection be extended to all races and ethnicities? Yet in the past when it has existed, hate speech laws have typically been used to oppress racial minorities rather than protect them. Finally, there is a disturbingly large element of vagueness in such legislation. Precisely what counts as "hate speech" and what doesn't?

Common Ground

The elimination, or at least reduction, of inequalities caused by racial and ethnic discrimination is a complex matter, and here we find, even among people of good will who are committed to eradicating the legacy of racism in our society, there is deep disagreement about how this can best be accomplished. Certain programs, most notably strong affirmative action programs, have elicited great controversy and resentment. If there is a common ground here, it is probably to be found in searching for other means that promote the same goal with fewer liabilities.

The Arguments

Howard McGary
"Achieving Democratic Equality: Forgiveness, Reconciliation, and Reparations"

Howard McGary is a Professor of Philosophy at Rutgers University, where his current research centers around critique of liberal theories of distributive justice and an examination of the alleged connection between racial identification and moral and political theories. His books include Race and Social Justice *(Blackwell, 1999) and an anthology on* Reparations for African Americans *(forthcoming from Rowman and Littlefield).*

In this article, McGary begins by providing an account of reparations in general, and then discusses the reasons why some African Americans believe they are entitled to reparations from the U.S. government. He argues that this claim of African Americans is plausible and, furthermore, that reparations might serve to heal the breech that is perceived by many African Americans to exist between themselves and their government.

As You Read, Consider This:

1. What does McGary mean by the assimilationist-separatist debate?

2. McGary distinguishes between the material and the psychological dimensions of reparations. Which does he think is more important? Why?

3. Why does McGary maintain that forgiveness is important for African Americans? For society as a whole?

4. According to McGary, what must wrongdoers do before genuine forgiveness and reconciliation are possible?

In *Achieving Our Country: Leftist Thought in Twentieth Century America,*[1] Richard Rorty explores two passages from James Baldwin's *The Fire Next Time.*[2] One of the passages deals with the subject that is the title of Rorty's book and the other addresses forgiveness:

> This is the crime of which I accuse my country and my country men, and for which I nor time nor history will ever forgive them, that they have destroyed and are destroying hundreds and thousands of lives and do not know it and do not want to know it.[3]
>
> If we—and now I mean the relatively conscious whites and the relatively conscious blacks, who must, like lovers, insist on, or create, the consciousness of the others—do not falter in our duty now, we

The Journal of Ethics 7: 93–113, 2003. © 2003 Kluwer Academic Publishers.

may be able, the handful that we are, to end the racial nightmare. And achieve our country, and change the history of the world.[4]

Rorty uses Baldwin to raise two questions that have been a fundamental part of African American thought: Should African Americans forget and forgive the horrible legacy of Slavery and Jim Crow and affirm their U.S. citizenship? Or should they treat the U.S. as a false ideal that will never achieve its promise? Baldwin, of course, sides with people like Frederick Douglass[5] and Martin Luther King Jr.[6] who believed that the U.S. should be treated as an ideal in progress that can help us transform the present to a morally preferable future. Baldwin was optimistic about the possibility of achieving the U.S. ideal even though he believed that certain parts of U.S. history were unforgivable.

The issue that Baldwin and Rorty worry about can be recast in terms of the assimilationist vs. the separatist debates in African American social and political thought. Howard Brotz[7] does a good job of gathering writers on both sides of this debate. The separatists are doubtful that blacks and whites in the U.S. can work together to positively influence the consciousness of those people who would opt out of the U.S. ideal: one people, one nation.

Assimilationists are more optimistic about what people of different races can achieve by co-operating with each other even against a background of a tragic history of slavery, Jim Crow, and racism. Some racial assimilationists in this group even believe that the way to achieve such cooperation is to do away with the very idea of races and move forward from this point under some version of a race-blind principle.[8] However, others claim that we must still acknowledge racial identities, and the experiences that have accompanied those identities, though we should not let our painful memories prevent us from achieving a more inclusive and just U.S.[9]

But even some of the supporters of the assimilationist ideal are skeptical of the view that African Americans should forgive and forget their awful history. Like Baldwin they support working towards one U.S., but they reject the idea that Africans must forgive and give up their racial identities before they can engage in such a transformative effort. But before we can say whether African Americans should forgive and forget, we must have an adequate account of forgiveness. I have attempted to provide such an account in *Between Slavery and Freedom: Philosophy and American Slavery*.[10] There I argue that the reasons for forgiving or failing to forgive are "self-pertaining" and that forgiving or refusing to forgive primarily involves the agent's feeling about the elimination of her resentment that is caused by wrongdoing. Eliminating this resentment is often a way of getting on with one's life and shaping a different future. On my account, it might make sense for African Americans to forgive those who have caused harmed to them individually and as a people. However, some ways of understanding forgiveness are such that in the case of certain wrongs that are so awful and far reaching that the victims should never forgive the wrongdoers. How we decide this question has an important bearing on achieving democratic equality?

As we shall see, there are various proposals and ways of conceptualizing how we can move from our present situation to a more democratic society. Rorty's neo-pragmatist way of understanding this transformative effort expresses a lack of interest in the usefulness of viewing this project in terms of knowledge and truth. He rejects any philosophical basis for assessing competing claims about how to understand and achieve genuine human flourishing. His strategy is to use the pragmatist tradition as a way of assisting intellectuals in places like Central and Eastern Europe who are struggling to shape the post-totalitarian democratic institutions and public policies. Judith Green[11] has applauded Rorty's efforts at revising American pragmatism, particularly the work of John Dewey, but she criticizes him for distorting Dewey's message. In particular, she criticizes him for his swift dismissal of multicultural education and other related diversity efforts in the U.S. for promoting understanding across racial differences. However, it is not my purpose hear to evaluate Rorty's neo-pragmatism or Green's criticisms of it. I mention them only to point out that even amongst philosophers who believe that working towards an inclusive democracy is a laudable goal, there is serious disagreement over how this task should be conceptualized.

Any viable account of how to achieve democratic equality in the U.S. must address group domination. And, I believe, any realistic account of group domination must be holistic. It cannot be explained only by reference to the attitudes or psychologies of the dominant group. Nor can it be explained by reference to economic forces. Nor can it be explained by reference only to the political structure. Nor can it be explained by reference only to culture. It is instead to be explained by the complex interplay of all of these determinants. Nonetheless, it is clear that the political structures and processes have played an important role in any viable explanation of why certain groups are dominated. Given the horrible legacy of U.S. slavery and Jim Crow, is it realistic to think that the U.S. can eliminate the vestige of racism without adopting policies and programs that give moral and legal significance to racial identities? This question is complicated by the fact that the vestige of racism still haunts us.

I wish to explore some of the difficulties that racial assimilationist encounter as they attempt to move from the present reality to one that more clearly approximates a just society for all. Andrew Hacker has documented the disparities that continue to exist between the races in U.S. society.[12] But it is important to note that these disparities do not fully explain the alienation that many African Americans report, irrespective of their socioeconomic circumstances. This alienation prevents many of them from fully embracing the idea of a race-blind society.[13] They believe that abandoning racial identities at this time would be to "throw the baby out with the bath water." According to these critics, before racial identities can be judged as insignificant or irrelevant, certain things need to be addressed, and these things cannot be addressed without giving some significance to race.[14]

Surveys reveal that African Americans feel strongly about the following concerns: (1) settling the historical debt of justice to the descendants of slavery and (2) changing the democratic process in a way to make it more responsive to the interests of African Americans.[15] But can these two concerns be addressed while at the same time keeping us on the track towards the racially assimilated society? If reparations or a public apology for slavery and its aftermath are necessary for African Americans to truly put this horrible history behind them, will a society that is still divided along racial lines be able to make such an apology?

On one reading, the role of a philosopher in the controversy over an apology or reparations for U.S. slavery should be to clarify the meaning and moral status of the concepts involved in the debate. The philosopher might also show how concepts are different from, but related to each other. This is all on the conceptual or theoretical level. However, the philosopher can also clarify and examine various arguments offered for and against specific demands for reparations. It is here where the philosopher moves into applied or practical normative discourse.

I will begin with an account of reparations in general and then present briefly one explanation of why many present day African Americans believe they are entitled to reparations from the U.S. Government. This explanation should not be seen as a final justification, but only as an indication why the demand for reparations for African Americans might be seen a plausible. Next, if it is reasonable to assume that reparations to African Americans are plausible, I then go on to explain why reparations might be necessary to fill the breech that is perceived to exist between many African Americans and their government. This explanation will involve an examination of the relationship between three concepts: forgiveness, reconciliation, and reparations. Then I explore why an apology or reparations for slavery and Jim Crow might be necessary for reconciliation between many African Americans and their government. Finally, I examine the contention that the legislative process can be used to obtain an apology or reparations from the government. An important part of this examination is a fairly close reading of Lani Guinier's proposals for making the democratic process responsive to the perceived interests of African Americans as a group.[16] I close with some skeptical remarks about the efficacy of using Guinier's proposals to obtain an apology or reparations from the U.S. Government for the injustices of slavery and Jim Crow and about the likelihood that members of the majority will see the demand for reparations as something they can endorse.

I

There are three ways that such an apology or black reparations might come about: (1) by executive order (2) by judicial decision and (3) through the legislative process. Former U.S. President Bill Clinton suggested the executive order route and met with great opposition.[17] And a number of groups and individuals are trying to pursue reparation claims in the courts[18] and some legislators[19] have endorsed legislation that would address these concerns. But to date none of these efforts have been successful.

Given the importance of the legislative process, I would like to spend some time discussing Guinier's proposal for changing this process to make it more responsive to the perceived interests of African Americans. I will not attempt to give necessary and sufficient conditions for democratic equality. However, I will assume for the sake of argument that democratic equality has not been achieved when there is the existence of permanent minorities. A permanent minority exists when the majority is in agreement on all or most of the important issues and the minority disagree with the majority. And where the consequence is that the minority is unable to achieve its important ends through the political process. I will also assume that this can occur even when the minority is not denied its political or economic rights in a *de jure* sense.

II

But before we turn to Guinier's proposals, I want to say a few things about how the United States as a society has come to be where it is. For a country that is hundreds of years old, African Americans secured the right to vote only a few decades ago. And this right to vote did not come about because the majority saw it simply as the right thing to do. Quite to the contrary, it came about because of a process of political struggle and turmoil in which many people sacrificed their lives to obtain the right to vote. So even though there have been legal and economic changes for the better in U.S. society, many African Americans still believe that the U.S. owes them a debt of justice for what they and their ancestors have endured. The historic and present demand for black reparations is a call for the settling of this debt.

Above I claimed that many African Americans believe that they cannot fully embrace the U.S. Government until these negative feelings and rightful resentment are addressed. As the title of this article suggests, forgiveness, reconciliation, and reparations are possible ways to overcome this resentment felt by many African Americans. But do present day African Americans have to receive reparations before they can forgive and reconcile with those who they deem to be responsible for the transgressions? Is forgiveness for slavery a necessary part of a program of reconciliation? Before we answer, let us briefly review the argument for black reparations.

According to the argument for black reparations, African Americans are owed reparations because some transgression has occurred. And those who have a transgressed have a moral duty to repair the results of their transgressions. Unlike a compensation argument, the reparation argument depends upon identifying the wronged party and the wrongdoer. A principle of reparation is not a principle designed to promote social utility or promote an egalitarian outcome of economic goods. It is designed to rectify violations of people's rights.

For John Locke and other liberal political theorists to deny a person's right to reparation amounts to a refusal to recognize the full moral status of the person.[20] In fact, acknowledging a duty of reparation is good evidence that one views the wronged party as a bonafide member of the moral and political communities. According to Lockeans, a political morality is rights-based and the proper role of the legitimate state is to protect rights and address rights violations. Locke did not believe that the state should use its coercive powers to promote social utility if this involved violating people's rights. It is clear that the political morality in the U.S. is strongly influenced by Lockean ideas. As U.S. citizens, African Americans also have strong Lockean intuitions. So they often frame their political concerns in Lockean rights-based terms. The demand for black reparations is no exception.

Very few contemporary U.S. citizens would deny that U.S. slaves deserved reparations for slavery. The debate over reparations for slavery focuses on whether present day African Americans are entitled to reparations and on whom would be obliged to settle this debt; not on whether slaves were the victims of a terrible injustice. The critics question whether it would be just and wise for the U.S. Government to use tax dollars, tax exemptions or some other means to settle a debt of justice to present day African Americans.

The thoughtful and sincere criticisms of reparations for African Americans rest on the complications involved in providing a compelling case. The critics of reparations question the legitimacy of the demand because all present day African Americans are not the descendants of chattel slaves. In fact, some are fairly recent immigrants. Critics argue that the call for reparations conflates the following groups: (1) the willing perpetrators of injustice, (2) the culpable beneficiaries of injustice, (3) the non-culpable beneficiaries, and (4) the innocent bystanders. Or put in another way, all African Americans are not victims and all white Americans are not perpetrators.[21]

I believe that these complications can be addressed and I have tried to address them in some of my other work.[22] However, in this discussion, I do not wish to take up those issues. I want to focus on why the debt of justice, if owed to African Americans, ought to have some priority. As I have claimed elsewhere, a duty of reparations has two dimensions: a material and a psychological dimension. Both are important, but I wish to explore why reparations are very important and necessary.

Perhaps too much attention has been given to the material aspects of the demand for reparations. The psychological aspect of reparations may be more important. The call for reparation can be seen in part as an apology for slavery and as a way of overcoming victimization and, in the minds of some supporters, as a way moving closer to the ideal of a racially assimilated society.

If putting the victimization behind one is an indispensable first step in achieving forgiveness and reconciliation, a failure to do this may cause many African Americans to sit on the fence and not fully embrace their U.S. identity because the U.S. Government has not acknowledged in an official way its role in the victimization of African American people. This is not to say that African Americans have not served their country in times of need. Clearly they have supported the country in numerous ways, and they have fought and died in defense of U.S. ideals, but, nonetheless, many have remained ambivalent about fully identifying as U.S. citizens.

Many African Americans believe that they still suffer because of the legacies of U.S. slavery and Jim Crow, but they realize that we live in political climate that stigmatizes black victimization. In fact, a prevalent view is that a person who sees herself as a victim of past discrimination is someone who is unwilling to take advantage of existing opportunities. Acknowledging black victimization is often described in pejorative terms as "playing the race card,"[23] or as a "victim's mentality."[24] And playing the race card is a practice that is taken to be at odds with the U.S. ideal of judging persons by their deeds rather than their racial identities. This practice is taken to be incompatible with genuinely working to achieve a racially assimilated society.

There is not a logical or practical incompatibility between acknowledging a history of racial discrimination and working hard to be successful in life. However, because of their life circumstances, people deal with discrimination and injustice in different ways. Some people are able to succeed in spite of it while others may be broken by it. But success and failure is usually not an individual achievement—it often depends upon networks and support systems. African American children who live in poverty need to know that they bear no responsibility for being born into a family that lives in a poor black community with inadequate schools and other services. Acknowledging the historical conditions that contributed to the formulation of such communities is not to coddle these children. Nor does it blind them to real opportunities.

In the debate over how to remedy the effects of past racial discrimination we find two approaches: backward-looking and forward-looking justifications. Reparations are an example of the former approach. Those who are called upon to give up holdings that they presently have in their possession because they have a duty of reparations are only asked to do so because they have been wrongdoers. And those who receive these holdings are entitled to them only because they have been wronged. Supporters of black reparations want to change the status quo, but they do so for different reasons than egalitarians or utilitarians.

III

Many of the supporters of reparations believe that the only way to achieve genuine reconciliation between the races is for the U.S. Government to acknowledge its debt of justice to African Americans. And a similar acknowledgement has been an important ingredient of reconciliation programs in Australia and South Africa.[25] Furthermore, they believe that there cannot be any hope for forgiveness unless this debt is acknowledged. Therefore, it is extremely difficult for those who believe this debt has not been acknowledged to fully embrace the ideal of one nation and one people. They believe that there must be some truth and reconciliation before this ideal can be made real. But why do they believe that settling a debt of reparations is necessary for this truth and reconciliation to occur?

In Australia and South Africa there are active movements to bring about reconciliation between the victims of state sanctioned racial discrimination and the beneficiaries of this institutional racism. Individuals and institutions in these countries have acknowledged the wrongness and the detrimental consequences of prolonged state sanctioned racism, and their guilt either by association or participation. We find letters of apology from white Australians and white South Africans that reveal in quite moving terms the regret that they feel for not actively opposing their country's unjust policies and practices.

These letters are nice, but, clearly by themselves, they do not constitute reconciliation. And a relevant questions that is often asked is "what more is needed?" The call for more than an apology is connected to the idea that there must be truth in the expression of regret and remorse, but it must also be true that there is an accurate accounting of what actually took place. In other words, the apology must be genuine and there should be no doubt about why the apology was necessary. Since we cannot see into the hearts and minds of others, we have to rely on less direct evidence to establish that an apology is genuine or that a person is truly regretful or remorseful for past wrongdoing. So, a pertinent question is "what are these other forms of evidence?" For minor wrongs or infractions mere words may be enough, but when serious wrongdoing has occurred, speech acts are not sufficient. Why not?

It is common belief that it is easy to utter words of regret or remorse, but that some non-verbal demonstration of one's sincerity give us greater assurance that our words are genuine. Sometimes the shedding of a tear, or our facial expressions can provide further evidence of a person's sincerity. These things are useful, but in the case of serious wrongs, they are usually not enough to convince the victim that the apology is genuine. This is especially true when there has been some unjust enrichment as a result of the wrongdoing. In such cases, relinquishing the unjust gains is a further sign of one's sincerity. To apologize, but not to offer to return one's unfair benefits, cast doubt on one's sincerity. Of course, I am not maintaining that an offer to return one's ill-gotten gains entails that a person's apology is genuine, but it can count as evidence. However, where the victim is entitled to reparation, this may be the best available evidence that the wrongdoer's apology is genuine.

So far we have discussed what can count as reliable evidence for the sincerity of a wrongdoer's expression of remorse. Now I would like to turn to a related, but different concern: the requirement that the wrongdoer give a truthful account of what he did and why he did it. It is important for the victims of wrongdoing to know that the perpetrators realize what they have done and how the victims have been affected by their actions. This is why convicted criminals are given the opportunity to speak after the verdict in a criminal trial. They are given the opportunity to speak in order to show that they appreciate the gravity of what they have done. Their statements can influence the judge in the sentencing process.

Reparations, when they are conceived properly, involve reassessment. The reassessment requires the alleged victims to examine their victimization, the alleged wrongdoers to come to grips with what they have done, and the victims and the wrongdoers to explore their relationship with one another. In a like manner, when a wrongdoer, be it the state or some other perpetrator, shows that there is an appreciation for the consequences of their wrongdoing, this helps to make reconciliation more likely. And reconciliation requires that the wronged and the wrongdoers be able to interact as moral equals. So reconciliation requires the parties to be as fully informed as possible.

Given that we are focusing on reconciliation between the victims of U.S. slavery and Jim Crow and their transgressors, it is proper to see the wrongs as rights violations. However, it would be a mistake to assume that all cases of forgiveness and reconciliation are rights violations. For example, I may feel especially close to a person who has been wronged through a violation of his rights and thus I may feel that I have been wronged even though my rights have not been violated. And, as a consequence, I experience anger and resentment. This may be the case in the case of slavery. I may feel wronged by the institution of slavery because my ancestors who were held as slaves had their rights violated.

If this is so, present-day African Americans may correctly feel that they are warranted in having negative feelings towards the perpetrators of past injustices even though they were not personally treated in these unjust ways. Of course, it is not my contention that each and every African American will respond to the injustice of slavery in this way. Some may not harbor negative feelings like anger or resentment, but instead feel hurt or disappointed. But in either case, it seems proper to say whether it is anger or hurt feelings, the wronged party has a grievance against the wrongdoers that needs to be overcome.

But why should present day African Americans who have these feelings think that they are morally justified in having them? Following Jeffrey Murphy's[26] lead, one might argue that these negative feelings are morally justified because when they occur in response to wrongdoing they are tied to a healthy self-concept. Or, put in another way, people who do not have these feelings do not have the appropriate regard for their status as moral beings.

Let us begin with the latter question. If forgiveness can be seen as the overcoming of negative feelings caused by wrongdoing, one might wonder what the proper relationship should be between forgiveness and reconciliation. Remember that both Australia and South Africa instituted reconciliation commissions. These commissions define "reconciliation" as overcoming a breech in a valued relationship where a person or group has been wronged by another person or group.[27] In the case of Australia and South Africa, the valued relationship that was breeched was equal citizenship. Reconciliation occurs when the valued relationship is restored. So if there is a breech between present day African Americans and their government due to slavery and Jim Crow, must African Americans forgive their government before reconciliation can occur? Is forgiveness a necessary condition of reconciliation?

Uma Narayan has argued that reconciliation can occur without forgiveness.[28] If she is right, then perhaps African Americans and the U.S. Government can reconcile their differences without forgiveness. But is forgiveness a necessary part of reconciliation? Here is Narayan's argument that it is not. She claims that through a process of resignation that people can resign themselves to a situation that they once resented by adopting lower expectations. She illustrates her point with the following example: A woman and a man are in a relationship where they both agree about what is expected of them in the relationship. But unfortunately, the man is repeatedly unable to keep his end of the bargain. The woman feels anger and resentment about his failings and this leads to a breech in their relationship. But on reflection, she comes to see that she values their relationship in spite of the shortcomings, so she lowers her expectations and once again restores and values her relationship and no longer resents her partner.[29]

Is Narayan correct in identifying this as an example of reconciliation? If she is, then this is not a case where one has eliminated or overcome one's resentment, but rather case where one has resigned oneself to live with it. If forgiveness is the overcoming of righteous resentment, then we have a case where reconciliation has occurred without forgiveness. A crucial part of her example and point is that resignation through lowered expectations can occur without us holding the person who engages in this type of resignation in contempt or disgust. In other words, the resignation can be seen as morally appropriate.

But even if Narayan is right about this case, it does not appear that African Americans who believe that they have been wronged as a result of slavery can lower their expectations about how the U.S. Government should act without raising serious questions about whether they have the proper regard for the demands of morality or themselves. Thus it does not appear that reconciliation can occur in this case without forgiveness.

IV

If reparations for Africans are justified, and they have the psychological value that I have given to them, can the democratic process serve as a vehicle for giving African Americans reparations and the recognition and respect that they feel they deserve? If reparations play the important role that I argued for earlier, can African Americans use the ballot box to obtain them?

According to procedural democracy, rule by the majority is both necessary and sufficient for filling the requirements of a democracy. Or, put in another way, it is a fair procedure for determining which conflicting interests should be given priority. However, many African American authors have argued that this procedure is not fair to their group. They contend that focusing on procedural democracy rather than substantive democracy will not give the appropriate regard to their interests, and as a consequence, they are not in any substantive way true participants in the democratic process.

Guinier gives clear articulation of this criticism.[30] She argues that the present political democracy in the U.S. tyrannizes certain racial minority groups, in particular African Americans. Here is her argument in the first part of the book.

P1: If a political system is to count as a genuine democracy, it must be responsive to the interests of all of it citizens.

P2: If a political system is responsive to its citizens, it must (i) protect the interests of all its citizens, (ii) avoid the problem of perpetual losers in the democratic process, (iii) engender a sense of faith in the system by all of the citizens, and (iv) serve as a tool for self-determination for each and every citizen.

P3: The political democracy in the United States has failed to be responsive to all citizens.

C1: The political system in the U.S. is not a genuine democracy.

Guinier's support for P1 follows traditional thinking, but controversy arises in regards to P2. There is widespread disagreement about what constitutes responding to the interests of all of the citizens. Guinier believes that without authentic black leaders it is doubtful that African American interests will be considered.

Guinier faces a dilemma shared by all racial assimilationists who provisionally adopt race-conscious policies in order to reach a race blind society. The dilemma is as follows: endorsing the moral ideal of a race-blind society, while at the same time maintaining that it will be necessary for a time to give significance to racial identity as a means to achieve the ideal of racial blindness.

Many in the majority might innocently believe that slaves were wronged in grievous ways, but they also believe there must be some limit on the time that a person or group has for seeking redress, and clearly this time has passed in the case for African American reparations. They appeal to something like the statute of limitations principle to support their position. The purpose of the statute of limitations principle is "to require diligent prosecution of know claims, thereby providing finality and predictability in legal affairs and ensuring that claims will be resolved while evidence is reasonably available and fresh."[31] The statute of limitations principle has its most common application in the law, but the debate over reparations for slavery is thought to have some moral currency. Since this is a paper about the morality of reparations, I will briefly explore what this moral currency might be.

In the law there are two basic reasons offered in support of the statute of limitations principle. One reason has to do with the reliability of the evidence that is at issue in a legal case and the other is the belief that people can change over time and that if we wait too long the person who committed a crime may not be the same person who is being prosecuted for the crime at some much later time. The idea is that the person at the later time is no longer the lawbreaker that committed the crime.

However this rationale for the statute of limitations principle appears to depend upon a theory of punishment or compensation that focuses on the motives of the actor rather than outcomes. If we adopt this rationale, then people who have committed the most horrendous crimes could avoid punishment because they have managed to turn their lives around. This way of viewing things would be at odds with punishing because of its deterrence value.

Most people in the controversy over reparations for slavery interpret the statute of limitations principle in a way that raises problems about the reliability of the evidence. For example, in a criminal trial the testimony of an eye-witness becomes less reliable over time because their memories fade. But with a greater reliance on things like DNA evidence, the passage of time becomes less relevant. However is the case of reparations for slavery, the critics believe that the passage of time does call into question the reliability of the evidence that is being used to make the case.

This criticism is most forceful when the case for reparations is being brought against individual persons who are the heirs of slaveholders. But when the liable party is thought to be the U.S. Government, the passage of time is not as relevant. This is because we have a more comprehensive public record about the actions of the U.S. Government than we do about individual citizens. Therefore, the passage of time does not weaken our ability to know what happened. In fact, in some cases we actually know more about what the U.S. government did two hundred years ago than the persons who were alive at the time. So when all the evidence is presented, I do not think the people who refuse to vote for reparations can say that they are justified in doing so by appeal to this interpretation of the statute of limitations principle.

But perhaps there is another interpretation of the principle that may better serve their purposes. Maybe the statute of limitations principle tells us that if we do not practice due diligence in bringing a case in a timely fashion, then we should not bring the case at all. For instance, in small claims court there is a specified period of time (usually two years) to bring a suit for damages.

However, even if the critics use this interpretation of the statute of limitations principle, their argument cannot succeed. The present demand for reparations is not the first time African Americans have demanded reparations from their government for slavery. Through the years they have made such a demand, but it has always fallen on deaf ears.[32] However, the present demand has created a public debate that did not accompany previous demands. Whether the supporters of reparations can convince the majority that their demand is a reasonable and worthy one is yet to be seen. On the merits, I think a strong case has been made. However, given the tendency by the majority to distort and misrepresent the facts when the subjects are black people,[33] I am skeptical that even a quite compelling case for reparations will have sway. But hopefully the discussion in the pages of this journal, along with other thoughtful commentary on both sides of this issue, will help to give the demand by African Americans for reparations the public and legislative discussion that it deserves.

References

1. Richard Rorty, *Achieving Our Country: Leftist Thought in Twentieth Century America* (New York: Penguin Putnam, 1999), pp. 11–14.
2. James Baldwin, *The Fire Next Time* (New York: A Laurel Book, 1985).
3. Baldwin, *The Fire Next Time*, p. 15.

4. Baldwin, *The Fire Next Time,* p. 141.

5. See, for example, Frederick Douglass, "The Meaning of July Fourth for the Negro," in Philip S. Foner (ed.), *The Life and Writings of Frederick Douglass,* Vol. 2 (New York: International Publishers, 1950–1975), pp. 181–204.

6. Martin Luther King, Jr., *Why We Can't Wait* (New York: Mass Market Paperback/ NAL, 2002).

7. Howard Brotz (ed.), *African American Social and Political Thought From 1850–1915* (New Brunswick: Transaction Books, 1991).

8. See K. Anthony Appiah and Amy Gutmann, *Color Conscious: The Political Morality of Race* (Princeton: Princeton University Press, 1996), pp. 30–74 and Richard Wasserstrom, "On Racism and Sexism," in R. Wasserstrom (ed.), *Philosophy and Social* Issues (Notre Dame: Notre Dame University Press, 1980), pp. 11–50.

9. Lucius Outlaw, *On Race and Philosophy* (New York: Routledge, 1996) and Iris Young, *Justice and the Politics of Difference* (Princeton: Princeton University Press, 1990).

10. Howard McGary and Bill Lawson, *Between Slavery and Freedom: Philosophy and American Slavery* (Bloomington: Indiana University Press, 1992), Chapter 6.

11. Judith Green, *Deep Democracy* (Lanham: Rowman and Littlefield Publishers, 1999), pp. 149–152.

12. Andrew Hacker, *Two Nations: Black and White, Separate, Hostile, Unequal* (New York: Scribner's, 1992).

13. Howard McGary, *Race and Social Justice* (London: Blackwell Publishers, 1999), Chapter 1.

14. See, for example, Outlaw, *On Race and Philosophy.*

15. Roy L. Brooks (ed.), *When Sorry Isn't Enough: The Controversy over Apologies and Reparations for Human Injustice* (New York: New York University Press, 1999).

16. Lani Guinier, *The Tyranny of the Majority: Fundamental Fairness in Representative Democracy* (New York: The Free Press, 1994).

17. See *The Source Magazine,* October 1997.

18. Several lawyers have been assembled by Professor Charles Ogletree of Harvard University to prepare reparations litigation for African Americans. There have also been a number of recent articles published in law journals supporting the idea of reparations for African Americans, e.g., Robert Westley, "Many Billions Gone: Is It Time to Reconsider the Case for Black Reparations?," *Boston College Law Review* 40 (1998), pp. 429–476.

19. Representative Tony Hall (D-Ohio) has introduced legislation calling for an official apology for slavery and representative John Conyers (D-Michigan) has consistently introduced legislation calling for reparations to African Americans.

20. John Locke, *The Second Treatise of Government,* ed. Thomas P. Peardon (New York: Bobbs-Merril, 1968), pp. 7–9.

21. David Horowitz, *Uncivil Wars: The Controversy over Reparations for Slavery* (New York: Encounter Books, 2001).

22. McGary, *Race and Social Justice.*

23. Tali Mendleberg, *The Race Card* (Princeton: Princeton University Press, 2001).

24. Shelby Steele, *The Content of Our Character: A New Vision of Race in America* (New York: Saint Martin's Press, 1990), Chapters 3 and 4.

25. Timothy George Lobert Smith, Jr., *A Mighty Long Journey: Reflections on Racial Reconciliation* (New York: Broadman & Holman Publishers, 2000).

26. Jeffrey Murphy and Jean Hampton, *Forgiveness and Mercy* (Cambridge: Cambridge University Press, 1994).

27. See, e.g., "Words, Symbols and Actions: Reconciliation Report Card 2002," A Report from the Reconciliation Australia Organization.

28. Uma Narayan, "Forgiveness, Moral Reassessment, and Reconciliation," in Thomas Magnell (ed.), *Explorations of Value* (Amsterdam: Rodopi, 1997), pp. 169–178.

29. Narayan, "Forgiveness, Moral Reassessment, and Reconciliation," p. 177.

30. Guinier, *The Tyranny of the Majority.*

31. *Black's Law Dictionary,* 7th ed. (St. Paul: West Group, 1999), p. 1422.

32. Randall Robinson, *The Debt: What America Owes to Blacks* (New York: Dutton, 2000).

33. See Irving Thalberg, "Visceral Racism," *The Monist* 56 (1972), pp. 43–63.

Journal/Discussion Questions

1. McGary asks whether "Given the horrible legacy of U.S. slavery and Jim Crow, is it realistic to think that the U.S. can eliminate the vestige of racism without adopting policies and programs that give moral and legal significance to racial identities?" What is your answer to this question? What implications for social policy follow from your answer?

2. Does reconciliation necessarily involve forgiveness? What is McGary's position on this issue? What do you think? Why?

3. On what basis does Guinier maintain that the United States is not a genuine democracy? Do you agree with her? Why or why not?

4. How does McGary respond to the claim that there should be a statute of limitations on reparations, and that in the United States that time limit has been passed? Do you agree with McGary?

David A. Reidy
"Hate Crimes Laws: Progressive Politics or Balkanization?"

David Reidy is an assistant professor at the University of Tennessee, where he teaches a course in the philosophy of law as well as ethics and social and political philosophy. He holds a degree in law as well as philosophy and has published widely in those areas. His recent work has centered on several different themes, including Rawls and international justice.

Civility and Its Discontents: Civic Virtue, Toleration, and Cultural Fragmentation, edited by Christine T. Sistare (Lawrence: University of Kansas Press, 2004).

In this article, Reidy is interested in pursuing the question of the justification of hate crime laws. He argues that the standard attempts to justify these laws fail and explores an alternative justification that he feels is more promising.

As You Read, Consider This:

1. Reidy identifies three main arguments in favor of hate crime laws. What are they? What flaws does he find in each?

2. Reidy presents and defends what he calls the argument from oppression. Briefly summarize that argument. How does it avoid the objections Reidy raises against the previous three arguments?

3. According to Reidy, in what ways does hate crime legislation threaten to be divisive in our society?

I. Introduction

In 1981 the Anti-Defamation League of B'nai B'rith published the model for what have now become known as hate crimes laws. Hate crimes laws are "penalty enhancement" laws. They enhance the penalties for a variety of crimes (most commonly assault, homicide, arson, trespass and vandalism) provided certain triggering conditions are met. Some hate crimes laws apply to specified crimes any time the perpetrator selects his victim because of her race, ethnicity, religion, sexual orientation or other specified characteristic. Others apply to specified crimes only if the perpetrator selects his victim out of a special animus toward a racial, ethnic, religious, or other specified group to which she belongs. So, a law of the first sort but not the second would apply to a criminal who commits one of the specified crimes against a Black victim not out of any particular hostility toward Blacks as a racial group, and not randomly, but because he believes the police less likely to investigate crimes committed against Blacks and thinks judges sentencing those convicted of such crimes less likely to impose harsh sentences.

Hate crimes laws are now common in the United States; they have even worked their way into federal law. Notwithstanding significant public and academic support, these laws have been subject to strong, serious and persistent criticism. And much of it is well-deserved, for the arguments standardly made in favor of hate crimes laws are either unsound or weak. Demonstrating as much is the first aim of this paper.

Its second aim, however, is to offer a non-standard argument for hate crimes laws that is neither unsound nor weak. This argument I call the argument from oppression. It captures and expresses better than any of the standard arguments the moral basis for the sentiments or intuitions many people have in favor of hate crimes laws, and the objections to the standard arguments do not apply to it. But one objection (or perhaps it is a family of objections) must still be addressed. This objection posits hate crimes laws (along with, perhaps, affirmative action policies, the expansion of sexual harassment laws, slavery reparations initiatives, and the like) as the balkanizing result of an identity or interest group politics of resentment inconsistent with progressive liberal democratic values.

II. The Standard Arguments

There are three standard arguments for hate crimes laws. The first is the argument from greater harm. The second is the argument from more culpable mental states. The third is the argument from liberal democratic values. Each of these arguments is either unsound or weak.

A. The Argument from Greater Harm

Whether crimes satisfying the trigger conditions of hate crimes laws cause greater harm, physical or psychological, either to victims or non-victim third parties, than similar but non-hate crimes is, of course, an empirical question. This is often forgotten and a priori pronouncements regarding the greater harmfulness of hate crimes are not uncommon. Unhappily, as prima facie plausible as these pronouncements may be, they are not supported by the available empirical evidence.

Crimes said to be hate crimes do often cause physical harm to their direct and immediate victims. But that is because they are very often assaults and homicides, not because they are committed by perpetrators who satisfy the relevant statutory trigger conditions for hate crimes penalty enhancements. As a class the crimes that satisfy these conditions are no more violent or physically harmful to their victims than the class that do not. And, in any event, existing laws already scale punishment to reflect the nature and degree of physical harm of assaults and homicides to victims.

Because there is little evidence to support the claim that crimes falling within the scope of hate crimes laws are more physically harmful to victims (or, for that matter, to non-victim third parties) than those otherwise similar crimes that do not, the argument is often made that these crimes, those that fall within the scope of hate crimes laws, cause greater psychological harm to their direct and immediate victims, or to non-victim third parties, than those that do not. This greater psychological harm justifies, so the argument goes, the additional punishment imposed by hate crimes laws.

Crimes said to be hate crimes do cause psychological harm both to their direct and immediate victims and to non-victim third parties. But so do virtually all crimes. The question is whether candidate hate crimes cause greater psychological harm than otherwise similar non-hate crimes. With respect to direct and immediate victims, the available empirical evidence suggests that they do not. Indeed, it suggests that candidate hate crimes may cause their direct and immediate victims marginally less psychological harm than similar crimes that would not count as hate crimes under typical hate crimes laws.

This evidence is admittedly counter-intuitive. There is, consequently, a temptation to dismiss it in favor of arm chair psychological speculation. But the evidence ought not be dismissed (although pending further studies it ought to be regarded as tentative). Most candidate hate crimes are committed against persons belonging to historically oppressed groups: Blacks, gays, Jews, ethnic minorities and the like. It is not implausible to suppose that many of these victims will possess preferences and other psychological mechanisms adapted to their condition, and that these may mitigate their subjective experience of psychological distress when made victim to a candidate hate crime. It is also not implausible to suppose that the nature of many candidate hate crimes will make it clear to the victim that she was targeted because of her race, or sexual orientation, or religion, etc., thus giving her a way of making a kind of sense of the crime committed against her she would not be able to make were she randomly victimized. These suppositions, admittedly unconfirmed, are sufficiently plausible as explanations of the admittedly counter-intuitive empirical evidence regarding the psychological harm caused by candidate hate crimes to their direct and immediate victims that that evidence ought not be simply dismissed.

As with direct and immediate victims, there is little evidence to support the claim that candidate hate crimes cause non-victim third parties greater psychological harm than similar crimes that fall outside the scope of hate crimes laws. The psychological harm of any crime to non-victim third parties is determined primarily by the proximity and visibility of the crime to such parties. This, of course, does not preclude additional psychological harms to non-victim third parties arising from the fact that the victim was selected because of or out of animosity toward her membership in a racial, religious, ethnic or other specified group. Or, at least it does not preclude such additional psychological harms when the crime visibly manifests an animosity toward a group with which the non-victim third parties strongly self-identify. While there is no substantial body of empirical evidence to confirm the claim that candidate hate crimes cause such harms to non-victim third parties, the claim (that obvious gay-bashings "terrorize" the gay community generally, etc.) is prima facie plausible. (Of course, even if there were empirical evidence confirming the claimed psychological harms, it would still be necessary to argue that those harms are serious enough to justify the relevant penalty enhancements.) It should not surprise, then, that this argument has been made to do much of the justificatory work in the case for hate crimes laws. Given the absence of compelling empirical evidence establishing the claimed psychological harms, however, it is at present a weak argument. It is also just the sort of argument that invites the characterization of hate crimes laws as the fruit of a balkanizing, identity group, politics of resentment. But that is a matter the discussion of which must be temporarily postponed in the interest of completing a review of the standard arguments. The upshot here is that the best version of the argument from greater harm is the argument from psychological harms to non-victim third parties, and that that argument is, as things stand, not very compelling.

There is, however, an additional difficulty with the argument from psychological harms to non-victim third parties that bears mentioning here. And that is that when we think about the mechanism through which such psychological harms are said to arise, we can see that it is not the harms themselves that explain the moral intuition or sentiment in favor of enhanced penalties for hate crimes. It is rather the membership of the victim in an oppressed group, or, better, the special moral wrong done by targeting for criminal conduct persons already disproportionately vulnerable to harm, whether by virtue of belonging to an oppressed group or for some other reason.

If hate crimes cause greater psychological harm to non-victim third parties than non-hate crimes, it is because they cause psychological harms (e.g., fear or terror) to persons who identify strongly through group membership with the victim and thus feel themselves to be vicariously targeted by the crime. This sort of self-identification through group membership is not uncommon among members of oppressed groups. And thus it is not implausible to assert that paradigm hate crimes cause greater psychological harms to non-victim third parties, and that these harms justify enhancing the penalties for such crimes. After all, paradigm hate crimes are committed against members of oppressed groups.

But the members of oppressed groups do not always self-identify through group membership. While self-identification through group membership is common within oppressed groups, it is not necessary or inevitable. It is usually the contingent result of strategic political resistance to oppression. Only through concrete political efforts have Blacks, women and gays, for example, produced such a group-based self-identification as a political resource. There was a time when few members of each group would have identified themselves primarily through their group membership. Yet, Blacks, women and gays were each oppressed groups (and thus disproportionately vulnerable to certain so-cial harms) prior to and independent of members self-identifying through group membership. And it is this deeper more basic fact about paradigm hate crimes, that they are selectively committed against members of oppressed groups, that generates the moral intuitions or sentiments in favor of penalty enhancements, not the contingent if often concomitant fact of psychological harm to non-victim third parties.

This can be seen by considering two alternative sorts of cases. The first involves crimes com-mitted selectively against the members of a group who strongly self-identify through group mem-bership but who are not oppressed and thus disproportionately vulnerable to social harm. Suppose (what may in fact be true) that many or most prostitutes self-identify with other prositittutes and that those who serially attack prostitutes specifically cause special psychological harms (e.g., fear and terror) to non-victim third party prostitutes. Do such crimes merit enhanced penalties as hate crimes? Few will have the intuition or feel the sentiment that they do. Or, suppose a criminal who serially and selectively attacks only Deadheads (the legendary followers of the Grateful Dead), a group the mem-bers of which strongly self-identify through group membership. Does he commit a hate crime? Again, few if any will think he does. In both cases it is likely that the crimes will cause special psycholog-ical harms to non-victim third parties. And these special harms may be noteworthy at the time of sen-tencing as an aggravating factor of some import. But they are not harms sufficient in moral weight to justify the non-discretionary legislative imposition of enhanced penalties through hate crimes laws. This is one important reason why hate crimes advocates do not propose statutory language cov-ering such cases.

The second sort of case involves crimes committed selectively against members of a group dis-proportionately vulnerable to social harm but not oppressed who do not self-identify through group membership. Such crimes cannot cause the relevant special psychological harms to non-victim third parties. But like crimes committed selectively against members of oppressed groups they generate powerful intuitions or sentiments in favor of penalty enhancement. Consider, for example, crimes committed selectively against the cognitively impaired. Such crimes generate strong moral intuitions or sentiments in favor of penalty enhancement. But not because of psychological harms to non-victim third parties, but rather because of the disproportionate vulnerability to harm of the cognitively im-paired and the additional moral wrong done by those who specifically target them for criminal con-duct. In terms of the moral logic in favor of penalty enhancement, these cases present a closer analogy to paradigm hate crimes than do those selectively committed against the members of non-oppressed groups who nevertheless strongly self-identify through group-membership.

Crimes committed selectively against Jews in the United States present an interesting difficulty here. Jews self-identify through group membership for both religious reasons and reasons rooted in resistance to a history of oppression. It is quite plausible to assert that crimes committed selectively against Jews in the United States cause greater psychological harm to non-victim third parties than similar crimes not so selectively committed. But there is a question as to whether we should assim-ilate such crimes to the class of crimes selectively committed against, say, Blacks and other groups currently oppressed (the members of which may or may not self-identify strongly through group membership) or to the class of crimes selectively committed against, say, DeadHeads and other groups the members of which self-identify through, but are not oppressed by virtue of, group-membership. This question turns, I think, on the empirical question of whether Jews constitute an oppressed group today in the United States. If they do, then crimes committed selectively against Jews belong in the same category as those committed selectively against Blacks. If they do not, then they belong in the same category as crimes committed against the members of other non-oppressed groups that nevertheless strongly self-identify through group membership.

What these cases show, I think, is that even if, or where, paradigm hate crimes cause greater psychological harm to non-victim third parties, it is not the greater psychological harms that justifies the penalty enhancements imposed by hate crimes laws. It is rather the special moral wrong done by those who selectively target members of oppressed groups. But this argument must wait for further development. There are other more standard arguments still waiting to be examined first.

B. The Argument from More Culpable Mental States

The criminal law in the United States already scales punishment according to whether an offender acts intentionally, knowingly, recklessly or negligently. Thus, if hate crimes laws are to be justified by appeal to the more culpable mental states of those who commit crimes satisfying their trigger conditions, it must be that those who commit such crimes act from a more culpable mental state than those who commit crimes otherwise identical but outside the scope of such laws.

This is straightforwardly implausible with respect to those hate crimes laws that apply to perpetrators who simply select their victims because of their race, or religion, or ethnicity, or sexual orientation, etc. Recall that hate crimes laws of this sort would apply to a criminal who selects only Protestant victims because he believes only Protestants will in fact enjoy the sort of salvation that might redeem their suffering here on earth. He selects his victims because of their religion. But does he act from a mental state more culpable than the criminal who randomly selects his victims just because he likes the experience of anonymous power, or the criminal who carefully selects his victims based on who is most likely to suffer the greatest from his crime? Obviously not.

To be sure, it may be that some criminals who commit crimes against victims selected because of their race, or religion, or ethnicity, etc., act from mental states more culpable than those who commit otherwise identical crimes against victims selected for other reasons. But this is not true of all criminals who commit crimes against victims selected for such reasons. It follows that where the mental state of a criminal who selects his victim because of her race, or religion, or ethnicity is in fact more culpable than it would be had he selected his victim for some other reason, the additional culpability must be a function of something beyond the fact that he selected his victim because of her race, or religion, or ethnicity, etc. What that something else is I will turn to later. For now, it is enough to note that the argument from more culpable mental states fails as an argument for those hate crimes laws that enhance penalties whenever the criminal selects his victim because of her race, or religion, or ethnicity, or sexual orientation, etc.

The argument from more culpable mental states is perhaps more plausible as a justification for those hate crimes laws that apply to perpetrators who select their victims out of one or another specified group-based animosity. After all, to act from racist, anti-Semitic, homophobic, or xenophobic hatred or animosity is clearly to act from a very culpable mental state, indeed a mental state more culpable than many still significantly culpable alternatives. And this greater culpability can be explained by reference to the evil of targeting individuals solely out of a group-based animosity.

But is it obvious that the mental state of a criminal who selects his victims out of racist animosity is more culpable than that of the criminal who selects his victims out of a desire to see the weak suffer, or to impose the greatest harm possible on a non-victim third party, or to display his superiority to the ordinary run of humanity, or to salve an ego all too easily bruised. That is less clear. Indeed, once adequate attention is given to the range of vicious and evil reasons that lead persons to commit crimes against others, it is not obvious that racist, anti-Semitic, homophobic or xenophobic reasons are significantly more vicious or evil than other familiar reasons criminals have for selecting victims which the law largely ignores when it comes to scaling punishment for crimes. In fact, the whole idea of correctly scaling criminal punishments to reflect the culpability of the reasons for which the criminal selected his victim looks to be beyond the reach of ordinary human abilities once the full range of reasons that lead people to commit crimes against particular victims is fully in view. It is, perhaps, no accident that for the most part the criminal law has limited its inquiry into the culpability of mental states to whether the act in question was done intentionally, knowingly, recklessly or negligently.

Like the argument from psychological harms to non-victim third parties, the argument from the greater culpability of racist, anti-Semitic, homophobic, xenophobic or similar mental states has been pressed into active and regular service by proponents of hate crimes laws. But it too is a weak argument. The problem is not that an empirical premise remains unconfirmed, but rather that an axiological premise—that to select a victim out of racist animosity, say, is worse, ceteris paribus, than to select a victim for virtually any other reason—appears either dubious or unjustifiable through argument available to ordinary human intellect. And this weakness renders the argument from more culpable mental states vulnerable, like the argument from psychological harms to non-victim third parties, to the charge that it arises out of and affirms an undesirable balkanizing, identity group, politics of resentment. What else, the objectors ask, could explain the vigor and confidence with which proponents of this argument assert the greater culpability of selecting a victim because he's Black, or gay, or Jewish, or Latino as compared to selecting a victim for any number of other reasons? This charge aside, the upshot here is that the argument from more culpable mental states is not a very compelling argument for either of the two sorts of hate crimes laws in force in the United States today.

C. The Argument from Liberal Democratic Values

Hate crimes laws are sometimes defended on the grounds that they are needed to give adequate public and symbolic expression to the fundamental liberal democratic values of nondiscrimination and tolerance. Crimes committed against particular victims because of or out of a group-based animosity for their race, or religion, or ethnicity or sexual orientation violate these values in a manner and to a degree calling for special public condemnation. Or so the argument goes.

There are many difficulties with this argument. The first is that it is weak as an argument for hate crimes laws that apply just in case the criminal selects his victim because of but not necessarily out of animosity toward her race, religion, ethnicity, etc. The criminal who decides just to assault Catholics, not because he has any group-based animosity toward them, but rather because he wants to systematize his victims in some fashion and attacking only Catholics enables him to do so, does not violate the liberal democratic values of nondiscrimination and tolerance in any significant way, or at least he violates those values no more so than does any other criminal guilty of assault. So, the argument is best taken as an argument for hate crimes laws that apply just in case the criminal selects his victim out of one or another specified group-based animosity.

But even so taken the argument is not strong. Even if a criminal who so selects his victim violates the liberal democratic values of nondiscrimination and tolerance, and even if that violation calls for a special and visible public condemnation, it does not follow that that condemnation must take the form of enhanced criminal penalties. A special concern with and condemnation of such conduct may be publicly and visibly expressed in a variety of ways within and through public political culture. Given the seriousness of enhancing criminal penalties (a limitation of liberty after all), the argument from liberal democratic values is weak as an argument for hate crimes laws unless it can be shown that enhancing penalties is the only or the best way publicly and visibly to express a special concern with and condemnation of such conduct.

But suppose this can be shown. Is the argument from liberal democratic values then a strong argument for hate crimes laws, or at least those laws triggered when a victim is selected out of a specified group-based animosity? Well, yes and no. It all depends on what we mean when we speak of the liberal democratic values of nondiscrimination and tolerance.

Suppose we mean that persons ought not impose avoidable harms on others for irrational, irrelevant or indefensible reasons. Employers ought not deny jobs to otherwise qualified persons solely because of their race. Children ought not exclude from their circle of friends perfectly kind and fun but very heavy or bespectacled peers. And the like. If this is what we mean when we speak of the values of nondiscrimination and tolerance, then the argument from liberal democratic values justifies hate crimes laws applicable not only to criminals who select their victims because they are Black or gay or Jewish, but also to criminals who select their victims because they are fat, or skinny, or ugly, or exceedingly beautiful, or socially awkward, or socially adept, and so on, including all irrational, irrelevant or indefensible reasons for which a criminal might select his victim. But if this is what we mean then it is hard to see how to limit hate crimes laws to any manageable list of specified group-based animosities the selecting of a victim from which will trigger the laws' application. And if the list of group-based animosities triggering the application of hate crimes laws is to include hatred of the fat, the skinny, the ugly, the tattooed, the homeless, the socially awkward, the excessively wealthy, etc., then what is the point of having hate crimes laws? Why not simply enhance the penalties for all crimes of the targeted type, e.g., all assaults, all vandalisms?

Suppose what we mean by the values of nondiscrimination and tolerance is instead that persons ought not impose avoidable harms on others because of some attribute or trait that either cannot be changed or can be changed only at an unreasonable cost. Employers, again, ought not deny jobs to otherwise qualified persons solely because of their race, or their religion, or ethnicity. And children, again, ought not exclude from their circle of friends perfectly kind and fun but very heavy or bespectacled peers. But, again, if this is what we mean by the values of nondiscrimination and tolerance, the list of specified group-based animosities the selecting of a victim from which will trigger the enhancing of criminal penalties will be long indeed. Those who target the tall, or the exceedingly intelligent, or the stutterers ought to be subject, on this understanding of nondiscrimination and tolerance values, to the penalty enhancements of hate crimes laws.

If hate crimes laws of the sort proponents advocate are to be justified by the argument from liberal democratic values, then the values of nondiscrimination and tolerance must be tied specially to race, religion, ethnicity, sexual orientation and the like. After all, the sentiments and intuitions felt by the supporters of hate crimes laws are aroused by lynchings and cross-burnings, gay-bashings, vandalisms of Jewish businesses or cemeteries, arsons in Latino neighborhoods and the like. These are the paradigmatic hate crimes that call for enhanced penalties. Not attacks against the fat, the skinny, the tattooed, the shabbily dressed, the ugly, or the glamorous, even when they are specifically targeted out of a generalized animosity for such persons.

So, suppose what we mean when we speak of the values of nondiscrimination and tolerance is just that persons ought not impose avoidable harms on others because of their race, religion, sexual orientation, ethnicity and the like. If this is what we mean, then we might be able to argue from these liberal democratic values to hate crimes laws of the typical sort. The question is whether this is what we do, or should, mean by these values.

The advantage of this account of nondiscrimination and tolerance values, or at least of these values as they are invoked as part of a justification for hate crimes laws, is that it captures the idea that there is something special about race, ethnicity, religion, sexual orientation and the like and thus something special about imposing avoidable harms on others because of their race, or ethnicity, etc. If I refuse to date tall people or to purchase goods from persons who bear tattoos, I irrationally and indefensibly impose an avoidable harm on others, perhaps even because of a characteristic or trait that cannot be easily altered. But it would be a stretch at best to say that I violate the fundamental liberal democratic values of nondiscrimination and tolerance, at least insofar as we are talking about those values as violated by paradigmatic hate crimes. To be sure, my conduct may be rightly criticized, even perhaps morally criticized through a loose use of the language of nondiscrimination and tolerance. But the basis of that criticism cannot really be that I violate the values of nondiscrimination and tolerance insofar as we take those values to be essential to a just and stable liberal democratic order. But if we substitute Blacks for tall people or Jews for persons who bear tattoos, then the picture changes, at least for those of us living in the United States, with its history.

It is tempting here to say that what the core values of nondiscrimination and tolerance demand is that we ignore race, religion, ethnicity or sexual orientation in our interactions with others. That we be color-blind, etc., when it comes to social life, even in our criminal conduct, should we endeavor such conduct. But this is a view that many if not most proponents of hate crimes laws will have reason to reject. It implies that there is no significant moral difference between a White criminal who selects his victims because they are Black and a Black criminal who selects his victims because they are White, or between a Protestant criminal who selects his victims because they are Jewish and a Jewish criminal who selects his victims because they are Protestant. But many if not most proponents of hate crimes laws begin with the intuition that there is a moral difference, even if there are also moral similarities, between these cases. In each example, the prior but not the latter case reflects, expresses and arguably serves to reconstitute existing historical patterns of structural, group-based oppression. To treat the two cases as if they are not morally distinct in any significant way is to fail to attend to the realities of longstanding, structural, group-based oppression at which hate crimes laws are aimed as a partial remedial social response. It is to view the issue of hate crimes from the point of view of the non-oppressed.

It is racially motivated crimes against Blacks, not racially motivated crimes generally, religiously motivated crimes against non-Christians, not religiously motivated crimes generally, that generate the intuitions and sentiments many feel in favor of hate crimes laws. It is crimes against members of already oppressed groups precisely because they are members of already oppressed groups that call for enhanced penalties. Given the realities and history of structural, group-based oppression, a racially motivated murder committed by a Black man against a White man is, for the purposes of punishment, not very different from any other murder, or at least not very different from a murder motivated by a hatred of brunettes committed by a blonde. But a racially motivated murder committed by a White man against a Black man is different from other murders. It connects with those realities and presses that history forward in ways other murders cannot.

At their core and as affirmed and protected by law, the values of nondiscrimination and tolerance must be understood in terms of race, religion, ethnicity, sexual orientation and the like. There is indeed something special, morally speaking, about these specific kinds of social groupings: they point us toward some of the most pressing historical cases of structural group-based oppression that call for a remedial social response. What we mean, then, when we speak of the fundamental values of nondiscrimination and tolerance is not that race, religion, ethnicity or sexual orientation ought always to be ignored in social life, but rather that social life ought to be reorganized so as to eliminate the real, specific, long-lived, structural group-based oppression of Blacks and other non-Whites, Jews and other non-Christians, gays, lesbians and other nonheterosexuals, and non-European ethnic groups. These are the great, structural and evil instances of discrimination and intolerance we want to end, not the more general fact that we notice and sometimes are moved in our social interactions by the race, religion, ethnicity or sexual orientation (or height, IQ, or handsomeness, for that matter) of others. The intuition or sentiment that racially motivated assaults on Blacks, for example, deserve more punishment than other assaults in the United States arises out of a strong desire to end a real, particular case of structural group-based oppression and an awareness of how such crimes affirms and threatens to reconstitute that very oppression.

The argument from liberal democratic values, then, is strongest if the values of nondiscrimination and tolerance are understood not just to be specially connected and limited to race, religion, ethnicity, sexual orientation and the like, but to be so connected and limited in a particular way—proscribing the imposition of avoidable harms on Blacks because they are Black, or Jews because they are Jews, etc., where the imposition of those harms reflects, expresses or serves to reconstitute the real, historical oppression of Blacks, Jews, etc. Of course, this version of the argument, like the strongest versions of the arguments from greater harm and from more culpable mental states, invites the objection that those who advocate hate crimes laws are engaging in a balkanizing, identity-group, politics of resentment.

There is, consequently, a temptation to retreat to the position that while it is not true that a murder is always just a murder, it is true that a racially motivated murder is always just a racially motivated murder. All racially motivated murders violate the liberal democratic values of nondiscrimination and tolerance equally, and thus if any call for enhanced penalties, all call equally for the same enhanced penalties. This version of the argument from liberal democratic values is weak, however. It presupposes a basic social structure within which Blacks and Whites, gays and straights, non-Christians and Christians are situated or positioned symmetrically as groups. But this presupposition is false. Indeed, it is from an awareness that this presupposition is false that the moral intuitions and sentiments that most strongly favor hate crimes laws arise. Even if this presupposition were true, however, this version of the argument from liberal democratic values would still be weak insofar as it offers no account of why selecting a victim on the basis of her race, religion, ethnicity or sexual orientation is so bad as to merit enhanced penalties (rather than some other sort of special public condemnation) as compared to selecting a victim on the basis of her height, weight, IQ or occupation. Only one such account is plausible, of course, and that is that some of the most dramatic and damaging cases of oppression in the United States have involved race (Blacks and other non-Whites), religion (Jews and other non-Christians), ethnicity (non-European) and sexual orientation (gays, lesbians and other non-heterosexuals). But to admit this is to admit that not all racially motivated crimes, for example, are morally equal, for not all racially motivated crimes reflect, express or potentially reconstitute such oppression. Oppression is always asymmetric. So, racially motivated

attacks by Whites on Blacks connect with historic and ongoing oppression in ways that racially motivated attacks by Blacks on Whites never could.

The upshot then is two-fold. The strongest version of the argument from liberal democratic
values invites the same balkanization objection as the strongest versions of the other standard arguments for hate crimes laws. And the strongest version of the argument from liberal democratic
values rides piggy back on, indeed is perhaps best understood as an imperfect articulation of, a
deeper argument from oppression. It is that argument to which we turn now.

III. The Argument from Oppression

The argument from oppression goes like this:

> P1: Structural group-based oppression is a fact of history and contemporary life in the
> United States;
> P2: Those who belong to oppressed groups are disproportionately and systemically more vul-
> nerable to a wide range of structurally and socially produced but avoidable harms;
> P3: Those who by virtue of their social positioning vis-à-vis the vulnerable members of an op-
> pressed group enjoy a special capacity to protect them from the harms to which they are vul-
> nerable, or to help to reorder social life so as to minimize (and eventually eliminate) their
> structurally produced, group-based vulnerability, have a special moral obligation to do so;
> P4: Those who intentionally select a member of an oppressed group, because they are a mem-
> ber of that group (but not necessarily out of a group-based animus), as their victim for a
> crime the harm of which reflects, expresses or contributes distinctively to the social re-
> constitution of the disproportionate vulnerabilities from which members of that group suf-
> fer, and who do so notwithstanding their being positioned socially such that they enjoy a
> special capacity to protect or aid the members of that group, fail to live up to a special
> moral obligation they owe to their victim;
> P5: It is the violation of this special moral obligation that makes paradigmatic hate crimes
> morally worse than otherwise similar crimes;
> P6: In general levels of criminal punishment should be scaled to reflect degrees of moral
> wrongfulness;
> C: The additional moral wrongfulness of paradigmatic hate crimes justifies the extra punish-
> ment imposed by hate crimes laws (of a suitably revised sort).

This argument differs from the standard arguments in important ways. While it appeals to the
place of hate crimes in a social order that systemically works a certain kind of harm on members of
oppressed groups, it is not an argument from the greater harm caused by hate crimes to direct and
immediate victims or non-victim third parties. And while it appeals to the greater moral culpability
of hate crimes offenders, it is not an argument from the greater culpability of motives grounded in
one or another group-based animosity. And finally, while it rests ultimately on and aims at the vin-
dication of liberal democratic values, it casts itself fundamentally as an argument from structural
group-based oppression, not from the values of nondiscrimination and tolerance as values applicable

to interactions between individuals assumed to be symmetrically positioned as group members by and within their basic social structure.

Central to the argument from oppression are the ideas of oppressed groups, disproportionate vulnerabilities, and special moral obligations to protect or aid. Explicating some of these ideas may help to avoid misunderstanding. And so it is to that task I turn now.

Oppressed groups are first social groups. Social groups are more than mere aggregates. Insurance companies may aggregate persons with one or another genetic trait for actuarial purposes. But taken together persons so aggregated do not constitute a social group. To constitute a social group members must stand in determinate relations with one another constituted through their interactions with one another and with those at the margins or outside the group. There are many different kinds of social groups, including associations, cultural or identity groups, and structural groups. Oppressed groups are necessarily structural groups, although as such they sometimes overlap with cultural or identity groups, or with associations.

Associations are social groups within which the determinate relations group members stand in with respect to themselves and to those at the margins or outside the group are a function of the group's shared aims, purposes or ends (e.g., families, the Catholic Church). Cultural or identity groups are social groups within which the relevant relations are a function of how group members construct their identity or self-understanding at its most basic levels (e.g., Chicanos, Southerners). Cultural or identity groups need not share any aim, purpose or end, although sometimes they do. But they must share something by way of tradition, history, language, social practice or cultural forms, and the like sufficient for members to constitute themselves as an "us" or "we" to which they belong. Structural groups are social groups within which the determinate relations group members stand in with respect to themselves and those at the margins or outside the group are a function of how they are positioned by the basic social structure of their society when it comes to access to fundamental goods and resources. Structural groups are produced through the institutional mechanisms through which authority, power, labor and production, desire and sexuality, prestige and the like are socially constituted and organized. Oppressed groups are structural groups the members of which are systematically disadvantaged in the distribution of or their access to the basic goods and resources needed to develop and exercise capacities for self-expression, self-development, and self-determination. The members of oppressed groups (e.g., African Americans in the United States) are thus disproportionately vulnerable to a wide and serious range of socially produced and avoidable harms (among the most serious, poverty, illiteracy, economic marginalization, violence, incarceration, avoidable illness, early mortality, and the like). Describing accurately these disproportionate vulnerabilities and marking out the many and interrelated ways in which they arise out of a basic social structure that systematically disadvantages some but not others is a key task of oppression theory.

The members of structural groups need share no common aim, purpose or end. And they need neither find nor construct their identity or self-understanding at basic levels through appeal to their membership in the group. Indeed, they may (and unhappily sometimes do) belong to the group without even knowing it. The existence of and membership within structural groups is a function of how persons are objectively positioned socially relative to one another within and through their basic social structure. The differentiation of structural groups is distinct, then, from the differentiation of associationist groups and cultural or identity groups, for in the latter cases group members must affirm their membership to be group members. In the United States, Blacks, gays, Jews and various ethnic groups, as well as women, have been and remain to various degrees oppressed structural groups.

This social fact does not depend at all on whether Blacks, gays, Jews, etc., think of themselves as a group. Of course, it also does not preclude them constituting associationist groups or cultural or identity groups more or less identical in terms of their membership.

It bears emphasizing that the existence of and membership within structural groups generally, or oppressed groups more particularly, is a function of reiterated patterns of social relations and interactions over time. Three things follow from this. First, membership within structural groups is something that may come in degrees, depending on the degree to which one is, over time and in general, implicated structurally in a web of systematically advantageous or disadvantageous social relations. So, particular persons may be more or less Black with respect to their membership in the structural group called Blacks. Second, membership within, indeed the existence of, a structural group may change over time. So, membership within and even the existence of Jews as a structural group in the United States has and continues to undergo significant change. Third membership in a structural group is logically independent of membership in associationist groups and cultural or identity groups. So, a particular individual may be marginally (perhaps not even) Black with respect to Blacks as a structural group but be centrally Black with respect to Blacks as a cultural or identity group, or vice versa.

Individual members of oppressed groups do not all suffer the same particular, individual socially produced and avoidable harms by virtue of their social positioning. But they are all disproportionately vulnerable to them. And for many, this vulnerability will itself constitute an actualized harm, a sort of psychological weight rooted in a deep sense of anxiety, insecurity, or powerlessness.

To be vulnerable is to be in a distinctively or especially precarious position, to be exposed or at risk to an unusual degree to some injury or harm. To be vulnerable is not the same as simply belonging to a class the members of which merely satisfy some precondition for a particular harm. Only women get ovarian cancer. So, only women are at risk of ovarian cancer. It doesn't follow that to be a woman is to be vulnerable to ovarian cancer. Similarly, only the employed can lose their jobs during an economic recession. It doesn't follow that to be employed is to be vulnerable to unemployment during a recession.

Vulnerabilities can arise from many sources. Some women are vulnerable to ovarian cancer by virtue of their genetic endowment. So, nature is one source of vulnerabilities. The disproportionate vulnerabilities that mark oppressed groups as oppressed groups arise from the "normal" functioning of the basic social structure of the society in which they exist. So, given the structure of labor markets and of authority within most employment contexts today, Blacks are more vulnerable to unemployment during an economic slowdown than are Whites. They are more likely to be laid off, and more likely to suffer adversely from being laid off. And given the historical exclusion of Blacks from political processes (something which continues informally today), Blacks are more vulnerable to the legislative sacrifice of their interests for the "common good." They are more likely to have their interests ignored during ordinary legislative processes, and then to be accused of and marginalized for divisiveness for asserting their interests once ordinary legislative processes are complete. The multiplication of these disproportionate vulnerabilities, ranging across wide ranges of social life, produce what Marilyn Frye has called the "bird cage" effect: Blacks and other oppressed groups find themselves caged by an intersecting network of constraints arising out of the "normal" operation of the basic social structure that limit or undermine their self-development, self-expression and self-determination.

   Disproportionate vulnerabilities are commonly understood to impose special obligations on those especially well-placed to prevent harm to, to protect, or to aid the vulnerable, and these special obligations are often legally enforced. So, adults have various special obligations to children. Providers of various services have various special obligations to the elderly, as do providers of medical services to the terminally ill. Those not cognitively impaired have special obligations to those who are cognitively impaired. These obligations arise as moral obligations in each case out of the asymmetry of the respective parties' social relationship or relative positionings. They are given legal backing because (although not exclusively because consequentialist considerations will have a role to play here) of the moral gravity of their violation. Similarly, the special obligations violated in paradigmatic hate crimes arise as moral obligations out of the asymmetry of the respective parties' social relationship or positioning (their group-based relationship or positioning within or through the "normal" functioning of the basic social structure) and are given legal backing because (although, again, not exclusively because consequentialist considerations will again have a role to play here) of the moral gravity of their violation. The moral intuition or sentiment at work here in the case of paradigmatic hate crimes belongs to the same family as that at work when we judge that stealing from a blind man is morally worse, and thus deserving of or at least eligible for greater punishment, than stealing from a sighted man.

   A full defense of the argument from oppression would require much more than the foregoing. However, I hope the foregoing sufficient to give a clear enough sense of how the argument goes and how it differs from and improves on the standard arguments.

V. Conclusion

Critics of hate crimes laws are correct about two things. First, the standard arguments given as justification for these laws are either unsound or weak. Second, these laws and the standard justifications given for them at least appear to arise out of and affirm a balkanizing, identity/interest-group politics of resentment. But the critics of hate crimes laws are incorrect in concluding that there is no compelling moral case for such laws. The argument from oppression is sufficiently compelling to constitute a prima facie justification for such laws. And hate crimes laws justified by appeal to and suitably revised in light of it cannot be saddled with the charge that they arise out of and affirm a balkanizing, identity/interest-group politics of resentment.

   Nevertheless, hate crimes laws and the politics from which they arise are undeniably divisive. But that is to be expected and by itself is unobjectionable; democratic initiatives aimed at responding to and remedying structural group-based oppression are almost always divisive. The question with all such initiatives is whether they are so divisive that their cost in terms of social unity outweighs whatever moral and political gains they promise. That is a complex question I have neither asked nor answered in this paper.

   But two points bear emphasizing, as a final thought, here. First, among the moral and political gains promised by hate crimes laws and the politics which surround them is a broader, deeper and more accurate understanding of social and political life. And that is a gain perhaps worth pursuing, even at the (one must hope temporary) cost of an increase in social tension and division between groups. Second, no proponent of hate crimes laws imagines them as a silver bullet capable of working significant social change by themselves. They are just one part of a broader set of social, political and legal initiatives aimed at responding to and remedying structural group-based oppression. Ultimately, their merits and demerits ought to be assessed within the context of that larger set of initiatives of which they are a part.

Journal/Discussion Questions

1. Have you had any experience with hate crimes at your school or university? How were these handled? Relate the response to such hate crimes to Reidy's discussion.

2. Reidy tells us that "racially motivated attacks by Whites on Blacks connect with historic and ongoing oppression in ways that racially motivated attacks by Blacks on Whites never could." What conclusions does he draw from this? Do you agree with him? Why or why not?

3. What are the principal objections to hate crimes laws? Critically assess the merits of those objections from your own standpoint.

Gregory Velazco y Trianosky
"Beyond Mestizaje: The Future of Race in America"

Gregory Velazco y Trianosky is a professor of philosophy at California State University at Northridge. He has published widely in the area of ethics, especially virtue ethics.

In this article, Velazco addresses the often-neglected question of mixed race in a society that often seems to force people to be either black or white. He argues against the assimilationist ideal that many immigrant groups (such as the Irish) accepted wholeheartedly.

As You Read, Consider This:

1. What is a phenotype? Explain what is meant by racist assumptions about phenotypic differences.

2. What does Velazco mean by calling American racial identity "bipolar"? What role does the *Nuevo Mestizaje* play in this regard?

3. Velazco draws several implications from his "tale of two cultures" for the construction of culturally mixed identities. What are these implications?

Since its inception, the United States has been obsessed with the idea of race. Moreover, despite many subtle transformations and variations, our dominant racial ideology has remained bipolar. We have always conceived ourselves, in the well-known words of the Kerner Commission, as two na-

New Faces in a Changing America: Multiracial Identity in the 21st Century, edited by Loretta I. Winters and Herman L. DeBose (Thousand Oaks, CA: Sage Publications, 2002), pp. 176–88.

tions, "one black, one white—separate and unequal" (National Advisory Commission on Civil Disorders, 1968; O'Brien, 1996; Schwarz, 1997).

There are some who think that the increasing presence and visibility of Latino/as in our society will help to cure this "bipolar disorder." In its more romantic versions, the thought is that somehow "brown" helps to bridge the gap between "black" and "white": that our mere presence as *a mestizo* or mixed-race people can perhaps help Americans to see black and white as at best endpoints on a continuum rather than as eternal and irreconcilable opposites. In this chapter I explore a less romanticized, more critical version of this thought primarily by examining the relationship between Latinos and the dominant Anglo culture in the United States.

Mestizaje in Latin America

It is true that the central racial and cultural reality of Latino life is that everyone is *mestizo*. Most of us are mixed by blood: descendants of Spanish conquerors and either African slaves or American Indian peoples or both. Even those who claim not to be mixed by blood are plainly mixed by culture; Latino cultures are clearly and fundamentally distinct from their Spanish ancestors. Even the newest immigrants to Latin America are mixed by language, for the Spanish that Latino/as speak always reflects, although not always honestly and without shame, the words, concepts, and accents of the three great cultural streams whose tragic and powerful coming-together was *la conquista,* the Conquest, the birth of Latino peoples.

It is important not to romanticize the racial ideologies of Latin America, however. *Mestizaje* in all its protean forms is a central reality; however, this does not mean it is an openly acknowledged reality. Many Latino/as live in a curious state of "doublethink," which Orwell described as the ability to believe something while simultaneously acknowledging the conditions that establish its falsehood. There is a well-known saying in Cuba and Puerto Rico: *"El que no tiene de Congo es de Carabali; y para el que no sabe na', to abuela 'donde 'sta?"* Although my family has been in Puerto Rico at least since the 1500s, my mother always insisted that we were "Spanish, not Puerto Rican," and she and my grandmother never went out in the sun without parasols, lest we "out" our Yoruba ancestry by a too-brown skin. Thus, in Latin America, the acknowledgment of our *mestizo* character frequently coexists with its denial, disarming its power to subvert our racialized understandings of ourselves.

Mestizaje in the United States

Will our presence in the United States help to undermine racist ideology here? It is certainly true that Latino/as are an increasingly large part of the American population. Our birth rate is the highest of any ethnic and racial group in the United States, and by some estimates one third of the American population will have some Latino/a blood by the year 2040. The 2000 Census indicates that we may already constitute the largest minority in the United States, depending on how the final results are tabulated.

As we thus move into the mainstream of American society, we become doubly mixed, doubly *mestizo.* We are mixed for the second time by culture, through our encounter with the dominant culture in this new land. We are mixed for the second time by race, as we inter-mingle with our new Anglo-European cousins. Thus, we become Puerto Rican-Americans, Mexican-Americans, Cuban-Americans.

"Una mano pa' 'lante, y una mano pa "tras," as Celia Cruz sings. This racial and cultural second mixing I call the *Nuevo Mestizaje.* Aurora Levins Morales describes it well:

> I am a child of the Americas,
> a light-skinned *mestiza* of the
> Caribbean,
> a child of many diaspora, born
> into this continent
> at a crossroads.
> I am a U.S. Puerto
> Rican Jew,
> a product of the ghettos of
> New York I have never
> known.
> An immigrant and the daughter and
> granddaughter of immigrants.
> I speak English with passion: it's the
> tongue of my
> consciousness,
> a flashing knife blade of crystal, my tool,
> my craft.
>
> I am Caribena, island grown.
> Spanish is in my
> flesh,
> ripples from my tongue, lodges in
> my hips:
> the language of garlic
> and mangoes
> the singing in my poetry, the flying
> gestures of my
> hands.
> I am of Latinoamerica, rooted in the
> history of my
> continent:
> I speak from that body.
>
> I am not African. Africa is in me, but I
> cannot return.
> I am not Taina. Taino is in me,
> but there is no way
> Back.
> I am not European. Europe lives in me,
> but I have
> no home there.

> I am new. History made me.
> My first language
> was spanglish.
> I was born at the crossroads
> and I am whole.
> —*Aurora Levins Morales (1990)*

Of course, the *Nuevo Mestizaje* is only new for us Latino/as, because race mixing has always been widespread in the United States (see, e.g., Ball, 1998; Gordon-Reed, 1998; Piper, 1992). Nonetheless, the idea of *mestizaje* remains radical here. The American bipolar racial ideology continues to deny the reality of widespread race mixing between white and nonwhite; and America's continuing fascination, if not obsession, with miscegenation reveals that conceptions of white racial purity remain a significant feature of American culture.

Perhaps for this reason, in the 19th century, as immigrant groups that historically were conceived as nonwhite began to mix with earlier Anglo European settlers, racial categories flexed so that while these groups were slowly assimilated, the line between white and non-white remained relatively clear. Thus, the Irish, the Slavs, and the Italians (and southern Mediterraneans generally), who were typically not seen as white when they arrived, have "become white," to use Noel Ignatiev's vivid phrase. The color line in the United States is like the national boundary between the United States and Mexico. It has moved around, but no matter where it locates itself it almost always remains clearly defined.

If this is right, however, then it is difficult to believe that either the mere presence of Latino/as in increasingly visible numbers or our continued mixing into the already-white population will yield any different result. We will, over time, simply become "white." Failing that, we will be assigned to the "black" category.

It follows that the *Nuevo Mestizaje* will not automatically provide a cure for America's bipolar disorder. Nonetheless, perhaps a more critical deployment of the notion of *mestizaje* can accomplish this goal.

Cultural Identity in a Strange Land

We can begin with a fundamental and widely recognized truth: Racial categories are socially constructed. This much should already have been suggested by the historical malleability of the concept of race. The construction of racial categories in America in particular is typically organized around several familiar racist assumptions:

- Putative, salient phenotypic differences are taken to signal underlying differences in "nature."
- Putative, salient differences in character and behavior (culture) are taken to signal under-lying differences in "nature."
- An essential, underlying difference in "nature" is posited between blacks and whites.

Because of the emphasis that everyday racial epistemology places on phenotypic difference, it is easy to take it for granted that the first assumption is the most fundamental. In point of fact, however, it is the second assumption about culture and its relation to underlying nature that is the most powerful determinant of how racial categories are constructed in America. In fact, the first assumption, central as it is to our familiar racist epistemology, can even be discarded depending on how cultural differences are understood. For example, Noel Ignatiev (1996) quotes the well-known and vicious 19th-century American canard, "An Irishman is a nigger turned inside out." On the surface, this intended slander against the Irish seems to involve discounting what to us are obvious phenotypic points of contrast between Irish immigrants and black Americans in favor of putative similarities in character and behavior. At a deeper level, however, this attempted slander puts pressure on the first assumption about racial categories, for the "inside-out" trope suggests that the alleged cultural similarities are rooted in biological isomorphisms that are obscured by mere phenotypic differences. "Inside" the trope implies, Irish immigrants are really the same as black Americans. Thus, because the perceived similarities in culture and behavior are reified—made to appear manifestations of a shared nature—the trope presses us to divest salient differences in phenotype of their familiar role as signs of divergent natures.

Now it might seem as though what happens ultimately is that race follows phenotype, because despite their putatively shared inner nature, Irish immigrants were not placed in the same racial category as black Americans. This, in turn, might suggest that it is our (culturally intransigent) perceptions of phenotypic salience that always trump in the construction of race. However, this puts the emphasis in the wrong place. The touchstone of American racial ideology is always the distinction between whites and nonwhites. The point of the canard under discussion is not that the Irish are black but that they are *not white.*

In short, I am suggesting that the key supposition in the racial ideology that divided Irish immigrants from whites in the late 19th century was the notion that the character and behavior that the former supposedly shared with black Americans revealed an underlying essential "nature" also shared with black Americans. Given this notion, then, the third assumption mentioned previously settles the matter: No group that shares the essential nature of black people could possibly be white. This is the deep insight suggested by the provocative title of Ignatiev's well-known book, *How the Irish Became White.* Irish immigrants became white not by changing their appearance or phenotype—still less by changing whatever underlying nature one might think they possessed—but by redefining their relationship to the dominant culture. As a group, they internalized its racial attitudes, particularly toward black people, and they found places for themselves in the dominant culture as border guards along the racial divide: in unions, on police forces, in class-rooms, and in the church. Once their character and behavior had assimilated to the dominant culture in these and many other ways, however, it became possible for white society to reinterpret their phenotype, and their underlying nature, as simply another variation on the theme of whiteness. In this way, they came to be seen as phenotypically—and essentially—white. I conjecture that the same sort of story could be told about other immigrants to the United States who were initially categorized as nonwhite (e.g., Arabs, Greeks, Italians, and perhaps Slavs). They became white by a transmogrification of culture or patterns of character and behavior, and not by some objectively describable change in phenotype. Perhaps, therefore, we can understand the logic of *mestizaje* or mixed-race identities by exploring the logic of the mixed-cultural identities that define the experience of Latino/as and many other immigrants to the United States.

For immigrants and other exiles, culture is mixed from the moment they arrive in this new world. The home culture is shared against the backdrop of a new, alien culture. However much "Little Italy" or "Mexicantown" is like the old country, it is almost always defined by a small space in comparison to the one staked out by the dominant culture. Moreover, that small space is almost inevitably one that, despite the best efforts of the elder generation, is pervaded by the influence of the new world that surrounds it.

The contrast between the home culture of the ghetto or the *barrio* and the dominant alien culture is particularly acute for the children of immigrants in a mass-media society. In a strange land the home culture is characteristically transmitted by personal contact. It is the parish deacon who runs the Ukrainian-language school. It is the grandmother and her sisters who know how to make the traditional Syrian dishes or tell fortunes in the trails left by the coffee grounds in one's cup. It is the corner grocer who will speak to the children only in Spanish or who corrects their too-casual, Americanized manners.

Thus, in the first instance, the tie between the children of immigrants and the home culture is hardly ever abstract or impersonal. It typically consists of concrete memories of sights, sounds and smells, words and phrases, and the faces, the voices and the touch of the people we grew up with. This is why Mario Puzo, who grew up in Brooklyn, upon visiting his parents' home town in Sicily for the first time when he was in his 30s, said that the faces, the accents, the gestures, and the actions of the people he met there seemed so very familiar to him. He was tied to them and so to the lived culture of that Sicilian town by the intensely personal experiences and emotions in the small space that was the center of his Brooklyn childhood.

This explains why, for the immigrant child, a child of parents cast ashore in a strange land, our emotional attachment to the home culture is typically some function of our emotional attachments to those who brought it to us. Our relationship to the home culture is thus shot through with the feelings, neuroses, and ambivalence that define our relationships with those in whose lives we first intimately experienced that culture. In living with us, and so in living out their culture with us, they became its embodiment in our lives. It should not be surprising then that what we learn to love, hate, fear, and admire in the home culture are the ways of that culture as they are embodied in the people who bring it intimately to life for us.

This is the lesson that Adrienne Rich's father understood, perhaps instinctively but too well. Rich is the daughter of a Jewish father and an Anglo southern mother. In her powerful essay, "Split at the Root: An Essay on Jewish Identity," Rich (1986) describes her embrace of a Jewish identity and heritage that her father had quite deliberately rejected both for himself and for his children. Her father's emotional absence is one of the dominant themes in Rich's descriptions of him. This absence is apparently the result of deliberate choice. Arnold Rich's mother came from a Sephardic family that, it appears, had already become highly assimilated in Vicksburg, Mississippi. His father, however, was an Ashkenazic immigrant from Austria-Hungary. Arnold Rich, himself a professor of pathology at Johns Hopkins University, was driven by a commitment to assimilation. Perhaps, like so many children of immigrants, he had come to see his father's home culture through the eyes of this new world, and so, having learned to be ashamed of it, did not wish to visit it on his children. Perhaps he thought more strategically, believing that taking on the traditions and manners of his father's home culture would only serve to set his daughter apart from the Gentile world in which he expected her, like him, to make her way. In any case, he does not even mention his father or his father's relatives. His Sephardic-Southern mother lives with them 6 months out of each year. However, she, Adrienne Rich says, "was a model of circumspect behavior . . . ladylike to an extreme," and "always tuned down to some WASP level [that] my father believed, surely, would protect us all"

(p. 111). Rich comments, "If you did not effectively deny [your Jewish] family and community, there would always be a remote cousin claiming kinship with you who was the 'wrong kind' of Jew . . . uneducated, aggressive, loud" (p. 112).

To ensure that his daughter—and he himself—will be at home in the "tuned-down," genteel, Gentile public world, Adrienne Rich's father obscures the Jewish elements in his own upbringing and their natural expression in his day-to-day life. He cannot celebrate the High Holy Days or even acknowledge them in any fashion, however secularized. He cannot sing the songs, tell the jokes, or speak the languages he must have heard in his youth from his father or his father's relatives. He cannot reminisce about the stories he probably heard from his own father about his grandparents or other relatives. He cannot share the books or the wisdom that one imagines his father shared with him.

Emotional intimacy and attachment are characteristic and very powerful modes of the transmission of culture for the children of immigrants. For this reason, it is perhaps inevitable that to silence his Jewish heritage, Rich's father must silence himself. Perhaps it is only through the death of emotional intimacy with his daughter and his wife that he is able to suffocate the reproduction of his home culture in her life and the life of his household. Perhaps it is only through the effort to reconnect with the withheld culture that Rich can find an intimate emotional connection to the father, now deceased, in whose person it was withheld.

The contrast between the modes of transmission of the home culture and of the dominant American culture for the children of immigrants is striking. The influence of the mass media is primary in the transmission of the dominant culture in the United States; and this influence is as impersonal as it is pervasive.

Eritrean children learn about Teletubbies from the television show, and Korean children learn about McDonald's from Ronald McDonald and the ubiquitous golden arches.

The culture that is transmitted by personal means is always altered, often in minute and unpredictable ways, by the personal character of its transmission. It is constantly reinterpreted by those who embody it and police it for one another and for their children. The transmission of culture by personal means is like a highly complex, multivoiced version of the children's party game of "Telephone," in which each hears in an intimate whisper the substance of what the other has learned from those who went before. The end result is always a humorous surprise, precisely because it is recognizably a transmogrification—a morph, although usually a barely coherent one—of the message with which the game began.

In contrast, the memories and impressions that enable mass culture to reproduce itself in the lives of immigrant communities are not idiosyncratic. They do not fade or get reinterpreted like personal memories. Instead, they are continually remanufactured, reproduced, and corrected in a uniform, mechanical (or electronic) way that is virtually impossible to duplicate through the everyday activities of ordinary people. This was Andy Warhol's great insight into the nature of mainstream American culture. In mass culture, although there is constant change, there is also a constant, dunning repetition of literally the same lessons. Moreover, the work of correcting misinterpretations and managing people's responses is almost automatic; consequently, our attachment to mass culture will in all probability lack the depth and emotional resonance of our attachments to a culture embodied primarily in the unique and idiosyncratic lives of those close to us.

This simple tale of two cultures has several implications for the construction of culturally mixed identities.

For us, the children of immigrant parents, the struggle over who we are is almost always a personal one. To embrace the home culture is to embrace the people who embodied it for you. On the other hand, to be angry or ambivalent toward those people is inevitably to experience the home culture with anger and ambivalence as well.

For me as the child of a Nuyorican mother and Puerto Rican grandparents, for example, to embrace the culture and the heritage that my mother's family gave me is to embrace her and the experiences that her presence framed for me. The defining memories of *la cultura nuestra* (our culture) for me will always be listening to the *coquis* (tree frogs) from the screen door of my grandmother's house in Yauco, *"el pueblito de cafe"* (the town of coffee); encountering the sharp wit and the passionate, even melodramatic, gestures that accompanied the retelling of any event; smelling *"cafe y pan"* (coffee and bread) in the morning, with the underlying sweetness of heavily sugared, milky coffee; finding in a Miami schoolyard in the fall of 1963 that for the first time, I had peers who also spoke Spanish. When my mother died 16 years ago, I began to understand that if I continued to "pass," speaking only English and living (as best I could) as a member of the dominant culture—if I put aside all of these powerful and intimate memories, burying them as nothing more than fragments of the past—then I would have lost her truly and completely. My resolution to reclaim the heritage and the language of my childhood—to own the cultural identity embodied in my childhood memories, and to endow it with positive significance—is a reconfiguration of my determination to keep her alive in my life. My love for the Spanish language, my pride in being part of *La Raza,* and my devotion to its children and its future are thus reconfigurations of my love, pride, and devotion to my mother and to her Puerto Rican family.

Yet silence, ambivalence, and anger can constitute emotional attachments as powerful as love and respect. Richard Rodriguez's father is for him the living agent of *el machismo,* the traditional culture of the Mexican man who is, as the old *dicho* (saying) quoted by Rodriguez (1983, p. 128) has it, *"feo, fuerte y formal"* (rugged, strong, and reserved). However, this understanding of who his father is takes a cruel twist for the young Rodriguez. When he is 7 or so, his parents accede to a request from his teachers that they speak only English at home. Suddenly deprived of the language in which intimacy has always been expressed, the child of 7 is "increasingly angry," "pushed away," "[his] throat twisted by unsounded grief":

> In an instant, they agreed to give *up* the language (the sounds) that had revealed and accentuated our family's closeness. The moment after the [teachers] left, the change was observed. *'Ahora,* speak to *us en ingles,'* my father and mother united to tell us. (Rodriguez, 1998, pp. 21–22)

The hesitation and the silence that this reliance on an alien and poorly understood language introduced into a previously voluble and expressive household henceforth define much of his relationship to his father. Yet despite the title of his extended and perceptive narrative, *Days of Obligation: An Argument with My Mexican Father,* even there we are given only glimpses of the elder Rodriguez, and we are left to infer the character of his son's relationship to him. Rodriguez is more forthcoming, however, in his expressions of contempt and hatred for the Mexico from which his father came. In one discussion of *machismo,* he says:

> In its male, in its public, in its city aspect, Mexico is an archtransvestite, *a* tragic buffoon. Dogs and babies cry when Mother Mexico walks abroad in the light of day. The policeman, the Marxist mayor—

Mother Mexico doesn't even bother to shave her mustachios. Swords and rifles and spurs and bags of money chink and clatter beneath her skirts. A chain of martyred priests dangles from her waist, for she is an austere, pious lady. Ay, how much—clutching her jangling bosoms; spilling cigars—how much she has suffered! (Rodriguez, 1992, p. 62)

If this is how he sees Mexico when it is figured as a man, then what is he to make of his own father's identity as a Mexican man, *el Mexicano, el macho?* On the one hand, Rodriguez himself is tied to this identity because of the power of the emotions that bind him so tightly to his father. Yet at the same time he himself is silenced in his discussion of his father, just as his father remains rugged, strong, and silent even with his own son. Even the betrayal of intimacy that occurred when the younger Rodriguez was 7—perhaps that most of all—cannot be discussed between father and son. The traditional identity by which they are both shaped in different ways, reinforced by the unnamed reality of that intimate betrayal that tore away the very language in which they could communicate intimacy, will not permit anything else between them. Perhaps it is the expressions of anger and resentment at this loss that are represented in his adult life as contempt and hatred for the culture that his father embodies, when that culture is imagined as a man. Perhaps it is such transmogrified anger and resentment that are expressed in Rodriguez' felt distance from the culture of his parents, his near-neurotic inability even to pronounce Spanish words correctly, let alone speak the language (Rodriguez, 1983, p. 23), and in his insistent opposition to bilingual education programs that might preserve the language of his childhood.

I suggest that for both Rodriguez and me, the depth and the character of our attachments to our home cultures—our identities as Chicano, *boricua,* Latino, *Mexicano,* Nuyorican—are a function of the emotional depth and the valence—positive or negative—that we find in our intimate relationships to those in whom this culture came alive for us: mother, father, grandmother, uncle, and aunt.

The culture so learned is characteristically idiosyncratic, and never exclusionary. This is the second implication of our tale of two cultures. The idiosyncratic nature of the newly reproduced immigrant culture is a consequence of the disruptive force of emigration. This is particularly true if the first immigrants live in small, fragmentary communities. Here the reproduction of the home culture may well take place *sans* the policing or homogenizing function exercised by larger, more well-entrenched versions of the home culture. What is typical among the few families in a small, struggling community may turn out to be quite different from what was typical back home. For instance, traditional public rituals that require churches, large groups of people, and the use of public space may be absent, and in their absence, children may grow up without a life that revolves around the religiosity that such rituals confirm. To take another example, "dating outside one's group" may be a much more viable option than it would ever have been "back home"; and the sense of identification with the romantic and marital values of one's parents may be correspondingly weakened.

Furthermore, in a mass culture like this one, even in large, comparatively stable immigrant communities, the character of the home culture as it is reproduced here is suffused with the tensions and ambiguities of the ongoing negotiations between the new generation who is being taught the home culture, the older generation who is teaching it, and the dominant mass culture that now pervades all their lives.

The transmission of culture from immigrants to their children is, of course, only one example of a tendency toward the chaotic and idiosyncratic that is characteristic of cultural reproduction during times of social, political, and economic upheaval. However, because change is the only constant, the character of a culture is almost constantly in flux. A culture is like a great river system. From its headwaters to the delta, there is not one major characteristic of the Amazon that does not vary as the river progresses: its rate of flow, its depth, its area, the habitats it forms, and the quantity and variety of life it sustains. Yet despite these profound transformations, it is always the Amazon.

This metaphor for cultural identity should also suggest the nonexclusionary character of the home culture as reproduced in the new world, for two such river systems will not always be discrete. In South Carolina, for example, the Ashley and the Cooper Rivers share a mouth, the Quiganonsett Bay; and yet they remain two different rivers, each with its own origin and path. In the same way, no child of immigrant parents—and particularly no child living within the larger mass culture of the United States—can possibly belong only to the home culture. Every child of the Americas is, like Levins Morales, Rich, Rodriguez, myself, and all the millions of others who grew up here in immigrant families, a child of many cultural streams at once. Almost all Puerto Rican Americans, for instance, are part of a living and continually evolving Puerto Rican culture. Thus, almost every Puerto Rican American is, culturally speaking, a Latino. At the same time, we are the latest in a long line of inheritors of the dominant, mass Anglo culture. Thus, we are Latino/as and we are also Anglos. We, the children of immigrants, are, perforce, the *Nuevos Mestizos*. We live in a newly mixed culture that is continuous with two distinct cultural traditions. We have two cultural identities; or rather one identity that is at once a recognizable morph of two very different cultural inheritances.

The Nuevo Mestizaje is constantly threatened by assimilation. Here is the third implication of my prior remarks. I have stressed that the *Nuevo Mestizaje is* not simply the offspring of the coming together of two cultures. For this reason the metaphor of the two streams is too simple. To vary the metaphor, the gravitational field of the mass culture that surrounds us exerts a constant and powerful pull. Thus, to take only one example, which elements of our home cultures are most easily preserved in a mass culture depends in part on which elements are most easily commodified at this particular historical juncture. After all, it is much easier to teach children to celebrate *El Dia de los Muertos* when it is front-page news in the "Style" section of the local paper every October and November. It is much easier to appreciate Frida Kahlo's self-martyrdom when it resonates so facilely, if falsely, with a self-obsessed, self-mutilating mass culture. We learn about ourselves through the eyes of others; and quick, powerful lessons are learned when electronic eyes so tirelessly represent the saleable part of us to ourselves: We are creative, we are emotional; we are good gardeners, good dancers; our food has "zest" (that pallid English translation of *"sabor"*); we are loyal and family oriented. We are in constant danger of becoming nothing more than animated promos that sell CDs, Hallmark cards, and Pace Picante Sauce.

The danger is particularly acute, however, when what we represent in the mass market are the fears and anxieties of the dominant culture. When the electronic eyes reflect back to us images of drug dealers, gang-bangers, convicts, welfare mothers, lazy, dishonest workers, sex-crazed Romeos, and all the rest of the sorry litany of images of Latino/as that still fill the screens, we may too easily learn to become what we see, this time at great cost in human suffering.

These images are sadly familiar. They are simple variations of the dominant culture's entrenched and stereotyped portrayals of African American people. Thus, although this is not usually understood, they all invite one or another form of assimilation. After all, for us to assimilate is for us to come to define ourselves by some niche that is established for us by this New World in which we have come to labor and to live. We can assimilate by becoming white, or by becoming what the dominant culture represents as black, or by becoming Carmen Miranda and *salsa picante*. If we choose the third of these options, we find ourselves in danger of being engulfed by a mass culture that has been busily defining a place for people like us at least since the time of the Mexican-American War by making commodities out of caricatures of our culture. Perhaps the second of these options is even more obviously destructive; and the first may even seem innocuous by comparison. However, to vary the metaphor, all three describe forms of assimilation that herald the death of that branch of the home culture that was newly born here in America, and its reanimation as a zombie, a creature without a soul or will of its own.

Race and Culture: Resistance Is Not Futile

The challenge of the *Nuevo Mestizaje* is the forging of a lived racial identity, the very terms of whose existence undercut the bipolar ideology of black and white. The key to meeting this challenge is to live out the conception of racial identity expressed in the rich, extended metaphor of the river. Thus, the new identity we negotiate in this new world must be, and represent itself as being, a part of several different streams, at once continuous with several distinct racialized identities. How does our discussion of the culture of immigrants help us do this?

Let us return to the story of how culture triumphed over phenotype in the case of the Irish. The lesson here for us Latino/as, as for so many immigrant groups in the last 150 years, is that we can cross the color line by crossing the culture line. If we become acculturated to being in the world as Anglos are, then for us as for Sicilians and Neapolitans, for example, our phenotype will be reinterpreted as a variant of white. Thus, the color of our skins need constitute a racial barrier for us to no greater an extent than it did for them.

It follows that for us, as for other immigrant groups that were originally seen as racially distinct, our racial identity as either white or nonwhite rests on a complex series of choices and responses that we negotiate between the dominant culture and our home culture. Here the contrast with the position of black people in America is profound; for black people as such cannot become white. As elastic as the American notion of whiteness has been, it has always been anchored in one firm and invariant truth: To be white is not to be black. Hence, no degree or variety of assimilation to Anglo culture can authorize the reinterpretation of black phenotypes as white. Black people in the United States cannot do what the Irish, the Italians, and various other immigrant groups have done, namely transform their racial identity by altering their behavior and character. In fact, for black people the constant struggle to define their own racial identity is constituted in no small measure by the struggle not to become the stereotype, assimilating to the degrading and dehumanizing roles set aside by the dominant culture for those of African descent.

In short, our determined refusal as Latino/as to become white is the refusal to allow our home cultures to be drowned in the Ocean Sea of American mass culture. This refusal constitutes a decision to set ourselves apart, to define our racial identity as distinct from that of white people in a way that the Irish and the Italians and various other immigrants to the United States chose not to do. This refusal positions us with African Americans, facing "a common struggle," to adapt DuBois' famous phrase: the struggle to resist assimilation to the stereotypes of black character and behavior, and instead to define our own racial identity.

This commonality of struggle with black people is more than just an alliance of disparate groups, however. Our mutual struggle to define ourselves against these stereotypes should remind us of the companion phrase that DuBois used: "a common history." It should remind us that our own history as Latino/as is as much the history of Africans in the new world as it is of the Spanish. In the identity we define for ourselves here, therefore, we must not reproduce the characteristically Latin American misrepresentations, subordinations, and erasures of the African elements in our history and our culture. Our double refusal to either become white or become the black stereotypes should thus serve to affirm our intimate relationship to African American peoples.

At the same time, this double refusal points to our potential to undermine America's racial ideology of black and white. We do this by living out a new, nonexclusionary conception of race that expresses the notion that a people can be real and legitimate descendants of several distinct, racialized cultural streams at one and the same time. This is the conception of race embodied in the metaphor of the river. Thus, I have said that we must refuse to become white, thereby losing all but a nostalgic connection to our home cultures, and alleging our cultural and racial distance from peoples of African descent. On the other hand, we must also affirm that we are indeed among the new and legitimate inheritors of Anglo culture. As we negotiate our relationships with the dominant culture, we become part of the stream that defines it. As DuBois (1989) said in *Souls of Black Folk:*

> I sit with Shakespeare and he winces not. Across the color line I move arm in arm with Balzac and Dumas. . . . I summon Aristotle and Aurelius and what soul I will, and they come all graciously with no scorn nor condescension. (p. 76)

In the same way, I have said that we must refuse to become the stereotype by assimilating to the roles that Anglo culture defines for black (and Latino/a) people. However, we must at the same time acknowledge and embrace our status by birth, by culture, and by language as a part of the great stream of the African diaspora; and so our intimate relationship to the African diaspora communities of the United States.

Finally, of course, we must weave these elements into an identity that is also a recognizable part of the Latino/a cultural stream. There is no one right way to live out a racial identity that is at once continuous with three distinct racialized streams. Nor is the prospect an easy one. Each of us must live out the challenge of weaving together multiple strands of identity in a world that always tries either to unravel them or to dye them all a single color. This is the site of the struggle and creative tension that Anzaldua (1987) describes so powerfully in *Borderlands/La Frontera.* Yet by living in this way, we embody a rejection of the idea of racial identities as mutually exclusive. By openly living out several racial identities at once, we can perhaps transform the character of each, so that black and white will no longer be mutually exclusive, polarized identities.

Elements of Successful Resistance

Perhaps this will sound less utopian if I close with some very brief remarks about the conditions required for successful resistance to assimilation in all its forms, with particular attention to the risks of commodification.

First, successful resistance to assimilation in all its forms requires recognizing the true nature of the conflict that defines our lives as *nuevos mestizos.* Our case is not the same as that of the Armenian refugees settling in early 20th-century Persia, for example, or the enslaved Yoruba brought to the Dahomey court in the early 19th century. The power of American mass culture to shape our understanding of ourselves, and thus our understanding of the cultures that we brought with us, is perhaps unequalled in human history. Bilingual education, Spanish-language newspapers, and our own foods will not suffice—although they may be necessary—to create a space in which we can nurture a genuinely new *mestizo* culture. We must also find ways to subvert mass culture or at least to shatter the flickering glamour it casts over us.

Second, given the nature of the conflict, the constant renewal of strong, positively valenced, personal and emotional attachments to our home culture is essential. After all, if it is through the depth of our positive emotional attachments that we children and grandchildren of immigrants acquired our commitments to the home culture, then it is surely through nurturing and expanding these attachments that we can strengthen and renew them. It is for this reason that to "forget where we came from" is the surest path toward assimilation in some form and thus toward being co-opted by bipolar ideology rather than resisting it. Moreover, if our resistance is to have a real impact on the racist ideology that is America's own bipolar disorder, then we Latinos/as must also prize, valorize, and constantly renew strong personal and emotional attachments to African American communities. If we allow the pressure to become white to divide us from our African American kin, we will have come here only to repeat the betrayals of our own past. Race ideology in America can only be destroyed if Latino/as and others like us confront directly the question of whether to leave African American people behind in our struggles to define who we are. Third, successful resistance requires finding ways to sustain endlessly creative responses to the endlessly creative lust of mass culture for commodification. There is no element of any home culture, however sacred or intimate, that cannot be commodified. This means that whenever some element of our home culture calls attention to itself, for instance by being wielded as an instrument of resistance, it is immediately in danger of commodification. This is one disturbing aspect of the increasingly widespread use of traditional images of *la Virgen de Guadalupe* as *objets d'art* (e.g., alongside pastel colors and Georgia O'Keefe prints in mass-marketed southwestern home fashion). Successful resistance requires constant, vigilant reinvention of the symbols of resistance, in the present example, for instance, through the kinds of creative reworkings of the image of *la Virgencita* found in the work of many contemporary Chicana/o artists.

Finally, just as our resistance to assimilation and the racial ideology that informs it requires a new understanding of the fluidity of race, so also it requires a more subtle understanding of culture. To regard the changes in our traditions that are fomented by mass culture as a loss of authenticity is to misunderstand the nature of culture. There is no single form or morph of our culture that can claim to be more truly and essentially Latino/a than any other. Cultures are constantly altered by their interactions with each other. Indeed, to all outward appearances, a culture sometimes disappears entirely, continuing only as a current beneath the surface, like the great westerly streams in the Atlantic that brought Columbus across the Ocean Sea from the coasts of Africa to the new world of the Caribbean. The prospect of our cultures being swallowed up by a mass culture that engulfs us from every side is indeed a horrifying one. However, the horror is not that the result would be something ersatz, a mere simulacrum that is somehow less truly Latino/a than what preceded it. Instead, what makes the prospect of being engulfed by mass culture so disturbing is the threat it represents to the autonomy of our culture. Cultural change has always been proceeded by the endless elaboration of creative, individual responses to and interpretations of what has gone before. The evil of mass culture is that it straitjackets this creativity and dulls our individuality. This is what I meant by saying that our assimilation in any form would leave Latino/as in America only a zombie culture. It is precisely the fear that Latino/a/a culture will continue, its soul replaced by the animus of a dead racial ideology, that should mobilize our greatest and most noble efforts.

> The most beautiful word in
> the American language is
> Resist.
> *(Tyler, 1994)*

References

Anzaldua, G. (1987). *Borderlands/La Frontera: The new mestiza.* San Francisco: Spinster/Aunt Lute Books.

Ball, E. (1998). *Slaves in the family.* New *York:* Farrar, Strauss, & Giroux.

Beltran, G. A. (1948–1949). *Los Negros en Mexico* [*Blacks in Mexico*]. Retrieved August 8, 2002, from www.folklorico.com/peoples/negros.html

Burton, R. D. E. (1997). *Afro-Creole: Power, opposition and play in the Caribbean.* Ithaca, NY: Cornell University Press.

DuBois, W. E. B. (1989). Of the training of black men. In W. E. B. DuBois (Ed.), *Souls of black folk* (p. 76). New York: Bantam Books.

Esteva-Fabregat, C. (1995). *Mestizaje in Ibero-America.* Tucson: University of Arizona Press.

Gordon-Reed, A. (1998). *Thomas Jefferson and Sally Hemings: An American controversy.* Charlottesville: University Press of Virginia.

Hudlin, R. (Director). (1996). *The great white hope.* Los Angeles: Twentieth-Century Fox.

Ignatiev, N. (1996). *How the Irish became white.* London: Routledge.

McDonald, A. (1996). *Turner diaries: A novel.* Fort Lee, NJ: Barricade Books.

Morales, A. L. (1990). *Getting borne alive.* Milford, CT: Firebrand Books.

National Advisory Commission on Civil Disorders. (1968). *Report of the National Advisory Commission on Civil Disorders.* New York: Bantam Books.

O'Brien, C. C. (1996). Thomas Jefferson: Radical and racist. *Atlantic Monthly, 278,* 53–74.

Omi, M., & Winant, H. (1986). *Racial formation in the United States: From the* 1960s *to the* 1980s. New York: Routledge.

Piper, A. M. S. (1992). Passing for white, passing for black. *Transition, 58,* 4–32.

Rich, A. (1986). *Split at the root: An essay on Jewish identity.* In A. Rich (Ed.), *Blood, bread, and poetry* (pp. 100–123). New York: W. W. Norton.

Rodriguez, R. (1983). *Hunger of memory: The education of Richard Rodriguez.* New York: Bantam Books.

Rodriguez, R. (1992). *Days of obligation: An argument with my Mexican father.* New York: Penguin Books.

Schwarz, B. (1997). What Jefferson helps to explain. *Atlantic Monthly, 279,* 60–72.

Tyler, M. (1994). The most beautiful word in the American language. In M. Algarin & B. Holman (Eds.), *Aloud! Voices from the Nuyorican Poets' Cafe.* New York: Owlet Books.

Velazco y Trianosky, G. (2002). *Radical race: Redefining our conception of race.* Unpublished manuscript, available from the author.

Journal/Discussion Questions

1. Discuss the ways in which your own experiences either resonate, or do not resonate, with the themes that Velazco y Trianosky is discussing.

2. Velazco writes, *"For us, the children of immigrant parents, the struggle over who we are is almost always a personal one."* What does he mean by this? Do you agree? Discuss.

Concluding Discussion Questions

Where Do You Stand Now?

Instructions

You have already answered the following questions in your moral problems self-quiz at the beginning of this book. Now that you have studied the material in this section, take a moment to answer the same questions again.

	Strongly Agree	Agree	Undecided	Disagree	Strongly Disagree	*Chapter 6: Race and Ethnicity*
21.	❏	❏	❏	❏	❏	African Americans are still often discriminated against in employment.
22.	❏	❏	❏	❏	❏	Affirmative action helps African Americans and other minorities.
23.	❏	❏	❏	❏	❏	Racial separatism is wrong.
24.	❏	❏	❏	❏	❏	Hate speech should be banned.
25.	❏	❏	❏	❏	❏	We should encourage the development of racial and ethnic identity.

Compare your answers to this self-quiz with the answers to the initial self-quiz. How, if at all, have your answers changed? How have the reasons for your answers changed?

Journal/Discussion Questions

✍ *In light of the readings in this chapter, would you change the way in which you understand any of your personal experiences in regard to issues of race or ethnicity?*

1. Do you think that their racially based injustices still occur in our society? If so, how do you think these can best be rectified and eliminated in the future?

2. What is your vision of a future ideal society in the United States in regard to the issues of race and ethnicity? How does that ideal relate to some of the ideals we have seen in this chapter? How do you think we can best move toward your ideal? What are the greatest possible objections to your ideal?

For Further Reading

Web Resources

For Web-based resources, including the major Supreme Court decisions on race and affirmative action, see the Race and Ethnicity page of Ethics Updates (http://ethics.SanDiego.edu).

Review Article

Bernard R. Boxill's "Racism and Related Issues," *Encyclopedia of Ethics,* edited by Lawrence and Charlotte Becker (New York: Garland, 1992), Vol. II, pp. 1056–1059 provides an excellent overview of work on race and related issues.

Racism

There is an extensive and often powerful literature dealing with the prevalence of racism in our society. Derrick Bell's *Faces at the Bottom of the Well: The Permanence of Racism* (New York: Basic Books, 1992) provides a penetrating look at the pervasiveness of racism in the United States today. Patricia J. Williams's *The Alchemy of Race and Rights* (Cambridge: Harvard University Press, 1991) is part autobiography, part feminist legal philosophy, and part cultural critique. Cornel West's *Race Matters* (Boston: Beacon Press, 1993) and his *Prophetic Thought in Postmodern Times* (Monroe, Maine: Common Courage Press, 1993) are both well-argued analyses by one of the foremost contemporary African American thinkers. Shelby Steele's *The Content of Our Character: A New Vision of Race in America* (New York: Harper Collins, 1990) offers a much more conservative interpretation of these phenomena. Stephen L. Carter's *Reflections of an Affirmative Action Baby* (New York: Basic Books, 1991) stresses the ambiguity of affirmative action for African Americans. *Lure and Loathing: Essays on Race, Identity, and the Ambivalence of Assimilation,* edited by Gerald Early (New York: Penguin Press, 1993), contains a number of insightful autobiographical essays on the ambivalence toward assimilation experienced by many contemporary African Americans. Naomi Zack's *Race and Mixed Race* (Philadelphia: Temple University Press, 1993), *Thinking About Race* (Wadsworth, 1998), and *American Mixed Race: The Culture of Diversity* (Roman & Littlefield, 1995) offer a perceptive analysis of many of the issues surrounding mixed race in our society.

Several anthologies contain shorter selections on these issues. See, especially, *Race, Class, and Gender in the United States,* 3rd ed., edited by Paula S. Rothenberg (New York: St. Martin's Press, 1995), which is a gold mine of eloquent selections; *Bigotry, Prejudice, and Hatred: Definitions, Causes, and Solutions,* edited by Robert M. Baird and Stuart E. Rosenbaum (Buffalo: Prometheus Books, 1993), which contains an number of excellent philosophical selections; and *Anatomy of Racism,* edited by David Theo Goldberg (Minneapolis: University of Minnesota Press, 1990), which contains pieces by Appiah, Outlaw, Fanon, Barthes, Kristeva, Said, Goldberg, and Gates. Also see *Women of Color in U.S. Society,* edited by Maxine Baca Zinn and Bonnie Thornton Dill (Philadelphia: Temple University Press, 1994), a collection of 16 essays, largely from social scientific standpoints.

Among the specifically philosophical approaches to racism and related issues, see the issue of *Philosophia,* Vol. 8, Nos. 2–3 (November 1978) that contains several articles on racism, including Marcus George Singer, "Some Thoughts on Race and Racism," pp. 153–183; Kurt Baier, "Merit and Race," pp. 121–151; and Peter Singer, "Is Racial Discrimination Arbitrary?", pp. 185–203; also see the double issue of *Philosophical Forum,* Vol. 9, Nos. 2–3 (1977–1978), entitled "Philosophy and the Black Experience" and the triple issue, "African-American Perspectives and Philosophical Traditions," Vol. XXIV, Nos. 1–3 (Fall-Spring 1992–1993). See Kwama Anthony Appiah, "Illusions of Race," *In My Father's House: Africa in the Philosophy of Culture* (New York: Oxford University Press, 1992), pp. 28–46, for a discussion of the slipperiness of the concept of race.

Multiculturalism

For an excellent discussion of the philosophical and political dimensions of multiculturalism, see Amy Gutmann, "The Challenge of Multiculturalism in Political Ethics," *Philosophy and Public Affairs,* Vol. 22, No. 3 (1993), pp. 171–206, and the essays in *Defending Diversity: Contemporary Philosophical Perspectives on Pluralism and Multiculturalism,* edited by Lawrence Foster and Patricia Herzog (Amherst, MA: University of Massachusetts Press, 1994). For a philosophically sophisticated account of the question of identity within this context, see Charles Taylor, *Multiculturalism and "The Politics of Recognition,"* with commentary by Amy Gutman, Steven C. Rockefeller, Michael Walzer, and Susan Wolf (Princeton: Princeton University Press, 1992). On the issue of identity, also see the papers by Anthony Appiah and others at the APA Symposium on Gender, Race, and Ethnicity, *Journal of Philosophy,* Vol. 87, No. 10 (October 1990), pp. 493–499. Also see the articles on multiculturalism and philosophy that appeared in *Teaching Philosophy,* Vol. 14, No. 2 (June 1991). See, more recently, Will Kymlicka, *Multicultural Citizenship: A Liberal Theory of Minority Rights* (New York: Oxford, 1995) and K. Anthony Appiah and Amy Gutmann, *Color Conscious: The Political Morality of Race* (Princeton, NJ: Princeton University Press, 1996).

The issue of banning hate speech has received a lot of attention in the past decade. Some of the most influential essays are gathered together in Mari J. Matsuda, et al., *Words That Wound: Critical Race Theory, Assaultive Speech, and the First Amendment* (Boulder, CO: Westview Press, 1993) and Henry Louis Gates, Jr., et al., *Speaking of Race, Speaking of Sex, Hate Speech, Civil Rights, and Civil Liberties,* with an Introduction by Ira Glesser (New York: New York University Press, 1994); also see Gates's "Let Them Talk: Why Civil Liberties Pose No Threat to Civil Rights," *The New Republic,* Vol. 209, Nos. 12–13 (September 20, 1993), p. 37 ff. Andrew Altman, "Liberalism and Campus Hate Speech: A Philosophical Examination," *Ethics,* Vol. 103, No. 2 (January 1993), pp. 302–317. Also see, Catharine A. MacKinnon, *Only Words* (Cambridge: Harvard University Press, 1993). More recently, see James B. Jacobs and Kimberly Potter, *Hate Crimes: Criminal Law and Identity Politics* (New York: Oxford, 1998) and Andrew Sullivan, "What's So Bad About Hate?" *New York Times Magazine* (September 26, 1999), pp. 50 ff.

Affirmative Action

See especially William G. Bowen and Derek Bok, T*he Shape of the River: Long-Term Consequences of Considering Race in College and University Admissions* (Princeton, NJ: Princeton University Press, 1998); this book, by the former presidents of Princeton and Harvard, respectively, provides a strong empirical case for the benefits of affirmative action in higher education; also see Bernard R. Boxill, *Blacks and Social Justice* (Totowa, NJ: Rowman & Allanheld, 1984); Gertrude Ezorsky, *Racism and Justice: The Case for Affirmative Action* (Ithaca: Cornell University Press, 1991); *The Reverse Discrimination Controversy: A Moral and Legal Analysis,* by Robert K. Fullinwider (Totowa, NJ: Rowman and Littlefield, 1980); *Invisible Victims: White Males and The Crisis of Affirmative Action,* by Frederick R. Lynch (New York: Greenwood Press, 1989); and Iris Marion Young, *Justice and the Politics of Difference* (Princeton: Princeton University Press, 1990), especially the chapter on "Affirmative Action and the Myth of Merit," pp. 192–225; and Thomas E. Hill, Jr., "The Message of Affirmative Action" *Social Philosophy and Policy,* Vol. 8 (Spring 1991), pp. 108–129.

CHAPTER 7

Gender

An Introduction to the Moral Issues

As we turn to a consideration of the issue of gender, we discover that a wide range of moral issues presents itself. Some have to do with equality and the various ways in which women have been denied equality in our society: sex discrimination, sexist language, sexual harassment, rape, pornography, hate speech, and reproductive rights. Others have to do with issues of diversity: not only diverse ideals of the place of gender in society but also the issue of whether women have a distinctive moral voice. In this introduction, we survey these issues, seeking to illuminate what is at stake in each of these areas and highlighting the questions each of us must answer in regard to this issue. Then we turn to a discussion of competing models of the place of gender in society and conclude with a discussion of the means of remedying some of the problems discussed here. First, however, let's take a quick look at the ways in which the issue of gender is similar to, and different from, ethnicity.

Defining the Problems: Issues of Sexism

Sexism is a notoriously difficult term to define precisely, but its overall elements are clear. It refers to both *attitudes* and *behavior*. Sexist attitudes are attitudes that see individuals, solely because of their gender, as being less than their male or female counterparts. For example, although both are equally competent, Jane is seen by her employer as less competent than her coworker John; the employer is exhibiting a sexist attitude. If the employer then goes ahead and, on the basis of this distorted perception, promotes John but does not promote Jane, then the employer is behaving in a sexist manner. Sexist *attitudes* refer to our perceptions and feelings; sexist *behavior* refers to our actions.

Overt and Institutional Sexism

Just as we did with racism, we can distinguish between overt and institutional sexism. *Overt sexism* is the intentional discrimination against a person because of that person's gender. For example, if a person is denied a job because that person is a male or female, that is an act of overt sexism. In contrast to this, *institutional sexism* occurs when a person is (perhaps unintentionally) discriminated against because of factors that pertain to that person's gender. For example, in some college sports such as basketball and football, women would be underrepresented if teams were open to both male and female applicants; if athletic scholarship money was given only to those who made the team, the indirect result would be that far fewer women would receive athletic scholarships than men. Although there may be no intent to discriminate in athletic scholarships against women, the net result might be precisely such institutional sexism.

Sexist Language

One of the more contentious areas of discussion in regard to sexism is language. There are two distinct aspects to this issue: (a) the gendered structure of our language and (b) its specific vocabulary. In regard to linguistic structure, many have pointed out that English, like many other languages, is gendered; we often are forced by our language to identify a person as either male or female, even when we don't know the person's gender. Because the masculine gender is the default gender in cases where we don't know, we usually supply the masculine pronouns and adjectives. It is very awkward to say, "The pioneer rode on his or her wagon." Instead, we usually say, "The pioneer rode on his wagon," thereby giving the false impression that the only pioneers were men. Advocates of a gender-neutral language have tried, with only partial success, to encourage us to use language in gender-neutral ways. This demands that we pay attention to our use of language, but that is usually something good. With some degree of care, it is usually possible to reformulate our language in gender-neutral ways. I have often used plural constructions in this book precisely for this reason.

Sexist vocabulary abounds in our language. Sometimes it is rooted in differential perceptions: a man is seen as "assertive," a woman behaving in exactly the same way is perceived as "aggressive." Sometimes the specific words tell us a lot. Obscene, transitive verbs describing sexual intercourse (e.g., "screw") are usually used in such a way as to place women as the direct object and are usually synonymous in English with "to harm or to hurt." This suggests a view of sexual intercourse that few of us would commend. Sexist language is often used to exert power. In the interview with Dr. Frances Conley, we see some of the ways in which her male colleagues used sexist language to intimidate and establish their own superior position of power.

Although it is easy to parody some attempts to eliminate sexist language, the point underlying such attempts is both clear and commendable. When we respect and care about someone, we speak both to them and about them in ways that manifest that respect and concern. In the final analysis, we try to avoid sexist language because we care about persons and respect them, and such language is incompatible with such caring and respect. If, on the other hand, we do not care for and respect others, our sexist language only solidifies and exacerbates that lack of caring and respect. The language is not the root problem, but the symptom of something deeper that has gone wrong. But just as it is valuable in medicine to reduce symptoms of disease, so too, there is a value in reducing sexist language, even though such reductions are far from a cure for the underlying ailment.

Sex Discrimination

Discrimination based on gender has certainly diminished over the years, but it still remains an important issue in American society. Although the Equal Rights Amendment (ERA) was never ratified by the required number of states, there are a number of legal guarantees available to individuals, especially women, who are the objects of sex discrimination. Moreover, numerous affirmative action programs have helped to increase the representation of women in places where they had previously been discriminated against.

Overt job discrimination. Overt discrimination, where a woman is denied a job or promotion solely because she is a woman or is paid less than her male counterpart in the same job, has decreased significantly in recent years. In the 1960s, women made 59 cents for every dollar earned by men. In 1990, this figure was 72 cents, and, for younger women during that year, it was 80 cents. How much of this remaining discrepancy is due to discrimination and how much is due to other factors (women, on the average, work fewer hours per week than their male counterparts, many have fewer years of work experience than men of the same age, some leave the job force earlier when the family no longer needs the second income, etc.) is unclear, but it is clear that the relative position of women to men in the marketplace—although still subordinate—is definitely improving. Those who are discriminated against in these ways have legal recourse, even without the ERA, and there is an increasingly wide consensus in American society that we ought not to discriminate against people on the basis of gender. Although we may fail to live up to our ideals in this area, clearly equal pay for equal work has become one of our accepted ideals.

Comparable worth.   One of the more subtle ways in which sex discrimination occurs is when predominantly female occupations are paid less than comparable occupations whose employees are predominantly male. Examples come easily enough to mind: plumbers and truck drivers versus cleaning staff and secretaries. Although intuitively this seems true (at least to me), there are two significant problems in translating this intuition into something more concrete and effective. First, the notion of "comparable," although intuitively plausible, is very difficult to make precise. Second, many (especially market conservatives) are very wary of intervening in the market to regulate wages.

Legal protection: Theory and implementation.   Finally, it is important to note that it is often insufficient simply to pass legislation prohibiting something like sex discrimination unless there is a monitoring and enforcement structure to implement the legislation. Often, the impact of the legislation can be undermined if there is insufficient funding for its implementation.

Sexual Harassment

Harassment in general consists of using undue and unwelcome *means*—usually short of outright violence—to pressure someone to some *end,* usually to do something that the harrassee does not want to do. Thus there are two crucial components of harassment: the means and the end. Workers might try to force a fellow worker to quit by pouring coffee in his locker, letting the air out of his car's tires, or calling him on the phone repeatedly in the middle of the night. Such actions would be the means of harassment, while the end would be forcing the other worker to quit.

Sexual harassment is usually sexual in two senses: (a) the *end* is usually to pressure someone (usually a woman) to have sexual intercourse with the harasser and (b) the *means* to this end are usually things such as repeated sexual innuendoes, unwanted fondling, showing pictures, and so on. Sometimes, however, the means may be comparatively unrelated to sex; they may be threats about losing one's job, a promotion, a raise, or something else that the harasser controls. Sometimes, too, the end may not even really be sexual: it may simply be about power. In the interview with Dr. Frances Conley, she speculates that her male harassers were primarily concerned with establishing their own dominance.

Several points need to be made about sexual harassment. First, most of us would agree that the less harassment in society, the better. This applies to all types of harassment, not just sexual harassment. Second, we are particularly wary of harassment of those who are most vulnerable to the intimidation of harassment: individuals of little power (usually women, often financially vulnerable) who have something (sex) that the harasser wants. Third, it is sometimes difficult to make judgments about incidents of harassment, especially when dealing with a single incident in isolation and without witnesses. However, in practice, harassment is often repeated and often done in front of other people. Fourth, sometimes appropriate expressions of sexual interest may cross the line into sexual harassment, either due to the insensitivity of the harasser or to the oversensitivity of the harrassee.

Given these general points about harassment, the central question facing us as a society in this regard is the extent to which we actively want to discourage sexual harassment, to provide special protection to those who may be victimized by it, and to punish those who harass. Sexual harassment can be discouraged through educational programs (beginning in schools, continuing on the job), the media, and the like. This is by no means limited to government initiatives; individuals can decide to provide appropriate models for dealing with harassment in their personal and public lives, in their business dealings, and so on. Potential victims can be afforded special protection through tough anti-harassment laws and through vigorous prosecution of those laws. Yet again, this is not simply a matter of legislation. Individuals can speak out against harassment when they witness it, even though it does not directly affect them. Companies can have strong internal policies against it, and it can be a serious factor in personnel decisions. Finally, we can pass strong legislation at various levels of government that discourage and punish sexual harassment.

Models of the Place of Gender in Society

Just as we saw that there was disagreement about the role of race in society, so too, we find that there is a significant degree of disagreement about precisely what the role of gender ought to be in society. The fundamental question that we face here is how we envision a future ideal society in regard to gender. Would it be one in which men and women occupy relatively traditional roles such as were common a generation ago? Is it one in which all references to gender have been banished, a unisex society? Is it one in which we still have some traditional roles but individuals—whether male or female—are free to choose whatever roles they want? Let's turn to a closer consideration of each of these three models of the place of gender in society.

The Traditional Model

Advocates of the traditional model of gender roles see the place of women as primarily in the home and the place of men as primarily in the workplace. Even within the home, the husband is seen as head of the family and the wife is viewed as subservient to him. For a man, his home is his castle; for his wife, the home is all too often something to be cleaned and a place of unpaid work. In the workplace, traditionalists usually—either explicitly in earlier times, or now implicitly—advocate a gender-based division of labor in which women occupy only low-paying (maids), menial (cleaning women), subservient (secretaries), and child-related (elementary school teachers) jobs that typically receive less pay than their male counterparts.

Critics of the traditional model argue that it places women in an inferior position in the home and in the workplace as well. Women's work in the home is unpaid and their labor in the workplace is underpaid. Moreover, women's options are most severely limited in this model, and they are especially limited from jobs that bring wealth and power. Moreover, in an age when men are freer to divorce their wives in midlife and marry younger women after their family is grown, and in an age when all too many fathers ignore child support, women are especially vulnerable to financial abandonment in middle age. In a society that is reluctant to hire middle-aged people, especially those without a strong employment history, such women face great challenges when they try to return to the workforce. Some critics of this model also add that the model is also injurious to men, forcing them into an emotionally constricting gender-based stereotype that denies them the joys of close relationships and places the burdens of financial support squarely on their shoulders.

Defenders of the traditional model center around the necessity of this model for a strong family life and the importance of strong family life for society as a whole. Although talk about family values is often vague and misleading, there is clearly a sound point here: The most effective juncture for dealing with many widespread social problems is before they begin, and the best time to do this is when children are young and in the home. We return to a discussion of this topic later when we consider gender roles and the family.

The Androgynous Model

At the other extreme from the traditional model, some have advocated a model of society in which gender would be as irrelevant as, for example, eye color presently is. Just as eye color makes no difference in job selection, salary, voting, child care, or anything else remotely similar, so, too—according to the androgynous model—gender should make no differences in these things either. Defenders of androgyny differ about how extensive the domain of the androgynous ought to be. The most extreme position, *strong androgyny,* maintains that sex- and gender-based distinctions ought to be eliminated whenever possible in all areas of life. *Weak androgyny* maintains that gender-based discrimination ought to be eliminated in the public realm (i.e., the workplace and the political realm), but in the private realm of personal relationships it may be unobjectionable.

Among the objections raised to androgyny, three stand out. First, many argue that strong androgyny is impossible. There are simply too many differences between men and women for it to be possible to fit all into the same inevitably constricting mold. Indeed, recent research—which is quickly echoed in pop psychology and therapy—seems to suggest that there are many such differences, including areas such as communication styles. Trying to cram everyone into a single model would undo the progress we have made in understanding and appreciating our differences. The merit of this claim is discussed later in the section of the nature-nurture controversy. Second, many claim that, even if strong androgyny were possible, it is hardly desirable. Just as we seek to encourage diversity and difference in society as a whole, so too, such critics argue, we should try to encourage diversity and difference in the domain of gender. Finally, some have argued that strong androgyny is part of a larger view that sees men primarily as oppressors and women primarily as victims.

Some defenders of strong androgyny reply to such criticisms by defending a weaker version of their position, which simply seeks to abolish sex-based stereotyping and prohibit, at least within the realm of work and politics, discrimination based on gender. At the juncture, androgyny comes increasingly close to the next model, which emphasizes the importance of freedom of choice for all persons.

The Maximal Choice Model

Finally, many have argued in favor of a model that seeks to eliminate any gender-based restrictions on individual choice. In contrast to advocates of strict androgyny, supporters of the maximal choice model do not seek a unisex society. They are willing to accept that men and women may typically develop different personality traits and that there might even be typical differences in behavior. However, they stress the centrality of establishing a society that promotes *freedom of choice,* so that individuals can make whatever choices they want in both public and private life irrespective of their gender. Gender-based discrimination in the workplace and in the political realm would be abolished, and equally qualified men and women would have equal accessibility to any job, profession, or office they desire. Similarly, within the family, men and women would be equally free to occupy any combination of roles traditionally associated with either men or women.

Criticisms of this model come from both sides. Traditionalists maintain that this model leads to great confusion in roles for everyone, and that social coherence is reduced as a result. Strong androgynists claim that, unless freedom of choice is reinforced with a strong restructuring of gender-based societal roles and expectations, the "freedom" is illusory: People will be subtly shifted into roles that correspond to the majority's expectations. Only a more radical form of androgyny will establish the social order necessary to ensure genuine freedom of choice.

The Nature-Nurture Controversy

Obviously, the choice of models in this realm will depend in part on the extent to which a choice is possible. Some have argued that choice is limited by human nature, and that nature fixes (at least to some extent) our gender roles. Others have claimed that these roles are established primarily (perhaps even exclusively) through nurture and are thus open to change. Advocates of change support the nurture side of this controversy, whereas advocates of the status quo (or, in some cases, an idealized version of it) support the nature side of the debate.

Although this controversy obviously cannot be settled here, it is important to distinguish three questions when evaluating arguments in this area. First, to what extent do differences between the sexes actually exist? This is an empirical question best answered through careful research, especially in the natural and social sciences. Second, if differences do exist, what is their basis? Are they genetically based, "hard-wired" differences that remain unaffected by environmental changes or are they part of our "software" that can be reprogrammed through changes in child rearing, education, and the like? This is also an empirical question, but a more difficult one because it is asking about the *causes* of certain empirical conditions, not simply whether the empirical conditions exist. Third, whether there are differences or not, we must ask whether there *ought* to be differences and, if so, what those differences ought to be.

Gender Roles and the Family

The place of gender in the family is one of the most difficult and controversial areas in which to seek common ground. As we indicated earlier in the discussion of the traditional model of gender roles, women pay a high price in their lives for their commitment to family—often a higher price than their male counterparts. As women have sought more equal access to the rewards of the workplace and more equal distribution of the responsibilities of home and family life, many men and women have been forced to rethink the ideal of the family and the way in which responsibilities have been apportioned by gender.

As Susan Moller Okin shows in the selection from her "Justice, Gender, and the Family," we would have to reorganize the family significantly if we were to make the family a just institution. In particular, responsibilities for the home and for children would have to be distributed evenly, and this entails a significant restructuring of roles. Such restructuring need not conflict with important social values, but it certainly involves a significant reordering of priorities and responsibilities for men.[1,2]

Endnotes

1. Lawrence Kohlberg, *The Philosophy of Moral Development* (San Francisco: Harper & Row, 1981).
2. Christina Hoff Sommers, *Who Stole Feminism?* (New York: Simon and Schuster, 1994).

The Arguments

Catharine MacKinnon
"What Is Sexual Harassment?"

Catharine MacKinnon, a professor at the Law School of the University of Michigan, pioneered the development of the legal concept of sexual harassment. Her book, Sexual Harassment of Working Women, *pioneered the application of civil rights law to sexual harassment. She was co-counsel in the first sexual harassment case heard by the Supreme Court. Her other books include* Toward a Feminist Theory of the State, Only Words, *and, with Andrea Dworkin,* In Harm's Way.

In this short interview, MacKinnon outlines the main components of sexual harassment.

As You Read, Consider This:

1. How exactly does MacKinnon define sexual harassment? To what extent is it subjective? To what extent is it objective?
2. Why is sexual harassment often so difficult to prove?

Q: What is sexual harassment?

A: In its broadest definition, it is sexual pressure that you are not in a position to refuse. In its verbal form, it includes a working environment that is saturated with sexual innuendoes, propositions, and advances. Other forms include leering, for example, at a woman's breasts while she talks, or staring up her skirt while she is bending over to get files. In its physical form, it includes unwanted sexual touching and rape.

Q: When was sexual harassment first recognized as a legal concept?

A: There were earlier cases, but the breakthrough occurred in 1977 when the Court of Appeals for the District of Columbia decided that Paulette Barnes was discriminated against when her government job was abolished in retaliation for her refusal to grant sexual favors to her boss. The Barnes case established that sexual harassment is sex discrimination under the Civil Rights Act. The 1986 Supreme Court case not only ratified the Barnes result but recognized as well that sexual harassment also encompasses a sexually hostile working environment.

Q: How does a woman prove she has been subjected to harassment?

A: A woman may have kept records or confided in friends, or she may have exhibited behavior—she may act upset, for example—consistent with having been aggressed against sexually. But the primary evidence is what the woman says happened.

Time Magazine, October 28, 1991, Cover; p. 48. Byline: Catharine A. MacKinnon, Peggy Brawley.

Q: But if all she has is her word, isn't she in a very difficult position?

A: Unfortunately, yes. It is very difficult for a woman to go up against a man's denial. Based on my experience with complaints at all levels, the rule of thumb is that it takes at least three women who are victims to counteract the simple stonewalling of a man. In matters of sexual abuse, women have one-third of a man's credibility, at best.

Q: It must be hard, then, for a woman to come forward with complaints of sexual harassment?

A: It was clearly difficult for Anita Hill. It should be noted that most of the women who have brought forward claims that have advanced the laws of sexual harassment have been black. Because racism is often sexualized, black women have been particularly clear in identifying this behavior as a violation of their civil rights.

Q: Do you think Professor Hill's appearance before the Judiciary Committee will encourage other women to come forward?

A: I don't know how many women will want to be subjected to the kind of brutal cross-examination Professor Hill withstood with such grace. Still, I think more women will see that Anita Hill did survive and will understand that what she did she did for all women. They will see that if they come forward with these kinds of allegations, they will not only survive but change the world for women, like she did.

Journal/Discussion Questions

✍ *Have you ever been involved in, or witnessed, an incident of sexual harassment? How well does MacKinnon's definition apply to that incident?*

1. What is MacKinnon's definition of sexual harassment? Do you agree with it? Is it too narrow or too broad?

2. What are the issues surrounding the question of proving sexual harassment? Develop and defend your own position on this issue.

David Benatar
"The Second Sexism"

David Benatar is an Associate Professor in the Department of Philosophy at the University of Cape Town, South Africa. He has published widely in the area of moral and political philosophy.

In this article, Benatar challenges traditional beliefs about sexism, arguing that there is significant sex discrimination against men that is largely neglected, even by those who otherwise take sex discrimination seriously.

As You Read, Consider This:

1. Benatar describes three underlying prejudicial attitudes toward males. What are those three attitudes?
2. What does Benatar mean by the "no-discrimination argument"?
3. Explain what Benatar means by the "distraction argument."
4. Explain what Benatar means by the "inversion argument."
5. Explain what Benatar means by the "cost of dominance argument."

In societies in which sex discrimination has been recognized to be wrong, the assault on this form of discrimination has targeted those attitudes and practices that (directly) disadvantage women and girls. At the most, there has been only scant attention to those manifestations of sex discrimination of which the primary victims are men and boys. What little recognition there has been of discrimination against males has very rarely resulted in amelioration. For these reasons, we might refer to discrimination against males as the "second sexism," to adapt Simone de Beauvoir's famous phrase. The second sexism is the neglected sexism, the sexism that is not taken seriously even by most of those who oppose sex discrimination. This is regrettable not only because of its implications for ongoing unfair male disadvantage, but also, as I shall argue later, because discrimination against *women* cannot fully be addressed without attending to all forms of sexism.

So unrecognized is the second sexism that the mere mention of it will appear laughable to some. For this reason, some examples of male disadvantage need to be provided. Although I think that all the examples I shall provide happen to be, to a considerable extent, either instances or consequences of sex discrimination, there is a conceptual and moral distinction to be drawn between disadvantage and discrimination. I shall follow the convention of understanding discrimination as the *unfair* disadvantaging of somebody on the basis of some morally irrelevant feature such as a person's sex.

Discrimination need not be intentional. It is the *effect* rather than the intent of a law, policy, convention, or expectation that is relevant to determining whether somebody is unfairly disadvantaged. Discrimination also need not be direct, as it is when one sex is explicitly prohibited from occupying some position. There are powerful social forces that shape the expectations or preferences of men and women so that significantly disproportionate numbers of men and women aspire to particular positions. Here indirect or subtle discrimination is operative. I shall not defend the claims that discrimination can be indirect and need not be intentional. These are accepted by many. Given that many other claims I shall make will be widely disputed, I shall focus on defending those more contentious claims.

Given the distinction between discrimination and disadvantage, outlining the examples of male disadvantage below is, at least for some of the examples, only the first step in the argument. I shall later consider and reject the view that these examples are not instances of discrimination.

Male Disadvantage

Perhaps the most obvious example of male disadvantage is the long history of social and legal pressures on men, but not on women, to enter the military and to fight in war, thereby risking their lives and bodily and psychological health. Where the pressure to join the military has taken the form of conscription, the costs of avoidance have been either self-imposed exile, imprisonment, or, in the most extreme circumstances, execution. At other times and places, where the pressures have been social rather than legal, the costs of not enlisting have been either shame or ostracism, inflicted not infrequently by women. Even in those few societies where women have been conscripted, they have almost invariably been spared the worst of military life—combat.

Some have noted, quite correctly, that the definition of "combat" often changes, with the result that although women are often formally kept from combat conditions, they are sometimes effectively engaged in risky combat activity. Nevertheless, it remains true that in those relatively few situations in which women are permitted to take combat roles, it is a result of their choice rather than coercion and that even then women are kept as far as possible from the worst combat situations. Others have noted that the exclusion of women from combat roles has not resulted in universal protection for women in times of war. Where wars are fought on home territory, women are regularly amongst the casualties of the combat. It remains true, however, that such scenarios are viewed by societies as being a deviation from the "ideal" conflict in which (male) combatants fight at a distance from the women and children whom they are supposed to be protecting. A society attempts to protect its own women but not its men from the life-threatening risks of war.

If we shift our attention from combat itself to military training, we find that women are generally not treated in the same demeaning ways reserved for males. Why, for instance, should female recruits not be subject to the same de-individualizing crewcuts as male recruits? There is nothing outside of traditional gender roles that suggests such allowances. If it is too degrading for a woman, it must be judged also to be too degrading for a man. That the same judgment is not made is testimony to a double standard. Permitting women longer hair as an expression of their "femininity" assumes a particular relationship between hair length and both "femininity" and "masculinity." These special privileges simply reinforce traditional gender roles.

Men are much more likely to be the targets of aggression and violence. Both men and women have been shown, in a majority of experimental studies, to behave more aggressively against men than toward women. Outside the laboratory, men are also more often the victims of violence. Consider some examples. Data from the U.S.A. show that nearly double the number of men than women are the victims of aggravated assault and more than three times more men than women are murdered. In the Kosovo conflict of 1998–99, according to one study, 90% of the war-related deaths were of men, and men constituted 96% of people reported missing. In South Africa, the Truth and Reconciliation Commission found that the overwhelming majority of victims of gross violations of human rights— killing, torture, abduction, and severe ill-treatment—during the Apartheid years (at the hands of both the government and its opponents) were males. Testimony received by the Commission suggests that the number of men who died was six times that of women. Non-fatal gross violations of rights were inflicted on more than twice the number of men than women. Nor can the Commission be accused of having ignored women and their testimony. The majority of the Commission's deponents (55.3%) were female, and so sensitive was the Commission to the relatively small proportion of women amongst the victims of the most severe violations that it held a special hearing on women.

The lives of men are more readily sacrificed in non-military and non-conflict contexts too. Where some lives must be endangered or lost, as a result of a disaster, men are the first to be sacrificed or put at risk. There is a long, but still thriving tradition (at least in Western societies) of "women and children first," whereby the preservation of adult female lives is given priority over the preservation of adult male lives.

Although corporal punishment has been inflicted on both males and females, it has been imposed, especially in recent times, on males much more readily than on females. Both mothers and fathers are more likely to hit sons than daughters. Where corporal punishment is permitted in schools, boys are hit much more often than girls are hit. Obvious sex role stereotypes explain at least some of the difference. These stereotypes also explain why, in some jurisdictions, physical punishment imposed by schools and courts has been restricted by law to male offenders.

Sexual assault on men is also often taken less seriously than such assault on women. For instance, the extent of sexual abuse of males is routinely underestimated. Sexual assaults upon boys are less likely to be reported than are those upon girls. Moreover, while rape by a male of a female is a crime everywhere, there are only a few jurisdictions in which forcing a male to have sex is regarded as rape. In these latter jurisdictions it is only recently that the definition of rape has been broadened to include the possibility of rape of a male. Before that, non-consensual sex with a man carried less severe penalties than non-consensual sex with a woman.

In a divorce, men are less likely to gain custody of their children than are women. Mothers gain custody of children in 90% of cases. Some have suggested that this is because very few men want child custody. The evidence does indeed suggest that a smaller percentage of fathers than mothers want custody and that even fewer fathers actually request custody. However, even taking this into account, fathers fare worse than mothers with regard to child custody. In one study, for instance, in 90% of cases where there was an uncontested request for maternal physical custody of the children, the mother was awarded this custody. However, in only 75% of cases in which there was an uncontested request for paternal physical custody was the father awarded such custody. In cases of conflicting requests for physical custody, mothers' requests were granted twice as often as fathers' requests. Similarly, when children were residing with the father at the time of the separation the father was more likely to gain custody than when the children were living with the mother at the time of separation, but his chances were not as high as a mother with whom children were living at the time of separation. This study was undertaken in California, which is noted for its progressive legislation and attitudes about both men and women and is thus a state in which men are less likely to be disadvantaged.

Fathers are not the only males to suffer disadvantage from post-divorce and other custodial arrangements. In one important study, divorced mothers showed their sons less affection than their daughters, "treated their sons more harshly and gave them more threatening commands—though they did not systematically enforce them . . ." "Even after two years . . . boys in . . . divorced families were . . . . more aggressive, more impulsive and more disobedient with their mothers than either girls in divorced families or children in intact families." In another study, "a significant proportion of boys who developed serious coping problems in adolescence, had lived in families in which their father was absent temporarily, either because of family discord or work." The same was not true of girls who grew up with an absent father. In short, boys tend to suffer more than girls as a result of divorce and of living with a single parent. This may be because children fare better when placed with the parent of their own sex, at least where that parent is amenable to having custody.

Homosexual men suffer more discrimination than do lesbians. For instance, male homosexual sex has been and continues to be criminalized or otherwise negatively targeted in more jurisdictions than is lesbian sex. Male homosexuals have a harder time adopting children than do lesbians, even in those places where same sex couples are permitted to adopt. Male homosexuals are much more frequently the victims of "gaybashing" assaults than are lesbians.

In addition to the above examples, for which the evidence is clear, there are also others for which there is only equivocal evidence. For instance, capital punishment is inflicted on men hundreds of times more often than it is inflicted on women. While it is true that men commit more capital crimes than women do, it is not clear that this fully explains the vast disparity in the number of men and women executed. The sex of the criminal may itself influence whether a criminal is executed. Consider also the broader criminal justice system. There is at least some evidence that, controlling for the number and nature of offenses, men are convicted more often and punished more harshly than are women (or, at least, than those women who conform to gender stereotypes). Given that there is conflicting evidence about these latter examples, we cannot be sure that they really are examples of unfair male disadvantage. Nevertheless, they are worth mentioning at least as topics suitable for further investigation.

Underlying Attitudes

These are not negligible forms of disadvantage. In seeking to explain how they arise, one can point to at least three related prejudicial attitudes about males. First, male life is often, but not always, valued less than female life. I do not mean by this that every society unequivocally values male lives less than female lives. This cannot be true, because there are some societies in which female infants are killed precisely because they are female. However, even in such societies, the lives of adult males seem to be valued less than those of adult females. The situation is less ambiguous in liberal democracies. It is not my claim that every single person in these societies values male life less, but that these societies generally do. Although, of course, there are countless examples in liberal democracies of fatal violence against women, this tends to be viewed as worse than the killing of men. If violence or tragedy takes the lives of "women and children," that is thought to be worthy of special mention. We are told that X number of people died, including Y number of women and children. That betrays a special concern, the depravity of which would be more widely denounced if newsreaders, politicians, poets, and others commonly saw fit to note the number of "men and children" who had lost their lives in a tragedy.

Sometimes the special concern for female lives is less overt and more sophisticated. Consider, for example, an argument of Amartya Sen and Jean Dreze, who have drawn attention to the number of female lives that have been lost as a result of advantages accorded men. They have spoken about the world's 100 million "missing women." To reach this figure they first observe that everywhere in the world there are around 105 boys born for every 100 girls. However, more males die at every age. For this reason, in Europe, North America, and other places where females enjoy basic nutrition and health care, the proportion of males and females inverts—around 105 females for every 100 males. Thus, the overall female-male ratio in these societies is 1.05. Amartya Sen and Jean Dreze observe, however, that in many countries the ratio falls to 0.94 or even lower. On this basis, they calculate the number of "missing women"—the number of women who have died because they have received less food or less care than their male counterparts. This is indeed an alarming and unacceptable inequity.

It is interesting, however, that no mention is made of "missing men." The implication is that there are only women who are missing. There are, however, millions of missing men, as should be most obvious from the greater number of men than women who die violently. However, there are other less obvious ways in which men become "missing." To highlight these, consider how the figure of 100 million missing women is reached. Amartya Sen says that if we took an equal number of males and females as the baseline, then "the low ratio of 0.94 women to men in South Asia, West Asia and China would indicate a 6 percent deficit in women." However, he thinks it is inappropriate to set the baseline as an equal number of males and females. He says that "since, in countries where men and women receive similar care the ratio is about 1.05, the real shortfall is about 11 percent." This, he says, amounts to 100 million missing women.

Now, I think it is extremely enlightening that the baseline is set as a female to male ratio of 1.05. Why start from that point rather than from the ratio that obtains at birth? The assumption is that the female-male ratio of 1.05 is the one that obtains in societies in which men and women are treated equally in the ways relevant to mortality—and these are taken to be basic nutrition and health care. But clearly males are not faring as well as females in those societies, so why not think that there are relevant inequalities, disadvantageous to males, operative in those societies? One answer might be biology—males seem to be not as resilient as females. I cannot see, however, why that would warrant setting the baseline at the female-male ratio of 1.05. Some distributive theories—those that claim that natural inequalities are undeserved—recommend distributing social resources in a way that compensates for natural inequalities. If males are biologically prone to die earlier, perhaps the ideal distribution is the one whereby the mortality imbalance is equalized (by funding research and medical practice that lowers the male mortality level to the female level). This certainly seems to be what feminists would advocate if biology disadvantaged women in the way it does men. If, for instance, 105 girls were born for every 100 boys, but various factors, including parturition, caused more females to die, there would be strong arguments for diverting resources to preventing those deaths. At the very least, the baseline for determining "missing people" would certainly not be thought to be set after the parturition deaths were excluded.

If we accept the male-female sex ratio at birth—105 males for every 100 females—as a baseline, then at birth there is a female-male ratio of 0.95. From that baseline there are millions of missing men, at least in those societies in which the female-male ratio inverts to 1.05, who go unseen in the Sen-Dreze analysis. This analysis fails to take account of the connection between its baseline ratio and how our health resources are currently distributed. That the Sen-Dreze analysis highlights the missing women of the world, but notes nothing about the missing men, is extremely revealing. It is a sophisticated form of the view that lost female lives are more noteworthy than lost male lives.

It might be suggested that the stronger concern to avoid female deaths rather than male deaths is best explained not by a greater valuing of women's lives but by social and economic considerations. Since the reproduction of a population requires more women than it does men, a society can less afford to lose large numbers of women (in combat, for example). This explanation, however, is not at odds with the claim that female lives are valued more. In fact, it is a possible explanation of why female lives are valued more. Note, however, that this explanation does not excuse the differential treatment. If it did, then excluding women from work outside the home, where they might be tempted to delay or abandon procreative activities, could also be excused.

The second prejudicial attitude underlying the examples I have given of male disadvantage is the greater social acceptance of non-fatal violence against males. This is not to deny the obvious truth that women are frequently the victims of such violence. Nor is it to deny that there are *some* ways in which violence against women is accepted. I suggest only that violence against men is much more socially accepted.

At least one author has taken issue with the claim that violence against men is regarded as more acceptable. He has said that those who think it is so regarded "never offer a criterion for determining when a social practice is acceptable." He says that "sometimes they slide from the fact that violence with men as victims is very widespread to the conclusion that it is acceptable." He notes, quite correctly, that a practice can be widespread without its being deemed acceptable. He also thinks that the "penalties for violent acts, social instructions against violent acts, and moral codes prohibiting violent acts" constitute evidence that violence against men is not acceptable.

It is doubtful that a single criterion of the greater acceptability of violence can be provided. However, there can be various kinds of evidence for such a claim. For instance, although violent acts against men do usually carry penalties (as do violent acts against women), the law does reveal bias. When the law prohibits physical punishment of women but permits such punishment of men, it indicates a level of greater societal acceptance of violence against men. Similarly, when the law does not punish male homosexual rape with the same severity as it punishes heterosexual rape of women, it sends a similar message. But the law is not the only evidence of societal bias. There are penalties for wifebatterers and for rape, yet this (appropriately) has not stopped feminists from showing how both legal and extra-legal factors can indicate societal tolerance of such activities. If, for instance, police do not take charges of wife-battery or rape seriously or if there are social impediments to the reporting of such crimes, this can sometimes constitute evidence of a societal complacency and therefore some implicit acceptance of such violence. If that can be true when women are the victims, why can it not be true when men are? There *are* differences in the way people view violence against men and women. For example, a man who strikes a woman is subject to much more disapproval than a man who strikes another man (even if the female victim is bigger and the male victim smaller than he is, which suggests that it is sex not size that counts).

The third prejudicial attitude is the belief that the instances of male disadvantage to which I have pointed are fully explicable by men's being naturally more aggressive, more violent, less caring, and less nurturing than women are. Some—perhaps most—people will take this to be not so much a prejudice as a truism. I shall assess this view shortly and will show that even if there are such natural behavioral differences between the sexes, the magnitude and significance of these differences is exaggerated. At the very least, those exaggerations constitute prejudices.

Responding to Objections

Some will recognize the value of attending to these prejudices and the forms of disadvantage to which they give rise. Among these people will be those feminists who acknowledge that opposition to instances of the second sexism, far from being incompatible with feminism, is an expression of feminism's best impulses. This, for reasons I shall make clear, is the view that I think all those opposed to sex discrimination ought to adopt. Regrettably, however, there will be others who will oppose combating what I have called the second sexism. These will include conservatives who endorse traditional gender roles, but also those feminists who will regard attention to the second sexism as threatening. I shall now consider and respond to four possible objections to concern about the second sexism.

1. The No-Discrimination Argument

What I call the no-discrimination argument suggests that the examples I have provided are not instances of discrimination (against men). The argument denies that there is a second sexism, by suggesting that it is not discrimination that accounts for these phenomena, but rather other factors. On this view, there may indeed be examples of male disadvantage, but these are not instances of *unfair* disadvantage.

I cannot offer a detailed application of this argument to all of the examples of male disadvantage. Therefore, although my discussion will have relevance to a number of them, I shall focus on the unequal pressures on men and women with regard to entering the military and engaging in combat. Many feminists do not question such inequalities. If pressed to explain their silence, some (but not others) might argue that these inequalities are an inevitable consequence of males' greater natural (rather than socially-produced) aggression. We might call this "the biological explanation." Insofar as they do not offer a similar explanation of the disproportionate number of men in the legislature, in specific professions, and in senior academic or management positions, and instead decry these inequalities, they selectively invoke the biological explanation to the advantage of females. Such selectivity is itself a kind of sexism. A similar charge could be laid against those feminists who would attribute both inequalities that disadvantage men and those that disadvantage women to natural differences between the sexes, but who call for an end only to those that adversely affect women.

The biological explanation does have a more consistent application in the hands of evolutionary psychologists and their followers. They argue that natural, evolutionarily explained differences between the sexes account, at least to a considerable extent, for social inequalities between men and women. They are careful to grant that environment also plays a role in psychological differences between the sexes and to acknowledge that no normative implications follow (directly) from the biological explanation. Notwithstanding such disclaimers, however, they regularly use the biological explanation to support conservative views that little if anything can or should be done to address sex inequalities, irrespective of which sex is disadvantaged. I shall now consider the common assumption that males are naturally more aggressive and then consider what implications this assumption, even if true, would really have for the sex inequalities I am considering.

The first point to note is that although males do account for more aggression and violence than females, the difference is not as great as it is usually thought to be. This is borne out by some laboratory studies. In real life, we find that there are at least some circumstances, most notably within the family, in which women behave as aggressively and violently as men and sometimes even more so than men. A number of studies have shown that wives use violence against their husbands at least as much as husbands use violence against their wives. Given the counter-intuitive and controversial nature of these findings, at least one well-known author (who shared the prevailing prejudices prior to his quantitative research) examined the data in multiple ways in order to determine whether these could be reconciled with common views. On almost every score, women were as violent as men. It was found that half the violence is mutual, and in the remaining half there were an equal number of female and male aggressors. When a distinction was drawn between "normal violence" (pushing, shoving, slapping, and throwing things) and "severe violence" (kicking, biting, punching, hitting with an object, "beating-up," and attacking the spouse with a knife or gun), the rate of mutual violence dropped to a third, the rate of violence by only the husband remained the same, but the rate of violence by only the wife increased. Wives have been shown to initiate violence as often as husbands do. At least some studies have suggested that there is a higher rate of wives assaulting husbands than husbands assaulting wives and most studies of dating violence show higher rates of female-inflicted violence.

Most authors agree that the *effects* of spousal violence are not equivalent for husbands and wives. Husbands, probably because they are generally bigger and stronger, cause more damage than wives. This is an important observation, of course, but in determining whether women are less violent than men are, it would be a mistake to point to the lesser effectiveness of their violence.

Recognizing that the sex differences in aggression and violence are less marked than commonly thought is important for the following reason. Any attempt to explain a phenomenon must be preceded by an accurate understanding of the phenomenon that is to be explained. To the extent that the sex differences in aggression are exaggerated, the posited explanations will be misdirected.

Because there are different possible explanations of the *actual* (that is, unexaggerated) sex differences in aggression, we need to consider next the evidence for the *biological* explanation of these differences. There are considerably divergent readings of the body of evidence on whether males are naturally more aggressive than females. The evolutionary psychologists understand the evidence clearly to support the biological explanation, while many feminists and others take the opposite view. Authoritatively assessing which of these interpretations is correct is too large a task to undertake here. Fortunately, for reasons I shall explain later, it is not necessary to do so. Nevertheless, for those who think that the evidence for the biological explanation is stronger than it really is, I shall first show that at the very least there is considerable room for doubt.

Consider first the alleged connections between aggression and circulating androgens, particularly testosterone. The administering of antiandrogens (and the resultant reduction of circulating testosterone levels) has been successful in curbing compulsive paraphilic sexual thoughts and impulsive and violent sexual behaviors. However, the drugs were not very effective in reducing nonsexual violence. Increasing testosterone levels in women or hypogonadal men to normal or supranormal levels has not been shown to increase aggression consistently. Lowering testosterone levels in men, by castration or antiandrogens, does not consistently decrease aggression.

Some of those reviewing the literature have concluded that the evidence does not support a link between circulating testosterone and human aggression. Some authors claim that the inability to establish this link stands in striking contrast to the ease with which relations have been shown between testosterone and other phenomena, including sexual activity. In those few studies that do suggest connections between circulating testosterone and human aggression, the links are correlational and there is some reason to think that it is the aggressive and dominant behaviors that cause testosterone levels to rise, rather than vice versa.

Now it might be argued that the evidence for androgenic causes of aggression is strongest not in the case of circulating androgens but in the case of prenatal androgen exposure. The suggestion is that exposure to androgens in utero causes the fetal brain to be organized in a way that causes increased aggression in the person that develops. On this view, since males are typically exposed to higher prenatal levels of androgens, they become naturally more aggressive.

There are clearly moral constraints on experimentally altering the androgen levels to which fetuses and infants are exposed. As a result, one of the few ways of testing the above hypothesis is by examining girls with congenital adrenal hyperplasia (CAH), a condition causing them to be exposed to unusually high levels of androgens in utero and until diagnosis soon after birth. Some studies have indeed found CAH girls to be more aggressive than control females, but some found "the difference was not significant." Other studies found no difference in aggression levels between CAH females and control females, even though affected females were, in other ways, found to be behaviorally similar to boys and unlike control females. The latter studies suggest that even if prenatal androgen exposure has other behavioral effects, an influence on aggression is not demonstrated.

There is, in any event, a significant problem that plagues the CAH studies. Given that the external genitalia of CAH girls tend to become virilized to some degree and parents know of their daughters' condition, one cannot discount social factors as a cause or partial cause of those behavioral differences that are found. One author has suggested that this objection can be rejected because normal children exposed prenatally to higher levels of testosterone have greater brain lateralization. However, unless cerebral lateralization can be shown to affect aggression, we cannot extrapolate from studies about the relationship between testosterone and lateralization to a relationship between testosterone and aggression.

None of this is to deny a biological basis for human aggression. It is possible, for example, that human aggression is rooted in some biological phenomenon other than androgens. There is some evidence that human aggression has many features in common with what is called "defensive aggression" (as distinct from "hormone-dependent aggression") in non-primate mammals and that this kind of aggression is rooted in the limbic system of the brain. One of the distinctive features of defensive aggression in non-primate mammals, however, is that it is quantitatively similar in males and females.

It is also possible that there is a connection between androgens and aggression even though none has yet been demonstrated. One possible explanation for this is that the posited connection is a complex one. One obvious feature of this complexity is the interaction with environmental factors. Even those who argue that there are (proven) hormone-related differences in aggression between the sexes agree that the environment, including the social environment, plays a significant role. Evolutionary psychologists often ignore the importance of this in drawing normative conclusions. Even if human aggression were shown to be influenced by androgens, current inequalities (in conscription and combat, for example) would still be cause for concern. One reason for this is that at least some of the inequality would be attributable to social factors rather than to natural hormonal differences between the sexes. Any natural differences in aggression that might exist could give rise to, but would also be greatly exaggerated by, sex-role expectations and conventions. This is one reason why conservatism is not a fitting response to current inequalities even if one thinks that natural differences account for some of the inequality. Another reason is that even if men are naturally more aggressive than women, it does not follow that women are not aggressive enough for military purposes or that they cannot be subject to environmental influences that would make them so.

Some feminists make much of how war is carried out by men, implying and sometimes even explicitly claiming that women are above this kind of behavior. But there are obvious social and gender role explanations that can account for why men become soldiers. Where women have had the opportunity to kill, torture, and perpetrate other cruel acts, they have proved very capable of doing so. There is a disingenuity in the arguments of those feminists who will discount the opportunity differentials between men and women for the violence of war, but who rush to explain the greater incidence of (non-sexual) child abuse by women as being a function of sexism. It is women, they correctly note, who have most contact with children and therefore have the greatest opportunity to abuse children. Moreover, we are told that female abusers of children "would probably not have become child abusers had the culture offered them viable alternatives to marriage and motherhood." If this line of argument (contrary to my own view) is acceptable, why can a similar explanation for participation in war not be given for young men "whose culture does not offer them viable alternatives" to machismo and the military?

Some feminists not only refuse to excuse men the violence of war (in the way they excuse women's violence) but, unlike other feminists, they also resist the very changes which would make it a less male affair—namely, parity in enlistment of the sexes. They oppose conscription of women. Feminist defenders of women's absence from combat assume that women are different and unsuited to war. They maintain that so long as there is (or must be) war, it is men who must wage it. There are a number of problems with this view. First, by seeking to preserve the status quo, they suppress the most effective test of whether men really are better suited to war. Notice how the real test of female competence to perform other tasks has been most unequivocally demonstrated by women actually performing those tasks. Whereas when there were almost no female lawyers people could have appealed to that fact to support claims of female unsuitability to the legal profession, that same line of argument is simply not available when there are vast numbers of successful female lawyers. Second, those who argue that women are ill-suited to war assume that men (unlike women) want to participate in war. Alternatively, male preferences on this score are a matter of indifference to them. The overwhelming majority of men do not wish to be part of the military. Were it otherwise, conscription would never be necessary. Why should these men be forced into the military, while women are not? It simply will not do, as I have explained, to justify this by saying that men are naturally more aggressive than women and thus more suitable to military activity.

Nor will it do, as some have tried, to justify the female exemption-exclusion from combat in other ways. I do not have space here to consider and respond to all the arguments for female exclusion from combat, but I shall examine two by way of illustration. Some have claimed that because women have less strength, stamina, and muscle than men, they are less suited than men to the physical demands of ground combat. There are numerous problems with this argument. For instance, much combat activity, at least in our time, does not require strength. But even if it did, that would not be a reason for excluding all women. Some women are stronger than some men are. If strength were really what counted, that and not sex would be the appropriate criterion.

Others have defended the combat exemption-exclusion as a way of protecting women from the greater risk of being raped which they would bear if captured by the enemy. It might be noted in response to this that it is far from clear that sexual abuse is not experienced by many male prisoners of war. Second, males may well stand a greater chance of being tortured in non-sexual ways than women. Why should there be such rigid (often paternalistic) exclusions of women from combat allegedly to protect them from rape, while men are not only not protected, but often forced into combat situations where they can face harms (including maiming and torture) that are arguably as traumatizing as rape? Finally, the argument that women should be exempted from combat because they need to be protected from rape (or because they are less aggressive or less strong) is one that feminists can advance only at their peril. If some such reason for exempting women were (thought to be) true, it could equally support the exclusion of women from functions they do wish to fulfill. Indeed, such reasons have been used regularly by the conservative defenders of traditional gender roles, including those who have sought to exclude from combat those women who do want such roles.

2. The Distraction Argument

Not all those opposed to highlighting the second sexism will deny that men are sometimes the victims of sex discrimination. However, those who are willing to grant this may argue that attention to the second sexism will distract us from the much greater discrimination against women. On this view, until there is parity between the extent of disadvantage suffered by men and women, we must devote our attention and energies to opposing the greater discrimination—that experienced by females.

This argument presupposes that the position of women is worse than that of men. I do not deny this, if it is a global claim that is being made. In most places, women are generally worse off than men. This is because the traditional gender roles for women are much more restrictive than those for men, and most of the world's human population continues to live in societies that are characterized by traditional gender roles. But what about contemporary liberal democracies, from whose ranks most feminists are drawn and to which substantial (but not exclusive) feminist attention is devoted?

In the light of the substantial inroads against sexism made in such societies, as well as the examples of the second sexism that I have outlined, are women worse off than men in such countries? Many people will confidently offer an affirmative answer. I cannot say that their answer is wrong. Nevertheless, the answer cannot be offered with confidence in a society that has viewed so lightly the serious forms of discrimination against men. The extent of discrimination against men is probably seriously underestimated and this makes fair comparison unlikely. Fortunately, I think that the question of which sex suffers the greater discrimination is simply irrelevant to the question of whether attention should be given to the second sexism. This brings me to my first response to the distraction argument.

Sex discrimination is wrong, irrespective of the victim's sex. It is not only the most severe manifestations of injustice that merit our attention. If it were wrong to focus on lesser forms of discrimination when greater forms were still being practiced, then we would have to attend to racial discrimination rather than sex discrimination, at least in those places in which racial discrimination is worse than sex discrimination. Moreover, where one opposed sex discrimination, one would have to ignore some forms of sex discrimination if one accepted the view that only the most serious injustices deserve our attention. Not all forms of sexism are equally severe. Using the word "man" to refer to people of both sexes, for example, is not as damaging as clitoridectomy or even as unfair as unequal pay. Feminists who think that we should devote our energies only to eliminating the worst forms of sex discrimination would be committed to a very restricted agenda. But if both major and minor forms of discrimination against women deserve attention, why should major forms of discrimination against men not be equally deserving of concern? How can it be acceptable to want an end to sexist speech while males die because of their sex? If one is opposed to injustice, then it is injustice that counts, not the sex of the victim. Even if it is the case that in general women are the greater victims of sex discrimination, it is still the case that some men suffer more from sex discrimination than some women. A young man on the Titanic who is denied a place in a lifeboat because of his sex is worse off than the young woman whose life is saved because of her sex. A young man, conscripted and killed in battle, is worse off than his sister who is not. It does not matter here that had he survived, the man would have had greater access to higher education or could have earned more. If he is made to lose his life because of his sex and she has her life spared because of her sex, then this man is the greater victim of sex discrimination than this woman. Countering sex discrimination against men will remove some relative advantages that women enjoy, but that is fair in the same way that it is fair that countering sex discrimination against women removes relative advantages that men enjoy.

There is a second important response to the distraction argument. Far from distracting one from those discriminatory practices that disadvantage females, confronting the second sexism can help undo discrimination against women. This is because ending discrimination against one sex is inseparable from ending discrimination against the other sex. One reason for this is that the same sets of stereotypes underlie both kinds of discrimination. For example, the very attitudes that prevent women from being conscripted and from being sent into combat, thereby discriminating against those males and protecting those women who have no wish to be part of the military, also favor those males but disadvantage those females who desire a military career and who do not want to be excluded from combat. Similarly, the stereotypes of men as aggressive and violent and of women as caring and gentle lead to only males' being sent into battle but also entail assumptions that it is women who must bear primary responsibility for child-caring. Or consider the small proportion of women amongst the victims of gross human rights violations in South Africa. This is attributable to gender roles that discouraged women from engaging in political activity, especially dangerous political activity in which men were encouraged or expected to participate. Although these gender roles had beneficial effects for women in protecting them from the violence of adversaries, these same gender roles disadvantaged women in other regards. The "women and children first" mentality is another, related, example. It disadvantages men in life-and-death situations but has obvious disadvantages for women in other circumstances. Women are protected, to be sure, but in the same way and for relics of the same reasons that children are—they are assumed to be weak and to be unable to look after themselves. Similarly, the battered woman syndrome defense, under which the criminal law (at least in the United States) allows evidence of abuse of women, but not of men, to constitute an excuse from criminal responsibility, has the effect of reaffirming prejudices about women as lacking the capacity for rational self control.

3. The Inversion Argument

By the "inversion argument," I mean the argument that what I have suggested are instances of discrimination against men are instead forms of discrimination against women. On this view, what I have called the second sexism is instead just another form of discrimination against women. Rarely is such an argument explicitly presented. That is to say, those employing this sort of argument do not argue that matters ought to be inverted. Rather they simply invert them. They do not argue that what might be thought to constitute discrimination against men is rather discrimination against women. Instead, they simply present the data as instances of anti-female bias. To this extent, my presentation of the inversion as an argument is a construction of an argument out of a practice. The absence of an explicit argument for inversion is understandable. Were an argument for inversion explicitly presented, its weakness would be much more apparent.

Consider, for example, those authors who present attempts at excluding women from the military as forms of discrimination against women. They say, for instance, that the military, faced with an increase in the number of women soldiers, "seems to have an exaggerated need to pursue more and more refined measures of sexual difference in order to *keep women in their place,*" noting that Western armed forces "search for a difference which can justify women's continued exclusion from the military's ideological core—combat. If they can find this difference, they can also exclude women from the senior command promotions that are open only to officers who have seen combat." As I have argued, excluding women from combat does indeed disadvantage some women. That it is a minority of women whom this exclusion disadvantages—those who seek combat opportunities and the career benefits that come with this in the military—does not alter the fact that *these* women are indeed the victims of sex discrimination. But to present the exclusion exclusively in terms of the negative effects it has on women is to ignore the much greater disadvantage suffered by vast numbers of men who are forced into combat against their wills. It is well and good to note, as I have done, how an instance of sex discrimination can cut both ways. It is quite another to present everything as disadvantaging only women.

Even those with a more balanced approach tend to make much more of the negative impact on women of those discriminatory practices whose primary victims are men. Thus, one author who notes that war is "often awful and meaningless," observes that there are advantages that combatants enjoy. She cites a prisoner of war graffito "freedom—a feeling the protected will never know" and "the feelings of unity, sacrifice and even ecstasy experienced by the combatant." Moreover, she notes that women "who remain civilians will not receive the post-war benefits of veterans, and those [women] who don uniforms will be a protected, exempt-from-combat subset of the military. Their accomplishments will likely be forgotten." Although true, the significance of these advantages is overdone—even to the point of depravity. Certainly, those who never experience its loss may not have the same acute appreciation of freedom, but that acute appreciation is, at most, a positive side effect of an immensely traumatic and damaging experience. Imagine how we would greet the observation that although paraplegia is "often awful and meaningless" it is only those who have lost the use of some limbs who can truly appreciate the value of having those limbs functional. Next, although veterans do have benefits denied to others, this is a form of compensation for sacrifice made. It is hardly unfair that compensation is not given to those to whom no compensation is due. People should be free, of course, to decide whether they want to accept the sacrifices of joining the military and the compensation that goes with it, but the absence of that choice is the disadvantage rather than the mere absence of the compensation. Finally, while the tasks of non-combatants are indeed less likely to be remembered, this observation grossly underplays the extent to which the tasks and sacrifices of most combatants are unremembered. Many of these who die in battle lie in unmarked graves or are memorialized in monuments to the "Unknown Soldier." In exceptional cases, as with the Vietnam War Memorial, a deceased combatant's memorial consists of an engraving of his name, along with thousands of others—hardly a remembrance proportionate to the sacrifice.

Consider another example of the inversion argument. Males, I noted earlier in my discussion of the Sen-Dreze argument, tend to die earlier than females. Although life expectancy has increased in developed countries over the last century, men have consistently lagged behind women. This suggests that the earlier death of males is (or, at least, was) not attributable to a biologically determined life-expectancy ceiling. As social conditions improved, men lived to be older, but never (on average) as old as women. If it were the case that men tended to live longer than women, we would be told that this inequality would need to be addressed by devoting more attention and resources to women's health. By means of the inversion argument, the call for more attention and resources to women's health is exactly what some people offer even though it is in fact men who die earlier. Such claims do not result from a belief that more is spent on the health care of men than women. A Canadian study on sex differences in the use of health care services showed that the "crude annual per capita use of health care resources (in Canadian dollars) was greater for female subjects ($1,164) than for male subjects ($918)" but that expenditures "for health care are similar for male and female subjects after differences in reproductive biology and higher age-specific mortality rates among men have been accounted for." Accepting that there is indeed an equal distribution of health-care dollars between men and women, one practitioner of the inversion argument suggested that such expenditure was not equitable. This, we are told, is because the greater longevity (of females) is "associated with a greater lifetime risk of functional disability and chronic illness, including cancer, cardiovascular disease, and dementia, and a greater need for long-term care." I shall assume that that is indeed so. Living longer does carry some costs, but on condition that those costs are not so great as to render the increased longevity a harm rather than a benefit, the infirmities that often accompany advanced age cannot be seen in isolation from the benefit of the longer life-span. An equitable distribution of health-care resources is not one that both favors a longer life-span for one sex and increases the quality of the additional years of that extra increment of life. Such a distribution would constitute a double favoring of one sex. A genuinely equitable distribution would be one that aimed at parity of life expectancy and the best quality of life for both sexes within that span of life. The proponents of the inversion argument, by contrast, are unsatisfied with any perceived trends that lessen the gap between men and the healthier sex. Thus we are told, disapprovingly, that at "a time when there have been improvements in the health status of men, the health status of women does not appear to be improving."

Another example of inversion is the common argument that the educational system disadvantages girls. It is widely thought that girls fare worse than boys in school and university. This is just the message proclaimed by a report from the Wellesley College Center for Research on Women. Sponsored by the American Association of University Women, the report, entitled "How Schools Shortchange Girls," has been widely cited. Indeed, there are some ways in which girls fare less well than boys in the educational system. For instance, boys tend to do better in mathematics and science tests and more doctoral degrees are awarded to men than to women. However, there are other ways in which boys are clearly at a disadvantage. In the U.S.A., girls outscore boys on reading and writing by a much greater margin than boys outscore girls in science and mathematics tests. And although boys do better on science and mathematics tests, girls get better class marks for these subjects. Some have suggested that this differential is to be explained by gender bias in the standardized tests. Christina Hoff Sommers suggests, however, that it could be better explained by a grading bias in schools against boys. Since Taiwanese and Korean girls score much higher than American boys on the same tests, it would seem that the gender-biased explanation of the standardized tests is not entirely satisfactory. Boys are educationally disadvantaged in other ways too. More boys miss classes, fail to do homework, have disciplinary problems, and drop out of school. The higher dropout rate for boys may partially explain the better average performance by boys on standardized tests. The academically weakest boys tend not to write. Boys are also "more likely to be robbed, threatened, and attacked in and out of school." Females now constitute a majority of college graduates and M.A.s in the U.S.A. Only in doctoral degrees are men still in the majority, but now by a much smaller margin than before. Females are worse off in some ways, but these disadvantages are diminishing. The inverters, ignoring the serious ways in which males are disadvantaged, present the educational institutions as disadvantaging only girls and women.

Sometimes the inversion argument or technique applies to a phenomenon that both discriminates against men and against women, but it presents the situation as discriminating only against women. We might call this a hemi-inversion argument. It inverts only that aspect that discriminates against men, thus presenting the phenomenon as disadvantaging only women. One example of this is the pair of authors who presented the exclusion of women in the sports media from male locker rooms after matches as an instance of blatant discrimination against those women. As they correctly observe, such sportswriters who "cannot get immediate access to athletes after a game . . . may miss deadlines and will likely be 'scooped' by the competition." They entirely ignore the other side of the issue, however, and quote with disapproval the coach who stated "I will not allow women to walk in on 50 naked men." Had it been a male sports writer seeking access to a locker room of 50 naked female athletes, we can be sure that a different tone would have been evident in feminist commentary on the matter. There are alternative solutions to such equity issues—such as denying all journalists, both male and female, from entering locker rooms. These authors ignore such options just as they ignore the invasion of privacy that would be experienced by the male athletes, who would surely be discriminated against if their female counterparts would not also be subject to such invasions. Instead, the authors view the matter entirely from the perspective of the female sports writers. I am fully aware that for other unfortunate reasons male sports draw more attention, and that female writers thus lose more in not having access to male locker rooms than male writers do in not having access to female locker rooms. However, if this is used to justify female access to male locker rooms but not male access to female locker rooms, then the intensity of the writer's interest rather than the athlete's privacy is taken to be the determining factor. And if that is so, then male journalists should be allowed to corner female politicians, actors, and other public personalities in female-only toilets and locker rooms if that is how they can scoop an important story. If this would not be acceptable, then neither is the intrusion by female sports writers on the privacy of male athletes, irrespective of the writers' interests in getting a story.

The inversion argument is a crass form of partiality. It presents *all* sex inequality as disadvantaging primarily or only women. This is unfair to those males who are the primary victims of some forms of sex discrimination. It also strategically compromises the case against those forms of discrimination that do in fact disadvantage women more than men. Unfairly presenting the relative disadvantages of different practices leads to one's legitimate claims being taken less seriously.

4. The Costs-of-Dominance Argument

A fourth kind of argument suggests that although there may indeed be costs to being a man, these are the costs of dominance—the costs that come with being the privileged sex. Unlike the inversion argument, the costs-of-dominance argument does not suggest that the costs of being a man are *themselves* actually advantages. Instead, this argument recognizes that they are indeed costs, but suggests that they should be seen merely as the by-products of a dominant position and thus not evidence of discrimination against males. In the words of one author, it "is a twist of logic to try to argue . . . that because there are costs in having power, one does not have power."

Clearly there are some situations in which the costs-of-dominance argument would be sound. Where a cost really is inseparable from one's position of power or (overall) advantage, then it is true that the cost is not a cause for complaint *on behalf of* the power-holder. However, it does not follow from this that all the costs experienced by males really are connected to their having power or privilege. For example, although the exemption-exclusion of women from the military is the result of females' perceived military incapacity, it is hardly obvious that male power would be impossible without this exemption-exclusion. For example, the rich have succeeded in preserving (even enhancing) their privilege while the poor, for various reasons, have endured a disproportionately heavy military burden. Thus, it need not be the case that those with the power in a society must be those who bear arms. Bearing arms is dirty work and there is no shortage of examples of underdogs being forced or enticed to do the dirty work. Similarly, it is far from clear that the higher rates of capital and corporal punishment of males is an inevitable by-product of male power.

It is sometimes alleged that the higher rates of male suicide, the tendency of males to die younger than women, the greater chance that men have of being killed, becoming alcoholic, and so forth, are side-effects of the stresses that come with privilege. It might be argued in response that alleged privileges that have these consequences are not real privileges for those who succumb. Although some men may benefit, many others experience only the costs. However, even if it were true that these were costs of genuine privilege, it would not follow that these costs were inevitable results. Those with power can divert resources in order to combat such side-effects of their power, thereby further improving their position.

Moreover, it is curious that as male power has surely (and appropriately) diminished in western democracies, the costs of being male have (inappropriately) increased, not decreased. For example, whereas a century or more ago men were almost guaranteed, following divorce, to gain custody of their children, today they are at a distinct disadvantage. As custody practices were better for men when they really did enjoy more power than they do now, it is clear that the current custody biases are not inevitable by-products of male power.

Thus, although it is true that the powerful cannot complain about having to bear the costs of that power, it does not follow that all disadvantages they suffer are such costs. Even if it is true that men in our society enjoy overall advantage—and I am not convinced that this is true any longer—it can still be true that they suffer genuine discrimination that is not an inevitable consequence of their privilege.

Now some will ask why those who hold most positions of power in a society could be the victims of pervasive discrimination. Why would those with power allow themselves to be treated in this way? Although there are a number of possible answers, the most important one is that insofar as discrimination is indirect and non-intentional, those who hold positions of power may not recognize it for what it is. They might take their disadvantage to be inevitable, perhaps because they share the very prejudices that contribute to their own disadvantage. A captain and officers clearly hold the powerful positions on a ship. Yet when it sinks and they adhere to and enforce a policy of saving "women and children," the social conventions lead them to use their power in a way that advantages women and disadvantages men (including themselves).

Taking the Second Sexism Seriously

The fitting response to the second sexism is to oppose it in the same way that we oppose those sexist attitudes and practices of which women are the primary victims. To date, however, there has been an asymmetrical assault on sexism. Practices that disadvantage women have steadily been uprooted, while very few disadvantages of men have been confronted. Male disadvantage is thought hardly worthy of mention. When it is mentioned it is often excused even by those who purport to oppose sex discrimination. In academic research into gender issues, the trend is to examine ways in which women are disadvantaged. Relatively little research examines the other side of the sexist coin. Because of this, we have every reason to think that the full extent of male disadvantage has not been revealed. If it has taken all the research it has to show the many facets of discrimination against women and girls, it surely will take as much to show the many ways in which men and boys suffer disadvantage.

Recognition of the second sexism sheds some light on the claim that all societies are structured to the exclusive benefit of men and are thus "patriarchal." So powerful is patriarchy, we are told, that women themselves internalize its values and serve its ends. Consider, for instance, female genital excision, which is widespread in some parts of the world. This ritual is almost always performed by women and many women are amongst the most vigorous defenders of the practice. Nevertheless, it is argued, entirely appropriately, that given how damaging the procedure is to the girls on whom it is performed, it cannot reasonably be claimed to serve the interests of women (except, perhaps, those few female performers of the ritual, as they may have a vested interest in it). What is curious, though, is that similar reasoning is not applied to the conscription of only males. Here some feminists are at pains to emphasize that it is men who make wars and men who conscript other men to fight them. This is true, but no less so than the claim that it is females who perform genital excision on little girls. Why is it not the case that the whole system of male-only conscription and combat serves women's interests? Why are the female agents of genital excision serving the interests of men, while the male—

and now also female—agents of government, the bureaucracy and the military who send *men* to war, are serving *men's* interests? Why are women not complicit in and partly culpable for the perpetuation of gender role stereotypes that lead to male disadvantage? Once one recognizes the second sexism, claims about universal patriarchy become either absurd or unfalsifiable. The evidence suggests that not *everything* counts against women and in favor of men. Society often favors men, but it also sometimes (perhaps even often) favors women. To the extent that claims about the existence of patriarchy deny this and explain away any conceivable example of male disadvantage, they are unfalsifiable and accordingly unscientific.

Understanding the second sexism also has consequences for the debate about affirmative action for women (qua women, rather than qua some other class of beings). For instance, one objection to strong affirmative action policies is that rather than redressing past disadvantage by making restitution to an identifiably disadvantaged person, such policies make restitution to a person who belongs to a class that has been disadvantaged. This, it is said, sometimes leads to somebody who has not been disadvantaged receiving the benefit of affirmative action. In response to this argument, defenders of affirmative action sometimes argue that given how society works, *all* women have been disadvantaged and thus an affirmative action policy favoring women cannot in practice favor somebody who has not been disadvantaged. What the second sexism shows is that this response will not work. It will sometimes—even often—be the case that a man has been more disadvantaged than a woman. This woman may not have had her career interrupted by childbearing and rearing, but this man may have had his career interrupted by a period of military service. This woman may have had every educational advantage during childhood schooling, while this man may have been one of the many who suffered educational disadvantage.

Moreover, asymmetrical attention has been given to how sexist attitudes lead to lopsiding in social institutions. Feminists regularly tell us that anything less than proportionate representation of the sexes in government, the professions, and other socially desirable positions is an indication of discrimination (whether subtle or otherwise). Although there are relatively few female engineers, for example, despite formal equality of opportunity, we are told that this is due to subtle sexist influences that discourage young girls from aspiring to be engineers. Yet, this sort of reasoning is not used to explain why the vast majority of prisoners or soldiers are male. It is not said that sexist stereotypes dispose (or force) young males to enlist or to behave in ways that make them more susceptible to imprisonment. The proportion of male prisoners and soldiers, for example, is simply taken as natural in a way that the proportion of male engineers or legislators is not.

If the under-representation of women in the academy, for example, must be redressed by affirmative action policies that ensure proportionality, why should similar policies not be used for the purposes of conscription and combat? Affirmative action conscription policies that aimed at enlisting equal numbers of males and females and insisted on sending equal numbers of men and women into battle would not only enforce the desired proportionality, it would also have an immense impact on the prejudicial views about gender roles. Similarly, notice that although women are now heavily represented in what were traditionally male jobs, men have not made comparable inroads into professions such as nursing, which (for about a century and a half) have traditionally been the preserve of women. Part of this is explicable by the lower status of traditionally female jobs, which makes them less attractive to men. But that, it seems to me, is just part of the sexist worldview that feminists are seeking to undo. If the aims of affirmative action include proportional representation of the sexes in each kind of work, and the overcoming of gender-linked jobs, then affirmative action has as much of a role to play in equalizing the nursing profession as it does in equalizing the sexes within the ranks of doctors. In fact, there is reason—including the actual success rates—to think that sexist stereotypes make it easier for women to enter traditionally male professions than for men to enter traditionally female professions. Accordingly, affirmative action policies, if justified, may be more needed in nursing than in medicine. I want to emphasize that I am not recommending affirmative action in the military, the nursing profession, and other such areas. My claim is only that the very arguments used to defend affirmative action in other contexts would apply equally here. To apply them selectively is disingenuous.

Conclusion

When one considers how much has been written about discrimination against women, it is clear that no one paper can address all aspects of the second sexism. It has not been possible for me to search for and probe all instances of the second sexism, and it has not been possible to consider and respond to all objections to the claim that there is a second sexism. Such constraints on a single paper are innocuous in themselves. Unfortunately, however, the paucity of papers giving attention to discrimination against men leads to those few that there are being taken less seriously. The absence of an extensive academic literature about discrimination against men both results from and further entrenches the neglect of such discrimination. That is to say, it is at least partly because such discrimination is not taken seriously that so little research time and money is devoted to it. But because it is not the vogue to examine such discrimination, much less is known about it and this perpetuates the impression that is not worthy of detailed consideration. The lopsided information we have about sexism creates a climate in which the research bias is preserved and reinforced. This is dangerous. We have every reason to think that academic neglect of a problem is not an indication of its absence. For example, it was not long ago that sexual abuse of children was thought to be an extremely rare phenomenon. That issue has since become a popular academic and social cause, with the result that we now know much more about it and it is now widely recognized to be more common than was previously thought.

But do (most) men feel as though they are victims of sexism? It has been noted that "women bent on escape from the female sphere do not usually run into hordes of oppressed men swarming in the opposite direction, trying to change places with their wives and secretaries" and that this is evidence for "where the real advantage lies." Notice that one could embrace the conclusion that overall advantage lies with men, while still acknowledging that men do experience some significant sexist discrimination. In this paper I have sought only to highlight this discrimination and to argue that it should be opposed. I have not sought to claim that men are worse off than women. Nevertheless, the observation that men (generally) do not want to change places with women should not be invested with too much significance. If people's satisfaction or dissatisfaction with their socially mandated roles were determinative (or even suggestive) of whether such roles were advantageous to their bearers, then a few conclusions that are unfortunate for feminists would follow. First, many women forced into traditional female roles could not be viewed as being the victims of sexism, so long as those roles were internalized by those women and found by them to be satisfying. Just such an attitude characterized most women until the dawn of the women's movement, and it is an attitude that is still widespread among women in more traditional societies, if not with respect to every feature of their position then at least to many of its features. Second, the women most dissatisfied with their condition are to be found in disproportionately large numbers amongst women who are subject to the least sexist discrimination and restrictions. For instance, female feminist professors in Western societies are arguably the most liberated women in the world—the women least restricted or disadvantaged by sexism. Yet they are also more concerned about the disadvantages they do face than are many less fortunate women. If the level of one's satisfaction with one's role is what determines the severity of the discrimination to which one is subjected, then the sexism experienced by contemporary Western feminists really is worse than that endured by those women in more traditional societies, past or present, who are satisfied with their position. Whether one takes that to be absurd will depend, at least in part, on what view one takes about such matters as adaptive preferences and false consciousness. It would be unwise to attempt to settle these issues here. All I wish to observe is that if men's apparent contentment with their position is taken to be evidence that they are not the victims of discrimination, then from that follow some conclusions that should be unsettling to most feminists. If, by contrast, it is thought that somebody might be the victim of discrimination without realizing it, then the way is opened to recognizing that even if most men are content with their position they might nonetheless be victims of a second sexism.

Journal/Discussion Questions

1. In your own experience, what have you seen that confirms Benatar's analysis of the second sexism? What have you seen that counts against his analysis? Overall, how would you assess the validity of his claims?

2. If Benatar is right, what conclusions follow for your own views about sexism in our society?

Susan Moller Okin
"Is Multiculturalism Bad for Women?"

Susan Moller Okin, the Marta Sutton Weeks Professor of Ethics in Society and Professor of Political Science at Stanford University, is the author of Women in Western Political Thought *and* Justice, Gender, and the Family.

In this article, Okin explores some of the tensions that arise between acceptance of diversity (a key tenet of multiculturalism) and concern for the rights and well-being of women.

As You Read, Consider This:

1. *"Feminism" and "multiculturalism" are two key terms in Okin's article. How does she define each of these terms?*

Originally published in the *Boston Review,* October/November 1997. Reprinted in Susan Moller Okin, *Is Multiculturalism Bad for Women?* edited by Joshua Cohen, Matthew Howard, and Martha C. Nussbaum (Princeton: Princeton University Press, 1999).

2. Why, according to Kymlicka, do certain minority groups deserve special group rights?
3. What is the liberal response to Okin's critique? What rejoinder does Okin offer to this response?

Until the past few decades, minority groups—immigrants as well as indigenous peoples—were typically expected to assimilate into majority cultures. This assimilationist expectation is now often considered oppressive, and many Western countries are seeking to devise new policies that are more responsive to persistent cultural differences. The appropriate policies vary with context: Countries such as England with established churches or state supported religious education find it hard to resist demands to extend state support to minority religious schools; countries such as France with traditions of strictly secular public education struggle over whether the clothing required by minority religions may be worn in the public schools. But one issue recurs across all contexts, though it has gone virtually unnoticed in current debate: What should be done when the claims of minority cultures or religions clash with the norm of gender equality that is at least formally endorsed by liberal states (however much they continue to violate it in their practice)?

In the late 1980s, for example, a sharp public controversy erupted in France about whether Magrbin girls could attend school wearing the traditional Muslim headscarves regarded as proper attire for postpubescent young women. Staunch defenders of secular education lined up with some feminists and far-right nationalists against the practice; much of the old left supported the multiculturalist demands for flexibility and respect for diversity, accusing opponents of racism or cultural imperialism. At the very same time, however, the public was virtually silent about a problem of vastly greater importance to many French Arab and African immigrant women: polygamy.

During the 1980s, the French government quietly permitted immigrant men to bring multiple wives into the country, to the point where an estimated 200,000 families in Paris are now polygamous. Any suspicion that official concern over headscarves was motivated by an impulse toward gender equality is belied by the easy adoption of a permissive policy on polygamy, despite the burdens this practice imposes on women and the warnings issued by women from the relevant cultures. On this issue, no politically effective opposition galvanized. But once reporters finally got around to interviewing the wives, they discovered what the government could have learned years earlier: that the women affected by polygamy regarded it as an inescapable and barely tolerable institution in their African countries of origin, and an unbearable imposition in the French context. Overcrowded apartments and the lack of each wife's private space lead to immense hostility, resentment, even violence both among the wives and against each other's children.

In part because of the strain on the welfare state caused by families with 20-30 members, the French government has recently decided to recognize only one wife and consider all the other marriages annulled. But what will happen to all the other wives and children? Having neglected women's view on polygamy for so long, the government now seems to be abdicating its responsibility for the vulnerability that women and children incurred because of its rash policy.

The French accommodation of polygamy illustrates a deep and growing tension between feminism and multiculturalist concerns to protect cultural diversity. I think we—especially those of us who consider ourselves politically progressive and opposed to all forms of oppression—have been too quick to assume that feminism and multiculturalism are both good things which are easily reconciled.

I shall argue instead that there is considerable likelihood of tension between them—more precisely, between feminism and a multiculturalist commitment to group rights for minority cultures.

A few words to explain the terms and focus of my argument. By "feminism," I mean the belief that women should not be disadvantaged by their sex, that they should be recognized as having human dignity equally with men, and the opportunity to live as fulfilling and as freely chosen lives as men can. "Multiculturalism" is harder to pin down, but the particular aspect that concerns me here is the claim, made in the context of basically liberal democracies, that minority cultures or ways of life are not sufficiently protected by ensuring the individual rights of their members and as a consequence should also be protected with special *group* rights or privileges. In the French case, for example, the right to contract polygamous marriages clearly constituted a group right, not available to the rest of the population. In other cases, groups claim rights to govern themselves, have guaranteed political representation, or be exempt from generally applicable law.

Demands for such group rights are growing—from indigenous native populations, minority ethnic or religious groups, and formerly colonized peoples (at least, when the latter immigrate to the former colonial state). These groups, it is argued, have their own "societal cultures" which—as Will Kymlicka, the foremost contemporary defender of cultural group rights, says—provide "members with meaningful ways of life across the full range of human activities, including social, educational, religious, recreational, and economic life, encompassing both public and private spheres."[1] Because societal cultures play so pervasive and fundamental a role in the lives of members, and because such cultures are threatened with extinction, minority cultures should be protected by special rights: That, in essence, is the case for group rights.

Some proponents of group rights argue that even cultures that "flout the rights of [their individual members] in a liberal society"[2] should be accorded group rights or privileges if their minority status endangers the culture's continued existence. Others do not claim that all minority cultural groups should have special rights, but rather that such groups—even illiberal ones, that violate their individual members' rights, requiring them to conform to group beliefs or norms—have the right to be "let alone" in a liberal society.[3] Both claims seem clearly inconsistent with the basic liberal value of individual freedom, which entails that group rights should not trump the individual rights of their members; thus, I will not address the problems they present for feminists here.[4] But some defenders of multiculturalism largely confine their defense of group rights to groups that are internally liberal.[5] Even with these restrictions, feminists—anyone, that is, who endorses the moral equality of men and women—should remain skeptical. So I will argue.

Gender and Culture

Most cultures are suffused with practices and ideologies concerning gender. Suppose, then, that a culture endorses and facilitates the control of men over women in various ways (even if informally, in the private sphere of domestic life). Suppose, too, that there are fairly clear disparities of power between the sexes, such that the more powerful, male members are those who are generally in a position to determine and articulate the group's beliefs, practices, and interests. Under such conditions, group rights are potentially, and in many cases actually, antifeminist. They substantially limit the capacities of women and girls of that culture to live with human dignity equal to that of men and boys, and to live as freely chosen lives as they can.

Advocates of group rights for minorities within liberal states have not adequately addressed this simple critique of group rights, for at least two reasons. First, they tend to treat cultural groups as monoliths—to pay more attention to differences between and among groups than to differences within them. Specifically, they give little or no recognition to the fact that minority cultural groups, like the societies in which they exist (though to a greater or lesser extent), are themselves *gendered,* with substantial differences of power and advantage between men and women. Second, advocates of group rights pay no or little attention to the private sphere. Some of the best liberal defenses of group rights urge that individuals need "a culture of their own," and that only within such a culture can people develop a sense of self-esteem or self-respect, or the capacity to decide what kind of life is good for them. But such arguments typically neglect both the different roles that cultural groups require of their members and the context in which persons' senses of themselves and their capacities are first formed *and* in which culture is first transmitted—the realm of domestic or family life.

When we correct for these deficiencies by paying attention to internal differences and to the private arena, two particularly important connections between culture and gender come into sharp relief, both of which underscore the force of the simple critique. First, the sphere of personal, sexual, and reproductive life provides a central focus of most cultures, a dominant theme in cultural practices and rules. Religious or cultural groups are often particularly concerned with "personal law"—the laws of marriage, divorce, child custody, division and control of family property, and inheritance. As a rule, then, the defense of "cultural practices" is likely to have much greater impact on the lives of women and girls than those of men and boys, since far more of women's time and energy goes into preserving and maintaining the personal, familial, and reproductive side of life. Obviously culture is not only about domestic arrangements, but they do provide a major focus of most contemporary cultures. Home is, after all, where much of culture is practiced, preserved, and transmitted to the young. In turn, the distribution of responsibilities and power at home has a major impact on who can participate in and influence the more public parts of the cultural life, where rules and regulations about both public and private life are made.

Second, most cultures have as one of their principal aims the control of women by men. Consider, for example, the founding myths of Greek and Roman antiquity, and of Judaism, Christianity, and Islam: they are rife with attempts to justify the control and subordination of women. These myths consist of a combination of denials of women's role in reproduction, appropriations by men of the power to reproduce themselves, characterizations of women as overly emotional, untrustworthy, evil, or sexually dangerous, and refusals to acknowledge mothers' rights over the disposition of their children. Think of Athena, sprung from the head of Zeus, and of Romulus and Remus, reared without a human mother. Or Adam, made by a male God, who then (at least according to one of the two biblical versions of the story) made Eve out of part of Adam. Consider Eve, whose weakness led Adam astray. Think of all those endless "begats" in Genesis, where women's primary role in reproduction is completely ignored, or of the textual justifications for polygamy, once practiced in Judaism, still practiced in many parts of the Islamic world and (though illegally) by Mormons in some parts of the United States. Consider, too, the story of Abraham, a pivotal turning point in the development of monotheism. God commands Abraham to sacrifice "his" greatly loved son. Abraham prepares to do exactly what God asks of him, without even telling, much less asking, Isaac's mother, Sarah. Abraham's absolute obedience to God makes him the central, fundamental model of faith, for all three religions.

While the powerful drive to control women—and to blame and punish them for men's difficulty controlling their own sexual impulses—has been softened considerably in the more progressive, reformed versions of Judaism, Christianity, and Islam, it remains strong in their more orthodox or fundamentalist versions. Moreover, it is by no means confined to Western or monotheistic cultures. Many of the world's traditions and cultures, including those practiced within formerly conquered or colonized nation states—certainly including most of the peoples of Africa, the Middle East, Latin America and Asia—are quite distinctly patriarchal. They too have elaborate patterns of socialization, rituals, matrimonial customs, and other cultural practices (including systems of property ownership and control of resources) aimed at bringing women's sexuality and reproductive capabilities under men's control. Many such practices make it virtually impossible for women to choose to live independently of men, to be celibate or lesbian, or not to have children.

Those who practice some of the most controversial such customs—clitoridectomy, the marriage of children or marriages that are otherwise coerced, or polygamy—sometimes explicitly defend them as necessary for controlling women, and openly acknowledge that the customs persist at men's insistence. In an interview with *New York Times* reporter Celia Dugger, practitioners of clitoridectomy in Côte d'Ivoire and Togo explained that the practice "helps insure a girl's virginity before marriage and fidelity afterward by reducing sex to a marital obligation." As a female exciser said, "[a] woman's role in life is to care for her children, keep house and cook. If she has not been cut, [she] might think about her own sexual pleasure."[6] In Egypt, where a law banning female genital cutting was recently overturned by a court, supporters of the practice say it "curbs a girl's sexual appetite and makes her more marriageable."[7] Moreover, in such contexts, many women have no economically viable alternative to marriage. Men in polygamous cultures, too, readily acknowledge that the practice accords with their self-interest and is a means of controlling women. As a French immigrant from Mali said in a recent interview: "When my wife is sick and I don't have another, who will care for me? . . . [O]ne wife on her own is trouble. When there are several, they are forced to be polite and well behaved. If they misbehave, you threaten that you'll take another wife." Women apparently see polygamy very differently. French African immigrant women deny that they like polygamy, and say not only that they are given "no choice" in the matter, but that their female forebears in Africa did not like it either.[8] As for child or otherwise coerced marriage: this practice is clearly a way not only of controlling whom the girls or young women marry, but also of ensuring that they are virgins at the time of marriage and, often, enhancing the husband's power by creating a significant age difference between husbands and wives.

Consider, too, the practice—common in much of Latin America, rural South East Asia and parts of West Africa—of encouraging or even requiring a rape victim to marry the rapist. In many such cultures—including fourteen countries of Latin America—rapists are legally exonerated if they marry or (in some cases) even offer to marry their victims. Clearly, rape is not seen in these cultures primarily as a violent assault on the girl or woman herself, but rather as a serious injury to her family and its honor. By marrying his victim, the rapist can help restore the family's honor and relieve it of a daughter who, as "damaged goods," has become unmarriageable. In Peru, this barbaric law was amended for the worse in 1991: the co-defendants in a gang rape are now all exonerated if one of them offers to marry the victim (feminists are fighting to get the law repealed). As a Peruvian taxi driver explained: "Marriage is the right and proper thing to do after a rape. A raped woman is a used item. No one wants her. At least with this law the woman will get a husband."[9] It is hard to imagine a worse fate for a woman than being pressured into marrying the man who has raped her. But worse fates do exist in some cultures—notably in Pakistan and parts of the Arab Middle East, where women who bring rape charges are quite frequently charged with the serious Muslim offense of *zina,* or sex outside of marriage. Law allows for the whipping or imprisonment of such a woman, and culture condones the killing or pressuring into suicide of a raped woman by relatives concerned to restore the family's honor.[10]

Thus, many culturally-based customs aim to control women and render them, especially sexually and reproductively, servile to men's desires and interests. Sometimes, moreover, "culture" or "traditions" are so closely linked with the control of women that they are virtually equated. In a recent news report about a small community of Orthodox Jews living in the mountains of Yemen—ironically, from a feminist point of view, the story was entitled "Yemen's small Jewish community thrives on mixed traditions"—the elderly leader of this small polygamous sect is quoted as saying: "We are Orthodox Jews, very keen on our traditions. If we go to Israel, we will lose hold over our daughters, our wives and our sisters." One of his sons added: "We are like Muslims, we do not allow our women to uncover their faces."[11] Thus the servitude of women is presented as virtually synonymous with "our traditions." (Only blindness to sexual servitude can explain the title; it is inconceivable that the article would have carried such a title if it were about a community that practiced any kind of slavery but sexual slavery.)

While virtually all of the world's cultures have distinctly patriarchal pasts, some—mostly, though by no means exclusively, Western liberal cultures—have departed far further from them than others. Western cultures, of course, still practice many forms of sex discrimination. They place far more stress on beauty, thinness, and youth in females and on intellectual accomplishment, skill, and strength in males; they expect women to perform for no economic reward far more than half of the unpaid work of their families, whether or not they also work for wages; partly as a consequence of this and partly because of workplace discrimination, women are far more likely than men to become poor; girls and women are also subjected by men to a great deal of (illegal) violence, including sexual violence. But women in more liberal cultures are, at the same time, legally guaranteed many of the same freedoms and opportunities as men. In addition, most families in such cultures, with the exception of some religious fundamentalists, do not communicate to their daughters that they are of less value than boys, that their lives are to be confined to domesticity and service to men and children, and that the only positive value of their sexuality is that it be strictly confined to marriage, the service of men, and reproductive ends. This, as we have seen, is quite different from women's situation in many of the world's other cultures, including many of those from which immigrants to Europe and Northern America come.

Group Rights?

Most cultures are patriarchal, then, and many (though not all) of the cultural minorities that claim group rights are more patriarchal than the surrounding cultures. So it is no surprise that the cultural importance of maintaining control over women shouts out to us in the examples given in the literature on cultural diversity and group rights within liberal states. Yet, though it shouts out, it is seldom explicitly addressed.

A 1986 paper about the legal rights and culture-based claims of various immigrant groups and gypsies in contemporary Britain mentions the roles and status of women as "one very clear example" of the "clash of cultures."[12] In it, Sebastian Poulter discusses claims put forward by members of such groups for special legal treatment on account of their cultural differences. A few are non-gender-related claims: about a Muslim schoolteacher's being allowed to be absent part of Friday afternoons in order to pray, and gypsy children having less stringent schooling requirements than others on account of their itinerant lifestyle. But the vast majority of the examples concern gender inequalities: child marriages, forced marriages, divorce systems biased against women, polygamy, and clitoridectomy. Almost all of the legal cases discussed stemmed from women's or girls' claims that their individual rights were being truncated or violated by the practices of their cultural groups. In a recent article by political philosopher Amy Gutmann, "The Challenge of Multiculturalism in Political Ethics," fully half the examples have do with gender issues—polygamy, abortion, sexual harassment, clitoridectomy, and purdah.[13] This is quite typical in the literature on subnational multicultural issues. Moreover, the same phenomenon occurs in practice in the international arena, where women's human rights are often rejected by the leaders of countries or groups of countries as incompatible with their various cultures.

Similarly, the overwhelming majority of "cultural defenses" that are increasingly being invoked in US criminal cases concerning members of cultural minorities are connected with gender—in particular with male control over women and children. Occasionally, cultural defenses come into play in explaining expectable violence among men, or the ritual sacrifice of animals. Much more common, however, is the argument that, in the defendant's cultural group, women are not human beings of equal worth but subordinates whose primary (if not only) functions are to serve men sexually and domestically. Thus, the four types of case in which cultural defenses have been used most successfully are: kidnap and rape by Hmong men who claim that their actions are part of their cultural practice of *zij poj niam* or "marriage by capture"; wife-murder by immigrants from Asian and Middle Eastern countries whose wives have either committed adultery or treated their husbands in a servile way; mothers who have killed their children but failed to kill themselves, and claim that because of their Japanese or Chinese backgrounds the shame of their husbands' infidelity drove them to the culturally condoned practice of mother-child suicide; and—in France, though not yet in the United States, in part because the practice was criminalized only in 1996—clitoridectomy. In a number of such cases, expert testimony about the accused's or defendant's cultural background has resulted in dropped or reduced charges, culturally-based assessments of *mens rea,* or significantly reduced sentences. In a well-known recent case, an immigrant from rural Iraq married his two daughters, aged 13 and 14, to two of his friends, aged 28 and 34. Subsequently, when the older daughter ran away with her 20-year-old boyfriend, the father sought the help of the police in finding her. When they located her, they charged the father with child abuse, and the two husbands and boyfriend with statutory rape. The Iraqis' defense is based in part, at least, on their cultural marriage practices.

As these examples show, the defendants are not always male, nor the victims always female. Both a Chinese immigrant man in New York who battered his wife to death for committing adultery and a Japanese immigrant woman in California who drowned her children and tried to drown herself because her husband's adultery had shamed the family, relied on cultural defenses to win reduced charges (from murder to second degree or involuntary manslaughter). It might seem, then, that cultural defense was biased toward the male in the first case, and the female in the second. But no such asymmetry exists. In both cases, the cultural message is similarly gender-biased: women (and children, in the second case) are ancillary to men, and should bear the blame and the shame for any departure from monogamy. Whoever is guilty of the infidelity, the wife suffers: in the first case, by being brutally killed on account of her husband's rage at her shameful infidelity; in the second, by being so shamed and branded a failure by his infidelity that she is driven to kill herself and her children.

Again, the idea that girls and women are first and foremost sexual servants of men whose virginity before marriage and fidelity within it are their preeminent virtues emerges in many of the statements made in defense of cultural practices.

Western majority cultures, largely at the urging of feminists, have recently made substantial efforts to avoid or limit excuses for brutalizing women. Well within living memory, American men were routinely held less accountable for killing their wives if they explained their conduct as a crime of passion, driven by jealousy on account of the wife's infidelity. Also not long ago, women who did not have completely celibate pasts or who did not struggle—even so as to endanger themselves— were routinely blamed when raped. Things have now changed to some extent, and doubts about the turn toward cultural defenses undoubtedly come in part from a concern to preserve recent advances. Another concern is that such defenses can distort perceptions of minority cultures by drawing excessive attention to negative aspects of them. But perhaps the primary concern is that, by failing to protect women and sometimes children of minority cultures from male and sometimes maternal violence, cultural defenses violate their rights to the equal protection of the laws. When a woman from a more patriarchal culture comes to the United States (or some other Western, basically liberal, state), why should she be less protected from male violence than other women are? Many women from minority cultures have protested the double standard that is being applied to their aggressors.

Liberal Defense

Despite all this evidence of cultural practices that control and subordinate women, none of the prominent defenders of multicultural group rights has adequately or even directly addressed the troubling connections between gender and culture, or the conflicts that arise so commonly between multiculturalism and feminism. Will Kymlicka's discussion is, in this respect, representative.

Kymlicka's arguments for group rights are based on the rights of individuals, and confine such privileges and protection to cultural groups that are internally liberal. Following John Rawls, Kymlicka emphasizes the fundamental importance of self-respect in a person's life. He argues that membership in a "rich and secure cultural structure,"[15] with its language and history, is essential both for the development of self-respect and for giving persons a context in which they can develop the capacity to make choices about how to lead their lives. Cultural minorities need special rights, then, because their culture may otherwise be threatened with extinction, and cultural extinction would likely undermine the self-respect and freedom of group members. Special rights, in short, put minorities on a footing of equality with the majority.

The value of freedom plays an important role in Kymlicka's argument. As a result, except in rare circumstances of cultural vulnerability, a group that claims special rights must govern itself by recognizably liberal principles, neither infringing on the basic liberties of its own members by placing internal restrictions on them, nor discriminating among them on grounds of sex, race, or sexual preference. This requirement is of great importance to a consistently liberal justification for group rights, since a "closed" or discriminatory culture cannot provide the context for individual development that liberalism requires and because collective rights might otherwise result in subcultures of oppression within and aided by liberal societies. As Kymlicka says: "To inhibit people from questioning their inherited social roles can condemn them to unsatisfying, even oppressive lives."[16]

As Kymlicka acknowledges, this requirement of internal liberalism rules out the justification of group rights for the "many fundamentalists of all political and religious stripes who think that the best community is one in which all but their preferred religious, sexual, or aesthetic practices are outlawed." For the promotion and support of *these* cultures "undermines the very reason we had for being concerned with cultural membership—that it allows for meaningful individual choice."[17] But the examples I cited earlier suggest that far fewer minority cultures than Kymlicka seems to think will be able to claim group rights under his liberal justification. Though they may not impose their beliefs or practices on others, and though they may appear to respect the basic civil and political liberties of women and girls, many cultures do not, especially in the private sphere, treat them with anything like the same concern and respect as men and boys, or allow them to enjoy the same freedoms. Discrimination against and control of the freedom of females is practiced, to a greater or lesser extent, by virtually all cultures, past and present, but especially religious ones and those that look to the past—to ancient texts or revered traditions—for guidelines or rules about how to live in the contemporary world. Sometimes more patriarchal minority cultures exist in the context of less patriarchal majority cultures; sometimes the reverse is true. In either case, the degree to which each culture is patriarchal and its willingness to become less so should be crucial factors in considering justifications for group rights—once we take women's equality seriously.

Clearly, Kymlicka regards cultures that discriminate overtly and formally against women—by denying them education, or the right to vote or to hold office—as not deserving special rights. But sex discrimination is often far less overt. In many cultures, strict control of women is enforced in the private sphere by the authority of either actual or symbolic fathers, often acting through, or with the complicity of, the older women of the culture. In many cultures in which women's basic civil rights and liberties are formally assured, discrimination practiced against women and girls within the household not only severely constrains their choices, but seriously threatens their well-being and even their lives. And such sex discrimination—whether severe or more mild—often has very powerful *cultural* roots.

Although Kymlicka rightly objects to the granting of group rights to minority cultures that practice overt sex discrimination, then, his arguments for multiculturalism fail to register what he acknowledges elsewhere: that the subordination of women is often informal and private, and that virtually no culture in the world today, minority or majority, could pass his "no sex discrimination" test if it were applied in the private sphere.[18] Those who defend group rights on liberal grounds need to address these very private, culturally reinforced kinds of discrimination. For surely self-respect and self-esteem require more than simple membership in a viable culture. Surely it is *not* enough, for one to be able to "question one's inherited social roles" and to have the capacity to make choices about the life one wants to lead, that one's culture be protected. At least as important to the development of self-respect and self-esteem is *our place within our culture*. And at least as important to our capacity to question our social roles is *whether our culture instills in and enforces particular social roles on us*. To the extent that their culture is patriarchal, in both these respects the healthy development of girls is endangered.

Part of the Solution?

It is by no means clear, then, from a feminist point of view, that minority group rights are "part of the solution." They may well exacerbate the problem. In the case of a more patriarchal minority culture in the context of a less patriarchal majority culture, no argument can be made on the basis of self-respect or freedom that the female members of the culture have a clear interest in its preservation. Indeed, they *may* be much better off if the culture into which they were born were either to become extinct (so that its members would become integrated into the less sexist surrounding culture) or, preferably, to be encouraged to alter itself so as to reinforce the equality of women—at least to the degree to which this is upheld in the majority culture. Other considerations would, of course, need to be taken into account, such as whether the minority group speaks a different language that requires protection, and whether the group suffers from prejudices such as racial discrimination. But it would take significant factors weighing in the other direction to counterbalance evidence that a culture severely constrained women's choices or otherwise undermined their well-being.

What some of the examples discussed above show us is how culturally endorsed practices that are oppressive to women can often remain hidden in the private or domestic sphere. In the Iraqi child marriage case mentioned above, if the father himself had not called in agents of the state, his daughters' plight might well not have become public. And in 1996 when Congress passed a law criminalizing clitoridectomy, a number of US doctors objected to the law as unjustified, since it concerned a private matter which, as one said, "should be decided by a physician, the family, and the child."[19] It can take more or less extraordinary circumstances for such abuses of girls or women to become public or for the state to be able to intervene protectively.

Thus it is clear that many instances of private sphere discrimination against women on cultural grounds are never likely to emerge in public, where courts can enforce their rights and political theorists can label such practices as illiberal and therefore unjustified violations of women's physical or mental integrity. Establishing group rights to enable some minority cultures to preserve themselves may not be in the best interests of the girls and women of the culture, even if it benefits the men.

When liberal arguments are made for the rights of groups, then, special care must be taken to look at within-group inequalities. It is especially important to consider inequalities between the sexes, since they are likely to be less public, and less easily discernible. Moreover, policies aiming to respond to the needs and claims of cultural minority groups must take seriously the need for adequate representation of less powerful members of such groups. Since attention to the rights of minority cultural groups, if it is to be consistent with the fundamentals of liberalism, must be ultimately aimed at furthering the well-being of the members of these groups, there can be no justification for assuming that the groups' self-proclaimed leaders—invariably mainly composed of their older and their male members—represent the interests of all of the groups' members. Unless women—and, more specifically, young women, since older women often become co-opted into reinforcing gender inequality—are fully represented in negotiations about group rights, their interests may be harmed rather than promoted by the granting of such rights.

References

1. Will Kymlicka, *Multicultural Citizenship: A Liberal Theory of Minority Rights* (Oxford: Oxford University Press, 1995), pp. 89, 76. See also Kymlicka, *Liberalism, Community, and Culture* (Oxford: The Clarendon Press, 1989). It should be noted that Kymlicka himself does not argue for extensive or permanent group rights for those who have voluntarily immigrated.

2. Avishai Margalit and Moshe Halbertal, "Liberalism and the Right to Culture," *Social Research* 61, 3 (Fall, 1994): 491.

3. For example, Chandran Kukathas, "Are There any Cultural Rights?" *Political Theory* 20, 1 (1992): 105–39.

4. Okin, "Feminism and Multiculturalism: Some Tensions," *Ethics* 108, 4 (1998): 661–684.

5. For example, Kymlicka, *Liberalism, Community, and Culture and Multicultural Citizenship,* especially chap. 8. Kymlicka does not apply his requirement that groups be internally liberal to those he terms "national minorities," but I will not address this aspect of his theory here.

6. *New York Times,* 5 October 1996, A4. The role that older women in such cultures play in perpetuating them is important but complex, and cannot be addressed here.

7. *New York Times,* 26 June 1997, A9.

8. *International Herald Tribune,* 2 February 1997, News section.

9. *New York Times,* 12 March 1997, A8.

10. This practice is discussed in Henry S. Richardson, *Practical Reasoning About Final Ends* (Cambridge: Cambridge University Press, 1994), especially pp. 240–43, 262–63, 282–84.

11. *Agence France Presse,* 18 May 1997, International News section.

12. Sebastian Poulter, "Ethnic Minority Customs, English Law, and Human Rights," *International and Comparative Law Quarterly* 36, 3 (1987): 589–615.

13. Amy Gutmann, "The Challenge of Multiculturalism in Political Ethics," *Philosophy and Public Affairs* 22, 3 (Summer 1993): 171–204. . . .

15. Kymlicka, *Liberalism, Community, and Culture,* p. 165.

16. Kymlicka, *Multicultural Citizenship,* p. 92.

17. Kymlicka, *Liberalism, Community, and Culture,* pp. 171–72.

18. Will Kymlicka, *Contemporary Political Philosophy: An Introduction* (Oxford: The Clarendon Press, 1990), pp. 239–62.

19. *New York Times,* 12 October 1996, A6. Similar views were expressed on public radio.

Journal/Discussion Questions

1. In your own experience, how have you seen the tension between women's interests and multiculturalism play itself out (if at all)?

2. Critically evaluate Okin's criticisms of multiculturalism.

Concluding Discussion Questions

Where Do You Stand Now?

Instructions

You have already answered the following questions in your moral problems self-quiz at the beginning of this book. Now that you have studied the material in this section, take a moment to answer the same questions again.

	Strongly Agree	*Agree*	*Undecided*	*Disagree*	*Strongly Disagree*	*Chapter 7: Gender*
31.	❏	❏	❏	❏	❏	Women's moral voices are different from men's.
32.	❏	❏	❏	❏	❏	Women are still discriminated against in the workplace.
33.	❏	❏	❏	❏	❏	Sexual harassment should be illegal.
34.	❏	❏	❏	❏	❏	Affirmative action helps women.
35.	❏	❏	❏	❏	❏	Genuine equality for women demands a restructuring of the traditional family.

Compare your answers to this self-quiz with the answers to the initial self-quiz. How, if at all, have your answers changed? How have the *reasons* for your answers changed?

Journal/Discussion Questions

✍ *Do you think the fact that you are a male or female has influenced your attitude toward any of the readings or ideas you encountered in this chapter? Discuss.*

1. What do you see as the ideal role of sex and gender in society? What do you think are the greatest liabilities associated with your view? The greatest assets? How does your view of this ideal relate to the views of the authors in this section?

2. Do you think that women are still discriminated against in today's society? Discuss the evidence for your position. If discrimination still exists, how should we as a society respond to it?

3. The issue of raising children is a central concern to many people, and is particularly troublesome to those who want to ensure equality between the sexes. Discuss the potential conflict between child-raising and sex equality and explain how you think our society should deal with this issue. Relate your position to those presented in this chapter.

For Further Reading

Web Resources

For Web-based resources, including the major Supreme Court decisions on gender issues, see the Gender and Sexism page of *Ethics Updates* (http://ethics.sandiego.edu). Among the resources are RealVideo of lectures by Carol Gilligan.

Journals

In addition to the standard journals in ethics discussed in the Appendix, there are several excellent journals devoted to issues of feminism. *Signs* is one of the oldest, and is a genuinely interdisciplinary journal devoted to issues relating to women; *Hypatia* is a philosophy journal created by members of the Society of Women in Philosophy; also see *Feminist Studies* and *Differences: A Journal of Feminist Cultural Studies.*

Review Articles and Overviews

For an excellent overview of feminist ethics, see Alison M. Jaggar, "Feminist Ethics," *Encyclopedia of Ethics,* edited by Lawrence C. Becker and Charlotte B. Becker (New York: Garland Publishing, 1992), Vol. I, pp. 361–370; Jane Grimshaw, "The Idea of a Female Ethic," *A Companion to Ethics,* edited by Peter Singer (Oxford: Blackwell, 1991), pp. 491–499. For a very helpful overview of various positions, see Rosemarie Tong, *Feminist Thought: A More Comprehensive Introduction* (Boulder, CO: Westview Press, 1998) and *Feminist Frameworks,* edited by Alison M. Jaggar and Paula S. Rothenberg, 2nd ed. (New York: McGraw-Hill, 1984).

Anthologies, Articles, and Books

There are a number of excellent anthologies on feminism and ethics, including Carole R. McCann and Seung-Kyung Kim, eds., *Feminist Theory Reader: Local and Global Perspectives* (London: Routledge, 2002); Claudia Card's *Feminist Ethics and Politics* (Lawrence, KS: University of Kansas Press, 1999); Eva Feder Kittay and Diana Meyer's *Women and Moral Theory* (Savage, MD: Rowman & Littlefield, 1987); *Feminism and Political Theory,* edited by Cass R. Sunstein (Chicago: University of Chicago Press, 1990); Claudia Card's *Feminist Ethics* (Lawrence, KS: University of Kansas Press, 1991), which contains an excellent bibliography; *Explorations in Feminist Ethics,* edited by Eva Browning Cole and Susan Coultrap-McQuin (Bloomington, IN: Indiana University Press, 1992), which also has an excellent bibliography; *Ethics: A Feminist Reader,* edited by Elizabeth Frazer, Jennifer Hornsby, and Sabina Lovibond (Oxford: Blackwell, 1992); also see Martha C. Nussbaum's excellent *Sex and Social Justice* (New York: Oxford, 1999) as well as *Women, Culture and Development: A Study of Human Capabilities,* edited by Martha Nussbaum and Jonathan Glover (New York: Oxford, 1995). Laurie J. Shrage, *Moral Dilemmas of Feminism: Prostitution,*

Adultery, and Abortion (New York: Routledge, 1994); Rita C. Manning, *Speaking from the Heart: A Feminist Perspective on Ethics* (Savage, MD: Rowman and Littlefield, 1992) is one of many excellent defenses of feminist perspectives in ethics. For a critical look at some elements in contemporary feminism, see Katie Roiphe, *The Morning After: Sex, Fear, and Feminism* (Boston: Little, Brown, 1993) and Christina Hoff Sommers, *Who Stole Feminism?* (New York: Simon and Schuster, 1994).

Pornography and Hate Speech

For a survey of the ethical issues surrounding pornography, see Lori Gruen, "Pornography and Censorship" in *A Companion to Applied Ethics: Blackwell Companions to Philosophy,* edited by R. G. Frey (Malden MA: Blackwell-Publishing, 2003), pp. 154–166 and Donald VanDeVeer, "Pornography," *Encyclopedia of Ethics,* edited by Lawrence C. Becker and Charlotte B. Becker (New York: Garland Publishing, 1992), Vol. II, pp. 991–993.

The philosophical issues surrounding pornography and censorship often take place within the context of a discussion of John Stuart Mill's work. See David Dyzanhaus, "John Stuart Mill and the Harm of Pornography," *Ethics,* Vol. 102, No. 3 (April 1992), pp. 534–551 and Robert Skipper, "Mill and Pornography," *Ethics,* Vol. 103, No. 5 (July 1993), pp. 726–730; Richard Vernon, "John Stuart Mill and Pornography: Beyond the Harm Principle," *Ethics,* Vol. 106, No. 3 (April 1996), pp. 621–32; Danny Scoccia, "Can Liberals Support a Ban on Violent Pornography?" *Ethics,* Vol. 106, No. 4 (July 1996), pp. 776–799. Rae Langton's "Speech Acts and Unspeakable Acts," *Philosophy and Public Affairs,* Vol. 22, No. 4 (Fall 1993), pp. 293–330, argues on the basis of speech act theory that pornography silences and subordinates women. Also see Catharine A. MacKinnon, "Sexuality, Pornography, and Method: 'Pleasure under Patriarchy'," *Ethics,* Vol. 99 (January, 1989), pp. 314–46.

Sexual Harassment

See the review articles by Ann E. Cudd and Leslie E. Jones, "Sexism" in *A Companion to Applied Ethics: Blackwell Companions to Philosophy,* edited by R. G. Frey (Malden, MA: Blackwell Publishing, 2003), pp. 102–117; and "Sexual Abuse and Harassment" by Naomi Scheman in *Encyclopedia of Ethics,* edited by Lawrence C. Becker and Charlotte B. Becker (New York: Garland Publishing, 1992), Vol. II, pp. 1139–1141. For an excellent starting point, see Linda LeMoncheck and James P. Sterba, *Sexual Harassment: Issues and Answers* (New York: Oxford University Press, 2001) and LeMoncheck and Mane Hajdin, *Sexual Harassment: A Debate* (Lanham, MD: Rowman and Littlefield, 1997). Also see Catharine MacKinnon, *Sexual Harassment of Working Women* (New Haven, CT: Yale University Press, 1979) for a view of sexual harassment as sex discrimination. Also see the excellent anthology, *Sexual Harassment: Confrontations and Decisions,* edited by Edmund Wall (Buffalo, NY: Prometheus Books, 1992).

CHAPTER
8

Sexual Orientation

Videotape

    Topic: "Gay Marriage"

    Source: *Nightline,* February 24, 2004

    Anchor: Ted Koppel, Michel Martin, Gary Langer, ABC News Polling Director

    Guest: President George W. Bush; Mayor Gavin Newsom (San Francisco); Senator John Kerry; Senator John Edwards; Matt Daniels (Alliance for Marriage); Patrick Guerrero (Log Cabin Republicans); Stanley Greenberg (Author/Political Consultant); Zachary Constantino (College Republicans); Dave Hodges (College Republicans); Allison Waithe (American University Queers and Allies)

An Introduction to the Moral Issues

Let's begin by considering what type of discrimination occurs against gays and lesbians in contemporary American society. Then we turn to a discussion of the arguments advanced against homosexuality, the competing ideals of the place of sexual orientation in society, and the means for attaining those ideals.

Discrimination Against Gays and Lesbians

Discrimination against gays and lesbians differs in several ways from the previous two types of discrimination we have considered: racism and sexism. One of the principal reasons for this is that sexual orientation is generally much less apparent than either race or sex. Because they are less easily identifiable, gays and lesbians are less likely to be subject to certain kinds of discrimination. Homosexuals have not formally been denied voting rights as women and African Americans have been, apparently do not suffer from a lower level of income than their heterosexual counterparts, and have not usually encountered restrictions on their individual right to hold property. In these ways, they are not in need of the same kinds of affirmative action programs that have been defended for racial minorities and women.

Despite these differences that favor gays and lesbians, they are discriminated against in ways that would not be tolerated today if such discrimination were directed against racial minorities or women. They are not permitted to serve openly in the military; they are not permitted to marry one another, with both the emotional and financial costs that such prohibitions incur; they are often discriminated against in child-related matters such as child custody during divorces, adoption, foster parenting, Big Brothers, the Boy Scouts, and the like. Consider, for example, the financial costs of not being permitted to marry. When a husband dies, his estate may pass to his wife without taxes; when a gay person's life partner dies, transferred assets are heavily taxed.

Moreover, gays and lesbians—and their families—usually experience a very painful process when they begin to let their sexual orientation become public. Again, there is nothing comparable for racial minorities or for women. Announcements of one's race or gender rarely come as surprises to one's family and loved ones in the way that revealing one's sexual orientation often does.

Finally, it is important to realize that some gays and lesbians experience discrimination because of the radical character of their beliefs and "lifestyles." Here it is difficult to draw the line, but it would seem that at least part of the criticism and opposition they experience is directed primarily against their radicalness, not their gayness.

Let's now turn to a consideration of two specific areas of discrimination—gays and lesbians in the military and homosexual marriage—and the more general issue raised by these particular problems, the issue of protection for gay rights.

Gays and Lesbians in the Military

After he was elected in 1992, President Clinton attempted to lift the ban against homosexuals in the military and thereby ignited a heated debate about whether open homosexuals should be officially allowed to serve in the armed forces. Various arguments were advanced against lifting the ban, many of which centered around the effect on heterosexual military personnel "unit cohesion" and "combat effectiveness." Interestingly, some of the same arguments advanced against gays could also be advanced against women in the armed forces and many of the arguments about the possibility of sexual harassment and unwanted sexual attention—if taken seriously—could certainly provide a welcome amount of protection for many women in the military.

Same-Sex Marriage

At the time this book was going to press (fall 2004), the question of same-sex marriage was an open issue in the courts and the legislature and there was a movement to pass a Defense of Marriage Act (DOMA) that would ban same-sex marriages. Some gay rights supporters have advocated the legalization of gay and lesbian marriages and same-sex marriage has been at least sporadically legally recognized in the United States. Opponents of the legalization of same-sex marriage often draw on religious sources. Many condemn gay and lesbian sexuality in general; others maintain that the traditionally religious meaning of marriage is incompatible with same-sex unions. Advocates of same-sex marriages see it as a matter of equal rights. They point to the many ways in which gays and lesbians have been disadvantaged because they have not been able to marry their partners. This has particularly been a source of anguish for gays since the onset of AIDS, when gays have cared for dying partners but have not been given the recognition of one who has lost a spouse. Some of the obstacles they face include denial of hospital visitation rights, challenges to durable power of attorney by blood-related family, the denial of rights to pass property without taxation, and challenges to the wills of the deceased by blood families. Other gay rights advocates have argued that marriage does not provide the path to liberation that Andrew Sullivan and others have claimed.

Models of the Place of Sexual Orientation in Society

When we envision the ideal society as we would like to see it, what place does sexual orientation have in it? Is it a society composed solely of heterosexuals, or at least one in which homosexuals are not tolerated as members in good standing? Is it a society in which gays and lesbians are not discriminated against, but whose presence is also not stressed in any way? Or is it a society in which difference is celebrated and encouraged?

Our picture here is a complex one, because we actually have two separate—and sometimes conflicting—factors at work as individuals develop their own position on this issue. First, there is the issue of the morality of homosexuality, which is part of an individual's overall views on sexual morality. Second, there is the issue of societal rights and governmental protection of those rights. Here the issue is the extent to which government ought to be involved in legislating matters of sexual morality.

Let's consider how both of these factors intersect to form the major positions in this ongoing societal debate.

The Traditional Model

Many conservatives espouse an ideal of society that has no room for gays and lesbians. In some versions, simply being homosexual is enough to eliminate a person from the community. In other versions, gays and lesbians would be allowed to have their sexual orientation, but not to engage in homosexual acts. They would, in other words, be sentenced to a life of involuntary chastity.

Defenders of conservative models offer two kinds of arguments. First, some maintain that homosexuality is intrinsically evil, and that therefore it should not be tolerated. Many defenders of this position cite religious sources as the foundation of their belief, whereas others appeal to some version of the "unnaturalness" argument discussed earlier. Second, some conservatives maintain that homosexuality contradicts important social and moral values—such as the value of family life—and should not be tolerated for that reason. Here the focus is not on homosexual *acts,* but on the *values* of homosexuals.

Critics of the traditional model offer several replies. First, many defenders of homosexuality argue that it is not unnatural, a point we have already discussed. Second, they point out that even if one believed something was unnatural and thus evil, it doesn't automatically follow that one is in favor of banning it. Many might think smoking cigarettes is bad, but that doesn't mean it should be completely banned. Third, they argue that it is consistent to support certain key social values, such as the value of family life, and yet not require that *everyone* live out that value in the same way. Many religious orders forbid their members from marrying, yet their presence is not seen in society as contradicting the value of family life. Fourth, many gays and lesbians support family life and in some cases would even like to have the option of marriage open to them.

Perhaps the most telling reply to supporters of the traditional model is one that does not address their specific arguments, but rather the plight of individuals who are ostracized from society simply on the basis of who they are. If the traditional model were to prevail, gays and lesbians would be excluded from presenting themselves honestly in society simply because of their sexual orientation, not because of any specific, nonsexual actions or values. Where can these people go? They can either pretend they are straight, and thus gain some acceptance, or stand by their sexual orientation and be excluded from society. They must choose, in other words, between acceptance through denial of their own identity or exclusion as a result of affirming their sexual identity. A model of society that excludes a significant group in this way seems to be both a cruel and an unjust model.

The Liberal Model

There is no single "liberal" position on the issue of gay and lesbian rights. However, there are two principal currents in the liberal tradition that discourage discrimination against homosexuals: the emphasis on individual autonomy and the importance of the right to privacy.

Autonomy arguments.   Liberals characteristically believe that individual liberty is a very high priority and consequently many hold that individuals should be free to have and express whatever sexual orientation they wish. In some versions of liberalism, this right is virtually absolute, limited only in those instances when its exercise infringes on someone else's autonomy, whereas other versions of liberalism believe that such rights may be restricted for other reasons as well.

Privacy arguments.   Many liberals place a high value on the right to privacy and see a person's sexual orientation as protected from public scrutiny by that right to privacy. A person's sexual orientation, they argue, is no one else's business, especially not the government's business. Privacy arguments are particularly important in regard to the issue of whether the state may forbid certain kinds of sexual acts between consenting adults in private.

The difference between toleration, acceptance, and support.   Liberal positions differ in the degree to which they are supportive of gay and lesbian rights. We can distinguish three levels here.

- *Tolerance:* Gays and lesbians should not be discriminated against, but they also should not be encouraged. The "don't ask, don't tell" policy of the military may fall into this category, although many gays and lesbians see it as less than tolerant. Also in this category are people who believe homosexuality is bad but who also believe sexual morality shouldn't be legislated. Supporters of this position would be in favor of abolishing laws that forbid homosexual acts between consenting adults in private.
- *Acceptance:* Gays and lesbians should be allowed to express their sexual orientation openly to the same extent that heterosexuals are allowed to express their sexual orientation openly and should not be discriminated against because of it. This would include support for legal protection against discrimination based on sexual orientation.
- *Endorsement:* Gay and lesbian sexual orientation and lifestyles should be presented as an option that is as valid and valuable as heterosexual orientation and lifestyles. This may include presenting gay and lesbian families as models in public school curricula, legally sanctioning gay marriages, and so on.

Within the liberal tradition, there is a wide variation in the level of support for gay and lesbian rights.

The Polymorphous Model

Finally, some in our society—and this includes some heterosexuals and some homosexuals—see sexuality as centered purely around pleasure, and they see no necessary link between sexuality and either procreation or intimacy. Whatever brings pleasure is good and pleasure may come in many forms—that is, it may be polymorphus. Advocates of this view of sexuality hold that people should be allowed to engage in whatever kind of sexual activity they want and with whomever they want.

Diversity and Consensus

Although there is relatively little common ground between the most extreme positions on this issue, there is the possibility of some reasonable consensus in the following way.

It seems reasonable that we, as a society, may want to encourage certain fundamental moral values in society. Although such encouragement need not take the form of legislating morality (in the sense of attempting to force people to hold particular moral values through legislative fiat), and although it need not deny individual freedom or the right to privacy (we can discourage something without outlawing it), we may indeed decide to encourage certain values (such as honesty, long-lasting commitment, monogamy, etc.) in our society as a whole, including both heterosexuals and homosexuals. We may further want to discourage certain values and their associated behaviors (such as treating people merely as sexual objects, anonymous sex, etc.), again for everyone, regardless of sexual orientation. The focus, in other words, for finding common ground is not on sexual orientation, but on values.

We can see how this could be applied to issues such as homosexuals in the military and to gay and lesbian marriages. Traditionally, the military has stood for certain values—patriotism, loyalty to one's unit, discipline, and so on—that could be affirmed for both homosexuals and heterosexuals. Indeed, this is in fact almost exactly the situation we have seen for decades (if not centuries). The gays and lesbians in the military have been committed first and foremost to military values, and have often served with great distinction. The only difference would be to allow them to acknowledge their sexual orientation while still retaining their commitment to the values of the military.

A similar approach can be taken to the question of gay and lesbian marriages. It seems reasonable that society as a whole would want to encourage certain values such as commitment, individual caring, intimacy, and the like. Insofar as marriage is one of the institutions that helps to support these values, extending this to include gays and lesbians would seem reasonable, for it gives them the opportunity to participate in a highly important societal institution.

The Arguments

Martha Nussbaum
"Gay Rights"

Martha Nussbaum is the Ernst Freund Professor of Law and Ethics at the University of Chicago, holding appointments in the Law School, Philosophy Department, and Divinity School, Associate in Classics. She is the author of numerous books and articles in philosophy, including The Fragility of Goodness, The Therapy of Desire, For Love of Country, Cultivating Humanity, *and* Sex and Social Justice.

Nussbaum looks at five rights that are at issue in the contemporary discussion of gay rights, the rights to: (1) protection from violence; (2) consensual adult sexual relations; (3) nondiscrimination in housing, employment, and education; (4) military service; and (5) custody and adoption of children.

As You Read, Consider This:

1. In each of the five areas of rights that Nussbaum considers, what justification does she offer for the rights claims she discusses?

Now in my own cases when I catch a guy like that I just pick him up and take him into the woods and beat him until he can't crawl. I have had seventeen cases like that in the last couple of years. I tell that guy if I catch him doing that again I will take him out to the woods and I will shoot him. I tell him that I carry a second gun on me just in case I find guys like him and that I will plant it in his hand and say that he tried to kill me and that no jury will convict me.

(Police officer in a large industrial city in the United States, being interviewed about his treatment of homosexuals; Westley, 'Violence and the Police,' quoted in Comstock, 1991, pp. 90–95)

Whose rights are we talking about when we talk about "gay rights," and what are the rights in question? I shall take on, first, the surprisingly difficult task of identifying the people. Next, I shall discuss a number of the most important rights that are at issue, including: (1) the right to be protected against violence and, in general, the right to the equal protection of the law; (2) the right to have consensual adult sexual relations without criminal penalty; (3) the right to nondiscrimination in housing, employment and education; (4) the right to military service; (5) the right to marriage and/or its legal benefits; (6) the right to retain custody of children and/or to adopt.

Martha Nussbaum, *Sex and Social Justice* (New York: Oxford University Press, 1999), pp. 184–206 (edited)

Whose Rights?

. . . Let us define gays, lesbians, and bisexuals, the class of persons with a "homosexual or bisexual orientation" (now the most common formulation in nondiscrimination law), as those who stably and characteristically desire to engage in sexual conduct with a member or members of the same sex (whether or not they also desire sexual conduct with the opposite sex) and let us adopt a difficult-to-ascertain but not impossibly broad definition of sexual conduct, namely that it is bodily conduct intended to lead to orgasm on the part of one or both parties. Notice, then, that we are talking about the rights both of people who frequently perform these acts and also of those who desire to but don't.

What Rights?

The Right to Be Protected Against Violence

Gays, lesbians and bisexuals are targets of violence in America. Twenty-four percent of gay men and ten percent of lesbians, in a recent survey, reported some form of criminal assault because of their sexual orientation during the past year (as compared to general population assault rates in a comparable urban area of 4 percent for women and 6 percent for men). A Massachusetts study found that 21 percent of lesbian and gay students, compared to 5 percent of the entire student body, report having been physically attacked. An average of five recent U.S. noncollege surveys on anti-gay/lesbian violence show that thirty-three percent of those surveyed had been chased or followed, 23 percent had had objects thrown at them, 18 percent had been punched, hit, kicked or beaten, 16 percent had been victims of vandalism or arson, 7 percent had been spat on, and 7 percent had been assaulted with a weapon (data from Comstock, 1991, pp. 31–55). To live as a gay or lesbian in America is thus to live with fear. As one might expect, such violence is not unknown in the military. Most famous, but not unique, was the 1992 death of navy radioman Allen Schindler at the hands of three of his shipmates who, unprovoked, stalked and then fatally beat him—and later blamed their crime on the presence of gays in the military.

Who are the perpetrators? They are more likely than average assault perpetrators are to be strangers to their victims. Ninety-four percent of them are male (as compared with 87 percent for comparable crimes of violence), 46 percent are under twenty-two years of age (as compared with 29 percent for comparable crimes); 67 percent are white. They do not typically exhibit what are customarily thought of as criminal attitudes. Many conform to or are models of middle-class respectability (Comstock, 1991, pp. 91–92). The arresting officer in a Toronto incident in which five youths beat a forty-year-old gay man to death remarked, "If you went to [a shopping mall] and picked up any group of young males about the same age as these boys—that is what they were like—average" (Comstock, 1991, p. 93). The data suggest that gay-beatings, including the most lethal, are often in essence "recreational": groups of adolescent men, bored and intoxicated, seek out gays not so much because they have a deep-seated hatred of them as because they recognize that this is a group society has agreed to dislike and not to protect fully (Comstock, 1991, p. 94). A California perpetrator of multiple anti-gay beatings, interviewed by Comstock, cited as reasons for his acts: boredom, the desire for adventure, a belief in the wrongness of homosexuality and, finally, attraction to the men he and his friends attacked. He told Comstock that [we] were probably attacking something within ourselves (Comstock, 1991, pp. 171–172).

Physical assaults are crimes as defined by the laws of every state in the U.S. In that sense, the right to be protected against them is a right that gays and lesbians have already. But there is ample evidence that the police often fail to uphold these rights. They may indeed actively perpetrate violence against gays, in unduly violent behavior during vice arrests, etc. Such violence is illegal if it exceeds the requirements of arrest, but it is widely practiced. Even more common is the failure of police to come promptly to the aid of gays and lesbians who are being assaulted. A Canadian study finds that in 56 percent of cases in which gays sought police protection the behavior of the responding officers was "markedly unsatisfactory" (Comstock, 1991, pp. 151–162).

In numerous U.S. jurisdictions, moreover, killers of gays have successfully pleaded "reasonable provocation," alleging that the revulsion occasioned by a (noncoercive and nonviolent) homosexual advance, or even by witnessing gay sexual acts, justified a homicidal response; there is no corresponding tradition of a "heterosexual advance" defense. In a 1990 Pennsylvania case in which a drifter murdered two lesbians whom he saw making love in the woods, the court refused to allow this defense, saying that the law "does not recognize homosexual activity between two persons as legal provocation sufficient to reduce an unlawful killing . . . from murder to voluntary manslaughter" (*Commonwealth v. Carr*). This is, however, the exception rather than the rule (Mison, 1992).

There is a good case for linking rights involving protection against violence to other facets of gay experience as yet not universally recognized. As long as no laws protect gays against discrimination in other areas of life and guarantee their equal citizenship, as long as their sex acts can be criminalized, as long they are disparaged as second-class citizens, we may expect the rights they do have to go on being underenforced, and violence against them to remain a common fact.

My discussion of violence has not addressed the emotional violence done to lesbians and gay people by the perception that they are hated and despised. This issue too can be addressed by law and public policy; for by enacting non-discrimination laws (such as the law recently enacted in my home state of Massachusetts, which forbids discrimination against lesbian and gay students in the school system) one can begin to alter the behavior that causes this harm. Perhaps eventually one may alter attitudes themselves.

The Right to Have Consensual Adult Sexual Relations Without Criminal Penalty

Consensual sexual relations between adult males were decriminalized in Britain in 1967. In the US, five states still criminalize only same-sex sodomy, while eighteen statutes (including the Uniform Code of Military Justice) criminalize sodomy for all. Five state sodomy laws have recently been judicially repealed, and, in addition, a Massachusetts law prohibiting "unnatural and lascivious act[s]." (But Massachusetts still has another law prohibiting "crime against nature," *Symposium*, 1993, p. 1774.) These laws are rarely enforced, but such enforcement as there is highly selective, usually against same-sex conduct. Penalties are not negligible: the maximum penalty for consensual sodomy in Georgia is twenty years' imprisonment.

Although sodomy laws are, as I have argued, both under- and over-inclusive for same-sex conduct, it is frequently assumed that sodomy defines gay or lesbian sexual life. Thus the laws, in addition to their use in targeting the consensual activities of actual sodomites, can also be used to discriminate against gay and lesbian individuals who have never been shown to engage in the practices in question—as when Robin Shahar lost her job in the Georgia Attorney General's office for announcing a lesbian marriage. It was claimed that she could not be a reliable enforcer of the state's sodomy statute (*Shahar v. Bowers*). (All heterosexual intercourse outside marriage is criminal "fornication" in Georgia, and yet there is no evidence that Bowers ever denied employment to heterosexual violators of either that law or the sodomy law.)

The case against sodomy laws is strong. Rarity of enforcement creates a problem of arbitrary and selective police behavior. Although neither all nor only homosexuals are sodomites, the laws are overwhelmingly used to target them; and the fact that some of their acts remain criminal is closely connected with the perception that they are acceptable targets of violence and with other social exclusions as well. For example, "[t]here is . . . a natural reluctance to appoint to judicial positions people who have committed hundreds or even thousands of criminal acts" (Posner, 1992, p. 311)—unjustified as this reluctance may be, and also arbitrary, given that the judiciary is no doubt full of heterosexual perpetrators of sodomy and criminal fornication. (Laumann shows that the frequency of both oral and anal sex among heterosexuals increases with level of education, Laumann et al., 1994.)

Most important, such adult consensual sexual activity does no harm. There is thus no public benefit to offset the evident burdens these laws impose. As Judge Posner concludes, such laws "express an irrational fear and loathing of a group that has been subjected to discrimination" (1992, p. 346). We have no need of such laws in a country all too full of incitements to violence.

Should the age of consent be the same for same-sex as for opposite-sex activity? I am inclined to think that, in current American and European nations, 16 is a reasonable age for both. The biggest problem with age of consent law generally is the failure to discriminate between the act of two 15-year-olds and an act between a 30-year-old and a 15-year-old. In both same and opposite-sex relations, the law should (and often does) address itself to this issue.

The Right to Be Free from Discrimination in Housing, Employment, and Education

Gays, lesbians and bisexuals suffer discrimination in housing and employment. Many U.S. states and local communities have responded to this situation by adopting non-discrimination laws. (Such laws have for some time been in effect in some European countries and in some Australian states.) Recently in the U.S., efforts have also been made to prevent local communities from so legislating, through referenda amending the state's constitution to forbid the passage of such a local law. The most famous example is that of Amendment 2 in the State of Colorado, which nullified anti-discrimination laws in three cities in the state, and prevented the passage of any new ones. I believe that there is no good argument for discrimination against gays and lesbians in housing and employment. (The repeated suggestion that such protection against discrimination would lead to quotas for this group and would therefore injure the prospects of other minorities was especially invidious and misleading; none of the local ordinances had even suggested quota policies.)

Along with the Supreme Court of Colorado (when it upheld a preliminary injunction against the law, laying the legal basis for the trial court judgment that found the law unconstitutional), I would make a further point. Such referenda, by depriving gays and lesbians of the right to organize at the local level to secure the passage of laws that protect them, thereby deprive them of equality with respect to the fundamental right of political participation. They, and they alone, have to amend the state constitution in order to pass a fair housing law in some town. Similar state laws have long been declared unconstitutional in the area of race. I believe that they are morally repugnant in this area as well.

The most serious issue that arises with regard to non-discrimination laws is that of religious freedom. Both institutions and individuals may sincerely believe that to be required to treat lesbians and gays as equal candidates for jobs (or as equal prospective tenants) is to be deprived of the freedom to exercise their religion. This argument seems more pertinent to some occupations than others. To hire someone as a teacher may plausibly be seen as conferring a certain role-model status on that person; to hire someone as an accountant can hardly be seen in this light. And it is not clear to me that a landlord's religious freedom is compromised by being forced to consider on an equal basis tenants he may deem immoral. (The U.S. Supreme Court recently refused to hear an appeal of an Alaska decision against a landlord who refused to rent on religious grounds to an unmarried heterosexual couple.)

Various responses are possible. The Denver statute exempted religious organizations from its non-discrimination provisions. The American Philosophical Association refused to exempt religious institutions from its (non-binding) non-discrimination policy for hiring and promotion, except in the case of discrimination on the basis of religious membership. I believe that we should combine these two approaches: religious organizations should in some cases be allowed greater latitude to follow their own beliefs; but in publicly funded and in large professional organizations, with sexuality as with race, freedom to discriminate should be limited by shared requirements of justice. I recognize, however, that many people of good faith with deep religious convictions are likely to disagree.

Even in the sensitive area of education, there is no evidence to show that the presence of gay and lesbian teachers harms children or adolescents. Gays are at least no more likely, and in some studies less likely to molest children than are heterosexual males; nor is there evidence to show that knowing or respecting a gay person has the power to convert children to homosexuality (any more than being taught by heterosexuals has converted gay youths to heterosexuality). The sexual harassment of students or colleagues should be dealt with firmly wherever it occurs. Beyond that, what one's colleagues do in bed should be irrelevant to their employment.

One further educational issue remains: this is the right to have opportunities to learn about lesbian and gay people. This right is of special interest to lesbian and gay students, but it is also, importantly, a right of all students, all of whom are citizens and need to learn something about their fellow citizens, especially as potential voters in referenda such as the one in Colorado. The study of homosexuality—historical, psychological, sociological, legal, literary—is now a burgeoning field of research. Do students of various ages have the right to learn about this work? In the U.S. the First Amendment makes a flat prohibition of such teaching unlikely (not impossible, since the First Amendment is not binding on private institutions), though teachers may be subtly penalized for introducing such material into their courses. In Britain, a 1986 law forbids local government to "intentionally promote homosexuality or publish material with the intention of promoting homosexuality" or to "promote the teaching in any maintained school of the acceptability of homosexuality as a pretended family relationship" (Local Government Act 1986, cited in *Symposium,* 1993, p. 7). This law would very likely be unconstitutional in the U.S. It is also, I think, morally repugnant for several reasons. First, it inhibits the freedom of inquiry. Second, it inhibits the freedom of political debate. Third, it creates just the sort of atmosphere of taboo and disgust that fosters discrimination and violence against gays and lesbians. Furthermore, I believe it to be counterproductive to the proponents' own ostensible goals of fostering morality as they understand it. For a moral doctrine to announce publicly that it needs to be backed up by informational restrictions of this sort is a clear confession of weakness. And Judge Richard Posner has cogently argued that such policies actually increase the likelihood that gay sex will be casual and promiscuous, presumably something the law's partisans wish to avoid. Deprived of the chance to learn about themselves in any way other than through action, Posner argues, young gay people will in all likelihood choose action earlier than they might have otherwise (Posner, 1992, p. 302). The atmosphere of concealment also makes courtship and dating difficult—so "they will tend to substitute the sex act, which can be performed in a very short time and in private, for courtship, which is public and protracted" (Posner, 1992, p. 302).

The Right to Military Service

It is clear enough that gays and lesbians can serve with distinction in the military, since many of them have done so (Shilts, 1992, *passim;* Posner, 1992, p. 317). Furthermore, the armies of quite a few nations have successfully integrated open homosexuals into the service: France, Germany, Israel, Switzerland, Sweden, Denmark, Norway, Finland, the Netherlands, Belgium, Australia, Spain and recently Canada. As Posner writes, "The idea that homosexuals will not or cannot fight seems a canard, on a par with the idea that Jews or blacks will not or cannot fight" (Posner, 1992, p. 317). Nor are they security risks, if they openly announce their homosexuality. Nor are they to be excluded because they might commit acts of sexual harassment. (If this were so, in the wake of recent sexual harassment scandals in the U.S. military we should first exclude all heterosexual males.) Sexual harassment should be dealt with firmly wherever it occurs; this has nothing to do with our issue.

The real issue that keeps coming up is that heterosexual males do not want to be forced to associate intimately with gay males, especially to be seen naked by them. The psychology of this intense fear of the gaze of the homosexual is interesting. (It has even been attempted as a legal defense in gay-bashing cases, under the description "homosexual panic.") This fear may have something to do with the idea expressed by Comstock's gay-basher, when he perceptively noted that his aggression assailed something within himself. It may also be connected with the thought that this man will look at me in the way I look at a woman—i.e. not in a respectful or personal way, but a way that says "I want to fuck you"—and that this gaze will somehow humiliate me. What should be noted, however, is that this fear goes away when it needs to, and quite quickly too. As a frequenter of health clubs, I note that in that setting both males and females undress all the time in front of other patrons, many of whom they can be sure are gay; frequently it is clear through conversation who the gays and lesbians are. Nonetheless, we do not observe an epidemic of muscular failure. Straight men do not leap off the treadmill or drop their barbells in panic. They know they cannot root out and eject these people, so they forget about the issue. Moving on, we note that openly gay officers have been included in the police forces of New York City, Chicago, San Francisco, Los Angeles and probably others by now, without incident. During wartime, moreover, when the need for solidarity and high morale is greatest, toleration of gay and lesbian soldiers has gone up, not down (see Shilts, 1992). It seems likely that gays could be integrated relatively painlessly into the U.S. Armed Forces, if firm leadership were given from the top. The unfortunate fact, however, is that, here as with the harassment of women, high-ranking officers do not give the requisite leadership. As Judge Posner writes, "it is terrible to tell people they are unfit to serve their country, unless they really are unfit, which is not the case here" (Posner, 1992, p. 321).

The Right to Marriage and/or the Legal and Social Benefits of Marriage

Gays and lesbians in Denmark, Sweden and Norway can form a registered partnership that gives all the tax, inheritance and other civic benefits of marriage; similar legislation is soon to be passed in Finland. Many businesses, universities, and other organizations within other nations, including the U.S., have extended their marriage benefits to registered same-sex domestic partners. Gay marriage is currently a topic of intense debate in Judaism and in every major branch of Christianity.

Why are marriage rights important to gays? Legally, marriage is a source of many benefits, including favorable tax, inheritance and insurance status; immigration rights; custody rights; the right to collect unemployment benefits if one partner quits a job to move to be where his or her partner has found employment; the spousal privilege exception when giving testimony; the right to bring a wrongful death action upon the negligent death of a spouse; the right to the privileges of next-of-kin in hospital visitations, decisions about burial, etc. (Mohr, 1994, pp. 72-73, Nava and Dawidoff, 1994, p. 155, citing Hawaii Sup. Ct, *Baehr v. Lewin*). Many gays and lesbians have discovered in the most painful way that they lack these rights, although they may have lived together loyally for years.

Emotionally and morally, being able to enter a legally recognized form of marriage means the opportunity to declare publicly an intent to live in commitment and partnership. Although many lesbian and gay people consider themselves married and have frequently solemnized their commitment in ceremonies not recognized by the state, they still seek to do so in a recognized manner, because they attach importance to the public recognition of their union.

As the Norwegian Ministry of Children and Family Affairs writes, supporting Norway's 1993 law: "It can be detrimental for a person to have to suppress fundamental feelings concerning attachment and love for another person. Distancing oneself from these feelings or attempts to suppress them may destroy one's self-respect" (Norwegian Act on Registered Partnerships for Homosexual Couples, 1993). Noting that 92 percent of gays and lesbians polled in a comprehensive Swedish survey were either part of a registered couple or stated that they would like to be, the Ministry concluded that the primary obstacle to stable marital unions in the gay community is negative attitudes from the social environment.

These seem to be very plausible views. And yet gay marriage is widely opposed. On what grounds? On what account of marriage is it an institution that should remain closed to lesbians and gay men? The basis of marriage in the U.S. and Europe is generally taken to be a stated desire to live together in intimacy, love and partnership, and to support one another, materially and emotionally, in the conduct of daily life. Of course many people enter marriage unprepared, and many marriages fail; but the law cannot and should not undertake a stringent inquiry into the character and behavior of the parties before admitting them to the benefits of that status.

Many people do believe that a central purpose of marriage is to have and educate children. But (apart from the fact that many lesbian and gay people do have and raise children, whether their own from previous unions or conceived by artificial insemination within the relationship) nobody has seriously suggested denying marriage rights to postmenopausal women, to sterile individuals of any age or to people who simply know (and state) that they don't want children and won't have them. It therefore seems flatly inconsistent and unjust to deny these rights to other individuals who wish to form exactly this type of committed yet childless union.

No doubt the extension of marriage rights to gays and lesbians will change the way we think about "the family." On the other hand, "the family" has never been a single thing in western, far less in world, history, and its nuclear heterosexual form has been associated with grave problems of child abuse and gender inequality, so there is no reason to sentimentalize it as a morally perfect institution. Studies have shown that homosexual households have a more equal division of domestic labor than heterosexual ones (Blumstein and Schwartz, 1983). So they may even have valuable contributions to make to our understanding of what personal commitment and marital fairness are.

The Right to Retain Custody of Children and/or to Adopt

Gays and lesbians have and raise children. In a 1970s California survey, 20 percent of male homosexuals and more than a third of female homosexuals have been married (Posner, 1992, p. 417), and many of those have had children. Lesbian couples can have children through artificial insemination or sex with a male; a gay man can obtain a child through some sort of surrogacy arrangement. Should these things be (or remain) legal? Experience shows that children raised in homosexual households showed no differences from other groups, either in sexual orientation or in general mental health or social adjustment. Indeed, there was evidence that children raised by an unmarried heterosexual woman had more psychological problems than others (Posner, 1992, p. 418). We need more research on these issues, clearly; samples have been small and have covered a relatively short time-span. But so far there is no evidence to justify a court in removing a child from its parent's custody on the grounds that he or she is living in a homosexual union. If one were to argue that such a child will inevitably be the target of social prejudice, no matter how well its parent is doing, it seems plausible that the Constitution will intervene to block that argument. In a 1984 case, *Palmore v. Sidoti*, in which a child was removed from its (white) mother's custody because she had remarried to a black man—grounds for change of custody being that such a child will suffer from public racial prejudice—the U.S. Supreme Court returned custody to the child's mother, holding that the law may not give public legitimacy to private prejudices. This case was cited as a precedent in a 1985 Alaska decision granting custody to a gay parent (Mison, 1992, p. 175). In general, it seems especially important that children should not be removed from the custody of parents who love and care for them successfully, without compelling reason.

As for adoption and foster-parenting, I concur with Judge Posner that courts should take a case-by-case approach, rejecting a flat ban. Frequently, especially where foster-parenting is concerned, such a placement might be a child's best chance for a productive home life (Posner, 1992, p. 420). Once again, the reason for refusing a homosexual couple must not be the existence of public prejudice against homosexuality; and yet, no feature intrinsic to homosexuality as such has been demonstrated to have a detrimental effect on children.

Journal/Discussion Questions

✍ *Nussbaum's essay covers a wide range of issues relating to gay and lesbian life. Which of these areas did you find particularly interesting? Controversial? Discuss.*

1. What arguments does Nussbaum advance against anti-sodomy laws? Critically evaluate her claims.

2. What arguments does Nussbaum present for the right to marriage for gays and lesbians? What do you think is the strongest argument? Do you agree with her?

3. Discuss Nussbaum's analysis of the right to military service for homosexuals in light of the essay, "A Quiet Siege," at the beginning of this chapter.

James Q. Wilson
"Against Homosexual Marriage"

*James Q. Wilson is Collins professor of management and public policy at UCLA. His books in-
clude* The Moral Sense, On Character, Moral Judgment: Does the Abuse Excuse Threaten Our Legal
System?, *and* Thinking about Crime.

   Using Andrew Sullivan's Virtually Normal *as a counterpoint, Wilson develops his arguments
against homosexual marriage.*

As You Read, Consider This:

   1. What, according to Wilson, are the prohibitionist, conservative, and liberal positions on the
       issue of homosexual marriage? Which of these is closest to Wilson's position?

Our courts, which have mishandled abortion, may be on the verge of mishandling homosexuality. As
a consequence of two pending decisions, we may be about to accept homosexual marriage.

   In 1993 the supreme court of Hawaii ruled that, under the equal-protection clause of that state's
constitution, any law based on distinctions of sex was suspect, and thus subject to strict judicial
scrutiny. Accordingly, it reversed the denial of a marriage permit to a same-sex couple, unless the state
could first demonstrate a "compelling state interest" that would justify limiting marriages to men
and women. A new trial is set for early this summer. But in the meantime, the executive branch of
Hawaii appointed a commission to examine the question of same-sex marriages; its report, by a vote
of five to two, supports them. The legislature, for its part, holds a different view of the matter, having responded to the court's decision by passing a law unambiguously reaffirming the limitation of
marriage to male-female couples.

   No one knows what will happen in the coming trial, but the odds are that the Hawaiian version
of the equal-rights amendment may control the outcome. If so, since the United States Constitution
has a clause requiring that "full faith and credit shall be given to the public acts, records, and judicial proceedings of every other state," a homosexual couple in a state like Texas, where the population is overwhelmingly opposed to such unions, may soon be able to fly to Hawaii, get married, and
then return to live in Texas as lawfully wedded. A few scholars believe that states may be able to impose public-policy objections to such; out-of-state marriages—Utah has already voted one in, and
other states may follow—but only at the price of endless litigation.

   That litigation may be powerfully affected by the second case. It concerns a Colorado statute,
already struck down by that state's supreme court, that would prohibit giving to homosexuals "any
claim of minority status, quota preferences, protected status, or claim of discrimination." The U.S.
Supreme Court is now reviewing the appeals. If its decision upholds the Colorado Supreme Court
and thus allows homosexuals to acquire a constitutionally protected status, the chances will decline
of successful objections to homosexual marriage based on considerations of public policy.

Commentary, March, 1996, Vol. 101, No. 3; pp, 34–39.

Contemporaneous with these events, an important book has appeared under the title *Virtually Normal.* In it, Andrew Sullivan, the editor of the *New Republic,* makes a strong case for a new policy toward homosexuals. He argues that "all public (as opposed to private) discrimination against homosexuals be ended. . . . And that is all." The two key areas where this change is necessary are the military and marriage law. Lifting bans in those areas, while also disallowing anti-sodomy laws and providing information about homosexuality in publicly supported schools, would put an end to the harm that gays have endured. Beyond these changes, Sullivan writes, American society would need no "cures of homophobia or reeducations, no wrenching private litigation, no political imposition of tolerance."

It is hard to imagine how Sullivan's proposals would, in fact, end efforts to change private behavior toward homosexuals, or why the next, inevitable, step would not involve attempts to accomplish just that purpose by using cures and reeducations, private litigation, and the political imposition of tolerance. But apart from this, Sullivan—an English Catholic, a homosexual, and someone who has on occasion referred to himself as a conservative—has given us the most sensible and coherent view of a program to put homosexuals and heterosexuals on the same public footing. His analysis is based on a careful reading of serious opinions and his book is written quietly, clearly, and thoughtfully. In her review of it in *First Things* (January 1996), Elizabeth Kristol asks us to try to answer the following question: What would life be like if we were not allowed to marry? To most of us, the thought is unimaginable; to Sullivan, it is the daily existence of declared homosexuals. His response is to let homosexual couples marry.

Sullivan recounts three main arguments concerning homosexual marriage, two against and one for. He labels them prohibitionist, conservative, and liberal. (A fourth camp, the liberationist, which advocates abolishing all distinctions between heterosexuals and homosexuals, is also described—and scorched for its "strange confluence of political abdication and psychological violence.") I think it easier to grasp the origins of the three main arguments by referring to the principles on which they are based.

The prohibitionist argument is in fact a biblical one; the heart of it was stated by Dennis Prager in an essay in the *Public Interest* ("Homosexuality, the Bible, and Us," Summer 1993).

When the first books of the Bible were written, and for a long time thereafter, heterosexual love is what seemed at risk. In many cultures—not only in Egypt or among the Canaanite tribes surrounding ancient Israel but later in Greece, Rome, and the Arab world, to say nothing of large parts of China, Japan, and elsewhere—homosexual practices were common and widely tolerated or even exalted. The Torah reversed this, making the family the central unit of life, the obligation to marry one of the first responsibilities of man, and the linkage of sex to procreation the highest standard by which to judge sexual relations. Leviticus puts the matter sharply and apparently beyond quibble:

> Thou shalt not live with mankind as with womankind; it is an abomination. . . . If a man also lie with mankind, as he lieth with a woman, both of them have committed an abomination; they shall surely be put to death; their blood shall be upon them.

Sullivan acknowledges the power of Leviticus but deals with it by placing it in a relative context. What is the nature of this "abomination" Is it like killing your mother or stealing a neighbor's bread, or is it more like refusing to eat shellfish or having sex during menstruation? Sullivan suggests that all of these injunctions were written on the same moral level and hence can be accepted or ignored as a whole. He does not fully sustain this view, and in fact a refutation of it can be found in Prager's essay. In Prager's opinion and mine, people at the time of Moses, and for centuries before him, understood that there was a fundamental difference between whom you killed and what you ate, and in all likelihood people then and for centuries earlier linked whom you could marry closer to the principles that defined life than they did to the rules that defined diets.

The New Testament contains an equally vigorous attack on homosexuality by St. Paul. Sullivan partially deflects it by noting Paul's conviction that the earth was about to end and the Second Coming was near; under these conditions, all forms of sex were suspect. But Sullivan cannot deny that Paul singled out homosexuality as deserving of special criticism. He seems to pass over this obstacle without effective retort.

Instead, he takes up a different theme, namely, that on grounds of consistency many heterosexual practices—adultery, sodomy, premarital sex, and divorce, among others—should be outlawed equally with homosexual acts of the same character. The difficulty with this is that it mistakes the distinction alive in most people's minds between marriage as an institution and marriage as a practice. As an institution, it deserves unqualified support; as a practice, we recognize that married people are as imperfect as anyone else. Sullivan's understanding of the prohibitionist argument suffers from his unwillingness to acknowledge this distinction.

The second argument against homosexual marriage—Sullivan's conservative category—is based on natural law as originally set forth by Aristotle and Thomas Aquinas and more recently restated by Hadley Arkes, John Finnis, Robert George, Harry V Jaffa, and others. How it is phrased varies a bit, but in general its advocates support a position like the following: man cannot live without the care and support of other people; natural law is the distillation of what thoughtful people have learned about the conditions of that care. The first thing they have learned is the supreme importance of marriage, for without it the newborn infant is unlikely to survive or, if he survives, to prosper. The necessary conditions of a decent family life are the acknowledgment by its members that a man will not sleep with his daughter or a woman with her son and that neither will openly choose sex outside marriage.

Now, some of these conditions are violated, but there is a penalty in each case that is supported by the moral convictions of almost all who witness the violation. On simple utilitarian grounds it may be hard to object to incest or adultery; if both parties to such an act welcome it and if it is secret, what differences does it make? But very few people, and then only ones among the overeducated, seem to care much about mounting a utilitarian assault on the family. To this assault, natural-law theorists respond much as would the average citizen—never mind "utility," what counts is what is right. In particular, homosexual uses of the reproductive organs violate the condition that sex serve solely as the basis of heterosexual marriage.

To Sullivan, what is defective about the natural-law thesis is that it assumes different purposes in heterosexual and homosexual love: moral consummation in the first case and pure utility or pleasure alone in the second. But in fact, Sullivan suggests, homosexual love can be as consummatory as heterosexual. He notes that as the Roman Catholic Church has deepened its understanding of the involuntary—that is, in some sense genetic—basis of homosexuality, it has attempted to keep homosexuals in the church as objects of affection and nurture, while banning homosexual acts as perverse.

But this, though better than nothing, will not work, Sullivan writes. To show why, he adduces an analogy to a sterile person. Such a person is permitted to serve in the military or enter an unproductive marriage; why not homosexuals? If homosexuals marry without procreation, they are no different (he suggests) from a sterile man or woman who marries without hope of procreation. Yet people, I think, want the form observed even when the practice varies; a sterile marriage, whether from choice or necessity, remains a marriage of a man and a woman. To this Sullivan offers essentially an aesthetic response, just as albinos remind us of the brilliance of color and genius teaches us about moderation, homosexuals are a "natural foil" to the heterosexual union, "a variation that does not eclipse the theme." Moreover, the threat posed by the foil to the theme is slight as compared to the threats posed by adultery, divorce, and prostitution. To be consistent, Sullivan once again reminds us, society would have to ban adulterers from the military as it now bans confessed homosexuals.

But again this misses the point. It would make more sense to ask why an alternative to marriage should be invented and praised when we are having enough trouble maintaining the institution at all. Suppose that gay or lesbian marriage were authorized; rather than producing a "natural foil" that would "not eclipse the theme," I suspect such a move would call even more seriously into question the role of marriage at a time when the threats to it, ranging from single-parent families to common divorces, have hit record highs. Kenneth Minogue recently wrote of Sullivan's book that support for homosexual marriage would strike most people as "mere parody," one that could farther weaken an already strained institution.

To me, the chief limitation of Sullivan's view is that it presupposes that marriage would have the same, domesticating, effect on homosexual members as it has on heterosexuals, while leaving the latter largely unaffected. Those are very large assumptions that no modern society has ever tested.

Nor does it seem plausible to me that a modern society resists homosexual marriages entirely out of irrational prejudice. Marriage is a union, sacred to most, that unites a man and woman together for life. It is a sacrament of the Catholic Church and central to every other faith. Is it out of misinformation that every modern society has embraced this view and rejected the alternative? Societies differ greatly in their attitude toward the income people may have, the relations among their various races, and the distribution of political power. But they differ scarcely at all over the distinctions between heterosexual and homosexual couples. The former are overwhelmingly preferred over the latter. The reason, I believe, is that these distinctions involve the nature of marriage and thus the very meaning—even more, the very possibility—of society.

The final argument over homosexual marriage is the liberal one, based on civil rights.

As we have seen, the Hawaiian Supreme Court ruled that any state-imposed sexual distinction would have to meet the test of strict scrutiny, a term used by the U.S. Supreme Court only for racial and similar classifications. In doing this, the Hawaiian court distanced itself from every other state court decision—there are several—in this area so far. A variant of the suspect-class argument, though, has been suggested by some scholars who contend that denying access to a marriage license by two people of the same sex is no different from denying access to two people of different sexes but also different races. The Hawaiian Supreme Court embraced this argument as well, explicitly comparing its decision to that of the U.S. Supreme Court when it overturned state laws banning marriages involving miscegenation.

But the comparison with black-white marriages is itself suspect. Beginning around 1964, and no doubt powerfully affected by the passage of the Civil Rights Act of that year, public attitudes toward race began to change dramatically. Even allowing for exaggerated statements to pollsters, there is little doubt that people in fact acquired a new view of blacks. Not so with homosexuals. Though the campaign to aid them has been going on vigorously for about a quarter of a century, it has produced few, if any, gains in public acceptance, and the greatest resistance, I think, has been with respect to homosexual marriages.

Consider the difference. What has been at issue in race relations is not marriage among blacks (for over a century, that right has been universally granted) or even miscegenation (long before the civil-rights movement, many Southern states had repealed such laws). Rather, it has been the routine contact between the races in schools, jobs, and neighborhoods. Our own history, in other words, has long made it clear that marriage is a different issue from the issue of social integration.

There is another way, too, in which the comparison with race is less than helpful, as Sullivan himself points out. Thanks to the changes in public attitudes I mentioned a moment ago, gradually race was held to be not central to decisions about hiring, firing, promoting, and schooling, and blacks began to make extraordinary advances in society. But then, in an effort to enforce this new view, liberals came to embrace affirmative action, a policy that said that race was central to just such issues, in order to ensure that real mixing occurred. This move created a crisis, for liberalism had always been based on the proposition that a liberal political system should encourage, as John Stuart Mill put it, "experiments in living" free of religious or political direction. To contemporary liberals, however, being neutral about race was tantamount to being neutral about a set of human preferences that in such matters as neighborhood and schooling left groups largely (but not entirely) separate.

Sullivan, who wisely sees that hardly anybody is really prepared to ignore a political opportunity to change lives, is not disposed to have much of this either in the area of race or in that of sex. And he points out with great clarity that popular attitudes toward sexuality are anyway quite different from those about race, as is evident from the fact that wherever sexual orientation is subject to local regulations, such regulations are rarely invoked. Why? Because homosexuals can "pass" or not, as they wish; they can and do accumulate education and wealth; they exercise political power. The two things a homosexual cannot do are join the military as an avowed homosexual or marry another homosexual.

The result, Sullivan asserts, is a wrenching paradox. On the one hand, society has historically tolerated the brutalization inflicted on people because of the color of their skin, but freely allowed them to marry; on the other hand, it has given equal opportunity to homosexuals, while denying them the right to marry. This, indeed, is where Sullivan draws the line. A black or Hispanic child, if heterosexual, has many friends, he writes, but a gay child "generally has no one." And that is why the social stigma attached to homosexuality is different from that attached to race or ethnicity—"because it attacks the very heart of what makes a human being human: the ability to love and be loved." Here is the essence of Sullivan's case. It is a powerful one, even if (as I suspect) his pro-marriage sentiments are not shared by all homosexuals.

Let us assume for the moment that a chance to live openly and legally with another homosexual is desirable. To believe that, we must set aside biblical injunctions, a difficult matter in a profoundly religious nation. But suppose we manage the diversion, perhaps on the grounds that if most Americans skip church, they can as readily avoid other errors of (possibly) equal magnitude. Then we must ask on what terms the union shall be arranged. There are two alternatives—marriage or domestic partnership.

Sullivan acknowledges the choice, but disparages the domestic-partnership laws that have evolved in some foreign countries and in some American localities. His reasons, essentially conservative ones, are that domestic partnerships are too easily formed and too easily broken. Only real marriages matter. But—aside from the fact that marriage is in serious decline, and that only slightly more than half of all marriages performed in the United States this year will be between never-before-married heterosexuals—what is distinctive about marriage is that it is an institution created to sustain child-rearing. Whatever losses it has suffered in this respect, its function remains what it has always been.

The role of raising children is entrusted in principle to married heterosexual couples because after much experimentation—several thousand years, more or less—we have found nothing else that works as well. Neither a gay nor a lesbian couple can of its own resources produce a child; another party must be involved. What do we call this third party? A friend? A sperm or egg bank? An anonymous donor? There is no settled language for even describing, much less approving of, such persons.

Suppose we allowed homosexual couples to raise children who were created out of a prior heterosexual union or adopted from someone else's heterosexual contact. What would we think of this? There is very little research on the matter. Charlotte Patterson's famous essay, "Children of Gay and Lesbian Parents" (*Journal of Child Development,* 1992), begins by conceding that the existing studies focus on children born into a heterosexual union that ended in divorce or that was transformed when the mother or father "came out" as a homosexual. Hardly any research has been done on children acquired at the outset by a homosexual couple. We therefore have no way of knowing how they would behave. And even if we had such studies, they might tell us rather little unless they were conducted over a very long period of time.

But it is one thing to be born into an apparently heterosexual family and then many years later to learn that one of your parents is homosexual. It is quite another to be acquired as an infant from an adoption agency or a parent-for-hire and learn from the first years of life that you are, because of your family's position, radically different from almost all other children you will meet. No one can now say how grievous this would be. We know that young children tease one another unmercifully; adding this dimension does not seem to be a step in the right direction.

Of course, homosexual "families," with or without children, might be rather few in number. Just how few, it is hard to say. Perhaps Sullivan himself would marry, but, given the great tendency of homosexual males to be promiscuous, many more like him would not, or if they did, would not marry with as much seriousness.

That is problematic in itself. At one point, Sullivan suggests that most homosexuals would enter a marriage "with as much (if not more) commitment as heterosexuals." Toward the end of his book, however, he seems to withdraw from so optimistic a view. He admits that the label "virtually" in the title of his book is deliberately ambiguous, because homosexuals as a group are not "normal." At another point, he writes that the "openness of the contract" between two homosexual males means that such a union will in fact be more durable than a heterosexual marriage because the contract contains an "understanding of the need for *extramarital outlets*" (emphasis added). But no such "understanding" exists in heterosexual marriage; to suggest that it might in homosexual ones is tantamount to saying that we are now referring to two different kinds of arrangements. To justify this difference, perhaps, Sullivan adds that the very "lack of children" will give "gay couples greater freedom." Freedom for what? Freedom, I think, to do more of those things that heterosexual couples do less of because they might hurt the children.

The courts in Hawaii and in the nation's capital must struggle with all these issues under the added encumbrance of a contemporary outlook that makes law the search for rights, and responsibility the recognition of rights. Indeed, thinking of laws about marriage as documents that confer or withhold rights is itself an error of fundamental importance—one that the highest court in Hawaii has already committed. "Marriage," it wrote, "is a state-conferred legal-partnership status, the existence of which gives rise to a multiplicity of rights and benefits. . ." A state-conferred legal partnership? To lawyers, perhaps; to mankind, I think not. The Hawaiian court has thus set itself on the same course of action as the misguided Supreme Court in 1973 when it thought that laws about abortion were merely an assertion of the rights of a living mother and an unborn fetus.

I have few favorable things to say about the political systems of other modern nations, but on these fundamental matters—abortion, marriage, military service—they often do better by allowing legislatures to operate than we do by deferring to courts. Our challenge is to find a way of formulating a policy with respect to homosexual unions that is not the result of a reflexive act of judicial rights-conferring, but is instead a considered expression of the moral convictions of a people.

Journal/Discussion Questions

✍ *Wilson refers briefly to the experience of adolescents who are gay and the difficulties they encounter in coming of age in our society. Have your own experiences and observations confirmed Wilson's observations? What moral significance do those experiences have?*

1. At several points in his essay, Wilson discusses the relationship between issues of race and ethnicity and issues of sexual orientation. In what ways are they similar? In what ways are they different?

2. Some have offered "domestic partnership laws" as an alternative to legalizing homosexual marriages. What is Wilson's position on this alternative? Do you agree or disagree?

Concluding Discussion Questions

Where Do You Stand Now?

Instructions

You have already answered the following questions in your moral problems self-quiz at the beginning of this book. Now that you have studied the material in this section, take a moment to answer the same questions again.

Strongly Agree	Agree	Undecided	Disagree	Strongly Disagree	*Chapter 8: Sexual Orientation*
31. ❏	❏	❏	❏	❏	Gays and lesbians should be allowed to serve openly in the military.
32. ❏	❏	❏	❏	❏	Gays and lesbians should not be discriminated against in hiring or housing.
33. ❏	❏	❏	❏	❏	Homosexuality is unnatural.
34. ❏	❏	❏	❏	❏	Same-sex marriages should be legal.
35. ❏	❏	❏	❏	❏	Homosexuality is a matter of personal choice.

Compare your answers to this self-quiz with the answers to the initial self-quiz. How, if at all, have your answers changed? How have the *reasons* for your answers changed?

Journal/Discussion Questions

✎ *How well do you think the articles in this section have understood the experience of being gay? How well do you think they have understood the experience of being heterosexual? What do you think they have left out or misunderstood?*

1. Imagine that you have been hired by a congressional committee charged with the responsibility of drafting new legislation to articulate the place of gays and lesbians in society. How would you advise the committee? What laws, if any, would you propose to add? To delete?

2. Should prominent gays and lesbians publicly reveal their sexual orientation? If they refuse to do so, are others—either gay or not—entitled to reveal it against their wishes?

3. Imagine a round table discussion of the issue of whether openly gay individuals should be allowed to serve in the military. The participants include you, Senator Goldwater, and Professors Nussbaum and Wilson. Recount the dialogue that would occur in such a discussion.

For Further Reading

Web Resources

For Web-based resources on sexual orientation, see the Sexual Orientation page of *Ethics Updates* (http://ethics.sandiego.edu). This page includes court decisions relating to sexual orientation.

Review Articles and Bibliographies

For a short overview of some of the philosophical issues about homosexuality, see Richard D. Mohr, "Homosexuality," *Encyclopedia of Ethics,* edited by Lawrence C. Becker and Charlotte B. Becker (New York: Garland, 1992), Vol. I, pp. 552–554.

General Books, Anthologies, and Articles

Perhaps the best sympathetic philosophical approach to these issues is to be found in Richard D. Mohr's *A More Perfect Union: Why Straight America Must Stand Up for Gay Rights* (Boston: Beacon Press, 1995). For a much different perspective, see Roger Scruton, *Sexual Desire* (London: Weidenfeld and Nicolson, 1985). For the exchange between Scruton and Martha Nussbaum, see *The Liberation Debate: Rights at Issue,* edited by Michael Leahy and Dan Cohn-Sherbok (London: Routledge, 1996), pp. 89–133. Also see Michael Ruse, *Homosexuality: A Philosophical Inquiry* (New York: Basil Blackwell, 1968); *Homosexuality and Ethics,* edited by Edward Batchelor, Jr. (New York: Pilgrim Press, 1980); Roger J. Magnuson *Are Gay Rights Right? Making Sense of the Controversy,* Updated Edition (Portland, OR: Multnomah, 1990); *Homosexuality: Debating the Issues,* edited by Robert M. Baird and M. Katherine Baird (New York: Prometheus Books, 1995); and, for shorter and more popular readings, *Homosexuality: Opposing Viewpoints,* edited by William Dudley (San Diego: Greenhaven Press, 1993).

On the "social construction" of the concept of homosexuality, see Edward Stein, *Forms of Desire: Sexual Orientation and the Social Constructionist Controversy* (New York: Routledge, 1992); David Halperin's *One Hundred Years of Homosexuality* (London: Routledge, 1992); and John Thorp's "The Social Construction of Homosexuality," *Phoenix,* Vol. 46, No. 1 (Spring 1992), pp. 54–61.

Homosexual Marriage

On the issue of gay and lesbian marriages, see David Moats, *Civil Wars: Gay Marriage in America* (Austin, TX: Harcourt, 2004) for a history of the Vermont legislation; Evan Gerstmann, *Same-Sex Marriage and the Constitution* (Cambridge: Cambridge University Press, 2003). For a lively exchange between two conservatives on opposite sides of this issue, see Shelby Steele, "Selma to San Francisco? Same-sex marriage is not a civil rights issue," *The Wall Street Journal* (March 20, 2004), reply by Andrew Sullivan, "Civil Rites," *The New Republic Online* (Post date 03/30/04) (http://www.tnr.com/doc.mhtml?i=fisking&s=sullivan033004); and rejoinder by Shelby Steele,

"Married with Children," *The New Republic Online* (Post date 04/14/04) http://www .tnr.com/doc.mhtml?i=express&s=steele041304). Roger Scruton, "The Moral Birds and Bees: Sex and Marriage, Properly Understood," *National Review,* Volume LV, No. 17 (September 15, 2003) argues against same-sex marriage; Jason A. Beyer, "Public Dilemmas and Gay Marriage: Contra Jordan," *Journal of Social Philosophy,* Vol. 33, No. 1 (Spring 2002), pp. 9–16; M. D. A. Freeman, "Not Such a Queer Idea: Is There a Case for Same Sex Marriages?" *Journal of Applied Philosophy,* Vol 16, No. 1 (1999), pp. 1–17; Angela Bolte, "Do Wedding Dresses Come in Lavender? The Prospects and Implications of Same-Sex Marriage," *Social Theory and Practice,* Vol. 24, No. 1 (Spring, 1998), pp. 111–131; Andrew M. Roth, "Sociological, Political, and Legal Contexts Regarding the Current Debate on Gay Marriage," *Public Affairs Quarterly,* Vol. 12, No. 3 (July, 1998), pp. 347–61; Claudia Card, "Against Marriage and Motherhood," *Hypatia,* Vol. 11, No. 3 (Summer 1996), pp. 1–23; Christine Pierce, "Gay Marriage," *Journal of Social Philosophy,* Vol 26, No. 2 (Fall 1995), pp. 5–16. Also see the essays in Andrew Sullivan, *Same-Sex Marriage: Pro and Con. A Reader* (Boston: Vintage, 1997); Timothy F. Murphy, ed., *Gay Ethics: Controversies in Outing, Civil Rights, and Sexual Science* (West Hazleton, PA: Haworth Press, 1994) and John Corvino, *Same Sex* (Lanham, MD: Rowman and Littlefield, 1997); on the implications of this discussion for the family, see *Sex, Preference, and Family: Essays on Law and Nature,* edited by Avid M. Estlund and Martha C. Nussbaum (New York: Oxford, 1997).

PART THREE

Expanding the Circle

In the final section of this book, we turn to a consideration of the scope of our moral duties. Although both classical deontological and utilitarian thought seem in principle largely neutral in regard to things such as national borders, in fact the boundaries of our nation often mark the boundaries of our moral obligation for many people. Egoistic theories seem to make the boundaries of our obligation much narrower yet.

In Part Three, we are asking the question of how far beyond our border our obligations extend. Chapter 9 deals with issues of world hunger and whether we have obligations to impoverished nations often far distant from our own. Chapter 10 asks whether our obligations extend yet further, to include nonhuman animals, the sentient world as a whole. Chapter 11 pursues the question of our obligations to the earth itself and the environment on which we constantly depend. Chapter 12 looks at ethical issues arising in the virtual world.

The following diagram illustrates the various ways of expanding the circle of morality that philosophers have proposed:

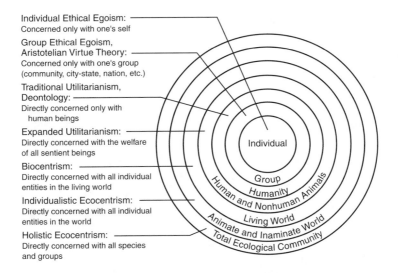

Individual Ethical Egoism:
Concerned only with one's self

Group Ethical Egoism,
Aristotelian Virtue Theory:
Concerned only with one's group
(community, city-state, nation, etc.)

Traditional Utilitarianism,
Deontology:
Directly concerned only with
human beings

Expanded Utilitarianism:
Directly concerned with the welfare
of all sentient beings

Biocentrism:
Directly concerned with all individual
entities in the living world

Individualistic Ecocentrism:
Directly concerned with all individual
entities in the world

Holistic Ecocentrism:
Directly concerned with all species
and groups

Individual

Group

Humanity

Human and Nonhuman Animals

Living World

Animate and Inanimate World

Total Ecological Community

As you consider each of the topics in the next four chapters, try to situate yourself within this map and see where you think the boundaries of our moral obligation should be drawn.

CHAPTER 9

World Hunger and Poverty

Narrative Account

Lawrence B. Salander
"The Hunger"

The author is president of Salander-O'Reilly Galleries in New York. He is also a painter with many solo and group exhibitions to his credit. He lives in New York.

In this article, Salander describes his experiences accompanying a CARE relief team to a famine-ridden town west of Mogadishu.

Baidoa is a provincial town approximately 120 miles west of Mogadishu. The pre-famine population of this godforsaken place is anyone's guess. I've read figures that range from 40,000 to 60,000. There are more people than that here now. The place is teeming with refugees who have made their way here because they have heard that it is better. Better than what?

You don't see many young children in Baidoa, because most of them are dead. One report commissioned by the United Nations estimates that 71 percent of the children of Baidoa under 5 years old have died. The accuracy of the figure is debatable, but whatever the true number, it is clearly horrific. And it's not as though these kids are dying from anything exotic. The two biggest killers are diarrhea and the measles. The medicine and food they need sits in storage in Mogadishu.

Rancid, disease-carrying water. Life in a six-foot-square grass-covered hut, home to eight people. Mothers and fathers driven mad by the hopelessness of their situation, watching their children die. Many of them seem to refuse to believe it, and carry on as if everything were normal. Human feces are everywhere, and swarms of flies surround the children not yet sick enough to be out of pain, their hair turned orange by malnutrition before falling out in clumps. Many have silver-dollar-size oozing sores caused by a lice-like animal that bores through their skin to the bone. These children with their distended stomachs, half-naked and filthy. Each one coughing a death cough.

I traveled here under the auspices of CARE. With machine-gun fire as background music, one of the organization's employees, Mary Jane Hammond, who for the last several months has been a resident of Baidoa, began what seemed to be a daily exercise with these kids. Surrounded by thirty or forty of them, she started to count to ten, out loud in English. The children picked up the count. When they reached ten they all gave themselves a round of applause, and then all of them broke into the most wonderful smiles—made larger, it seemed, by their emaciated faces. The few optimistic moments in Baidoa clearly defined the almost unbearable misery. Death was not the worst of it.

I went to the "hospital" to visit the dying. As terrible as it was, it was almost a relief to see these kids out of pain. It's their parents who need our compassion. Two dark and damp ten-by-twenty-foot adjoining rooms serve as the "pediatric ward." Each room contains seven or eight beds—

The New Republic Vol. 208, No. 1–2 (January 4, 1993), pp. 9–10.

wooden platforms that two children often share. One mother pointed out her dying infant, who was too small to see at first. She searched my eyes for the hope I could not give her. A father took my arm and led me to the bed where his 5-year-old boy lay moments from death. He pulled back the cover to show me the boy's dissipated body, and then took my hand and placed it on what was left of his son's stomach.

We climbed back into our Jeep-like vehicle, with a crew of "security men" hired for the day by CARE. A 15-year-old manned the machine gun on the roof while two other riflemen rode shotgun. The driver was the boss, the oldest and the biggest. They were high from chewing khat all day. The next stop was the airstrip, and the man was in a hurry to get there. Moving targets must be harder to hit. The dust was flying as people scattered to avoid us. A young boy made a run for it, to join his friends across the street. The driver hit the brakes, and the kid froze. We missed him by inches.

This thug, the driver, got out of the car with a bamboo stick and chased the boy down. He hit him twice. I turned away in rage and disgust. But then I realized that this single, barbaric act was the most hopeful thing I'd seen all day. This guy was beating the child to teach him to be more careful. And that implies a belief in tomorrow, which in Baidoa is no small thing.

Journal/Discussion Questions

✎ *Have you had any direct experience with relief efforts in counties with famines? If so, discuss those experiences in light of Salander's description of his own.*

1. Why did Salander describe the beating on the child as "hopeful"? Discuss your reactions to this description.

An Introduction to the Moral Issues

The Problem

We cannot help but be struck by the vast differences in standards of living between the United States (and other comparable industrialized nations) and developing countries. We have only to turn on the evening news to see clips of famine and starvation, natural disasters, and other political turmoil throughout the world. We may believe the political disagreements are best resolved among the disputants themselves. The natural disasters are transitory, but perhaps more evenly distributed among all the countries of the world. The hunger and starvation, however, are more disturbing, especially when we look around at our own affluence as a nation.

Should we help other nations, especially those in great poverty whose population is starving? Let's look more closely at these issues, beginning with the arguments in favor of helping other countries that are impoverished and whose population is starving.

The Case for Helping Other Countries

There are a number of strong reasons for helping countries that are impoverished and starving. The first of these centers on our character and in particular on the virtue of compassion. Others center on consequences, rights, and the duty to beneficence.

The Argument from Virtue

The moral force of suffering.   The mere sight of the deep suffering associated with poverty and starvation has a moral force all its own: It touches the deepest roots of human compassion to see such suffering. Anyone who possesses the virtue of compassion cannot help but respond to such suffering. To turn our backs in the face of such human misery would be cold-hearted indeed. Such a response would not only fail to relieve the suffering of others, but it would also diminish us, revealing a disturbing moral indifference. A virtuous person *must* respond to such suffering.

The issue of luck.   Our moral disquiet about this poverty and hunger is intensified by the fact that we know we as individuals do not deserve this affluence any more or less than those in famine-ridden countries deserve their destitution and hunger. This is not to deny that we work hard. But if we had been born in Rwanda or Somalia, we could be working just as hard and starving to death. The overall affluence of our society is not something we have because of our merit; it is largely a matter of luck.

The place of the children.   The children have a special place in all of this, but if there are any innocents left in the world, it is the children. Whatever we may say about the political and economic leaders of a country, we cannot help but feel that the children deserve better. In a sea of suffering, their suffering stands out as having a special and undeniable moral force. It pulls us out of our moral complacency and demands a response from us.

The statistics.   When we begin to look at the statistics, we realize that our impressionistic view of global inequalities and suffering is born out by the facts. The United States possesses a startling share of the world's wealth, consumes a highly disproportionate amount of its resources, and even produces an excessive percentage of its waste.

The Issue of Complicity

We don't deserve to be born into an affluent society any more than we deserve to be born into an impoverished one. It is simply a matter of luck. But is it purely a matter of luck that some societies are rich and others are poor? Here the issue becomes more complex. The argument, put forth by many, is that the affluence of countries like the United States is built in part on the impoverishment of developing nations. The natural resources and labor of such nations are often exploited by major industrial nations in ways that are profoundly destructive to the social, economic, and political well-being of developing nations.

The Group Egoist Argument

The compassionate response demands that we set aside self-interest and respond directly to relieve the suffering of others, even when we must make sacrifices to do so. This is a morally demanding response, and some have argued that we may not always be able or willing to respond so selflessly. Some in this tradition have argued that there are still good, self-centered moral reasons for trying to relieve the suffering of other countries.

The Strict Utilitarian Argument

Utilitarianism, as we have said before, is a very demanding moral doctrine, for it asserts (1) that we should give our own happiness and pain no special weight and (2) that we should always do what produces the *greatest* overall amount of utility. When we combine these principles, we begin to get a strong argument that morally requires rich nations to reduce the gap between themselves and poor nations until they are relatively equal. Once one accepts the strongly impartialist premise that anyone else's suffering counts just as much as your own in the moral calculus, then it is a comparatively short step to concluding that we should reduce everyone else's suffering to the same level as our own.

The Basic Rights Argument

Some authors, including Henry Shue in *Basic Rights,* have argued that everyone has a right to minimal subsistence, and that this is a positive right. Recall the difference between a negative right and a positive one. If I have a negative right, that simply prohibits others from interfering with me in the exercise of that right. A negative right to free speech prevents others from silencing me, but it does not require them to give me a microphone, even if they have an extra one. A positive right, in contrast, obligates other people to assist me in the exercise of my right. If I have a positive right to free speech, others (usually the state) must provide me with the opportunity and means for exercising that right. The right to subsistence, Shue argues, is a positive right that obligates others (particularly those with an overabundance of food) to assist me in continuing to subsist.

The Kantian Imperfect Duty Argument

In his discussion of moral duties, Immanuel Kant distinguished between two types of duties. *Perfect duties* are those that require specific actions and that must be met all the time. The duty to tell the truth, for example, is a perfect duty. We must always tell the truth. *Imperfect duties,* in contrast, require that we perform some among a group of actions but do not mandate each and every action. The duty to benevolence is an imperfect duty. We are morally required, Kant says, to perform acts of benevolence toward those in need, but this does not mean that we are required to act benevolently toward each and every person in need and on each and every occasion of such need. We are morally obligated to act benevolently, but we have a considerable amount of moral freedom to decide about the particular occasions of such benevolence.

One of the strengths of Kant's position is that it allows us to find a middle ground between those who maintain that we have no duties to other countries and those who claim that we have seemingly overwhelming obligations to them. We have a duty to some benevolence, but we do not have a duty to reduce our standard of living to the point of equality with the poor of the world. In this respect, Kant's position seems to correspond with the moral intuitions of many people today.

The Case Against Helping Other Countries

Several different types of arguments have been advanced against claims that we should provide aid to impoverished and starving peoples.

The Lifeboat Argument

In one of the most controversial articles ever written on this subject, Garrett Hardin in "Lifeboat Ethics" argues that we have a duty *not* to help the poor and starving of other countries. This is a strong and startling claim. Hardin is not simply saying that it was acceptable not to aid the poor—he was saying that it was *wrong* to help them.

The lifeboat metaphor.   Hardin suggests that rich nations are like lifeboats, and swimming around them are the poor of the world, who are clambering to get into the lifeboat. If we let them into the lifeboat—that is, if we provide aid or permit immigration in significant degrees—then we will surely swamp the lifeboat and everyone, not just the poor already in the water, will be adrift. The answer—at least from the standpoint of those in the lifeboat—is not to take as many people in as possible until it is on the verge of sinking, but rather to preserve the integrity and long-term survivability of the boat itself. Hardin admits that it is purely a matter of luck that one is born in the lifeboat rather than in the water, but he does not see this as changing his position. Those who really feel it is unfair can give up their places in the lifeboat to people in the water.

The Effectiveness Argument

Arguments that wealthy nations are obligated to aid poor nations contain not only a moral premise about obligation but also an implicit pragmatic premise that such aid can be effective. Some critics of aid have maintained that this issue can be settled on pragmatic grounds: aid, they argue, just doesn't *work*. And since it doesn't, we are under no moral obligation to do it.

The Libertarian Argument

Some claim that we have only negative rights and thus only negative duties. Libertarianism is the clearest political expression of this doctrine, and the work of Ayn Rand is the most popular literary expression of it. For a libertarian, the right to life is purely a negative one. No one is entitled to take my life away from me, but certainly no one is obligated to support my existence. Each person is solely responsible for his or her own existence, and society as a whole owes me nothing positive.

Furthermore, many in this tradition hold the right to property to be practically as strong as the right to life. This has important implications for any analysis of the unequal distribution of wealth. The libertarians maintain that the government has very few, if any, rights to deprive individuals of their property. (Many, for this reason, are strongly opposed to most taxes.) Thus libertarians see this issue as a conflict between an extremely weak or nonexistent claim (the right of the poor to aid) against a very strong claim (the right of individuals to acquire and retain their own property). For them, the choice is easy.

The Particularity Argument

Special moral obligation to take care of our own. As we indicated earlier, there is something suspicious about a moral theory that requires us to care so much about strangers that we diminish the quality of life for those nearest and dearest to us. Consider this in relation to children. I love my daughter dearly and I work hard to try to ensure that she has the opportunities for a good life. If I am a utilitarian, am I obligated to give up money I would spend on my daughter to relieve the (admittedly, quite worse) suffering of complete strangers on the other side of the globe?

To raise this question is to call into doubt one of the most fundamental premises of most ethical theories: impartiality. Both Kantians and utilitarians would agree that the moral point of view is one of strict impartiality. I should not give more weight to the suffering of those I love than I do to the suffering of strangers. Yet in recent years this premise has come under increasing challenge and some have argued that particularity may have more positive significance in the moral life than previously thought. In fact, some in this tradition would argue that there is something morally alienating about individuals who do not put the interests of those they love above the interests of strangers. This continues to be a point of great controversy among philosophers.

The Liberal State Argument

The final argument that has been advanced against claims of obligations to impoverished and starving nations could be considered a political version of the particularity argument or a type of group egoism argument. The argument is a simple one. The liberal state can only function well—that is, provide the services to its citizens that it promises—if it rests on a solid economic foundation. If that foundation is threatened either through massive foreign aid or through massive immigration, then the state may no longer be able to provide any of its members with the traditional benefits of a liberal state. Education, defense, health care, construction, and maintenance of infrastructure—all of these things would be drastically reduced if the liberal state were suddenly paying out huge sums for foreign aid or trying to meet the needs of a vast influx of immigrants.

Diversity and Consensus

Short-Term Relief

Many of the issues surrounding relief, both short-term and long-term, are empirical issues concerning effectiveness. As we have already seen in our earlier discussion of efficiency, critics of even short-term relief often express their greatest doubts about the *efficacy* of such relief. One of the principal challenges to supporters of such aid is to show that such aid does more good than harm in the long run.

Despite these criticisms, the moral bottom line about short-term relief centers around the issue of compassion. How can we, in the face of such suffering and in the midst of our relative affluence, turn away in indifference? To fail to respond seems inhumane. The moral challenge is to discern how to respond wisely and effectively.

Long-Term Assistance

Assistance programs are generally oriented toward helping recipient countries to become self-sustaining, rather than at establishing a long-term relationship of aid and dependency. How we can do this with skill and efficiency is an extremely complex question, but one that must be answered. In the process of answering it, we must also deal with questions about exploitation, population control, human rights, and respect for diverse cultural traditions. Moreover, we must figure out a way of determining how far we should go in offering assistance and support. The two extremes—Hardin, who advocates not helping at all, and Singer, who says we should help to the point of relative equality—leave a vast middle ground. Presumably the truth is somewhere in the middle here.

A Common World

What kind of world do we envision for our future? Is it a world of vast inequities, the superfluously rich and the starving poor? Or is it a world in which all human beings have the minimal conditions of a good life? And if it is the latter type of world that we hope for, then we must ask ourselves how we shall achieve it.

The Arguments

Garrett Hardin
"Lifeboat Ethics: The Case Against Helping the Poor"

Garrett Hardin was a professor of biology at the University of California, Santa Barbara. A collection of his essays, Naked Emperors, *appeared in 1983. He died in 2003.*

This is one of the most controversial articles published about the problem of world hunger, for in it Hardin argues that rich nations should not try to help poor, starving ones. Rich nations, Hardin suggests, are like lifeboats, sailing in a sea amid drowning poor people who want to get into their boats. If the poor get in the boats, they will only sink them and everyone will perish.

As You Read, Consider This:

1. Much of what Hardin says depends on acceptance of the lifeboat metaphor. What are the strengths of this metaphor? In what ways is it misleading? In what ways is it different from the spaceship metaphor?

2. What does Hardin mean by "the tragedy of the commons"? What support is there for his claim that those who own property will care for it responsibly? What evidence is there against that claim?

Environmentalists use the metaphor of the earth as a "spaceship" in trying to persuade countries, industries and people to stop wasting and polluting our natural resources. Since we all share life on this planet, they argue, no single person or institution has the right to destroy, waste, or use more than a fair share of its resources.

But does everyone on earth have an equal right to an equal share of its resources? The spaceship metaphor can be dangerous when used by misguided idealists to justify suicidal policies for sharing our resources through uncontrolled immigration and foreign aid. In their enthusiastic but unrealistic generosity, they confuse the ethics of a spaceship with those of a lifeboat.

A true spaceship would have to be under the control of a captain, since no ship could possibly survive if its course were determined by committee. Spaceship Earth certainly has no captain; the United Nations is merely a toothless tiger, with little power to enforce any policy upon its bickering members.

Psychology Today, Vol. 8 (1974), pp. 38–43, 123–126.

If we divide the world crudely into rich nations and poor nations, two thirds of them are desperately poor, and only one third comparatively rich, with the United States the wealthiest of all. Metaphorically each rich nation can be seen as a lifeboat full of comparatively rich people. In the ocean outside each lifeboat swim the poor of the world, who would like to get in, or at least to share some of the wealth. What should the lifeboat passengers do?

First, we must recognize the limited capacity of any lifeboat. For example, a nation's land has a limited capacity to support a population and as the current energy crisis has shown us, in some ways we have already exceeded the carrying capacity of our land.

Adrift in a Moral Sea

So here we sit, say fifty people in our lifeboat. To be generous, let us assume it has room for ten more, making a total capacity of sixty. Suppose the fifty of us in the lifeboat see 100 others swimming in the water outside, begging for admission to our boat or for handouts. We have several options: we may be tempted to try to live by the Christian ideal of being "our brother's keeper," or by the Marxist ideal of "to each according to his needs." Since the needs of all in the water are the same, and since they can all be seen as "our brothers," we could take them all into our boat, making a total of 150 in a boat designed for sixty. The boat swamps, everyone drowns. Complete justice, complete catastrophe.

Since the boat has an unused excess capacity of ten more passengers, we could admit just ten more to it. But which ten do we let in? How do we choose? Do we pick the best ten, the neediest ten, "first come, first served"? And what do we say to the ninety we exclude? If we do let an extra ten into our lifeboat, we will have lost our "safety factor," an engineering principle of critical importance. For example, if we don't leave room for excess capacity as a safety factor in our country's agriculture, a new plant disease or a bad change in the weather could have disastrous consequences.

Suppose we decide to preserve our small safety factor and admit no more to the lifeboat. Our survival is then possible, although we shall have to be constantly on guard against boarding parties.

While this last solution clearly offers the only means of our survival, it is morally abhorrent to many people. Some say they feel guilty about their good luck. My reply is simple: "Get out and yield your place to others." This may solve the problem of the guilt-ridden person's conscience, but it does not change the ethics of the lifeboat. The needy person to whom the guilt-ridden person yields his place will not himself feel guilty about his good luck. If he did, he would not climb aboard. The net result of conscience-stricken people giving up their unjustly held seats is the elimination of that sort of conscience from the lifeboat.

This is the basic metaphor within which we must work out our solutions. Let us now enrich the image, step by step, with substantive additions from the real world, a world that must solve real and pressing problems of overpopulation and hunger.

The harsh ethics of the lifeboat become even harsher when we consider the reproductive differences between the rich nations and the poor nations. The people inside the lifeboats are doubling in numbers every eighty-seven years; those swimming around outside are doubling, on the average, every thirty-five years, more than twice as fast as the rich. And since the world's resources are dwindling, the difference in prosperity between the rich and the poor can only increase.

As of 1973, the U.S. had a population of 210 million people, who were increasing by 0.8 percent per year. Outside our lifeboat, let us imagine another 210 million people (say the combined populations of Colombia, Ecuador, Venezuela, Morocco, Pakistan, Thailand and the Philippines), who are increasing at a rate of 3.3 percent per year. Put differently, the doubling time for this aggregate population is twenty-one years, compared to eighty-seven years for the U.S.

Multiplying the Rich and the Poor

Now suppose the U.S. agreed to pool its resources with those seven countries, with everyone receiving an equal share. Initially the ratio of Americans to non-Americans in this model would be one-to-one. But consider what the ratio would be after eighty-seven years, by which time the Americans would have doubled to a population of 420 million. By then, doubling every twenty-one years, the other group would have swollen to 354 billion. Each American would have to share the available resources with more than eight people.

But, one could argue, this discussion assumes that current population trends will continue, and they may not. Quite so. Most likely the rate of population increase will decline much faster in the U.S. than it will in the other countries, and there does not seem to be much we can do about it. In sharing with "each according to his needs," we must recognize that needs are determined by population size, which is determined by the rate of reproduction, which at present is regarded as a sovereign right of every nation, poor or not. This being so, the philanthropic load created by the sharing ethic of the spaceship can only increase.

The Tragedy of the Commons

The fundamental error of spaceship ethics, and the sharing it requires, is that it leads to what I call "the tragedy of the commons." Under a system of private property, the men who own property recognize their responsibility to care for it, for if they don't they will eventually suffer. A farmer, for instance, will allow no more cattle in a pasture than its carrying capacity justifies. If he overloads it, erosion sets in, weeds take over, and he loses the use of the pasture.

If a pasture becomes a commons open to all, the right of each to use it may not be matched by a corresponding responsibility to protect it. Asking everyone to use it with discretion will hardly do, for the considerate herdsman who refrains from overloading the commons suffers more than a selfish one who says his needs are greater. If everyone would restrain himself, all would be well; but it takes only one less than everyone to ruin a system of voluntary restraint. In a crowded world of less than perfect human beings, mutual ruin is inevitable if there are no controls. This is the tragedy of the commons.

One of the major tasks of education today should be the creation of such an acute awareness of the dangers of the commons that people will recognize its many varieties. For example, the air and water have become polluted because they are treated as commons. Further growth in the population or per-capita conversion of natural resources into pollutants will only make the problem worse. The same holds true for the fish of the oceans. Fishing fleets have nearly disappeared in many parts of the world, technological improvements in the art of fishing are hastening the day of complete ruin. Only the replacement of the system of the commons with a responsible system of control will save the land, air, water and oceanic fisheries.

In recent years there has been a push to create a new commons called a World Food Bank, an international depository of food reserves to which nations would contribute according to their abilities and from which they would draw according to their needs. This humanitarian proposal has received support from many liberal international groups, and from such prominent citizens as Margaret Mead, U.N. Secretary General Kurt Waldheim, and Senators Edward Kennedy and George McGovern.

A world food bank appeals powerfully to our humanitarian impulses. But before we rush ahead with such a plan, let us recognize where the greatest political push comes from, lest we be disillusioned later. Our experience with the "Food for Peace program," or Public Law 480, gives us the answer. This program moved billions of dollars worth of U.S. surplus grain to food-short, population-long countries during the past two decades. But when P.L. 480 first became law, a headline in the business magazine *Forbes* revealed the real power behind it: "Feeding the World's Hungry Millions: How It Will Mean Billions for U.S. Business."

And indeed it did. In the years 1960 to 1970, U.S. taxpayers spent a total of $7.9 billion on the Food for Peace program. Between 1948 and 1970, they also paid an additional $50 billion for other economic-aid programs, some of which went for food and food-producing machinery and technology. Though all U.S. taxpayers were forced to contribute to the cost of P.L. 480, certain special interest groups gained handsomely under the program. Farmers did not have to contribute the grain; the government, or rather the taxpayers, bought it from them at full market prices. The increased demand raised prices of farm products generally. The manufacturers of farm machinery, fertilizers and pesticides benefited by the farmers' extra efforts to grow more food. Grain elevators profited from storing the surplus until it could be shipped. Railroads made money hauling it to ports, and shipping lines profited from carrying it overseas. The implementation of P.L. 480 required the creation of a vast government bureaucracy, which then acquired its own vested interest in continuing the program regardless of its merits.

Extracting Dollars

Those who proposed and defended the Food for Peace program in public rarely mentioned its importance to any of these special interests. The public emphasis was always on its humanitarian effects. The combination of silent selfish interests and highly vocal humanitarian apologists made a powerful and successful lobby for extracting money from taxpayers. We can expect the same lobby to push now for the creation of a World Food Bank.

However great the potential benefit to selfish interests, it should not be a decisive argument against a truly humanitarian program. We must ask if such a program would actually do more good than harm, not only momentarily but also in the long run. Those who propose the food bank usually refer to a current "emergency" or "crisis" in terms of world food supply. But what is an emergency? Although they may be infrequent and sudden, everyone knows that emergencies will occur from time to time. A well-run family, company, organization or country prepares for the likelihood of accidents and emergencies. It expects them, it budgets for them, it saves for them.

Learning the Hard Way

What happens if some organizations or countries budget for accidents and others do not? If each country is solely responsible for its own well-being, poorly managed ones will suffer. But they can learn from experience. They may mend their ways, and learn to budget for infrequent but certain emergencies. For example, the weather varies from year to year, and periodic crop failures are certain. A wise and competent government saves out of the production of the good years in anticipation of bad years to come. Joseph taught this policy to Pharaoh in Egypt more than 2,000 years ago. Yet the great majority of the governments in the world today do not follow such a policy. They lack either the wisdom or the competence, or both. Should those nations that do manage to put something aside be forced to come to the rescue each time an emergency occurs among the poor nations?

"But it isn't their fault!" some kindhearted liberals argue. "How can we blame the poor people who are caught in an emergency? Why must they suffer for the sins of their governments?" The concept of blame is simply not relevant here. The real question is, what are the operational consequences of establishing a world food bank? If it is open to every country every time a need develops, slovenly rulers will not be motivated to take Joseph's advice. Someone will always come to their aid. Some countries will deposit food in the world food bank, and others will withdraw it. There will be almost no overlap. As a result of such solutions to food shortage emergencies, the poor countries will not learn to mend their ways, and will suffer progressively greater emergencies as their populations grow.

Population Control the Crude Way

On the average, poor countries undergo a 2.5 percent increase in population each year; rich countries, about 0.8 percent. Only rich countries have anything in the way of food reserves set aside, and even they do not have as much as they should. Poor countries have none. If poor countries received no food from the outside, the rate of their population growth would be periodically checked by crop failures and famines. But if they can always draw on a world food bank in time of need, their population can continue to grow unchecked, and so will their "need" for aid. In the short run, a world food bank may diminish that need, but in the long run it actually increases the need without limit.

Without some system of worldwide food sharing, the proportion of people in the rich and poor nations might eventually stabilize. The overpopulated poor countries would decrease in numbers, while the rich countries that had room for more people would increase. But with a well-meaning system of sharing, such as a world food bank, the growth differential between the rich and the poor countries will not only persist, it will increase. Because of the higher rate of population growth in the poor countries of the world, 88 percent of today's children are born poor, and only 12 percent rich. Year by year the ratio becomes worse, as the fast-reproducing poor outnumber the slow-reproducing rich.

A world food bank is thus a commons in disguise. People will have more motivation to draw from it than to add to any common store. The less provident and less able will multiply at the expense of the abler and more provident, bringing eventual ruin upon all who share in the commons. Besides, any system of "sharing" that amounts to foreign aid from the rich nations to the poor nations will carry the taint of charity, which will contribute little to the world peace so devoutly desired by those who support the idea of a world food bank.

As past U.S. foreign-aid programs have amply and depressingly demonstrated, international charity frequently inspires mistrust and antagonism rather than gratitude on the part of the recipient nation.

Chinese Fish and Miracle Rice

The modern approach to foreign aid stresses the export of technology and advice, rather than money and food. As an ancient Chinese proverb goes: "Give a man a fish and he will eat for a day; teach him how to fish and he will eat for the rest of his days." Acting on this advice, the Rockefeller and Ford Foundations have financed a number of programs for improving agriculture in the hungry nations. Known as the "Green Revolution," these programs have led to the development of "miracle rice" and "miracle wheat," new strains that offer bigger harvests and greater resistance to crop damage. Norman Borlaug, the Nobel Prize winning agronomist who, supported by the Rockefeller Foundation, developed miracle wheat, is one of the most prominent advocates of a world food bank.

Whether or not the Green Revolution can increase food production as much as its champions claim is a debatable but possibly irrelevant point. Those who support this well-intended humanitarian effort should first consider some of the fundamentals of human ecology. Ironically, one man who did was the late Alan Gregg, a vice president of the Rockefeller Foundation. Two decades ago he expressed strong doubts about the wisdom of such attempts to increase food production. He likened the growth and spread of humanity over the surface of the earth to the spread of cancer in the human body, remarking that "cancerous growths demand food; but, as far as I know, they have never been cured by getting it."

Overloading the Environment

Every human born constitutes a draft on all aspects of the environment: food, air, water, forests, beaches, wildlife, scenery and solitude. Food can, perhaps, be significantly increased to meet a growing demand. But what about clean beaches, unspoiled forests, and solitude? If we satisfy a growing population's need for food, we necessarily decrease its per capita supply of the other resources needed by men.

India, for example, now has a population of 600 million, which increases by 15 million each year. This population already puts a huge load on a relatively impoverished environment. The country's forests are now only a small fraction of what they were three centuries ago, and floods and erosion continually destroy the insufficient farmland that remains. Every one of the 15 million new lives added to India's population puts an additional burden on the environment, and increases the economic and social costs of crowding. However humanitarian our intent, every Indian life saved through medical or nutritional assistance from abroad diminishes the quality of life for those who remain, and for subsequent generations. If rich countries make it possible, through foreign aid, for 600 million Indians to swell to 1.2 billion in a mere twenty-eight years, as their current growth rate threatens, will future generations of Indians thank us for hastening the destruction of their environment? Will our good intentions be sufficient excuse for the consequences of our actions?

My final example of a commons in action is one for which the public has the least desire for rational discussion—immigration. Anyone who publicly questions the wisdom of current U.S. immigration policy is promptly charged with bigotry, prejudice, ethnocentrism, chauvinism, isolationism or selfishness. Rather than encounter such accusations, one would rather talk about other matters, leaving immigration policy to wallow in the crosscurrents of special interests that take no account of the good of the whole, or the interests of posterity.

Perhaps we still feel guilty about things we said in the past. Two generations ago the popular press frequently referred to Dagos, Wops, Polacks, Chinks and Krauts, in articles about how America was being "overrun" by foreigners of supposedly inferior genetic stock. But because the implied inferiority of foreigners was used then as justification for keeping them out, people now assume that restrictive policies could only be based on such misguided notions. There are other grounds.

A Nation of Immigrants

Just consider the numbers involved. Our government acknowledges a net inflow of 400,000 immigrants a year. While we have no hard data on the extent of illegal entries, educated guesses put the figure at about 600,000 a year. Since the natural increase (excess of births over deaths) of the resident population now runs about 1.7 million per year, the yearly gain from immigration amounts to at least 19 percent of the total annual increase, and may be as much as 37 percent if we include the estimate for illegal immigrants. Considering the growing use of birth-control devices, the potential effect of educational campaigns by such organizations as Planned Parenthood Federation of America and Zero Population Growth, and the influence of inflation and the housing shortage, the fertility rate of American women may decline so much that immigration could account for all the yearly increase in population. Should we not at least ask if that is what we want?

For the sake of those who worry about whether the "quality" of the average immigrant compares favorably with the quality of the average resident, let us assume that immigrants and native-born citizens are of exactly equal quality, however one defines that term. We will focus here only on quantity; and since our conclusions will depend on nothing else, all charges of bigotry and chauvinism become irrelevant.

Immigration vs. Food Supply

World food banks *move food to the people,* hastening the exhaustion of the environment of the poor countries. Unrestricted immigration, on the other hand, *moves people to the food,* thus speeding up the destruction of the environment of the rich countries. We can easily understand why poor people should want to make this latter transfer, but why should rich hosts encourage it?

As in the case of foreign-aid programs, immigration receives support from selfish interests and humanitarian impulses. The primary selfish interest in unimpeded immigration is the desire of employers for cheap labor, particularly in industries and trades that offer degrading work. In the past, one wave of foreigners after another was brought into the U.S. to work at wretched jobs for wretched wages. In recent years the Cubans, Puerto Ricans and Mexicans have had this dubious honor. The interests of the employers of cheap labor mesh well with the guilty silence of the country's liberal intelligentsia. White Anglo-Saxon Protestants are particularly reluctant to call for a closing of the doors to immigration for fear of being called bigots.

But not all countries have such reluctant leadership. Most educated Hawaiians, for example, are keenly aware of the limits of their environment, particularly in terms of population growth. There is only so much room on the islands, and the islanders know it. To Hawaiians, immigrants from the other forty-nine states present as great a threat as those from other nations. At a recent meeting of Hawaiian government officials in Honolulu, I had the ironic delight of hearing a speaker, who like most of his audience was of Japanese ancestry, ask how the country might practically and constitutionally close its doors to further immigration. One member of the audience countered: "How can we shut the doors now? We have many friends and relatives in Japan that we'd like to bring here some day so that they can enjoy Hawaii too." The Japanese-American speaker smiled sympathetically and answered: "Yes, but we have children now, and someday we'll have grandchildren too. We can bring more people here from Japan only by giving away some of the land that we hope to pass on to our grandchildren some day. What right do we have to do that?"

At this point, I can hear U.S. liberals asking: "How can you justify slamming the door once you're inside? You say that immigrants should be kept out. But aren't we all immigrants, or the descendants of immigrants? If we insist on staying, must we not admit all others?" Our craving for intellectual order leads us to seek and prefer symmetrical rules and morals: a single rule for me and everybody else; the same rule yesterday, today, and tomorrow. Justice, we feel, should not change with time and place.

We Americans of non-Indian ancestry can look upon ourselves as the descendants of thieves who are guilty morally, if not legally, of stealing this land from its Indian owners. Should we then give back the land to the now living American descendants of those Indians? However morally or logically sound this proposal may be, I, for one, am unwilling to live by it and I know no one else who is. Besides, the logical consequence would be absurd. Suppose that, intoxicated with a sense of pure justice, we should decide to turn our land over to the Indians. Since all our wealth has also been derived from the land, wouldn't we be morally obliged to give that back to the Indians too?

Pure Justice vs. Reality

Clearly, the concept of pure justice produces an infinite regression to absurdity. Centuries ago, wise men invented statutes of limitations to justify the rejection of such pure justice, in the interest of preventing continual disorder. The law zealously defends property rights, but only relatively recent property rights. Drawing a line after an arbitrary time has elapsed may be unjust, but the alternatives are worse.

We are all the descendants of thieves, and the world's resources are inequitably distributed. But we must begin the journey to tomorrow from the point where we are today. We cannot remake the past. We cannot safely divide the wealth equitably among all peoples so long as people reproduce at different rates. To do so would guarantee that our grandchildren, and everyone else's grandchildren, would have only a ruined world to inhabit.

To be generous with one's own possessions is quite different from being generous with those of posterity. We should call this point to the attention of those who, from a commendable love of justice and equality, would institute a system of the commons, either in the form of a world food bank, or of unrestricted immigration. We must convince them if we wish to save at least some parts of the world from environmental ruin.

Without a true world government to control reproduction and the use of available resources, the sharing ethic of the spaceship is impossible. For the foreseeable future, our survival demands that we govern our actions by the ethics of a lifeboat, harsh though they may be. Posterity will be satisfied with nothing less.

Journal/Discussion Questions

✍ *Hardin's article is one that usually elicits strong emotional reactions. What did you feel when you read his article? To what extent are your feelings supported by your arguments?*

1. Hardin argues that programs such as the World Food Bank appear humanitarian in motivation, but in fact are highly beneficial to many commercial interests. What is the force of this kind of objection? Does it undermine the value of such programs? Why? Why not?

2. Hardin cites Alan Gregg as saying that the spread of humanity is like a cancer. Discuss the strengths and weaknesses of this metaphor. What conclusions does acceptance of this metaphor lead to? Do you agree with those conclusions? Why or why not?

3. On what basis does Hardin object to current U.S. immigration policies? Critically evaluate his position on this issue?

4. Hardin concludes that "the concept of pure justice produces an infinite regression to absurdity." Explain what he means by this conclusion. Discuss the reasons why you agree with him and why you disagree with him. Is his concept of "pure justice" a straw man?

Peter Singer
"Rich and Poor"

Peter Singer, DeCamp Professor in Princeton University's Center for Human Values, is the author of numerous works in ethics, especially in applied ethics. His books include The Expanding Circle, Animal Liberation, Practical Ethics, *and, most recently,* Rethinking Life and Death *and* How Are We to Live? *He has also edited a number of books, including* A Companion to Ethics. *In his work, Singer sees himself as holding our conventional moral beliefs to a standard of consistency, coherence, and the avoidance of arbitrary distinctions. He finds that many of these traditional beliefs are remnants of earlier, religiously inspired doctrines that he believes many people no longer accept, whereas other beliefs survive only because they promote some form of group selfishness.*

Writing from a strict utilitarian standpoint, Singer argues that rich nations have an obligation to aid poor and starving ones up to the point of relative equality between rich and poor. Letting people starve to death when we could prevent it without giving up our own lives, Singer argues, is the moral equivalent of actively killing them—and because killing them is clearly wrong, so too is letting them starve to death under the present conditions. Singer considers various objections to his position, but finds none of them sufficiently strong to undermine his position.

Practical Ethics, Second Edition (New York: Cambridge University Press, 1993), pp. 218–46, 372–74 (notes).

As You Read, Consider This:

1. Singer maintains that "If we stopped feeding animals on grains and soybeans, the amount of food saved would—if distributed to those who need it—be more than enough to end hunger throughout the world." How do you think the issue of vegetarianism is related to world hunger? If people are asked to give up eating meat, are they being asked to give up something morally signficant, something to which they have a strong right?

2. Singer maintains that if "allowing someone to die is not intrinsically different from killing someone, it would seem that we are all murderers." What is the moral difference between actively killing someone and passively letting someone die whom you could save? How does this issue play a role in the development of Singer's position? Do you agree with his principle, "if it is in our power to prevent something very bad from happening, without thereby sacrificing anything of comparable moral significance, we ought to do it"?

Some Facts about Poverty

Consider these facts: by the most cautious estimates, 400 million people lack the calories, protein, vitamins and minerals needed to sustain their bodies and minds in a healthy state. Millions are constantly hungry; others suffer from deficiency diseases and from infections they would be able to resist on a better diet. Children are the worst affected. According to one study, 14 million children under five die every year from the combined effects of malnutrition and infection. In some districts half the children born can be expected to die before their fifth birthday.

Nor is lack of food the only hardship of the poor. To give a broader picture, Robert McNamara, when president of the World Bank, suggested the term "absolute poverty." The poverty we are familiar with in industrialized nations is relative poverty—meaning that some citizens are poor, relative to the wealth enjoyed by their neighbors. People living in relative poverty in Australia might be quite comfortably off by comparison with pensioners in Britain, and British pensioners are not poor in comparison with the poverty that exists in Mali or Ethiopia. Absolute poverty, on the other hand, is poverty by any standard. In McNamara's words:

> Poverty at the absolute level . . . is life at the very margin of existence. The absolute poor are severely deprived human beings struggling to survive in a set of squalid and degraded circumstances almost beyond the power of our sophisticated imaginations and privileged circumstances to conceive.
>
> Compared to those fortunate enough to live in developed countries, individuals in the poorest nations have:
>
> An infant mortality rate eight times higher;
> A life expectancy one-third lower;
> An adult literacy rate 60 percent less;
> A nutritional level, for one out of every two in the population, below acceptable standards;
> And for millions of infants, less protein than is sufficient to permit optimum development of the brain.

McNamara has summed up absolute poverty as "a condition of life so characterized by malnutrition, illiteracy, disease, squalid surroundings, high infant mortality and low life expectancy as to be beneath any reasonable definition of human decency."

Absolute poverty is, as McNamara has said, responsible for the loss of countless lives, especially among infants and young children. When absolute poverty does not cause death, it still causes misery of a kind not often seen in the affluent nations. Malnutrition in young children stunts both physical and mental development. According to the United Nations Development Programme, 180 million children under the age of five suffer from serious malnutrition. Millions of people on poor diets suffer from deficiency diseases, like goitre, or blindness caused by a lack of vitamin A. The food value of what the poor eat is further reduced by parasites such as hookworm and ringworm, which are endemic in conditions of poor sanitation and health education.

Death and disease apart, absolute poverty remains a miserable condition of life, with inadequate food, shelter, clothing, sanitation, health services and education. The Worldwatch Institute estimates that as many as 1.2 billion people—or 23 percent of the world's population—live in absolute poverty. For the purposes of this estimate, absolute poverty is defined as "the lack of sufficient income in cash or kind to meet the most basic biological needs for food, clothing, and shelter." Absolute poverty is probably the principal cause of human misery today.

Some Facts about Wealth

This is the background situation, the situation that prevails on our planet all the time. It does not make headlines. People died from malnutrition and related diseases yesterday, and more will die tomorrow. The occasional droughts, cyclones, earthquakes, and floods that take the lives of tens of thousands in one place and at one time are more newsworthy. They add greatly to the total amount of human suffering; but it is wrong to assume that when there are no major calamities reported, all is well.

The problem is not that the world cannot produce enough to feed and shelter its people. People in the poor countries consume, on average, 180 kilos of grain a year, while North Americans average around 900 kilos. The difference is caused by the fact that in the rich countries we feed most of our grain to animals, converting it into meat, milk, and eggs. Because this is a highly inefficient process, people in rich countries are responsible for the consumption of far more food than those in poor countries who eat few animal products. If we stopped feeding animals on grains and soybeans, the amount of food saved would—if distributed to those who need it—be more than enough to end hunger throughout the world.

These facts about animal food do not mean that we can easily solve the world food problem by cutting down on animal products, but they show that the problem is essentially one of distribution rather than production. The world does produce enough food. Moreover, the poorer nations themselves could produce far more if they made more use of improved agricultural techniques.

So why are people hungry? Poor people cannot afford to buy grain grown by farmers in the richer nations. Poor farmers cannot afford to buy improved seeds, or fertilizers, or the machinery needed for drilling wells and pumping water. Only by transferring some of the wealth of the rich nations to the poor can the situation be changed.

That this wealth exists is clear. Against the picture of absolute poverty that McNamara has painted, one might pose a picture of "absolute affluence." Those who are absolutely affluent are not necessarily affluent by comparison with their neighbors, but they are affluent by any reasonable definition of human needs. This means that they have more income than they need to provide themselves adequately with all the basic necessities of life. After buying (either directly or through their taxes) food, shelter, clothing, basic health services, and education, the absolutely affluent are still able to spend money on luxuries. The absolutely affluent choose their food for the pleasures of the palate, not to stop hunger; they buy new clothes to look good, not to keep warm; they move [into a new] house to be in a better neighborhood or have a playroom for the children, not to keep out the rain; and after all this there is still money to spend on stereo systems, video-cameras, and overseas holidays.

At this stage I am making no ethical judgments about absolute affluence, merely pointing out that it exists. Its defining characteristic is a significant amount of income above the level necessary to provide for the basic human needs of oneself and one's dependents. By this standard, the majority of citizens of Western Europe, North America, Japan, Australia, New Zealand, and the oil-rich Middle Eastern states are all absolutely affluent. To quote McNamara once more:

> The average citizen of a developed country enjoys wealth beyond the wildest dreams of the one billion people in countries with per capita incomes under $200. These, therefore, are the countries—and individuals—who have wealth that they could, without threatening their own basic welfare, transfer to the absolutely poor.

At present, very little is being transferred. Only Sweden, the Netherlands, Norway, and some of the oil-exporting Arab states have reached the modest target, set by the United Nations, of 0.7 percent of gross national product (GNP). Britain gives 0.31 percent of its GNP in official development assistance and a small additional amount in unofficial aid from voluntary organizations. The total comes to about £2 per month per person, and compares with 5.5 percent of GNP spent on alcohol, and 3 percent on tobacco. Other, even wealthier nations, give little more: Germany gives 0.41 percent and Japan 0.32 percent. The United States gives a mere 0.15 percent of its GNP.

The Moral Equivalent of Murder?

If these are the facts, we cannot avoid concluding that by not giving more than we do, people in rich countries are allowing those in poor countries to suffer from absolute poverty, with consequent malnutrition, ill health, and death. This is not a conclusion that applies only to governments. It applies to each absolutely affluent individual, for each of us has the opportunity to do something about the situation; for instance, to give our time or money to voluntary organizations like Oxfam, Care, War on Want, Freedom from Hunger, Community Aid Abroad, and so on. If, then, allowing someone to die is not intrinsically different from killing someone, it would seem that we are all murderers.

Is this verdict too harsh? Many will reject it as self-evidently absurd. They would sooner take it as showing that allowing to die cannot be equivalent to killing than as showing that living in an affluent style without contributing to an overseas aid agency is ethically equivalent to going over to Ethiopia and shooting a few peasants. And no doubt, put as bluntly as that, the verdict is too harsh.

There are several significant differences between spending money on luxuries instead of using it to save lives, and deliberately shooting people.

First, the motivation will normally be different. Those who deliberately shoot others go out of their way to kill; they presumably want their victims dead, from malice, sadism, or some equally unpleasant motive. A person who buys a new stereo system presumably wants to enhance her enjoyment of music—not in itself a terrible thing. At worst, spending money on luxuries instead of giving it away indicates selfishness and indifference to the sufferings of others, characteristics that may be undesirable but are not comparable with actual malice or similar motives. Second, it is not difficult for most of us to act in accordance with a rule against killing people: it is, on the other hand, very difficult to obey a rule that commands us to save all the lives we can. To live a comfortable, or even luxurious life it is not necessary to kill anyone; but it is necessary to allow some to die whom we might have saved, for the money that we need to live comfortably could have been given away. Thus the duty to avoid killing is much easier to discharge completely than the duty to save. Saving every life we could would mean cutting our standard of living down to the bare essentials needed to keep us alive.[1] To discharge this duty completely would require a degree of moral heroism utterly different from that required by mere avoidance of killing.

A third difference is the greater certainty of the outcome of shooting when compared with not giving aid. If I point a loaded gun at someone at close range and pull the trigger, it is virtually certain that the person will be killed; whereas the money that I could give might be spent on a project that turns out to be unsuccessful and helps no one.

Fourth, when people are shot there are identifiable individuals who have been harmed. We can point to them and to their grieving families. When I buy my stereo system, I cannot know who my money would have saved if I had given it away. In a time of famine I may see dead bodies and grieving families on television reports, and I might not doubt that my money would have saved some of them; even then it is impossible to point to a body and say that had I not bought the stereo, that person would have survived.

Fifth, it might be said that the plight of the hungry is not my doing, and so I cannot be held responsible for it. The starving would have been starving if I had never existed. If I kill, however, I am responsible for my victims' deaths, for those people would not have died if I had not killed them.

These differences need not shake our previous conclusion that there is no intrinsic difference between killing and allowing to die. They are extrinsic differences, that is, differences normally but not necessarily associated with the distinction between killing and allowing to die. We can imagine cases in which someone allows another to die for malicious or sadistic reasons; we can imagine a world in which there are so few people needing assistance, and they are so easy to assist, that our duty not to allow people to die is as easily discharged as our duty not to kill; we can imagine situations in which the outcome of not helping is as sure as shooting; we can imagine cases in which we can identify the person we allow to die. We can even imagine a case of allowing to die in which, if I had not existed, the person would not have died—for instance, a case in which if I had not been in a position to help (though I don't help) someone else would have been in my position and would have helped.

Our previous discussion of euthanasia illustrates the extrinsic nature of these differences, for they do not provide a basis for distinguishing active from passive euthanasia. If a doctor decides, in consultation with the parents, not to operate on—and thus to allow to die—a Down's syndrome infant with an intestinal blockage, her motivation will be similar to that of a doctor who gives a lethal injection rather than allow the infant to die. No extraordinary sacrifice or moral heroism will be required in either case. Not operating will just as certainly end in death as administering the injection. Allowing to die does have an identifiable victim. Finally, it may well be that the doctor is personally responsible for the death of the infant she decides not to operate upon, since she may know that if she had not taken this case, other doctors in the hospital would have operated.

Nevertheless, euthanasia is a special case, and very different from allowing people to starve to death. (The major difference being that when euthanasia is justifiable, death is a good thing.) The extrinsic differences that *normally* mark off killing and allowing to die do explain why we *normally* regard killing as much worse than allowing to die.

To explain our conventional ethical attitudes is not to justify them. Do the five differences not only explain, but also justify, our attitudes? Let us consider them one by one:

1. Take the lack of an identifiable victim first. Suppose that I am a traveling salesperson, selling tinned food, and I learn that a batch of tins contains a contaminant, the known effect of which, when consumed, is to double the risk that the consumer will die from stomach cancer. Suppose I continue to sell the tins. My decision may have no identifiable victims. Some of those who eat the food will die from cancer. The proportion of consumers dying in this way will be twice that of the community at large, but who among the consumers died because they ate what I sold, and who would have contracted the disease anyway? It is impossible to tell; but surely this impossibility makes my decision no less reprehensible than it would have been had the contaminant had more readily detectable, though equally fatal, effects.

2. The lack of certainty that by giving money I could save a life does reduce the wrongness of not giving, by comparison with deliberate killing; but it is insufficient to show that not giving is acceptable conduct. The motorist who speeds through pedestrian crossings, heedless of anyone who might be on them, is not a murderer. She may never actually hit a pedestrian; yet what she does is very wrong indeed.

3. The notion of responsibility for acts rather than omissions is more puzzling. On the one hand, we feel ourselves to be under a greater obligation to help those whose misfortunes we have caused. (It is for this reason that advocates of overseas aid often argue that Western nations have created the poverty of third world nations, through forms of economic exploitation that go back to the colonial system.) On the other hand, any consequentialist would insist that we are responsible for all the consequences of our actions, and if a consequence of my spending money on a luxury item is that someone dies, I am responsible for that death. It is true that the person would have died even if I had never existed, but what is the relevance of that? The fact is that I do exist, and the consequentialist will say that our responsibilities derive from the world as it is, not as it might have been.

One way of making sense of the non-consequentialist view of responsibility is by basing it on a theory of rights of the kind proposed by John Locke or, more recently, Robert Nozick. If everyone has a right to life, and this right is a right *against* others who might threaten my life, but not a right to assistance from others when my life is in danger, then we can understand the feeling that we are responsible for acting to kill but not for omitting to save. The former violates the rights of others, the latter does not. Should we accept such a theory of rights? If we build up our theory of rights by imagining, as Locke and Nozick do, individuals living independently from each other in a "state of nature," it may seem natural to adopt a conception of rights in which as long as each leaves the other alone, no rights are violated. I might, on this view, quite properly have maintained my independent existence if I had wished to do so. So if I do not make you any worse off than you would have been if I had had nothing at all to do with you, how can I have violated your rights? But why start from such an unhistorical, abstract and ultimately inexplicable idea as an independent individual? Our ancestors were—like other primates—social beings long before they were human beings, and could not have developed the abilities and capacities of human beings if they had not been social beings first. In any case, we are not, now, isolated individuals. So why should we assume that rights must be restricted to rights against interference? We might, instead, adopt the view that taking rights to life seriously is incompatible with standing by and watching people die when one could easily save them.

4. What of the difference in motivation? That a person does not positively wish for the death of another lessens the severity of the blame she deserves; but not by as much as our present attitudes to giving aid suggest. The behavior of the speeding motorist is again comparable, for such motorists usually have no desire at all to kill anyone. They merely enjoy speeding and are indifferent to the consequences. Despite their lack of malice, those who kill with cars deserve not only blame but also severe punishment.

5. Finally, the fact that to avoid killing people is normally not difficult, whereas to save all one possibly could save is heroic, must make an important difference to our attitude to failure to do what the respective principles demand. Not to kill is a minimum standard of acceptable conduct we can require of everyone; to save all one possibly could is not something that can realistically be required, especially not in societies accustomed to giving as little as ours do. Given the generally accepted standards, people who give, say, $1,000 a year to an overseas aid organization are more aptly praised for above average generosity than blamed for giving less than they might. The appropriateness of praise and blame is, however, a separate issue from the rightness or wrongness of actions. The former evaluates the agent: the latter evaluates the action. Perhaps many people who give $1,000 really ought to give at least $5,000, but to blame them for not giving more could be counterproductive. It might make them feel that what is required is too demanding, and if one is going to be blamed anyway, one might as well not give anything at all.

(That an ethic that puts saving all one possibly can on the same footing as not killing would be an ethic for saints or heroes should not lead us to assume that the alternative must be an ethic that makes it obligatory not to kill, but puts us under no obligation to save anyone. There are positions in between these extremes, as we shall soon see.)

Here is a summary of the five differences that normally exist between killing and allowing to die, in the context of absolute poverty and overseas aid. The lack of an identifiable victim is of no moral significance, though it may play an important role in explaining our attitudes. The idea that we are directly responsible for those we kill, but not for those we do not help, depends on a questionable notion of responsibility and may need to be based on a controversial theory of rights. Differences in certainty and motivation are ethically significant and show that not aiding the poor is not to be condemned as murdering them; it could, however, be on a par with killing someone as a result of reckless driving, which is serious enough. Finally, the difficulty of completely discharging the duty of saving all one possibly can makes it inappropriate to blame those who fall short of this target as we blame those who kill; but this does not show that the act itself is less serious. Nor does it indicate anything about those who, far from saving all they possibly can, make no effort to save anyone.

These conclusions suggest a new approach. Instead of attempting to deal with the contrast between affluence and poverty by comparing not saving with deliberate killing, let us consider afresh whether we have an obligation to assist those whose lives are in danger, and if so, how this obligation applies to the present world situation.

The Obligation to Assist

The Argument for an Obligation to Assist

The path from the library at my university to the humanities lecture theater passes a shallow ornamental pond. Suppose that on my way to give a lecture I notice that a small child has fallen in and is in danger of drowning. Would anyone deny that I ought to wade in and pull the child out? This will mean getting my clothes muddy and either canceling my lecture or delaying it until I can find something dry to change into; but compared with the avoidable death of a child this is insignificant.

A plausible principle that would support the judgment that I ought to pull the child out is this: if it is in our power to prevent something very bad from happening, without thereby sacrificing anything of comparable moral significance, we ought to do it. This principle seems uncontroversial. It will obviously win the assent of consequentialists; but non-consequentialists should accept it too, because the injunction to prevent what is bad applies only when nothing comparably significant is at stake. Thus the principle cannot lead to the kinds of actions of which non-consequentialists strongly disapprove—serious violations of individual rights, injustice, broken promises, and so on. If non-consequentialists regard any of these as comparable in moral significance to the bad thing that is to be prevented, they will automatically regard the principle as not applying in those cases in which the bad thing can only be prevented by violating rights, doing injustice, breaking promises, or whatever else is at stake. Most non-consequentialists hold that we ought to prevent what is bad and promote what is good. Their dispute with consequentialists lies in their insistence that this is not the sole ultimate ethical principle: that it is an ethical principle is not denied by any plausible ethical theory.

Nevertheless the uncontroversial appearance of the principle that we ought to prevent what is bad when we can do so without sacrificing anything of comparable moral significance is deceptive. If it were taken seriously and acted upon, our lives and our world would be fundamentally changed. For the principle applies, not just to rare situations in which one can save a child from a pond, but to the everyday situation in which we can assist those living in absolute poverty. In saying this I assume that absolute poverty, with its hunger and malnutrition, lack of shelter, illiteracy, disease, high infant mortality, and low life expectancy, is a bad thing. And I assume that it is within the power of the affluent to reduce absolute poverty, without sacrificing anything of comparable moral significance. If these two assumptions and the principle we have been discussing are correct, we have an obligation to help those in absolute poverty that is no less strong than our obligation to rescue a drowning child from a pond. Not to help would be wrong, whether or not it is intrinsically equivalent to killing. Helping is not, as conventionally thought, a charitable act that it is praiseworthy to do, but not wrong to omit; it is something that everyone ought to do.

This is the argument for an obligation to assist. Set out more formally, it would look like this.

First premise:	If we can prevent something bad without sacrificing anything of comparable significance, we ought to do it.
Second premise:	Absolute poverty is bad.
Third premise:	There is some absolute poverty we can prevent without sacrificing anything of comparable moral significance.
Conclusion:	We ought to prevent some absolute poverty.

The first premise is the substantive moral premise on which the argument rests, and I have tried to show that it can be accepted by people who hold a variety of ethical positions.

The second premise is unlikely to be challenged. Absolute poverty is, as McNamara put it, "beneath any reasonable definition of human decency" and it would be hard to find a plausible ethical view that did not regard it as a bad thing.

The third premise is more controversial, even though it is cautiously framed. It claims only that some absolute poverty can be prevented without the sacrifice of anything of comparable moral significance. It thus avoids the objection that any aid I can give is just "drops in the ocean" for the point is not whether my personal contribution will make any noticeable impression on world poverty as a whole (of course it won't) but whether it will prevent some poverty. This is all the argument needs to sustain its conclusion, since the second premise says that any absolute poverty is bad, and not merely the total amount of absolute poverty. If without sacrificing anything of comparable moral significance we can provide just one family with the means to raise itself out of absolute poverty, the third premise is vindicated.

I have left the notion of moral significance unexamined in order to show that the argument does not depend on any specific values or ethical principles. I think the third premise is true for most people living in industrialized nations, on any defensible view of what is morally significant. Our affluence means that we have income we can dispose of without giving up the basic necessities of life, and we can use this income to reduce absolute poverty. Just how much we will think ourselves obliged to give up will depend on what we consider to be of comparable moral significance to the poverty we could prevent: stylish clothes, expensive dinners, a sophisticated stereo system, overseas holidays, a (second?) car, a larger house, private schools for our children, and so on. For a utilitarian, none of these is likely to be of comparable significance to the reduction of absolute poverty; and those who are not utilitarians surely must, if they subscribe to the principle of universalisability, accept that at least some of these things are of far less moral significance than the absolute poverty that could be prevented by the money they cost. So the third premise seems to be true on any plausible ethical view—although the precise amount of absolute poverty that can be prevented before anything of moral significance is sacrificed will vary according to the ethical view one accepts.

Objections to the Argument

Taking care of our own. Anyone who has worked to increase overseas aid will have come across the argument that we should look after those near us, our families, and then the poor in our own country, before we think about poverty in distant places.

No doubt we do instinctively prefer to help those who are close to us. Few could stand by and watch a child drown; many can ignore a famine in Africa. But the question is not what we usually do, but what we ought to do, and it is difficult to see any sound moral justification for the view that distance, or community membership, makes a crucial difference to our obligations.

Consider, for instance, racial affinities. Should people of European origin help poor Europeans before helping poor Africans? Most of us would reject such a suggestion out of hand, and our discussion of the principle of equal consideration of interests in Chapter 2 [of *Practical Ethics*] has shown why we should reject it: people's need for food has nothing to do with their race, and if Africans need food more than Europeans, it would be a violation of the principle of equal consideration to give preference to Europeans.

The same point applies to citizenship or nationhood. Every affluent nation has some relatively poor citizens, but absolute poverty is limited largely to the poor nations. Those living on the streets of Calcutta, or in the drought-prone Sahel region of Africa, are experiencing poverty unknown in the West. Under these circumstances it would be wrong to decide that only those fortunate enough to be citizens of our own community will share our abundance. We feel obligations of kinship more strongly than those of citizenship. Which parents could give away their last bowl of rice if their own children were starving? To do so would seem unnatural, contrary to our nature as biologically evolved beings—although whether it would be wrong is another question altogether. In any case, we are not faced with that situation, but with one in which our own children are well-fed, well-clothed, well-educated, and would now like new bikes, a stereo set, or their own car. In these circumstances any special obligations we might have to our children have been fulfilled, and the needs of strangers make a stronger claim upon us.

The element of truth in the view that we should first take care of our own, lies in the advantage of a recognized system of responsibilities. When families and local communities look after their own poorer members, ties of affection and personal relationships achieve ends that would otherwise require a large, impersonal bureaucracy. Hence it would be absurd to propose that from now on we all regard ourselves as equally responsible for the welfare of everyone in the world; but the argument for an obligation to assist does not propose that. It applies only when some are in absolute poverty, and others can help without sacrificing anything of comparable moral significance. To allow one's own kin to sink into absolute poverty would be to sacrifice something of comparable significance; and before that point had been reached, the breakdown of the system of family and community responsibility would be a factor to weigh the balance in favor of a small degree of preference for family and community. This small degree of preference is, however, decisively outweighed by existing discrepancies in wealth and property.

Property myths.   Do people have a right to private property, a right that contradicts the view that they are under an obligation to give some of their wealth away to those in absolute poverty? According to some theories of rights (for instance, Robert Nozick's), provided one has acquired one's property without the use of unjust means like force and fraud, one may be entitled to enormous wealth while others starve. This individualistic conception of rights is in contrast to other views, like the early Christian doctrine to be found in the works of Thomas Aquinas, which holds that since property exists for the satisfaction of human needs, "whatever a man has in superabundance is owed, of natural right, to the poor for their sustenance." A socialist would also, of course, see wealth as belonging to the community rather than the individual, while utilitarians, whether socialist or not, would be prepared to override property rights to prevent great evils.

Does the argument for an obligation to assist others therefore presuppose one of these other theories of property rights, and not an individualistic theory like Nozick's? Not necessarily. A theory of property rights can insist on our *right* to retain wealth without pronouncing on whether the rich *ought* to give to the poor. Nozick, for example, rejects the use of compulsory means like taxation to redistribute income, but suggests that we can achieve the ends we deem morally desirable by voluntary means. So Nozick would reject the claim that rich people have an "obligation" to give to the poor, in so far as this implies that the poor have a right to our aid, but might accept that giving is something we ought to do and failing to give, though within one's rights, is wrong—for there is more to an ethical life than respecting the rights of others.

The argument for an obligation to assist can survive, with only minor modifications, even if we accept an individualistic theory of property rights. In any case, however, I do not think we should accept such a theory. It leaves too much to chance to be an acceptable ethical view. For instance, those whose forefathers happened to inhabit some sandy wastes around the Persian Gulf are now fabulously wealthy, because oil lay under those sands; while those whose forefathers settled on better land south of the Sahara live in absolute poverty, because of drought and bad harvests. Can this distribution be acceptable from an impartial point of view? If we imagine ourselves about to begin life as a citizen of either Bahrein or Chad—but we do not know which—would we accept the principle that citizens of Bahrein are under no obligation to assist people living in Chad?

Population and the ethics of triage.   Perhaps the most serious objection to the argument that we have an obligation to assist is that since the major cause of absolute poverty is overpopulation, helping those now in poverty will only ensure that yet more people are born to live in poverty in the future.

In its most extreme form, this objection is taken to show that we should adopt a policy of "triage." The term comes from medical policies adopted in wartime. With too few doctors to cope with all the casualties, the wounded were divided into three categories: those who would probably survive without medical assistance, those who might survive if they received assistance, but otherwise probably would not, and those who even with medical assistance probably would not survive. Only those in the middle category were given medical assistance. The idea, of course, was to use limited medical resources as effectively as possible. For those in the first category, medical treatment was not strictly necessary; for those in the third category, it was likely to be useless. It has been suggested that we should apply the same policies to countries, according to their prospects of becoming self-sustaining. We would not aid countries that even without our help will soon be able to feed their populations. We would not aid countries that, even with our help, will not be able to limit their population to a level they can feed. We would aid those countries where our help might make the difference between success and failure in bringing food and population into balance. Advocates of this theory are understandably reluctant to give a complete list of the countries they would place into the "hopeless" category; Bangladesh has been cited as an example, and so have some of the countries of the Sahel region of Africa. Adopting the policy of triage would, then, mean cutting off assistance to these countries and allowing famine, disease, and natural disasters to reduce the population of those countries to the level at which they can provide adequately for all. In support of this view Garrett Hardin has offered a metaphor: we in the rich nations are like the occupants of a crowded lifeboat adrift in a sea full of drowning people. If we try to save the drowning by bringing them aboard, our boat will be overloaded and we shall all drown. Since it is better that some survive than none, we should leave the others to drown. In the world today, according to Hardin, "lifeboat ethics" apply. The rich should leave the poor to starve, for otherwise the poor will drag the rich down with them.

Against this view, some writers have argued that overpopulation is a myth. The world produces ample food to feed its population, and could, according to some estimates, feed ten times as many. People are hungry not because there are too many but because of inequitable land distribution, the manipulation of third world economies by the developed nations, wastage of food in the West, and so on. Putting aside the controversial issue of the extent to which food production might one day be increased, it is true, as we have already seen, that the world now produces enough to feed its inhabitants—the amount lost by being fed to animals itself being enough to meet existing grain shortages. Nevertheless population growth cannot be ignored. Bangladesh could, with land reform and using better techniques, feed its present population of 115 million; but by the year 2000, according to United Nations Population Division estimates, its population will be 150 million. The enormous effort that will have to go into feeding an extra 35 million people, all added to the population within a decade, means that Bangladesh must develop at full speed to stay where it is. Other low-income countries are in similar situations. By the end of the century, Ethiopia's population is expected to rise from 49 to 66 million; Somalia's from 7 to 9 million, India's from 853 to 1041 million, Zaire's from 35 to 49 million.[2]

What will happen if the world population continues to grow? It cannot do so indefinitely. It will be checked by a decline in birth rates or a rise in death rates. Those who advocate triage are proposing that we allow the population growth of some countries to be checked by a rise in death rates—that is, by increased malnutrition, and related diseases; by widespread famines; by increased infant mortality; and by epidemics of infectious diseases.

The consequences of triage on this scale are so horrible that we are inclined to reject it without further argument. How could we sit by our television sets, watching millions starve while we do nothing? Would not that be the end of all notions of human equality and respect for human life? (Those who attack the proposals for legalizing euthanasia discussed in Chapter 7 [of *Practical Ethics*], saying that these proposals will weaken respect for human life, would surely do better to object to the idea that we should reduce or end our overseas aid programs, for that proposal, if implemented, would be responsible for a far greater loss of human life.) Don't people have a right to our assistance, irrespective of the consequences? Anyone whose initial reaction to triage was not one of repugnance would be an unpleasant sort of person. Yet initial reactions based on strong feelings are not always reliable guides. Advocates of triage are rightly concerned with the long-term consequences of our actions. They say that helping the poor and starving now merely ensures more poor and starving in the future. When our capacity to help is finally unable to cope—as one day it must be—the suffering will be greater than it would be if we stopped helping now. If this is correct, there is nothing we can do to prevent absolute starvation and poverty, in the long run, and so we have no obligation to assist. Nor does it seem reasonable to hold that under these circumstances people have a right to our assistance. If we do accept such a right, irrespective of the consequences, we are saying that, in Hardin's metaphor, we should continue to haul the drowning into our lifeboat until the boat sinks and we all drown. If triage is to be rejected it must be tackled on its own ground, within the framework of consequentialist ethics. Here it is vulnerable. Any consequentialist ethics must take probability of outcome into account. A course of action that will certainly produce some benefit is to be preferred to an alternative course that may lead to a slightly larger benefit, but is equally likely to result in no benefit at all. Only if the greater magnitude of the uncertain benefit outweighs its uncertainty should we choose it. Better one certain unit of benefit than a 10 percent chance of five units; but better a 50 pecent chance of three units than a single certain unit. The same principle applies when we are trying to avoid evils.

The policy of triage involves a certain, very great evil: population control by famine and disease. Tens of millions would die slowly. Hundreds of millions would continue to live in absolute poverty, at the very margin of existence. Against this prospect, advocates of the policy place a possible evil that is greater still: the same process of famine and disease, taking place in, say, fifty years' time, when the world's population may be three times its present level, and the number who will die from famine, or struggle on in absolute poverty, will be that much greater. The question is: how probable is this forecast that continued assistance now will lead to greater disasters in the future?

Forecasts of population growth are notoriously fallible, and theories about the factors that affect it remain speculative. One theory, at least as plausible as any other, is that countries pass through a "demographic transition" as their standard of living rises. When people are very poor and have no access to modern medicine their fertility is high, but population is kept in check by high death rates. The introduction of sanitation, modern medical techniques, and other improvements reduces the death rate, but initially has little effect on the birth rate. Then population grows rapidly. Some poor countries, especially in sub-Saharan Africa, are now in this phase. If standards of living continue to rise, however, couples begin to realize that to have the same number of children surviving to maturity as in the past, they do not need to give birth to as many children as their parents did. The need for children to provide economic support in old age diminishes. Improved education and the emancipation and employment of women also reduce the birthrate, and so population growth begins to level off. Most rich nations have reached this stage, and their populations are growing only very slowly, if at all. If this theory is right, there is an alternative to the disasters accepted as inevitable by supporters of triage. We can assist poor countries to raise the living standards of the poorest members of their population. We can encourage the governments of these countries to enact land reform measures, improve education, and liberate women from a purely child-bearing role. We can also help other countries to make contraception and sterilization widely available. There is a fair chance that these measures will hasten the onset of the demographic transition and bring population growth down to a manageable level. According to United Nations estimates, in 1965 the average woman in the third world gave birth to six children, and only 8 percent were using some form of contraception; by 1991 the average number of children had dropped to just below four, and more than half the women in the third world were taking contraceptive measures. Notable successes in encouraging the use of contraception had occurred in Thailand, Indonesia, Mexico, Colombia, Brazil, and Bangladesh. This achievement reflected a relatively low expenditure in developing countries—considering the size and significance of the problem—of $3 billion annually, with only 20 percent of this sum coming from developed nations. So expenditure in this area seems likely to be highly cost-effective. Success cannot be guaranteed; but the evidence suggests that we can reduce population growth by improving economic security and education, and making contraceptives more widely available. This prospect makes triage ethically unacceptable. We cannot allow millions to die from starvation and disease when there is a reasonable probability that population can be brought under control without such horrors.

Population growth is therefore not a reason against giving overseas aid, although it should make us think about the kind of aid to give. Instead of food handouts, it may be better to give aid that leads to a slowing of population growth. This may mean agricultural assistance for the rural poor, or assistance with education, or the provision of contraceptive services. Whatever kind of aid proves most effective in specific circumstances, the obligation to assist is not reduced. One awkward question remains. What should we do about a poor and already overpopulated country that, for religious or nationalistic reasons, restricts the use of contraceptives and refuses to slow its population growth? Should we nevertheless offer development assistance? Or should we make our offer conditional on effective steps being taken to reduce the birthrate? To the latter course, some would object that putting conditions on aid is an attempt to impose our own ideas on independent sovereign nations. So it is—but is this imposition unjustifiable? If the argument for an obligation to assist is sound, we have an obligation to reduce absolute poverty; but we have no obligation to make sacrifices that, to the best of our knowledge, have no prospect of reducing poverty in the long run. Hence we have no obligation to assist countries whose governments have policies that will make our aid ineffective.

This could be very harsh on poor citizens of these countries—for they may have no say in the government's policies—but we will help more people in the long run by using our resources where they are most effective. (The same principles may apply, incidentally, to countries that refuse to take other steps that could make assistance effective—like refusing to reform systems of land holding that impose intolerable burdens on poor tenant farmers.)

Leaving it to the government.   We often hear that overseas aid should be a government responsibility, not left to privately run charities. Giving privately, it is said, allows the government to escape its responsibilities. Since increasing government aid is the surest way of making a significant increase to the total amount of aid given, I would agree that the governments of affluent nations should give much more genuine, no-strings-attached, aid than they give now. Less than one-sixth of one per cent of GNP is a scandalously small amount for a nation as wealthy as the United States to give. Even the official UN target of 0.7 percent seems much less than affluent nations can and should give—though it is a target few have reached. But is this a reason against each of us giving what we can privately, through voluntary agencies? To believe that it is seems to assume that the more people there are who give through voluntary agencies, the less likely it is that the government will do its part. Is this plausible? The opposite view—that if no one gives voluntarily the government will assume that its citizens are not in favor of overseas aid, and will cut its programme accordingly—is more reasonable. In any case, unless there is a definite probability that by refusing to give we would be helping to bring about an increase in government assistance, refusing to give privately is wrong for the same reason that triage is wrong: it is a refusal to prevent a definite evil for the sake of a very uncertain gain. The onus of showing how a refusal to give privately will make the government give more is on those who refuse to give.

This is not to say that giving privately is enough. Certainly we should campaign for entirely new standards for both public and private overseas aid. We should also work for fairer trading arrangements between rich and poor countries, and less domination of the economies of poor countries by multinational corporations more concerned about producing profits for shareholders back home than food for the local poor. Perhaps it is more important to be politically active in the interests of the poor than to give to them oneself—but why not do both? Unfortunately, many use the view that overseas aid is the government's responsibility as a reason against giving, but not as a reason for being politically active.

Too high a standard?   The final objection to the argument for an obligation to assist is that it sets a standard so high that none but a saint could attain it. This objection comes in at least three versions. The first maintains that, human nature being what it is, we cannot achieve so high a standard, and since it is absurd to say that we ought to do what we cannot do, we must reject the claim that we ought to give so much. The second version asserts that even if we could achieve so high a standard, to do so would be undesirable. The third version of the objection is that to set so high a standard is undesirable because it will be perceived as too difficult to reach, and will discourage many from even attempting to do so.

Those who put forward the first version of the objection are often influenced by the fact that we have evolved from a natural process in which those with a high degree of concern for their own interests, or the interests of their offspring and kin, can be expected to leave more descendants in future generations, and eventually to completely replace any who are entirely altruistic. Thus the biologist Garrett Hardin has argued, in support of his "lifeboat ethics," that altruism can only exist "on a small scale, over the short term, and within small, intimate groups"; while Richard Dawkins has written, in his provocative book *The Selfish Gene:* "Much as we might wish to believe otherwise, universal love and the welfare of the species as a whole are concepts which simply do not make evolutionary sense." I have already noted, in discussing the objection that we should first take care of our own, the very strong tendency for partiality in human beings. We naturally have a stronger desire to further our own interests, and those of our close kin, than we have to further the interests of strangers. What this means is that we would be foolish to expect widespread conformity to a standard that demands impartial concern, and for that reason it would scarcely be appropriate or feasible to condemn all those who fail to reach such a standard. Yet to act impartially, though it might be very difficult, is not impossible. The commonly quoted assertion that "ought" implies "can" is a reason for rejecting such moral judgments as "You ought to have saved all the people from the sinking ship," when in fact if you had taken one more person into the lifeboat, it would have sunk and you would not have saved any. In that situation, it is absurd to say that you ought to have done what you could not possibly do. When we have money to spend on luxuries and others are starving, however, it is clear that we can all give much more than we do give, and we can therefore all come closer to the impartial standard proposed in this chapter. Nor is there, as we approach closer to this standard, any barrier beyond which we cannot go. For that reason there is no basis for saying that the impartial standard is mistaken because "ought" implies "can" and we cannot be impartial.

The second version of the objection has been put by several philosophers during the past decade, among them Susan Wolf in a forceful article entitled "Moral Saints." Wolf argues that if we all took the kind of moral stance defended in this chapter, we would have to do without a great deal that makes life interesting: opera, gourmet cooking, elegant clothes, and professional sport, for a start. The kind of life we come to see as ethically required of us would be a single-minded pursuit of the overall good, lacking that broad diversity of interests and activities that, on a less demanding view, can be part of our ideal of a good life for a human being. To this, however, one can respond that while the rich and varied life that Wolf upholds as an ideal may be the most desirable form of life for a human being in a world of plenty, it is wrong to assume that it remains a good life in a world in which buying luxuries for oneself means accepting the continued avoidable suffering of others. A doctor faced with hundreds of injured victims of a train crash can scarcely think it defensible to treat fifty of them and then go to the opera, on the grounds that going to the opera is part of a well-rounded human life. The life-or-death needs of others must take priority. Perhaps we are like the doctor in that we live in a time when we all have an opportunity to help to mitigate a disaster. Associated with this second version of the objection is the claim that an impartial ethic of the kind advocated here makes it impossible to have serious personal relationships based on love and friendship; these relationships are, of their nature, partial. We put the interests of our loved ones, our family, and our friends ahead of those of strangers; if we did not do so, would these relationships survive? I have already indicated, in the response I gave when considering the objection that we should first take care of our own, that there is a place, within an impartially grounded moral framework, for recognizing some degree of partiality for kin, and the same can be said for other close personal relationships. Clearly, for most people, personal relationships are among the necessities of a flourishing life, and to give them up would be to sacrifice something of great moral significance. Hence no such sacrifice is required by the principle for which I am here arguing.

The third version of the objection asks: might it not be counterproductive to demand that people give up so much? Might not people say: "As I can't do what is morally required anyway, I won't bother to give at all." If, however, we were to set a more realistic standard, people might make a genuine effort to reach it. Thus setting a lower standard might actually result in more aid being given.

It is important to get the status of this third version of the objection clear. Its accuracy as a prediction of human behavior is quite compatible with the argument that we are obliged to give to the point at which by giving more we sacrifice something of comparable moral significance. What would follow from the objection is that public advocacy of this standard of giving is undesirable. It would mean that in order to do the maximum to reduce absolute poverty, we should advocate a standard lower than the amount we think people really ought to give. Of course we ourselves—those of us who accept the original argument, with its higher standard—would know that we ought to do more than we publicly propose people ought to do, and we might actually give more than we urge others to give. There is no inconsistency here, since in both our private and our public behavior we are trying to do what will most reduce absolute poverty.

For a consequentialist, this apparent conflict between public and private morality is always a possibility, and not in itself an indication that the underlying principle is wrong. The consequences of a principle are one thing, the consequences of publicly advocating it another. A variant of this idea is already acknowledged by the distinction between the intuitive and critical levels of morality, of which I have made use in previous chapters. If we think of principles that are suitable for the intuitive level of morality as those that should be generally advocated, these are the principles that, when advocated, will give rise to the best consequences. Where overseas aid is concerned, those will be the principles that lead to the largest amount being given by the affluent to the poor.

Is it true that the standard set by our argument is so high as to be counterproductive? There is not much evidence to go by, but discussions of the argument, with students and others have led me to think it might be. Yet, the conventionally accepted standard—a few coins in a collection tin when one is waved under your nose—is obviously far too low. What level should we advocate? Any figure will be arbitrary, but there may be something to be said for a round percentage of one's income like, say, 10 percent—more than a token donation, yet not so high as to be beyond all but saints. (This figure has the additional advantage of being reminiscent of the ancient tithe, or tenth, that was traditionally given to the church, whose responsibilities included care of the poor in one's local community. Perhaps the idea can be revived and applied to the global community.) Some families, of course, will find 10 percent a considerable strain on their finances. Others may be able to give more without difficulty. No figure should be advocated as a rigid minimum or maximum; but it seems safe to advocate that those earning average or above average incomes in affluent societies, unless they have an unusually large number of dependents or other special needs, ought to give a tenth of their income to reducing absolute poverty. By any reasonable ethical standards this is the minimum we ought to do, and we do wrong if we do less.

Endnotes

1. Strictly, we would need to cut down to the minimum level compatible with earning the income which, after providing for our needs, left us most to give away. Thus if my present position earns me, say, $40,000 a year, but requires me to spend $5,000 a year on dressing respectably and maintaining a car, I cannot save more people by giving away the car and clothes if that will mean taking a job that, although it does not involve me in these expenses, earns me only $20,000.

2. Ominously, in the twelve years that have passed between editions of this book, the signs are that the situation is becoming even worse than was then predicted. In 1979, Bangladesh had a population of 80 million and it was predicted that by 2000 its population would reach 146 million; Ethiopia's was only 29 million, and was predicted to reach 54 million; and India's was 620 million and predicted to reach 958 million.

Journal/Discussion Questions

✍ *In the concluding pages of his essay, Singer deals with the issue of whether his position is too demanding. On a personal level, do you feel that Singer's position places too high a set of expectation on you? Discuss this issue in light of his comments.*

1. Singer maintains that affluent *individuals* as well as affluent societies are obligated to help poor nations. What is the relationship between individual responsibility and collective responsibility? If we as a *nation* have an obligation to poorer nations, does it follow that each of us as *individuals* also has such an obligation? Discuss.

2. Singer considers five possible ways in which killing is morally different from letting die. What are these five possible differences? What reasons does Singer give for claiming that they do not undermine his claim that letting die is the moral equivalent of killing?

3. Singer maintains that "any consequentialist would insist that we are responsible for all the consequences of our actions." Do you think this is true? Can you imagine a situation in which you might not be responsible for all the consequences of your acts, even if those consequences are foreseeable?

4. How does Singer explain that "taking care of our own" argument? Do you think his presentation of the argument puts that argument in its best light? What objections does Singer offer to this argument? Critically assess his objections.

5. What objections does Singer offer to the triage argument—and the related argument about population expansion—advanced by Hardin and others? Critically evaluate his objections.

Hugh LaFollette and Larry May
"Suffer the Little Children"

Hugh LaFollete is a professor of philosophy at East Tennessee State University. He has published widely in the area of ethics, including Personal Relationships: Love, Friendship and Morality *and (with Niall Shanks)* Brute Science: The Dilemmas of Animal Experimentation. *Larry May is a professor of philosophy at Washington University, and his books include* The Morality of Groups, Sharing Responsibility, *and* The Socially Responsible Self.

World Hunger and Morality, Second Edition, edited by William Aiken and Hugh LaFollette (Upper Saddle River, NJ: Prentice-Hall, 1996), pp. 70–84.

When we see pictures of starving children, we want to help. LaFollette and May explore the philosophical foundations of this immediate reaction and argue that "those of us who are in a position to help are responsible to the malnourished and starving children of the world." They consider several counterarguments to their position.

As You Read, Consider This:

1. What are the two characteristics of starving children that account for our initial sense of responsibility toward them?
2. What, according to LaFollette and May, is the purpose of morality?
3. What is the difference between acute need and chronic need? What role does this distinction play in LaFollette and May's argument?

Children are the real victims of world hunger: at least 70 percent of the malnourished people of the world are children. By best estimates forty thousand children a day die of starvation (FAO 1989: 5). Children do not have the ability to forage for themselves and their nutritional needs are exceptionally high. Hence, they are unable to survive for long on their own, especially in lean times. Moreover, they are especially susceptible to diseases and conditions which are the staple of undernourished people: simple infections and simple diarrhea (UNICEF 1993, p. 22). Unless others provide adequate food, water, and care, children will suffer and die (WHO 1974, 677, 679). This fact must frame any moral discussions of the problem.

And so it does—at least pre-philosophically. When most of us first see pictures of seriously undernourished children, we want to help them, we have a sense of responsibility to them, we feel sympathy toward them (Hume 1978: 368–71). Even those who think we needn't or shouldn't help the starving take this initial response seriously: they go to great pains to show that this sympathetic response should be constrained. They typically claim that assisting the hungry will demand too much of us, or that assistance would be useless and probably detrimental. The efforts of objectors to undermine this natural sympathetic reaction would be pointless unless they saw its psychological force.

We want to explain and bolster this sympathetic reaction—this conviction that those of us in a position to help are responsible to the malnourished and starving children of the world. We contend that we have this responsibility to starving children unless there are compelling reasons which show that this sympathetic reaction is morally inappropriate (Ibid.: 582). This requires, among other things, that we seek some "steady and general point of view" from which to rebut standard attempts to explain away this instinctive sympathetic response. By showing that assistance is neither too demanding nor futile, we think more people will be more inclined to act upon that pre-philosophical sense of responsibility. And, by philosophically championing that sense of responsibility, we will make most people feel more justified in so acting.

Vulnerability and Innocence

Our initial sense of responsibility to the starving and malnourished children of the world is intricately tied to their being paradigmatically vulnerable and innocent. They are paradigmatically vulnerable because they do not have the wherewithal to care for themselves; they must rely on others to care for them. All children are directly dependent on their parents or guardians, while children whose parents cannot provide them food—either because of famine or economic arrangements—are also indirectly dependent on others: relief agencies or (their own or foreign) governments. Children are paradigmatically innocent since they are neither causally nor morally responsible for their plight. They did not cause drought, parched land, soil erosion, and over-population; nor are they responsible for social, political, and economic arrangements which make it more difficult for their parents to obtain food. If anyone were ever an innocent victim, the children who suffer and die from hunger are.

Infants are especially vulnerable. They temporarily lack the capacities which would empower them to acquire the necessities of life. Thus, they are completely dependent on others for sustenance. This partly explains our urge to help infants in need. James Q. Wilson claims that our instinctive reaction to the cry of a newborn child is demonstrated quite early in life.

As early as ten months of age, toddlers react visibly to signs of distress in others, often becoming agitated; when they are one and a half years old they seek to do something to alleviate the other's distress; by the time they are two years old they verbally sympathize . . . and look for help (Wilson 1993: 139–140).

Although this response may be partly explained by early training, available evidence suggests that humans have an "innate sensitivity to the feelings of others" (Wilson 1993: 140). Indeed, Hans Jonas claims the parent-child relationship is the "archetype of responsibility," where the cry of the newborn baby is an ontic imperative "in which the plain factual 'is' evidently coincides with an 'ought'" (1983: 30).

This urge to respond to the infant in need is, we think, the appropriate starting point for discussion. But we should also explain how this natural response generates or is somehow connected to moral responsibility.

The Purpose of Morality

The focus of everyday moral discussion about world hunger is on the children who are its victims. Yet the centrality of children is often lost in more abstract debates about rights, obligations, duties, development, and governmental sovereignty. We do not want to belittle either the cogency or the conclusions of those arguments. Rather, we propose a different way of conceptualizing this problem. Although it may be intellectually satisfying to determine whether children have a right to be fed or whether we have an obligation to assist them, if those arguments do not move us to action, then it is of little use—at least to the children in need. So we are especially interested in philosophical arguments which are more likely to motivate people to act. We think arguments which keep the spotlight on starving children are more likely to have that effect.

Moreover, by thinking about hunger in these ways we can better understand and respond to those who claim we have no obligation to assist the starving. For we suspect that when all the rhetoric of rights, obligations, and population control are swept away, what most objectors fear is that asking people to assist the starving and undernourished is to ask too much. Morality or no, people are unlikely to act in ways they think require them to substantially sacrifice their personal interests. Thus, as long as most people think helping others demands too much, they are unlikely to provide help.

John Arthur's critique of Peter Singer highlights just this concern. Arthur objects to moral rules which require people to abandon important things to which they have a right.

> Rights or entitlements to things that are our own reflect important facts about people. Each of us has only one life and it is uniquely valuable to each of us. Your choices do not constitute my life, nor do mine

yours. . . . It seems, then, that in determining whether to give aid to starving persons . . . [agents must assign] special weight to their own interests (1977: 43).

Thus, people need not assist others if it requires abandoning something of substantial moral significance. Since what we mean by "substantial moral significance" has an ineliminable subjective element (Ibid.: 47), some individuals may conclude that sending *any* money to feed the starving children would be to ask too much of them. Arthur thereby captures a significant element of most people's worries about assisting the needy. The concern for our own projects and interests is thought to justify completely repressing, or at least constraining, our natural sympathies for children in need.

At bottom, we suspect that what is at issue is the proper conception and scope of morality. Some philosophers have argued that morality should not be exceedingly demanding; indeed, one of the stock criticisms of utilitarianism is that it is far too demanding. On the other hand, some theorists, including more than a few utilitarians, have bitten the proverbial bullet and claimed that morality is indeed demanding, and that its demandingness in no way counts against its cogency (Parfit, 1984; Kegan, 1988). On the former view, morality should set expectations which all but the most weak-willed and self-centered person can satisfy; on the latter view, morality makes demands which are beyond the reach of most, if not all, of us.

We wish to take the middle ground and suggest that morality is a delicate balancing act between Milquetoast expectations which merely sanctify what people already do, and expectations which are *excessively* demanding and, thus, are psychologically impossible—or at least highly improbable. Our view is that the purpose of morality is not to establish an edifice which people fear, but to set expectations which are likely to improve us, and—more relevant to the current issue—to improve the lot of those we might assist. Morality would thus be like any goals which enable us to grow and mature: they must be within reach, yet not easily reachable (LaFollette 1989: 503–6). Of course, what is within reach changes over time; and what is psychologically probable depends, in no small measure, on our beliefs about what is morally expected of us. So by expecting ourselves to do more and to be more than we currently do and are, we effectively stimulate ourselves to grow and improve. But all that is part of the balancing act of which we speak.

Thus, we frame the moral question in the following way: what should responsible people do? Our initial sympathetic response is to help the starving children. Are there any compelling reasons to think our compassion should, from some "steady and general point of view," be squelched? We think the answer is "No." Are there additional reasons which bolster this initial reaction? We think the answer is "Yes." In short, we think our initial conviction that we are responsible to malnourished children is not only undefeated, it is also rationally justified.

Moral Responsibility

We "instinctively" respond to the needs of starving and malnourished children. But are we, in fact, morally responsible for their plight? There are, of course, two different questions intermingled here: (1) Are we *causally* responsible *for* their condition—did we, individually or collectively, cause their hunger or create the environment which made their hunger and malnourishment more likely? (2) Are we *morally* responsible *to* these children, whether or not we are causally responsible for the conditions which make them hungry?

It is a commonplace of moral argument that people are morally responsible to those to whom they cause harm. If I run a stoplight and hit your auto, then I must pay any medical bills and either repair or replace your auto. If I trip you, causing you to break your arm, then I am expected to carry any resulting financial burden. The principle here is that we should respond to those whose cry for help results from our actions. If others are contributing causes to the harm, we may be jointly responsible to you (Hart and Honore 1959: 188–229). Or, if my action was itself caused by the actions of some other agent—e.g., if someone shoved me into you—then this other person is both causally and morally responsible for the harm. But, barring such conditions, a person is morally responsible for harms he or she causes.

Some commentators have argued that the affluent nations, especially colonial powers, are morally responsible to the starving because they created the conditions which make world-wide starvation possible, and perhaps inevitable (O'Neill 1993: 263–4). We find such claims plausible. But, such claims, although plausible, are contentious. Hence, for purposes of argument, we will assume that we in affluent nations are in no way causally responsible for the plight of the starving. If we can show we are (morally) responsible to the children, even if we are not (causally) responsible for their plight, then our responsibility to them will be all the stronger if, as we suspect, these causal claims are true.

Shared Responsibility

If we are the cause of harm, then we are responsible *to* the "victim" because we are responsible *for* their condition. For instance, we assume biological parents have *some* responsibility *to* children because they were responsible *for* bringing them into the world. However, being the cause of harm is not the only condition which creates a responsibility *to* someone. We are also responsible to those whom we have explicitly agreed or promised to help. For instance, by assuming a job as a lifeguard, I have agreed to care for those who swim at my beach or pool, even if they, through lack of care or foresight, put themselves into jeopardy.

More important for the current argument, responsibilities also arise from actions which, although not explicit agreements, nonetheless create reasonable expectations of care. For example, although *some* of the parents responsibilities to their children is explained by their being the cause of the children's existence, this clearly does explain the full *range* of parental responsibilities. For even when an agent is indisputably responsible *for* the harm to another, we would *never* think the agent is obliged to change the "victim's" soiled pants, to hold her at night when she is sick, or to listen patiently as she recounts her afternoon's activities. Yet we *do* expect this—and much more—of parents.

Our ordinary understanding of parental responsibilities makes no attempt to ground specific responsibilities *to* the child on any causal claims about the parents' responsibility *for* the child's condition. Rather, this understanding focuses on the needs of the child, and the fact that the parents are in the best position to respond to those needs. This is exactly where the focus should be.

Although for any number of reasons these responsibilities typically fall to the child's biological parents, the responsibilities are not limited to the parents. Others of us (individually or collectively) have a responsibility to care for children whose parents die or abandon them. It matters not that we neither brought these children into the world nor did we voluntarily agree to care for them. Rather, as responsible people we should care for children in need, especially since they are paradigmatically vulnerable and innocent. This is our natural sympathetic reaction. "No quality of human nature is more remarkable, both in itself and in its consequences, than the propensity we have to sympathize with others" (Hume 1978: 316).

This helps explain our shared moral responsibility to care for children who are not being cared for by their parents. Since the range of parental responsibilities cannot be explained either by the parents' being the cause of the child's existence or by their explicitly agreeing to care for the child, it should not be surprising that our shared responsibility likewise does not depend on an explicit agreement or an implicit assumption of responsibility. We assume responsible people will, in fact, care for abandoned children. This shared responsibility springs from our common vulnerability and from our ability to respond to others who are similarly situated.

Acute Need

Until now we have spoken as if all starvation and malnutrition were created equal. They are not. The hunger with which we are most familiar—the hunger whose images often appear on our television sets—is hunger caused by famine. And famines tend to be episodic; often they are unpredictable. An extended drought or a devastating flood may destroy crops in a region, so that the people of that region can no longer feed themselves. (Or, as is more often the case, these environmental catastrophes may not destroy all crops, but primarily that portion of the crop which is used to feed the local population; crops used for export may be protected in some way.) In these cases the problem may emerge quickly and, with some assistance, may disappear quickly. Such need is acute.

The nature of our responsibility to the starving arguably depends on the nature of their need. Peter Singer offers a vivid example of acute need and claims his example shows we have a serious moral obligation to relieve world starvation.

> If I am walking past a shallow pond and see a child drowning in it, I ought to wade in and pull the child out. That will mean getting my clothes muddy, but this is insignificant when the death of the child would presumably be a very bad thing. (1971: 231)

This case, Singer claims, illustrates the intuitive appeal of the following moral principle: "if it is in our power to prevent something bad from happening, without thereby sacrificing something of comparable moral importance, we ought, morally, to do it." In the case in question, this is sage moral advice. If muddying my clothes saves the life of an innocent child, then it is time for me to send the cleaners some additional business.

Singer's example vividly illustrates our fundamental moral responsibility to meet acute need, especially the acute need of children—those who are paradigmatically vulnerable and innocent. In Singer's example, the child is in immediate danger; with relatively little effort we can remove her from danger. As we argued earlier, we have a shared moral responsibility which arises from our common vulnerability. None of us has complete control over our lives. All of us are vulnerable to circumstances beyond our control: floods, hurricanes, droughts, etc. Through no fault of our own, our lives and welfare may be jeopardized. Admittedly some acute need results from our ignorance or stupidity. Even so, others should assist us when feasible, at least if the cost to them is slight. After all, even the most careful person occasionally makes mistakes. When need is caused by natural disaster or personal error, we each want others to come to our aid. Indeed, we think they *should* come to our aid. If, upon reflection, our desire for assistance is reasonable when *we* are in need, then, by extension, we should acknowledge that we should help others in similar need. Shared responsibility and sympathy conspire to create the sense that we should go to the aid of those who cannot alleviate their own acute needs.

Although we are here emphasizing responsibility rather than justice (narrowly defined), it is noteworthy that the conditions which generate responsibility to help others in acute need resemble the conditions Hume cites as generating our sense of justice: *". . .'tis only from selfishness and confin'd generosity of man, along with the scanty provision nature has made for his wants, that justice derives its origin"* (1978: 495; emphasis his). Our common vulnerability to circumstances and to the "scanty provision nature has made" leads us to seek ways to protect ourselves against misfortune and error. Natural disasters occur. They may occur where I live; they may not. Prudent people will recognize that we are all more secure, and thus, better off, if we recognize a shared responsibility to assist others in acute need.

As we have suggested throughout this essay, this responsibility is all the more apparent when those in need cannot care for themselves and are in no way responsible for their plight. In short, the responsibility is greatest (and less contentious) when children are the victims. In fact, when children are in acute need, especially when many are in a position to help, there's little moral difference between the responsibility of biological parents and others. If a child is drowning, then even if the parents (or some third party) tossed the child into the pond (and are thus singularly responsible for the child's plight), we should still rescue her if we can. Likewise, if a child is starving, and her need is acute, then even if the child's parents and its government have acted irresponsibly, we should still feed the child if we can.

Arguably the problem is different if the acute need is so substantial and so widespread as to require us to make considerable sacrifices to help those in need. In this case our responsibilities to the children in acute need may resemble our responsibilities to children in chronic need.

Chronic Need

Acute need arises once (or at least relatively infrequently). It requires immediate action, which, if successful, often alleviates the need. But most hunger is not acute, it is chronic. Chronic hunger is the hunger of persistently malnourished children, where the causes of hunger are neither episodic nor easily removed. If the need can be met at all, it can be met only through more substantial, sustained effort, and often only by making numerous (and perhaps fundamental) institutional changes, both within our countries, and the other countries in need of aid.

That is why Singer's case is disanalogous with most world hunger. The drowning child is in acute need. Suppose, however, that Singer's fictional child lives on the edge of a pond where she is relatively unsupervised. We cannot protect this child by simply dirtying our clothes once. Rather, we must camp on the pond's edge, poised to rescue her whenever she falls or slips into the water. However, can we reasonably expect anyone to devote her entire life (or even the next six years) as this child's lifeguard? It is difficult to see how. The expectation seems even less appropriate if there are many children living beside the pond.

Likely the only sensible way to protect the child from harm is to relocate her away from the pond. Or perhaps we could teach her to swim. But are we responsible to make these efforts? Do we have the authority to forcibly relocate the child or to erect an impregnable fence around the pond? Can we *require* her to take swimming lessons? Can we *force* her government to make substantial internal economic and political changes? In short, even though we are morally responsible to assist those in acute need (and especially children), we cannot straightforwardly infer that we must assist those (even children) in chronic need.

For instance, if we try to save a child from famine, we may have reason to think that quick action will yield substantial results. Not so with chronic hunger. Since we are less likely to see the fruits of our efforts, we may be less motivated to assist. Moreover, some have argued that we can alleviate chronic need only if we exert enormous effort, over a long period of time. If so, expecting someone to respond to chronic need arguably burdens her unduly. Responsible people need not spend all their time and resources helping those in chronic need, especially if there is only a small chance of success. This is surely the insight in Arthur's view.

Consider the following analogy which illuminates that insight. Suppose an adult builds a house by the side of a river that floods every few years. After the first flood we may help them, thinking we should respond to someone who appears to be in acute need. However, after the second or third flood, we will feel it is asking too much of us to continue to help. We would probably conclude that this adult has intentionally chosen a risky lifestyle. They have made their own bed; now they must sleep in it. Although this case may well be disanalogous to the plight of starving adults—since most have little control over the weather, soil erosion, or governmental policy—nonetheless, many people in affluent nations think it is analogous.

What is indisputable, however, is the case is totally disanalogous to the plight of children. Children did not choose to live in an economically deprived country or in a country with a corrupt government. Nor can they abandon their parents and relocate in a land of plenty, or in a democratic regime. Hence, they are completely innocent—in no sense did they cause their own predicament. Moreover, they are paradigms of vulnerability.

Since they are the principal victims of chronic malnutrition, it is inappropriate to refuse to help them unless someone can show that assisting them would require an unacceptable sacrifice. That, of course, demands that we draw a line between reasonable and unreasonable sacrifice. We do not know how to draw that line. Perhaps, though, before drawing the line we should ask: if it were our child who was starving, where would we want the line to be drawn?

A Dose of Reality

Evidence suggests, however, that this whole line of inquiry is beside the point. Although it would be theoretically interesting to determine how to draw the line between reasonable and unreasonable sacrifices, this is not a determination we need make when discussing world hunger. Doomsayers like Garrett Hardin claim we have long-since crossed that line: that feeding starving children requires more than we can reasonably expect even highly responsible people to do; indeed, Hardin claims such assistance is effectively suicide (1974; reprinted here). However, the doomsayers are mistaken. Current efforts to alleviate hunger have been far short of efforts which would require a substantial sacrifice from any of us. Nonetheless, even these relatively measly efforts have made a noticeable dent in the problem of world hunger. And these successes have been achieved with smaller than anticipated growth in population. According to the FAO:

> The number of chronically undernourished people in developing countries with populations exceeding 1 million is estimated at 786 million for 1988–90, reflecting a decline from 941 million in 1969–71 and a lowering of their proportion of the population from 36 to 20 percent . . ." (FAO 1992b: 1)
>
> During the same period, the average number of calories consumed per person per day went from 2430 to 2700—more than a 10 percent increase. (FAO 1992b: 3)

Since the relatively meager efforts to assist the starving has made a noticeable dent in the incidence of world hunger, then, although enormous problems clearly remain, we have good reason to think that heightened efforts—efforts still *far* short of those requiring substantial sacrifices from the affluent—could seriously curtail, if not completely eliminate, world starvation. If so, we do not need to decide where the line should be drawn. We are still some distance from that line. Put differently, many of the world's poor are not like the unsupervised child who lives on the side of the lake. Even though their need may be chronic, their needs can be met short of the enormous efforts that would require us to camp next to the pond for the remainder of our days. To that extent, our responsibility to chronically starving children is, despite first appearances, similar to our responsibility to children in acute need.

How to Act Responsibly

Many people are already motivated to help others (and especially children) in need. Indeed, this helps explain the influence and appeal of Singer's essay more than two decades after its publication. Thus, the claim that we have a shared responsibility to meet the needs of others in acute need is psychologically plausible. Even so, it is often difficult to motivate people to respond to others in chronic need. Many in affluent nations feel or fear that aid just won't do anything more than line the pockets of charitable organizations or corrupt governments. Doubtless some money sent for aid does not reach its intended source. But that may simply reflect our inability to determine which relief agencies are most effective. Moreover, even if some aid does not reach those in need, it is even more obvious that most relief aid *does* reach its desired target. That is what the statistics cited in the last section demonstrate.

We suspect that the strongest barrier to helping those in chronic need is more psychological than philosophical: most people just don't feel any connection with someone starving half-way around the world (or, for that matter, in the ghetto across town). As Hume noted, most of us do tend to feel more sympathy for what we see than for what we do not see. This at least partly explains why many of us are less willing to help starving children in foreign lands—we don't see them, and thus, don't feel a tie or connection to them. As we have argued through the paper, this is the core insight in Arthur's view: moral obligations which require us to abandon what is important to us, especially in the absence of some connection with those in need, will rarely be met by many people—and thus, will make no moral difference. Someone might argue, on more abstract philosophical grounds, that we should not need that link. Perhaps that is true. But, whether we should need to feel this connection, the fact is, most people do need it. And our concern in this paper is how to help meet the needs of the children. Thus, we want to know what will *actually* motivate people to act.

Of course, just as we should not take our initial sense of responsibility *to* children as *determining* our moral obligations, neither should we put too much weight on the unanalyzed notion of "normal ties." Doing so ignores ways in which our moral feelings can be shaped for good and for ill. So perhaps the better question is not whether we have such feelings, but whether we could cultivate them in ourselves and perhaps all humanity, and, if so, whether that would be appropriate. We suspect, though, that many of us cannot develop a sense of shared responsibility for *every* person in need. More likely we must rely on a more limited sense of shared responsibility; certainly that is not beyond the psychological reach of most of us. Indeed, it is already present in many of us. Thus, working to cultivate this sense of responsibility in ourselves and others would increase the likelihood that we could curtail starvation.

Since people have a natural sympathetic response to the cry of children, the best way to cultivate this connection is to keep people focused on children as the real victims of starvation and malnutrition. If we keep this fact firmly in the fore of our minds, we are more likely, individually and collectively to feel and act upon this sense of shared responsibility.

But even if we acknowledge this responsibility, how should we meet it? Should we provide food directly? Perhaps sometimes. But this direct approach will not solve chronic starvation. More likely we should empower the children's primary caretakers so they can feed and care for their children. To this extent our shared responsibility to hungry children is mediated by the choices and actions of others. Thus, it might be best conceptualized as akin to (although obviously not exactly like) our responsibility to provide education. Our responsibility is not to ensure that each child receives an education (although we will be bothered if a child "slips through the cracks"). Rather, our responsibility is to establish institutions which make it more likely that all will be educated. By analogy, since it is virtually impossible to feed children directly, our responsibility is not to particular children, but a responsibility to change the circumstances which make starvation likely.

Changing those circumstances might occasionally require that we be a bit heavy-handed. Perhaps such heavy-handedness is unavoidable if we wish to achieve the desired results. OXFAM, for example, provides aid to empower people in lands prone to famine and malnutrition to feed themselves and their children. If the recipients do not use the aid wisely, then OXFAM will be less likely to provide aid again. This is only a bit Draconian, but perhaps not so much as to be morally objectionable.

Conclusion

In both cases of chronic and acute need, we must remember the children who are the real victims of world hunger. The suffering child is paradigmatically vulnerable and innocent. Since we can, without serious damage to our relatively affluent lifestyles, aid these children, we should help. We share a responsibility *to* them because we are well-placed to help them, and because we can do so without substantially sacrificing our own interests. This is so even if we in *no way* caused or sustained the conditions which make their hunger likely.

However, if the stronger claim that we *caused* their starvation (or created the conditions which made their starvation more likely) can be defended—as we think it probably can—this responsibility becomes a stronger imperative. Thus, if the views of Sen, Crocker, and others are correct—and we suspect they are—then most of our responsibility is to cease supporting national and international institutions which cause and sustain conditions which make hunger likely. And *this* responsibility could be explained much more simply as a responsibility to not harm others.[1]

Endnote

1. We wish to thank William Aiken, John Hardwig, and Carl Wellman for helpful comments on earlier drafts of this paper.

References

Aiken, William and LaFollette, Hugh. *World Hunger and Morality.* 2nd ed. (Englewood Cliffs, NJ: Prentice Hall, 1996).

Arthur, J. "Rights and the Duty to Bring Aid." In W. Aiken and H. LaFollette, *World Hunger and Moral Obligation* (Englewood Cliffs, NJ: Prentice Hall, 1977).

Brown, L. *The State of the World 1994: A World Watch Institute Report on Progress Toward a Sustainable Society* (New York: W.W. Norton, 1994).

—. *In the Human Interest* (New York: W.W. Norton, 1974).

Food and Agricultural Organization (FAO) *World Food Supplies and Prevalence of Chronic Undernutrition in Developing Regions as Assessed in 1992.* (Rome: FAO Press, 1992).

—. FAO News Release. (Rome: FAO Press, 1992).

—. *World Hunger.* (Rome: FAO Press, 1989).

Hardin, G. *Exploring a New Ethics for Survival* (New York: Penguin, 1975).

—. "Lifeboat Ethics: The Case Against Helping the Poor." *Psychology Today,* 8: 38–43, 123–6.

Hart, H. and Honore, A. *Causation in the Law* (Oxford: Oxford University Press, 1959).

Hume, D. *A Treatise of Human Nature,* L.A. Selby-Bigge (ed.) (Oxford: Oxford University Press, 1976).

Jonas, H. *The Imperative of Responsibility* (Chicago: University of Chicago Press, 1984).

Kegan, S. *The Limits of Morality* (Oxford: Oxford University Press, 1988).

LaFollette, H. "The Truth in Psychological Egoism." In J. Feinberg (ed.), *Reason and Responsibility* (Belmont, CA: Wadsworth, 1989).

May, L. 1996: *Socially Responsible Self,* forthcoming.

—. *Sharing Responsibility* (Chicago: University of Chicago Press, 1992).

Mesarovic, M. and Pestel, E. *Mankind at the Turning Point* (New York: Signet Books, 1974).

O'Neill, O. "Ending World Hunger." In T. Regan (ed.), *Matters of Life and Death* (New York: McGraw Hill, 1993).

Parfit, D. *Reasons and Persons* (Oxford: Oxford University Press, 1984).

Singer, P. "Famine, Affluence, and Morality." *Philosophy and Public Affairs,* 1: 229–43.

United Nations Children's Fund (UNICEF) *The State of the World's Children 1993* (Oxford: Oxford University Press, 1993).

Wilson, J. *The Moral Sense* (New York: The Free Press, 1993).

World Health Organization (WHO) *Health Statistics Report* (Geneva: World Health Organization, 1974).

Journal/Discussion Questions

✎ *All of us have seen posters of starving children? How do you react to these pictures? What moral significance do they have?*

   Do you agree with LaFollette and May's analysis?

1. Peter Singer introduces the example of the drowning child. What criticisms do LaFollette and May offer of this example? Do you agree with their critique of Singer?

2. How do chronic need and acute need differ from one another? Which is more common in world hunger? What moral implications do LaFollette and May draw from this distinction?

3. What criticisms do LaFollette and May offer of Hardin's lifeboat ethics? Do you agree with their assessment of Hardin's position? Discuss.

Concluding Discussion Questions

Where Do You Stand Now?

Instructions

You have already answered the following questions in your moral problems self-quiz at the beginning of this book. Now that you have studied the material in this section, take a moment to answer the same questions again.

	Strongly Agree	*Agree*	*Undecided*	*Disagree*	*Strongly Disagree*	*Chapter 9: World Hunger and Poverty*
41.	❏	❏	❏	❏	❏	Only the morally heartless would refuse to help the starving.
42.	❏	❏	❏	❏	❏	We should help starving nations until we are as poor as they are.
43.	❏	❏	❏	❏	❏	In the long run, relief aid to starving nations does not help them.
44.	❏	❏	❏	❏	❏	Overpopulation is the main cause of world hunger and poverty.
45.	❏	❏	❏	❏	❏	The world is gradually becoming a better place.

Compare your answers to this self-quiz with the answers to the initial self-quiz. How, if at all, have your answers changed? How have the *reasons* for your answers changed?

Journal/Discussion Questions

✍ *Let's return to rock-bottom experiences. We are left with the fact that there are people throughout the world who are starving to death, slowly and painfully. We are—at least as a nation, and at least comparatively as individuals—affluent. How do you re-* spond as a compassionate human being to the fact of such suffering?

1. Imagine that you have been asked to address the Annual Convention of Ethical Egoists (ACEE) on the issue of world hunger. What could you say about world

hunger to those who believe that their only moral duty is to promote their own welfare?

2. Imagine that you have been asked to address the annual convention of compassionate persons on the issue of world hunger and the *dangers* of compassion. What would you have to say to this audience of compassionate people about the dangers and pitfalls of compassionate responses to world hunger?

3. Imagine that you have been asked by the president of the United States to draft a policy statement on the question of how the United States should respond to world hunger. What main elements would it contain?

For Further Reading

Web Resources

The World Hunger and Poverty page of *Ethics Updates* (http://ethics.sandiego.edu) contains numerous online resources relating to poverty and world hunger. In addition to extensive statistical information and a PowerPoint presentation on World Hunger, this page includes links to online texts by Amartya Sen and others, as well as RealVideo lectures by Amartya Sen, Oscar Arias, and the 2004 APA Mini-Conference on Global Justice.

Journals

In addition to the standard ethics journals mentioned in the bibliographical essay at the end of Chapter 1, also see the journals *Ethics and International Affairs* and *World Development.*

Review Articles

For excellent, very recent introductions to the issues of world hunger, see Hugh LaFollette, "World Hunger," *A Companion to Applied Ethics: Blackwell Companions to Philosophy,* edited by R. G. Frey (Malden, MA: Blackwell Publishing, 2003), pp. 238–253 and Nigel Dower, "World Hunger," *The Oxford Handbook of Practical Ethics,* edited by Hugh LaFollette (Oxford England: Oxford University Press, 2003), pp. 643–659. Nigel Dower's "World Poverty" in *A Companion to Ethics,* edited by Peter Singer (Cambridge England: Blackwell, 1991), surveys the literature and argues "for a moderate but significant duty of caring in response to the evils of extreme poverty." Onora O'Neill, "International Justice: Distribution," *Encyclopedia of Ethics,* edited by Lawrence C. Becker and Charlotte B. Becker (New York: Garland, 1992), Vol. I, pp. 624–628 provides an insightful and nuanced discussion of the issues of distributive justice, especially insofar as they relate to world hunger.

Reports

Several reports on the state of the world have helped to share the international discussion of these issues. The Unicef report, *The State of the World's Children 2004* (http://www.unicef.org/sowc04/) is one of the most recent. Also see the excellent Worldwatch Institute Reports on Progress Toward a Sustainable Society, *State of the World 2004* (New York: W.W. Norton, 2004) and Lester Brown's *Plan B* (New York: W.W. Norton, 2003). For a contrasting view, see Bjorn Lomborg, *The Skeptical Environmentalist: Measuring the Real State of the World* (Cambridge, England: Cambridge University Press, 2001).

Among the popular books that have been influential in this discussion, see Albert Gore, *Earth in the Balance: Ecology and the Human Spirit* (Boston: Houghton Mifflin: 1992). Frances Moore Lappe and Joseph Collins, *Food First: Beyond the Myth of Scarcity,* revised and updated (New

York: Ballantine Books, 1978) and also their *World Hunger: Twelve* Myth, 2nd ed. (New York: Grove Press, 1998). For a much more optimistic view, see Julian Simon, *The Ultimate Resource* (Princeton, NJ: Princeton University Press, 1981) and Julian Simon and Herman Kahn, *The Resourceful Earth* (Oxford, England: Blackwell, 1984).

Anthologies

Several valuable anthologies are available. William Aiken and Hugh LaFollette's *World Hunger and Moral Obligation,* 2nd ed. (Englewood Cliffs, NJ: Prentice Hall, 1996) contains all the classic papers and a number of excellent recent articles; see especially the pieces by Hardin, Singer, Arthur, Narveson, Slote, and O'Neill; if you read just one book on world hunger, this should be it. *International Justice and the Third World,* edited by Robin Attfield and Barry Wilkins (New York: Routledge, 1992) contains eight papers discussing notions of global justice and its implications for the Third World; the papers also relate Third World development to sustainability, issues of gender, environmentalism, and Third World debt.

Responses to Hardin

Garrett Hardin's "Lifeboat Ethics" (and relate versions of the same piece) stirred extensive discussion. A number of the articles in Aiken and LaFollette, *World Hunger and Moral Obligation,* respond to Hardin; see especially Onora O'Neill's "Lifeboat Earth" in this collection. Also see some of the articles in *Problems of International Justice,* especially Onora O'Neill's "Hunger, Needs, and Rights" and William Aiken's "World Hunger, Benevolence, and Justice." Robert Coburn's "On Feeding the Hungry," *Journal of Social Philosophy,* Vol. 7 (Spring 1976), pp. 11–16, and Daniel Callahan's "Garrett Hardin's 'Lifeboat Ethic,'" *Hastings Center Report,* Vol. 4 (December 1974), pp. 1–4, both strongly criticize Hardin's position.

General Defenses of the Duty to Aid Poor and Starving Nations

Peter Singer, *One World: The Ethics of Globalization* (New Haven, CT: Yale University Press, 2002), deals with poverty and world hunger especially in Chapter 5; Thomas Pogge, *World Poverty and Human Rights: Cosmopolitan Responsibilities and Reforms* (Cambridge: Polity Press, 2002); Thomas Pogge, ed. (Global Justice (Malden, MA: Blackwell, 2002); Pablo DeGreiff and Ciaran P. Cronin, eds., *Global Justice and Transnational Politics* (Boston: MIT Press, 2002); David Leslie Miller and Sohail H. Hashmi, eds., *Boundaries and Justice: Diverse Ethical Perspectives* (Princeton, NJ: Princeton University Press, 2001); Darrel Moellendorf, *Cosmopolitan Justice* (Boulder, CO: Westview Press, 2002). Henry Shue, *Basic Rights: Subsistence, Affluence, and U.S. Foreign Policy,* 2nd ed. (Princeton, NJ: Princeton University Press, 1996), offers a strong conceptual foundation for positive basic rights; also see his anthology (co-edited with Peter G. Brown), *Food Policy* (New York: The Free Press, 1977). Peter Unger's *Living High and Letting Die: Our Illusion of Innocence* (New York: Oxford, 1996) offers a strong case for much greater responsibility toward impoverished peoples. Robert Goodin's *Protecting the Vulnerable* (Chicago: University of Chicago Press, 1986) is very carefully argued. Nicholas Dower, in *What Is Development? A Philosopher's Answer* (Glasgow

University Centre for Development Studies: Occasional Paper Series No. 3, 1988) argues for significant but not overpowering obligation to aid poor nations. Onora O'Neill's *Faces of Hunger* (London: Allen & Unwin, 1986) derives the obligation to aid from people's right not to be killed. Amartya Sen, *Poverty and Famines: An Essay on Entitlement and Deprivation* (New York: Oxford University Press, 1981) stresses the way in which famines are rarely due to natural causes alone; also see Jean Drèze and Amartya Sen, *Hunger and Public Action* (Oxford, England: Clarendon Press, 1989).

Arguments Against the Duty to Aid

Jennifer Trusted, "The Problem of Absolute Poverty," in *The Environment in Question: Ethics and Global Issues,* edited by David E. Cooper (New York: Routledge, 1992), pp. 13–27, discusses the obligations of individuals in affluent countries to the Third World, arguing that there can be no duty of general beneficence and that it is not wrong to favor those who are near and dear to us. James S. Fishkin, *The Limits of Obligation* (New Haven: Yale University Press, 1982), especially Chapter 9: The Famine Review Argument, on the limits of the obligations of rich nations to poor ones. Ruth Lucier, "Policies For Hunger Relief: Moral Considerations" in *Inquiries into Values,* edited by Sander H. Lee (Lewiston: Mellen Press), pp. 477–493 suggests that food aid has moral ramifications stemming from present limitations on the aid available for distribution.

CHAPTER 10

Living Together with Animals

Narrative Account

Robert B. White
"Beastly Questions"

Robert B. White, a physician, chronicles his own personal experiences with the benefits of research involving animals.

We wept and watched, my wife and I, as a little girl fought for her life. She was tiny, frail, helpless, and so very vulnerable. Motionless except as her chest rose and fell spasmodically, there lay Lauren, our first grandchild, born so prematurely that each breath was a desperate and failing effort. We wept, our hearts torn by the growing realization that Lauren might not live. The next day she died. The best care that medicine could offer was not enough. The research on baby lambs and kittens that has given life to many premature infants such as Lauren was still in the future and would come too late for her.

In time, two grandsons, Jonathan and Bryan, were born. Premature babies, they also had to struggle for life. Our pain of uncertainty and of waiting was all to be endured twice again. But the little boys lived. The knowledge gained through research on lambs and kittens gave them life, a gift that Lauren could not have.

The memories of despair and grief at the death of one grandchild and of relief and hope and joy at the life of two others, all of these memories came back to me as I sat at my desk preparing to write this essay in defense of the moral and scientific necessity for the use of animals in medical research. And as I thought of the numerous advances in medical care that would have been impossible without experiments on cats and sheep and baby lambs, on dogs and pigs and monkeys and mice, on cows and horses and even armadillos, as I thought of all these advances in medical care that have given health and life to countless people, including my grandsons, my mind was flooded by a host of memories.

First was the memory of an esteemed colleague whose recovery from a near-fatal heart attack was made possible by the use of a newly discovered enzyme that dissolved the clot that fouled his arteries. Later he was restored to nearly perfect health by a coronary arteriogram and a percutaneous transluminal coronary angioplasty. He owes his life to scores of dogs on whom the studies were done to perfect the use of streptokinase, the enzyme that was used to dissolve the clotted blood from his coronary arteries. And he also owes his life to yet other dogs on whom the techniques of coronary arteriography and angioplasty were developed and perfected.

Another colleague whom I recently saw at a medical meeting came next to mind. He had developed disabling arthritis of one hip, but now was able to walk again, thanks to the surgical replacement of his crippled joint. He now walks with a limp, but he walks—only because of dogs that were operated on in the course of research that developed and perfected the artificial hip.

Hastings Center Report (March/April 1989):39–40.

One memory evoked another and then another and then another. I recalled patients who were devastated by poliomyelitis in the terrible epidemic of the 1940s, an epidemic in which one of my closest friends and colleagues contracted the disease and nearly died. He survived miraculously after being confined for many days in a respirator, or, as it was called in those days, an iron lung.

And then came memories from the 1950s when I helped give Salk vaccine to the children in a small town in New England. The little ones howled when I approached them with the syringe and needle. A few years later such children were immunized without screams of fear and pain because by then vaccination against poliomyelitis involved nothing more than sucking on a little cube of sugar containing a few drops of vaccine. In his very moving history of the development of the oral vaccine against poliomyelitis, Albert Sabin gave a graphic description of the thirty years of research that were needed to develop his highly effective vaccine. He made clear that this outstanding contribution to the welfare of mankind would not have been possible without experiments on "many thousands of monkeys and hundreds of chimpanzees."[1] Dr. Sabin's vaccine, since its introduction in 1960, has provided nearly complete protection against poliomyelitis to hundreds of millions of people all over the world. The monkeys and chimps to which he referred have saved thousands of lives and spared hundreds of thousands of children a lifetime marred by paralyzed limbs. Poliomyelitis has been very nearly eradicated throughout the industrialized world and could be eradicated in developing nations if those countries had the resources to do so.

These memories were soon followed by recollection of my experience as a consultant on the burn wards here at my medical school and of the scores of severely burned children and adults whose survival often depended on care perfected through the study of burns experimentally inflicted on pigs and sheep and dogs in the research laboratory. In addition, some of those patients who survived did so because the skin of pigs was used as a temporary graft to cover the raw, oozing areas of their seared flesh.

Then came more recent recollections of my work as a consultant in the care of patients with the acquired immune deficiency syndrome, better known as AIDS. They die slowly and pathetically, these patients with AIDS, and we physicians stand by helplessly as they die because as yet we do not know enough about the virus that causes this dread disease. Thousands are dying from that virus now, and tens of thousands will die in this epidemic in the coming few years unless current research leads to an effective vaccine. This research must include the study of monkeys that are deliberately infected with the AIDS virus. Will the opponents of experimentation on animals prevent present-day researchers from eradicating the AIDS virus, as Dr. Sabin and others, conquered the virus of poliomyelitis?

And finally, I thought of another friend and colleague whose belly was ripped by machine gun fire as he parachuted into Europe during the second world war. Without plasma and blood transfusions, this young medical officer would have died before he could be flown to a hospital in England. If those who oppose the use of animals in medical research had prevailed some fifty years ago, there would have been no research on hemorrhagic shock in dogs. This research cost the life of many dogs that were bled into a state of severe and, at times, fatal shock. But the knowledge gained through the sacrifice of these animals gave medicine the means to save this soldier when he nearly bled to death as he dangled helplessly in his parachute in the French sky in 1944. And there is no counting the number of others, soldiers and civilians, who owe their lives to these experiments on dogs.

And so my memories came, one after the other, but they all led to the same question: "How can any rational, compassionate, and thoughtful person oppose the use of animals in medical research?" Have those who oppose such research watched one grandchild die because of lack of medical

knowledge and then, a few years later, watched two other grandchildren be saved by medical procedures that could not have been developed without research on animals? Would they have a young
medical officer bleed to death somewhere in war-torn France rather than allow the experiments on
dogs that were essential to the development of effective treatment of shock due to massive loss of
blood? Are they so blindly opposed to the use of animals in medical research that they would prevent Dr. Sabin's experiments on his "thousands of monkeys and hundreds of chimpanzees" that were
necessary to perfect the vaccine that conquered poliomyelitis? Will they tell the thousands of patients
who today suffer from AIDS to give up hope because monkeys should not be used in the laboratory
in our fight against this plague? Are those who oppose my view on the use of animals in medical research willing to tell my grandsons that it would have been preferable to let them and thousands of
other children die rather than allow research on animals? I hope not.

But the fact is, there are people who would let my grandsons die rather than allow any animal
to be used in medical research. These are not people who press only for the humane treatment of animals in the laboratory, a cause that no reasonable person can oppose. These are antivivisectionists
who will, if they have their way, put a stop to all experimentation on animals no matter the cost to
the advancement of health care. The number and the political influence of people in this movement
have grown alarmingly in recent years. They have lobbied successfully for a law in Massachusetts
to forbid the use of pound animals in biomedical research. And now they are pressing Congress to impose similar restrictions nationwide. If such federal legislation is passed, it will seriously hamper all
medical research in this country and will make the cost of some research prohibitively high, as it already has done in Massachusetts.[2]

Those who oppose the use of pound animals in biomedical studies make little or no mention of
the fact that only two percent of those animals are used in scientific experiments, while the other ten
to fifteen million meet a meaningless and useless death at the pound each year.

And the comments of some of the leaders in the antivivisectionist movement suggest that they
are motivated more by personal needs to win a power struggle against the leaders of the biomedical
community than by humanitarian concerns for either people or animals. For example, John McAr-
dle, a nationally prominent antivivisectionist, has stated that he believes medical researchers have
been placed by the public on a pedestal and he comments: "we're whacking away at the base of that
pedestal, and it is going to fall."[3] He also has made the rather macabre suggestion that medical researchers should perform their experiments on brain-dead humans rather than animals. He stated, "It
may take people awhile to get used to the idea, but once they do, the savings in animal lives will be
substantial."

Another leading antivivisectionist is Ingrid Newkirk, the codirector of PETA, or People for
the Ethical Treatment of Animals. She has said that scientists who experiment on animals have been
"lying and misleading the public" about the value of research on animals.[4] She stated that the objective
of PETA is to attack "the whole grubby system of biomedical research, because if you jeopardize an
animal one iota [in doing research] . . . you're doing something immoral. Even painless research is
fascism . . ." And, she added, "Animal liberationists do not separate out the human animal, so there
is no rational basis for saying that a human being has special rights. A rat is a pig is a dog is a boy."
Jonathan and Bryan, my grandsons, disagree.

Endnotes

1. Albert B. Sabin, "Oral Poliovirus Vaccine: History of Its Development and Prospects for Eradication of Poliomyelitis," *Journal of the American Medical Association* 194, no. 8 (1965): 872–76.

2. Katie McCabe, "Who Will Live, Who Will Die," *The Washingtonian* 21, no. 11(1986): 112–18.

3. Ibid.

4. Ibid.

Journal/Discussion Questions

1. Have you had any experiences with the benefits of medical research? How has it affected your life? Do you think you may have benefited from it in ways that you do not realize?

2. White presents a lot of evidence, primarily by way of examples, of his central claim. What is the *argument* that he is advancing? Critically evaluate the argument.

Peter Singer
"Down on the Factory Farm"

Peter Singer, currently Ira W. DeCamp Professor of Bioethics, University Center for Human Values, Princeton University, is the author of numerous works in ethics, especially in applied ethics. His books include The Expanding Circle, Animal Liberation, Practical Ethics, *and most recently,* Rethinking Life and Death *and* How Are We to Live? *He has also edited a number of books, including* A Companion to Ethics. *In his work, Singer sees himself as holding our conventional moral beliefs to a standard of consistency, coherence, and the avoidance of arbitrary distinctions. He finds that many of these traditional beliefs are remnants of earlier, religiously inspired doctrines that he believes many people no longer accept; other beliefs survive only because they promote some form of group selfishness.*

One of the ways in which we avoid dealing with the issue of animal suffering is simply and literally by not seeing it. In this article, Peter Singer describes a number of the practices that are common in contemporary animal farming, concentrating on the treatment of chickens and veal calves.

As Your Read, Consider This:

1. How much of the animal suffering that Singer describes were you aware of? Do you think your views on eating meat and factroy farming would be changed if you had more direct contact with the reality of such situations?

From *Animal Liberation* (Random House), reprinted in Tom Regan and Peter Singer, *Animal Rights and Human Obligations,* 2nd ed. (Englewood Cliffs, NJ: Prentice-Hall, 1989)

2. How much does animal suffering count in your life? What moral weight does it have? Are your views on this changing as you read this article?

For most humans, especially those in modern urban and suburban communities, the most direct form of contact with non-human animals is at meal time: we eat them. This simple fact is the key to our attitudes to other animals, and also the key to what each one of us can do about changing these attitudes. The use and abuse of animals raised for food far exceeds, in sheer numbers of animals affected, any other kind of mistreatment. Hundreds of millions of cattle, pigs, and sheep are raised and slaughtered in the United States alone each year; and for poultry the figure is a staggering 3 billion. (That means that about 5,000 birds—mostly chickens—will have been slaughtered in the time it takes you to read this page.) It is here, on our dinner table and in our neighborhood supermarket or butcher's shop, that we are brought into direct touch with the most extensive exploitation of other species that has ever existed.

In general, we are ignorant of the abuse of living creatures that lies behind the food we eat. Consider the images conjured up by the word "farm": a house, a barn, a flock of hens, overseen by a strutting rooster, scratching around the farmyard, a herd of cows being brought in from the fields for milking, and perhaps a sow rooting around in the orchard with a litter of squealing piglets running excitedly behind her.

Very few farms were ever as idyllic as that traditional image would have us believe. Yet we still think of a farm as a pleasant place, far removed from our own industrial, profit-conscious city life. Of those few who think about the lives of animals on farms, not many know much of modern methods of animal raising. Some people wonder whether animals are slaughtered painlessly, and anyone who has followed a truckload of cattle must know that farm animals are transported in very crowded conditions; but few suspect that transportation and slaughter are anything more than the brief and inevitable conclusion of a life of ease and contentment, a life that contains the natural pleasures of animal existence without the hardships that wild animals must endure in the struggle for survival.

These comfortable assumptions bear little relation to the realities of modern farming. For a start, farming is no longer controlled by simple country folk. It is a business, and big business at that. In the last thirty years the entry of large corporations and assembly-line methods of production have turned farming into "agribusiness." . . .

The first animal to be removed from the relatively natural conditions of the traditional farms and subjected to the full stress of modern intensive farming was the chicken. Chickens have the misfortune of being useful to humans in two ways: for their flesh and for their eggs. There are now standard mass-production techniques for obtaining both these products.

Agribusiness enthusiasts consider the rise of the chicken industry to be one of the great success stories of farming. At the end of World War II chicken for the table was still relatively rare. It came mainly from small independent farmers or from the unwanted males produced by egg-laying flocks. Today "broilers"—as table chickens are now usually called—are produced literally by the million from the highly automated factory-like plants of the large corporations that own or control 98 percent of all broiler production in the United States.[1]

The essential step in turning the chicken from a farmyard bird into a manufactured item was confining them indoors. A broiler producer today gets a load of 10,000, 50,000, or even more day-old chicks from the hatcheries, and puts them straight into a long, windowless shed—usually on the floor, although some producers use tiers of cages in order to get more birds into the same size shed. Inside the shed, every aspect of the birds' environment is controlled to make them grow faster on less feed. Food and water are fed automatically from hoppers suspended from the roof. The lighting is adjusted according to advice from agricultural researchers: for instance, there may be bright light 24 hours a day for the first week or two, to encourage the chicks to gain quickly; then the lights may be dimmed slightly and made to go off and on every two hours, in the belief that the chickens are readier to eat after a period of sleep; finally there comes a point, around six weeks of age, when the birds have grown so much that they are becoming crowded, and the lights will then be made very dim at all times. The point of this dim lighting is to reduce the effects of crowding. Toward the end of the eight- or nine-week life of the chicken, there may be as little as half a square foot of space per chicken—or less than the area of a sheet of quarto paper for a 3.5-lb. bird. Under these conditions with normal lighting the stress of crowding and the absence of natural outlets for the bird's energies lead to outbreaks of fighting, with birds pecking at each other's feathers and sometimes killing and eating one another. Very dim lighting has been found to reduce this and so the birds are likely to live out their last weeks in near-darkness.

Feather-pecking and cannibalism are, in the broiler producer's language, "vices." They are not natural vices, however—they are the result of the stress and crowding to which the modern broilerman subjects his birds. Chickens are highly social animals, and in the farmyard they develop a hierarchy, sometimes called a "pecking order." Every bird yields, at the food trough or elsewhere, to those above it in rank, and takes precedence over those below. There may be a few confrontations before the order is firmly established but more often than not a show of force, rather than actual physical contact, is enough to put a chicken in its place. As Konrad Lorenz, a renowned figure in the field of animal behavior, wrote in the days when flocks were still small:

> Do animals thus know each other among themselves? They certainly do. . . . Every poultry farmer knows that . . . there exists a very definite order, in which each bird is afraid of those that are above her in rank. After some few disputes, which need not necessarily come to blows, each bird knows which of the others she has to fear and which must show respect to her. Not only physical strength, but also personal courage, energy, and even the self-assurance of every individual bird are decisive in the maintenance of the pecking order.[2]

Other studies have shown that a flock of up to 90 chickens can maintain a stable social order, each bird knowing its place; but 10,000 birds crowded together in a single shed is obviously a different matter.[3] The birds cannot establish a social order, and as a result they fight frequently with each other. Quite apart from the inability of the individual bird to recognize so many other birds, the mere fact of extreme crowding probably contributes to irritability and excitability in chickens, as it does in humans and other animals. This is something farming magazines are aware of, and they frequently warn their readers:

> Feather-pecking and cannibalism have increased to a formidable extent of late years, due, no doubt, to the changes in technique and the swing towards completely intensive management of laying flocks and table poultry. . . . The most common faults in management which may lead to vice are boredom, overcrowding in badly ventilated houses. . . . Lack of feeding space, unbalanced food or shortage of water, and heavy infestation with insect pests.[4]

Clearly the farmer must stop "vices," because they cost him money; but although he may know that overcrowding is the root cause, he cannot do anything about this, since in the competitive state of the industry, eliminating overcrowding could mean eliminating his profit margin at the same time. He would have fewer birds to sell, but would have had to pay the same outlay for his building, for the automatic feeding equipment, for the fuel used to heat and ventilate the building, and for labor. So the farmer limits his efforts to reducing the consequences of the stress that costs him money. The unnatural way in which he keeps his birds causes the vices; but to control them the poultryman must make the conditions still more unnatural. Very dim lighting is one way of doing this. A more drastic step, though one now almost universally used in the industry, is "de-beaking." This involves inserting the chick's head in a guillotine-like device which cuts off part of its beak. Alternatively the operation may be done with a hot knife. Some poultrymen claim that this operation is painless, but an expert British Government committee under zoologist Professor F.W. Rogers Brambell appointed to look into aspects of intensive farming found otherwise:

> . . . between the horn and the bone is a thin layer of highly sensitive soft tissue, resembling the "quick" of the human nail. The hot knife used in de-beaking cuts through this complex of horn, bone and sensitive tissue, causing severe pain.[5]

De-beaking, which is routinely performed in anticipation of cannibalism by most poultrymen, does greatly reduce the amount of damage a chicken can do to other chickens. It also, in the words of the Brambell Committee, "deprives the bird of what is in effect its most versatile member" while it obviously does nothing to reduce the stress and overcrowding that lead to this unnatural cannibalism in the first place. . . .

"A hen," Samuel Butler once wrote, "is only an egg's way of making another egg." Butler, no doubt, was being humorous; but when Fred C. Haley, president of a Georgia poultry firm that controls the lives of 225,000 laying hens, describes the hen as "an egg producing machine" his words have more serious implications. To emphasize his businesslike attitude Haley adds: "The object of producing eggs is to make money. When we forget this objective, we have forgotten what it is all about."[6]

Nor is this only an American attitude. A British farming magazine has told its readers:

> The modern layer is, after all, only a very efficient converting machine, changing the raw material—feedingstuffs—into the finished product—the egg—less, of course, maintenance requirements.[7]

Remarks of this kind can regularly be found in the egg industry trade journals throughout the United States and Europe, and they express an attitude that is common in the industry. As may be anticipated, their consequences for the laying hens are not good.

Laying hens go through many of the same procedures as broilers, but there are some differences. Like broilers, layers have to be de-beaked, to prevent the cannibalism that would otherwise occur in their crowded conditions; but because they live much longer than broilers, they often go through this operation twice. So we find a poultry specialist at the New Jersey College of Agriculture advising poultrymen to de-beak their chicks when they are between one and two weeks old because there is, he says, less stress on the chicks at this time than if the operation is done earlier, and in addition "there are fewer culls in the laying flock as a result of improper de-beaking." In either case, the article continues, the birds must be de-beaked again when they are ready to begin laying, at around twenty weeks of age.[8]

Laying hens get no more individual attention than broilers. Alan Hainsworth, owner of a poultry farm in upstate New York, told an inquiring local reporter that four hours a day is all he needs for the care of his 36,000 laying hens, while his wife looks after the 20,000 pullets (as the younger birds not yet ready to lay are called): "It takes her about 15 minutes a day. All she checks is their automatic feeders, water cups and any deaths during the night."

This kind of care does not make for a happy flock as the reporter's description shows:

> Walk into the pullet house and the reaction is immediate—complete pandemonium. The squawking is loud and intense as some 20,000 birds shove to the farthest side of their cages in fear of the human intruders.[9]

Julius Goldman's Egg City, 50 miles northwest of Los Angeles, is one of the world's largest egg producing units, consisting of 2 million hens divided into block long buildings containing 90,000 hens each, five birds to a 16 by 18 inch cage. When the *National Geographic* magazine did an enthusiastic survey of new farming methods, Ben Shames, Egg City's executive vice-president, explained to its reporter the methods used to look after so many birds:

> We keep track of the food eaten and the eggs collected in 2 rows of cages among the 110 rows in each building. When production drops to the uneconomic point, all 90,000 birds are sold to processors for potpies or chicken soup. It doesn't pay to keep track of every row in the house, let alone indivdual hens; with 2 million birds on hand you have to rely on statistical samplings.[10]

Nearly all the big egg producers now keep their laying hens in cages. Originally there was only one bird to a cage; and the idea was that the farmer could then tell which birds were not laying enough eggs to give an economic return on their food. Those birds were then killed. Then it was found that more birds could be housed and costs per bird reduced if two birds were put in each cage. That was only the first step, and as we have seen, there is no longer any question of keeping a tally of each bird's eggs. The advantages of cages for the egg producer now consist in the greater number of birds that can be housed, warmed, fed, and watered in one building, and in the greater use that can be made of labor-saving automatic equipment.

The cages are stacked in tiers, with food and water troughs running along the rows, filled automatically from a central supply. They have sloping wire floors. The slope—usually a gradient of 1 in 5—makes it more difficult for the birds to stand comfortably, but it causes the eggs to roll to the front of the cage where they can easily be collected by hand or, in the more modern plants, carried by conveyor belt to a packing plant.

When a reporter from the *New York Daily News* wanted to see a typical modern egg farm, he visited Frenchtown Poultry Farm, in New Jersey, where he found that

> Each 18 by 24 inch cage on the Frenchtown farm contains nine hens who seemed jammed into them by some unseen hand. They barely have enough room to turn around in the cages.
> "Really, you should have no more than eight birds in a cage that size," conceded Oscar Grossman, the farm's lessor. "But sometimes you have to do things to get the most out of your stock."[11]

Actually, if Mr. Grossman had put only eight birds in his cages they would still have been grossly overcrowded; at nine to a cage they have only 1/3 square foot per bird.

In 1968 the farm magazine *American Agriculturalist* advised its readers in an article headed "Bird Squeezing" that it had been found possible to stock at 1/3 square foot per bird by putting four birds in a 12-by 16-inch cage. This was apparently a novel step at the time; the steady increase in densities over the years is indicated by the fact that a 1974 issue of the same magazine describing the Lannsdale Poultry Farm, near Rochester, New York, mentions the same housing density without any suggestion that it is unusual.[12] In reading egg industry magazines I have found numerous reports of similar high densities, and scarcely any that are substantially lower. My own visits to poultry farms in the United States have shown the same pattern. The highest reported density that I have read about is at the Hainsworth farm in Mt. Morris, New York, where four hens are squeezed into cages 12 inches by 12 inches, or just one square foot—and the reporter adds: "Some hold five birds when Hainsworth has more birds than room."[13] This means 1/4, and sometimes 1/5, square foot per bird. At this stocking rate *a single sheet of quarto paper represents the living area of two to three hens.*

Under the conditions standard on modern egg farms in the United States and other "developed nations" every natural instinct the birds have is frustrated. They cannot walk around, scratch the ground, dustbathe, build a nest, or stretch their wings. They are not part of a flock. They cannot keep out of each other's way and weaker birds have no escape from the attacks of stronger ones, already maddened by the unnatural conditions. . . .

Intensive production of pigs and cattle is now also common; but of all the forms of intensive farming now practiced, the quality veal industry ranks as the most morally repugnant, comparable only with barbarities like the force-feeding of geese through a funnel that produces the deformed livers made into pate de foie gras. The essence of veal raising is the feeding of a high-protein food (that should be used to reduce malnutrition in poorer parts of the world) to confined, anemic calves in a manner that will produce a tender, pale-colored flesh that will be served to gourmets in expensive restaurants. Fortunately this industry does not compare in size with poultry, beef, or pig production; nevertheless it is worth our attention because it represents an extreme, both in the degree of exploitation to which it subjects its animals and in its absurd inefficiency as a method of providing people with nourishment.

Veal is the flesh of a young calf, and the term was originally reserved for calves killed before they had been weaned from their mothers. The flesh of these very young animals was paler and more tender than that of a calf that had begun to eat grass; but there was not much of it since calves begin to eat grass when they are a few weeks old and still very small. So there was little money in veal, and the small amount available came from the unwanted male calves produced by the dairy industry. These males were a nuisance to the dairy farmers, since the dairy breeds do not make good beef cattle. Therefore they were sold as quickly as possible. A day or two after being born they were trucked to market where, hungry and frightened by the strange surroundings and the absence of their mothers, they were sold for immediate delivery to the slaughterhouse.

Once this was the main source of veal in the United States. Now, using methods first developed in Holland, farmers have found a way to keep the calf longer without the flesh becoming darker in color or less tender. This means that the veal calf, when sold, may weigh as much as 325 lbs., instead of the 90-odd lbs. that newborn calves weigh. Because veal fetches a premium price, this has made rearing veal calves a profitable occupation.

The trick depends on keeping the calf in highly unnatural conditions. If the calf were left to grow up outside, its playful nature would lead it to romp around the fields. Soon it would begin to develop muscles, which would make its flesh tough. At the same time it would eat grass and its flesh would lose the pale color that the flesh of newborn calves has. So the specialist veal producer takes his calves straight from the auction ring to a confinement unit. Here, in a converted barn or purpose-built shed, he will have rows of wooden stalls. Each stall will be 1 foot 10 inches wide and 4 feet

6 inches long. It will have a slatted wooden floor, raised above the concrete floor of the shed. The calves will be tethered by a chain around the neck to prevent them from turning around in their stalls. (The chain may be removed when the calves grow too big to turn around in such narrow stalls.) The stall will have no straw or other bedding, since the calf might eat it, spoiling the paleness of his flesh.

Here the calves will live for the next thirteen to fifteen weeks. They will leave their stalls only to be taken out to slaughter. They are fed a totally liquid diet, based on non-fat milk powder with added vitamins, minerals, and growth-promoting drugs. . . .

The narrow stalls and their slatted wooden floors are a serious source of discomfort for the calves. The inability to turn around is frustrating. When he lies down, the calf must lie hunched up, sitting almost on top of his legs rather than having them out to one side as he would do if he had more room. A stall too narrow to turn around in is also too narrow to groom comfortably in; and calves have an innate desire to twist their heads around and groom themselves with their tongues. A wooden floor without any bedding is hard and uncomfortable; it is rough on the calves' knees as they get up and lie down. In addition, animals with hooves are uncomfortable on slatted floors. A slatted floor is like a cattle grid, which cattle will always avoid, except that the slats are closer together. The spaces, however, must still be large enough to allow manure to fall or be washed through, and this means that they are large enough to make the calves uncomfortable.[14]

The special nature of the veal calf has other implications that show the industry's lack of genuine concern for the animals' welfare. Obviously the calves sorely miss their mothers. They also miss something to suck on. The urge to suck is strong in a baby calf, as it is in a baby human. These calves have no teat to suck on, nor do they have any substitute. From their first day in confinement—which may well be only the third or fourth day of their lives—they drink from a plastic bucket. Attempts have been made to feed calves through artificial teats, but the problems of keeping the teats clean and sterile are apparently too great for the farmer to try to overcome. It is common to see calves frantically trying to suck some part of their stalls, although there is usually nothing suitable; and if you offer a veal calf your finger he will immediately begin to suck on it, as a human baby sucks its thumb.

Later on the calf develops a desire to ruminate—that is, to take in roughage and chew the cud. But roughage is strictly forbidden and so, again, the calf may resort to vain attempts to chew the sides of its stall. Digestive disorders, including stomach ulcers, are common in veal calves, as are chronically loose bowel movements.

As if this were not enough, there is the fact that the calf is deliberately kept anemic. As one veal producers' journal has said,

> Color of veal is one of the primary factors involved in obtaining "topdollar" returns from the fancy veal market . . . "light color" veal is a premium item much in demand at better clubs, hotels and restaurants. "Light color" or pink veal is partly associated with the amount of iron in the muscle of the calves.[15]

So veal feeds are deliberately kept low in iron. A normal calf would obtain iron from grass or other forms of roughage, but since a veal calf is not allowed this he becomes anemic. Pale pink flesh is in fact anemic flesh. The demand for flesh of this color is a matter of snob appeal. The color does not affect the taste and it certainly does not make the flesh more nourishing—rather the opposite.

Calves kept in this manner are unhappy and unhealthy animals. Despite the fact that the veal producer selects only the strongest, healthiest calves to begin with, uses a medicated feed as a routine measure, and gives additional injections at the slightest sign of illness, digestive, respiratory and infectious diseases are widespread. It is common for a veal producer to find that one in ten of a batch of calves do not survive the fifteen weeks of confinement. Ten percent mortality over such a short period would be disastrous for anyone raising calves for beef, but the veal producer can tolerate this loss because of the high price restaurants are prepared to pay for his product. If the reader will recall that this whole laborious, wasteful, and painful process exists for the sole purpose of pandering to would-be gourmets who insist on pale, soft veal, no further comment should be needed.

Endnotes

1. Harrison Wellford, *Sowing the Wind: The Politics of Food, Safety and Agribusiness* (New York: Grossman Press, 1971), p. 104.
2. K. Lorenz, *King Solomon's Ring* (London: Methuen, 1964), p. 147.
3. Ian Duncan, "Can the Psychologist Measure Stress?" *New Scientist,* October 18, 1973.
4. *The Smallholder,* January 6, 1962; quoted by Ruth Harrison, *Animal Machines* (London: Vincent Stuart, 1964), p. 18.
5. *Report of the Technical Committee to Enquire into the Welfare of Animals Kept Under Intensive Livestock Husbandry Systems* (London: Her Majesty's Stationery Office, 1965), para. 97.
6. *Poultry Tribune,* January 1974.
7. *Farmer and Stockbreeder,* January 30, 1962; quoted by Ruth Harrison, *Animal Machines,* p. 50.
8. *American Agriculturist,* July 1966.
9. *Upstate,* August 5, 1973, report by Mary Rita Kiereck.
10. *National Geographic,* February 1970.
11. *New York Daily News,* September 1, 1971.
12. *American Agriculturist,* August 1968, April 1974.
13. *Upstate,* August 5, 1973.
14. Ruth Harrison, *Animal Machines,* p. 72.
15. *The Wall Street Journal,* published by Provimi, Inc., Watertown, Wisconsin, November 1973.

Journal/Discussion Questions

✍ *Do you have any direct experience with the raising and slaughtering of animals for food? (Did you grow up on a farm or have you ever visited an animal farm or a slaughterhouse?) How have these experiences affected your views on animal rights? If you have not had any of these experiences, do you think this lack has affected your views? Discuss.*

1. If chickens are raised under the conditions that Singer describes, what implica-

tions—if any—does that have for eating eggs and meat from chickens under those conditions?

2. Singer stresses that modern animal agriculture is "big business," not the product of many small farmers. What moral implications, if any, does this have?

3. Why does Singer single out the "quality veal industry as the most morally repugnant" form of animal farming? Do you agree with his assessment? Discuss.

An Introduction to the Moral Issues

The Scope of the Moral Circle

In this chapter, we shall examine whether the circle of morality ought to be extended to include animals—and, if so, how this would transform our world. Certainly there are many areas of our daily lives that involve animals either directly or indirectly. Many of us have pets, ride horses, visit zoos and places like Sea World, and perhaps even go hunting or fishing. All of these involve animals directly. Many of us eat meat or fish, wear leather belts and shoes, use prescription medications, and ride in cars with seat belts. Many of these involve animals indirectly as sources of food, as subjects of medical and safety research, and the like. Our relationship with animals pervades our daily lives in numerous, often unnoticed, ways.

Many of these relationships with animals must be revised if we discover that animals are persons, or even that they have a moral status beyond the little that has traditionally been accorded to them. A variety of different types of concern—religious, rights, consequentialist, and character-based—have been offered as reasons for either modifying or retaining our present view of the moral status of animals. Let's consider each of these issues.

Consequentialist Concerns

For many people, morality is primarily about consequences, about doing the thing that creates the most happiness and the least unhappiness. Yet the crucial question, at least in this context, is happiness *for whom?* Is it only happiness for human beings, or does the circle extend beyond this?

Utilitarian Concerns

From its origins in the work of Jeremy Bentham, utilitarianism has shown a sensitivity to the suffering of animals not found in, for example, the Kantian tradition. For Bentham, the notable moral fact is suffering, whether that be the suffering of animals or of human beings.

Not all versions of utilitarianism share the sensitivity to animal suffering that Bentham had. But even when utilitarianism is concerned only with the happiness or pleasure of human beings and such, it does not consign animals to moral oblivion. When we consider consequences solely for human beings, we notice that this by no means justifies all of our harmful treatment of animals in the past. Consider two examples: eating meat and cruelty to animals.

First, consider eating meat. Although vegetarianism is often espoused for the sake of animals, there may well be a strong, human-centered case for vegetarianism. What are the consequences of a diet rich in meat, especially red meat, for human beings? This is an empirical question, but it may well be the case that the overall effects of vegetarianism are significantly more healthful than the effects of a diet that contains meat. *Second,* consider cruelty to animals. Even if we leave aside for the moment the harmful effects on the animals themselves, it may well be the case that treating animals cruelly has harmful effects on human beings. Immanuel Kant, for example, argued that such cruelty makes us less morally sensitive beings and less likely to respond appropriately to the suffering of human beings. Cruelty to animals may well lead to cruelty to human beings, and is therefore to be avoided.

Thus, even when we assume a purely human-centered consequentialist approach to moral matters, we do not have to conclude that "anything goes" in regard to our treatment of animals. There may be important, human-centered constraints on our treatment of animals that have nothing to do with the moral status of the animals themselves.

Speciesism

The fundamental moral question that was raised in the 1970s by Peter Singer in his book *Animal Liberation* was whether utilitarianism was being arbitrary when it considered the pleasure and pain of only human beings. If utilitarianism is fundamentally a doctrine about increasing pleasure and reducing pain and suffering, then shouldn't *all* pleasure and *all* pain and suffering count, not just the pleasure and pain of one species?

Considerations about Rights

Concerns about the strength of Singer's proposed utilitarian foundation for our attitude toward animals has led some philosophers, most notably Tom Regan, to shift the focus from the *liberation* of animals to animal *rights*. Nonhuman animals, Regan argues in our selection, "The Case for Animal Rights," and in his book of the same name, have rights, just as human animals do. The crucial factor about rights is that they are, as Ronald Dworkin once suggested, like "trump cards." In other words, they take precedence over anything else, including considerations of utility. Thus, even if from a utilitarian point of view the killing of animals was sometimes justified, they still may be protected because they have a right to life.

Who Has Rights?

Imagine that you were on a Star Trek mission to an unexplored planet and that through a fluke accident you find yourself marooned on a planet that you know nothing about. Able to breathe the atmosphere, but lacking food and water, you are immediately faced with the question of what in your environment you may—both safely and morally—consume. Let's imagine that there is little plant matter, and the little that is available lacks nutritional content. You turn toward the living beings on the planet that are crawling, walking, hopping, running, and flying around. Leaving aside the question of safety, how would you decide which creatures had a right to be respected and which creatures—if any—you were morally justified in eating?

As we tried to answer this question, presumably we would look for certain things—such as intelligence, language, culture, and the like—that would indicate these beings are deserving of respect and are not to be used as a mere means to our nutritional goals. Similarly, when we look on earth at the nonhuman animal world around us, we must ask which animals have rights. The answer that animal rights advocates give is simple: the ability to feel pain (sentience) is what confers rights. What if the criterion is the ability to think and use language? Then certain kinds of animals—dolphins, chimps, and others—may qualify for rights, whereas other kinds of animals—slugs, worms, and so on—would not qualify, nor would certain human beings—most notably, those with severe mental disabilities and those in deep comas. The extent of animal rights depends directly on the criterion for conferring rights.

How Do We Resolve Conflicts of Rights?

Authors such as Alasdair MacIntyre and Mary Ann Glendon have criticized the growing philosophical and political preoccupation with rights and they have argued that the language of rights is only a fiction and that it leads to polarization and increased conflict. Certainly one of the difficulties is that rights are often presented as absolute, although the philosophically more defensible situation is to see virtually all rights as less than absolute. Otherwise we are left with the irresolvable situation of what to do when one absolute right conflicts with another absolute right. Obviously, we need some kind of hierarchy, some ordering of rights.

These considerations have a particular relevance in the area of animal rights. Advocates of animal rights have to answer three questions. *First,* what particular rights do all animals have? Do all animals have the right to life? The right not to suffer needlessly? The right to liberty? *Second,* do rights vary by species or do all types of animals have equal rights? Does a worm have the same rights as a chimp and as a baby human being? *Third,* how do we resolve interspecies conflicts of rights? Is the right to life of a worm equal in moral standing to the right to life of a chimp and the right to life of a human infant? These are difficult questions, although not necessarily unanswerable. A strong defense of animal rights must, however, provide a plausible answer to these questions. In "The Case for Animal Rights," Tom Regan addresses each of these questions.

Concerns about Character

In addition to concerns about religion, consequences, and rights, defenders of animals have often pointed to the issue of *moral character* as providing a foundation for changing our attitudes toward animals. The argument has been that compassionate people will be more responsive to the suffering of animals and that continuing mistreatment of animals in our society dulls our capacity for compassion in regard to all beings.

Compassion

Almost everyone has had the experience of seeing an animal in pain and for most of us our immediate response is to want to relieve the animal's suffering. We may nurse an injured bird back to health, wash the wounds of a dog that has been in a fight, even try to set the broken leg of a kitten. Sometimes, whether rightly or wrongly, we may conclude that the animal cannot recover, and kill it to end its suffering. (Issues of animal rights prompt a reconsideration of euthanasia, not just abortion.)

Yet compassion initially seems to be a shaky foundation for our moral attitude toward animals. Sometimes, sympathy and compassion can turn into mere sentimentality—and some have criticized the animal rights movement for falling into the trap of sentimentality.

Proximity

Most people who eat meat in modern industrialized societies don't slaughter their own animals to do so, and this simple fact has important implications for the issue of character. If the cruelty of animal agriculture is kept from view, then sensitive and compassionate people may participate in such cruelty through ignorance. Of course, some would maintain that such ignorance is itself morally blameworthy, and some of the more visible protests by animal rights activists have been aimed at making cruelty to animals inescapably visible.

Common Ground

The various moral concerns outlined in the preceding pages come directly into play when we seek a common ground on a number of pressing issues in regard to our moral attitude toward animals. Let's briefly consider several of these areas: medical experimentation on animals, commercial agriculture, the keeping of pets, and our interactions with wild animals.

Medical Experimentation: Balancing Competing Concerns

One of the most difficult areas in which to assert animal rights is medical experimentation. When the choice is simply between preserving the lives of animals *versus* being able to save the lives of human beings, for most people the choice is easy: the human takes priority over the animal. Few would agree with Ingrid Newkirk, the national director of PETA, who claims that "Animal liberationists do not separate out the human animal, so there is no rational basis for saying that a human being has special rights. A rat is a pig is a dog is a boy. They're all mammals."[1]

The difficulty is that we are rarely, if ever, presented with such a stark choice between the life of one human being and the life of one animal. The choices are more likely to be between the lives of hundreds of animals and the *possible* beneficial effects of some new drug for human beings. Often the issue of animal experimentation is about further confirmation of experimental results that are already available or about determining what changes would occur if some small variable were altered. Sometimes the issue is simply training students and laboratory workers in experimental techniques.

The middle ground.   *How much* should animal suffering count? If we are discontent with the wholesale endorsement of the use of animals in research, and if we have rejected the claim that there is no morally significant difference between human suffering and animal suffering, then where do we stand? The middle ground here would seem to be that animal suffering should be reduced whenever possible. Questions should be raised about whether the research is really necessary, whether it absolutely has to include animals, whether it can involve fewer animals, and whether the suffering of the animals can be reduced in any way.

Commercial Animal Agriculture and Eating Meat

The cruelty of animal farming.   In his selection "Down on the Factory Farm," Peter Singer gives us a glimpse of what commercial animal agriculture is like, and it is a disturbing picture indeed. Animals are raised under extremely harsh and unnatural conditions that deprive them of many of the natural consolations of their lives, such as sucking, grooming, pecking, and the like. Even if we leave aside the fact that their lives eventually end in slaughter, many of us would find much to object to in the way in which such animals are treated.

The vegetarian option.   Many supporters of animal rights respond to this situation by espousing vegetarianism, because this is clearly the option that eliminates the need to raise and kill animals under these conditions. As we indicated earlier, vegetarianism has much to recommend in addition to the issue of animal suffering. However, if vegetarianism for the entire world is not a realistic option at this time, it is important to ask whether there would be any conditions under which the raising of animals for food would be morally acceptable.

Common ground.   Two distinct issues arise in regard to raising animals for food: their deaths and their lives. Presumably it is morally better to kill animals painlessly (including a minimum of anticipatory fear as well as a minimum of physical pain) than painfully. If animals are slaughtered, it should be done in a way that minimizes their pain. Second, their lives should be (a) as free as possible from pain inflicted by human beings and (b) as natural as possible. The first requirement is clearly utilitarian in character, whereas the second relates to what we might call "quality of life." Part of respecting a being is that we recognize the natural rhythms and contours of that being's life and we try to avoid unnecessarily disturbing them. For example, many animals groom themselves and such grooming activity provides them with comfort on a variety of levels, psychological as well as physical. Whenever possible, we should raise animals in ways that allow them to follow their own natural inclinations.

Endnotes

1. K. McCabe, "Who Will Live, Who Will Die?" *Washingtonian Magazine* (August 1986), p. 115.

The Arguments

Tom Regan
"The Case for Animal Rights"

Tom Regan is one of the most articulate and powerful spokepersons for animal rights. He has published widely on a range of different topics, but his most influential work has been in the area of animal rights. His book, Animal Rights, *is one of the foundational works in that area.*

In this article, Regan argues a case for animal rights, maintaining that those who take animal rights seriously must be committed to abolishing the use of animals in science, animal agriculture, and commercial hunting and trapping. "The fundamental wrong," he writes, "is the system that allows us to view animals as our resources, here for us—to be eaten, or surgically manipulated, or exploited for sport or money." Regan considers and rejects several approaches to understanding our relationship to animals: indirect duty, contractarianism, and utilitarianism. Only a rights approach is able to recognize the inherent value of the individual, including the individual animal.

As You Read, Consider This:

1. Regan distinguishes between things that "make things worse" and the "fundamental wrong." If we could eliminate the factors that "make things worse" for animals, do you think that would be enough? Which of Regan's arguments supports the claim that there is a "fundamental wrong" here?

2. Regan sees the animal rights movement as "cut from the same cloth" as human rights movements that oppose racism and sexism. Are the kinds of arguments that Regan advances for animal rights the same kinds of arguments that were advanced for human rights?

I regard myself as an advocate of animal rights—as a part of the animal rights movement. That movement, as I conceive it, is committed to a number of goals, including:

- the total abolition of the use of animals in science;
- the total dissolution of commercial animal agriculture;
- the total elimination of commercial and sport hunting and trapping.

There are, I know, people who profess to believe in animal rights but do not avow these goals. Factory farming, they say, is wrong—it violates animals' rights—but traditional animal agriculture is

From *In Defence of Animals,* edited by Peter Singer (Oxford: Basil Blackwell, 1985), pp. 13–26.

all right. Toxicity tests of cosmetics on animals violates their rights, but important medical research—cancer research for example—does not. The clubbing of baby seals is abhorrent, but not the harvesting of adult seals. I used to think I understood this reasoning. Not any more. You don't change unjust institutions by tidying them up.

What's wrong—fundamentally wrong—with the way animals are treated isn't the details that vary from case to case. It's the whole system. The forlornness of the veal calf is pathetic, heart wrenching; the pulsing pain of the chimp with electrodes planted deep in her brain is repulsive; the slow, torturous death of the raccoon caught in the leg-hold trap is agonizing. But what is wrong isn't the pain, isn't the suffering, isn't the deprivation. These compound what's wrong. Sometimes—often—they make it much, much worse. But they are not the fundamental wrong.

The fundamental wrong is the system that allows us to view animals as our resources, here for us—to be eaten, or surgically manipulated, or exploited for sport or money. Once we accept this view of animals—as our resources—the rest is as predictable as it is regrettable. Why worry about their loneliness, their pain, their death? Since animals exist for us, to benefit us in one way or another, what harms them really doesn't matter—or matters only if it starts to bother us, makes us feel a trifle uneasy. . . .

In the case of animals in science, whether and how we abolish their use . . . are to a large extent political questions. People must change their beliefs before they change their habits. Enough people, especially those elected to public office, must believe in change—must want it—before we will have laws that protect the rights of animals. This process of change is very complicated, very demanding, very exhausting, calling for the efforts of many hands in education, publicity, political organization and activity, down to the licking of envelopes and stamps. As a trained and practicing philosopher, the sort of contribution I can make is limited but, I like to think, important. The currency of philosophy is ideas—their meaning and rational foundation—not the nuts and bolts of the legislative process, say, or the mechanics of community organization. That's what I have been exploring over the past ten years or so in my essays and talks and, most recently, in my book, *The Case for Animal Rights.* I believe the major conclusions I reach in the book are true because they are supported by the weight of the best arguments. I believe the idea of animal rights has reason, not just emotion, on its side.

In the space I have at my disposal here I can only sketch, in the barest outline, some of the main features of the book. Its main themes—and we should not be surprised by this—involve asking and answering deep, foundational moral questions about what morality is, how it should be understood, and what is the best moral theory, all considered. I hope I can convey something of the shape I think this theory takes. The attempt to do this will be (to use a word a friendly critic once used to describe my work) cerebral, perhaps too cerebral. But this is misleading. My feelings about how animals are sometimes treated run just as deep and just as strong as those of my more volatile compatriots. Philosophers do—to use the jargon of the day—have a right side to their brains. If it's the left side we contribute (or mainly should), that's because what talents we have reside there.

How to proceed? We begin by asking how the moral status of animals has been understood by thinkers who deny that animals have rights. Then we test the mettle of their ideas by seeing how well they stand up under the heat of fair criticism. If we start our thinking in this way, we soon find that some people believe that we have no duties directly to animals, that we owe nothing to them, that we can do nothing that wrongs them. Rather, we can do wrong acts that involve animals, and so we have duties regarding them, though none to them. Such views may be called indirect duty views. By way of illustration: suppose your neighbor kicks your dog. Then your neighbor has done something wrong. But not to your dog. The wrong that has been done is a wrong to you. After all, it is wrong to upset people, and your neighbor's kicking your dog upsets you. So you are the one who is wronged, not your dog. Or again: by kicking your dog your neighbor damages your property. And since it is wrong to damage another person's property, your neighbor has done something wrong—to you, of course, not to your dog. Your neighbor no more wrongs your dog than your car would be wronged if the wind-shield were smashed. Your neighbor's duties involving your dog are indirect duties to you. More gen-erally, all of our duties regarding animals are indirect duties to one another—to humanity.

How could someone try to justify such a view? Someone might say that your dog doesn't feel anything and so isn't hurt by your neighbor's kick, doesn't care about the pain since none is felt, is as unaware of anything as is your windshield. Someone might say this, but no rational person will, since, among other considerations, such a view will commit anyone who holds it to the position that no human being feels pain either—that human beings also don't care about what happens to them. A second possibility is that though both humans and your dog are hurt when kicked, it is only human pain that matters. But, again, no rational person can believe this. Pain is pain wherever it occurs. If your neighbor's causing you pain is wrong because of the pain that is caused, we cannot rationally ignore or dismiss the moral relevance of the pain that your dog feels.

Philosophers who hold indirect duty views—and many still do—have come to understand that they must avoid the two defects just noted: that is, both the view that animals don't feel anything as well as the idea that only human pain can be morally relevant. Among such thinkers the sort of view now favored is one or other form of what is called contractarianism.

Here, very crudely, is the root idea: morality consists of a set of rules that individuals volun-tarily agree to abide by, as we do when we sign a contract (hence the name contractarianism). Those who understand and accept the terms of the contract are covered directly; they have rights created and recognized by, and protected in, the contract. And these contractors can also have protection spelled out for others who, though they lack the ability to understand morality and so cannot sign the contract themselves, are loved or cherished by those who can. Thus young children, for example, are unable to sign contracts and lack rights. But they are protected by the contract nonetheless because of the sentimental interests of others, most notably their parents. So we have, then, duties involving these children, duties regarding them, but no duties to them. Our duties in their case are indirect du-ties to other human beings, usually their parents.

As for animals, since they cannot understand contracts, they obviously cannot sign; and since they cannot sign, they have no rights. Like children, however, some animals are the objects of the sen-timental interest of others. You, for example, love your dog or cat. So those animals that enough peo-ple care about (companion animals, whales, baby seals, the American bald eagle), though they lack rights themselves, will be protected because of the sentimental interests of people. I have, then, ac-cording to contractarianism, no duty directly to your dog or any other animal, not even the duty not to cause them pain or suffering; my duty not to hurt them is a duty I have to those people who care about what happens to them. As for other animals, where no or little sentimental interest is pres-ent—in the case of farm animals, for example, or laboratory rats—what duties we have grow weaker and weaker, perhaps to a vanishing point. The pain and death they endure, though real, are not wrong if no one cares about them.

When it comes to the moral status of animals, contractarianism could be a hard view to refute if it were an adequate theoretical approach to the moral status of human beings. It is not adequate in this latter respect, however, which makes the question of its adequacy in the former case, regarding animals, utterly moot. For consider: morality, according to the (crude) contractarian position before us, consists of rules that people agree to abide by. What people? Well, enough to make a difference—enough, that is, collectively to have the power to enforce the rules that are drawn up in the contract. That is very well and good for the signatories but not so good for anyone who is not asked to sign. And there is nothing in contractarianism of the sort we are discussing that guarantees or requires that everyone will have a chance to participate equally in framing the rules of morality. The result is that this approach to ethics could sanction the most blatant forms of social, economic, moral and political injustice, ranging from a repressive caste system to systematic racial or sexual discrimination. Might, according to this theory, does make right. Let those who are the victims of injustice suffer as they will. It matters not so long as no one else—no contractor, or too few of them—cares about it. Such a theory takes one's moral breath away . . . as if, for example, there would be nothing wrong with apartheid in South Africa if few white South Africans were upset by it. A theory with so little to recommend it at the level of the ethics of our treatment of our fellow humans cannot have anything more to recommend it when it comes to the ethics of how we treat our fellow animals.

The version of contractarianism just examined is, as I have noted, a crude variety, and in fairness to those of a contractarian persuasion it must be noted that much more refined, subtle and ingenious varieties are possible. For example, John Rawls, in his *A Theory of Justice,* sets forth a version of contractarianism that forces contractors to ignore the accidental features of being a human being—for example, whether one is white or black, male or female, a genius or of modest intellect. Only by ignoring such features, Rawls believes, can we ensure that the principles of justice that contractors would agree upon are not based on bias or prejudice. Despite the improvement a view such as Rawls's represents over the cruder forms of contractarianism, it remains deficient: it systematically denies that we have direct duties to those human beings who do not have a sense of justice—young children, for instance, and many mentally retarded humans. And yet it seems reasonably certain that, were we to torture a young child or a retarded elder, we would be doing something that wronged him or her, not something that would be wrong if (and only if) other humans with a sense of justice were upset. And since this is true in the case of these humans, we cannot rationally deny the same in the case of animals.

Indirect duty views, then, including the best among them, fail to command our rational assent. Whatever ethical theory we should accept rationally, therefore, it must at least recognize that we have some duties directly to animals, just as we have some duties directly to each other. . . .

Some people think that the theory we are looking for is utilitarianism. A utilitarian accepts two moral principles. The first is that of equality: everyone's interests count, and similar interests must be counted as having similar weight or importance. White or black, American or Iranian, human or animal—everyone's pain or frustration matters, and matters just as much as the equivalent pain or frustration of anyone else. The second principle a utilitarian accepts is that of utility: do the act that will bring about the best balance between satisfaction and frustration for everyone affected by the outcome.

As a utilitarian, then, here is how I am to approach the task of deciding what I morally ought to do: I must ask who will be affected if I choose to do one thing rather than another, how much each individual will be affected, and where the best results are most likely to lie—which option, in other words, is most likely to bring about the best results, the best balance between satisfaction and frustration. That option, whatever it may be, is the one I ought to choose. That is where my moral duty lies.

The great appeal of utilitarianism rests with its uncompromising egalitarianism: everyone's interests count and count as much as the like interests of everyone else. The kind of odious discrimination that some forms of contractarianism can justify—discrimination based on race or sex, for example—seems disallowed in principle by utilitarianism, as is speciesism, systematic discrimination based on species membership.

The equality we find in utilitarianism, however, is not the sort an advocate of animal or human rights should have in mind. Utilitarianism has no room for the equal moral rights of different individuals because it has no room for their equal inherent value or worth. What has value for the utilitarian is the satisfaction of an individual's interests, not the individual whose interests they are. A universe in which you satisfy your desire for water, food and warmth is, other things being equal, better than a universe in which these desires are frustrated. And the same is true in the case of an animal with similar desires. But neither you nor the animal have any value in your own right. Only your feelings do.

Here is an analogy to help make the philosophical point clearer: a cup contains different liquids, sometimes sweet, sometimes bitter, sometimes a mix of the two. What has value are the liquids: the sweeter the better, the bitterer the worse. The cup, the container, has no value. It is what goes into it, not what they go into, that has value. For the utilitarian you and I are like the cup; we have no value as individuals and thus no equal value. What has value is what goes into us, what we serve as receptacles for; our feelings of satisfaction have positive value, our feelings of frustration negative value.

Serious problems arise for utilitarianism when we remind ourselves that it enjoins us to bring about the best consequences. What does this mean? It doesn't mean the best consequences for me alone, or for my family or friends, or any other person taken individually. No, what we must do is, roughly, as follows: we must add up (somehow!) the separate satisfactions and frustrations of everyone likely to be affected by our choice, the satisfactions in one column, the frustrations in the other. We must total each column for each of the options before us. That is what it means to say the theory is aggregative. And then we must choose that option which is most likely to bring about the best balance of totaled satisfactions over totaled frustrations. Whatever act would lead to this outcome is the one we ought morally to perform—it is where our moral duty lies. And that act quite clearly might not be the same one that would bring about the best results for me personally, or for my family or friends, or for a lab animal. The best aggregated consequences for everyone concerned are not necessarily the best for each individual.

That utilitarianism is an aggregative theory—different individuals' satisfactions or frustrations are added, or summed, or totaled—is the key objection to this theory. My Aunt Bea is old, inactive, a cranky, sour person, though not physically ill. She prefers to go on living. She is also rather rich. I could make a fortune if I could get my hands on her money, money she intends to give me in any event, after she dies, but which she refuses to give me now. In order to avoid a huge tax bite, I plan to donate a handsome sum of my profits to a local children's hospital. Many, many children will benefit from my generosity, and much joy will be brought to their parents, relatives and friends. If I don't get the money rather soon, all these ambitions will come to naught. The once-in-a-lifetime opportunity to make a real killing will be gone. Why, then, not kill my Aunt Bea? Oh, of course I might get caught. But I'm no fool and, besides, her doctor can be counted on to cooperate (he has an eye for the same investment and I happen to know a good deal about his shady past). The deed can be done . . . professionally, shall we say. There is very little chance of getting caught. And as for my conscience being guilt-ridden,

I am a resourceful sort of fellow and will take more than sufficient comfort—as I lie on the beach at Acapulco—in contemplating the joy and health I have brought to so many others.

Suppose Aunt Bea is killed and the rest of the story comes out as told. Would I have done anything wrong? Anything immoral? One would have thought that I had. Not according to utilitarianism. Since what I have done has brought about the best balance between totaled satisfaction and frustration for all those affected by the outcome, my action is not wrong. Indeed, in killing Aunt Bea the physician and I did what duty required.

This same kind of argument can be repeated in all sorts of cases, illustrating, time after time, how the utilitarian's position leads to results that impartial people find morally callous. It is wrong to kill my Aunt Bea in the name of bringing about the best results for others. A good end does not justify an evil means. Any adequate moral theory will have to explain why this is so. Utilitarianism fails in this respect and so cannot be the theory we seek.

What to do? Where to begin anew? The place to begin, I think, is with the utilitarian's view of the value of the individual—or, rather, lack of value. In its place, suppose we consider that you and I, for example, do have value as individuals—what we will call inherent value. To say we have such value is to say that we are something more than, something different from, mere receptacles. Moreover, to ensure that we do not pave the way for such injustices as slavery or sexual discrimination, we must believe that all who have inherent value have it equally, regardless of their sex, race, religion, birthplace and so on. Similarly to be discarded as irrelevant are one's talents or skills, intelligence and wealth, personality or pathology, whether one is loved and admired or despised and loathed. The genius and the retarded child, the prince and the pauper, the brain surgeon and the fruit vendor, Mother Teresa and the most unscrupulous used-car salesman—all have inherent value, all possess it equally, and all have an equal right to be treated with respect, to be treated in ways that do not reduce them to the status of things, as if they existed as resources for others. My value as an individual is independent of my usefulness to you. Yours is not dependent on your usefulness to me. For either of us to treat the other in ways that fail to show respect for the other's independent value is to act immorally, to violate the individual's rights.

Some of the rational virtues of this view—what I call the rights view—should be evident. Unlike (crude) contractarianism, for example, the rights view in principle denies the moral tolerability of any and all forms of racial, sexual or social discrimination; and unlike utilitarianism, this view in principle denies that we can justify good results by using evil means that violate an individual's rights—denies, for example, that it could be moral to kill my Aunt Bea to harvest beneficial consequences for others. That would be to sanction the disrespectful treatment of the individual in the name of the social good, something the rights view will not—categorically will not—ever allow.

The rights view, I believe, is rationally the most satisfactory moral theory. It surpasses all other theories in the degree to which it illuminates and explains the foundation of our duties to one another—the domain of human morality. On this score it has the best reasons, the best arguments, on its side. Of course, if it were possible to show that only human beings are included within its scope, then a person like myself, who believes in animal rights, would be obliged to look elsewhere.

But attempts to limit its scope to humans only can be shown to be rationally defective. Animals, it is true, lack many of the abilities humans possess. They can't read, do higher mathematics, build a bookcase or make baba ghanoush. Neither can many human beings, however, and yet we don't (and shouldn't) say that they (these humans) therefore have less inherent value, less of a right to be treated with respect, than do others. It is the similarities between those human beings who most clearly, most non-controversially have such value (the people reading this: for example) not our differences, that matter most. And the really crucial, the basic similarity is simply this: we are each of us the experiencing subject of a life, a conscious creature having an individual welfare that has importance to us whatever our usefulness to others. We want and prefer things, believe and feel things, recall and expect things. And all these dimensions of our life, including our pleasure and pain, our enjoyment and suffering, our satisfaction and frustration, our continued existence or our untimely death—all make a difference to the quality of our life as lived, as experienced, by us as individuals. As the same is true of those animals that concern us, . . . they too must be viewed as the experiencing subjects of a life, with inherent value of their own.

Some there are who resist the idea that animals have inherent value. "Only humans have such value," they profess. How might this narrow view be defended? Shall we say that only humans have the requisite intelligence, or autonomy, or reason? But there are many, many humans who fail to meet these standards and yet are reasonably viewed as having value above and beyond their usefulness to others. Shall we claim that only humans belong to the right species, the species Homo sapiens? But this is blatant speciesism. Will it be said, then, that all—and only—humans have immortal souls? Then our opponents have their work cut out for them. I am myself not ill-disposed to the proposition that there are immortal souls. Personally, I profoundly hope I have one. But I would not want to rest my position on a controversial ethical issue on the even more controversial question about who or what has an immortal soul. That is to dig one's hole deeper, not to climb out. Rationally, it is better to resolve moral issues without making more controversial assumptions than are needed. The question of who has inherent value is such a question, one that is resolved more rationally without the introduction of the idea of immortal souls than by its use.

Well, perhaps some will say that animals have some inherent value, only less than we have. Once again, however, attempts to defend this view can be shown to lack rational justification. What could be the basis of our having more inherent value than animals? Their lack of reason, or autonomy, or intellect? Only if we are willing to make the same judgment in the case of humans who are similarly deficient. But it is not true that such humans—the retarded child, for example, or the mentally deranged—have less inherent value than you or I. Neither, then, can we rationally sustain the view that animals, like them in being the experiencing subjects of a life, have less inherent value. All who have inherent value have it equally, whether they be human animals or not.

Inherent value, then, belongs equally to those who are the experiencing subjects of a life. Whether it belongs to others—to rocks and rivers, trees and glaciers, for example—we do not know and may never know. But neither do we need to know, if we are to make the case for animal rights. We do not need to know, for example, how many people are eligible to vote in the next presidential election before we can know whether I am. Similarly, we do not need to know how many individuals have inherent value before we can know that some do. When it comes to the case for animal rights, then, what we need to know is whether the animals that, in our culture, are routinely eaten, hunted and used in our laboratories, for example, are like us in being subjects of a life. And we do know this. We do know that many—literally, billions and billions—of these animals are the subjects of a life in the sense explained and so have inherent value if we do. And since, in order to arrive at the best theory of our duties to one another, we must recognize our equal inherent value as individuals, reason—not sentiment, not emotion—reason compels us to recognize the equal inherent value of these animals and, with this, their equal right to be treated with respect.

That, *very* roughly, is the shape and feel of the case for animal rights. Most of the details of the supporting argument are missing. They are to be found in the book to which I alluded earlier. Here, the details go begging, and I must, in closing, limit myself to four final points.

The first is how the theory that underlies the case for animal rights shows that the animal rights movement is a part of, not antagonistic to, the human rights movement. The theory that rationally grounds the rights of animals also grounds the rights of humans. Thus those involved in the animal rights movement are partners in the struggle to secure respect for human rights—the rights of women, for example, or minorities, or workers. The animal rights movement is cut from the same moral cloth as these.

Second, having set out the broad outlines of the rights view, I can now say why its implications for . . . science, among other fields, are both clear and uncompromising. In the case of the use of animals in science, the rights view is categorically abolitionist. Lab animals are not our tasters; we are not their kings. Because these animals are treated routinely, systematically as if their value were reducible to their usefulness to others, they are routinely, systematically treated with a lack of respect, and thus are their rights routinely, systematically violated. This is just as true when they are used in trivial, duplicative, unnecessary or unwise research as it is when they are used in studies that hold out real promise of human benefits. We can't justify harming or killing a human being (my Aunt Bea, for example) just for these sorts of reason. Neither can we do so even in the case of so lowly a creature as a laboratory rat. It is not just refinement or reduction that is called for, not just larger, cleaner cages, not just more generous use of anesthetic or the elimination of multiple surgery, not just tidying up the system. It is complete replacement. The best we can do when it comes to using animals in science is—not to use them. That is where our duty lies, according to the rights view. . . .

My last two points are about philosophy, my profession. It is, most obviously, no substitute for political action. The words I have written here and in other places by themselves don't change a thing. It is what we do with the thoughts that the words express—our acts, our deeds—that changes things. All that philosophy can do, and all I have attempted, is to offer a vision of what our deeds should aim at. And the why. But not the how.

Finally, I am reminded of my thoughtful critic, the one I mentioned earlier, who chastised me for being too cerebral. Well, cerebral I have been: indirect duty views, utilitarianism, contractarianism—hardly the stuff deep passions are made of. I am also reminded, however, of the image another friend once set before me—the image of the ballerina as expressive of disciplined passion. Long hours of sweat and toil, of loneliness and practice, of doubt and fatigue: those are the discipline of her craft. But the passion is there too, the fierce drive to excel, to speak through her body, to do it right, to pierce our minds. That is the image of philosophy I would leave with you, not "too cerebral" but disciplined passion. Of the discipline enough has been seen. As for the passion: there are times, and these not infrequent, when tears come to my eyes when I see, or read, or hear of the wretched plight of animals in the hands of humans. Their pain, their suffering, their loneliness, their innocence, their death. Anger. Rage. Pity. Sorrow. Disgust. The whole creation groans under the weight of the evil we humans visit upon these mute, powerless creatures. It is our hearts, not just our heads, that call for an end to it all, that demand of us that we overcome, for them, the habits and forces behind their systematic oppression. All great movements, it is written, go through three stages: ridicule, discussion, adoption. It is the realization of this third stage, adoption, that requires both our passion and our discipline, our hearts and our heads. The fate of animals is in our hands. God grant we are equal to the task.

Journal/Discussion Questions

✍ *In your own life, what moral standing or importance do animals have? What difference does animal suffering make to you? How were you affected by Regan's article?*

1. What does Regan mean by "indirect duty views"? What criticisms does he offer of them? In what ways do you agree/disagree with his criticisms?

2. According to Regan, what is "contractarianism"? What criticisms does he offer of the contractarian approach to morality?

3. Why, according to Regan, should we reject utilitarian approaches to the issue of our relationship to animals?

4. Why, according to Regan, is the rights view superior to all other approaches to the issue of our relationship to animals? Do you agree with Regan's assessment?

Carl Cohen
"The Case for the Use of Animals in Biomedical Research"

Cohen offers a strong defense of the moral appropriateness of using animals in biomedical research. He offers arguments against those who maintain that animals have rights and suggests that, if we consider consequences, we will realize that these too permit animal use in research.

As You Read, Consider This:
1. What arguments does Cohen advance against the claim that animals have rights?
2. Defenders of animal rights and welfare often charge their opponents with "speciesism." How does Cohen respond to that criticism?
3. What is Cohen's position on substitution and reduction of animal use in biomedical research?

Using animals as research subjects in medical investigations is widely condemned on two grounds: first, because it wrongly violates the rights of animals,[1] and second, because it wrongly imposes on sentient creatures much avoidable suffering.[2] Neither of these arguments is sound. The first relies on a mistaken understanding of rights; the second relies on a mistaken calculation of consequences. Both deserve definitive dismissal.

Why Animals Have No Rights

A right, properly understood, is a claim, or potential claim, that one party may exercise against another. The target against whom such a claim may be registered can be a single person, a group, a community, or (perhaps) all humankind. The content of rights claims also varies greatly: repayment

Carl Cohen, "The Case for the Use of Animals in Biomedical Research," *New England Journal of Medicine 315,* pp. 865–870. Reprinted with the permission of the author.

of loans, nondiscrimination by employers, noninterference by the state, and so on. To comprehend any genuine right fully, therefore, we must know who holds the right, against whom it is held, and to what it is a right.

Alternative sources of rights add complexity. Some rights are grounded in constitution and law (e.g., the right of an accused to trial by jury); some rights are moral but give no legal claims (e.g., my right to your keeping the promise you gave me); and some rights (e.g., against theft or assault) are rooted both in morals and in law.

The differing targets, contents, and sources of rights, and their inevitable conflict, together weave a tangled web. Notwithstanding all such complications, this much is clear about rights in general: they are in every case claims, or potential claims, within a community of moral agents. Rights arise, and can be intelligibly defended, only among beings who actually do, or can, make moral claims against one another. Whatever else rights may be, therefore, they are necessarily human; their possessors are persons, human beings.

The attributes of human beings from which this moral capability arises have been described variously by philosophers, both ancient and modern: the inner consciousness of a free will (Saint Augustine)[3]; the grasp, by human reason, of the binding character of moral law (Saint Thomas)[4]; the self-conscious participation of human beings in an objective ethical order (Hegel)[5]; human membership in an organic moral community (Bradley)[6]; the development of the human self through the consciousness of other moral selves (Mead)[7]; and the underivative, intuitive cognition of the rightness of an action (Prichard).[8] Most influential has been Immanuel Kant's emphasis on the universal human possession of a uniquely moral will and the autonomy its use entails.[9] Humans confront choices that are purely moral; humans—but certainly not dogs or mice—lay down moral laws, for others and for themselves. Human beings are self-legislative, morally autonomous.

Animals (that is, nonhuman animals, the ordinary sense of that word) lack this capacity for free moral judgment. They are not beings of a kind capable of exercising or responding to moral claims. Animals therefore have no rights, and they can have none. This is the core of the argument about the alleged rights of animals. The holders of rights must have the capacity to comprehend rules of duty, governing all including themselves. In applying such rules, the holders of rights must recognize possible conflicts between what is in their own interest and what is just. Only in a community of beings capable of self-restricting moral judgments can the concept of a right be correctly invoked.

Humans have such moral capacities. They are in this sense self-legislative, are members of communities governed by moral rules, and do possess rights. Animals do not have such moral capacities. They are not morally self-legislative, cannot possibly be members of a truly moral community, and therefore cannot possess rights. In conducting research on animal subjects, therefore, we do not violate their rights, because they have none to violate.

To animate life, even in its simplest forms, we give a certain natural reverence. But the possession of rights presupposes a moral status not attained by the vast majority of living things. We must not infer, therefore, that a live being has, simply in being alive, a "right" to its life. The assertion that all animals, only because they are alive and have interests, also possess the "Right to life"[10] is an abuse of that phrase, and wholly without warrant.

It does not follow from this, however, that we are morally free to do anything we please to animals. Certainly not. In our dealings with animals, as in our dealings with other human beings, we have obligations that do not arise from claims against us based on rights. Rights entail obligations, but many of the things one ought to do are in no way tied to another's entitlement. Rights and obligations are not reciprocals of one another, and it is a serious mistake to suppose that they are.

Illustrations are helpful. Obligations may arise from internal commitments made: physicians have obligations to their patients not grounded merely in their patients' rights. Teachers have such obligations to their students, shepherds to their dogs, and cowboys to their horses. Obligations may arise from differences of status: adults owe special care when playing with young children, and children owe special care when playing with young pets. Obligations may arise from special relationships: the payment of my son's college tuition is something to which he may have no right, although it may be my obligation to bear the burden if I reasonably can; my dog has no right to daily exercise and veterinary care, but I do have the obligation to provide these things for her. Obligations may arise from particular acts or circumstances: one may be obliged to another for a special kindness done, or obliged to put an animal out of its misery in view of its condition—although neither the human benefactor nor the dying animal may have had a claim of right.

Plainly, the grounds of our obligations to humans and to animals are manifold and cannot be formulated simply. Some hold that there is a general obligation to do no gratuitous harm to sentient creatures (the principle of nonmaleficence); some hold that there is a general obligation to do good to sentient creatures when that is reasonably within one's power (the principle of beneficence). In our dealings with animals, few will deny that we are at least obliged to act humanely—that is, to treat them with the decency and concern that we owe, as sensitive human beings, to other sentient creatures. To treat animals humanely, however, is not to treat them as humans or as the holders of rights.

A common objection, which deserves a response, may be paraphrased as follows:

> If having rights requires being able to make moral claims, to grasp and apply moral laws, then many humans—the brain-damaged, the comatose, the senile—who plainly lack those capacities must be without rights. But that is absurd. This proves [the critic concludes] that rights do not depend on the presence of moral capacities.[11]

This objection fails; it mistakenly treats an essential feature of humanity as though it were a screen for sorting humans. The capacity for moral judgment that distinguishes humans from animals is not a test to be administered to human beings one by one. Persons who are unable, because of some disability, to perform the full moral functions natural to human beings are certainly not for that reason ejected from the moral community. The issue is one of kind. Humans are of such a kind that they may be the subject of experiments only with their voluntary consent. The choices they make freely must be respected. Animals are of such a kind that it is impossible for them, in principle, to give or withhold voluntary consent or to make a moral choice. What humans retain when disabled, animals have never had.

A second objection, also often made, may be paraphrased as follows:

> Capacities will not succeed in distinguishing humans from the other animals. Animals also reason; animals also communicate with one another; animals also care passionately for their young; animals also exhibit desires and preferences.[12] Features of moral relevance—rationality, interdependence, and love— are not exhibited uniquely by human beings. Therefore [this critic concludes], there can be no solid moral distinction between humans and other animals.[13]

This criticism misses the central point. It is not the ability to communicate or to reason, or dependence on one another, or care for the young, or the exhibition of preference, or any such behavior that marks the critical divide. Analogies between human families and those of monkeys, or between human communities and those of wolves, and the like, are entirely beside the point. Patterns of conduct are not at issue. Animals do indeed exhibit remarkable behavior at times. Conditioning, fear, instinct, and intelligence all contribute to species survival. Membership in a community of moral agents nevertheless remains impossible for them. Actors subject to moral judgment must be capable of grasping the generality of an ethical premise in a practical syllogism. Humans act immorally often enough, but only they—never wolves or monkeys—can discern, by applying some moral rule to the facts of a case, that a given act ought or ought not to be performed. The moral restraints imposed by humans on themselves are thus highly abstract and are often in conflict with the self-interest of the agent. Communal behavior among animals, even when most intelligent and most endearing, does not approach autonomous morality in this fundamental sense.

Genuinely moral acts have an internal as well as an external dimension. Thus, in law, an act can be criminal only when the guilty deed, the actus reus, is done with a guilty mind, mens rea. No animal can ever commit a crime; bringing animals to criminal trial is the mark of primitive ignorance. The claims of moral right are similarly inapplicable to them. Does a lion have a right to eat a baby zebra? Does a baby zebra have a right not to be eaten? Such questions, mistakenly invoking the concept of right where it does not belong, do not make good sense. Those who condemn biomedical research because it violates "animal rights" commit the same blunder.

In Defense of "Speciesism"

Abandoning reliance on animal rights, some critics resort instead to animal sentience—their feelings of pain and distress. We ought to desist from the imposition of pain insofar as we can. Since all or nearly all experimentation on animals does impose pain and could be readily forgone, say these critics, it should be stopped. The ends sought may be worthy, but those ends do not justify imposing agonies on humans, and by animals the agonies are felt no less. The laboratory use of animals (these critics conclude) must therefore be ended—or at least very sharply curtailed.

Argument of this variety is essentially utilitarian, often expressly so;[14] it is based on the calculation of the net product, in pains and pleasures, resulting from experiments on animals. Jeremy Bentham, comparing horses and dogs with other sentient creatures, is thus commonly quoted: "The question is not, Can they reason? nor Can they talk? but, Can they suffer?"[15]

Animals certainly can suffer and surely ought not to be made to suffer needlessly. But in inferring, from these uncontroversial premises, that biomedical research causing animal distress is largely (or wholly) wrong, the critic commits two serious errors.

The first error is the assumption, often explicitly defended, that all sentient animals have equal moral standing. Between a dog and a human being, according to this view, there is no moral difference; hence the pains suffered by dogs must be weighed no differently from the pains suffered by humans. To deny such equality, according to this critic, is to give unjust preference to one species over another; it is "speciesism." The most influential statement of this moral equality of species was made by Peter Singer:

> The racist violates the principle of equality by giving greater weight to the interests of members of his own race when there is a clash between their interests and the interests of those of another race. The sexist violates the principle of equality by favoring the interests of his own sex. Similarly the speciesist

allows the interests of his own species to override the greater interests of members of other species. The pattern is identical in each case.[16]

This argument is worse than unsound; it is atrocious. It draws an offensive moral conclusion from a deliberately devised verbal parallelism that is utterly specious. Racism has no rational ground whatever. Differing degrees of respect or concern for humans for no other reason than that they are members of different races is an injustice totally without foundation in the nature of the races themselves. Racists, even if acting on the basis of mistaken factual beliefs, do grave moral wrong precisely because there is no morally relevant distinction among the races. The supposition of such differences has led to outright horror. The same is true of the sexes, neither sex being entitled by right to greater respect or concern than the other. No dispute here.

Between species of animate life, however—between (for example) humans on the one hand and cats or rats on the other—the morally relevant differences are enormous and almost universally appreciated. Humans engage in moral reflection; humans are morally autonomous; humans are members of moral communities, recognizing just claims against their own interest. Human beings do have rights; theirs is a moral status very different from that of cats or rats.

I am a speciesist. Speciesism is not merely plausible; it is essential for right conduct, because those who will not make the morally relevant distinctions among species are almost certain, in consequence, to misapprehend their true obligations. The analogy between speciesism and racism is insidious. Every sensitive moral judgment requires that the differing natures of the beings to whom obligations are owed be considered. If all forms of animate life—or vertebrate animal life?—must be treated equally, and if therefore in evaluating a research program the pains of a rodent count equally with the pains of a human, we are forced to conclude (1) that neither humans nor rodents possess rights, or (2) that rodents possess all the rights that humans possess. Both alternatives are absurd. Yet one or the other must be swallowed if the moral equality of all species is to be defended.

Humans owe to other humans a degree of moral regard that cannot be owed to animals. Some humans take on the obligation to support and heal others, both humans and animals, as a principal duty in their lives; the fulfillment of that duty may require the sacrifice of many animals. If biomedical investigators abandon the effective pursuit of their professional objectives because they are convinced that they may not do to animals what the service of humans requires, they will fail, objectively, to do their duty. Refusing to recognize the moral differences among species is a sure path to calamity. (The largest animal rights group in the country is People for the Ethical Treatment of Animals; its co-director, Ingrid Newkirk, calls research using animal subjects "fascism" and "supremacism." "Animal liberationists do not separate out the human animal," she says, "so there is no rational basis for saying that a human being has special rights. A rat is a pig is a dog is a boy. They're all mammals.")[17]

Those who claim to base their objection to the use of animals in biomedical research on their reckoning of the net pleasures and pains produced make a second error, equally grave. Even if it were true—as it is surely not—that the pains of all animate beings must be counted equally, a cogent utilitarian calculation requires that we weigh all the consequences of the use, and of the non-use, of animals in laboratory research. Critics relying (however mistakenly) on animal rights may claim to ignore the beneficial results of such research, rights being trump cards to which interest and advantage must give way. But an argument that is explicitly framed in terms of interest and benefit for all over the long run must attend also to the disadvantageous consequences of not using animals in research, and to all the achievements attained and attainable only through their use. The sum of the benefits of their use is utterly beyond quantification. The elimination of horrible disease, the increase of longevity, the avoidance of great pain, the saving of lives, and the improvement of the quality of lives (for humans and for animals) achieved through research using animals is so incalculably great that the argument of these critics, systematically pursued, establishes not their conclusion but its reverse: to refrain from using animals in biomedical research is, on utilitarian grounds, morally wrong.

When balancing the pleasures and pains resulting from the use of animals in research, we must not fail to place on the scales the terrible pains that would have resulted, would be suffered now, and would long continue had animals not been used. Every disease eliminated, every vaccine developed, every method of pain relief devised, every surgical procedure invented, every prosthetic device implanted—indeed, virtually every modern medical therapy is due, in part or in whole, to experimentation using animals. Nor may we ignore, in the balancing process, the predictable gains in human (and animal) well-being that are probably achievable in the future but that will not be achieved if the decision is made now to desist from such research or to curtail it.

Medical investigators are seldom insensitive to the distress their work may cause animal subjects. Opponents of research using animals are frequently insensitive to the cruelty of the results of the restrictions they would impose.[18] Untold numbers of human beings—real persons, although not now identifiable-would suffer grievously as the consequence of this well-meaning but shortsighted tenderness. If the morally relevant differences between humans and animals are borne in mind, and if all relevant considerations are weighed, the calculation of long-term consequences must give overwhelming support for biomedical research using animals.

Concluding Remarks

Substitution

The humane treatment of animals requires that we desist from experimenting on them if we can accomplish the same result using alternative methods—in vitro experimentation, computer simulation, or others. Critics of some experiments using animals rightly make this point.

It would be a serious error to suppose, however, that alternative techniques could soon be used in most research now using live animal subjects. No other methods now on the horizon—or perhaps ever to be available—can fully replace the testing of a drug, a procedure, or a vaccine, in live organisms. The flood of new medical possibilities being opened by the successes of recombinant DNA technology will turn to a trickle if testing on live animals is forbidden. When initial trials entail great risks, there may be no forward movement whatever without the use of live animal subjects. In seeking knowledge that may prove critical in later clinical applications, the unavailability of animals for inquiry may spell complete stymie. In the United States, federal regulations require the testing of new drugs and other products on animals, for efficacy and safety, before human beings are exposed to them.[19] We would not want it otherwise.

Every advance in medicine—every new drug, new operation, new therapy of any kind—must sooner or later be tried on a living being for the first time. That trial, controlled or uncontrolled, will be an experiment. The subject of that experiment, if it is not an animal, will be a human being. Prohibiting the use of live animals in biomedical research, therefore, or sharply restricting it, must result either in the blockage of much valuable research or in the replacement of animal subjects with human subjects. These are the consequences—unacceptable to most reasonable persons—of not using animals in research.

Reduction

Should we not at least reduce the use of animals in biomedical research? No, we should increase it, to avoid when feasible the use of humans as experimental subjects. Medical investigations putting human subjects at some risk are numerous and greatly varied. The risks run in such experiments are usually unavoidable, and (thanks to earlier experiments on animals) most such risks are minimal or moderate. But some experimental risks are substantial.

When an experimental protocol that entails substantial risk to humans comes before an institutional review board, what response is appropriate? The investigation, we may suppose, is promising and deserves support, so long as its human subjects are protected against unnecessary dangers. May not the investigators be fairly asked, Have you done all that you can to eliminate risk to humans by the extensive testing of that drug, that procedure, or that device on animals? To achieve maximal safety for humans we are right to require thorough experimentation on animal subjects before humans are involved.

Opportunities to increase human safety in this way are commonly missed; trials in which risks may be shifted from humans to animals are often not devised, sometimes not even considered. Why? For the investigator, the use of animals as subjects is often more expensive, in money and time, than the use of human subjects. Access to suitable human subjects is often quick and convenient, whereas access to appropriate animal subjects may be awkward, costly, and burdened with red tape. Physician-investigators have often had more experience working with human beings and know precisely where the needed pool of subjects is to be found and how they may be enlisted. Animals, and the procedures for their use, are often less familiar to these investigators. Moreover, the use of animals in place of humans is now more likely to be the target of zealous protests from without. The upshot is that humans are sometimes subjected to risks that animals could have borne, and should have borne, in their place. To maximize the protection of human subjects, I conclude, the wide and imaginative use of live animal subjects should be encouraged rather than discouraged. This enlargement in the use of animals is our obligation.

Consistency

Finally, inconsistency between the profession and the practice of many who oppose research using animals deserves comment. This frankly ad hominem observation aims chiefly to show that a coherent position rejecting the use of animals in medical research imposes costs so high as to be intolerable even to the critics themselves.

One cannot coherently object to the killing of animals in biomedical investigations while continuing to eat them. Anesthetics and thoughtful animal husbandry render the level of actual animal distress in the laboratory generally lower than that in the abattoir. So long as death and discomfort do not substantially differ in the two contexts, the consistent objector must not only refrain from all eating of animals but also protest as vehemently against others eating them as against others experimenting on them. No less vigorously must the critic object to the wearing of animal hides in coats and shoes, to employment in any industrial enterprise that uses animal parts, and to any commercial development that will cause death or distress to animals.

Killing animals to meet human needs for food, clothing, and shelter is judged entirely reasonable by most persons. The ubiquity of these uses and the virtual universality of moral support for them confront the opponent of research using animals with an inescapable difficulty. How can the many common uses of animals be judged morally worthy, while their use in scientific investigation is judged unworthy?

The number of animals used in research is but the tiniest fraction of the total used to satisfy assorted human appetites. That these appetites, often base and satisfiable in other ways, morally justify the far larger consumption of animals, whereas the quest for improved human health and understanding cannot justify the far smaller, is wholly implausible. Aside from the numbers of animals involved, the distinction in terms of worthiness of use, drawn with regard to any single animal, is not defensible. A given sheep is surely not more justifiably used to put lamb chops on the supermarket counter than to serve in testing a new contraceptive or a new prosthetic device. The needless killing of animals is wrong; if the common killing of them for our food or convenience is right, the less common but more humane uses of animals in the service of medical science are certainly not less right.

Scrupulous vegetarianism, in matters of food, clothing, shelter, commerce, and recreation, and in all other spheres, is the only fully coherent position the critic may adopt. At great human cost, the lives of fish and crustaceans must also be protected, with equal vigor, if speciesism has been forsworn. A very few consistent critics adopt this position. It is the reductio ad absurdum of the rejection of moral distinctions between animals and human beings.

Opposition to the use of animals in research is based on arguments of two different kinds—those relying on the alleged rights of animals and those relying on the consequences for animals. I have argued that arguments of both kinds must fail. We surely do have obligations to animals, but they have, and can have, no rights against us on which research can infringe. In calculating the consequences of animal research, we must weigh all the long-term benefits of the results achieved—to animals and to humans—and in that calculation we must not assume the moral equality of all animate species.

Endnotes

1. T. Regan, *The Case for Animal Rights* (Berkeley, Calif.: University of California Press, 1983).

2. P. Singer, *Animal Liberation* (New York: Avon Books, 1977).

3. Augustine (A.D. 397), *Confessions* (New York: Pocketbooks, 1957), bk. 7, pp. 104–26.

4. Aquinas (A.D. 1273), *Summa Theologica* (Philosophic Texts) (New York: Oxford University Press, 1960), pp. 353–66.

5. G. W. F. Hegel (1821), *Philosophy of Right* (London: Oxford University Press, 1952), pp. 105–10.

6. F. H. Bradley, "Why Should I Be Moral?" in *Ethical Theories,* ed. A. I. Melden (New York: Prentice-Hall, 1950), pp. 345–59.

7. G. H. Mead (1925), "The Genesis of the Self and Social Control" in *Selected Writings,* ed. A. J. Reck (Indianapolis: Bobbs-Merrill, 1964), pp. 264–93.

8. H. A. Prichard (1912), "Does Moral Philosophy Rest on a Mistake?" in *Readings in Ethical Theory,* ed. W. Cellars and J. Hospers (New York: Appleton-Century-Crofts, 1952), pp. 149–63.

9. I. Kant (1785), *Fundamental Principles of the Metaphysic of Morals* (New York: Liberal Arts Press, 1949).

10. B. E. Rollin, *Animal Rights and Human Morality* (Buffalo, N.Y.: Prometheus Books, 1981).

11. [See note 1 and] C. Hoff, "Immoral and Moral Uses of Animals," *New England Journal of Medicine* 302 (1980): 115–18.

12. [See note 11 and] D. Jamieson, "Killing Persons and Other Beings," in *Ethics and Animals,* ed. H. B. Miller and W. H. Williams (Clifton, N.J.: Humana Press, 1983), pp. 135–46.

13. B. E. Rollin, *Animal Rights and Human Morality.*

14. P. Singer, "Ten Years of Animal Liberation," *New York Review of Books* 31 (1985): 46–52.

15. J. Bentham, *Introduction to the Principles of Morals and Legislation* (London: Athlone Press, 1970).

16. P. Singer, *Animal Liberation.*

17. K. McCabe, "Who Will Live, Who Will Die?" *Washingtonian Magazine,* August 1986, 115.

18. P. Singer, *Animal Liberation.*

19. U. S. Code of Federal Regulations, Title 21, Sect. 505(i). Food, Drug, and Cosmetic Regulations. U. S. Code of Federal Regulations, Title 16, Sect. 1500.40-2. Consumer Product Regulations.

Journal/Discussion Questions

1. Cohen maintains that there are many morally relevant differences between humans and other animals. What are they, according to Cohen? Critically evaluate his argument.

2. Many moderates maintain that, although animals may sometimes be used in biomedical research, this ought to be avoided as much as possible. What does Cohen have to say about this argument?

Concluding Discussion Questions

Where Do You Stand Now?

Instructions

You have already answered the following questions in your moral problems self-quiz at the beginning of this book. Now that you have studied the material in this section, take a moment to answer the same questions again.

	Strongly Agree	Agree	Undecided	Disagree	Strongly Disagree	*Chapter 10: Living Together with Animals*
46.	❏	❏	❏	❏	❏	There's nothing morally wrong with eating veal.
47.	❏	❏	❏	❏	❏	It's morally permissible to cause animals pain to do medical research that benefits human beings.
48.	❏	❏	❏	❏	❏	All animals have the same moral standing.
49.	❏	❏	❏	❏	❏	Zoos are a morally good thing.
50.	❏	❏	❏	❏	❏	There is nothing morally wrong with hunting.

Compare your answers to this self-quiz with the answers to the initial self-quiz. How, if at all, have your answers changed? How have the *reasons* for your answers changed?

Journal/Discussion Questions

✍ *In light of the material in this chapter, how have your views changed on the ethical treatment of animals in regard to issues such as keeping pets, eating meat, wearing fur and animal products (such as leather shoes), using animals for testing shampoos, and using animals for medical research?*

1. In light of all the readings in this chapter, what changes (if any) do you think we should make in the ways in which animals are treated in our society? Why should peo- ple be motivated to make these changes if they involve some degree of sacrifice on their part?

2. If we grant animals rights, then we are accepting the general principle that non-humans can have rights. One of the issues in the abortion debate has been the claim that the fetus is not (yet) a human being and thus does not have rights. If animals have rights, does this have moral implications for the rights of fetuses?

3. Drawing on the readings in this and the previous chapter, discuss the relationship between animals rights, vegetarianism, and world hunger. To what extent could problems of world hunger be solved by vegetarianism, an option that would at the same time reduce animal suffering? How would a utilitarian answer this question? How do you answer it?

For Further Reading

Web Resources

For extensive resources on ethical issues in our relationships with animals, see the animal rights page of *Ethics Updates* (http://ethics.sandiego.edu).

Journals

In addition to the standard journals in ethics discussed in the bibliographical essay at the end of Chapter 1, there are two journals devoted solely to issues related to animals: *Ethics and Animals* and *Between the Species.*

Survey Articles

For an overview of the issues relating to animals, see R. G. Frey, "Animals"*The Oxford Handbook of Practical Ethics,* edited by Hugh LaFollette (Oxford: Oxford University Press, 2003), pp. 161–187 and Jeff McMahan, "Animals," *A Companion to Applied Ethics: Blackwell Companions to Philosophy,* edited by R. G. Frey, (Malden, MA: Blackwell Publishing, 2003), pp. 525–536. Tom Regan's "Treatment of Animals," in *Encyclopedia of Ethics,* edited by Lawrence Becker (New York: Garland, 1992), Vol. I, pp. 42–46 provides an excellent, short survey of the principal ethical issues surrounding the treatment of animals; it includes a bibliography. Lori Gruen's "Animals," in *A Companion to Ethics,* edited by Peter Singer (Oxford: Blackwell, 1991), pp. 343–353 also provides an excellent summary of these issues along with a bibliography. For a broader social history of the animal rights movement, see "Man's Mirror; History of Animal Rights," *The Economist,* Vol. 321, No. 7733 (November 16, 1991) p. 21 ff. For an overview of issues relating to moral status, see Mary-Anne Warren, "Moral Status," *A Companion to Applied Ethics: Blackwell Companions to Philosophy,* edited by R. G. Frey (Malden MA: Blackwell Publishing, 2003), pp. 439–50.

Anthologies

There are a number of excellent anthologies dealing with issues of the moral status of animals, including the issue entitled "In the Company of Animals," *Social Research,* Vol. 62, No. 1 (Fall 1995), with articles by Vikki Hearne, Stephen Jay Gould, Daniel Dennett, Cora Diamond, Colin McGinn, Wendy Doniger, and others. Also see Susan J. Armstrong and Richard G. Botzler, eds., *The Animal Ethics Reader* (New York: Routledge, 2003); Justine Burley and John Harris, eds., *A Companion to Genethics* (Cambridge: Blackwell, 2002); *Animal Rights: Opposing Viewpoints,* edited by Andrew Harnack (San Diego, CA: Greenhaven Press, 1996) contains an excellent collection of short articles; it also includes a list of organizations involved in the animal rights issue and how to contact them. *Animal Rights and Welfare,* edited by Jeanne Williams (New York: H.W. Wilson Company, 1991), in the series The Reference Shelf, Vol. 63, No. 4., is a well-edited, short (168 pages) collection of short and often popular articles on the issues of animal rights, animals in research, and changes in the animal rights movement. *Ethics and Animals,* edited by Harlan B. Miller and William H. Williams (Clifton, NJ: Humana Press, 1983) is an excellent anthology of philosophical articles by well-known philosophers (including Tom Regan, Jan Narveson, Annette Baier, Bernard Rollin, Dale Jamieson, Lawrence Becker, James Rachels, R. G. Frey, and many others) and includes a very good bibliography. *On the Fifth Day: Animal Rights and Human Ethics,* edited by Richard Knowles Morrow and Michael W. Fox (Washington, DC: Acropolis Books, 1978) is a volume sponsored by the Humane Society of the United States and contains 12 essays on the moral status of animals and a statement of the Principles of the Humane Society. *The Animal Rights/Environmental Ethics Debate,* edited by Eugene C. Hargrove (Albany: State University of New York Press, 1992) contains 11 very good articles dealing specifically with the question of the relationship between animals rights issues and issues about environmental ethics. On the issue of animal experimentation, see F. Barbara Orlans, Tom L. Beauchamp, Rebecca Dresser, David B. Morton, and John P. Gluck, *The Human Use of Animals* (New York: Oxford, 1997) and *Animal Experimentation: The Moral Issues,* edited by Robert M. Baird and Stuart E. Rosenbaum (Buffalo, NY: Prometheus Books, 1991) contains 15 articles on animal rights and experimentation and a short bibliography. Also see R. G. Frey, *Rights, Killing, and Suffering: Moral Vegetarianism and Applied Ethics* (Oxford: Basil Blackwell, 1983); *Animal Sacrifices: Religious Perspectives on the Use of Animals in Science,* edited by Tom Regan (Philadelphia: Temple University Press, 1986); *In Defense of Animals,* edited by Peter Singer (New York: Blackwell, 1985); and *Animals' Rights: A Symposium,* edited by David Paterson and Richard Ryder (Fontwell, Sussex: Centaur, 1979). Tom Regan and Peter Singer co-edited *Animal Rights and Human Obligations* (Englewood Cliffs: Prentice Hall, 1976). Peter Singer's *Ethics* (New York: Oxford, 1994) is not an anthology about animal rights, but rather a very interesting anthology about ethics from the standpoint of a strong advocate of animal rights.

Single-Author Works

One of the most interesting recent works to raise questions about the moral status of animals is J. M. Coetzee, *The Lives of Animals* (Princeton: Princeton University Press, 2001). These are Coetzee's Tanner Lectures, and they are followed by responses by Amy Gutmann, Peter Singer, Wendy Doniger, and others.

Although there are certainly some early works that defended the rights of animals, such as Lewis Gompertz's *Moral Inquiries on the Situation of Man and of Brutes* (1824) and Henry S. Salt, *Animals' Rights* (1892), it was not until the past three decades that strong defenses of animal rights gained significant ground. Peter Singer's *Animal Liberation,* now in its second edition (New York: Avon Books, 1990), first appeared in 1976. Also see his *Practical Ethics,* 2nd ed. (New York: Cambridge University Press, 1993). Equally influential has been the work of Tom Regan, whose *The Case for Animal Rights* (Berkeley, CA: University of California Press, 1983) and *The Thee Generation: Reflections on the Coming Revolution* (Philadelphia: Temple University Press, 1991), a collection of his recent essays, including "Christians Are What Christians Eat," have both had a wide impact. Mary Midgley, *Animals and Why They Matter* (Athens, GA: University of Georgia Press, 1983) is admirably argued, as is James Rachels, *Created from Animals: The Moral Implications of Darwinism* (Oxford: Oxford University Press, 1991). Bernard E. Rollin, *The Unheeded Cry: Animal Consciousness, Animal Pain, and Science,* with a Foreword by Jane Goodall (Oxford: Oxford University

Press, 1989) surveys changing attitudes toward animal consciousness and deals specifically with the issue of how we can know and measure animal pain, and his *Animal Rights and Human Morality,* revised edition (Buffalo, NY: Prometheus Books, 1992) is a well-written, articulate defense of animal rights. In *The Animals Issue* (Cambridge: Cambridge University Press, 1992), Peter Carruthers defends a contractualist account of ethics and argues that animals do not have direct moral significance. Michael P.T. Leahy's *Against Liberation: Putting Animals in Perspective* (London and New York: Routledge, 1991) offers a Wittgensteinian critique of contemporary defenses of animal rights. In *Interests and Rights: The Case Against Animals* (Oxford: Clarendon Press, 1980), R. G. Frey argues that animals are part of the moral community, but that their lives are not of equal value to adult human lives. For a nuanced discussion of these issues by a philosopher whose primary concern is with the concept of rights rather than animals, see Chapter 6 of A.I. Melden, *Rights in Moral Lives* (Berkeley: University of California Press, 1988). Also see Steven F. Sapontzis, *Morals, Reason, and Animals* (Philadelphia: Temple University Press, 1987); Richard Ryder, *Victims of Science* (London: David-Poynter, 1975); Marian Stamp Dawkins, *Animal Suffering: The Science of Animal Welfare* (London and New York: Chapman and Hall, 1980). In *The Case for Animal Experimentation* (Berkeley: University of California Press, 1986), Michael A. Fox argues that animals lack the critical self-awareness necessary for membership in the moral community; however, he renounced this view almost immediately after publication of the book. See Michael A. Fox, "Animal Experimentation: A Philosopher's Changing Views," *Between the Species,* Vol. 3 (1987), pp. 55–60. On the historical origins of the Western dabate, see Richard Sorabji, *Animal Minds and Human Morals* (Ithaca NY: Cornell, 1993).

More recently, please note Dale Jamieson, *Morality's Progress: Essays on Humans, Other Animals, and the Rest of Nature* (Oxford: Clarendon Press, 2002); John Dupre, *Humans and Other Animals* (Oxford: Clarendon Press, 2002); Tom Regan, *Empty Cages: Facing the Challenge of Animal Rights* (Lannam, MD: Rowman & Littlefield Publishing, 2004); Steven M. Wise, *Drawing the Line: Science and the Case for Animal Rights* (Boulder, CO: Perseus, 2002); Steven M. Wise and Jane Goodall, *Rattling the Cage: Toward Legal Rights for Animals* (Boulder, CO: Perseus 2001). Matthew Scully's *Dominion: The Power of Man, the Suffering of Animals, and the Call to Mercy* (New York: St. Martin's Griffin, 2003) is probably the only book by a former Bush administration member to deal exclusively with the issue of animal suffering.

Environmental Ethics

Narrative Account

N. Scott Momaday
"Native American Attitudes Toward the Environment"

N. Scott Momaday is the author of numerous works, including House Made of Dawn *and* The Way to Rainy Mountain.

In an informal context, Mr. Momaday discusses the ways in which Native Americans understand their relationship to the natural environment. He focuses on several key ideas: the ways in which the relationship between human beings and the environment is one of mutual appropriation, the ways in which Native Americans understand what an "appropriate" relationship is between a person and the environment, and the important role played by imagination in understanding these issues.

As You Read, Consider This:

1. How does Mr. Momaday use stories to develop his ideas? Would you draw the same conclusions from his stories that Mr. Momaday does?
2. What does Mr. Momaday mean by "appropriateness"?

The first thing to say about the Native American perspective on environmental ethics is that there is a great deal to be said. I don't think that anyone has clearly understood yet how the Indian conceives of himself in relation to the landscape. We have formulated certain generalities about that relationship, and the generalities have served a purpose, but they have been rather too general. For example, take the idea that the Indian reveres the earth, thinks of it as the place of his origin and thinks of the sky also in a personal way. These statements are true. But they can also be misleading because they don't indicate anything about the nature of the relationship which is, I think, an intricate thing in itself.

I have done much thinking about the "Indian worldview," as it is sometimes called. And I have had some personal experience of Indian religion and Indian societies within the framework of a worldview. Sometime ago I wrote an essay entitled "An American Land Ethic" in which I tried to talk in certain ways about this idea of a Native American attitude toward the landscape. And in that essay I made certain observations. I tried to express the notion first that the Native American ethic with

Seeing with a Native Eye: Essays on Native American Religion, edited by Walter Holden Capps (New York: Harper and Row, 1976), pp. 79–85.

respect to the physical world is a matter of reciprocal appropriation: appropriations in which man invests himself in the landscape, and at the same time incorporates the landscape into his own most fundamental experience. That suggests a dichotomy, or a paradox, and I think it is a paradox. It is difficult to understand a relationship which is defined in these terms, and yet I don't know how better to define it.

Secondly, this appropriation is primarily a matter of the imagination. The appropriation is realized through an act of the imagination which is moral and kind. I mean to say that we are all, I suppose, at the most fundamental level what we imagine ourselves to be. And this is certainly true of the American Indian. If you want a definition, you would not go, I hope, to the stereotype which has burdened the American Indian for many years. He is not that befeathered spectacle who is always chasing John Wayne across the silver screen. Rather, he is someone who thinks of himself in a particular way and his idea comprehends his relationship to the physical world, among other things. He imagines himself in terms of that relationship and others. And it is that act of the imagination, that moral act of the imagination, which I think constitutes his understanding of the physical world.

Thirdly, this imagining, this understanding of the relationship between man and the landscape, or man and the physical world, man and nature, proceeds from a racial or cultural experience. I think his attitude toward the landscape has been formulated over a long period of time, and the length of time itself suggests an evolutionary process perhaps instead of a purely rational and decisive experience. Now I am not sure that you can understand me on this point; perhaps I should elaborate. I mean that the Indian has determined himself in his imagination over a period of untold generations. His racial memory is an essential part of his understanding. He understands himself more clearly than perhaps other people, given his situation in time and space. His heritage has always been rather closely focused, centered upon the landscape as a particular reality. Beyond this, the Native American has a particular investment in vision and in the idea of vision. You are familiar with the term "vision quest" for example. This is another essential idea to the Indian worldview, particularly that view as it is expressed among the cultures of the Plains Indians. This is significant. I think we should not lose the force of the idea of seeing something or envisioning something in a particular way. I happen to think that there are two visions in particular with reference to man and his relationship to the natural world. One is physical and the other is imaginative. And we all deal in one way or another with these visions simultaneously. If I can try to find an analogy, it's rather like looking through the viewfinder of a camera, the viewfinder which is based upon the principle of the split image. And it is a matter of trying to align the two planes of that particular view. This can be used as an example of how we look at the world around us. We see it with the physical eye. We see it as it appears to us, in one dimension of reality. But we also see it with the eye of the mind. It seems to me that the Indian has achieved a particularly effective alignment of those two planes of vision. He perceives the landscape in both ways. He realizes a whole image from the possibilities within his reach. The moral implications of this are very far-reaching. Here is where we get into the consideration of religion and religious ideas and ideals.

There is another way in which I think one can very profitably and accurately think of the Indian in relation to the landscape and in terms of his idea of that relationship. This is to center on such a word as *appropriate*. The idea of "appropriateness" is central to the Indian experience of the natural world. It is a fundamental idea within his philosophy. I recall the story told to me some years ago by a friend, who is not himself a Navajo, but was married for a time to a Navajo girl and lived with her family in Southern Utah. And he said that he had been told this story and was passing it on to me.

There was a man living in a remote place on the Navajo reservation who had lost his job and was having a difficult time making ends meet. He had a wife and several children. As a matter of fact, his wife was expecting another child. One day a friend came to visit him and perceived that his situation was bad. The friend said to him "Look, I see that you're in tight straits, I see you have many mouths to feed, that you have no wood and that there is very little food in your larder. But one thing puzzles me. I know you're a hunter, and I know, too, there are deer in the mountains very close at hand. Tell me, why don't you kill a deer so that you and your family might have fresh meat to eat?" And after a time the man replied, "No, it is inappropriate that I should take life just now when I am expecting the gift of life."

The implications of that idea, and the way in which the concept of appropriateness lies at the center of that little parable is a central consideration within the Indian world. You cannot understand how the Indian thinks of himself in relation to the world around him unless you understand his conception of what is appropriate; particularly what is morally appropriate within the context of that relationship.

Question: Could you probe a little deeper into what lies behind the idea of appropriate or inappropriate behavior regarding the natural world. Is it a religious element? Is it biological or a matter of survival? How would you characterize what makes an action appropriate or inappropriate?

Momaday: It is certainly a fair question but I'm not sure that I have the answer to it. I suspect that whatever it is that makes for the idea of appropriateness is a very complex thing in itself. Many things constitute the idea of appropriateness. Basically, I think it is a moral idea as opposed to a religious one. It is a basic understanding of right within the framework of relationships, and, within the framework of that relationship I was talking about a moment ago, between man and the physical world. That which is appropriate within this context is that which is *natural*. This is another key word. My father used to tell me of an old man who has lived a whole life. I have often thought of this image. The old man used to come to my grandfather's house periodically to pay visits, and my father has very vivid recollections of this man whom I never knew. But his name was Chaney. Father says that Chaney would come to the house and he would make himself perfectly at home. He would be passing by going from one place to another, exercising his ethnic prerogative for nomadism. But he would make my grandfather's house a kind of resting place. He stayed there on many occasions. My father says that every morning when Chaney was there as a guest he would get up in the first light, paint his face, go outside, face the east, and bring the sun out of the horizon. Then he would pray. He would pray aloud to the rising sun. He did that because it was appropriate that he should do that. He understood. Or perhaps I should say that in terms of his own understanding, the sun was the origin of his strength. He understood the sun, within a more formal religious context, similar to the way someone else understands the presence of a deity. And in the face of that recognition, he acted naturally or appropriately. Through the medium of prayer, he returned some of his strength to the sun. He did this everyday. It was a part of his daily life. It was as natural and appropriate to him as anything could be. There is in the Indian worldview this kind of understanding of what is and what is not appropriate. It isn't a matter of intellection. It is respect for the understanding of one's heritage. It is a kind of racial memory and it has its origin beyond any sort of historical experience. It reaches back to the dawn of time.

Question: When talking about vision, you said that the Indians saw things physically and also with the eye of the mind, I think this is the way you put it. You also said that this was a whole image, and that it had certain moral implications. Would you elaborate further?

Momaday: I think there are different ways of seeing things. I myself am particularly interested in literature, and in the traditions of various peoples, the Indians in particular. I understand something of how this works within the context of literature. For example, in the nineteenth century in America, there were poets who were trying very hard to see nature and to write about it. This is one kind of vision. They succeeded in different ways, some succeeding more than others. They succeeded in seeing what was really there on the vision plain of the natural world and they translated that vision, or that perception of the natural world, into poetry. Many of them had a kind of scientific training. Their observations were trained through the study of botany, astronomy, or zoology, etc. This refers, of course, to one kind of vision.

But, obviously, this is not the sort of view of the landscape which characterizes the Indian world. His view rather is of a different and more imaginative kind. It is a more comprehensive view. When the Native American looks at nature, it isn't with the idea of training a glass upon it, or pushing it away so that he can focus upon it from a distance. In his mind, nature is not something apart from him. He conceives of it, rather, as an element in which he exists. He has existence within that element, much in the same way we think of having existence within the element of air. It would be unimaginable for him to think of it in the way the nineteenth century "nature poets" thought of looking at nature and writing about it. They employed a kind of "esthetic distance," as it is sometimes called. This idea would be alien to the Indian. This is what I meant by trying to make the distinction between two sides of a split image.

Question: So then, presumably in moral terms, the Indian would say that a person should not harm nature because it's something in which one participates oneself.

Momaday: This is one aspect of it. There is this moral aspect, and it refers to perfect alignment. The appropriation of both images into the one reality is what the Indian is concerned to do: to see what is really there, but also to see what is *really* there. This reminds me of another story. It is very brief. It was told to me by the same fellow who told me about the man who did not kill the deer. (To take a certain liberty with the title of a novel that I know well.) He told me that while he himself was living in southern Utah with his wife's family, he became very ill. He contracted pneumonia. There was no doctor, no physician nearby. But there was a medicine man close at hand. The family called in a diagnostician (the traditional thing to do), who came and said that my friend was suffering from a particular malady whose cure would be the red-ant ceremony. So a man who is very well versed in that ceremony, a seer, a kind of specialist in the red-ant ceremony, came in and administered it to my friend. Soon after that my friend recovered completely. Not long after this he was talking to his father-in-law, and he was very curious about what had taken place. He said, "I wonder about the red-ant ceremony. Why is it that the diagnostician prescribed that particular ceremony for me?" His father-in-law looked at him and said, "Well, it was obvious to him that there were red ants in your system, and so we had to call in a seer to take the red ants out of your system." At this point, my friend became very incredulous, and said, "Yes, but surely you don't mean that there were red ants inside of me." His father-in-law looked at him for a moment, then said, "Not ants, but ants." Unless you understand this distinction, you might have difficulty understanding something about the Indian view of the natural world.

Endnote

This paper was adapted from transcriptions of oral remarks Professor Momaday made on this subject, informally, during a discussion with faculty and students.

Journal/Discussion Questions

✍ *Mr. Momaday suggests that "appropriateness" is a central concept in terms of which Native Americans understand their relationship to the natural world. In your own life, what role—if any—does this notion play in your understanding of your own relationship to the natural world. Does this concept shed light on any parts of your experience that you hadn't reflected on before?*

1. Explain what Mr. Momaday means by appropriateness. How could this idea be used to develop environmental policies?

2. Think about the way in which Mr. Momaday responds to questions. He usually tells a story. What does this suggest about the way in which Native Americans maintain and transmit moral wisdom? How does this relate to the role of imagination?

An Introduction to the Moral Issues

Perhaps more than any of the other issues that we have considered in this book, questions about our relationships with animals and the environment take us to the heart of a fundamental clash of world-views. It is, moreover, not like the familiar clashes between liberal and conservative, theist and atheist, or the like; it is, rather, a clash between a *scientific* and *technological worldview*—that encompasses liberal and conservative, theist and atheist, and other divisions familiar to us—and a diverse set of *natural worldviews*—many of them echoing the cultures of indigenous peoples—that emphasize the continuity and interdependence of human beings and the natural world.

One of the by-products of this clash of worldviews is that much of environmental ethics calls into question the foundations of traditional (i.e., Western European) ethics. This has been both an asset and a liability for the development of environmental ethics. On the plus side, it has resulted in a number of interesting discussions that illuminate aspects of the foundations of Western ethics that might not otherwise be brought as sharply into focus. In particular, it has called attention to the ways in which Western ethics conceptualizes the natural world and understands the place of human beings in it. On the negative side, however, the concern with such foundational questions has detracted, at least in the eyes of some, from environmental ethic's principal task as *applied* ethics. Rather than concentrating on specific moral issues facing those concerned with the environment (as well as those who are not concerned with it!), environmental ethics has concentrated on issues that exist on such a high level of abstraction that they are not immediately fruitful for making decisions about the specific environmental issues.

The Central Questions

As we turn toward a consideration of environmental ethics, three questions present themselves:

1. *Who,* or what, *has moral weight* (i.e., is deserving of direct moral consideration)?
2. *How much* moral weight does each (type of) entity have?
3. How do we make *decisions* when there are *conflicts* among different types of beings, each of which have moral weight?

An adequate environmental ethic must eventually provide answers to all three of these questions. In recent work by environmentalists, considerable attention has been paid to the first of these questions. Here the debate has centered around the question of whether individual animals, species, plants, rivers, and the like have moral weight (i.e., whether we should give moral consideration to the question of their well-being or continued flourishing). Sometimes this question is posed in relation to individuals (e.g., this specific plant) and sometimes it is posed in relation to species (e.g., the spotted owl). In the next section of this introduction, we examine a number of specific answers to these questions.

The second question—how much moral standing something has—is both crucial and usually neglected. It is crucial because ethics must eventually provide guidance for our actions, and if we have no way of ranking how much moral consideration a given entity merits, we are left without assistance in resolving conflicts among morally considerable beings. The answer to the third question obviously presupposes an answer to the first two questions. We shall consider each of these three questions here, but first sketch out an overview of the main schools of thought in environmental ethics.

An Overview

Because this is relatively uncharted territory for many of us, it may be helpful to see an overview of the conceptual terrain and the various positions that have been marked out on it by the current participants in the discussion of environmental ethics. We may initially divide these approaches into two categories. *Human-centered approaches* to the environment take human beings as their moral point of reference and consider questions of the environment solely from that perspective. They ask, in other words, environmental questions from the standpoint of the effects of the answers to such questions on human beings in one way or another. In contrast to these approaches, we find in recent years that a number of *expanded-circle approaches* (to borrow a term from the title of Peter Singer's *The Expanding Circle*) have come into the circle of morally considerable beings—that is, entities deserving of moral respect in some way—with an increasingly wide radius. Let's examine each of these in somewhat more detail.[1]

Human-Centered Approaches

Human-centered approaches to the environment do not necessarily neglect the environment, but typically they recognize as valid moral reasons only those reasons acceptable to traditional moral theories. These theories are of the various types we discussed in the Introduction to this book.

Ethical egoists recognize only reasons of self-interest as an adequate moral justification for treating the environment in a particular way. For example, ethical egoists could well imagine people wanting a particular landscape preserved because it provided them personally with an aesthetically pleasing view, but it would also see those who wanted to strip mine that particular landscape as morally justified if it maximized their own self-interest.

Group egoists are also concerned with self-interest, but the net of self-interest is more broadly cast to include not only one's personal interests, but the interests of the group with which one most strongly affiliates. The boundaries of the group may be comparatively narrow (one's family), intermediate (one's neighborhood, one's corporation, one's church group), or quite broad (one's nation, all those who share one's religious beliefs). What is characteristic of these approaches is that only the interests of one's group are to be given moral weight in making decisions. Similarly, there are approaches in *virtue ethics* that concentrate on developing those character traits that contribute to the welfare of the group: loyalty, a spirit of self-sacrifice, obedience to authority, and so on. Aristotle, for example, sought to determine those character traits that would make a person a good member of the *polis,* the Greek city-state. Much more recently, William Bennett and others have sought to determine the virtues we should foster to have a better civic and communal life in the United States. One of the principal differences between group egoist and virtue ethics is that egoism focuses on the question of what actions we should perform, whereas virtue ethics looks at the kind of person we should be.

Utilitarians, like egoists, are consequentialists; that is, they determine whether particular actions are right or wrong by looking at their consequences. However, whereas the ethical egoist looks at consequences only insofar as they affect the egoist personally, the utilitarian looks at consequences insofar as they affect all human beings. Often courses of action that would be justified from the standpoint of ethical egoism are not morally justified from a utilitarian standpoint, because they may benefit the egoist but not provide sufficient benefit to humanity as a whole (when judged in relation to competing courses of action).

Preserving the natural environment may be an important value to utilitarians if doing so provides the maximal benefit to humanity. There are a variety of ways in which this could be so. For example, preservation—or at least careful management—of the natural environment may provide long-term resources for all of humanity. Thus, we may want to preserve the rain forests because, even though destroying them might bring short-term profit to a small group of people, preserving them provides irreplaceable benefits to humanity in terms of air quality, natural resources, and the like. Notice that there is no claim here that the rain forest is valuable in itself; its value derives from the ways in which it contributes to human well-being. If in the long-run human well-being would best be served by destroying the rain forests, then utilitarianism would not only permit this, it would require it.

Expanded-Circle Approaches

Expanded utilitarianism. Utilitarianism has often been concerned with the effects of various actions on the well-being of human beings. The underlying rationale has been that the whole point of ethics is to increase pleasure or happiness and to decrease pain, suffering, or unhappiness. As we saw in the previous chapter, a number of philosophers, most notably Peter Singer, have taken the next step and asked why only *human* suffering counts in the utilitarian calculus. If we are concerned with reducing suffering, should we be concerned with reducing the suffering of *all* sentient beings. Thus this version of utilitarianism has expanded the circle of morally considerable beings to include nonhuman animals. Although this is far from a full-fledged environmental ethic, it is an important step beyond a purely anthropocentric ethic.

Biocentrism. Biocentrism represents the first step toward a genuinely environmental ethic, for it maintains that all living beings—this includes plants, fauna, and so on, as well as human and nonhuman animals—are deserving of moral consideration in their own right. Biocentric approaches focus on individual entities and the premise here seems to be primarily a teleological one. All living beings have some *telos* or final goal, and this is usually understood in terms of flourishing or growing in some sense. They are thus entitled to moral consideration from us—that is, we should not act in ways that thwart their movement toward their natural goal.

Ecocentrism. Ecocentrism, which is often called deep ecology by its supporters, expands the circle to its maximal terrestrial limits by taking the entirety of what exists on the earth as morally considerable, inanimate as well as animate. It comes in two versions, the latter of which is much more plausible than the former. *Individualistic ecocentrism* gives moral weight to each and every entity within the ecosystem. The difficulty with this approach flows from the fact that individualistic ecocentrism has been unable to provide a criterion for assigning different weights to different individuals—and if everything has an equal moral weight, then it is virtually impossible to arrive at a decision procedure in particular cases in which precedence must be given to one individual over another.

The more plausible variant of ecocentrism is to be found in *holistic ecocentrism,* which gives moral weight to each species, type, and so forth in the ecosystem. Thus holistic ecocentrism is concerned with the preservation of species, and concern about individuals is only a means to the end of species-preservation. Similarly, ecocentric environmentalists may be concerned about the preservation of particular types of environments—wetlands, sand dunes, rain forest—both in their own right and insofar as they are parts of larger ecosystems. The ultimate ecosystem is the earth as a whole.

As we saw in Chapter 9, many philosophers argued that the moral circle ought to be expanded to include nonhuman animals. As we see in this chapter, some philosophers want to expand this circle even further to include all of the natural environment.

Endnotes

1. This typology draws on several sources, most notably Carolyn Merchant's "Environmental Ethics and Political Conflict," and J. Baird Callicott's "Environmental Ethics," *Encyclopedia of Ethics,* edited by Lawrence and Charlotte Becker (New York: Garland, 1992), Vol. I, pp. 311–315.

2. Kenneth E. Goodpaster, "On Being Morally Considerable," *Journal of Philosophy,* Vol. LXXV, No. 6 (June 1978), pp. 308–324.

3. W. Murray Hunt, "Are Mere Things Morally Considerable?" *Environmental Ethics,* Vol. 2 (Spring 1980), pp. 59–65.

The Arguments

Holmes Rolston III
"Challenges in Environmental Ethics"

Holmes Rolston III is University Distinguished Professor at Colorado State University. Rolston's research covers a variety of areas but he is especially known for his work in environmental ethics, including Philosophy Gone Wild, Environmental Ethics, *and* Conserving Natural Value. *He is also a cofounder and associate editor of the* Journal of Environmental Ethics *and founding past-president of the International Society of Environmental Ethics. Rolston is also a backpacker, a field naturalist, and a bryologist.*

Rolston presents a biocentric view of environmental ethics, arguing that all living things are intrinsically valuable. He argues, however, that this is a matter of degree, with sentient beings having more intrinsic value than plants and nonsentient animals, and with self-conscious rational animals (human beings) having more intrinsic value than those which are not self-conscious. He also accords a special value to species and to ecosystems.

As You Read, Consider This:

1. What, according to Rolston, does environmental ethics teach us about ethics in general?
2. What, according to Rolston, is radically wrong with anthropencentric value?

Ethicists had settled on at least one conclusion as ethics became modern in Darwin's century: that the moral has nothing to do with the natural. To argue otherwise commits the naturalistic fallacy, moving without justification from what *is* in nature *ought to be* in culture. Science describes natural history, natural law; ethics prescribes human conduct, moral law; and to confuse the two makes a category mistake. Nature simply *is*, without objective value; the preferences of human subjects establish value; and these human values, appropriately considered, generate human duties. Only humans are ethical subjects and only humans are ethical objects. Nature is amoral; the moral community is interhuman.

In the last third of this century, unsettled as we enter the next millennium, there is foreboding revolution. Only the human species contains moral agents, but perhaps conscience on such an earth ought not be used to exempt every other form of life from consideration, with the resulting paradox that the sole moral species acts only in its collective self-interest toward all the rest. There is something

Environmental Philosophy, edited by Michael Zimmerman et al., Third Edition (Upper Saddle River, New Jersey: Prentice Hall, 2001), pp. 126–46.

overspecialized about an ethic, held by the dominant class of *Homo sapiens,* that regards the welfare of only one of several million species as an object and beneficiary of duty. We need an interspecific ethics. Whatever ought to be in culture, this biological world that *is* also *ought to be;* we must argue from the natural to the moral.

If this requires a paradigm change about the sorts of things to which duty can attach, so much the worse for those humanistic ethics no longer functioning in, nor suited to, their changing environment. The anthropocentrism associated with them was fiction anyway. There is something Newtonian, not yet Einsteinian, besides something morally naive, about living in a reference frame where one species takes itself as absolute and values everything else relative to its utility. If true to their specific epithet, ought not *Homo sapiens* value this host of life as something with a claim to care in its own right? Man may be the only measurer of things, but is man the only measure of things? The challenge of environmental ethics is a principled attempt to redefine the boundaries of ethical obligation.

Still there is the sense of anomaly that forebodes paradigm overthrow. An ecological conscience? Sometimes this seems to be a category mistake, joining a scientific adjective with an ethical noun, rather like Christian biochemistry mismatches a religious adjective and a scientific noun. With analysis, we suspect that the relation is three-place. Person A has a duty to person B concerning the environment C, and no one has ever denied that natural things have instrumental value to humans. Humans are helped or hurt by the condition of their environment, and we have duties to humans that concern their valuable environment, an environment they are able to value. So conservatives may shrink back into the persistent refusal of philosophers to think biologically, to naturalize ethics in the deep sense. They will fear that it is logically incoherent to suppose there is a nonanthropogenic value, or that this is too metaphysically speculative ever to be operational and that it does not make any pragmatic difference anyway, claiming that an adequate environmental ethic can be anthropogenic, even anthropocentric.

When we face up to the crisis, however, we undergo a more direct moral encounter. Environmental ethics is not a muddle; it is an invitation to moral development. All ethics seeks an appropriate respect for life, but respect for human life is only a subset of respect for all life. What ethics is about, in the end, is seeing outside your own sector of self-interest, of class interest. A comprehensive ethic will find values in and duties to the natural world. The vitality of ethics depends on our knowing what is really vital, and there will be found the intersection of value and duty. An ecological conscience requires an unprecedented mix of science and conscience, of biology and ethics.

1. Higher Animals

We have direct encounters with life that has eyes, at least where our gaze is returned by something that itself has a concerned outlook. The relation is two-place: I-thou, subject to subject. Compared with concern about soil and water, which are instrumentally vital but blind, when we meet the higher animals there is somebody there behind the fur and feathers. "The environment" is external to us all, but where there is inwardness in this environment, perhaps we ought to be conscious of other consciousness. Whatever matters to animals, matters morally.

Wild animals defend their own lives, because they have a good of their own. Animals hunt and howl, seek shelter, build nests and sing, care for their young, flee from threats, grow hungry, thirsty, hot, tired, excited, sleepy, seek out their habitats and mates. They suffer injury and lick their wounds. They can know security and fear, endurance and fatigue, comfort and pain. When they figure out their helps and hurts in the environment, they do not make man the measure of things at all; more, man is not the only measurer of things.

Still, man is the only moral measurer of things, and how should he count these wild, nonmoral things? One might expect classical ethics to have sifted well an ethics for animals. Our ancestors did not think about endangered species, ecosystems, acid rain, or the ozone layer, but they lived in closer association with wild and domestic animals than do we. Nevertheless, until recently, the scientific, humanistic centuries since the so-called Enlightenment have not been sensitive ones for animals. Animals were mindless, living matter; biology was mechanistic. Even psychology, rather than defending animal experience, was behaviorist. Philosophy, as we have already said, thought man the measure of things. Across several centuries of hard science and humanist ethics there has been little compassion for animals. We eat millions of them every year and we use many millions more in industry and research, as though little matters unless it matters to humans.

So far as we got ethically, we rather oddly said that we should be humane toward nonhuman animals. "The question is not," said Bentham, "Can they reason, nor Can they talk? but, Can they suffer?" These nonhumans do not share with humans the capacity to reason or talk, but they do share the capacity to suffer, and human ethics can be extended so far forth to our animal cousins. We may be unsure about insects and fish, but at least we will need an avian and a mammal ethics.

The progress of recent science itself has increasingly smeared the human-nonhuman boundary line. Animal anatomy, biochemistry, perception, cognition, experience, behavior, and evolutionary history are kin to our own. Animals have no immortal souls, but then persons may not either, or beings with souls may not be the only kind that count morally. Ethical progress further smeared the boundary. Sensual pleasures are a good thing, ethics should be egalitarian nonarbitrary, nondiscriminatory. There are ample scientific grounds that animals enjoy pleasures and suffer pains; and ethically no grounds to value these in humans and not in animals. The *is* in nature and the *ought* in ethics are not so far apart after all. We should treat animals humanely, that is, treat animals equally with ourselves where they have equal interests.

Recently, then, there has been a vigorous reassessment of human duties to sentient life. More has been written on this subject in the past fifteen years than in the previous fifteen centuries. The world cheered in the fall of 1988 when humans rescued two whales from the winter ice. A sign in Rocky Mountain National Park enjoins humans not to harass bighorn sheep: "Respect their right to life." We have passed animal welfare legislation and set up animal care committees in our universities. We have made a vital breakthrough past humans, and the first lesson in environmental ethics has been learned.

But the risk of ethical inadequacy here lies in a moral extension that expands rights as far as mammals and not much further, a psychologically based ethic that counts only felt experience. We respect life in our nonhuman but near-human animal cousins, a semi-anthropic and still quite subjective ethics. Justice remains a concern for just-us subjects. Extending our human ethics, we say that the sheep, too, have rights and that we should be humane to the whales. There has, in fact, not been much theoretical breakthrough, no paradigm shift. We do not yet have a biologically based ethics.

We certainly need an ethic for animals, but that is only one level of concern in a comprehensive environmental ethics. When we try to use culturally extended rights and psychologically based utilities to protect the flora or even the insentient fauna, to protect endangered species or ecosystems, we can only stammer. Indeed, we get lost trying to protect bighorns, because in the wild the cougar is not respecting the rights or utilities of the sheep she slays. There are no rights in the wild, and nature is indifferent to the welfare of particular animals. Further, in culture, humans slay sheep and eat them regularly, while humans have every right not to be eaten by either humans or cougars.

A bison fell through the ice into a river in Yellowstone Park; the environmental ethic there, letting nature take its course, forbade would-be rescuers from either saving or mercy killing the suffering animal. A drowning human would have been saved at once. It was as vital to the struggling bison as to any human to get out; the poor thing froze to death that night. Was the Yellowstone ethic callous to life, inhumane? Or had it other vitalities to consider? This ethic seems rather to have concluded that a moral extension is too nondiscriminating; we are unable to separate an ethics for humans from an ethics for wildlife. To treat wild animals with compassion learned in culture does not appreciate their wildness.

Man, said Socrates, is the political animal; humans maximally are what they are in culture, where the natural selection pressures (impressively productive in ecosystems) are relaxed without detriment to the species *Homo sapiens,* and indeed with great benefit to its member persons. Wild and even domestic animals cannot enter culture; they do not have that capacity. They cannot acquire language at sufficient levels to take part in culture; they cannot make their clothing, or build fires, much less read books or receive an education.

Worse, cultural protection can work to their detriment; with too much human or humane care their wildness is made over into a human artifact. A cow does not have the integrity of a deer, a poodle that of a wolf. Culture is a good thing for humans, often a bad thing for animals. Culture does make a relevant ethical difference, and environmental ethics has different criteria from interhuman ethics.

Can they talk? and, Can they reason? indicating cultural capacities, are relevant questions, not just, Can they suffer? Compassionate respect for life in its suffering is only part of the analysis. Sometimes in an environmental ethic we do need to follow nature, and not so much to treat animals humanely, like we do humans, as to treat animals naturally, for what they are by themselves. Even when we treat them humanely within culture, part of the ethic may also involve treating them naturally.

"Equality" is a positive word in ethics, "discriminatory" a pejorative one. On the other hand, simplistic reduction is a failing in the philosophy of science and epistemology; to be "discriminating" is desirable in logic and value theory. Something about treating humans as equals with bighorns and cougars seems to "reduce" humans to merely animal levels of value, a "no more" counterpart in ethics of the "nothing but" fallacy often met in science. Humans are "nothing but" naked apes. Something about treating sheep and cougars as the equals of humans seems to elevate them unnaturally, unable to value them for what they are. There is something insufficiently discriminating in such judgments—species blind in a bad sense, blind to the real differences between species, valuational differences that do count morally. To the contrary, a discriminating ethicist will insist on preserving the differing richness of valuational complexity, wherever found.

Two tests of discrimination are pain and diet. It might be thought that pain is a bad thing, whether in nature or culture. Perhaps when dealing with humans in culture, additional levels of value and utility must be protected by conferring rights that do not exist in the wild, but meanwhile at least we should minimize animal suffering. That is indeed a worthy imperative in culture where animals are removed from nature and bred, but it may be misguided where animals remain in ecosystems. When the bighorn sheep of Yellowstone caught pinkeye—blinded, injured, and starving in result—300 bighorns, over half the herd, perished. Wildlife veterinarians wanted to treat the disease, as they would have in any domestic herd, and as they did with Colorado bighorns infected with an introduced lungworm, but the Yellowstone ethicists left them to suffer, seemingly not respecting their life. Had they no mercy? Was this again inhumane?

They knew rather that, although intrinsic pain is a bad thing whether in humans or in sheep, pain in ecosystems is instrumental pain, through which the sheep are naturally selected for a more satisfactory adaptive fit. Pain in a medically skilled culture is pointless, once the alarm to health is sounded, but pain operates functionally in bighorns in their niche, even after it becomes no longer in the interests of the pained individuals. To have interfered in the interests of the blinded sheep would have weakened the species. The question, Can they suffer? is not as simple as Bentham thought. What we *ought* to do depends on what *is*. The *is* of nature differs significantly from the *is* of culture, even when similar suffering is present in both.

Some ethicists will insist that at least in culture we can minimize animal pain, and that will constrain our diet. There is predation in nature; humans evolved as omnivores. But humans, the only moral animals, should refuse to participate in the meat-eating phase of their ecology, just as they refuse to live merely by the rules of natural selection. Humans do not look to the behavior of wild animals as an ethical guide in other matters (marriage, truth telling, promise keeping, justice, charity). There they do not follow nature. Why should they justify their dietary habits by watching what animals do?

But the difference is that these other matters are affairs of culture; these are person-to-person events, not events at all in spontaneous nature. By contrast, eating is omnipresent in wild nature; humans eat because they are in nature, not because they are in culture. Eating animals is not an event between persons, but is a human-to-animal event; and the rules for this come from the ecosystems in which humans evolved and which they have no duty to remake. We must eat to live; nature absolutely requires that. We evolved to eat as omnivores; that animal nature underruns over human nature. Even in culture meat eating is still relatively natural; there is nothing immoral about fitting into one's ecology. We follow nature, treat animals naturally, capture nutritional values, and learn our place in the scheme of life and death. This respects life, profoundly so. Humans, then, can model their dietary habits from their ecosystems, though they cannot and should not so model their interpersonal justice or charity. When eating they ought to minimize animal suffering, and they also may gladly affirm their ecology. The boundary between animals and humans has not been rubbed out after all; only what was a boundary line has been smeared into a boundary zone. We have discovered that animals count morally, though we are only beginning to solve the challenge of how to count them.

2. Organisms

In college zoology I did an experiment on nutrition in rats, to see how they grew with and without vitamins. When the experiment was completed, I was told to take the rats out and drown them. I felt squeamish but did it. In college botany I did an experiment on seedlings to test how they grew with this or that fertilizer. The experiment over, I threw out the seedlings without a second thought. While there can be ethics about sentient animals, after that perhaps ethics is over. Respect for life ends somewhere in zoology; it is not part of botany. No consciousness, no conscience. Without sentience, ethics is nonsense.

Or do we want an ethic that is more objective about life? In Yosemite National Park for almost a century humans entertained themselves by driving through a tunnel cut in a giant sequoia. Two decades ago the Wawona tree, weakened by the cut, blew down in a storm. People said: Cut us another drive-through sequoia. The Yosemite environmental ethic, deepening over the years, said no! You ought not to mutilate majestic sequoias for amusement. Respect their life! Indeed, some ethicists count the value of redwoods so highly that they will spike redwoods, lest they be cut. In the Rawah

Wilderness in alpine Colorado, old signs read, "Please leave the flowers for others to enjoy" When they rotted out, the new signs urged a less humanist ethic: "Let the flowers live!"

But trees and flowers cannot care, so why should we? We are not considering animals that are close kin, nor can they suffer or experience anything. There are no humane societies for plants. Plants are not valuers with preferences that can be satisfied or frustrated. It seems odd to claim that plants need our sympathy, odd to ask that we should consider their point of view. They have no subjective life, only objective life.

Fishermen in Atlantic coastal estuaries and bays toss beer bottles overboard, a convenient way to dispose of trash. On the bottom, small crabs, attracted by the residual beer, make their way inside the bottles and become trapped, unable to get enough foothold on the slick glass neck to work their way out. They starve slowly. Then one dead crab becomes bait for the next victim, an indefinitely re-setting trap! Are those bottle traps of ethical concern, after fishermen have been warned about this effect? Or is the whole thing out of sight, out of mind, with crabs too mindless to care about? Should sensitive fishermen pack their bottle trash back to shore—whether or not crabs have much, or any, felt experience?

Flowers and sequoias live; they ought to live. Crabs have value out of sight, out of mind. Afraid of the naturalistic fallacy, conservative ethicists will say that people should enjoy letting flowers live or that it is silly to cut drive-through sequoias, aesthetically more excellent for humans to appreciate both for what they are. The crabs are out of sight, but not really out of mind; humans value them at a distance. But these ethically conservative reasons really do not understand what biological conservation is in the deepest sense. Nothing matters to a tree, but much is *vital.*

An organism is a spontaneous, self-maintaining system, sustaining and reproducing itself, executing its program, making a way through the world, checking against performance by means of responsive capacities with which to measure success. It can reckon with vicissitudes, opportunities, and adversities that the world presents. Something more than physical causes, even when less than sentience, is operating within every organism. There is *information* super-intending the causes; without it the organism would collapse into a sand heap. This information is a modern equivalent of what Aristotle called formal and final causes; it gives the organism a *telos,* "end," a kind of (nonfelt) goal. Organisms have ends, although not always ends-in-view.

All this cargo is carried by the DNA, essentially a *linguistic* molecule. By a serial "reading" of the DNA, a polypeptide chain is synthesized, such that its sequential structure determines the bioform into which it will fold. Ever-lengthening chains (like ever-longer sentences), are organized into genes (like paragraphs and chapters). Diverse proteins, lipids, carbohydrates, enzymes—all the life structures are "written into" the genetic library. The DNA is thus a *logical set,* not less than a biological set, informed as well as formed. Organisms use a sort of symbolic logic, use these molecular shapes as symbols of life. The novel resourcefulness lies in the epistemic content conserved, developed, and thrown forward to make biological resources out of the physicochemical cause and effect system, and partly something more: partly a historical information system discovering and evaluating ends so as to map and make a way through the world, partly a system of significances attached to operations, pursuits, resources. In this sense, the genome is a set of *conservation* molecules.

The genetic set is really a *propositional set*—to choose a provocative term—recalling how the Latin *proposition* is an assertion, a set task, a theme, a plan, a proposal, a project, as well as a cognitive statement. From this it is also a motivational set, unlike human books, since these life motifs are set to drive the movement from genotypic potential to phenotypic expression. Given a chance, these molecules seek organic self-expression. They thus proclaim a life way, and with this an organism, unlike an inert rock, claims the environment as source and sink, from which to abstract energy and materials and into which to excrete them. It "takes advantage" of its environment, life thus arises out of earthen sources (as do rocks), but life turns back on its sources to make resources out of them (unlike rocks). An acorn becomes an oak; the oak stands on its own.

So far we have only description. We begin to pass to value when we recognize that the genetic set is a *normative set;* it distinguishes between what *is* and what *ought to be.* This does not mean that the organism is a moral system, for there are no moral agents in nature; but the organism is an axiological, evaluative system. So the oak grows, reproduces, repairs its wounds, and resists death. The physical state that the organism seeks, idealized in its programmatic form, is a valued state. *Value* is present in this achievement. *Vital* seems a better word for it than *biological.* We are not dealing simply with an individual defending its solitary life but with an individual having situated fitness in an ecosystem. Still, we want to affirm that the living individual, taken as a "point experience" in the web of interconnected life, is *per se* an intrinsic value.

A life is defended for what it is in itself, without necessary further contributory reference, although, given the structure of all ecosystems, such lives necessarily do have further reference. The organism has something it is conserving, something for which it is standing: its life. Organisms have their own standards, fit into their niche though they must. They promote their own realization, at the same time that they track an environment. They have a technique, a know-how. Every organism has a *good-of-its-kind;* it defends its own kind as a *good kind.* In that sense, as soon as one knows what a giant sequoia tree is, one knows the biological identity that is sought and conserved. Man is neither the measurer nor the measure of things; value is not anthropogenic, it is biogenic.

There seems no reason why such own-standing normative organisms are not morally significant. A moral agent deciding his or her behavior, ought to take account of the consequences for other evaluative systems. This does not follow nature, if we mean by that to imitate ethical agents there, for nature is amoral. But it does follow nature, if we mean by that we respect these amoral organic norms as we shape our conduct. Such an ethic will be teleological, I suppose, since it values the *telos* in organisms, but it seems equally deontological, since it owes (Gk: *deont-*) respect for life in itself, intrinsically, and not just instrumentally, consequentially. (Frankly, the classical teleological/deontological distinction seems as troublesome as helpful in moral analysis here.)

Within the community of moral agents one has not merely to ask whether X is a normative system, but, since the norms are a personal option, to judge the norm and the consequences. But within the biotic community organisms are amoral normative systems, and there are no cases where an organism seeks a good of its own that is morally reprehensible. The distinction between having a good of its kind and being a good kind vanishes, so far as any faulting of the organism is concerned. To this extent, everything with a good of its kind is a good kind and thereby has intrinsic value.

One might say that an organism is a bad organism if, during the course of pressing its normative expression, it upsets the ecosystem or causes widespread disease, bad consequences. Remember though, that an organism cannot be a good kind without situated environmental fitness. By natural selection the kind of goods to which it is genetically programmed must mesh with its ecosystemic role. Despite the ecosystem as a perpetual contest of goods in dialectic and exchange, it is difficult to say that any organism is a bad kind in this instrumental sense either. The misfits are extinct, or soon will be. In spontaneous nature any species that preys upon, parasitizes, competes with, or crowds another will be a bad kind from the narrow perspective of its victim or competitor.

But if we enlarge that perspective it typically becomes difficult to say that any species is a bad kind overall in the ecosystem. An "enemy" may even be good for the "victimized" species, though harmful to individual members of it, as when predation keeps the deer herd healthy. Beyond this, the "bad kinds" typically play useful roles in population control, in symbiotic relationships, or in providing opportunities for other species. The *Chlamydia* microbe is a bad kind from the perspective of the bighorns, but when one thing dies, something else lives. After the pinkeye outbreak, the golden eagle population in Yellowstone flourished, preying on the bighorn carcasses. For them *Chlamydia* is a good kind instrumentally.

Some biologist-philosophers will say that, even though an organism evolves to have a situated environmental fitness, not all such situations are good arrangements; some can be clumsy or bad. True, the vicissitudes of historical evolution do sometimes result in ecological webs that are suboptimal solutions, within the biologically limited possibilities and powers of interacting organisms. Still, such systems have been selected over millennia for functional stability; and at least the burden of proof is on a human evaluator to say why any natural kind is a bad kind and ought not to call forth admiring respect. Something may be a good kind intrinsically but a bad kind instrumentally in the system; these will be anomalous cases, however, with selection pressures against them. These claims about good kinds do not say that things are perfect kinds, or that there can be no better ones, only that natural kinds are good kinds until proven otherwise.

What is almost invariably meant by a "bad" kind is that an organism is instrumentally bad when judged from the viewpoint of human interests, of humane interests. "Bad" so used is an anthropocentric word; there is nothing at all biological or ecological about it, and so it has no force evaluating objective nature, however much humanist force it may sometimes have.

A really *vital* ethic respects all life, not just animal pains and pleasures, much less just human preferences. In the Rawah, the old signs, "Leave the flowers for others to enjoy," were application signs using an old, ethically conservative, humanistic ethic. The new ones invite a change of reference frame—a wilder, more logical because more biological ethic, a radical ethic that goes down to the roots of life, that really is conservative because it understands biological conservation at depths. What the injunction, "Let the flowers live!" means is: "Daisies, marsh-marigolds, geraniums, larkspurs are evaluative systems that conserve goods of their kind, and, in the absence of evidence to the contrary, are good kinds. There are trails here by which you may enjoy these flowers. Is there any reason why your human interests should not also conserve these good kinds?" A drive-through sequoia causes no suffering; it is not cruel, but it is callous and insensitive to the wonder of life. The ethically conservative will complain that we have committed the naturalistic fallacy; rather, we invite a radical commitment to respect all life.

3. Species

Certain rare species of butterflies occur in hummocks (slightly elevated forested ground) on the African grasslands. It was formerly the practice of unscrupulous collectors to go in, collect a few hundred specimens, and then burn out the hummock with the intention of destroying the species, thereby driving up the price of their collections. I find myself persuaded that they morally ought not do this. Nor will the reason resolve into the evil of greed, but it remains the needless destruction of a butterfly species.

This conviction remains even when the human goods are more worthy. Coloradans are considering whether to build the Two Forks Dam to supply urban Denver with water. This would require destroying a canyon and altering the Platte River flow, with many negative environmental consequences, including endangering a butterfly, the Pawnee montane skipper, *Hesperia leonardus montana,* as well as endangering the whooping crane downstream. I doubt whether the good of humans who wish more water for development, both for industry and for bluegrass lawns, warrants endangering species of butterflies and cranes.

Sometimes the stakes are alleged to rise even higher. The Bay checkerspot, *Euphydryas editha bayensis,* proposed to be listed as an endangered species, inhabits peripheral tracts of a large facility on which United Technologies Corporation, a missile contractor, builds and tests Minuteman and Tomahawk propulsion systems. The giant defense contractor has challenged the proposed listing and thinks it airy and frivolous that a butterfly should slow the delivery of warhead missile propulsion systems, and so went ahead and dug a water pipeline through a butterfly patch. They operated out of the classical ethics that says that butterflies do not count but that the defense of humans does.

But a more radical, environmental ethics demurs. The good of humans might override the good of butterfly species but the case must be argued. Lest this seem the foolishness of a maverick philosopher, I point out that such conviction has been written into national law. The Endangered Species Act requires that the case must be argued before a high level "God" committee.

A species exists; a species ought to exist. Environmental ethics must make both claims and move from biology to ethics with care. Species exist only instantiated in individuals, yet are as real as individual plants or animals. The claim that there are specific forms of life historically maintained in their environments over time seems as certain as anything else we believe about the empirical world. At times biologists revise the theories and taxa with which they map these forms, but species are not so much like lines of latitude and longitude as like mountains and rivers, phenomena objectively there to be mapped. The edges of these natural kinds will sometimes be fuzzy, to some extent discretionary. One species will slide into another over evolutionary time. But it does not follow from the fact that speciation is sometimes in progress that species are merely made up, not found as evolutionary lines with identity in time as well as space.

A consideration of species is revealing and challenging because it offers a biologically based counterexample to the focus on individuals—typically sentient and usually persons—so characteristic in classical ethics. In an evolutionary ecosystem, it is not mere individuality that counts, but the species is also significant because it is a dynamic life form maintained over time. The individual represents (re-presents) a species in each new generation. It is a token of a type, and the type is more important than the token.

A species lacks moral agency, reflective self-awareness, sentience, or organic individuality. The older, conservative ethic will be tempted to say that specific-level processes cannot count morally. Duties must attach to singular lives, most evidently those with a psychological self, or some analogue to this. In an individual organism, the organs report to a center; the good of a whole is defended. The members of a species report to no center. A species has no self. It is not a bounded singular. There is no analogue to the nervous hookups or circulatory flows that characterize the organism.

But singularity, centeredness, selfhood, individuality, are not the only processes to which duty attaches. A more radically conservative ethic knows that having a biological identity reasserted genetically over time is as true of the species as of the individual. Identity need not attach solely to the centered organism; it can persist as a discrete pattern over time. Thinking this way, the life that the individual has is something passing through the individual as much as something it intrinsically possesses. The individual is subordinate to the species, not the other way around. The genetic set, in which is coded the *telos,* is as evidently the property of the species as of the individual through which it passes. A consideration of species strains any ethic fixed on individual organisms, much less on sentience or persons. But the result can be biologically sound even though it revises what was formerly thought logically permissible or ethically binding. This is a higher teleological ethic, finding now the specific *telos,* and concerned about consequences at that level; again, it is deontological, duty bound to the dynamic form of life for what it is in itself.

The species line is the *vital* living system, the whole, of which individual organisms are the essential parts. The species too has its integrity, its individuality, its "right to life" (if we must use the rhetoric of rights); and it is more important to protect this vitality than to protect individual integrity. The right to life, biologically speaking, is an adaptive fit that is right for life, that survives over millennia, and this generates at least a presumption that species in niche are good right where they are, and therefore that it is right for humans to let them be, to let them evolve.

Processes of value that we earlier found in an organic individual reappear at the specific level: defending a particular form of life, pursuing a pathway through the world, resisting death (extinction), regeneration maintaining a normative identity over time, creative resilience discovering survival skills. It is as logical to say that the individual is the species' way of propagating itself as to say that the embryo or egg is the individual's way of propagating itself. The dignity resides in the dynamic form; the individual inherits this, exemplifies it, and passes it on. If, at the specific level, these processes are just as evident, or even more so, what prevents duties arising at that level? The appropriate survival unit is the appropriate level of moral concern. This would be following nature specifically.

Sensitivity to this level, however, can sometimes make an environmental ethicist seem callous. On San Clemente Island, the U.S. Fish and Wildlife Service and the California Department of Fish and Game planned to shoot 2,000 feral goats to save three endangered plant species, *Malacothamnus clementinus, Castilleja grisea, Delphinium kinkiense,* of which the surviving individuals numbered only a few dozens. After a protest, some goats were trapped and relocated. But trapping all was impossible and many hundreds were killed. Is it inhumane to count plant species more than mammal lives, a few plants more than a thousand goats?

Those who wish to restore rare species of big cats to the wilds have asked about killing genetically inbred, inferior cats, presently held in zoos, in order to make space available for the cats needed to reconstruct and maintain a population genetically more likely to survive upon release. All the Siberian tigers in zoos in North America are descendants of seven animals; if these were replaced by others nearer to the wild type and with more genetic variability, the species could be saved in the wild. When we move to the level of species, we may kill individuals for the good of their kind.

Or we may now refuse to let nature take its course. The Yellowstone ethicists let the bison drown, callous to its suffering; they let the blinded bighorns die. But in the spring of 1984 a sow grizzly and her three cubs walked across the ice of Yellowstone Lake to Frank Island, two miles from shore. They stayed several days to feast on two elk carcasses, when the ice bridge melted. Soon afterward, they were starving on an island too small to support them. This time the Yellowstone ethicists promptly rescued the grizzlies and released them on the mainland, in order to protect an endangered species. They were not rescuing individual bears so much as saving the species. They thought that humans had already and elsewhere imperiled the grizzly, and that they ought to save this form of life.

Humans have more understanding than ever of the natural world they inhabit, of the speciating processes, more predictive power to foresee the intended and unintended results of their actions, and more power to reverse the undesirable consequences. The duties that such power and vision generate no longer attach simply to individuals or persons but are emerging duties to specific forms of life. The wrong that humans are doing, or allowing to happen through carelessness, is stopping the historical vitality of life, the flow of natural kinds.

Every extinction is an incremental decay in this stopping life, no small thing. Every extinction is a kind of superkilling. It kills forms (*species*), beyond individuals. It kills "essences" beyond "existences," the "soul" as well as the "body." It kills collectively, not just distributively. It kills birth as well as death. Afterward nothing of that kind either lives or dies. A shutdown of the life stream is the most destructive event possible. Never before has this level of question—superkilling by a superkiller—been deliberately faced. What is ethically callous is the malestrom of killing and insensitivity to forms of life and the sources producing them. What is required is principled responsibility to the biospheric earth.

Several billion years' worth of creative toil, several million species of teeming life, have been handed over to the care of this late-coming species in which mind has flowered and morals have emerged. Life on earth is a many splendored thing; extinction dims its luster. If, in this world of uncertain moral convictions, it makes any sense to claim that one ought not to kill individuals, without justification, it makes more sense to claim that one ought not to superkill the species, without superjustification. That moves from what *is* to what *ought to be;* and the fallacy is not committed by naturalists who so argue but by humanists who cannot draw these conclusions.

4. Ecosystems

"A thing is right," urged Aldo Leopold, concluding his land ethic, "when it tends to preserve the integrity, stability, and beauty of the biotic community; it is wrong when it tends otherwise." Again, we have two parts to the ethic: first that ecosystems exist, both in the wild and in support of culture; secondly that ecosystems ought to exist, both for what they are in themselves and as modified by culture. Again, we must move with care from the biological claims to the ethical claims.

Classical, humanistic ethics finds ecosystems unfamiliar territory. It is difficult to get the biology right, and, superimposed on the biology, to get the ethics right. Fortunately, it is often evident that human welfare depends on ecosystemic support, and in this sense all our legislation about clean air, clean water, soil conservation, national and state forest policy, pollution controls, oil spills, renewable resources, and so forth is concerned about ecosystem level processes. Further, humans find much of value for themselves in preserving wild ecosystems and our wilderness and park system is accordingly ecosystem oriented.

Still, a comprehensive environmental ethics needs the best, naturalistic reasons, as well as the good, humanistic ones, for respecting ecosystems. The ecosystem is the community of life; in it the fauna and flora, the species have entwined destinies. Ecosystems generate and support life, keep selection pressures high, enrich situated fitness, evolve congruent kinds in their places with sufficient containment. The ecologist finds that ecosystems are objectively satisfactory communities in the sense that organismic needs are sufficiently met for species long to survive, and the critical ethicist finds (in a subjective judgment matching the objective process) that such ecosystems are satisfactory communities to which to attach duty. Our concern must be for the fundamental unit of survival.

Giant forest fires raged over Yellowstone National Park in the summer of 1988, consuming nearly a million acres, despite the efforts of a thousand firefighters. By far the largest fires ever known in the park, the fires seemed a disaster. But the Yellowstone land ethic enjoins: Let nature take its course. Let it burn! So the fires were not fought at first, but in midsummer national authorities overrode that policy and ordered the fires put out. Even then, weeks later, fires continued to burn, partly because they were too big to control, but partly, too, because Yellowstone personnel did not altogether want the fires put out. Despite the evident destruction of trees, shrubs, and wildlife, they believe that fires are a good thing. Fires reset succession, release nutrients, recycle materials, renew the biotic community. (Nearby, in the Teton wilderness, a storm blew down 15,000 acres of trees, and some proposed that the area be declassified as wilderness for commercial salvage of the timber. But a similar environmental ethics said: No, let it rot.)

Aspen are important in the Yellowstone ecosystem. While some aspen stands are climax and self-renewing, many are seral and give way to conifers. Aspen groves support many birds and much wildlife, especially the beavers, whose activities maintain the riparian zones. Aspen are rejuvenated after fires, and the Yellowstone land ethic wants the aspen for its critical role in the biotic community. Elk browse the young aspen stems. To a degree this is a good thing, since it gives elk critical nitrogen, but in excess it is a bad thing. The elk have no predators, since the wolves are gone, and as a result they overpopulate. Excess elk also destroy the willows and this in turn destroys the beavers. Rejuvenating the aspen might require managers to cull hundreds of elk—all for the sake of a healthy ecosystem.

The Yellowstone ethic wishes to restore wolves to the greater Yellowstone ecosystem. At the level of species, this is partly for what the wolf is in itself, but it is partly because the greater Yellowstone ecosystem does not have its full integrity, stability, and beauty without this majestic animal at the top of the trophic pyramid. Restoring the wolf as a top predator would mean suffering and death for many elk, but that would be a good thing for the aspen and willows, for the beavers and riparian habitat, with mixed benefits for the bighorns and mule deer, whose food the overpopulating elk consume, but who would also be consumed by the wolves. The Yellowstone ethic demands wolves, as it does fires, in appropriate respect for life in its ecosystem.

Letting nature take its ecosystemic course is why the Yellowstone ethic forbade rescuing the drowning bison, but rescued the sow grizzly with her cubs, the latter to insure that the big predators remain. After the bison drowned, coyotes and magpies, foxes and ravens fed on the carcass. Later, even a grizzly bear fed on it. All this is a good thing because the system cycles on. On that account rescuing the whales trapped in the winter ice seems less of a good thing, when we note that rescuers had to drive away polar bears that attempted to eat the dying whales.

An ecosystem, the conservative ethicist will say, is too low a level of organization to be respected intrinsically. Ecosystems can seem little more than random, statistical processes. A forest can seem a loose collection of externally related parts, the collection of fauna and flora a jumble, hardly a community. The plants and animals within an ecosystem have needs, but their interplay can seem simply a matter of distribution and abundance, birth rates and death rates, population densities, parasitism and predation, dispersion, checks and balances, stochastic process. Much is not organic at all (rain, groundwater, rocks, soil particles, air), while some organic material is dead and decaying debris (fallen trees, scat, humus). These things have no organized needs. There is only catch-as-catch-can scrimmage for nutrients and energy—a game played with loaded dice, not really enough integrated process to call the whole a community.

Unlike higher animals, ecosystems have no experiences; they do not and cannot care. Unlike plants, an ecosystem has no organized center; no genome. It does not defend itself against injury or death. Unlike a species, there is no ongoing *telos,* no biological identity reinstantiated over time. The organismic parts are more complex than the community whole. More troublesome still, an ecosystem can seem a jungle where the fittest survive, a place of contest and conflict, beside which the organism is a model of cooperation. In animals, the heart, liver, muscles and brain are tightly integrated, as are the leaves, cambium, and roots in plants. But the ecosystem community is pushing and shoving between rivals, each aggrandizing itself or else indifference and haphazard juxtaposition, nothing to call forth our admiration.

Environmental ethics must break through the boundary posted by disoriented ontological conservatives, who hold that only organisms are "real," actually existing as entities, whereas ecosystems are nominal—just interacting individuals. Oak trees are real but forests are nothing but collections of trees. But any level is real if it shapes behavior on the level below it. Thus the cell is real because that pattern shapes the behavior of amino acids; the organism because that pattern coordinates the behavior of hearts and lungs. The biotic community is real because the niche shapes the morphology of the oak trees within it. Being real at the level of community only requires an organization that shapes the behavior of its members.

The challenge is to find a clear model of community and to discover an ethics for it—better biology for better ethics. Even before the rise of ecology, biologists began to conclude that the combative survival of the fittest distorts the truth. The more perceptive model is coaction in adapted fit. Predator and prey, parasite and host, grazer and grazed are contending forces in dynamic process where the well-being of each is bound up with the other—coordinated (orders that couple together) as much as heart and liver are coordinated organically. The ecosystem supplies the coordinates through which each organism moves, outside which the species cannot really be located. A species is what it is where it is.

The community connections are looser than the organism's internal interconnections—but not less significant. Admiring organic unity in organisms and stumbling over environmental looseness is like valuing mountains and despising valleys. The matrix the organism requires in order to survive is the open, pluralistic ecology. Internal complexity—heart, liver, muscles, brain—arises as a way of dealing with a complex, tricky environment. The skin-out processes are not just the support, they are the subtle source of the skin-in processes. In the complete picture, the outside is as *vital* as the inside. Had there been either simplicity or lock-step concentrated unity in the environment, no organismic unity could have evolved. Nor would it remain. There would be less elegance in life.

To look at one level for what is appropriate at another makes a categorical mistake. One should not look for a single center or program in ecosystems, much less for subjective experiences. Instead, one should look for a matrix, for interconnections between centers (individual plants and animals, dynamic lines of speciation), for creative stimulus and open-ended potential. Everything will be connected to many other things, sometimes by obligate associations, more often by partial and pliable dependencies and, among other things, there will be no significant interactions. There will be functions in a communal sense: shunts and criss-crossing pathways, cybernetic subsystems, and feedback loops. An order arises spontaneously and systematically when many self-concerned units jostle and seek their own programs, each doing their own thing and forced into informed interaction.

An ecosystem is a productive, projective system. Organisms defend only their selves, with individuals defending their continuing survival and species increasing the numbers of kinds. But the evolutionary ecosystem spins a bigger story, limiting each kind, locking it into the welfare of others, promoting new arrivals, bringing forth kinds and the integration of kinds. Species *increase their kind;* but ecosystems *increase kinds,* superimposing the latter increase onto the former. *Ecosystems are selective systems, as surely as organisms are selective systems.* The natural selection comes out of the system and is imposed on the individual. The individual is programmed to make more of its kind, but more is going on systemically than that; the system is making more kinds.

This extends natural selection theory beyond the merely tautological formulation that the system selects the best adapted to survive. Ecosystems select for those features that appear over the long ranges, for individuality, for diversification, for sufficient containment, for quality supervening on quantity of life. They do this, appropriately to the community level, by employing conflict, decenteredness, probability, succession, spontaneous generation of order, and historicity. Communal processes—the competition between organisms, more or less probable events, plant and animal successions, speciation over historical time—generate an ever-richer community.

Hence the evolutionary toil, elaborating and diversifying the biota, that once began with no species and results today in five million species, increasing over time the quality of lives in the upper rungs of the tropic pyramids. One-celled organisms evolved into many-celled, highly integrated organisms. Photosynthesis evolved and came to support locomotion—swimming, walking, running, flight. Stimulus-response mechanisms became complex instinctive acts. Warm-blooded animals followed cold-blooded ones. Complex nervous systems, conditioned behavior and learning emerged. Sentience appeared—sight, hearing, smell, tastes, pleasure, pain. Brains coupled with hands. Consciousness and self-consciousness arose. Culture was superimposed on nature.

These developments do not take place in all ecosystems or at every level. Microbes, plants, and lower animals remain, good of their kinds, and serving continuing roles, good for other kinds. The understories remain occupied. As a result, the quantity of life and its diverse qualities continue—from protozoans to primates to people. There is a push-up, lock-up, ratchet effect that conserves the upstrokes and the outreaches. The later we go in time the more accelerated are the forms at the top of the tropic pyramids, the more elaborated are the multiple tropic pyramids of earth. There are upward arrows over evolutionary time.

The system is a game with loaded dice, but the loading is a prolife tendency, not mere stochastic process. Though there is no *nature* in the singular, the system has a nature, a loading that pluralizes, putting *natures* into diverse kinds, nature$_1$, nature$_2$, natures . . . nature$_n$. It does so using random elements (in both organisms and communities), but this is a secret of its fertility, producing steadily intensified interdependencies and options. An ecosystem has no head, but it has a "heading" for species diversification, support, and richness. Though not a superorganism, it is a kind of vital field.

Instrumental value uses something as a means to an end; *intrinsic value* is worthwhile in itself. No warbler eats insects to become food for a falcon; the warbler defends its own life as an end in itself and makes more warblers as it can. A life is defended intrinsically without further contributory reference. But neither of these traditional terms is satisfactory at the level of the ecosystem. Though it has value *in* itself, the system does not have any value *for* itself. Though a value producer, it is not a value owner. We are no longer confronting instrumental value, as though the system were of value instrumentally as a fountain of life. Nor is the question one of intrinsic value, as though the system defended some unified form of life for itself. We have reached something for which we need a third term: *systemic value.* Duties arise in an encounter with the system that projects and protects these member components in biotic community. If you like, that is an ethic that is teleological again, but since we are respecting both processes and products, perhaps a better word for it now is communitarian. We follow nature, this time ecologically.

Ethical conservatives, in the humanist sense, will say that ecosystems are of value only because they contribute to human experiences. But that mistakes the last chapter for the whole story, one fruit for the whole plant. Humans count enough to have the right to flourish there, but not so much that they have the right to degrade or shut down ecosystems, not at least without a burden of proof that there is an overriding cultural gain. Earlier, environmental ethics will say that ecosystems are of value because they contribute to animal experiences or to organismic life. Later, the deeper, more conservative and more radical view sees that the stability, integrity, and beauty of biotic communities are what are most fundamentally to be conserved.

5. Value Theory

In practice the ultimate challenge of environmental ethics is the conservation of life on earth. In principle the ultimate challenge is a value theory profound enough to support that ethic. We need an account of how nature carries value, and an ethics that appropriately respects those values. For subjectivists both the theory and the ethics will be nothing but human constructs; but objectivists in environmental ethics will use such theory to discover facts, how nature carries values, and from this sometimes there will follow what humans ought to do. The values that nature carries belong as much to the biology of natural history as to the psychology of human experience. Some of the values that nature carries are up to us, our assignment. But fundamentally there are powers in nature that move to us and through us. The splendors of earth do not simply lie in their roles as human resources, supports of culture, or stimulators of experience.

There is no value without an evaluator. So runs a well-entrenched dogma. Humans clearly evaluate their world; sentient animals may also. But plants cannot evaluate their environment; they have no options and make no choices. *A fortiori,* species and ecosystems, earth and nature cannot be bona fide evaluators. Value, like a tickle or remorse, must be felt to be there. Its *esse* is *percipi.* Nonsensed value is nonsense. There are no thoughts without a thinker, no percepts without a perceiver, no deeds without a doer, no targets without an aimer. Valuing is felt preferring; value is the product of this process.

If value arrives only with consciousness, experiences where humans find value then have to be dealt with as appearances of various sorts. The value has to be relocated in the valuing subject's creativity as a person meets a valueless world, or even a valuable one—one *able to be valued*—but which before the human bringing of value ability contains only possibility and not any actual value. Value can only be extrinsic to nature, never intrinsic to it. Nature offers but the standing possibility of valuation; value is not generated until humans appear with their valuing ability.

But the valuing subject in an otherwise valueless world is an insufficient premise for the experienced conclusions of those who respect all life. Conversion to a biological view seems truer to world experience and more logically compelling. Here the order of knowing reverses—and also enhances—the order of being. This, too, is a perspective, but ecologically better informed. Science has been steadily showing how the consequences (life, mind) are built on their precedents (energy, matter), however much they overlap them. Life and mind appear where they did not before exist, and with this levels of value emerge that did not before exist. But that gives no reason to say that all value is an irreducible emergent at the human (or upper animal) level. Nature does, of course, offer possibilities for human valuation, but the vitality of the system is not something that goes on in the human mind, nor is its value. The possibility of valuation is carried to us by evolutionary and ecological natural history, and such nature is already valuable before humans arrive to evaluate what is taking place.

How do we humans come to be charged up with values, if there was and is nothing in nature charging us up so? Some value is anthropogenic, generated by humans, but some is biogenic, in the natural genesis. A comprehensive environmental ethics reallocates value across the whole continuum. Value increases in the emergent climax, but is continuously present in the composing precedents. The system is *value-able, able* to produce *value*. Human evaluators are among its products. But when we value we must not forget our communal bonds. Sometimes we need to evaluate (appraise the worth of) what we ourselves may not value (personally prefer). Against the standard view that all value requires a beholder, some value requires only a holder, and some value is held within the historic system that carries value to and through individuals.

Here we do not want a subjective morality but an objective one, even though we find that subjectivity is the most valuable output of the objective system. Is there any reason for ethical subjects to discount the vital systemic processes unless and until accompanied by sentience? Perhaps to evaluate the entire biological world on the basis of sentience is as much a categorical mistake as to judge it according to whether justice and charity are found there. The one mistake judges biological places by extension from psychology, the other from culture. What is "right" about the biological world is not just the production of pleasures and positive experiences. What is "right" includes ecosystemic patterns, organisms in their generating, sustaining environments.

Some value depends on subjectivity, yet all value is generated within the geosystemic and ecosystemic community. Systemically, value fades from subjective to objective value, but also fans out from the individual to its role and matrix. Things do not have their separate natures merely in and for themselves, but they face outward and co-fit into broader natures. Value-in-itself is smeared out to become value-in-togetherness. Value seeps out into the system, and we lose our capacity to identify the individual as the sole locus of value.

Intrinsic value, that of an individual "for what it is in itself," becomes problematic in a holistic web. True, the system produces such values more and more with its evolution of individuality and freedom. Yet to decouple this from the biotic, communal system is to make value too internal and elementary; this forgets relatedness and externality. Every intrinsic value has leading and trailing *ands* pointing to value from which it comes and toward which it moves. Adapted fitness makes individualistic value too system independent. Intrinsic value is a part in a whole, not to be fragmented by valuing it in isolation. An isolated *telos* is biologically impossible; the ethic cannot be teleological in that sense, nor can we term it deontological either, if this requires respect for an intrinsic value regardless of ecosystemic consequences. (The classical distinction fails again.)

Everything is good in a role, in a whole, although we can speak of objective intrinsic goodness wherever a good kind defends itself. We can speak of subjective intrinsic goodness when such an event registers as a point experience, at which point humans pronounce both their experience and what it is of good without need to enlarge their focus. The system is a value transformer where form and being, process and reality, fact and value are inseparably joined. Intrinsic and instrumental values shuttle back and forth, parts-in-wholes and wholes-in-parts, local details of value embedded in global structures, gems in their settings, and their setting-situation a corporation where value cannot stand alone. Every good is in community.

This is what is radically wrong with anthropocentric or merely anthropogenic value. It arrogates to humans what permeates the community. Subjective self-satisfactions are, and ought to be, sufficiently contained within the objectively satisfactory system. The system creates life, selects for adaptive fit, constructs increasingly richer life in quantity and quality, supports myriads of species, escalates individually, autonomy, and even subjectivity, within the limits of decentralized community. When persons appraise this natural history if such land is not a valuable, satisfactory biotic community; why not? Does earth and its community of life not claim their concern and care?

In environmental ethics one's beliefs about nature, which are based upon but exceed science, have everything to do with beliefs about duty. The way the world *is* informs the way it *ought* to be. We always shape our values in significant measure in accord with our notion of the kind of universe that we live in, and this drives our sense of duty. Our model of reality implies a model of conduct. Perhaps we can leave open what metaphysics ultimately underlies our cosmos, but for an environmental ethics at least we will need an earthbound metaphysics, a metaecology. Differing models sometimes imply similar conduct, but often they do not. A model in which nature has no value apart from human preferences will imply different conduct from one where nature projects fundamental values, some objective and others that further require human subjectivity superposed on objective nature.

This evaluation is not scientific description; hence not ecology per se, but we do move to metaecology. No amount of research can verify that, environmentally, the right is the optimum biotic community. Yet ecological description generates this valuing of nature, endorsing the systemic rightness. The transition from *is* to *good* and thence to *ought* occurs here; we leave science to enter the domain of evaluation, from which an ethic follows.

What is ethically puzzling and exciting is that an *ought* is not so much *derived* from an *is* as discovered simultaneously with it. As we progress from descriptions of fauna and flora, of cycles and pyramids, of autotrophs coordinated with heterotrophs, of stability and dynamism, on to intricacy, planetary opulence and interdependence, to unity and harmony with oppositions in counterpoint and synthesis, organisms evolved within and satisfactorily fitting their communities, arriving at length of beauty and goodness, it is difficult to say where the natural facts leave off and where the natural values appear. For some at least, the sharp *is/ought* dichotomy is gone; the values seem to be there as soon as the facts are fully in, and both alike properties of the system. This conviction, and the conscience that follows from it, can yield our best adaptive fit on earth.

Journal/Discussion Questions

✍ *Rolston provides a number of examples of environmental incidents. Were any of these of particular interest to you? Discuss.*

1. Rolston writes, "I doubt whether the good of humans who wish more water for development, both for industry and for bluegrass lawns, warrants endangering species of butterflies and cranes." Do you agree with this statement? Discuss.

2. How does Rolston deal with the question of whether human beings should have greater moral weight than other living beings? Critically assess Rolston's position.

3. At several points in his essay, Rolston refers to *ought* and *is*. Traditionally, most moral philosophers have maintained that it is impossible to derive an "ought" from an "is," that is, to derive a statement about moral obligation from a set of merely factual statements. What is Rolston's position on this issue? Do you agree?

Peter S. Wenz
"Just Garbage"

Peter S. Wenz, Professor of Philosophy and Legal Studies at the University of Illinois at Springfield and Adjunct Professor of Medical Humanities at the Southern Illinois University School of Medicine, is author of four books, Environmental Justice *(SUNY 1988),* Abortion Rights as Religious Freedom *(Temple 1992),* Nature's Keeper *(Temple 1996), and* Environmental Ethics Today *(Oxford 2001). He is currently working on issues at the intersection of environmental protection, political philosophy, human rights, and globalization.*

In this article, Wenz examines some of the ways in which environmental policies place disproportionate burdens on the poor and people of color, exposing them to more potential harms and giving them fewer potential benefits. Wenz assesses these practices from the standpoint of justice, and suggests an alterative approach that more fully meets the demands of justice.

As You Read, Consider This:

1. What are LULUs?
2. What, precisely, is the principle of the double effect? What role does this principle play in the defense of current environmental policies?
3. What is the principle of commensurate burdens and benefits? What role does it play in Wenz's arguments?
4. What is Wenz's Lowerarchy of Worry?
5. What is NIMBYism?

Environmental racism is evident in practices that expose racial minorities in the United States, and people of color around the world, to disproportionate shares of environmental hazards.[1] These include toxic chemicals in factories, toxic herbicides and pesticides in agriculture, radiation from uranium mining, lead from paint on older buildings, toxic wastes illegally dumped, and toxic wastes legally stored. In this article, which concentrates on issues of toxic waste, both illegally dumped and legally stored, I will examine the justness of current practices as well as the arguments commonly given in their defense. I will then propose an alternative practice that is consistent with prevailing principles of justice.

A Defense of Current Practices

Defenders often claim that because economic, not racial, considerations account for disproportionate impacts on nonwhites, current practices are neither racist nor morally objectionable. Their reasoning recalls the Doctrine of Double Effect. According to that doctrine, an effect whose pro-

Faces of Environmental Racism, edited by Laura Westra and Bill E. Lawson, Second Edition (Lanham: Rowman & Littlefield, 2001), pp. 57–72.

duction is usually blameworthy becomes blameless when it is incidental to, although predictably conjoined with, the production of another effect whose production is morally justified. The classic case concerns a pregnant woman with uterine cancer. A common, acceptable treatment for uterine cancer is hysterectomy. This will predictably end the pregnancy, as would an abortion. However, Roman Catholic scholars who usually consider abortion blameworthy consider it blameless in this context because it is merely incidental to hysterectomy, which is morally justified to treat uterine cancer. The hysterectomy would be performed in the absence of pregnancy, so the abortion effect is produced neither as an end-in-itself, nor as a means to roach the desired end, which is the cure of cancer.

Defenders of practices that disproportionately disadvantage non-whites seem to claim, in keeping with the Doctrine of Double Effect, that racial effects are blameless because they are sought neither as ends in-themselves nor as means to reach a desired goal. They are merely predictable side effects of economic and political practices that disproportionately expose poor people to toxic substances. The argument is that burial of toxic wastes, and other locally undesirable land uses (LULUs), lower property values. People who can afford to move elsewhere do so. They are replaced by buyers (or renters) who are predominantly poor and cannot afford housing in more desirable areas. Law professor Vicki Been puts it this way: "As long as the market allows the existing distribution of wealth to allocate goods and services, it would be surprising indeed if, over the long run, LULUs did not impose a disproportionate burden upon the poor." People of color are disproportionately burdened due primarily to poverty, not racism.[2] This defense against charges of racism is important in the American context because racial discrimination is illegal in the United States in circumstances where economic discrimination is permitted.[3] Thus, legal remedies to disproportionate exposure of nonwhites to toxic wastes are available if racism is the cause, but not if people of color are exposed merely because they are poor.

There is strong evidence against claims of racial neutrality. Professor Been acknowledges that even if there is no racism in the process of siting LULUs, racism plays at least some part in the disproportionate exposure of African Americans to them. She cites evidence that "racial discrimination in the sale and rental of housing relegates people of color (especially African Americans) to the least desirable neighborhoods, regardless of their income level."[4]

Without acknowledging for a moment, then, that racism plays no part in the disproportionate exposure of nonwhites to toxic waste, I will ignore this issue to display a weakness in the argument that justice is served when economic discrimination alone is influential. I claim that even if the only discrimination is economic, justice requires re-dress and significant alteration of current practices. Recourse to the Doctrine of Double Effect presupposes that the primary effect, with which a second effect is incidentally conjoined, is morally justifiable. In the classic case, abortion is justified only because hysterectomy is justified as treatment for uterine cancer. I argue that disproportionate impacts on poor people violate principles of distributive justice, and so are not morally justifiable in the first place. Thus, current practices disproportionately exposing nonwhites to toxic substances are not justifiable even if incidental to the exposure of poor people.

Alternate practices that comply with acceptable principles of distributive justice are suggested below. They would largely solve problems of environmental racism (disproportionate impacts on nonwhites) while ameliorating the injustice of disproportionately exposing poor people to toxic hazards. They would also discourage production of toxic substances, thereby reducing humanity's negative impact on the environment.

The Principle of Commensurate Burdens and Benefit

We usually assume that, other things being equal, those who derive benefits should sustain commensurate burdens. We typically associate the burden of work with the benefit of receiving money, and the burdens of monetary payment and tort liability with the benefits of ownership.

There are many exceptions. For example, people can inherit money without working, and be given ownership without purchase. Another exception, which dissociates the benefit of ownership from the burden of tort liability, is the use of tax money to protect the public from hazards associated with private property, as in Superfund legislation. Again, the benefit of money is dissociated from the burden of work when governments support people who are unemployed. The fact that these exceptions require justification, however, indicates an abiding assumption that people who derive benefits should shoulder commensurate burdens. The ability to inherit without work is justified as a benefit owed to those who wish to bequeath their wealth (which someone in the line of inheritance is assumed to have shouldered burdens to acquire). The same reasoning applies to gifts.

Using tax money (public money) to protect the public from dangerous private property is justified as encouraging private industry and commerce, which are supposed to increase public wealth. The system also protects victims in case private owners become bankrupt as, for example, in Times Beach, Missouri, where the government bought homes made worthless due to dioxin pollution. The company responsible for the pollution was bankrupt.

Tax money is used to help people who are out of work to help them find a job, improve their credentials, or feed their children. This promotes economic growth and equal opportunity. These exceptions prove the rule by the fact that justification for any deviation from the commensuration of benefits and burdens is considered necessary.

Further indication of an abiding belief that benefits and burdens should be commensurate is grumbling that, for example, many professional athletes and corporate executives are overpaid. Although the athletes and executives shoulder the burden of work, the complaint is that their benefits are disproportionate to their burdens. People on welfare are sometimes criticized for receiving even modest amounts of taxpayer money without shouldering the burdens of work, hence recurrent calls for "welfare reform." Even though these calls are often justified as means to reducing government budget deficits, the moral issue is more basic than the economic. Welfare expenditures are minor compared to other programs, and alternatives that require poor people to work are often more expensive than welfare as we know it.

The principle of commensuration between benefits and burdens is not the only moral principle governing distributive justice, and may not be the most important, but it is basic. Practices can be justified by showing them to conform, all things considered, to this principle. Thus, there is no move to "reform" the receipt of moderate pay for ordinary work, because it exemplifies the principle. On the other hand, practices that do not conform are liable to attack and require alternate justification, as we have seen in the cases of inheritance, gifts, Superfund legislation, and welfare.

Applying the principle of commensuration between burdens and benefits to the issue at hand yields the following: In the absence of countervailing considerations, the burdens of ill health associated with toxic hazards should be related to benefits derived from processes and products that create these hazards.

Toxic Hazards and Consumerism

In order to assess, in light of the principle of commensuration between benefits and burdens, the justice of current distributions of toxic hazards, the benefits of their generation must be considered. Toxic wastes result from many manufacturing processes, including those for a host of common items and materials, such as paint, solvents, plastics, and most petrochemical-based materials. These materials surround us in the paint on our houses, in our refrigerator containers, in our clothing, in our plumbing, in our garbage pails, and elsewhere.

Toxins are released into the environment in greater quantities now than ever before because we now have a consumer-oriented society where the acquisition, use, and disposal of individually owned items is greatly desired. We associate the numerical dollar value of the items at our disposal with our "standard of living," and assume that a higher standard is conducive to, if not identical with, a better life. So toxic wastes needing disposal are produced as by-products of the general pursuit of what our society defines as valuable, that is, the consumption of material goods.

Our economy requires increasing consumer demand to keep people working (to produce what is demanded). This is why there is concern each Christmas season, for example, that shoppers may not buy enough. If demand is insufficient, people may be put out of work. Demand must increase, not merely hold steady, because commercial competition improves labor efficiency in manufacture (and now in the service sector as well), so fewer workers can produce desired items. More items must be desired to forestall labor efficiency-induced unemployment, which is grave in a society where people depend primarily on wages to secure life's necessities.

Demand is kept high largely by convincing people that their lives require improvement, which consumer purchases will effect. When improvements are seen as needed, not merely desired, people purchase more readily. So our culture encourages economic expansion by blurring the distinction between wants and needs.

One way the distinction is blurred is through promotion of worry. If one feels insecure without the desired item or service, and so worries about life without it, then its provision is easily seen as a need. Commercials, and other shapers of social expectations, keep people worried by adjusting downward toward the trivial what people are expected to worry about. People worry about the provision of food, clothing, and housing without much inducement. When these basic needs are satisfied, however, attention shifts to indoor plumbing, for example, then to stylish indoor plumbing. The process continues with needs for a second or third bathroom, a kitchen disposal, and a refrigerator attached to the plumbing so that ice is made automatically in the freezer, and cold water can be obtained without even opening the refrigerator door. The same kind of progression results in cars with CD players, cellular phones, and automatic readouts of average fuel consumption per mile.

Abraham Maslow was not accurately describing people in our society when he claimed that after physiological, safety, love, and (self-) esteem needs are met, people work toward self-actualization, becoming increasingly their own unique selves by fully developing their talents. Maslow's Hierarchy of Needs describes people in our society less than Wenz's Lowerarchy of Worry. When one source of worry is put to rest by an appropriate purchase, some matter less inherently or obviously worrisome takes its place as the focus of concern. Such worry-substitution must be amenable to indefinite repetition in order to motivate purchases needed to keep the economy growing without inherent limit. If commercial society is supported by consumer demand, it is worry all the way down. Toxic wastes are produced in this context.

People tend to worry about ill health and early death without much inducement. These concerns are heightened in a society dependent upon the production of worry, so expenditure on health care consumes an increasing percentage of the gross domestic product. As knowledge of health impairment due to toxic substances increases, people are decreasingly tolerant of risks associated with their proximity. Thus, the same mindset of worry that elicits production that generates toxic wastes, exacerbates reaction to their proximity. The result is a desire for their placement elsewhere, hence the NIMBY syndrome—Not In My Back Yard. On this account, NIMBYism is not aberrantly selfish behavior, but integral to the cultural value system required for great volumes of toxic waste to be generated in the first place.

Combined with the principle of Commensurate Burdens and Benefits, that value system indicates who should suffer the burden of proximity to toxic wastes. Other things being equal, those who benefit most from the production of waste should shoulder the greatest share of burdens associated with its disposal. In our society, consumption of goods is valued highly and constitutes the principal benefit associated with the generation of toxic wastes. Such consumption is generally correlated with income and wealth. So other things being equal, justice requires that people's proximity to toxic wastes be related positively to their income and wealth. This is exactly opposite to the predominant tendency in our society, where poor people are more proximate to toxic wastes dumped illegally and stored legally.

Rejected Theories of Justice

Proponents of some theories of distributive justice may claim that current practices are justified. In this section I will explore such claims. A widely held view of justice is that all people deserve to have their interests given equal weight. John Rawls's popular thought experiment in which people choose principles of justice while ignorant of their personal identities dramatizes the importance of equal consideration of interests. Even selfish people behind the "veil of ignorance" in Rawls's "original position" would choose to accord equal consideration to everyone's interests because, they reason, they may themselves be the victims of any inequality. Equal consideration is a basic moral premise lacking serious challenge in our culture, so it is presupposed in what follows. Disagreement centers on application of the principle.

Libertarianism

Libertarians claim that each individual has an equal right to be free of interference from other people. All burdens imposed by other people are unjustified unless part of, or consequent upon, agreement by the party being burdened. So no individual who has not consented should be burdened by burial of toxic wastes (or the emission of air pollutants, or the use of agricultural pesticides, etc.) that may increase risks of disease, disablement, or death. Discussing the effects of air pollution, libertarian Murray Rothbard writes, "The remedy is simply to enjoin anyone from injecting pollutants into the air, and thereby invading the rights of persons and property. Period."[5] Libertarians John Hospers and Tibor R. Machan seem to endorse Rothbard's position.[6]

The problem is that implementation of this theory is impractical and unjust in the context of our civilization. Industrial life as we know it inevitably includes production of pollutants and toxic substances that threaten human life and health. It is impractical to secure the agreement of every individual to the placement, whether on land, in the air, or in water, of every chemical that may adversely affect the life or health of the individuals in question. After being duly informed of the hazard, someone potentially affected is bound to object, making the placement illegitimate by libertarian criteria.

In effect, libertarians give veto power to each individual over the continuation of industrial society. This seems a poor way to accord equal consideration to everyone's interests because the interest in physical safety of any one individual is allowed to override all other interests of all other individuals in the continuation of modern life. Whether or not such life is worth pursuing, it seems unjust to put the decision for everyone in the hands of any one person.

Utilitarianism

Utilitarians consider the interests of all individuals equally, and advocate pursuing courses of action that promise to produce results containing the greatest (net) sum of good. However, irrespective of how "good" is defined, problems with utilitarian accounts of justice are many and notorious.

Utilitarianism suffers in part because its direct interest is exclusively in the sum total of good, and in the future. Since the sum of good is all that counts in utilitarianism, there is no guarantee that the good of some will not be sacrificed for the greater good of others. Famous people could receive (justifiably according to utilitarians) particularly harsh sentences for criminal activity to effect general deterrence. Even when fame results from honest pursuits, a famous felon's sentence is likely to attract more attention than sentences in other cases of similar criminal activity. Because potential criminals are more likely to respond to sentences in such cases, harsh punishment is justified for utilitarian reasons on grounds that are unrelated to the crime.

Utilitarianism suffers in cases like this not only from its exclusive attention to the sum total of good, but also from its exclusive preoccupation with future consequences, which makes the relevance of past conduct indirect. This affects not only retribution, but also reciprocity and gratitude, which utilitarians endorse only to produce the greatest sum of future benefits. The direct relevance of past agreements and benefits, which common sense assumes, disappears in utilitarianism. So does direct application of the principle of Commensurate Burdens and Benefits.

The merits of the utilitarian rejection of common sense morality need not be assessed, however, because utilitarianism seems impossible to put into practice. Utilitarian support for any particular conclusion is undermined by the inability of anyone actually to perform the kinds of calculations that utilitarians profess to use. Whether the good is identified with happiness or preference-satisfaction, the two leading contenders at the moment, utilitarians announce the conclusions of their calculations without ever being able to show the calculation itself.

When I was in school, math teachers suspected that students who could never show their work were copying answers from other students. I suspect similarly that utilitarians, whose "calculations" often support conclusions that others reach by recourse to principles of gratitude, retributive justice, commensuration between burdens and benefits, and so forth, reach conclusions on grounds of intuitions influenced predominantly by these very principles.

Utilitarians may claim that, contrary to superficial appearances, these principles are themselves supported by utilitarian calculations. But, again, no one has produced a relevant calculation. Some principles seem *prima facie* opposed to utilitarianism, such as the one prescribing special solicitude of parents for their own children. It would seem that in cold climates more good would be produced if people bought winter coats for needy children, instead of special dress coats and ski attire for their own children. But utilitarians defend the principle of special parental concern. They declare this principle consistent with utilitarianism by appeal to entirely untested, unsubstantiated assumptions about counterfactuals. It is a kind of "Just So" story that explains how good is maximized by adherence to current standards. There is no calculation at all.

Another indication that utilitarians cannot perform the calculations they profess to rely upon concerns principles whose worth is in genuine dispute. Utilitarians offer no calculations that help to settle the matter. For example, many people wonder today whether or not patriotism is a worthy moral principle. Detailed utilitarian calculations play no part in the discussion.

These are some of the reasons why utilitarianism provides no help to those deciding whether or not disproportionate exposure of poor people to toxic wastes is just.

Free Market Approach

Toxic wastes, a burden, could be placed where residents accept them in return for monetary payment, a benefit. Since market transactions often satisfactorily commensurate burdens and benefits, this approach may seem to honor the principle of commensuration between burdens and benefits.

Unlike many market transactions, however, whole communities, acting as corporate bodies, would have to contract with those seeking to bury wastes. Otherwise, any single individual in the community could veto the transaction, resulting in the impasse attending libertarian approaches.[7] Communities could receive money to improve such public facilities as schools, parks, and hospitals, in addition to obtaining tax revenues and jobs that result ordinarily from business expansion.

The major problem with this free market approach is that it fails to accord equal consideration to everyone's interests. Where basic or vital goods and services are at issue, we usually think equal consideration of interests requires ameliorating inequalities of distribution that markets tend to produce. For example, one reason, although not the only reason, for public education is to provide every child with the basic intellectual tools necessary for success in our society. A purely free market approach, by contrast, would result in excellent education for children of wealthy parents and little or no education for children of the nation's poorest residents. Opportunities for children of poor parents would be so inferior that we would say the children's interests had not been given equal consideration.

The reasoning is similar where vital goods are concerned. The United States has the Medicaid program for poor people to supplement market transactions in health care precisely because equal consideration of interests requires that everyone be given access to health care. The 1994 health care debate in the United States was, ostensibly, about how to achieve universal coverage, not about whether or not justice required such coverage. With the exception of South Africa, every other industrialized country already has universal coverage for health care. Where vital needs are concerned, markets are supplemented or avoided in order to give equal consideration to everyone's interests.

Another example concerns military service in time of war. The United States employed conscription during the Civil War, both world wars, the Korean War, and the war in Vietnam. When the national interest requires placing many people in mortal danger, it is considered just that exposure be largely unrelated to income and market transactions.

The United States does not currently provide genuine equality in education or health care, nor did universal conscription (of males) put all men at equal risk in time of war. In all three areas, advantage accrues to those with greater income and wealth. (During the Civil War, paying for a substitute was legal in many cases.) Imperfection in practice, however, should not obscure general agreement in theory that justice requires equal consideration of interests, and that such equal consideration requires rejecting purely free market approaches where basic or vital needs are concerned.

Toxic substances affect basic and vital interests. Lead, arsenic, and cadmium in the vicinity of children's homes can result in mental retardation of the children.[8] Navajo teens exposed to radiation from uranium mine tailings have seventeen times the national average of reproductive organ cancer.[9] Environmental Protection Agency (EPA) officials estimate that toxic air pollution in areas of South Chicago increase cancer risks 100 to 1,000 times.[10] Pollution from Otis Air Force base in Massachusetts is associated with alarming increases in cancer rates.[11] Non-Hodgkin's Lymphoma is related to living near stone, clay, and glass industry facilities, and leukemia is related to living near chemical and petroleum plants.[12] In general, cancer rates are higher in the United States near industries that use toxic substances and discard them nearby.[13]

In sum, the placement of toxic wastes affects basic and vital interests just as do education, health care, and wartime military service. Exemption from market decisions is required to avoid unjust impositions on the poor, and to respect people's interests equally. A child dying of cancer receives little benefit from the community's new swimming pool.

Cost-Benefit Analysis (CBA)

CBA is an economist's version of utilitarianism, where the sum to be maximized is society's wealth, as measured in monetary units, instead of happiness or preference satisfaction. Society's wealth is computed by noting (and estimating where necessary) what people are willing to pay for goods and services. The more people are willing to pay for what exists in society, the better off society is, according to CBA.

CBA will characteristically require placement of toxic wastes near poor people. Such placement usually lowers land values (what people are willing to pay for property). Land that is already cheap, where poor people live, will not lose as much value as land that is currently expensive, where wealthier people live, so a smaller loss of social wealth attends placement of toxic wastes near poor people. This is just the opposite of what the Principle of Commensurate Burdens and Benefits requires.

The use of CBA also violates equal consideration of interests, operating much like free market approaches. Where a vital concern is at issue, equal consideration of interests requires that people be considered irrespective of income. The placement of toxic wastes affects vital interests. Yet CBA would have poor people exposed disproportionately to such wastes.[14]

In sum, libertarianism, utilitarianism, free market distribution, and cost-benefit analysis are inadequate principles and methodologies to guide the just distribution of toxic wastes.

LULU Points

An approach that avoids these difficulties assigns points to different types of locally undesirable land uses (LULUs) and requires that all communities earn LULU points. In keeping with the Principle of Commensurate Benefits and Burdens, wealthy communities would be required to earn more LULU points than poorer ones. Communities would be identified by currently existing political divisions, such as villages, towns, city wards, cities, and counties.

Toxic waste dumps are only one kind of LULU. Others include prisons, half-way houses, municipal waste sites, low-income housing, and power plants, whether nuclear or coal fired. A large deposit of extremely toxic waste, for example, may be assigned twenty points when properly buried but fifty points when illegally dumped. A much smaller deposit of properly buried toxic waste may be assigned only ten points, as may a coal-fired power plant. A nuclear power plant may be assigned twenty-five points, while municipal waste sites are only five points, and one hundred units of low-income housing are eight points.

These numbers are only speculations. Points would be assigned by considering probable effects of different LULUs on basic needs, and responses to questionnaires investigating people's levels of discomfort with LULUs of various sorts. Once numbers are assigned, the total number of LULU points to be distributed in a given time period could be calculated by considering planned development and needs for prisons, power plants, low-income housing, and so on. One could also calculate points for a community's already existing LULUs. Communities could then be required to host LULUs in proportion to their income or wealth, with new allocation of LULUs (and associated points) correcting for currently existing deviations from the rule of proportionality.

Wherever significant differences of wealth or income exist between two areas, these areas should be considered part of different communities if there is any political division between them. Thus, a county with rich and poor areas would not be considered a single community for purposes of locating LULUs. Instead, villages or towns may be so considered. A city with rich and poor areas may similarly be reduced to its wards. The purpose of segregating areas of different income or wealth from one another is to permit the imposition of greater LULU burdens on wealthier communities. When wealthy and poor areas are considered as one larger community, there is the danger that the community will earn its LULU points by placing hazardous waste near its poorer members. This possibility is reduced when only relatively wealthy people live in a smaller community that must earn LULU points.

Practical Implications

Political strategy is beyond the scope of this chapter, so I will refrain from commenting on problems and prospects for securing passage and implementation of the foregoing proposal. I maintain that the proposal is just. In a society where injustice is common, it is no surprise that proposals for rectification meet stiff resistance.

Were the LULU points proposal implemented, environmental racism would be reduced enormously. To the extent that poor people exposed to environmental hazards are members of racial minorities, relieving the poor of disproportionate exposure would also relieve people of color.

This is not to say that environmental racism would be ended completely. Implementation of the proposal requires judgment in particular cases. Until racism is itself ended, such judgment will predictably be exercised at times to the disadvantage of minority populations. However, because most people of color currently burdened by environmental racism are relatively poor, implementing the proposal would remove 80 to 90 percent of the effects of environmental racism. While efforts to end racism at all levels should continue, reducing the burdens of racism is generally advantageous to people of color. Such reductions are especially worthy when integral to policies that improve distributive justice generally.

Besides improving distributive justice and reducing the burdens of environmental racism, implementing the LULU points proposal would benefit life on earth generally by reducing the generation of toxic hazards. When people of wealth, who exercise control of manufacturing processes, marketing campaigns, and media coverage, are themselves threatened disproportionately by toxic hazards, the culture will evolve quickly to find their production largely unnecessary. It will be discovered, for example, that many plastic items can be made of wood, just as it was discovered in the late 1980s that the production of many ozone-destroying chemicals is unnecessary. Similarly, necessity being the mother of invention, it was discovered during World War II that many women could work in factories. When certain interests are threatened, the impossible does not even take longer.

The above approach to environmental injustice should, of course, be applied internationally and intranationally within all countries. The same considerations of justice condemn universally, all other things being equal, exposing poor people to vital dangers whose generation predominantly benefits the rich. This implies that rich countries should not ship their toxic wastes to poor countries. Since many poorer countries, such as those in Africa, are inhabited primarily by nonwhites, prohibiting shipments of toxic wastes to them would reduce significantly worldwide environmental racism. A prohibition on such shipments would also discourage production of dangerous wastes, as it would require people in rich countries to live with whatever dangers they create. If the principle of LULU points were applied in all countries, including poor ones, elites in those countries would lose interest in earning foreign currency credits through importation of waste, as they would be disproportionately exposed to imported toxins.

In sum, we could reduce environmental injustice considerably through a general program of distributive justice concerning environmental hazards. Pollution would not thereby be eliminated, since to live is to pollute. But such a program would motivate significant reduction in the generation of toxic wastes, and help the poor, especially people of color, as well as the environment.

Notes

1. See the introduction to *Faces of Environmental Racism* for studies indicating the disproportionate burden of toxic wastes on people of color.

2. Vicki Been, "Market Forces, Not Racist Practices, May Affect the Siting of Locally Undesirable Land Uses," in *At Issue: Environmental Justice,* ed. by Jonathan Petrikin (San Diego, Calif.: Greenhaven Press, 1995), 41.

3. See *San Antonio Independent School District v. Rodriguez,* 411 R.S. 1 (1973) and *Village of Arlington Heights v. Metropolitan Housing Development Corporation,* 429 U.S. 252 (1977).

4. Been, 41.

5. Murray Rothbard, "The Great Ecology Issue," *The Individualist* 21, no. 2 (February 1970): 5.

6. See Peter S. Wenz, *Environmental Justice* (Albany, N.Y.: State University of New York Press, 1988), 65–67 and associated endnotes.

7. Christopher Boerner and Thomas Lambert, "Environmental Justice Can Be Achieved Through Negotiated Compensation," in *At Issue: Environmental Justice.*

8. F. Diaz-Barriga et al., "Arsenic and Cadmium Exposure in Children Living Near to Both Zinc and Copper Smelters," summarized in *Archives of Environmental Health* 46, no. 2 (March/April 1991): 119.

9. Dick Russell, "Environmental Racism," *Amicus Journal* (Spring 1989): 22–32, 24.

10. Marianne Lavelle, "The Minorities Equation," *National Law Journal* 21 (September 1992): 3. Christopher Hallowell, "Water Crisis on the Cape," *Audubon* (July/August 1991): 65–74, especially 66 and 70.

11. Athena Linos et al., "Leukemia and Non-Hodgkin's Lymphoma and Residential Proximity to Industrial Plants," *Archives of Environmental Health* 46, no. 2 (March/April 1991): 70–74.

12. L. W. Pickle et al., *Atlas of Cancer Mortality among Whites: 1950—1980*, HHS publication # (NIH) 87-2900 (Washington, D.C.: U.S. Department of Health and Human Services, Government Printing Office: 1987).

13. Wenz, 216–18.

14. The idea of LULU points comes to me from Frank J. Popper, "LULUs and Their Blockage," in *Confronting Regional Challenges: Approaches to LULUs, Growth, and Other Vexing Governance Problems,* ed. by Joseph DiMento and Le Roy Graymer (Los Angeles, Calif.: Lincoln Institute of Land Policy, 1991), 13–27, especially 24.

Journal/Discussion Questions

1. What examples of environmental racism have you witnessed in your own community? What was the general reaction to these cases? Do you perceive them at the as instances of environmental racism?

2. Wenz criticizes utilitarian approaches to toxic waste management. On what basis? Do you agree? Discuss.

3. Wenz offers an alternative approach to the issue of the distribution of burdens such as toxic waste, one that centers on what he calls LULU points. Critically evaluate his approach.

Ramachandra Guha
"Radical American Environmentalism and Wilderness Preservation:
A Third World Critique"

Ramachandra Guha is a member of the Centre for Ecological Sciences, Indian Institute of Science, Bangalore, India.

In this essay, Professor Guha presents a Third World critique of the trend in American environmentalism known as deep ecology, analyzing each of deep ecology's central tenets: the distinction between anthropocentrism and biocentrism, the focus on wilderness preservation, the invocation of Eastern traditions, and the belief that it represents the most radical trend within environmentalism. He argues that the anthropocentrism-biocentrism distinction is of little use in understanding the dynamics of environmental degradation, that the implementation of the wilderness agenda is causing serious deprivation in the Third World, that the deep ecologist's interpretation of

Environmental Ethics, Vol. 11 (Spring 1989), pp. 71–83.

Eastern traditions is highly selective, and that in other cultural contexts (e.g., West Germany and India) radical environmentalism manifests itself quite differently, with a far greater emphasis on equity and the integration of ecological concerns with livelihood and work. He concludes that despite its claims to universality, deep ecology is firmly rooted in American environmental and cultural history and is inappropriate when applied to the Third World.

As You Read, Consider This:

1. Often, those outside our own culture can help us see things about ourselves that would not otherwise have been visible to us. In what ways does Guda help you to see things about the American environment movement more clearly?

2. According to Guha, many of us in the West have misperceptions of Eastern spirituality. What are some of these misperceptions?

> Even God dare not appear to the poor man except in the form of bread.
>
> —Mahatma Gandhi

I. Introduction

The respected radical journalist Kirkpatrick Sale recently celebrated "the passion of a new and growing movement that has become disenchanted with the environmental establishment and has in recent years mounted a serious and sweeping attack on it—style, substance, systems, sensibilities and all."[1] The vision of those whom Sale calls the "New Ecologists"—and what I refer to in this article as deep ecology—is a compelling one. Decrying the narrowly economic goals of mainstream environmentalism, this new movement aims at nothing less than a philosophical and cultural revolution in human attitudes toward nature. In contrast to the conventional lobbying efforts of environmental professionals based in Washington, it proposes a militant defense of "Mother Earth," an unflinching opposition to human attacks on undisturbed wilderness. With their goals ranging from the spiritual to the political, the adherents of deep ecology span a wide spectrum of the American environmental movement. As Sale correctly notes, this emerging strand has in a matter of a few years made its presence felt in a number of fields: from academic philosophy (as in the journal *Environmental Ethics*) to popular environmentalism (for example, the group Earth First!).

In this article I develop a critique of deep ecology from the perspective of a sympathetic outsider. I critique deep ecology not as a general (or even a foot soldier) in the continuing struggle between the ghosts of Gifford Pinchot and John Muir over control of the U.S. environmental movement, but as an outsider to these battles. I speak admittedly as a partisan, but of the environmental movement in India, a country with an ecological diversity comparable to the U.S., but with a radically dissimilar cultural and social history.

My treatment of deep ecology is primarily historical and sociological, rather than philosophical, in nature. Specifically, I examine the cultural rootedness of a philosophy that likes to present itself in universalistic terms. I make two main arguments: first, that deep ecology is uniquely American, and despite superficial similarities in rhetorical style, the social and political goals of radical environmentalism in other cultural contexts (e.g., West Germany and India) are quite different; second, that the social consequences of putting deep ecology into practice on a worldwide basis (what its practitioners are aiming for) are very grave indeed.

II. The Tenets of Deep Ecology

While I am aware that the term deep ecology was coined by the Norwegian philosopher Arne Naess, this article refers specifically to the American variant.[2] Adherents of the deep ecological perspective in this country, while arguing intensely among themselves over its political and philosophical implications, share some fundamental premises about human-nature interactions. As I see it, the defining characteristics of deep ecology are fourfold:

First, deep ecology argues, that the environmental movement must shift from an "anthropocentric" to a "biocentric" perspective. In many respects, an acceptance of the primacy of this distinction constitutes the litmus test of deep ecology. A considerable effort is expended by deep ecologists in showing that the dominant motif in Western philosophy has been anthropocentric—i.e., the belief that man and his works are the center of the universe—and conversely, in identifying those lonely thinkers (Leopold, Thoreau, Muir, Aldous Huxley, Santayana, etc.) who, in assigning man a more humble place in the natural order, anticipated deep ecological thinking. In the political realm, meanwhile, establishment environmentalism (shallow ecology) is chided for casting its arguments in human-centered terms. Preserving nature, the deep ecologists say, has an intrinsic worth quite apart from any benefits preservation may convey to future human generations. The anthropocentric-biocentric distinction is accepted as axiomatic by deep ecologists, it structures their discourse, and much of the present discussion remains mired within it.

The second characteristic of deep ecology is its focus on the preservation of unspoilt wilderness—and the restoration of degraded areas to a more pristine condition—to the relative (and sometimes absolute) neglect of other issues on the environmental agenda. I later identify the cultural roots and portentous consequences of this obsession with wilderness. For the moment, let me indicate three distinct sources from which it springs. Historically, it represents a playing out of the preservationist (read radical) and utilitarian (read reformist) dichotomy that has plagued American environmentalism since the turn of the century. Morally, it is an imperative that follows from the biocentric perspective; other species of plants and animals, and nature itself, have an intrinsic right to exist. And finally, the preservation of wilderness also turns on a scientific argument—viz., the value of biological diversity in stabilizing ecological regimes and in retaining a gene pool for future generations. Truly radical policy proposals have been put forward by deep ecologists on the basis of these arguments. The influential poet Gary Snyder, for example, would like to see a 90 percent reduction in human populations to allow a restoration of pristine environments, while others have argued forcefully that a large portion of the globe must be immediately cordoned off from human beings.[3]

Third, there is a widespread invocation of Eastern spiritual traditions as forerunners of deep ecology. Deep ecology, it is suggested, was practiced both by major religious traditions and at a more popular level by "primal" peoples in non-Western settings. This complements the search for an authentic lineage in Western thought. At one level, the task is to recover those dissenting voices within the Judeo-Christian tradition; at another, to suggest that religious traditions in other cultures are, in contrast, dominantly if not exclusively "biocentric" in their orientation. This coupling of (ancient)

Eastern and (modern) ecological wisdom seemingly helps consolidate the claim that deep ecology is a philosophy of universal significance.

Fourth, deep ecologists, whatever their internal differences, share the belief that they are the "leading edge" of the environmental movement. As the polarity of the shallow/deep and anthropocentric/biocentric distinctions makes clear, they see themselves as the spiritual, philosophical, and political vanguard of American and world environmentalism.

III. Toward a Critique

Although I analyze each of these tenets independently, it is important to recognize, as deep ecologists are fond of remarking in reference to nature, the interconnectedness and unity of these individual themes.

1. Insofar as it has begun to act as a check on man's arrogance and ecological hubris, the transition from an anthropocentric (human-centered) to a biocentric (humans as only one element in the ecosystem) view in both religious and scientific traditions is only to be welcomed.[4] What is unacceptable are the radical conclusions drawn by deep ecology, in particular, that intervention in nature should be guided primarily by the need to preserve biotic integrity rather than by the needs of humans. The latter for deep ecologists is anthropocentric, the former biocentric. This dichotomy is, however, of very little use in understanding the dynamics of environmental degradation. The two fundamental ecological problems facing the globe are (i) overconsumption by the industrialized world and by urban elites in the Third World and (ii) growing militarization, both in a short-term sense (i.e., on-going regional wars) and in a long-term sense (i.e., the arms race and the prospect of nuclear annihilation). Neither of these problems has any tangible connection to the anthropocentric-biocentric distinction. Indeed, the agents of these processes would barely comprehend this philosophical dichotomy. The proximate causes of the ecologically wasteful characteristics of industrial society and of militarization are far more mundane: at an aggregate level, the dialectic of economic and political structures, and at a micro-level, the life style choices of individuals. These causes cannot be reduced, whatever the level of analysis, to a deeper anthropocentric attitude toward nature; on the contrary, by constituting a grave threat to human survival, the ecological degradation they cause does not even serve the best interests of human beings! If my identification of the major dangers to the integrity of the natural world is correct, invoking the bogey of anthropocentrism is at best irrelevant and at worst a dangerous obfuscation.

2. If the above dichotomy is irrelevant, the emphasis on wilderness is positively harmful when applied to the Third World. If in the U.S. the preservationist/utilitarian division is seen as mirroring the conflict between "people" and "interests," in countries such as India the situation is very nearly the reverse. Because India is a long settled and densely populated country in which agrarian populations have a finely balanced relationship with nature, the setting aside of wilderness areas has resulted in a direct transfer of resources from the poor to the rich. Thus, Project Tiger, a network of parks hailed by the international conservation community as an outstanding success, sharply posits the interests of the tiger against those of poor peasants living in and around the reserve. The designation of tiger reserves was made possible only by the physical displacement of existing villages and their inhabitants; their management requires the continuing exclusion of peasants and livestock. The initial impetus for setting up parks for the tiger and other large mammals such as the rhinoceros and elephant came from two social groups: first, a class of ex-hunters turned conservationists belonging

mostly to the declining Indian feudal elite and, second, representatives of international agencies, such as the World Wildlife Fund (WWF) and the International Union for the Conservation of Nature and Natural Resources (IUCN), seeking to transplant the American system of national parks onto Indian soil. In no case have the needs of the local population been taken into account, and as in many parts of Africa, the designated wildlands are managed primarily for the benefit of rich tourists. Until very recently, wildlands preservation has been identified with environmentalism by the state and the conservation elite; in consequence, environmental problems that impinge far more directly on the lives of the poor—e.g., fuel, fodder, water shortages, soil erosion, and air and water pollution—have not been adequately addressed.[5]

Deep ecology provides, perhaps unwittingly, a justification for the continuation of such narrow and inequitable conservation practices under a newly acquired radical guise. Increasingly, the international conservation elite is using the philosophical, moral, and scientific arguments used by deep ecologists in advancing their wilderness crusade. A striking but by no means atypical example is the recent plea by a prominent American biologist for the takeover of large portions of the globe by the author and his scientific colleagues. Writing in a prestigious scientific forum, the *Annual Review of Ecology and Systematics,* Daniel Janzen argues that only biologists have the competence to decide how the tropical landscape should be used. As "the representatives of the natural world," biologists are "in charge of the future of tropical ecology," and only they have the expertise and mandate to "determine whether the tropical agroscape is to be populated only by humans, their mutualists, commensals, and parasites, or whether it will also contain some islands of the greater nature—the nature that spawned humans, yet has been vanquished by them." Janzen exhorts his colleagues to advance their territorial claims on the tropical world more forcefully, warning that the very existence of these areas is at stake: "if biologists want a tropics in which to biologize, they are going to have to buy it with care, energy, effort, strategy, tactics, time, and cash."[6]

This frankly imperialist manifesto highlights the multiple dangers of the preoccupation with wilderness preservation that is characteristic of deep ecology. As I have suggested, it seriously compounds the neglect by the American movement of far more pressing environmental problems within the Third World. But perhaps more importantly, and in a more insidious fashion, it also provides an impetus to the imperialist yearning of Western biologists and their financial sponsors, organizations such as the WWF and IUCN. The wholesale transfer of a movement culturally rooted in American conservation history can only result in the social uprooting of human populations in other parts of the globe.

3. I come now to the persistent invocation of Eastern philosophies as antecedent in point of time but convergent in their structure with deep ecology. Complex and internally differentiated religious traditions—Hinduism, Buddhism, and Taoism—are lumped together as holding a view of nature believed to be quintessentially biocentric. Individual philosophers such as the Taoist Lao Tzu are identified as being forerunners of deep ecology. Even an intensely political, pragmatic, and Christian influenced thinker such as Gandhi has been accorded a wholly undeserved place in the deep ecological pantheon. Thus the Zen teacher Robert Aitken Roshi makes the strange claim that Gandhi's thought was not human-centered and that he practiced an embryonic form of deep ecology which is "traditionally Eastern and is found with differing emphasis in Hinduism, Taoism and in Theravada and Mahayana Buddhism."[7] Moving away from the realm of high philosophy and scriptural religion, deep ecologists make the further claim that at the level of material and spiritual practice "primal" peoples subordinated themselves to the integrity of the biotic universe they inhabited.

I have indicated that this appropriation of Eastern traditions is in part dictated by the need to construct an authentic lineage and in part a desire to present deep ecology as a universalistic philosophy. Indeed, in his substantial and quixotic biography of John Muir, Michael Cohen goes so far as to suggest that Muir was the "Taoist of the [American] West."[8] This reading of Eastern traditions is selective and does not bother to differentiate between alternate (and changing) religious and cultural traditions; as it stands, it does considerable violence to the historical record. Throughout most recorded history the characteristic form of human activity in the "East" has been a finely tuned but nonetheless conscious and dynamic manipulation of nature. Although mystics such as Lao Tzu did reflect on the spiritual essence of human relations with nature, it must be recognized that such ascetics and their reflections were supported by a society of cultivators whose relationship with nature was a far more *active* one. Many agricultural communities do have a sophisticated knowledge of the natural environment that may equal (and sometimes surpass) codified "scientific" knowledge; yet, the elaboration of such traditional ecological knowledge (in both material and spiritual contexts) can hardly be said to rest on a mystical affinity with nature of a deep ecological kind. Nor is such knowledge infallible; as the archaeological record powerfully suggests, modern Western man has no monopoly on ecological disasters.

In a brilliant article, the Chicago historian Ronald Inden points out that this romantic and essentially positive view of the East is a mirror image of the scientific and essentially pejorative view normally upheld by Western scholars of the Orient. In either case, the East constitutes the Other, a body wholly separate and alien from the West; it is defined by a uniquely spiritual and nonrational "essence," even if this essence is valorized quite differently by the two schools. Eastern man exhibits a spiritual dependence with respect to nature—on the one hand, this is symptomatic of his prescientific and backward self, on the other, of his ecological wisdom and deep ecological consciousness. Both views are monolithic, simplistic, and have the characteristic effect—intended in one case, perhaps unintended in the other of denying agency and reason to the East and making it the privileged orbit of Western thinkers.

The two apparently opposed perspectives have then a common underlying structure of discourse in which the East merely serves as a vehicle for Western projections. Varying images of the East are raw material for political and cultural battles being played out in the West; they tell us far more about the Western commentator and his desires than about the "East." Inden's remarks apply not merely to Western scholarship on India, but to Orientalist constructions of China and Japan as well:

> Although these two views appear to be strongly opposed, they often combine together. Both have a similar interest in sustaining the Otherness of India. The holders of the dominant view, best exemplified in the past in imperial administrative discourse (and today probably by that of "development economics"), would place a traditional, superstition-ridden India in a position of perpetual tutelage to a modern, rational West. The adherents of the romantic view, best exemplified academically in the discourses of Christian liberalism and analytic psychology, concede the realm of the public and impersonal to the positivist. Taking their succor not from governments and big business, but from a plethora of religious foundations and self-help institutes, and from allies in the "consciousness industry," not to mention the important industry of tourism, the romantics insist that India embodies a private realm of the imagination and the religious which modern, Western man lacks but needs. They, therefore, like the positivists, but for just the opposite reason, have a vested interest in seeing that the Orientalist view of India as "spiritual," "mysterious," and "exotic" is perpetuated.[9]

4. How radical, finally, are the deep ecologists? Notwithstanding their self-image and strident rhetoric (in which the label "shallow ecology" has an opprobrium similar to that reserved for "social democratic" by Marxist-Leninists), even within the American context their radicalism is limited and it manifests itself quite differently elsewhere.

To my mind, deep ecology is best viewed as a radical trend within the wilderness preservation movement. Although advancing philosophical rather than aesthetic arguments and encouraging political militancy rather than negotiation, its practical emphasis—viz., preservation of unspoilt nature—is virtually identical. For the mainstream movement, the function of wilderness is to provide a temporary antidote to modern civilization. As a special institution within an industrialized society, the national park "provides an opportunity for respite, contrast, contemplation, and affirmation of values for those who live most of their lives in the workaday world."[10] Indeed, the rapid increase in visitations to the national parks in postwar America is a direct consequence of economic expansion. The emergence of a popular interest in wilderness sites, the historian Samuel Hays points out, was "not a throwback to the primitive, but an integral part of the modern standard of living as people sought to add new 'amenity' and 'aesthetic' goals and desires to their earlier preoccupation with necessities and conveniences."[11]

Here, the enjoyment of nature is an integral part of the consumer society. The private automobile (and the lifestyle it has spawned) is in many respects the ultimate ecological villain, and an untouched wilderness the prototype of ecological harmony; yet, for most Americans it is perfectly consistent to drive a thousand miles to spend a holiday in a national park. They possess a vast, beautiful, and sparsely populated continent and are also able to draw upon the natural resources of large portions of the globe by virtue of their economic and political dominance. In consequence, America can simultaneously enjoy the material benefits of an expanding economy and the aesthetic benefits of unspoilt nature. The two poles of "wilderness" and "civilization" mutually coexist in an internally coherent whole, and philosophers of both poles are assigned a prominent place in this culture. Paradoxically as it may seem, it is no accident that Star Wars technology and deep ecology both find their fullest expression in that leading sector of Western civilization, California.

Deep ecology runs parallel to the consumer society without seriously questioning its ecological and sociopolitical basis. In its celebration of American wilderness, it also displays an uncomfortable convergence with the prevailing climate of nationalism in the American wilderness movement. For spokesmen such as the historian Roderick Nash, the national park system is America's distinctive cultural contribution to the world, reflective not merely of its economic but of its philosophical and ecological maturity as well. In what Walter Lippman called the American century, the "American invention of national parks" must be exported worldwide. Betraying an economic determinism that would make even a Marxist shudder, Nash believes that environmental preservation is a "full stomach" phenomenon that is confined to the rich, urban, and sophisticated. Nonetheless, he hopes that "the less developed nations may eventually evolve economically and intellectually to the point where nature preservation is more than a business."[12]

The error which Nash makes (and which deep ecology in some respects encourages) is to equate environmental protection with the protection of wilderness. This is a distinctively American notion, borne out of a unique social and environmental history. The archetypal concerns of radical environmentalists in other cultural contexts are in fact quite different. The German Greens, for example, have elaborated a devastating critique of industrial society which turns on the acceptance of environmental limits to growth. Pointing to the intimate links between industrialization, militarization, and conquest, the Greens argue that economic growth in the West has historically rested on the economic and ecological exploitation of the Third World. Rudolf Bahro is characteristically blunt:

> The working class here [in the West] is the richest lower class in the world. And if I look at the problem from the point of view of the whole of humanity, not just from that of Europe, then I must say that the metropolitan working class is the worst exploiting class in history. . . . What made poverty bearable in eighteenth or nineteenth-century Europe was the prospect of escaping it through exploitation of the periphery. But this is no longer a possibility, and continued industrialism in the Third World will mean poverty for whole generations and hunger for millions.[13]

Here the roots of global ecological problems lie in the disproportionate share of resources consumed by the industrialized countries as a whole *and* the urban elite within the Third World. Since it is impossible to reproduce an industrial monoculture worldwide, the ecological movement in the West must begin by cleaning up its own act. The Greens advocate the creation of a "no growth" economy, to be achieved by scaling down current (and clearly unsustainable) consumption levels.[14] This radical shift in consumption and production patterns requires the creation of alternate economic and political structures—smaller in scale and more amenable to social participation—but it rests equally on a shift in cultural values. The expansionist character of modern Western man will have to give way to an ethic of renunciation and self-limitation, in which spiritual and communal values play an increasing role in sustaining social life. This revolution in cultural values, however, has as its point of departure an understanding of environmental processes quite different from deep ecology.

Many elements of the Green program find a strong resonance in countries such as India, where a history of Western colonialism and industrial development has benefited only a tiny elite while exacting tremendous social and environmental costs. The ecological battles presently being fought in India have as their epicenter the conflict over nature between the subsistence and largely rural sector and the vastly more powerful commercial-industrial sector. Perhaps the most celebrated of these battles concerns the Chipko (Hug the Tree) movement, a peasant movement against deforestation in the Himalayan foothills. Chipko is only one of several movements that have sharply questioned the nonsustainable demand being placed on the land and vegetative base by urban centers and industry. These include opposition to large dams by displaced peasants, the conflict between small artisan fishing and large-scale trawler fishing for export, the countrywide movements against commercial forest operations, and opposition to industrial pollution among downstream agricultural and fishing communities.[15]

Two features distinguish these environmental movements from their Western counterparts. First, for the sections of society most critically affected by environmental degradation—poor and landless peasants, women, and tribals—it is a question of sheer survival, not of enhancing the quality of life. Second, and as a consequence, the environmental solutions they articulate deeply involve questions of equity as well as economic and political redistribution. Highlighting these differences, a leading Indian environmentalist stresses that "environmental protection per se is of least concern to most of these groups. Their main concern is about the use of the environment and who should benefit from it."[16] They seek to wrest control of nature away from the state and the industrial sector and place it in the hands of rural communities who live within that environment but are increasingly denied access to it. These communities have far more basic needs, their demands on the environment are far less intense, and they can draw upon a reservoir of cooperative social institutions and local ecological knowledge in managing the "commons"—forests, grasslands, and the waters—on a

sustainable basis. If colonial and capitalist expansion has both accentuated social inequalities and signaled a precipitous fall in ecological wisdom, an alternate ecology must rest on an alternate society
and polity as well.

This brief overview of German and Indian environmentalism has some major implications for
deep ecology. Both German and Indian environmental traditions allow for a greater integration of ecological concerns with livelihood and work. They also place a greater emphasis on equity and social
justice (both within individual countries and on a global scale) on the grounds that in the absence of
social regeneration environmental regeneration has very little chance of succeeding. Finally, and
perhaps most significantly, they have escaped the preoccupation with wilderness preservation so
characteristic of American cultural and environmental history.[17]

IV. A Homily

In 1958, the economist J.K. Galbraith referred to overconsumption as the unasked question of the
American conservation movement. There is a marked selectivity, he wrote, "in the conservationist's
approach to materials consumption. If we are concerned about our great appetite for materials, it is
plausible to seek to increase the supply, to decrease waste, to make better use of the stocks available,
and to develop substitutes. But what of the appetite itself? Surely this is the ultimate source of the
problem. If it continues its geometric course, will it not one day have to be restrained? Yet in the literature of the resource problem this is the forbidden question. Over it hangs a nearly total silence."[18]

The consumer economy and society have expanded tremendously in the three decades since
Galbraith penned these words; yet his criticisms are nearly as valid today. I have said "nearly," for
there are some hopeful signs. Within the environmental movement several dispersed groups are working to develop ecologically benign technologies and to encourage less wasteful life styles. Moreover,
outside the self-defined boundaries of American environmentalism, opposition to the permanent war
economy is being carried on by a peace movement that has a distinguished history and impeccable
moral and political credentials.

It is precisely these (to my mind, most hopeful) components of the American social scene that
are missing from deep ecology. In their widely noticed book, Bill Devall and George Sessions make
no mention of militarization or the movements for peace, while activists whose practical focus is on
developing ecologically responsible life styles (e.g., Wendell Berry) are derided as "falling short of
deep ecological awareness."[19] A truly radical ecology in the American context ought to work toward
a synthesis of the appropriate technology, alternate life style, and peace movements.[20] By making the
(largely spurious) anthropocentric-biocentric distinction central to the debate, deep ecologists may
have appropriated the moral high ground, but they are at the same time doing a serious disservice to
American and global environmentalism.[21]

Acknowledgments

This essay was written while the author was a visiting lecturer at the Yale School of Forestry and
Environmental Studies. He is grateful to Mike Bell, Tom Birch, Bill Burch, Bill Cronon, Diane
Mayerfeld, David Rothenberg, Kirkpatrick Sale, Joel Seton, Tim Weiskel, and Don Worster for
helpful comments.

Endnotes

1. Kirkpatrick Sale, "The Forest for the Trees: Can Today's Environmentalists Tell the Difference," *Mother Jones* 11, no. 8 (November 1986): 26.

2. One of the major criticisms I make in this essay concerns deep ecology's lack of concern with inequalities *within* human society. In the article in which he coined the term *deep ecology,* Naess himself expresses concerns about inequalities between and within nations. However, his concern with social cleavages and their impact on resource utilization patterns and ecological destruction is not very visible in the later writings of deep ecologists. See Arne Naess, "The Shallow and the Deep, Long-Range Ecology Movement: A Summary," *Inquiry* 16 (1973): p. 96 (I am grateful to Tom Birch for this reference).

3. Gary Snyder, quoted in Sale, "The Forest for the Trees," p. 32. See also Dave Foreman, "A Modest Proposal for a Wilderness System," *Whole Earth Review,* no. 53 (Winter 1986–1987): 42–45.

4. See, for example, Donald Worster, *Nature's Economy: The Roots of Ecology* (San Francisco, Sierra Club Books, 1977).

5. See Centre for Science and Environment, *India: The State of the Environment 1982: A Citizens Report* (New Delhi: Centre for Science and Environment, 1982); R. Sukumar, "Elephant-Man Conflict in Karnataka," in Cecil Saldanha, ed., *The State of Karnataka's Environment* (Bangalore: Centre for Taxonomic Studies, 1985). For Africa, see the brilliant analysis by Helge Kjekshus, *Ecology Control and Economic Development in East African History* (Berkeley: University of California Press, 1977).

6. Daniel Janzen, "The Future of Tropical Ecology," *Annual Review of Ecology and Systematics* 17 (1986): 305–306; emphasis added.

7. Robert Aitken Roshi, "Gandhi, Dogen, and Deep Ecology," reprinted as appendix C in Bill Devall and George Sessions, *Deep Ecology: Living as if Nature Mattered* (Salt Lake City: Peregrine Smith Books, 1985). For Gandhi's own views on social reconstruction, see the excellent three volume collection edited by Raghavan Iyer, *The Moral and Political Writings of Mahatma Gandhi* (Oxford: Clarendon Press, 1986–1987).

8. Michael Cohen. *The Pathless Way* (Madison: University of Wisconsin Press, 1984), p. 120.

9. Ronald Inden, "Orientalist Constructions of India," *Modern Asian Studies* 20 (1986): 442. Inden draws inspiration from Edward Said's forceful polemic, *Orientalism* (New York: Basic Books, 1980). It must be noted, however, that there is a salient difference between Western perceptions of Middle Eastern and Far Eastern cultures respectively. Due perhaps to the long history of Christian conflict with Islam, Middle Eastern cultures (as Said documents) are consistently presented in pejorative terms. The juxtaposition of hostile and worshipping attitudes that Inden talks of applies only to Western attitudes toward Buddhist and Hindu societies.

10. Joseph Sax, *Mountains Without Handrails: Reflections on the National Parks* (Ann Arbor: University of Michigan Press, 1980), p. 42. Cf. also Peter Schmitt, *Back to Nature: The Arcadian Myth in Urban America* (New York: Oxford University Press, 1969), and Alfred Runte, *National Parks: The American Experience* (Lincoln: University of Nebraska Press, 1979).

11. Samuel Hays, "From Conservation to Environment: Environmental Politics in the United States since World War Two," *Environmental Review* 6 (1982): 21. See also the same author's book

entitled *Beauty, Health and Permanence: Environmental Politics in the United States, 1955–1985* (New York: Cambridge University Press, 1987).

12. Roderick Nash, *Wilderness and the American Mind,* 3rd ed. (New Haven: Yale University Press, 1982).

13. Rudolf Bahro, *From Red to Green* (London: Verso Books, 1984).

14. From time to time, American scholars have themselves criticized these imbalances in consumption patterns. In the 1950s, William Vogt made the charge that the United states, with one-sixteenth of the world's population, was utilizing one-third of the globe's resources. (Vogt, cited in E.F. Murphy, *Nature, Bureaucracy and the Rule of Property* [Amsterdam: North Holland, 1977, p. 29].) More recently, Zero Population Growth has estimated that each American consumes thirty-nine times as many resources as an Indian. See *Christian Science Monitor,* 2 March 1987.

15. For an excellent review, see Anil Agarwal and Sunita Narain, eds., *India: The State of the Environment 1984–1985: A Citizens Report* (New Delhi: Centre for Science and Environment, 1985). Cf. Also Ramachandra Guha, *The Unquiet Woods: Ecological Change and Peasant Resistance in the Indian Himalaya* (Berkeley: University of California Press, forthcoming).

16. Anil Agarwal, "Human-Nature Interactions in a Third World Country," *The Environmentalist* 6. no. 3 (1986): 167.

17. One strand in radical American environmentalism, the bioregional movement, by emphasizing a greater involvement with the bioregion people inhabit, does indirectly challenge consumerism. However, as yet, bioregionalism has hardly raised the questions of equity and social justice (international, intranational, and intergenerational) which I argue must be a central plank of radical environmentalism. Moreover, its stress on (individual) experience as the key to involvement with nature is also somewhat at odds with the integration of nature with livelihood and work that I talk of in this paper. Cf. Kirkpatrick Sale, *Dwellers in the Land: The Bioregional Vision* (San Francisco: Sierra Club Books, 1985).

18. John Kenneth Galbraith, "How Much Should a Country Consume?" in Henry Jarrett, ed., *Perspectives on Conservation* (Baltimore: Johns Hopkins Press, 1958), pp. 91–92.

19. Devall and Sessions, *Deep Ecology,* p. 122. For Wendell Berry's own assessment of deep ecology, see his "Amplications: Preserving Wildness," *Wilderness* 50 (Spring 1987): 39–40, 50–54.

20. See the interesting recent contribution by one of the most influential spokesmen of appropriate technology—Barry Commoner, "A Reporter at Large: The Environment," *New Yorker,* 15 June 1987. While Commoner makes a forceful plea for the convergence of the environmental movement (viewed by him primarily as the opposition to air and water pollution and to the institutions that generate such pollution) and the peace movement, he significantly does not mention consumption patterns, implying that "limits to growth" do not exist.

21. In this sense, my critique of deep ecology, although that of an outsider, may facilitate the reassertion of those elements in the American environmental tradition for which there is a profound sympathy in other parts of the globe. A global perspective may also lead to a critical reassessment of figures such as Aldo Leopold and John Muir, the two patron saints of deep ecology. As Donald Worster has pointed out, the message of Muir (and, I would argue, of Leopold

as well) makes sense only in an American context; he has very little to say to other cultures. See Worster's review of Sterchen Fox's *John Muir and His Legacy,* in *Environmental Ethics* 5 (1983): 277–281.

Journal/Discussion Questions

✍ *What experience have you had in third world countries? How does your experience shed light on what Guha says in this article?*

1. Explain the difference between an anthropocentric and a biocentric perspective.

2. What are Guha's principal objections to deep ecology? Critically assess his objections.

3. How do you think environmental issues should best be handled in developing countries? What are the principal factors to consider? How does your answer to this relate to Guha's?

Concluding Discussion Questions

Where Do You Stand Now?

Instructions

You have already answered the following questions in your moral problems self-quiz at the beginning of this book. Now that you have studied the material in this section, take a moment to answer the same questions again.

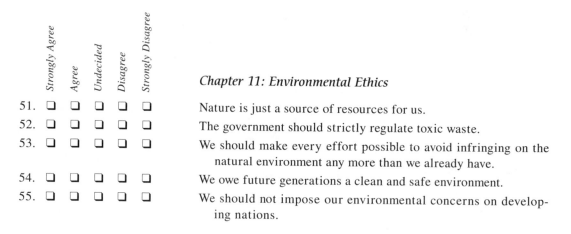

Chapter 11: Environmental Ethics

	Strongly Agree	Agree	Undecided	Disagree	Strongly Disagree	
51.	❑	❑	❑	❑	❑	Nature is just a source of resources for us.
52.	❑	❑	❑	❑	❑	The government should strictly regulate toxic waste.
53.	❑	❑	❑	❑	❑	We should make every effort possible to avoid infringing on the natural environment any more than we already have.
54.	❑	❑	❑	❑	❑	We owe future generations a clean and safe environment.
55.	❑	❑	❑	❑	❑	We should not impose our environmental concerns on developing nations.

Compare your answers to this self-quiz with the answers to the initial self-quiz. How, if at all, have your answers changed? How have the *reasons* for your answers changed?

For Further Reading

Journals

In addition to the standard journals in ethics discussed in the bibliographical essay at the end of Chapter 1, see especially *Environmental Ethics,* which has been a rich source of scholarship and theory on issues of environmental ethics; also see the journal *Environmental Values, Between the Species, The Journal of Agricultural and Environmental Ethics,* and *Philosophy and Geography.*

Review Articles

See the review articles by Kristin Shrader-Frechette, "Environmental Ethics," *The Oxford Handbook of Practical Ethics,* edited by Hugh LaFollette (Oxford: Oxford University Press, 2003), pp. 188–215; Andrew Light, "Environmental Ethics," *A Companion to Applied Ethics: Blackwell Companions to Philosophy,* edited by R. G. Frey (Malden, MA: Blackwell Publishing, 2003), pp. 633–649; Holmes Rolston III, "Environmental Ethics," *The Blackwell Companion to Philosophy,* 2nd ed., edited by Nicholas Bunnin (Malden, MA: Blackwell Publishing, 2003), pp. 517–530; J. Baird Callicott, "Environmental Ethics," *Encyclopedia of Ethics,* edited by Lawrence C. Becker and Charlotte B. Becker (New York: Garland Publishing, Inc., 1992), Vol. I, pp. 311–314; and Robert Elliot, "Environmental Ethics," *A Companion to Ethics,* edited by Peter Singer (Oxford: Blackwell, 1991), pp. 284–293. Also see the articles in *Environmental Philosophy: From Animal Rights to Radical Ecology,* discussed later, and John Passmore, "Environmentalism," *A Companion to Contemporary Political Philosophy,* edited by Robert E. Goodin and Philip Pettit (Oxford: Blackwell, 1993), pp. 471–488.

Anthologies

Andrew Light and Holmes Rolston III, eds., *Environmental Ethics: An Anthology* (Malden, MA: Blackwell Publishing, 2003) is a fine starting point for the literature in environmental ethics. *Environmental Philosophy: From Animal Rights to Radical Ecology,* edited by Michael E. Zimmerman et al., 3rd ed. (Englewood Cliffs, NJ: Prentice Hall, 2000) is a fine collection of essays, with introductions for individual sections done by representatives of each tradition, including ecofeminism, deep ecology, and social ecology. *Environmental Pragmatism,* edited by Andrew Light and Eric Katz (London: Routledge, 1998) stresses the importance of ethical pluralism and environmental pragmatism in understanding and resolving environmental issues.

    Responsibilities to Future Generations, edited by Ernest Partridge (Buffalo, NY: Prometheus, 1980), *Obligations to Future Generations,* edited by R. I Sikora and Brian Barry (Philadelphia: Temple University Press, 1978, reprinted by White horse Press, 2001), and *Obligations to Future Generations,* edited by E. Partridge (Buffalo, NY: Prometheus, 1981) all contain articles about the issue of our responsibility to future generations for not destroying the natural environment. *Why Posterity Matters: Environmental Policies and Future Generations,* edited by Avner De-Shalit

(London: Routledge, 1991) focuses specifically on the environmental dimensions of our obligations to future generations, and *Caring for Future Generations: Jewish, Christian and Islamic Perspectives* (Praeger Studies on the 21st Century), edited by Emmanuel Agius and Lionel Chircop (New York: Praeger, 1998) focuses on this issue in three major religious traditions.

Aldo Leopold's *A Sand County Almanac: With Essays on Conservation from Round River* (New York: Ballantine Books, 1970) is a classic of the environmental movement; J. Baird Callicott's *In Defense of the Land Ethic: Essays in Environmental Philosophy* (Albany: State University of New York Press, 1988) is a development of, and defense of, Leopold's land ethic. In this same tradition is Holmes Rolston III, *Environmental Ethics: Duties to and Values in the Natural World* (Philadelphia: Temple University Press, 1988) and *Philosophy Gone Wild: Essays in Environmental Ethics* (New York: Prometheus, 1986). J. Baird Callicott and Michael P. Nelson, *American Indian Environmental Ethics: An Ojibwa Case Study* (Upper Saddle River, NJ: Prentice Hall, 2003); Andrew Light and Avner De Shalit, *Moral and Political Reasoning in Environmental Practice* (Cambridge, MA: MIT Press, 2003).

Environmental Justice

For an excellent overview, see Claudia Mills and Robert Figueroa "Environmental Justice," *A Companion to Environmental Philosophy,* edited by Dale Jamieson (2001) as well as Jamieson's earlier article "Global Environmental Justice," *Philosophy and the Natural Environment,* edited by Robin Attfield and Andrew Belsey (New York: Cambridge University Press, 1994).

One of the first philosophical works in this area was Peter Wenz's *Environmental Justice* (Stony Brook: SUNY Press, 1988). Anthologies include *Environmental Racism and the Rise of the Environmental Justice Movement,* edited by Luke W. Cole and Sheila R. Foster, and *Faces of Environmental Racism: Confronting Issues of Global Justice,* edited by Laura Westra and Bill E. Lawson (2001); Gerald R. Visgilio and Diana M. Whitelaw, eds., *Our Backyard: A Quest for Environmental Justice* (Lanham, MD: Rowman & Littlefield, August 2003); Joni Adamson, Mei Mei Evans, and Rachel Stein, *The Environmental Justice Reader: Politics, Poetics, & Pedagogy* (Tucson: University of Arizona Press, 2002)

Kristin Shrader-Frechette's *Environmental Justice: Creating Equality, Reclaiming Democracy* (Oxford, Oxford University Press, 2002) provides an excellent starting point in this area. Also see David Schlosberg, "The Justice of Environmental Justice: Reconciling Equity, Recognition, and Participation in a Political Movement," *Moral and Political Reasoning in Environmental Practice,* edited by Andrew Light (Cambridge, MA: MIT Press, 2003), pp. 77–106; Ralph M. Perhac, Jr., "Environmental Justice: The Issue of Disproportionality," *Environmental Ethics,* Vol. 21, No. 1 (Spring 99), pp. 81–92; Roy W. Perrett, "Indigenous Rights and Environmental Justice," *Environmental Ethics,* Vol. 20, No. 4 (Winter 1998), pp. 377–91; Jace Weaver, ed., *Defending Mother Earth: Native American Perspectives on Environmental Justice* (Maryknoll, NY: Orbis, 1996); Kristin Shrader-Frechette and Daniel C. Wigley, "Environmental Justice: A Louisiana Case Study," Journal of Agricultural and Environmental Ethics, Vol. 9, No. 1 (1996), pp. 61–82; Holmes Rolston, III, "Environmental Justice," *Between the Species,* Vol. 5 (Summer 1989), pp. 147–53; Luke W. Cole and Sheila R. Foster, *From the Ground Up: Environmental Racism and the Rise of the Environmental Justice Movement* (New York: New York University Press, 2000). For an interesting case study, see David Naguib Pellow, *Garbage Wars: The Struggle for Environmental Justice in Chicago* (Urban and Industrial Environments; Cambridge, MA: MIT Press, 2002)

CyberEthics

Videotape

Topic:	Inundated by E-mail Spam
Source:	ABC *20/20,* August 1, 2003
Anchors:	Barbara Walters, John Stossel, Chris Cuomo
Guests:	Ronnie Scelson (bulk e-mailer); Ted Leonsis (Vice Chairman of AOL); Bill Waggoner (bulk e-mailer); Tom Coles (bulk e-mailer)

Narrative Account

Joseph Menn
"Hackers Live by Own Code"

This article considers some of the codes of ethics that hackers use to describe their own activities online and some of the various justifications they offer for their activities.

It wasn't Mary Ann Davidson's worst nightmare, but it was close.

A fax from a hacker in the Middle East landed on her desk at Oracle Corp., proclaiming the discovery of a hole in the company's database software through which he could steal crucial information from such customers as Boeing Co., Ford Motor Co. and the CIA. The fax warned Davidson, the company's chief security officer, to contact the hacker immediately—or else.

Luckily, the hacker hadn't found a real hole; he'd just misinterpreted a function of the program. More surprisingly, he meant no harm.

"The sort of threatening tone he took was really only to get our attention," Davidson said. "He actually turned out to be a nice guy."

The confrontational style of Davidson's hacker isn't unusual. As they troll through other people's computer networks, hackers abide by their own quirky rules of etiquette. What would strike most folks in corporate America as bad manners or worse may be considered the height of courtesy in hackerdom.

In large part, that disconnect stems from the fierce individualism of hackers—they are, after all, the sort of people who set aside the instruction manual and take a machine apart to see how it works. Though they inhabit a lawless domain where no data are considered private and "No Trespassing" signs are meaningless, they adhere to their own codes of ethics that vary depending largely on what motivates the hacker to hack.

Sometimes it's fame. Now and then it's money. Often it's a selfless desire to make software more secure. And occasionally it's a yearning to wreak senseless havoc.

The frequency of such attacks is on the rise, capped by the Blaster worm and SoBig virus that overpowered e-mail programs and crashed computer systems this summer. Computer Economics Inc. of Carlsbad, Calif., estimates that damage caused by hackers will cost companies and consumers $12.5 billion this year, up 13% from 2002.

Most hackers aren't malicious, security experts agree. But from afar, it can be difficult to distinguish the saboteurs from the merely curious, because they use the same tools, travel in the same virtual circles and often share a disdain for the rule of law.

Their philosophy predates personal computers, going back to the days when pranksters manipulated the telephone system to make free long-distance calls and cause other mischief. The personal rules that guide them today generally allow them to break laws, as long as they believe nobody will get hurt.

Los Angeles Times, November 19, 2003, page 1.

Firms Are Fair Game

This maverick outlook is best personified by Kevin Mitnick, either the most notorious hacker or the most demonized, depending on your point of view. He stole millions of dollars' worth of software after cracking into the computer systems of big companies such as Sun Microsystems Inc. and Motorola Inc. But he said he never sold any of it or otherwise profited from his electronic theft.

Mitnick, now 40, served five years in federal prison. Yet that hasn't deterred a younger generation of hackers who view private companies as fair game as long as no data are destroyed or profit turned. For many of them, hacking is just something their curiosity compels them to do.

Adrian Lamo, a 22-year-old hacker from Sacramento, always viewed his hacking habit as harmless at worst and helpful at best. If he has a chance to inform people about a security flaw in a company's internal network, he considers the disclosure a form of public service.

Lamo says he can't help it. He just starts wondering, then he looks for holes in a company's infrastructure, and he's in.

"When I'm curious about something, it's difficult to *not* seek out security problems," he said.

Working sporadically during long nights in Kinko's copy shops two years ago, Lamo used his battered Toshiba laptop computer to burrow deep into WorldCom Inc.'s internal networks. By the time he was done, he could have redirected the phone giant's employee paychecks to his own account or shut down the system of WorldCom customer Bank of America Corp.

Lamo did neither.

Instead, he recounted his exploits to a hacker turned journalist at SecurityFocus.com, a Web site devoted to tracking hacks, holes and fixes. SecurityFocus then called WorldCom executives and told them Lamo was happy to answer any of their questions. After Lamo showed WorldCom what he had done and how to prevent it from happening again, the company publicly thanked him for improving its security.

Part of Lamo's creed is a refusal to take financial advantage of anything he finds. The biggest compensation he's ever accepted from a company he's broken into, he said, was a bottle of water.

Chris Wysopal used to feel the same way when he worked at an outfit known as the L0pht, a band of security enthusiasts in a Boston apartment strewn with spare computer parts salvaged from area trash bins.

Claiming a dedication to telling software buyers the unvarnished truth, the L0pht crew published free security warnings on its Web site and in e-mail newsletters. Those warnings often were accompanied by programs to help people test whether their computers were vulnerable to attack.

In Wysopal's view, hacker etiquette didn't require him to give software makers advance warning before publishing his discoveries—even though his reports could aid the unscrupulous. Without the threat of public exposure and the fear that malicious hackers would use the newfound information, he figured, software makers wouldn't have incentive to make fixes in a timely manner.

"They dealt with security like a feature request—they would get around to it in the next version," Wysopal said.

The shaming tactics started working, so well that by 1999, Wysopal was forced to reconsider what constituted appropriate hacker behavior.

After the L0pht publicized a problem with a piece of Microsoft Corp. software for server computers, the company responded that it would have been happy to fix the mistake if only it had been given the chance. Instead, Microsoft had to race to develop a fix and get it to customers in time to head off an assault.

End to Free-for-All

Wysopal, along with a great number of his fellow hackers, realized the days of the free-for-all should end. It was no longer morally defensible to tell malicious teens how to hurt firms and their customers before they had the tools to defend themselves. Now he works with software makers to develop patches before blowing the whistle.

"It isn't as much fun," said Wysopal, who helped the L0pht morph into a computer security company called @stake Inc. "But if we publish right away, we are really arming the bad guys."

For other hackers, proper etiquette is dictated by the pursuit of money.

The most direct angle is simply to tell the software company there's a bug, then request a fee to explain it.

"If I come up with a vulnerability and I inform the source that I've discovered it, but I say, 'Would you mind paying me $5,000 to help you close it?' from my perspective that's a very reasonable request," said Bob Weiss, president of Password Crackers, Inc., in North Potomac, Md., which helps companies recover information hidden on their machines.

But what looks like a reasonable request to a hacker is often perceived as extortion by the company being asked to shell out. That's how one California software firm reacted after it heard from a hacker who had found a hole in its Web-messaging system and offered to explain it—for $10,000.

"The company got pretty mad," said Jennifer Granick, a cyber law specialist at Stanford University who represented the hacker in 2000. "It's very difficult for some cocky 18-year-old kid to approach a company without it feeling threatened." After Granick smoothed things over, the company agreed not to press charges.

There's also the loss-leader approach. After identifying a problem and explaining it, many hackers offer to look for additional glitches in exchange for a consulting fee.

Even that strategy backfired on a Boxboro, Mass., security group called SnoSoft. In 2002, SnoSoft researchers found a hole in a version of the Unix operating system made by Hewlett-Packard Co. The hackers told HP they would explain it for free, but they also asked to be paid for additional work.

"We made it clear we wouldn't charge [for the initial bug], because that would be extortion," SnoSoft co-founder Adriel Desautels said.

HP declined to offer SnoSoft a contract. Instead, the company threatened to sue under the Digital Millennium Copyright Act of 1998, which prohibits some attempts to tinker with programs to see how they work.

To computer security experts—including some inside HP—that threat amounted to a gross violation of etiquette on the part of HP. The company backed down and recently said it would never use the digital copyright law to stifle research. The Palo Alto computing giant declined to discuss the SnoSoft case.

For a few hackers, there is only one principle that matters: Do as much damage as possible.

That may have been the goal of a group of Chinese hackers who reverse-engineered a patch designed to fix a devastating hole in most versions of Microsoft's Windows operating system for PCs and servers. Within days, the hackers published a program to seize control of unsuspecting computers, which was used by others in the Blaster worm attack this summer.

Counterattacks Increase

With malevolent programs on the rise, large software companies are trying to get a handle on the problem. A consortium of software giants including Microsoft and Oracle has joined with security firms such as Symantec Corp. to formalize the etiquette of hacking so that software makers have time to patch holes before they are disclosed to the world at large.

The rules proposed by the new Organization for Internet Safety would give companies a month or so to develop and distribute a patch. Then another month is supposed to elapse before the hacker can disclose any details about the problem that the patch was designed to fix.

But hackers say they are unlikely to sign off on the rules, especially because they would neutralize the biggest weapon in their arsenal—the threat of public exposure.

In the meantime, companies that find themselves victimized by hackers are stepping up their counterattacks.

The New York Times wasn't amused when Lamo, the hacker who helped WorldCom beef up its network security, bragged to SecurityFocus that he had wriggled into the newspaper's computers.

Once inside, Lamo perused records of contributors to the paper's Op-Ed page (including the Social Security numbers and home phone numbers of former heads of state), conducted database searches using the paper's Lexis-Nexis account and added himself to a list of expert sources on hacking.

Unlike WorldCom, the New York Times called the FBI. In September, federal prosecutors in New York charged Lamo with the electronic equivalent of breaking and entering.

Out on bail, Lamo said he had no regrets about the way he hacked. "I always knew that the things I did could have consequences," he said.

Journal/Discussion Questions

1. What elements of the hacker's codes do you think are legitimate? Which ones do you reject? Why?

An Introduction to the Moral Issues

Introduction

Computer and information technologies have grown exponentially over the last two decades, and promise to continue to do so. Moore's law—developed by Gordon Moore, a co-founder of Intel—states that computing power will double every 18 months, and this has proved to be a conservative estimate. If you put $1000 in the bank in the year 2000, and it grew at the same rate as computing power, you would have over $250,000 at the end of the year 2012, and you would break the $1,000,000 mark three years later. Computing power is growing that fast.

Given this exponential growth, it is not surprising that computing has transformed our world; nor is it surprising that it has brought about changes so quickly that it has outstripped the ethical rules that usually guide our decisions. Computer ethics arises in response to what James H. Moor, a noted computer ethicist at Dartmouth, has called a policy vacuum. Technology gets out ahead of us, and we have to work hard on our policies and ethical guidelines to catch up with the new technology. In the area of computing, some of the challenges are novel enough that, in attempting to address them, we may find ourselves transforming, not just developing, ethical theory.

Although the area of computer ethics covers a wide range of topics, many of the specific issues fall into one or more of several major categories: privacy, ownership of information, and security. In addition, there are important, more general ethical questions about the ways in which computers and the Internet have transformed our lives. Some of these issues are treated in James Moor's article, reprinted here, "Should We Let Computers Get Under Our Skins?" Before looking at those, let's consider some of the specific moral problems raised by these technological advances.

Privacy and Control of Personal Information

The distinction between public and private is central to the American democratic tradition, for the private domain has long been considered the domain within which individual freedom is most fully exercised. In particular, the private has long been considered comparatively safe from government scrutiny.

Computers have changed all that, and they have done so in a very interesting way. Various computer-based technologies allow governments, corporations, and even individuals to collect an amazing amount of information about people. Imagine all the ways in which an average person leaves electronic footprints during the day. Using computers at home and work, individuals leave a vast amount of information about themselves, their reading and buying habits, their business dealings, their personal likes and dislikes, and so forth. Prior to the advent of computers, one person could perhaps have followed another person around, noting the other person's actions, contacts, and the like. The rise of computers now allows a single individual to track thousands of people simultaneously, finding a range of details about them that would previously been impossible.

What limits, if any, ought to be placed on the power of individuals, corporations, and governments to acquire such information? Often we see doomsday scenarios in which government—a virtual Big Brother—controls the lives of ordinary citizens through increasingly extensive data collection. Since September 11, 2001, there have been growing political pressures in the United States to combat terrorism, often at the price of removing restrictions to the government's acquisition of information. However, this is not an issue limited solely to governments. Private corporations often have access to information that could have a profound effect on the lives of individuals. Insurance companies and HMOs have been ethical hotspots for the privacy and control of information in recent years, and this has been a particularly thorny area insofar as insurance and health care are tied to employment. To what extent, if any, can insurance companies and employers and others share information about individuals with whom they deal? As the ability to share information increases, the need for clear and enforceable guidelines in this area increases as well.

Free Speech, Privacy, and Censorship

Consider some of the thorny issues relating to pornography. In the United States, pornography is defined in terms of the violation of local standards. But what counts as local? Is it the standards of the community of the person viewing the pornography? Or the standards of the community in which the purveyor of the pornography resides? What responsibility does the Internet Service Provider (ISP) have in hosting such a site? What restrictions, if any, ought to be placed on pornography sites?

What rights do individuals have to keep information about themselves off the internet? In one case, critics of a police chief started putting personal information about him on the Web—pictures of his house, his address and phone number, and anything else they could find. Does the police chief have a right to privacy? Or, to take another example, in some cases anti-abortion activists have posted similar information about abortion providers. Again, to what extent—if any—do individuals have a right to privacy?

Closely related to this issue is the problem of data mining. The tremendous growth of computer power and storage, coupled with the vast increase in the amount of information stored in databases, has opened the door to powerful database searches that reveal more about individuals than they would have believed possible. Think of the many ways in which average individuals leave information about themselves in computers during a typical day: all swipes of cards for credit or identification purposes, preferred customer cards at the grocery store, all use of any computer they are logged onto, all telephone calls made or received—not to mention the countless surveillance cameras that may have picked up their images during the day. If all these pieces can be put together (and this is what advances in computing power and storage make possible), then an amazingly detailed picture of an individual's day begins to emerge.

Encryption plays an important role in this discussion as well. To what extent should individuals be allowed to encrypt their communications? Some levels of encryption (e.g., 128 bit) are virtually impossible to break. If criminals and terrorists can use such encryption, they can effectively prevent the government from monitoring their communications. What restrictions, if any, should the government be allowed to impose on encryption programs?

Property Rights

The rapid rise of Napster and then KaZaA was the most dramatic signal of a change ushered in by the computer revolution: because digital media can be shared so easily and cheaply and without diminishing the original and without loss of quality, digitized property—most notably, music and video—began to speed around the Internet with increasing frequency.

As this happened, the traditional notion of private property—based on the paradigm of land and other physical objects—and property rights came under serious challenge. Our understanding of property rights was based on this traditional model, one in which giving a piece of property to someone else meant that you yourself lost something. For example, if I give a book to my friend, I no longer possess that book. I could, of course, Xerox a copy of the book, but that would be a lot of work and the copy would not be as good as the original. In the digital world, however, this is no longer the case. If I have an electronic copy of a book (or a piece of music), I can send that to *all* of my friends and still not lose anything, and the copy they receive will be as good as mine.

Intellectual property is not exactly like a physical object, but we still have laws and policies based on the old paradigm and there is significant disagreement about where to go from here. On the one hand, many maintain that the traditional laws of property ought to continue to apply unchanged and see all attempts to alter the law as a threat. On the other hand, some in the internet community are fervently committed to the idea that all information ought to be freely available—and that means, among other things, removing restrictions on copying and duplicating materials, including music and video.

Responsibility

In the age of the Internet, responsibility has become more diffuse in several ways. First, the Web allows the possibility of anonymity (or at least the illusion of anonymity), and this makes it easier for people to deny responsibility for their actions, even to themselves. On-line pornography and internet plagiarism are but two of the most obvious examples of the way in which the anonymity of the Web allows people to engage in behavior that, at least often, they would not perform in the public world of everyday life.

Moreover, the lines of responsibility in such cases are complex. What, for example, is the responsibility of ISPs for the actions of their clients? Do they, for example, have a responsibility to protect customers from cyber stalkers? From unwanted pornography? From unwanted advertisements? Or, to take another example, what responsibilities do college network administrators have if, for example, students are using college internet connections to download pirated music and video? To order plagiarized term papers?

Responsibility issues have been transformed in another way as well. Increasingly, computer systems perform actions. Computer systems often decide who gets credit for a loan, in some cases they even decide when a missile is to be fired (e.g., the Aegis Firing System used by the U.S. Navy). To whom do we attribute responsibility when something goes wrong? In the past, designers have built in a moment at which a human being must confirm the decision, but this is increasingly impractical. Even when a human being is involved, that person is often depending on information supplied by the computer. As computer-driven systems become increasingly autonomous, responsibility becomes more and more elusive.

A Computer-Mediated World

Some computer-related ethical issues can be fairly specific, even when we are unclear about the best answer. What, for example, are we going to do about spam? Other issues, however, are more diffuse, but perhaps even more important precisely because they are not as easily brought into focus in such a way that straightforward policy decisions can resolve them.

One of those diffused and pervasive issues relates to the ways in which computers have mediated the human world and, in the process, transformed it. Consider a simple example: presentation software such as PowerPoint has transformed at least certain segments of education, changing the nature of teaching in important ways. Some of these ways are good, others probably are not—but they largely escape notice precisely because they are transparent. Similarly, personal relationships have been transformed in an age of instant messaging—again, with bad as well as good consequences. Medicine has largely been reshaped into a computer-based technology of testing, and this too has had an impact of the relationship between physician and patient. Increasingly, our world is mediated by computers in ways that reshape the human world, but these changes are rarely the result of explicit decisions that take those consequences into account.

Some critics, reflecting on the eventual outcome of these changes, have painted nightmare scenarios. Will we, for example, reach a world in which human beings no longer know enough to understand what the computers are doing? Increasingly, we depend on computers to design and repair other computers themselves, as well as many pieces of equipment. (The day of the home garage mechanic is long gone.) Soon freeway driving will be managed by computers that will be able to pack cars much closer together, resulting in greatly increase traffic flow without the addition of new lanes to existing freeways. Recently, mathematicians used computers to prove a centuries-old mathematical theorem, but then they were divided on the question of whether this really constitutes a proof if no human being can directly understand it. Increasingly, we are turning to computerized voting machines, but then there is no original ballot against which to check votes—but computer checks assure us that there has been no tampering. Will computers reach the point where they are in charge?

The Digital Divide

This is not the only pervasive issue. While many (especially in education) find their lives permeated by computers in many ways, others are effectively barred from access to computers, primarily for economic reasons. The world is splitting into the haves and the have-nots, based in significant measure on access to computing power. Young children from middle and upper class families grow up comfortable with computers, happy to use them and confident of their own ability to figure out and solve problems. In an increasingly computerized world, they have an immediate advantage over children who do not grow up with such skills. Similarly, significant portions of the industrialized world are highly computerized, whereas many parts of the developing world lack even the basic necessities of life, much less access to computers.

The Arguments

James H. Moor
"Should We Let Computers Get Under Our Skins?"

James Moor is a Professor of philosophy at Dartmouth College, he is a primary figure in the growing area of computer ethics. His award winning article, "What is Computer Ethics?" is widely reprinted and regarded as a milestone for the study of computer ethics. He was an early pioneer in computer-assisted instruction in logic, including work on Bertie, Venn, and Proof Designer. He is co-author of The Logic Book *and has written widely on the philosophy of artificial intelligence. Most recently, he is co-editor of* The Digital Phoenix: How Computers Are Changing Philosophy.

In this article, Moor looks at the question of whether we are gradually becoming cyborgs—part human, part computer—and what ethical limits ought to be imposed on this.

As You Read, Consider This:

1. What are cyborgs? In what ways are we already moving toward becoming cyborgs?
2. Explain the therapy/enhancement distinction. What is its significance in this article? What criticisms of this distinction does Moor consider?
3. Explain what Moor means by "the Borg argument."
4. What, according to Moor, are the three main areas in which we should be particularly sensitive to the coming of age of cyborgs?

Being connected with the passions also, the moral virtues must belong to our composite nature; and the virtues of our composite nature are human; so, therefore, are the life and the happiness which correspond to these.

—Aristotle

Being a human was ok, I even enjoyed some of it. But being a Cyborg has a lot more to offer.

—Kevin Warwick

The Impact of the Internet on Our Moral Lives, edited by Robert Cavalier (Albany: SUNY Press, 2004).

The Case for Becoming a Cyborg

Aristotle suggests that human nature is fixed. Our human intellectual and moral virtues depend on our having this nature. If we changed our nature, we would change our virtues (excellences). Aristotle believed that if a friend became a god, for example, friendship with that person would cease because a god has a different nature than a human being. In the wake of evolutionary theory and modern genetics, the claim that human nature is fixed is not very plausible, but Aristotle's belief that shifting human nature might well alter moral virtue remains defensible. In today's scientifically changing world we need to confront this issue: if we change the kind of thing we are, what will be the consequences for ethics?

We will change ourselves genetically and we will change ourselves computationally as well. We will become cybernetic organisms—cyborgs—part human, part computer. The logical malleability of computers will allow us to go beyond what can be accomplished through genetic manipulation alone. The human body is the ultimate platform from which to launch new computer applications. It is likely that in the coming decades more and more computer hardware and software will be embedded in us. To what extent it should happen is the ultimate question, of course, but certainly there will be increasing pressure to produce cyborgs. Today the rationale and technology already coexist. First, we humans as creative creatures continually seek new ways to perform routine and not so routine tasks. Not infrequently our creative task solving involves the development of new tools. Second, the computer is the best master tool we have. The general-purpose computer is a meta-tool, a tool for making tools. If we have a task to do and we can express the task in terms of an appropriate algorithm to connect inputs to appropriate outputs, then in principle a computer can do it. In fact, even if we do not know an appropriate algorithm, computers using neural nets or genetic algorithms can sometimes evolve satisfactory computational structures for us. Third, considerable knowledge has been gained in recent years about interfaces between computers and living systems. We know that organic and inorganic structures can effectively interact at many levels—the organism level, the organ level, and the cell level. Someday nanomachines may interact in our bodies at the atomic level. Given that naturally curious humans love to find better solutions for problems, have a great master tool (the computer), and possess the perfect location (the human body) on which to store and operate the new devices, the gradual transformation of many humans into cyborgs, humans with computer parts, is all but certain.

Simply forbidding the implantation of computer chips because they are not natural, only artifacts, is not a plausible policy. This overly broad approach would not only prevent the use of beneficial computer implants but would rule out beneficial noncomputer implants such as artificial hip joints and dental crowns. Still, the thought of becoming a cyborg may seem rather repulsive. Who would want to have computer parts implanted? To become part computer? The idea of having a computer implanted may seem unnatural, possibly even grotesque, or at least something that undermines human dignity. But such a negative reaction is not defensible upon close examination. In fact, the transformation of humans into cyborgs has been taking place with no loss of dignity for years, although we do not commonly think of it in those terms.

For example, hundreds of thousands of people have cardiac pacemakers and defibrillators implanted to maintain regular heartbeats and heart rhythms (Lu, Anderson, and Steinhaus, 1995, Pinski and Trohman, 2000). Such implants not only promote life but also the quality of life. Totally implantable pacemakers have been in use since 1960, and programmable pacemakers were developed in the mid-1970s. The newest pacemakers can communicate via phone and the Internet. A patient needs only to wave a wand over his chest to pick up signals from the generator and then plug the wand into the phone line to send his physician an update on how the device and patient are doing. It would be hard to raise a principled objection against such beneficial devices. Implanting computerized cardiac devices is no more unnatural than putting other products of technology, like medicines or processed food, into our bodies. Given the alternatives for the cardiac patient, these vital, portable computer implants considerably enhance human dignity, not reduce it (Ocampo, 2000).

A similar case can be made for the benefits of implanting computer chips for vision. There are various projects underway to develop bionic eyes that will restore some level of vision to blind patients. Some approaches put chips on or under the retina and others connect computer chips to other parts of the visual system. In 2002, a Canadian farmer, who had lost his sight eighteen years earlier, had a bionic implant. A digital camera mounted on his glasses sent an image to a computer worn on his belt. The image was processed and sent to electrodes implanted in his visual cortex. His vision was not fully restored, but he was not totally blind anymore. He was able to see well enough to navigate through rooms and even drive a car to a limited extent (Gupta, and Petersen, 2002).

Some diseases, such as retinitis pigmentosa or age-related macular degeneration, damage the rods and cones in retinas but leave the rest of their visual wiring, the ganglia cells that process information from the rods and cones and the optic nerve, intact. The various visual bionics under development hold great promise for bypassing the damaged areas of the visual system and restoring vision to the patient. In the United States, over a million people are legally blind and worldwide millions more. These cutting-edge bionic implants will offer enormous benefit.

More examples of beneficial computer implants can be marshaled, but I believe the case for the benefits of some computer implants is established. The debate is not whether humans should ever become cyborgs because in some cases, particularly where beneficial implants help overcome severe disabilities, justification for becoming a cyborg is clear. The transformation of some humans into cyborgs will continue to happen and it should. People who wish to have such helpful computer implants should be allowed to have them.

But how far should the conversion of humans into cyborgs go? What are the ethical boundaries? Could we find ourselves in a position that we would want to get away from computer implants but couldn't? Could the implants be used to track us? Reduce our autonomy? Give us freakish powers? In this paper I want to explore some potential ethical pitfalls of computer implants as well as the impact that computer implants might have on ethical theory itself.

Therapy versus Enhancement

The therapy versus enhancement distinction suggests a basis for a policy that would limit unnecessary computer implants. Given that the human body has natural functions, it might be argued that implanting chips in the body is acceptable as long as such implants maintain or restore the body's natural functions. In this spirit, consider the remarks of Michael Dertrouzos, a director of the MIT Laboratory for Computer Science, regarding the possibility of implants connected to the brain:

> Even if it would someday be possible to convey such higher-level information to the brain—and that is a huge technical "if"—we should not do it. Bringing light impulses to the visual cortex of a blind person would justify such an intrusion, but unnecessarily tapping into the brain is a violation of our bodies, of nature, and for many, of God's design. (Dertrouzos, 1997, p. 77)

The distinction between therapeutic applications and enhancing applications offers a criterion for limiting computer implants. Under this policy, pacemakers, defibrillators, and bionic eyes that maintain and restore natural bodily functions are acceptable. But giving patients additional pairs of robotic arms or infrared vision would be prohibited. It would endorse the use of a chip that reduced dyslexia but would forbid the implanting of a deep blue chip for superior chess play. It would permit a chip implant to assist the memory of Alzheimer's patients but would not license the implanting of a miniature digital camera that would record and play back what the implantee had just seen and heard. In a later book Dertrouzos stresses his point again, "Few people would implant a chip into their brain for less than life-and-death reasons. We have wisely set a high threshold for tampering with the core of our being, not just because of fear, but because of natural, moral, and spiritual beliefs" (Dertrouzos, 2001, p. 46).

Of course, even therapeutic applications raise ethical questions if they are not safe and effective or the patient has not given informed consent. But, let us assume safety, effectiveness, and informed consent. Does the therapy/enhancement distinction give a proper limit to computer implants? Although this policy generally avoids unethical implants, I believe it is too conservative and cannot be defended.

First Objection: Unclear Distinction

The line between therapy and enhancement is not always agreed upon. Consider the example of cochlear implants (Spelman, 1999). A microphone is worn behind the ear and a microcomputer filters and analyzes the sound from the microphone converting the sound into digital signals. These signals are sent by radio waves to a receiver implanted under the skin, then via a wire to electrodes embedded in the cochlea in the patient's ear, which in turn stimulate nerves that carry sound to the brain. When cochlear implants became available in 1985, they could help approximately 35 percent of patients; today they can improve hearing in about 80%.

Receiving a cochlear implant, a bionic ear, may seem obviously therapeutic. However, within the deaf community the issue of whether to get a cochlear implant has been controversial. Some deaf individuals have questioned whether these implants are desirable or even therapeutic. Some challenge the standard assumption of the medical community that deafness is a disability that can be "fixed" by having a cochlear implant. At the heart of the debate is the importance and normalcy of the deaf culture. Within the deaf community many find solidarity with others who are deaf and share a common language of signing. Therefore, some in the deaf community believe the acquisition of hearing through cochlear implants needlessly threatens to undermine an adequately functioning culture. These views are held strongly as illustrated by the fact that one member of the deaf community found her tires slashed when she refused to speak out against cochlear implants (Yaffe, 1999).

Some in the deaf community believe that deafness is a disability, but they maintain that it is not worth correcting given the damaged caused to the deaf community. But another position is that deafness is not a disability at all given the availability and success of sign language within the community. Much of the debate about cochlear implants turns on whether one takes the absence of hearing as a disability. If it is, then having a cochlear implant is therapeutic, and, if it is not, then having a cochlear implant is an enhancement.

There are many things that we cannot do, and yet we do not classify them as disabilities. We cannot digest steel and we cannot breathe underwater without special equipment. It would be strange for someone, other than superman, to claim he had a disability because he could not leap tall buildings in a single bound. These sorts of actions are in the realm of inabilities, not disabilities. A disability is a lack of normal ability in reference to a class of individuals. Adults living today are disabled if they do not understand some language, but they are not disabled if they do not understand an extinct language. Those strongly opposed to cochlear implants might argue that within the deaf culture there is normal functioning with full use of language that happens to be a sign language, not an oral one. If the members of the deaf culture are picked as the reference class, then hearing should be regarded as an inability, not a disability. Given this standard, a cochlear implant would not be therapeutic and might be regarded as unnecessary and possibly detrimental.

My purpose here is not to argue for or against cochlear implants. Rather, it is to point out that the distinction between therapy and enhancement is not as straightforward as might be assumed. The decision about getting a cochlear implant is a personal choice and sometimes a difficult one that requires careful consideration of all the consequences. Families of deaf children may find themselves choosing between communities and are sometimes sharply divided within themselves on this issue. The decision can be agonizing because if the implant is to be most effective it must be implanted early in the deaf child's life, preferably before language development occurs.

The cochlear implant debate illustrates that the lack of agreement on what counts as a disability and what does not. However, even if there were agreement on what counts as therapy and what constitutes enhancement, implanted chips can offer a bit of both. For example, an implanted defibrillator can monitor a heart and deliver a shock within 30 seconds after life-threatening irregularities in rhythm are detected. The defibrillator restores normal heart function, but it does so through an enhancing functionality that people without defibrillators do not have. Or, consider an Alzheimer's patient who has a chip embedded that allows her to be located by others and perhaps even guides her back by global positioning satellites. Is this chip therapeutic or enhancing? Suppose a paralyzed patient has a chip implanted that allows him to control the lights in his room by shifting his neural patterns. Is this implant therapeutic or enhancing?

Second Objection: Limitation of Freedom

The second argument against the policy of allowing therapeutic but not enhancing implants is that it arbitrarily limits personal freedom. As long as the implantee and others are not being harmed by the implant, what is the objection to allowing it? In other matters we routinely allow, if not encourage, people to have enhancements. Generally speaking, education enhances as does exercise and a good diet. They enhance the body and the mind and we encourage all of them. Freedom is a core good and we properly allow people the freedom to exercise it. People, at least in a liberal state, are at liberty to have cosmetic surgery, belly-button rings, and tattoos. Enhancement is what many of us strive for much of the time. As a simple illustration, consider laser eye surgery guided by computer that can enhance vision beyond the normal 20/20. It would seem perverse to insist that a patient should not have the freedom to correct her vision to a better than normal 20/15 but had to stop at 20/20. Similarly, it seems perverse not to give people freedom to enhance themselves in other ways, including the implantation of computer chips if they wish.

In 1998, Kevin Warwick, a cybernetics professor from the University of Reading in the United Kingdom, had a chip implanted that permitted sensors in his laboratory to detect his location and motion. In March, 2002, he had a much more sophisticated computer implant (Warwick, 2002). An array with 100 spikes was implanted in Warwick's wrist to connect his median nerve with a computer. The median nerve travels along the arm and contains both sensory neurons that detect pressure and temperature and motor neurons that connect the spinal cord with muscle groups in the hand. The spikes of the array were implanted in these sensory and motor neurons in the median nerve. Wires from the array traveled up Warwick's arm and surface through a skin puncture in his forearm. The wires were connected to a gauntlet, a transmitting/receiving device, located externally on Warwick's arm. The gauntlet sent information about neural firing to an external computer. The computer, properly calibrated, distinguished neural impulses when Warwick's left hand was open and when it was closed. This provided sufficient binary information for Warwick to guide miniature robots, manipulate a robotic hand, light up specially wired jewelry, and steer an adapted wheelchair.

Warwick could feel the impulse if the information flow was reversed and the computer sent a signal to the gauntlet that transferred it to the implant in his median nerve. In an interesting experiment Warwick wore a baseball cap with an ultrasonic transmitter and receiver. Ultrasonic impulses were sent out from the cap and bounced back quickly if objects were close. In this situation a rapid series of pulses were sent to the computer, to the gauntlet, and to his median nerve. If objects were farther away, the pulses were less rapid. This gave Warwick an extrasensory input. When blindfolded, but hooked up to the ultrasonic device, he could guide himself around his laboratory using bat-like echolocation. In another experiment his wife, Irena, who had a simpler neural connection, and he could exchange binary information back and forth from one nervous system to the other via the Internet. Warwick has raised the possibility that one day more sophisticated information and possibly emotional responses could be communicated from nervous system to nervous system via the Internet.

Warwick's reports on his body image were interesting. Warwick makes it quite clear that having the implant under his skin was important as compared with simply putting on wearable computing that can easily be removed. "from the very start, I regarded the array and wires as being a part of me. Having it extracted, I knew, would be like losing part of my body, almost an amputation" (Warwick, 2002, p. 292). But he also had some sense of his body's being extended by the machine attachments like the robotic hand. "The articulated hand felt like a part of me, yet, because it was remote, in another sense it didn't" (Warwick, 2002, pp. 233–234).

Warwick acknowledges the potential risks but believes the eventual benefits of computer implant enhancements outweigh these risks. Ethically, should Warwick enhance himself with computer implants? Some believe not. Langdon Winter suggests that such experiments are "profoundly amoral" (Vogel, 2002, p. 1020). Although becoming a cyborg may eventually raise questions about human nature, it is hard to see how the experiments that Warwick performed are beyond straightforward moral judgment. If he is not causing harm to others and not violating any particular duties, why should he not have the freedom to do it? His wife is at some risk of harm, but she freely gave her informed consent. Both his implant procedure and her procedure passed hospital ethics committee evaluation. The experiments may strike some as grotesque, scientifically ill defined, or grandstanding, but such judgments, assuming they were correct, would still not make the experiments amoral or immoral.

The Borg Argument

The fear remains that allowing freedom of enhancement through computer chip implants will take us down a slippery slope to some very undesirable results. To imagine a worst case scenario, consider the Borg from the science fiction series *Star Trek*. The Borg is a collection of cyborgs that travels through space in a large cube that has the ability to assimilate new species that it encounters. The Borg's menacing conduct is indicated by its foreboding mottoes: "Resistance is futile" and "We will assimilate you." The inhabitants of the Borg have numerous unattractive appliances attached to them, have no personal autonomy, and are controlled by the directives of a collective consciousness. The inhabitants of the Borg do not have individual lives worth living, at least not as intelligent creatures. They neither examine their lives nor personally flourish. And so, the argument runs, we do not want to end up like the inhabitants of the Borg. How do we prevent sliding down the slope to such an existence once we give people the freedom to implant chips?

Slippery slope arguments are not very convincing, particularly if the slope is rather long and stopping along it seems possible. There is considerable slope between allowing people the freedom to implant chips and becoming a Borg culture. But can we easily brake on the slope? I believe we can, but the Borg argument has some force. A Borg culture in which people become slave cyborgs is not something that sane people would choose for themselves. However, other mechanisms might push us toward such a state. Here are two:

The Sleepwalking Scenario: We might inadvertently fall into a Borg-like state if we are not careful. Imagine that people for good reasons decide to have chips implanted in order to communicate with their children or do their jobs better or receive the latest music and sports information or have medication automatically released. Eventually, almost everyone is hooked up to the Web internally and wirelessly. It is the way life is conducted. Babies are given chips as routinely as vaccinations. Such interconnections are useful in organizing our lives. Gradually, for practical, not evil, motives the Web/human system begins to take on a life of its own, coordinating people's activities by sending information tantamount to instructions for where to be and when to be there. Under such a condition the population might look better than the inhabitants of the *Star Trek* Borg, but its behavior might have an uncanny similarity.

The Totalitarian State Scenario: The Borg culture might come into existence through the directives of a dictator of a totalitarian state. Dictators want to control their population. What better way than putting their subjects to work with implants that track their locations and force their labor? Neither the sleepwalking scenario nor the totalitarian state scenario is likely to happen in the immediate future, but these developments are real possibilities. We have yet to produce an Orwellian 1984 society, but that is probably due to a shortage of the right kind of information technology. That technological shortcoming is rapidly being overcome and a Borg culture is something to be on guard against.

Freedom with Responsibility

In general, I am advocating a policy of responsible freedom. People should have the freedom to implant computer chips in themselves, including implants for enhancements. As with all our actions, we should be alert if harm or the risk of harm is a factor. If harm or the risk of harm would occur to either the person being implanted or to others, we need to consider whether the action is justified. Harm does not automatically curtail freedom of action, but it does require justification. Exercising such freedom requires evaluating consequences and formulating relevant policies that can be advocated impartially and publicly so that anyone is permitted to follow them in similar circumstances (Moor, 1999).

Harm can result in many ways when implanting computer chips, but there are three general areas of major concern, three ethical hot spots, to which we should be particularly sensitive in the coming age of cyborgs. These areas are privacy, control, and fairness. Some computer implants will enhance privacy or control or fairness. Some will undermine them.

Privacy

In May 2002, Jeff and Leslie Jacobs and their son, Derek, were the first to have VeriChips implanted in their arms. These chips, little bigger than a grain of rice, store six lines of text. Information is read from the chip by a handheld computer. Such medical information could be lifesaving in giving emergency physicians information about allergies and special medical needs before they administered treatment. In the case of the Jacobs, the chips contain phone numbers and information about previous medications. The U.S. Federal Food and Drug Administration (FDA) ruled a month earlier that it did not regard the chip as a medical device and would not regulate it.

The chip is not very useful unless the implantee is at a hospital that has the appropriate handheld computer reader, but the technology is likely to spread because it is relatively inexpensive. The chip itself is dormant, but when the right radio frequency energy passes through the skin it activates the chip that in turn emits a radio signal containing an identification number. This number can be sent to an FDA secure data storage site via telephone or the Internet. Given our flourishing Information Age, the demand for implanted chips to store personal, medical, and financial information as well as any information whatsoever is likely to increase.

Implanted chips can be more sophisticated than memory chips. VeriChip is the product of Applied Digital Solutions (ADS) that has for several years been working on another product called the "Digital Angel." The Digital Angel is a tracking device that uses Global Positioning System (GPS) technology. The Digital Angel technology potentially can be used to track almost anyone or anything from children, convicts, and cats to lost hikers and lost luggage. ADS has a bold vision of what the chip might be able to do. According to one early projection, the future chip, if implanted, will be powered by a piezoelectric device that converts energy from normal bodily movements into electricity. The chip will send information to receivers connected to various networks. In addition, the device will be able to collect information about the possessor's body, such as temperature and blood pressure. Blood oxygen and glucose level detection are promised as well. Its designers propose that pulse detection will be based on infrared radiation naturally emitted from the bloodstream. In this vision of the future, solid state accelerometers and gyroscopes will allow the Digital Angel to sense the posture and gait of the possessor to detect sudden falls. EKG and EEG detection are claimed to be in the works. If this information gathering comes to fruition, the objective is to transmit the information to receivers that make it available on the Internet through Web-enabled desktop, laptop, or wireless devices. Depending on the configuration a Digital Angel device could be turned on or off by the possessor, the possessor's body, or remotely by radio signal. The device would not need to be on and transmitting at all times, but would have the ability to turn on automatically if it sensed, for example, a heart attack or was sent an instruction to do so.

Digital Angel is the brainchild of Peter Zhou, who is enthusiastic about the future of implanted chip technology. Despite Zhou's enthusiasm, critics have expressed concerns. Civil rights groups compared the use of implanting these chips to Nazi tattooing and some Christians compared the implanting of the chips to the mark of the beast mentioned in the Bible. Thus far, ADS has brought out the first generation of the Digital Angel as a product to be worn as a wristband or carried. Its initial capability is limited to establishing the location of its possessor.

Regardless of the current stage of development of this implant, the concept of a chip that actively gathers data about its owner as well as sending and receiving information is technologically feasible and such chips will come onto the market for particular uses at some point. Potential uses are plentiful. A person who suffers from arrhythmia could be assisted when the chip monitoring her pulse notifies medical authorities of her location and her condition. A firearm could be programmed to fire only when the chip identifies its user as the proper owner. Herds of animals, not to mention millions of pets, could be tracked so that no animal is lost. Every soldier in a battle unit could be monitored for his or her location and health status. A kidnapped child possessing such a chip could be located and checked for life signs. Such a chip could serve as an ID for business and other human interactions. A potential customer could be positively identified biometrically through transmissions from the chip. Her transaction then would be charged automatically to or deducted from her account based on information passed along by the chip.

A world with implanted personal data chips will generate an enormous flow of personal information in novel ways that will require new protection plans for the privacy of individuals. New policies will need to be created to safeguard the collection of all the up-to-the minute information about people's health, location, financial condition, and other matters transmitted and received by these chips. It is not that personal privacy cannot in principle be protected with the use of such chips. The concern is that the technology will be developed and deployed without establishing privacy protection.

Control

Another ethical hot spot in which implanted chips can provide enormous benefits but put us at risk is control. Respect for the agency of others is a hallmark of ethics. Implanted computer chips hold great promise for both giving and taking away human agency.

In the United States over a million patients suffer from Parkinson's disease, a degenerative neurological disorder that causes them to shake uncontrollably. Another two million suffer from essential tremor that causes similar violent shaking. The shaking is so debilitating that these patients often have trouble working, eating, and simply getting dressed. In the past the drug L-dopa has been given to Parkinson's patients, though its effectiveness wanes over time. Less than half of the patients with essential tremor are improved with medication. Sometimes patients undergo surgery to destroy parts of their brains that cause the shaking, but this procedure is not reversible and not always effective.

An alternative for these patients is to have a chip implanted. Physicians implant an electrode in a patient's thalamus and run a wire under the scalp to the patient's collarbone where a pulse generator is implanted. This device sends electrical signals customized for each patient to the electrode in the thalamus. A constant stream of electrical shocks blocks the tremors. The device is effective in stopping the shaking in both Parkinson's patients and essential tremor patients. The procedure is reversible and the device can be turned on and off by the patient.

The results of such an implant are nothing short of spectacular. A Parkinson's patient whose hands are shaking violently can run a magnet over his chest activating the pulse generator, and within a few seconds his hands become steady. With another swipe of the magnet, the device is turned off, and his hands will begin to shake again. In one case a typical Parkinson's patient, who had lost her mobility and whose medications made her arms and legs move out of control, could sit down and play complex pieces on the piano after her implant was installed (Freudenheim, 1997).

This Deep Brain Stimulation technique using the pulse generator is now being used for a variety of other medical conditions—even for psychiatric conditions such as obsessive compulsive disorder. One seriously ill patient had repetitive thoughts for hours and would wash his hands seventy times per day. After having a chip implant he stopped his compulsive hand washing and returned to work (Carmichael, 2002).

What is striking about these examples of implants is that they restore agency to the patients. Patients regain control of their lives. The sinister side is the threat that computer implants might be used to remove agency. Chips might be developed to induce uncontrollable shaking, cause obsessive-compulsive disorder.

Consider the recent development of a ratbot. Three electrodes were placed in a rat's brain: two in the somatosensory cortical where the rat's brain processes touch from its right and left whiskers, and one in the medial forebrain bundle where the rat processes pleasure. When one of the two electrodes in the sensory region is stimulated, the rat experiences an apparent touch. If it turns in the direction of its right or left whisker depending on which side is stimulated, it is electrically rewarded in its pleasure center. With this setup and some radio controls to send the signals researchers were able to guide the rat. Using a laptop, researchers maneuvered the rat through a difficult three-dimensional maze that included ladders, filing cabinets, and thin wooden boards. As one researcher appropriately remarked, "I certainly don't think it would be a good idea to put these in primates, or especially in humans" (Cook, 2002).

Rat brains are not human brains, but humans do have pleasure centers in their brains and one can easily imagine the use of implants to control humans. Could such a device be offered to help people stop smoking or lose weight? The military and the penal system might consider using the technology to produce loyal troops and obedient prisoners. Computer implants can potentially elevate human agency or severely reduce it. Continual vigilance regarding the deployment of such devices is necessary to ensure that respect for human agency is maintained.

Fairness

A final ethical hot spot to consider is fairness. Implanted chips can tip the scales of justice in various ways. For example, implanted chips can encourage fairness by giving those with disabilities more power to interact in the world. Consider the case of Johnny Ray who suffered a brainstem stroke in 1997. He has locked-in syndrome and no muscle control. Although he is cognitively intact, he is totally paralyzed and cannot make a motion. Researchers have inserted a subcranial cortical implant. Parts of the implant in the motor cortex are surrounded with tissue culture to encourage brain cells to grow toward the contacts. The patient is asked to think about distinctive conditions such as hot versus cold. The corresponding brain outputs are captured, amplified, and used to control an external device such as a cursor on a computer screen. "By reproducing the same brain pattern, Ray eventually was able to move the cursor at will to choose screen icons, spell, and even generate musical tones" (Hockenberry, 2001, p. 96).

When computer implants improve access and interactive capabilities for those who are disadvantaged, fairness is served. But there are easily imagined situations in which future implants might give the implantee unfair advantages. Just imagine a grandmaster chess chip that contained book openings and generated excellent chess moves. Suppose it were developed, giving its owner superior ability in playing chess. Presumably, such chips would need to be banned in championship play just as steroids are outlawed in Olympic competition. Chip implants that facilitated an athlete's coordination might be banned for similar reasons.

Fairness will be an ongoing concern as chip implants get better and more useful. Eventually, a chip implant divide will emerge between those who have chip implants versus those who do not (Macguire and McGee, 1999). Parents, as parents always do, will want to give their children the best abilities and opportunities possible. Those who can afford chip implants and chip upgrades will have a distinct advantage over those who cannot.

Viewing the Distant Future

Thus far I have been considering the matter of computer implants in light of common morality in the short run. I have been focusing on ethical concerns for and against implanting chips in the near future. Now I wish to reverse direction and consider the possible implications of computer implants on metaphysical issues and ethical theory in the long run.

The possibility of enhancing humans through computer implants raises the question of what human nature could and should be. Traditionally, essentialist philosophers like Aristotle maintain that humans have a fixed nature. Some existentialist philosophers like Sartre argue that existence precedes essence and that human nature is radically free. We can change our essence by making different choices. In an era of increasing understanding of genetics and neurology, neither position seems quite right. Human nature does not appear to be irrevocably fixed or completely open. Computer implants offer us an opportunity to adjust at least some of our nature. Our essence as humans may not be radically open, but, if we are clever enough in developing implants, we can, if we choose, significantly change our nature from what it is now.

Accurate prediction of what computer implants will be available in the distant future is, of course, impossible. But let's speculate a bit. With implants we can change our internal functioning in ways that are not possible, using variations of our genetic code. We might enhance our sense of sight to access parts of the electromagnetic spectrum far beyond what any humans or other animals can. Similarly our sense of hearing could be radically extended. Artificial devices for touch, taste, and smell already exist and these senses could be great enhanced. We could develop new senses. We might continue to experiment with implants for echolocation, for example, and discover at least in part what it is like to be a bat.

Communicating with other humans may be more direct than ever before. We could have sensors installed in our bodies that would let us know if our loved ones were in danger. We could lock and unlock doors, turn appliances on and off, and adjust the heat in our houses through computers that monitor neural patterns. And our cognition could be greatly enhanced with better memory and more accurate recall (Eisenberg, 2002). Perhaps education and physical conditioning could be done by downloads, not tedious schooling and training. Improving our abilities to create music or make inferences might be possible. Although all of this is speculation, nothing seems to preclude these possibilities. However the future develops, it seems likely that human nature as we currently conceive it could be modified.

Martha Nussbaum, defending an Aristotelean position, has argued against such aspirations.

> . . . What my argument urges us to reject as incoherent is the aspiration to leave behind altogether the constitutive conditions of our humanity, and to seek for a life that is really the life of another sort of being—as if it were higher and better life for *us*. It asks us to bound our aspirations by recalling that there are some very general conditions of human existence that are also necessary conditions for the values that we know, love, and appropriately pursue. (Nussbaum, 1990, p. 379)

Of course, everything depends on what constitutes the conditions of our humanity. The example she uses to illustrate the point is mortality. She cites Odysseus's decision to choose the life of a mortal human being who returns to his marriage to a mortal woman although Calypso has offered him immortality and agelessness, a life of no fatigue and no cessation of calm pleasure if only he would remain on the island with her. Nussbaum grants that we strive for excellence within our capabilities but we should not strive to change those constitutive conditions.

Aiming for immortality may be aiming a little high, but why shouldn't we change our nature if we have good reasons to believe we would be better off with an improved nature? There is the danger that if some changed and others did not there could be a division of the species or at least significant new groupings within them. Today we have Human Nature version 1.0, but why not use implants to move to Human Nature 2.0, especially if the latter gives us longer life, more happiness, and increased freedom of action? And if Human Nature 2.0 is acceptable, why not Human Nature 3.0 in which some of the traditional abilities of Human Nature 1.0 are given up and replaced with new ones. The judgment to move to Human Nature 3.0 is made from the vantage of Human Nature 2.0 that understands the importance of some modifications differently than Human Nature 1.0. We might through this process bootstrap ourselves into a condition in which Human Nature 17.3 was quite different from Human Nature 1.0.

Such a transition in human nature could have a serious impact on the application of ethical theories. First, there is the moral scope issue. By "moral scope" I mean what kind of entities are regarded as moral agents and what kind as moral patients. We usually count normally functioning adult humans as moral agents. We assign them duties and hold them accountable. But other less sophisticated entities are sometimes treated as moral patients, that is, entities deserving moral protection, such as small children, fetuses, animals, and the environment. For many, moral patients are thought to merit less protection than moral agents. It is better to kill a tree than take a human life. Would humans of nature 17.3 regard humans 1.0 as full-fledged moral agents or as merely moral patients or as entities outside the scope of moral protection altogether?

Another difficulty raised for ethical theory if human nature were transformed is the creation of new values and the assignment of new weights to old values. Now, although there is variation in how much weight we give to various values, there is a shared structure of human experience in which these values play a role. Other humans experience pain and pleasure as we do. When other humans speak of excruciating pain, we know the experience they are having, even if we haven't suffered exactly that kind of pain ourselves, and we know it is something to be avoided if possible. But if human nature is divergent, the understanding and sympathy factors so important in ethics may begin to wane. How values are weighted may differ enormously. In this regard consider J. S. Mill's test to establish that some states are better than others. Mill imagined that a human had only to try both states and would know which is better. As Mill put it in his very famous comparison, "It is better to be a human being dissatisfied than a pig satisfied; better to be Socrates dissatisfied than a fool satisfied. And if the fool, or the pig, are of a different opinion, it is because they only know their own side of the question. The other party to the comparison knows both sides" (Mill, 1979, p. 10). But, assuming radical differences in human nature, we, who come with original equipment (i.e., Human Nature 1.0) may find ourselves in the role of the pig or the fool. Indeed, if the differences are significant enough, then no party may be able to experience both states and compare them.

And some of the consequences of computer implants might be truly bizarre and a challenge for ethical theory. Imagine that with the right implants some humans contribute wirelessly to a group mind. Unlike the Borg scenario, each individual thinks and acts freely on his or her own but part of his brain is used by a group mind that is connected through a computer implant. Different parts of the brains of different individuals might make different contribution. The actions of the group person might be carried out through some computerized device connected to the network. Such a collective might be treated ethically as a group person in terms of responsibility—not simply in the sense that it is a group made out of individuals who cooperate, say, as the members of a corporation do, but as a group that is made up of closely interacting parts in the way the parts of the brain make up a normal individual person. Within such a group there might not be any easy assignment of responsibility and no particular individual who was in charge anymore than there is a homunculus guiding the activity of an individual brain. If this strange configuration of brain parts and computer implants were to develop, our accountability procedures would likely require adjustment.

Conclusion

Are there good reasons to limit the evolution of human nature with computer implants? Of course, there are good reasons to limit some kinds of implants. It would be ethically unacceptable to implant a chip that would do nothing other than put someone in intense pain. And there are good reasons to be extremely cautious in changing human nature that has been shaped by the merciless forces of evolution. Human nature is not arbitrary. Out of a history of seven million years of hominid evolution, Homo sapiens are the ones who are left. But limits and caution do not preclude carefully considered advancement. We advance ourselves in many ways. Computer implants are only one of the latest methods of development.

Simply put, ethical theory and computer implants may affect each other. On the one hand, our common morality allows us to assess the use of computer implants. It can instruct us about when and when not to implant and how and how not to use computer implants. On the other hand, the implantation of computer chips may gradually change human nature enough that ethical theories will need to be adjusted. Aristotle was right to emphasize the close dependence of ethics on human nature. What is less clear is whether we should pursue a path that leads to transformation of this nature. Ethically speaking, there may be no nonquestion-begging way of judging the proper direction for the evolution of human nature. At the very least, the development of chip implants will put pressure on our ethical considerations. The concept of life may be understood less in organic terms and more in functional terms as our bodies contain more inorganic computerized parts. Replacement parts may become easier to obtain and hence some severe disabilities may be considered much less harmful. Some new abilities may become essential in order to flourish. Distinctions between mental acts and physical acts may begin to blur as our minds directly influence and are influenced by physical objects around us. Our responsibility standards may shift if we regularly obtain information via daily Internet downloads into implanted memory chips or group identity gains precedence over individual identity.

Whatever our cyborg future will hold, it is coming. Many of us born human will die cyborgs. The question we must re-evaluate continually is not whether we should become cyborgs, but rather what sort of cyborgs should we become?

References

Carmichael, M. (2002). Healthy Shocks to the Head. Newsweek, June 24, pp. 56–57.

Cook, G. (2002). Scientists Produce "ratbot": First Radio-Controlled Animal. *The Boston Globe,* May 2, 2002, pp. A1 and A24.

Dertrouzos, M. L. (1997). *What Will Be: How the New World of Information Will Change Our Lives.* New York: HarperCollins.

Dertrouzos, M. L. (2001). *The Unfinished Revolution: Human-Centered Computers and What They Can Do for Us.* New York: HarperCollins.

Eisenberg, A. (2002). A Chip That Mimics Neurons, Firing Up the Memory. *The New York Times,* June 20, p. G7.

Freudenheim, M. (1997). New Technique Offers Promise in Treating Parkinson's Disease. *The New York Times,* October 28, p. F9.

Gupta, S., & Petersen, K. (2002). Could Bionic Eye End Blindness? http://www.cnn.com/2002/HEALTH/06/13/bionic.eye/index.html.

Hockenberry, J. (2001). The Next Brainiacs. Wired, 9, 94–105.

Lu, R., Anderson, J., & Steinhaus, B. 1995, The Evolution of the Implanted Pacemaker's Window to the World. *Biomedical Sciences Instrumentation, 31,* 241–246.

Macguire, Jr, G. Q., & McGee, E. M. (1999). Implantable Brain Chips. *Hastings Center Report, 29,* 7–13.

Mill, J. S. (1979). *Utilitarianism.* Indianapolis, IN: Hackett Publishing Company, Inc.

Moor, J. H. (1999). Just Consequentialism and Computing. *Ethics and Information Technology, 1,* 65–69.

Nussbaum, M. C. (1999). *Love's Knowledge: Essays on Philosophy and Literature,* England: Oxford: Oxford University Press.

Ocampo, C. M. (2000). Living with an Implantable Cardoverter Defibrillator. *Nursing Clinics of North America, 35,* 1019–1030.

Pinski, S. L., & Trohman, R. G. (2000). Permanent Pacing via Implantable Defibrillators. *Pacing and Clinical Electrophysiology, 23,* 1667–1682.

Spelman, F. A. (1999). The Past, Present, and Future of Cochlear Prostheses. *IEEE Engineering in Medicine and Biology,* May/June, 27–33.

Vogel, G. (2002). Part Man, Part Computer: Researcher Test the Limits. *Science, 29,* 1020.

Warwick, K. (2002). *I, Cyborg*. London: Century.

Yaffe, S. (1999). To Hear or Not to Hear. *Toronto Sun*, March 7, p. 4

Journal/Discussion Questions

1. Who do you know that has some computer components implanted under his or her skin? Talk with them. Are they disturbed by any of the considerations Moor discusses in this article?

2. It seems that we are headed almost inevitably toward a future in which computer implants are increasingly common. For yourself and for those you love, what limits—if any—would you impose on the use of computer implants? Why? Discuss.

Frances S. Grodzinsky and Herman T. Tavani
"Ethical Reflections on Cyberstalking"

Frances S. Grodzinsky is a Professor of Computer Science and Information Technology at Sacred Heart University in Fairfield, CT in the Computer Science/Information Technology department. She is a frequent contributor to computer ethics journals.

Herman T. Tavani is Professor and Chair of the Philosophy Department and Director of the Liberal Studies Program at Rivier College in Nashua, NH. The author of numerous publications in applied ethics, his recent books include Ethics and Technology: Ethical Issues in Information and Communication Technology *(John Wiley & Sons, 2004) and two anthologies co-edited with Richard Spinello:* Readings in CyberEthics *(Jones and Bartlett Publishers, 2004); and* Intellectual Property Rights in a Networked World: Theory and Practice *(forthcoming 2004).*

In this article, Grodzinsky and Tavani examine some ethical aspects of stalking behavior in cyberspace, concentrating on the implications that cyberstalking has for our notion of moral responsibility. They also examine questions about the moral responsibilities of Internet Service Providers.

As You Read, Consider This:

1. What is the difference between cyberstalking and harassment?
2. Who was Amy Boyer? Describe what happened to her.
3. In what ways, if any, does cybertechnology make a moral difference in assessing cases such as Amy Boyer's?
4. What is the Spinello view? How does that contrast with the Vedder view?

Ethics and Information Technology, Vol. 4(2) (2002), pp. 123–132.

1. Introduction: Stalking Incidents in Cyberspace

What is cyberstalking? And how do stalking incidents in cyberspace raise ethical concerns? In answering these questions, we begin with a definition of stalking in general. According to *Webster's New World Dictionary of the American Language,* to engage in stalking is "to pursue or approach game, an enemy, etc. stealthily, as from cover." In the context of criminal activities involving human beings, a stalking crime is generally considered to be one in which an individual ("the stalker") clandestinely tracks the movements of another individual or individuals ("the stalkee[s]"). Cyberstalking can be understood as a form of behavior in which certain types of stalking-related activities, which in the past have occurred in physical space, are extended to the online world. We should note, however, that criteria used in determining which kinds of behavior should count as stalking crimes in the physical realm has been neither consistent nor clear. Hence, it has been even more difficult to determine what the criteria should be for determining a stalking crime in the cyber-realm.

One difficulty in understanding some of the essential features of cyberstalking crimes is that they sometimes border on, and thus become confused with, broader forms of "harassment crimes" in cyberspace. Consider a recent incident involving twenty-year-old Christian Hunold, who was charged with terrorizing Timothy McGillicuddy, a high school principal in the state of Massachusetts. Hunold constructed a Web site that included "hit lists" of teachers and students at that Massachusetts school, on which he also included a picture of the school that was displayed through "the cross hairs of a rifle." Using various pseudonyms, Hunold corresponded with several eighth graders in the school. He then made specific threats to these Massachusetts students, who had no idea that they were communicating with a person who lived in Missouri ("The Web's Dark Side," 2000). Should this particular criminal incident be viewed as a case of cyberstalking? Or is it better understood under a different description such as "cyber-harassment?"

A criminal incident involving Randi Barber and Gary Dellapenta is sometimes also included under the category of cyberstalking. In 1996, Barber met Dellapenta, a security guard, through a friend. Although Dellapenta wanted a relationship with Barber, she spurned his advances. A few months later, Barber began to receive telephone solicitations from men; and in one instance, a "solicitor" actually appeared at the door of her residence. Barber seemed to be unaware of how potentially dangerous her situation had become. For example, she had no idea that Dellapenta had assumed her identity in various Internet chat rooms, when soliciting "kinky sex." Anonymity and pseudonymity tools, available to any Internet user, allowed Dellapenta to represent himself as Barber, via screen names such as a "playfulkitty4U" and "kinkygal30." Barber became aware of what was going on only after she asked one caller why he was phoning her (Foote, 1999). Note that in this alleged case of *cyber*stalking, Dellapenta engaged others to "stalk" his intended victim in physical space. So once again, we can ask whether the Barber/Dellapenta incident is a genuine case of cyberstalking or whether it can be more appropriately described as instance of a harassment involving the use of Internet technology.

Thus far we have briefly described two different criminal incidents that some authors have referred to as examples of cyberstalking. It is perhaps worth noting that no physical harm resulted to victims in either incident; and in both cases, it was difficult to separate certain harassment activities (in general) from stalking behavior in particular. Also, in the Barber/Dellapenta case, the stalking-related activities involved both physical space and cyberspace. We next examine a stalking incident involving Amy Boyer, which we believe is a clearer case of cyberstalking.

2. The Amy Boyer Cyberstalking Case

On October 15, 1999, Amy Boyer, a twenty-year-old resident of Nashua, NH, was murdered by a young man who had stalked her via the Internet. Her stalker, Liam Youens, was able to carry out most of the stalking activities that eventually led to Boyer's death by using a variety of online tools available to any Internet user. Through the use of online search facilities, for example, Youens was able to find out where Boyer lived, where she worked, what kind of vehicle she drove, and so forth. Youens was also able to use other kinds of online tools, typically provided by Internet service providers (ISPs), to construct two Web sites. On one site, he posted personal information about Boyer, including a picture of her; and on another site, Youens described, in explicit detail, his plans to murder Boyer.

The Amy Boyer case raises several ethical and social questions, independent of the important fact that the stalking behavior in this incident eventually led to Boyer's death. For example, some have argued that Boyer's privacy was violated. We could ask whether Boyer was the victim of online defamation. We could also ask whether Youens had a right to post information about Boyer on his Web site, and whether such a "right" is one that ought to be protected by free speech. Or should such "speech" be controlled in cyberspace? Also, we could ask whether issues raised in the Boyer case are more ethically significant than those in other online stalking incidents because of the physical harm caused to Boyer resulting in her death. Although the Amy Boyer case raises several ethical issues, we can ask whether there is anything unique or even special about these issues from a moral point of view.

3. What, if Anything, Is Ethically Significant about Cyberstalking Crimes?

From an ethical perspective, an interesting question is whether there is anything unique or even special about the Amy Boyer case in particular, or cyberstalking in general. On the one hand, we do not claim that cyberstalking is a new kind of crime; nor, for that matter, do we argue that cyberstalking is a "genuine" computer crime" (Tavani, 2000). Yet we can reasonably ask whether Internet technology has made a relevant difference in the stalking case involving Amy Boyer. Perhaps the more important question, however, is: Has cybertechnology made a moral difference? One might be inclined to answer *no*. For example, one could argue that "murder is murder," and that whether a murderer uses a computing device that included Internet tools to assist in carrying out a particular murder is irrelevant from an ethical point of view. One could further argue that there is nothing special about cyberstalking incidents in general—irrespective of whether or not those incidents result in the death of the victims—since stalking activities have had a long history of occurrence in the "off-line" world. According to this line of reasoning, the use of Internet technology could be seen as simply the latest in a series of tools or techniques that have become available to stalkers to assist them in carrying out their criminal activities.

However, it could also be argued that the Internet has made a relevant difference with respect to stalking-related crimes because of the ways in which stalking activities can now be carried out. For example, Internet stalkers can operate anonymously or pseudononymously while online. Also consider that a cyberstalker can stalk one or more individuals from the comfort of his or her home, and thus does not have to venture out into the physical world to stalk someone. So Internet technology has provided stalkers with a certain mode of stalking that was not possible in the pre-Internet era (Tavani, 2002).

It could also be argued that cyberstalking has made possible certain kinds of behavior that challenge our conventional moral and legal frameworks. These challenges have to do primarily with issues of *scale* and *scope*. For example, a cyberstalker can stalk multiple victims simultaneously through the use of multiple "windows" on his or her computer. The stalker can also stalk victims who happen to live in states and countries that are geographically distant from the stalker. So, potentially, both the number of stalking incidents and the range of stalking activities can increase dramatically because of the Internet. However, we leave open the question of whether any of these matters make a moral difference.

In the remainder of this essay, we focus on two questions involving issues of moral responsibility in the Boyer case: (1) Should the two ISPs that permitted Youens to post information about Amy Boyer on Web sites that reside in their Internet "space" be held morally accountable? (2) Do ordinary users who happen to come across a Web site that contains a posting of a death threat directed at an individual (or group of individuals) have a moral responsibility to inform those individuals whose lives are threatened?

4. Moral Responsibility and Internet Service Providers (ISPs)

As noted above, Youens set up two Web sites about Amy Boyer: one containing descriptive information about Boyer, as well as a photograph of her, and another on which he described in detail his plans to murder Boyer. To what extent, if any—either legally or morally, or both—should the ISPs that hosted the Web sites created by Youens be held responsible? Because this question is very complex, it would be beneficial to break it down into several shorter questions. For example, we first need to understand what is meant by "responsibility" in both its legal and moral senses. We also have to consider whether we can attribute moral blame (or praise) to an organization or collectivity (i.e., a group of individuals), such as an ISP. We begin by briefly examining some recent laws and court challenges that either directly or indirectly pertain to questions involving responsibility and liability for ISPs.

In *Stratton Oakmont v. Prodigy Services Company* (1995), the court determined that Prodigy could be held legally liable since it had advertised that it had "editorial control" over the content in the computer bulletin board system (BBS) it hosted. In the eyes of the court, Prodigy's claim to have editorial control over its BBS made that ISP seem similar to a newspaper, in which case the standard of strict legal liability used for original publishers could be applied. In response to the decision in the Prodigy case, many ISPs have since argued that they should not be understood as "original publishers," but rather as "common carriers," similar in relevant respects to telephone companies. Their argument for this view rested in part on the notion that ISPs provide the "conduits for communication but not the content." This view of ISPs would be used in later court decisions (such as *Zeran v. America Online Inc.* 1997).

In Section 230 of the Communications Decency Act (CDA), the function of ISPs was interpreted in such a way that would appear to protect them from lawsuits similar to the one filed against Prodigy. Here the court specifically stated, "No provider or user of an interactive computer service shall be treated as the publisher or speaker of any information provided by another information content provider." Although the U.S. Supreme Court eventually struck down CDA, Section 230 of that Act has remained intact. While ISPs are not legally liable for the content of their Web sites or for the content of other electronic forums that they also might host—e.g., forums such as bulletin boards, chat rooms, and list servers—they have nonetheless been encouraged to monitor and filter, to the extent that they can, the content of these electronic forums. But this has presented ISPs with a thorny legal problem. Consider, for example, that the more an ISP edits content, the more it becomes like a publisher (such as a newspaper). And the more it becomes like a publisher, with editorial control, the more liable an ISP becomes from a legal perspective. So, effectively, there could be some disincentive for ISPs to monitor and filter content. This, in turn, raises a moral dilemma for ISPs.

Should Internet Service Providers be held morally accountable for objectionable behavior that occurs in their forums? Deborah Johnson (2001) notes that while it might be easier to make a utilitarian case for holding ISPs legally liable in certain instances, it would be much more difficult to make the case that ISPs should be morally responsible for the behavior of their customers. Recently, however, Richard Spinello (2001) and Anton Vedder (2001) have tried to show, via different very different kinds of arguments, why ISPs also should be held morally accountable to some extent. Neither Spinello nor Vedder address the issue of cyberstalking per se; however, we believe that Spinello's remarks regarding "on-line defamation" and Vedders's comments regarding on-line "harm," both of which are associated with ISPs, can help shed some light on the question before us. We briefly examine both arguments.

4.1 The Spinello View

Arguing that ISPs should be held morally accountable in cases involving defamation, Spinello first distinguishes between "moral responsibility" and "moral accountability." In making this distinction, he uses a model advanced by Helen Nissenbaum (1994). According to Nissenbaum's scheme, accountability, unlike responsibility, does not require *causality* or a causal connection. Spinello points out that because ISPs do not *cause* defamation, they cannot be held responsible in the strict or narrow sense of the term. However, he argues that they could, nonetheless, be held accountable—i.e., "answerable"—in the sense that they "provide an occasion or forum" for defamation. Spinello is careful to point out that simply because an ISP presents an "occasion for defamation," it does not necessarily follow that an ISP is accountable. Rather, for an ISP to be accountable, two further conditions are required: (a) the ISP must also have some *capability* to do something about the defamation, and (b) the ISP failed to take action once it had been informed. Spinello believes that this standard of accountability takes into consideration what ISPs can reasonably do—i.e., what they are *capable* of doing—to prevent defamation or at least to limit its damage. So the fact that an ISP might not have caused the defamation does not rule out the possibility that the ISP can be held accountable in some sense for defamatory remarks.

Spinello concedes that technical and economic factors make it virtually impossible for ISPs to take preventative, or what he calls "pre-screening," measures that would detect or filter out defamatory messages. Thus we cannot hold ISPs responsible in a causal sense for defamation. Assuming that Spinello's overall argument is correct, however, we might hold ISPs accountable if they fail to take certain actions once they are informed that a victim has been defamed. For Spinello, these steps would include three actions: (i) prompt removal of the defamatory remarks; (ii) the issuance of a retraction on behalf of the victim; and (iii) the initiation of a good faith effort to track down the originator so that the defamation does not reoccur.

Does this threefold requirement provide us with a standard of accountability that is a "reasonable middle ground," as Spinello suggests? Or is it an unreasonable expectation for ISPs? Spinello notes that in the current system, a victim of defamation has no legal recourse because of the absolute immunity given to ISPs. On the other hand, the strict legal liability that was applied in the Prodigy case seems unduly harsh for ISPs. So Spinello believes that his alternative scheme provides the appropriate middle ground needed, because it grants some protection to victims of defamation without burdening the ISP. So even if the law does not require ISPs to take any action, Spinello believes that "post-screening" in a "diligent fashion" for content along the lines of the threefold criteria described above is the morally right thing to do. He concedes, however, that ISPs do not have the capability to "pre-screen" content for defamation.

4.2 The Vedder Argument

Anton Vedder (2001) has recently advanced a very different kind of argument for why we should consider holding ISPs morally responsible for harm caused to individuals. Vedder suggests that we begin by drawing an important distinction between two senses of moral responsibility: *prospective* and *retrospective* responsibility. Whereas retrospective responsibility tends to be "backward looking," prospective responsibility is "forward looking." Vedder believes that in the past, arguments that have been used to ascribe legal liability to ISPs have tended to be prospective in nature. This is because the primary objective of liability laws has been to deter future on-line abuses rather than punish past offenses.

Vedder also notes that even though ISPs are not legally liable for their content under current US law, the mere threat of legal liability can be used to deter ISPs from becoming lax about "policing" their electronic forums to some reasonable extent. So underlying the reasoning for arguments for applying strict legal liability to ISPs is the utilitarian principle that having liability laws in place will deter harm to ISP users in the future. And this legal argument, in turn, is based on a notion of moral responsibility that is essentially *prospective* in nature. Vedder also points out that we are hesitant to attribute a retrospective sense of responsibility to ISPs because this sense of moral responsibility:

(a) is usually applied to individuals (as opposed to organizations or what he calls "collectivities"), and

(b) it also often implies guilt.

And as Vedder correctly notes, the notion of guilt is typically attributed to individuals and not to organizations or collectivities. He suggests, however, that in some cases it also makes sense to attribute the notion of guilt to a collectivity such as an ISP.

Attributing some moral accountability to ISPs makes sense, in Vedder's scheme, because of the connection that exists between retrospective and prospective responsibility. Vedder argues that it makes no sense to hold an agent (i.e., either an individual or a collectivity) responsible for an act in a prospective sense if that agent could not also be held responsible for the act in a retrospective sense as well. So Vedder concludes that if we assume that collectivities such as ISPs can be held responsible in a prospective sense—a rationale that has been used as the basis for utilitarian arguments in attributing legal liability for ISPs—then we can also ascribe retrospective responsibility to ISPs. So, as in the case of Spinello, Vedder believes that ISPs can be held morally accountable to some extent for speech that is communicated in their electronic forums.

4.3 Implications for the Amy Boyer Case

We can now apply Vedder's and Spinello's arguments to the Amy Boyer cyberstalking case. Should Tripod and Geocities, the two ISPs that enabled Liam Youens to set up his Web sites about Boyer, be held morally accountable for the harm caused to Boyer and to her family? And should those two ISPs be held morally accountable, even if they were not responsible (in the narrow sense) for causing harm to Boyer and even if they can be exonerated from charges of strict legal liability? If the arguments by Vedder and Spinello succeed, then it is reasonable to hold these ISPs morally accountable if it also could be shown that Tripod and Geocities were capable of limiting the harm that resulted to Boyer. (Tim Remsberg, Amy Boyer's stepfather, has recently filed a wrongful death suit against both ISPs.)

Of course, one might ask what the purpose would be in attributing moral responsibility to ISPs if no legal action could be taken against them. At least two different replies are possible to this question, both of which might also cause us to be more careful in our thinking about moral issues involving cyberspace. First, an analysis of moral issues in this light could help us to distinguish further between moral and legal aspects of controversial cyberspace issues. Second, such an analysis can also help to consider some ways in which moral responsibility can be applied at the collective, as well as at the individual, level.

5. Individual Moral Responsibility at the Level of Ordinary Internet Users

We next examine questions of moral responsibility that apply at the individual level, i.e., at the level of individual users in online communities. For example, do ordinary Internet users have a moral responsibility to inform "would-be victims" of their imminent danger to online stalkers? If an Internet user had been aware of Boyer's situation, should that user have notified Boyer that she was being stalked? In other words, should that user be morally obligated to do so?

Various proposals for controlling individual behavior in online communities have resulted in a conflict between those who wish to regulate strictly by law and those who wish to preserve the practice of self-regulation. Of course, this dispute is sometimes also at the base of arguments involving claims having to do with a "safe" social space vs. a "restrictive" one. In the case of cyberstalking, should we assist others based strictly on formal legal regulations, or should we assist them because it is the morally right thing to do?

5.1 A Minimalist Sense of Moral Obligation vs. an "Ethic of Care"

Some have argued that while morality can demand of an agent that he or she "do no harm" to others, it cannot *require* that an agent actively "prevent harm," or "do good." In one sense, to do no harm is to act in accordance with the rules of a moral system. But is doing so always sufficient for complying with what is required of us as moral agents? In other words, if it is in our power to prevent harm and to do good, should we do so? Some theoretical frameworks suggest that individuals should prevent harm (and otherwise do good) whenever it is in their power to do so. For example, if one believes, as some natural law theorists assert, that the purpose of morality is to alleviate human suffering and to promote human flourishing, whenever possible, then clearly we would seem obligated to prevent harm in cyberspace. An interesting account of this view has been advanced by Louis Pojman (2001).

Unfortunately, we are not able to present Pojman's argument here in the detail that it deserves, since doing so would take us beyond the scope of this paper. But we can see how, based on a model like Pojman's, one might develop a fuller theory in which individuals have an obligation to "assist" others in the act of preventing harm from coming to those persons.

We recognize the difficulties of defending a natural law theory; and we are not prepared to do so here. However, we also believe that the kind of limited or "moderate" natural law theories that can be found in Pojman, and to some extent in James Moor (1998), can be very useful in making the case for an extended sense of moral obligation at the level of individuals.

Another moral framework that implies an expanded sense of moral responsibility on the part of individuals is the "ethic of care," introduced in a seminal work by Carol Gilligan (1982). Complying with a "care ethic," individuals would assist one another whenever it is in their power to do so. As such, an ethic based on care is more robust than a mere "non-interference" notion of ethics that simply involves "doing no harm to others"—i.e., it is concerned with a sense of commitment to others that Virginia Held (1995) describes as "above and beyond the floor of duty."

Gilligan's ethic of care has been contrasted with traditional ethical systems, such as utilitarian and Kantian theories. Alison Adam (2000) points out that traditional ethical theories are often based simply on following formal rules and that they tend to engender a sense of individualism (as opposed to community). Adam (2001, 2002) has also argued that an ethic of care, in particular, and feminist ethical theory in general, can help us to understand more clearly some of the social and ethical implications of cyberstalking behavior in ways that traditional ethical theories cannot.

Adopting an "ethic of care" in cyberspace would mean that individuals, i.e., ordinary Internet users, would be prone to assist others whenever they can help to prevent harm from coming to them. From this perspective, individuals would assist one another, even though there may be no specific laws or rules that require them to do so. In what sense would such an expectation on the part of individuals expand our conventional notion of moral obligation?

5.2 Expanding the Sphere of Moral Responsibility: A *Duty to Assist*

Questions concerning whether individuals have a "duty to assist" others often arise in the aftermath of highly publicized crimes such as the one involving in the Kitty Genovese case in 1964. Genovese, a young woman, was murdered on the street outside her apartment building in Queens, New York, as thirty-eight of her neighbors watched. None of her neighbors called the police during the 35-minute period of repeated stabbings. Some have since referred to this refusal to assist a neighbor in critical need as "the Genovese Syndrome." Police involved in the Genovese case believe that the witnesses were morally obligated to notify the police, even though there may have been no formal law or specific statute requiring them to do so.

Drawing an analogy between the Genovese and Boyer cases, we can ask whether users who might have been able to assist Boyer should have done so (i.e., whether they were morally obligated to assist her). We can also ask what kind of community cyberspace will become, if people refuse to assist users who may be at risk to predators and murderers. First, we need to consider the potential harm that could come to members of the online community if we fail to act to prevent harm from coming to those individuals, when it is in our power to help and when doing so would neither cause us any great inconvenience nor put our safety at risk. What would have happened to Randi Barber if no one had intervened in her behalf? In the cyberstalking case involving Barber and Dellapenta,

Barber's father, with the cooperation of the men who were soliciting her, provided evidence that led to Dellapenta's arrest. In the case of Amy Boyer, however, the same sense of individual moral responsibility and concern was not apparent. Consider that some Internet users had, in fact, viewed the Youens Web site but did not inform Boyer that she was being stalked and that her life was in imminent danger. Like Kitty Genovese, who received no assistance from members of her physical community, Amy Boyer received no assistance from members of the online community.

Because of what happened to Amy Boyer, and because of what could happen to future victims of online stalking, we argue that ordinary users, as members of an online community, should adopt a notion of moral responsibility that involves assisting fellow users. Doing so would help to keep cyberspace a safer place for everyone, but especially for women and children who are particularly vulnerable to stalking activities. Failing to embrace such a notion of moral responsibility, on the other hand, could result in users disconnecting themselves from their responsibilities towards fellow human beings.

6. Conclusion

We have examined some ethical concerns involving cyberstalking in general, and the Amy Boyer case in particular. We saw that stalking activities in cyberspace raise questions about the sphere of moral responsibility, both for ISPs and ordinary Internet users. We argued that ISPs and individual users, each in different ways, should assume a more robust sense of moral responsibility, which goes beyond a mere "non-interference ethic," in order to help to prevent harm from coming to individuals targeted by cyberstalkers.

Acknowledgments

We are grateful to Anton Vedder for some very helpful comments on an earlier version of this paper. We also wish to thank Detective Sergeant Frank Paison of the Nashua, NH Police Department, who was the chief investigator in the Amy Boyer cyberstalking case, for some helpful information that he provided during an interview with him.

Portions of this essay are extracted from Tavani (2004). We are grateful to John Wiley & Sons, Publishers for permission to reprint that material.

References

Adam, Alison (2000). "Gender and Computer Ethics." *Computers and Society,* Vol. 30, No. 4, pp. 17–24.

Adam, Alison (2001). "Cyberstalking: Gender and Computer Ethics." In Eileen Green and Alison Adam, eds. *Virtual Gender: Technology, Consumption, and Identity.* London: Routledge, pp. 209–234.

Adam, Alison (2002). "Cyberstalking and Internet Pornography: Gender and the Gaze." *Ethics and Information Technology,* Vol. 4, No. 2, pp. 133–142.

Foote, D. (1999). "You Could Get Raped," *Newsweek,* Vol. 133, No. 6, Feb. 8, pp. 64–65.

Gilligan, Carol (1982). *In a Different Voice.* Cambridge: Harvard University Press.

Grodzinsky, Frances S., and Herman T. Tavani (2001). "Is cyberstalking a Special Type of Computer crime?" In Terrell Ward Bynum, et al., eds, *Proceedings of ETHICPMP 2001: The Fifth International Conference on the Social and Ethical Impacts of Information and Communication Technology.* Vol. 2. Gdansk, Poland: Wydawnicktwo Mikom Publishers, pp.72–81.

Grodzinsky, Frances S., and Herman T. Tavani (2002). "Cyberstalking, Moral Responsibility, and Legal Liability Issues for Internet Service Providers." In Joseph Herkert, ed. *Proceedings of ISTAS 2002: The International Symposium on Technology and Society.* Los Alamitos, CA: IEEE Computer Society Press, pp. 331–339.

Held, Virginia (1995). "The Meshing of Care and Justice," *Hypatia,* University of Indiana Press, Spring.

Johnson, Deborah G. (2001). *Computer Ethics.* 3rd. ed. Upper Saddle River, NJ: Prentice Hall.

Moor, James H. (1998). "Reason, Relativity, and Responsibility in Computer Ethics." *Computers and Society,* Vol. 28, No. 1, 1998, pp. 14–21.

Nissenbaum, Helen (1994). "Computing and Accountability," *Communications of the ACM,* Vol. 37, No. 1, pp. 73–80.

Pojman, Louis P. (2001). *Ethics: Discovering Right and Wrong.* 4th ed. Belmont, CA: Wadsworth.

Spinello, Richard A. (2001). "Internet Service Providers and Defamation: New Standards of Liability." In R. A. Spinello and H. T. Tavani, eds. *Readings in CyberEthics.* Sudbury, MA: Jones and Bartlett, pp. 198–209.

Tavani, Herman T. (2000). "Defining the Boundaries of Computer Crime: Piracy, Break-ins and Sabotage in Cyberspace." *Computers and Society,* Vol. 30, No. 4, 2000, pp. 3–9.

Tavani, Herman T. (2002). "The Uniqueness Debate in Computer Ethics: What Exactly Is at Issue, and Why Does it Matter?" *Ethics and Information Technology,* Vol. 4, No. 1, pp. 37–54.

Tavani, Herman T. (2004). *Ethics and Technology: Ethical Issues in an Age of Information and Communication Technology.* New York: John Wiley and Sons.

Tavani, Herman T., and Frances S. Grodzinsky (2002). "Cyberstalking, Personal Privacy, and Moral Responsibility," *Ethics and Information Technology,* Vol. 4, No. 2, pp. 123–132.

"The Web's Dark Side: In the Shadows of Cyberspace, an Ordinary Week is a Frightening Time," *U.S. News & World Report,* Vol. 129, No. 8, Aug. 28, 2000.

Vedder, Anton H. (2001). "Accountability of Internet Access and Service Providers: Strict Liability Entering Ethics." *Ethics and Information Technology,* Vol. 3, No. 1, pp. 67–74.

Journal/Discussion Questions

1. Have you known anyone who was the object of cyberstalking? What special dimensions were present because the incident occurred in cyberspace?

2. Cyberstalking is only one of several questionable things that happen in cyberspace. What do you think the responsibilities of Internet Service Providers should be in this regard?

Richard A. Spinello
"Ethical Reflections on the Problem of Spam"

Richard Spinello teaches at the Carroll School of Management, Boston University. He has written extensively in the area of cyberethics and the law. His books include Cyberethics: Morality and Law in Cyberspace, Case Studies in Information Technology Ethics *(2nd edition),* Regulating Cyberspace: The Policies and Technologies of Control, *and, with Herman Tavani,* Intellectual Property Rights in a Networked World: Theory and Practice *and* Readings in Cyberethics.

In this article, Spinello looks at some of the legal and ethical issues surrounding spam.

As You Read, Consider This:

1. What is spam? Why does it make a difference how we define it?
2. What does Spinello mean by "significant externalities"?
3. What conclusions does Spinello draw about the legality of spam? Is it ethical? What limits should be placed on it?

1. Introduction

In a recent *New York Times* article spam was described as a "betrayal of all that mail once stood for" (Slatella, 1998). This quote captures the negative sentiment that most users have cultivated about spam, a derogatory name for unsolicited, promotional electronic mail. Spam messages flood into mailboxes all over the 'Net and sell everything from education to sex. Spam is communicated to users either by postings to Usenet newsgroups or through bulk electronic mail delivered to Internet mailing lists. Spam may seem to be a trivial matter, nothing more than a minor nuisance and hardly a serious ethical problem. However, many users regard it as an invasive form of commercial advertising that perversely shifts some of its costs from the advertiser to the consumer. This cost shifting along with the deceptive tactics of "spammers" has given spam a moral stigma that seems well deserved. Moreover, the problem of unsolicited advertisements in cyberspace is likely to intensify in light of two important and converging trends: the rapid growth of electronic commerce and the continued reliance on direct marketing techniques deployed by advertisers soliciting a targeted or select group of consumers.

The ethical propriety of sending bulk promotional e-mail is not a simple matter to adjudicate since it does represent a form of free speech. How do we balance the right of commercial free speech with other rights at stake in this controversy such as the privacy rights of users? In addition, is the right to free speech curtailed when certain costs are imposed on those to whom that speech is directed? Does my right to send someone an advertisement cease when the recipient has to incur some costs for receiving that ad? And if we agree that the consumer can absorb a trivial cost, where and

Ethics and Information Technology, Vol. 1(3) (1999), pp. 185–191.

how do we draw the line? At what point does cost shifting become truly burdensome for typical end users on the Internet?

We will attempt to address these and other salient moral issues about spam in this paper. Our primary theme is that the transmission of spam poses a considerable moral problem for two reasons: under some circumstances it constitutes a violation of personal autonomy, and because of its volume spam also has a disruptive effect on the fragile ecology of the Internet.

2. What's Wrong with Spam?

To begin with, how precisely should we define "spam"? Spam refers to unsolicited, promotional electronic mail usually sent in bulk to thousands or millions of Internet users. Quite simply, it is junk e-mail which is usually a significant annoyance to its recipients. But is all unsolicited commercial e-mail a form of spam? Spam has typically been associated with "get rich quick" schemes and other marginal businesses, but that is changing. As more and more individuals conduct business in cyberspace, mainstream advertisers and political organizations are beginning to rely on bulk e-mail to sell their products or solicit donations. The Democratic Party of California, for instance, uses e-mail to promote its activities and communicate endorsements. Do these unsolicited communications also constitute spam? We seem to be in a nebulous area and the deployment of unsolicited e-mail by legitimate groups surely compounds the problem. Obviously, some unsolicited communications will have more merit than others based upon the sender and the content. We should keep this in mind throughout the course of this discussion, but for our purposes in this paper we will consider all forms of unsolicited promotional e-mail as spam.

Some of those vendors which do rely on spam maintain that this whole controversy is blown out of proportion by purists who want to see the Internet liberated from excessive commercial use. They argue that spam is no different from conventional junk mail which does not receive the same level of scrutiny or the same trenchant criticism. Opponents of spam, on the other hand, complain that it robs users and Internet providers of resources and sullies the 'Net just as litter or pollutants sully the physical environment.

Do the pro-spammers have a point? After all, why single spam out when there are so many other forms of "junk" communication such as regular junk mail and unsolicited phone calls? What makes spam so pernicious and costly? The major difference between electronic junk mail and paper junk mail is that the per copy cost of sending the former is so much lower. There are paper, printing, and postage charges for each piece of regular junk mail but the marginal cost of sending an additional piece of junk e-mail is negligible. For instance, Jeffrey Slaton, a direct marketer who specializes in spam, charges his clients a flat fee of $425 to send out several million messages. As he explains in a recent interview in *Wired,* "It's just as cost effective to send to 6 million e-mail addresses as to 1 million e-mail addresses, so why bother being selective?" (Garfinkel, 1996).

But spam is not cost-free. The problem is that the lion's share of these costs are externalities, that is, they are costs borne involuntarily by others. As Raisch (1995) has observed, spam is "postage-due marketing." The biggest cost associated with spam is the consumption of computer resources. For example, when someone sends out spam the messages must sit on a disk somewhere, and this means that valuable disk space is being filled with unwanted mail. Also, many users must pay for each message received or for each disk block used. Others pay for the time they are connected to the Internet, time which can be wasted downloading and deleting spam. As the volume of spam grows and commercial use of the Internet expands, these costs will continue their steady increase.

Further, when spam is sent through Internet Service Providers (ISPs), they must bear the costs of delivery. This amounts to wasted network bandwith and the utilization of system resources such as disk storage space along with the servers and transfer networks involved in the transmission process. Despite its efforts to control junk e-mail, America Online reports that 2.5 million pieces of spam still engulf its system each day. According to the ISP/C (1997), the ISP's trade group, "Although the cost for a single UCE [unsolicited commercial e-mail] message may be small, when messages to be processed swell into the thousands or millions, that cost becomes both significant and burdensome."

In addition to these technical costs imposed by spam there are also administrative costs. Users who receive these unwanted messages are forced to waste time reading and deleting them. If a vendor sends out 6 million messages and it takes 6 seconds to delete each one, the total cost of this one mailing is 10,000 person hours of lost time. Spam is also a disutility because it clutters mailboxes and usegroup postings. If a business is forced to deal with and delete a large volume of electronic junk mail every day, that unwanted mail may be interfering with the timely receipt and disposition of its regular mail. If the volume of spam continues its rapid growth rate, it could seriously attenuate the utility of electronic mail.

Finally, junk mailers often use questionable practices to gather names and addresses. The spammers have been accused of violating privacy rights by distributing e-mail addresses without consent, by harvesting e-mail addresses left at web sites, by ignoring those who submit requests to have their names removed from mailing lists, and by making it virtually impossible to submit those requests by using forged addresses.

3. Defending Spam

Those who defend the right to send out unsolicited junk electronic mail might concede that spam does impose some costs on its recipients. They claim, however, that those costs are trivial and that many users enjoy and benefit from this form of advertising. Unsolicited advertising does not necessarily mean that it is unwanted. Spam represents an efficient and inexpensive way to advertise many worthwhile products. In addition, it stands to reason that if firms are going to do business in cyberspace they must be allowed to advertise there, and direct electronic mail campaigns are an effective means of accomplishing this.

Spam also makes it much easier for small entrepreneurs to get their message out in a cost effective way and to thereby compete on a more level playing field with their larger and more established counterparts. The chance to advertise to millions of prospective customers on the Internet represents a significant economic opportunity especially for the growth market of electronic commerce, and it should not be undermined by meddlesome and restrictive regulations.

Proponents of spam also contend that this is simply another form of commercial free speech which deserves the same level of First Amendment protection as traditional advertising. They point out, perhaps correctly, that a ban on spam would not only be impractical but also unconstitutional since it would violate their constitutional right to communicate. The right to commercial forms of speech has stood on tenuous ground and has never been seen as morally equivalent to political speech. In recent years, however, the Court has tended to offer more substantial protection for commercial speech than it did several decades ago. According to Carroll (1996), "With the development of our information economy, the Court has come to read the First Amendment to provide broader protection over the nexus between the marketplace of ideas and the marketplace for goods and services."

Finally, defenders of spam also support any legal, albeit questionable, methods of collecting e-mail addresses. They believe that they have every right to gather e-mail addresses from various sources (such as AOL's member directory) and to use them for commercial purposes. In a *Computerworld* interview David Silver, a direct marketer who uses spam, contends that e-mail addresses are just as public as phone numbers: "If I look up a phone number in the White Pages, I have the right to call that number because it's public information. So is the e-mail address that's posted anywhere on the 'net. If I had to break in with a password to get that address, that would be illegal. But what I do is the same as opening the phone book. If someone doesn't want bulk e-mail, they shouldn't place their address anywhere that's publicly accessible." (Goff, 1997).

4. The Legal Status of Spam

Prior to this current controversy over spam, unsolicited commercial advertisements transmitted by facsimile machines posed the same sort of challenge to public policy makers. The response was the Telephone Consumer Protection Act or TCPA (1991) which banned any such solicitations that contained advertising:

> It shall be unlawful for any person within the United States to use any telephone facsimile machine, computer, or other device to send an unsolicited advertisement to a telephone facsimile machine.

The rationale behind this legislation was based on a recognition of cost-shifting: there is some expense involved in receiving faxes (such as the consumption of paper and toner) so the recipient is implicitly subsidizing the advertiser. These costs are unavoidable and constitute enough of a burden to warrant regulatory protection.

The more significant problem with unsolicited faxes, however, was perceived to be message preclusion: faxes often involve the transmission of time sensitive material and that transmission might be disrupted if one is "forced" to consistently receive junk faxes. Thus, the primary difficulty with unsolicited faxes is that they can too easily prevent the timely reception of critically important material.

Although many see an analogy between these two forms of junk communication, electronic junk mail is not covered by the TCPA. There may be some cost shifting involved with spam especially for those who pay for their on-line services by the minute. But there are many others who pay a flat fee to be connected to the Internet. Hence from a legal point of view it is difficult to make a strong case that cost shifting is as serious a problem for spam as it is for junk faxes. Likewise, the preclusion problem poses a more notable difficulty for a fax machine than it does for electronic mail. If a fax machine is forced to receive a piece of junk mail all other incoming faxes are on hold. It is highly unlikely, however, that a critical piece of electronic mail could not be delivered because a user's mail box was filled with useless spam messages.

It seems evident that the Internet provides a more flexible mode of communication than telephones and fax machines, and hence it is difficult to draw an exact comparison between junk e-mail and junk faxes. As a result, since spam does not cause the same level of cost shifting and message preclusion as do junk faxes, and therefore is not as burdensome to individual users, legislators in the U.S. have concluded that it should not be subject to the restrictions imposed by the TCPA.

5. Ethical Issues and Spam

Spam may indeed be perfectly legal, but is the practice of sending bulk promotional e-mail within the bounds of ethical propriety? In my estimation, a strong case can be put forth demonstrating that spam is morally objectionable in its current form. There are two basic problems with spam—its negative effects on the Internet environment which can lead to an electronic version of a "tragedy of the commons," and its potential for violating the rights of the individual recipients of this junk mail.

Let us first deal with the latter concern. On one level this issue can be seen as a conflict of rights: the right of the vendor or advertiser to communicate with others by means of unsolicited electronic mail in conflict with the right to autonomy and privacy. Do vendors actually have such a right in this context? Let us assume for the sake of this argument that unsolicited, promotional e-mail is a rare occurrence in cyberspace and therefore does not amount to a widespread problem. Let us also assume that there are no measurable direct costs involved, i.e., the recipient pays a flat fee to be connected to the Internet.

Under these conditions, one can certainly argue that the isolated act of sending a piece of unsolicited electronic mail, advertising a legitimate product or service, is perfectly reasonable and hardly amounts to a transgression of commonly accepted ethical norms. Vendors are simply exercising their right of free expression within an open medium of communication.

Some anti-spammers have asserted that all Internet communications should be "consensual" (Harmon, 1998). But this is an extreme and untenable position that would be difficult to justify from any ethical standpoint. The heavy costs of such an exclusionary policy would far outweigh any benefits. Do the majority of Internet users really want to preclude any communications to which they have not given their consent? Wouldn't they be impoverished by such a restriction? For instance, if I'm a novelist and a colleague writes without my consent to offer some thoughtful reflections on my latest book, wouldn't I be quite eager to read his e-mail? How could such communications fall under the category of useless spam? The open communications and democratic expression enabled by the Internet would be seriously undermined if we insisted that all exchanges had to be consensual.

However, although advertisers do have a right to send this mail they do not have a right to force it upon someone. The right to communicate in this fashion must be balanced with the right of privacy which is essentially defined as the right to be left alone within one's own personal domain. In order to effect some compromise in this situation individuals must be allowed to maintain their autonomy by exercising some measure of control over this unwanted mail. Each individual should have the right to control his or her domain or private space. This should include the prerogative to protect it from unwanted mail whether it be regular mail sent to one's house or electronic mail sent to one's electronic mailboxes which should also be regarded as an extension of one's private physical space. This is derived from the more basic right of autonomy over one's person and possessions which is violated by the coercive activity of making someone a captive audience to another's communications. Of course, the user can exercise control simply by deleting the unwanted message. It also seems reasonable, however, that the user should be able to go a step further and tell the sender to stop sending any more messages or mailings. The right to communicate must be limited by the preferences of an unreceptive consumer.

Vendors and advertisers, therefore, must respect this right and not impose their mailings on unwilling recipients. For regular mail this amounts to providing people with the opportunity to have their names removed from a mailing list, and this same opportunity must be provided by spammers. At a minimum, they too must allow users a convenient opportunity to "opt out" of future mailings. Vendors should not send unsolicited electronic mail unless they have the facility and willingness to expediently remove names from their lists, enabling them to respect the rights of those who reject this mail. Thus, the transmission of spam could be an unethical act if (a) it is carelessly or intentionally sent to someone who has opted out or (b) there is no intention to comply with requests to opt out and thereby respect the rights and autonomy of the recipients.

What about the cost factor for the individual who receives junk e-mail? Should the right to commercial free speech be curtailed when that "speech" is not exactly free to its recipients? It must be recognized that most types of junk communication, including phone calls and regular mail, entail certain costs for the recipients. These might include time lost answering the phone or sifting through piles of junk mail. To some extent, they represent the cost of living in a free and open society and do not impose a heavy burden on the vast majority of individuals. An occasional piece of junk e-mail would also fall within this category. Even if users do pay for their Internet time by the minute, the miniscule costs involved in deleting a piece of unwanted mail does not seem to warrant the suppression of another's right to free speech. Such a solution would be disproportionate to the gravity of the problem. Thus, we still conclude that it is not really unethical for a vendor to send out unsolicited e-mail even if there is a minimal cost imposed upon the recipient. The real problem arises, of course, when users are forced to contend with a large volume of junk e-mail, but we have been assuming up to now that spam is an infrequent occurrence.

Even if we reach the conclusion that the transmission of electronic junk mail is not an unethical act per se as long as the mailer does not coerce his or her message and provides a reasonable opportunity to opt out, there are still problems with spam when one considers its overall collective effect in cyberspace. The conditions described above do not exist since spam is quite common on the Internet. Unfortunately, spam is growing at an exponential rate as direct mailers seek to capitalize on the Internet's expanding population, and this raises the ethical stakes quite considerably.

This brings us to the second moral issue concerning the social costs or externalities imposed by spam, that is, costs forced upon third parties in the Internet community as well as the direct recipients of spam. As we have already pointed out, spam shifts costs from the advertiser to several other parties including the recipients of the ad, the Internet Service Providers, and even to other users of the Internet who are indirectly inconvenienced by this practice.

In addition to this significant cost shifting, there is another externality involving a threat to the integrity and smooth functioning of the Internet. This is posed by the unabated growth of unsolicited commercial e-mail. There is a cumulative social cost to the sending of junk electronic mail, not unlike the social costs incurred when the environment is polluted.

Indeed the analogy between environmental degradation and the propagation of unsolicited junk e-mail in cyberspace is worth pursuing. Just as businesses have had a tendency to regard the environment (air, water, land) as a free and unlimited good, there has also been a tendency on the part of spammers to regard the Internet in the same way. But the conviction that these resources are unlimited and free sometimes promotes their wasteful consumption. The end result is what Garrett Hardin (1996) has characterized as a "tragedy of the commons":

> Picture a pasture open to all. It is expected that each herdsman will try to keep as many cattle as possible on the commons. As a rational being, each herdsman seeks to maximize his gain [and] . . . concludes that the only sensible course to pursue is to add another animal to the herd. And another, and another.

But this is the conclusion reached by each and every rational herdsman sharing a commons. Therein is the tragedy. Each man is locked into a system that compels him to increase his herd without limit—in a world that is limited. Ruin is the destination toward which all men rush, each pursuing his own best interest in a society that believes in the freedom of the commons. Freedom in commons brings ruin to all.

The moral of this story is clear enough: for any common good, problems can develop if individuals exclusively pursue their own rational self-interest and do not take into account the good of the whole (i.e., the commons). Each person rationalizes that their consumption of the resource is marginal and inconsequential but the combined result is the deterioration of that common resource. Thus, acting in concert they gradually destroy the natural environment or impair a pivotal public domain.

The situation in cyberspace is, of course, somewhat different since we are not talking about a physical resource that can be consumed or physically degraded. Nevertheless, like Hardin's pasture, the Internet is an open, free, and publicly accessible environment; just as there is no cost to use the pasture, there is virtually no cost to sending out a few extra pieces of junk e-mail. Consequently, if each small business in America and Europe decided to send out several hundred thousand advertising messages the cumulative effect of this on disk resources, bandwith, and the general Internet infrastructure would be devastating. The Internet's viability as a common resource for exchanging valuable information would be seriously eroded and millions of people would be adversely affected by much slower response time and cluttered mailboxes. Further, given the complicated interdependencies we find in our economy, the negative ramifications of widespread spamming will be diffuse, unpredictable, and potentially quite damaging.

The presence of both externalities, cost shifting and the erosion of the Internet's viability, cannot be casually ignored by spammers. Companies and individuals must assess and be accountable for *all* the short and long-range costs of their activities or transactions. It is morally unacceptable to thrust burdensome external costs on to third parties (such as the ISPs) against their will.

Moreover, all users have an obligation to respect the common good (in this case, the viability of Internet communications) which enables them to operate in the first place. They cannot maximize their short-term, private advantage by abetting the destruction of a common resource. There is no such thing as a purely private business that is not interconnected with and accountable to a greater whole. Instead there is a shared responsibility for preserving the efficiency and reliability of common communications systems such as the Internet. The Internet functions efficiently precisely because the majority of its users are cooperative and refrain from asocial activities like spamming. It is unfair, therefore, for spammers to dismiss or ignore the social costs of sending unsolicited bulk e-mail and to thereby benefit from the self restraint and moral decency of others.

We can undoubtedly find support for this position in several ethical frameworks, especially those that emphasize fairness or one's duty to abide by the legitimate norms of the community. For example, let us consider the nonconsequentialist framework of Immanuel Kant (1959). Spamming clearly violates the spirit of Kant's categorical imperative ("Act according to a maxim which is at the same time valid as a universal law"), which requires us to perform only those actions that can be universalized. According to Kant, the test of moral correctness is the rational acceptability of a hypothetical, but universal, conformity to a policy or practice. In other words, the universalization process usually demands that we imagine a counterfactual situation. In this case, we must imagine what would happen if all organizations and vendors which had an interest in on-line advertising adopted a policy of spamming, that is, transmitting large volumes of bulk e-mail through cyberspace on a regular basis. Beyond any doubt, the Internet would become hopelessly congested and the entire system would rapidly become dysfunctional. Spamming therefore is not a coherently universalizable practice, since it entails a pragmatic contradiction to the categorical imperative. To avoid such contradictions, one must not pursue actions "whose efficacy in achieving their purposes depends upon their being exceptional" (Korsgaard, 1996). Spamming, of course, can only be efficacious if it is an exception to the norm.

At the heart of Kant's ethical system is the notion that there are rational constraints on what we can do. We may want to engage in some action (such as sending millions of unsolicited electronic mail messages) but we are inconsistent and hence unethical unless we accept the implications of everyone doing the same thing. According to Kant, it is unethical to make arbitrary exceptions for ourselves, which is exactly what the spammers are implicitly doing. As a result, they are violating the basic rule of fair play which is expressed in the categorical imperative as well as in other ethical principles. In the simplest terms, the categorical imperative suggests the following question: what if everybody did what you are doing? In this case if everybody practiced spamming the end result would be a calamity for the Internet and a debilitating effect on electronic commerce. Hence from a Kantian perspective and from the perspective of similar theories that emphasize fairness and consistency, there is a moral duty to eschew this questionable activity.

We conclude therefore that because spamming does entail these substantial social costs that burden others and could bring about a tragedy of the commons, it is a morally objectionable activity. It unfairly exploits the Internet and the majority of its users who refrain from spamming, and it is disrespectful of the common good. Imprudent practices like spamming that ignore the good of the community and treat its members as commodities are certainly problematic from an ethical perspective.

In order to be morally and socially responsible, all Internet users must therefore be much more sensitive to the ecological nature of the 'Net, which, as the root of that word (Greek: *oikos* or house) connotes, is a sort of "household" or community. Such sensitivity precludes spamming and similar disruptive activities out of deference to the welfare of the community.

6. Conclusions

We might conclude by observing that spam is also a troubling public policy issue. From a public policy viewpoint spammers represent a classic example of *free riders,* since they do not pay for disseminating their advertising message the way traditional advertisers do. The individuals or companies who use spam benefit from the servers and transfer networks that make up the Internet and from the efforts of others to make it an environment hospitable to electronic commerce. But they "ride for free" by failing to contribute in a way that is proportionate to their consumption of Internet resources and by refusing to accept the obvious rules which enables the Internet and ISPs to function efficiently.

A discussion of the public policy issues associated with spam is well beyond the scope of this paper and we refer interested readers to Carroll (1996) for a thorough treatment of this issue. Suffice it to say that there should always be room for certain forms of advertising and promotional mailings on the Internet as long as users are willing to receive them and absorb their costs. But the exact limits on purely unsolicited commercial e-mail will be difficult to establish, and consequently the public policy debate on what to do about spam will not be settled any time soon.

We have simply tried to demonstrate here that if Internet users objectively reflect upon the moral implications of using spam they will reach the conclusion that its transmission is an asocial and selfish act. Even if the volume of spam were not an issue, spam would still be unethical if there is no intention of honoring the users request not to receive these mailings. This is based on the principle that no one should be forced to receive unwanted materials. Moreover, as we have been at pains to insist, because of the present and projected volume of spam it is also morally objectionable because it has the potential to bring about a tragedy of the commons for the Internet. It undermines the sense of shared responsibility which all users should assume for this important communications medium.

References

Carroll, M. (1996). Garbage In: Emerging Media and Regulation of Unsolicited Commercial Solicitations. *Berkeley Technology Law Journal, 11,* Fall.

Garfinkel, S. (1996). Spam King! Your Source for Spams Netwide. *Wired,* February, 84–92.

Goff, L. (1997). A Line in the SPAM. *Computerworld,* August, 88–89.

Hardin, G. (1996). The Tragedy of the Commons. In *Business and Society* (ed., B. Castro), Oxford University Press, New York.

Harmon, A. (1998). American Way of Spam: An E-Mail Battleground. *The New York Times,* May 7, E8.

Internet Service Providers Consortium (1997). ISP/C Position on Unsolicited Commercial E-Mail. (http://www.mids.org).

Kant, I. (1959). Foundations of the Metaphysics of Morals (trans. Lewis White Beck), Bobbs-Merrill Company, Indianapolis, IN.

Korsgaard, C. (1996). Creating the Kingdom of Ends, Cambridge University Press, New York.

Raisch, R. (1995). Postage Due Marketing: An Internet Company White Paper. (http://www.Internet.com:2010/marketing/postage.html).

Slatella, M. (1998). Hunting the Elusive Spammer. *The New York Times,* March 19, E 11.

The Telephone Consumer Protection Act (1991), 47 USC #227 (b) (1).

Journal/Discussion Questions

1. What new developments have occurred in regard to legal restrictions on spam? How effective have they been?

2. Has the issue of externalities grown more important in the last three years in regard to spam? What do you think is the best way of dealing with spam? Why?

Concluding Discussion Questions

Where Do You Stand Now?

Instructions

You have already answered the following questions in your moral problems self-quiz at the beginning of this book. Now that you have studied the material in this section, take a moment to answer the same questions again.

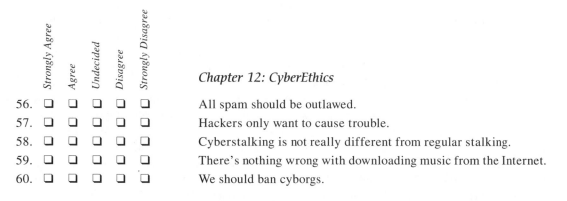

	Strongly Agree	Agree	Undecided	Disagree	Strongly Disagree	*Chapter 12: CyberEthics*
56.	❏	❏	❏	❏	❏	All spam should be outlawed.
57.	❏	❏	❏	❏	❏	Hackers only want to cause trouble.
58.	❏	❏	❏	❏	❏	Cyberstalking is not really different from regular stalking.
59.	❏	❏	❏	❏	❏	There's nothing wrong with downloading music from the Internet.
60.	❏	❏	❏	❏	❏	We should ban cyborgs.

Compare your answers to this self-quiz with the answers to the initial self-quiz. How, if at all, have your answers changed? How have the *reasons* for your answers changed?

For Further Reading

Much of the most important work in computer ethics has been done in the form of articles rather than books, and several journals have been particularly good resources in this area. These include: *Computers and Society; Ethics and Information Technology;* and *Communication and Ethics in Society.* In addition, the American Philosophical Association publishes a *Newsletter on Philosophy and Computing,* which often contains helpful articles in the area of computer ethics.

For an excellent overview, see Deborah G. Johnson, "Computer Ethics," *A Companion to Applied Ethics: Blackwell Companions to Philosophy,* edited by R. G. Frey (Malden, MA: Blackwell Publishing, 2003), pp. 608–619. Also see Johnson's *Computer Ethics,* Third Edition (Upper Saddle River, NJ: Prentice Hall, 2000).

Once of the classics in this field is Norbert Wiener, *The Human Use of Human Beings: Cybernetics and Society* (DaCapo Press, 1998). Much more recently, see Lawrence Lessig, *The Future of Ideas: The Fate of the Commons in a Connected World* (Vintage, 2002), as well as his *Code and Other Laws of Cyberspace* (Basic Books, 2000). For a brief history, see Terrell Ward Bynum, "Computer Ethics: Its Birth and Its Future," *Ethics and Information Technology,* vol. 3, No. 2 (2001), pp. 109–112.

There are a number of valuable anthologies that reprint key articles on many of the topics contained in this chapter. Among the most helpful are James H. Moor and Terrell Ward Bynum, *Cyberphilosophy: The Intersection of Philosophy and Computing* (Blackwell, 2003); Terrell Ward Bynum and Simon Rogerson, *Computer Ethics and Professional Responsibility: Introductory Text and Readings* (Blackwell, 2003); M. David Ermann and Michele S. Shauf, eds., *Computers, Ethics, and Society* (New York: Oxford University Press, 2002); Richard A. Spinello, *Case Studies in Information Technology Ethics* (2nd ed., Upper Saddle River, NJ: Prentice Hall, 2002); Richard Spinello and Herman T. Tavani, *Readings in CyberEthics* (Jones & Bartlett, 2001); Robert M. Baird, Reagan Mays Ramsower, and Stuart E. Rosenbaum, *Cyberethics: Social & Moral Issues in the Computer Age* (Prometheus Books, 2000); D. Micah Hester and Paul J. Ford, *Computers and Ethics in the Cyberage* (Upper Saddle River, NJ: Prentice Hall, 2000); Stacey L. Edgar and Genesco Suny *Morality and Machines: Perspectives on Computer Ethics* (Jones and Bartlett, 1997); Deborah G. Johnson and Helen Nissenbaum, eds., *Computers, Ethics and Social Values* (Upper Saddle River, NJ: Prentice Hall, 1995).

Among the textbooks in this area, see especially the Johnson text mentioned earlier; Herman T. Tavani, *Ethics and Technology: Ethical Issues in an Age of Information and Communication Technology* (New York: Wiley Text Books, 2001); and Sara Baase, *A Gift of Fire* (Upper Saddle River, NJ: Prentice Hall, 2002).

On the question of whether computer ethics is a unique field or, at least eventually, just a part of other branches of ethics (engineering ethics, business ethics, etc.), see James H. Moor, "What is computer ethics?", *Metaphilosophy,* vol. 16 (October, 1985), p. 266–75; Herman Tavani, "The Uniqueness Debate in Computer Ethics: What Exactly Is at Issue, and Why Does It Matter?" *Ethics and Information Technology,* vol. 4, No. 1 (2002), pp. 37–54; Luciano Floridi and J. W. Sanders, "Mapping the Foundationalist Debate in Computer Ethics," *Ethics and Information Technology,* Vol. 4, No. 1 (2002), pp. 1–9; James H, Moor, "The Future of Computer Ethics: You Ain't Seen Nothin' Yet!" *Ethics and Information Technology,* Vol. 3, No. 2 (2001), pp. 89–91.

NW

ZADIE SMITH

ISIS
LARGE PRINT
Oxford

First published in Great Britain 2012
by
Hamish Hamilton
an imprint of
Penguin Books Ltd.

Published in Large Print 2013 by ISIS Publishing Ltd.,
7 Centremead, Osney Mead, Oxford OX2 0ES
by arrangement with
Penguin Books Ltd.

CIP data is available for this title from the British Library

ISBN 978–0–7531–9214–6 (hb)
ISBN 978–0–7531–9215–3 (pb)

Printed and bound in Great Britain by
T. J. International Ltd., Padstow, Cornwall

For Kellas